In
Himalaya

Bradley Mayhew
Richard Plunkett   Michelle Coxall
Phillipa Saxton   Paul Greenway

LONELY PLANET PUBLICATIONS
Melbourne • Oakland • London • Paris

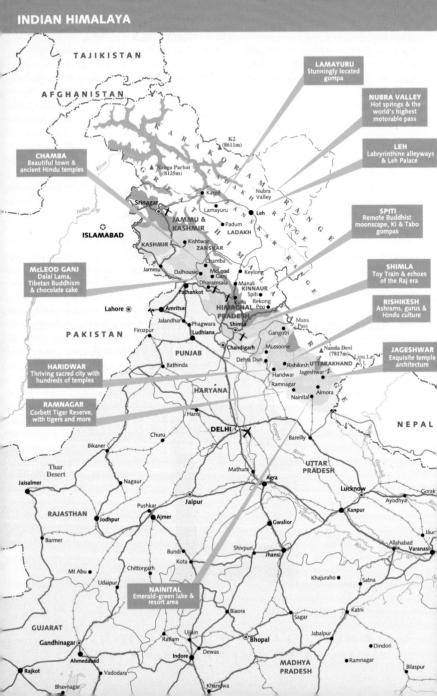

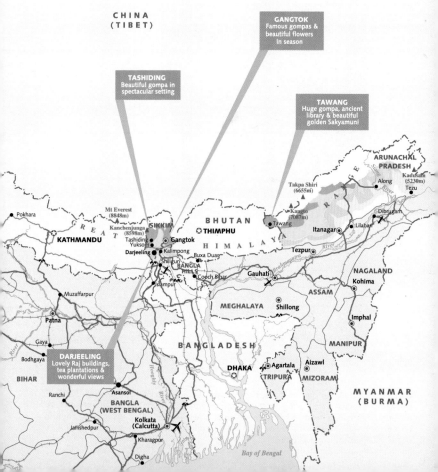

ELEVATION

3000 m

2000 m

1000 m

500 m

200 m

0

0   100   200 km

The external boundaries of India
on this map have not been authenticated
and may not be correct

CHINA
(TIBET)

GANGTOK
Famous gompas &
beautiful flowers
in season

TASHIDING
Beautiful gompa in
spectacular setting

TAWANG
Huge gompa, ancient
library & beautiful
golden Sakyamuni

ARUNACHAL
PRADESH

Kadusam
(5230m)
Along   Tezu

Takpa Shiri
(6655m)

Mt Everest
(8848m)   Kangto
(7087m)   Dibrugarh

Pokhara   SIKKIM   BHUTAN   Tawang   Lilabari

Kanchenjunga   ✿THIMPHU   Itanagar
(8598m)
KATHMANDU   Tashiding ◉Gangtok   Tezpur
Yuksom Kalimpong
Darjeeling   NAGALAND
BANGLA
Siliguri HILLS   Buxa Duar   Gauhati   Kohima
Islampur   Cooch Bihar   ◉

Muzaffarpur   MEGHALAYA   ASSAM

Patna   Shillong   Imphal
◉   ◉
MANIPUR
Gaya   BANGLADESH
Bodhgaya   Aizawl
DARJEELING   DHAKA   ◉Agartala ◉
Lovely Raj buildings,   ✞   TRIPURA MIZORAM
BIHAR   tea plantations &
wonderful views
Ranchi   MYANMAR
Asansol   (BURMA)
BANGLA
Jamshedpur   (WEST BENGAL)

Kolkata
(Calcutta)

Kharagpur

Digha   Bay of Bengal

Indian Himalaya
2nd edition – January 2000
First published – September 1996

Published by
Lonely Planet Publications Pty Ltd A.C.N. 005 607 983
192 Burwood Rd, Hawthorn, Victoria 3122, Australia

Lonely Planet Offices
Australia PO Box 617, Hawthorn, Victoria 3122
USA 150 Linden St, Oakland, CA 94607
UK 10a Spring Place, London NW5 3BH
France 1 rue du Dahomey, 75011 Paris

Photographs
Many of the images in this guide are available for licensing from
Lonely Planet Images.
email: lpi@lonelyplanet.com.au

Front cover photograph
A crisp morning at Tangboche Gompa, Ladakh (Bruce Mitchell)

ISBN 0 86442 688 7

text & maps © Lonely Planet 2000
photos © photographers as indicated 2000

Printed by SNP Printing Pte Ltd, Singapore

All rights reserved. No part of this publication may be reproduced,
stored in a retrieval system or transmitted in any form by any means,
electronic, mechanical, photocopying, recording or otherwise, except
brief extracts for the purpose of review, without the written permission
of the publisher and copyright owner.

**Although the authors
and Lonely Planet try
to make the informa-
tion as accurate as
possible, we accept
no responsibility for
any loss, injury or
inconvenience sus-
tained by anyone
using this book.**

Contents – Text

1

Contents – Maps

MAPS

TAJIKISTAN

PAKISTAN

CHINA
(TIBET)

NEPAL

INDIA

BHUTAN

BANGLADESH

INDIA

MYANMAR
(BURMA)

0   150   300 km

The external boundaries of India on this map have not been authenticated and may not be correct.

The Authors

Bradley Mayhew

Bradley started travelling in South-West China, Tibet and northern Pakistan while studying Chinese at Oxford University. Upon graduation he fled to Central America for six months to forget his Chinese and then worked in Beijing in a futile attempt to get it back. Since then he has spent two months in the Silk Road cities of Bukhara and Khiva, two months trekking in Kyrgyzstan and has enjoyed extended trips to Iran, eastern Turkey and Ladakh. He is also the co-author of Lonely Planet's *Pakistan*, *Karakoram Highway*, *South-West China*, *Central Asia* and *Tibet* guides.

Bradley is also the co-author and photographer of the *Odyssey Guide to Uzbekistan*, and has lectured on Central Asia at the Royal Geographical Society. He splits his time between Sevenoaks in south-east England and Las Vegas, Nevada.

Richard Plunkett

Richard grew up on a farm in central Victoria, Australia. A week after his high school exams he arrived alone in Kolkata (Calcutta), and was never quite the same again. Between subsequent jaunts to Asia and the Middle East he worked as a journalist at *The Age* in Melbourne and the Australian edition of *The Big Issue*.

He eventually landed a job at Lonely Planet largely on the strength of knowing the capital of Burkina Faso. After 18 months of armchair travel, he took to the hills to research Ladakh, Garhwal, Sikkim and Arunachal Pradesh, as well as Lonely Planet's *Delhi* city guide.

Phillipa Saxton

The seed was sown for a life of penury as a travel writer during a childhood living in several countries and probably germinated after receiving a cheque for £5 as 'Encouragement Fee' for two travel stories published at the age of 14. Intervening years included studying to become the world's greatest forensic scientist (abandoned), marriage (terminated) and raising three wonderful children (completed). On becoming a full-time writer, the natural progression was to visit India, the ancestral home of five previous generations and the subject of many childhood stories. As with many visitors, India became her passion, and publishing a magazine, *Saffron Road*, was her attempt to repay India for the vast joy the association has given her.

Michelle Coxall

Michelle fell under the spell of the Indian Himalaya when she spent seven months in Dharamsala, working with the Tibetan refugees in McLeod Ganj. She has worked on several LP titles, including the first editions of LP's *Indian Himalaya* and *Rajasthan*.

Paul Greenway

Paul caught his first tropical disease in 1985, and has had the 'travel bug' ever since. Gratefully plucked from the security and blandness of the Australian Public Service, he is now a full-time traveller and writer, who has written a diverse number of Lonely Planet guides, including *Mongolia*, *Madagascar & Comoros* and *Iran*. Paul is based in Adelaide, South Australia, where he supports his beloved Adelaide Crows football club, relaxes to tuneless heavy rock and will do anything (like go to Mongolia and Iran) to avoid settling down.

FROM THE AUTHORS

Bradley Mayhew Thanks to Mr Sah of Hotel Lake View for info and a lift to Naukuchi-yatal and Mr Yogunda at Shimla HPTDC Ignace Pollet for trek notes.

Richard Plunkett Big thanks to Linda and Elana in Ladakh, Nasir and friends in Leh, Franz and Trudi in the Nubra Valley, Jean-Claude and Martine in Zanskar, Mohammed Sadiq in Kargil, Gary and Pip in Badrinath, Avi and Steve in Rishikesh, Clay Youngkin and Ha-Jo in Sikkim, and Naved Chowdhury and Bina Lyngdoh in Meghalaya. Thanks also to the owners of Delhi's Hotel Namaskar, and to Sanjay Singh in Delhi and Asha in Sydney for their help with navigating Indian officialdom.

A very special thanks to Mr Chakraborty of Bandardewa for his help in getting me into Arunachal Pradesh. I'd probably still be at the checkpoint arguing with the border police if it weren't for you. Thanks also to the Buddhist community of Itanagar for being so helpful. Back in Melbourne, thanks to Hannah for letting me run away for so long, and to Geoff, Sue, Sharan and Adam at LP for the job.

Phillipa Saxton My thanks to the Director and staff of the Government of India Tourist Office in Kolkata (Calcutta), especially Bidisha Sengupta; Diamond & Nimmie Oberoi at Hotel New Elgin, and all my other friends in Darjeeling, for their warm hospitality and friendship; Kanta Talukdar Stanchina, a good friend and an absolute font of information on Bangali culture and art; fellow travellers Peter Hunt (ferret extraordinaire) and Martin Bradshaw who walked his legs off on my behalf; Bryn Thomas without whose advice I would have been completely lost (and probably still be in India looking for facts and figures); Swosti Travels who introduced me to Orissa and saved me from many onerous bus trips; Warwick Blacker and Sue Larsen of Thai Airways in Sydney who dealt with perpetual excess luggage requests and changing itineraries; Michael Halstead a loyal and generous friend; Dee Davison; my sisters and family for their unstinting support; and my partner Mike Ferris, who had to deal with calls home, general depression and the weeks of write-up on my return.

This Book

Michelle Coxall and Paul Greenway wrote and researched the first edition of this book.

Bradley Mayhew, Richard Plunkett and Phillipa Saxton updated this edition, which includes two new chapters – the virgin destination Arunachal Pradesh, and a Gateway Cities chapter, designed to help travellers reach the Indian Himalaya from Delhi and Kolkata (Calcutta).

Bradley coordinated this edition and updated the introductory chapters, Jammu & Kashmir, Himachal Pradesh and Uttarakhand. Richard updated Ladakh & Zanskar, Sikkim, Garhwal and wrote the new Arunachal Pradesh chapter. Phillipa updated the Bangla (West Bengal) Hills chapter, while Garry Weare, author of Lonely Planet's *Trekking in the Indian Himalaya*, updated the trekking sections.

FROM THE PUBLISHER

This second edition of *Indian Himalaya* was produced at Lonely Planet's Melbourne office. Thalia Kalkipsakis was the coordinating editor, with welcome assistance from Brigitte Ellemor, Adam Ford, Joyce Connolly and (previous author!) Michelle Coxall.

Shahara Ahmed coordinated the mapping, design and layout, with assistance from Maree Styles, Paul Piaia, Sarah Sloane and Mark Germanchis.

Illustrations were supplied by Martin Harris, Greg Herriman, William Mezzetti and Prof T. C. Majapuria. Quentin Frayne compiled the Language chapter and Simon Bracken designed the cover, while Darren Elder compiled the index.

Tim Uden and Andrew Tudor provided Quark support, while Sharan Kaur and Adriana Mammarella provided overall support.

Special thanks to Garry Weare for the trekking information.

Acknowledgment

The extract on page 14 from *Across the Top* by Sorrel Wilby is reprinted by kind permission of Pan Macmillan Australia Pty Limited. © Sorrel Wilby 1992.

THANKS
Many thanks to the travellers who used the last edition and wrote to us with helpful hints, advice and interesting anecdotes. Your names appear in the back of this book.

Foreword

ABOUT LONELY PLANET GUIDEBOOKS

The story begins with a classic travel adventure: Tony and Maureen Wheeler's 1972 journey across Europe and Asia to Australia. Useful information about the overland trail did not exist at that time, so Tony and Maureen published the first Lonely Planet guidebook to meet a growing need.

From a kitchen table, then from a tiny office in Melbourne (Australia), Lonely Planet has become the largest independent travel publisher in the world, an international company with offices in Melbourne, Oakland (USA), London (UK) and Paris (France).

Today Lonely Planet guidebooks cover the globe. There is an ever-growing list of books and there's information in a variety of forms and media. Some things haven't changed. The main aim is still to help make it possible for adventurous travellers to get out there – to explore and better understand the world.

At Lonely Planet we believe travellers can make a positive contribution to the countries they visit – if they respect their host communities and spend their money wisely. Since 1986 a percentage of the income from each book has been donated to aid projects and human rights campaigns.

Updates Lonely Planet thoroughly updates each guidebook as often as possible. This usually means there are around two years between editions, although for more unusual or more stable destinations the gap can be longer. Check the imprint page (following the colour map at the beginning of the book) for publication dates.

Between editions up-to-date information is available in two free newsletters – the paper *Planet Talk* and email *Comet* (to subscribe, contact any Lonely Planet office) – and on our Web site at www.lonelyplanet.com. The *Upgrades* section of the Web site covers a number of important and volatile destinations and is regularly updated by Lonely Planet authors. *Scoop* covers news and current affairs relevant to travellers. And, lastly, the *Thorn Tree* bulletin board and *Postcards* section of the site carry unverified, but fascinating, reports from travellers.

Correspondence The process of creating new editions begins with the letters, postcards and emails received from travellers. This correspondence often includes suggestions, criticisms and comments about the current editions. Interesting excerpts are immediately passed on via newsletters and the Web site, and everything goes to our authors to be verified when they're researching on the road. We're keen to get more feedback from organisations or individuals who represent communities visited by travellers.

Lonely Planet gathers information for everyone who's curious about the planet – and especially for those who explore it first-hand. Through guidebooks, phrasebooks, activity guides, maps, literature, newsletters, image library, TV series and Web site we act as an information exchange for a worldwide community of travellers.

Research Authors aim to gather sufficient practical information to enable travellers to make informed choices and to make the mechanics of a journey run smoothly. They also research historical and cultural background to help enrich the travel experience and allow travellers to understand and respond appropriately to cultural and environmental issues.

Authors don't stay in every hotel because that would mean spending a couple of months in each medium-sized city and, no, they don't eat at every restaurant because that would mean stretching belts beyond capacity. They do visit hotels and restaurants to check standards and prices, but feedback based on readers' direct experiences can be very helpful.

Many of our authors work undercover, others aren't so secretive. None of them accept freebies in exchange for positive write-ups. And none of our guidebooks contain any advertising.

Production Authors submit their raw manuscripts and maps to offices in Australia, USA, UK or France. Editors and cartographers – all experienced travellers themselves – then begin the process of assembling the pieces. When the book finally hits the shops, some things are already out of date, we start getting feedback from readers and the process begins again …

WARNING & REQUEST

Things change – prices go up, schedules change, good places go bad and bad places go bankrupt – nothing stays the same. So, if you find things better or worse, recently opened or long since closed, please tell us and help make the next edition even more accurate and useful. We genuinely value all the feedback we receive. Julie Young coordinates a well travelled team that reads and acknowledges every letter, postcard and email and ensures that every morsel of information finds its way to the appropriate authors, editors and cartographers for verification.

Everyone who writes to us will find their name in the next edition of the appropriate guidebook. They will also receive the latest issue of *Planet Talk*, our quarterly printed newsletter, or *Comet*, our monthly email newsletter. Subscriptions to both newsletters are free. The very best contributions will be rewarded with a free guidebook.

Excerpts from your correspondence may appear in new editions of Lonely Planet guidebooks, the Lonely Planet Web site, *Planet Talk* or *Comet*, so please let us know if you *don't* want your letter published or your name acknowledged.

Send all correspondence to the Lonely Planet office closest to you:

Australia: PO Box 617, Hawthorn, Victoria 3122
USA: 150 Linden St, Oakland, CA 94607
UK: 10A Spring Place, London NW5 3BH
France: 1 rue du Dahomey, 75011 Paris

Or email us at: talk2us@lonelyplanet.com.au

For news, views and updates see our Web site: www.lonelyplanet.com

HOW TO USE A LONELY PLANET GUIDEBOOK

The best way to use a Lonely Planet guidebook is any way you choose. At Lonely Planet we believe the most memorable travel experiences are often those that are unexpected, and the finest discoveries are those you make yourself. Guidebooks are not intended to be used as if they provide a detailed set of infallible instructions!

Contents All Lonely Planet guidebooks follow roughly the same format. The Facts about the Destination chapters or sections give background information ranging from history to weather. Facts for the Visitor gives practical information on issues like visas and health. Getting There & Away gives a brief starting point for researching travel to and from the destination. Getting Around gives an overview of the transport options when you arrive.

The peculiar demands of each destination determine how subsequent chapters are broken up, but some things remain constant. We always start with background, then proceed to sights, places to stay, places to eat, entertainment, getting there and away, and getting around information – in that order.

Heading Hierarchy Lonely Planet headings are used in a strict hierarchical structure that can be visualised as a set of Russian dolls. Each heading (and its following text) is encompassed by any preceding heading that is higher on the hierarchical ladder.

Entry Points We do not assume guidebooks will be read from beginning to end, but that people will dip into them. The traditional entry points are the list of contents and the index. In addition, however, some books have a complete list of maps and an index map illustrating map coverage.

There may also be a colour map that shows highlights. These highlights are dealt with in greater detail in the Facts for the Visitor chapter, along with planning questions and suggested itineraries. Each chapter covering a geographical region usually begins with a locator map and another list of highlights. Once you find something of interest in a list of highlights, turn to the index.

Maps Maps play a crucial role in Lonely Planet guidebooks and include a huge amount of information. A legend is printed on the back page. We seek to have complete consistency between maps and text, and to have every important place in the text captured on a map. Map key numbers usually start in the top left corner.

Although inclusion in a guidebook usually implies a recommendation we cannot list every good place. Exclusion does not necessarily imply criticism. In fact there are a number of reasons why we might exclude a place – sometimes it is simply inappropriate to encourage an influx of travellers.

Introduction

Not even in a hundred years of the gods could I tell you of the glories of the Himalaya.

The Puranas

Throughout the ages, sages and mystics have travelled to the mighty Indian Himalaya (Abode of Snow) to draw inspiration from its perennially snow-clad peaks, magnificent remote valleys and gorges and life-giving rivers for their meditations. The early sages who gave voice to their awe of this soul-stirring mountain chain referred to it as 'the expanse of the two arms of the Great Being' – an evocative description suggesting a world locked in the Himalaya's divine snowy embrace.

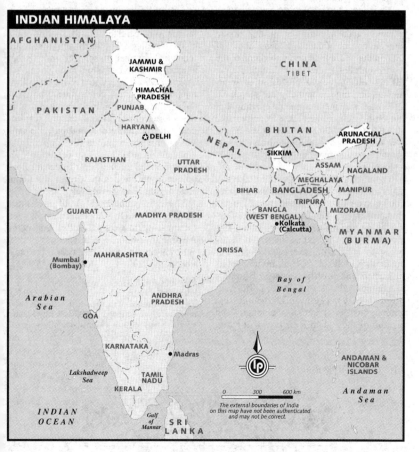

INDIAN HIMALAYA

AFGHANISTAN

JAMMU & KASHMIR

HIMACHAL PRADESH

PUNJAB

CHINA
TIBET

PAKISTAN

HARYANA

⬩DELHI

RAJASTHAN

UTTAR PRADESH

NEPAL

BHUTAN

SIKKIM

ARUNACHAL PRADESH

ASSAM

NAGALAND

MEGHALAYA

BIHAR

BANGLADESH

MANIPUR

TRIPURA

BANGLA (WEST BENGAL)

●Kolkata (Calcutta)

MIZORAM

GUJARAT

MADHYA PRADESH

MYANMAR (BURMA)

MAHARASHTRA

ORISSA

Mumbai (Bombay)●

ANDHRA PRADESH

Bay of Bengal

Arabian Sea

GOA

KARNATAKA

●Madras

ANDAMAN & NICOBAR ISLANDS

Lakshadweep Sea

TAMIL NADU

KERALA

Andaman Sea

INDIAN OCEAN

Gulf of Mannar

SRI LANKA

0   300   600 km

The external boundaries of India on this map have not been authenticated and may not be correct.

The Himalaya was also known as *Dhev-bumi* – the Abode of the Gods.

Once a pilgrimage to this remote lofty realm entailed a long, arduous journey on foot from the hot Indian plains, or across the formidable high passes that were the only means of passage from the Tibetan plateau. Today it is possible to penetrate the mountain fastnesses by bus or jeep, and to some areas, such as Ladakh, in the north-eastern region of the state of Jammu & Kashmir, by plane – a flight that affords some of the world's most stunning aerial scenery.

It is almost too easy to get carried away with superlatives when writing about the Indian Himalaya, but after all, this region *does* have some of the most beautiful mountains in the world (and certainly some of the world's highest); the most dramatic river valleys and gorges; a profusion of wildflowers and unique fauna; quiet places for reflection and meditation; fascinating hill stations; laidback travellers' centres like McLeod Ganj, Manali and Manikaran; exhilarating river rapids; extraordinary temple complexes and ornate and colourful *gompas* (monasteries).

If you enjoy trekking, you can take day hikes or three-week expeditions. Perhaps you're keen to learn more about Tibetan Buddhism; if so, McLeod Ganj, Leh or Darjeeling are the places to head. Rishikesh is *the* place to go if you're interested in aspects of Hindu philosophy. Wildflower buffs should head to Sikkim to see its renowned and prolific variety of orchids and rhododendrons, or to the beautiful Valley of Flowers in Garhwal. The temples and gompas scattered across the length and breadth of the Indian Himalaya will tempt those interested in architecture and manifestations of Hindu and Tibetan Buddhist culture. For rest and recreation there are always the hill stations, eminently accessible – some by tiny toy trains that wend their way up gravity-defying tortuous narrow-gauge lines.

For wild elephant, tiger or rhino spotting, you'll enjoy safaris at the Rajaji, Corbett and Jaldhapara wildlife sanctuaries respectively, and these places are also home to an astonishing array of mammals and a great variety of birdlife.

The hustle and bustle characteristic of life on the Indian plains rapidly evaporates the farther you ascend towards the soaring peaks of the Himalaya. The mountain villages are renowned for their hospitality and it's not unusual to be invited into a family home for a cup of *chai* (tea), or to a colourful village religious or harvest celebration. The Buddhist gompas of the Indian Himalaya remain repositories of rich Tibetan culture, resplendent with vibrantly coloured prayer rooms and exquisitely embroidered *thangkas* (religious paintings). Festivals celebrated according to the Tibetan lunar calendar afford unique opportunities to witness the pomp and pageant of this living religion.

There is something about the sheer grandeur of the Himalaya that inspires even the most world-weary traveller. For as the Australian author and adventurer Sorrel Wilby writes in her Himalayan travelogue *Across the Top*:

I do not know the meaning of existence; I do not know the answers; but here, in these mountains, for just one moment there is no need to ask questions. Life is understood. And that is why I return – will always return – to the abode of snows.

Facts about the Region

HISTORY

Fragments of implements dating from the early Stone Age (8000 BCE – before common era) have been recovered from the Alaknanda Valley in Uttarakhand (Uttar Pradesh), and prehistoric implements discovered near Srinagar (Jammu & Kashmir) as well as further evidence from Himachal Pradesh all testify to the antiquity of human habitation. With the expansion of the Indus Valley civilisation of proto-Dravidians (2500-1500 BCE), migrations to the foothills followed. The Aryan invasion over the north-west passes (1500-1000 BCE) drove the Dravidians back south. The four books of Aryan scriptures *(Vedas)* move from early worship of the Indus River eastwards to honour the Ganges. Where the Ganges rises in Uttarakhand is known as *Dhev-bumi* – the Land of the Gods.

The Aryans propitiated their nature gods through sacrificial rituals conducted by their hereditary priests, the Brahmans, who continued to dominate the social hierarchy, with indigenous inhabitants being relegated to humbler status. Thus originated India's complex caste system. Around 800 BCE the speculative *Upanishad* scriptures included the doctrines of Hindu philosophy and idealised the Himalayan ashram. Buddha (born c563 BCE) threatened Brahmanical orthodoxy by his rejection of the caste system. In 260 BCE the emperor Ashoka declared Buddhism the state religion and official patronage saw the new faith spread both to South-East Asia and over the Himalaya to China.

The great Hindu monist philosopher Shankaracharya (born c788 CE) restored the Brahmanical order aided by his energetic missionary pilgrimages in the Himalaya. Thanks to his teaching, orthodox Hindus view physical reality as illusory *(maya)*. Hypotheses such as the Aryan invasion are rejected in favour of belief in a golden age beyond the purview of history.

The popular scriptural epics of Hinduism began to be written down around 400 BCE. Specific references to the Himalaya are made in the *Mahabharata*. The semiscriptural *Puranas* are a mix of mythology and surprisingly detailed Himalayan geography. The Vedic gods were merged largely into Vishnu the preserver and Shiva the destroyer. Legendary heroes such as Rama and Krishna were deified as embodiments of Vishnu by the orthodox, but the majority of Hindus in the Himalaya stayed with the lingam (phallic symbol) worship of Shiva.

Ladakh & Zanskar

The first inhabitants of Ladakh were the nomadic Khampas who roamed the remote grazing areas of the Tibetan plateau. The Mons, who professed Buddhism, established the first settlements on the windswept plateau. Dards from the Indus Valley introduced irrigation to make agriculture possible in the higher reaches. The Dards were gradually displaced or assimilated by migrations from Guge, a province in western Tibet. The Indian teacher Padmasambhava (8th century CE) crossed the Himalaya to establish Tibetan Buddhism, which was enriched by the 11th century scholar Ringchen Zangpo who founded several famous *gompas* (monasteries). In the 14th century the Gelukpa order of monks was introduced to Ladakh.

With Islam spreading up the Indus Valley, the divided upper and lower realms of Ladakh united under the Buddhist ruler Tashi Namgyal. Later, however, the Muslim ruler of Baltistan forced the Ladakhi king to marry his daughter. Ladakh enjoyed stability under Singe Namgyal, the offspring of this union. He constructed the royal palace at Leh and established gompas of the Drukpa order in Ladakh and Zanskar. The Ladakhi kingdom now included Zanskar and Spiti in addition to the Indus Valley, but these territories diminished after a war with the forces of the fifth Dalai Lama sent from Lhasa. Relations with Tibet improved after the signing of a trade agreement.

In 1846 Ladakh became part of the territory of the maharaja of Jammu & Kashmir and remained under Kashmiri control until 1995 when it achieved partial administrative autonomy.

Jammu & Kashmir

Prior to its conversion to Islam in the 14th century, Kashmir was renowned as a repository of Buddhist and Brahmanical learning. Kashmiri pundits occupy a unique niche in Hindu affections and their wholesale displacement in the current agitation betrays the state's tradition of assimilation. During the Utpala and Karokta dynasties the influence of Kashmir was felt beyond the valley. Shah Mir arrived in Kashmir to found an Islamic dynasty that lasted to the Mughal era.

It was Sultan Sikandar who destroyed Kashmir's notable temples and imposed a tax on Hindus. The Mughals valued Kashmir as a reminder of their Central Asian roots. Following them the despotic Afghan Durranis held sway until the Sikh Maharaja Ranjit Singh took control. The British intervened and by the Treaty of Amritsar (1846) the Hindu maharaja of Jammu acquired Kashmir. The new state of Jammu & Kashmir (J&K) included Hindu Jammu, Buddhist Ladakh and Muslim Kashmir and Baltistan. (The bloody outcome of this union, in Kashmir's recent history, will be considered later in this chapter under Government & Politics.)

For 101 years the Dogras of Hindu Jammu ruled over Kashmir. The last maharaja, Hari Singh, ruled from 1923 and was reluctant to cede his territory to either India or Pakistan after Partition in 1947. While the maharaja vacillated, Pakistan dispatched Pathan tribesmen to capture Srinagar. Hari Singh called for Indian help to repel the aggressors, which resulted in war between India and Pakistan leading to a Line of Actual Control that continues to be a source of aggravated dispute.

Himachal Pradesh

In 1966, Himachal Pradesh comprised a nucleus of 31 'native states' that had combined their destinies in 1948 after a millennia of internecine strife. These tiny hill states enjoyed relative affluence owing to their strategic location on the trading routes between Central Asia and the Indian peninsula. Alexander the Great invaded north-west India in 327 BCE and penetrated as far as the Beas River but was pushed back by Chandragupta II, the founder of north India's classic Hindu dynasty.

Himachal's squabbling petty warlords overlooked the rise of Rajput power. Meru Varman had already installed himself as the Rajput ruler of the Chamba Valley in the mid-6th century. He established a kingdom with his headquarters at Brahmapuri (Brahmaur) and the Varman dynasty survived in the valley for over a thousand years. The beautiful temples at Brahmaur and at the later capital of Chamba (founded by Raja Sahil Varman in the 10th century) are a legacy of this dynasty. Chamba's strategic position between the high Himalaya and the Kangra Valley to the south was used to great advantage by its rulers. They controlled trade across the Pangi Range where a main route linked Kullu and Lahaul with Kishtwar and Kashmir along the Chandrabhaga River.

The Kangra Valley was the domain of the Katoch dynasty whose first capital was Nagarkot. Later it moved to Kangra. It was the fabled wealth of the Bajreshwari Temple in Kangra Fort (amassed by the rulers' trading activities) that lured the notorious despoiler of Hindu temples, Mahmud of Ghazni. In 1009 the Afghan raider carried off a vast fortune in gold, silver and jewels. The Kangra rulers were renowned for their refinement and later would commission miniature paintings which, although inspired by the Mughal court, developed their own distinctive Kangra style. This Pahari school of painting peaked under the patronage of Raja Sansar Chand (1775) who after the decline of Mughal influence had extended his claims, deposing the rulers of Chamba and Kullu.

The rise of Sikh ambitions now threatened the hill rulers. Their warrior guru Govind Singh had won the first battles based at Paonta Sahib in the south-east, site of a famous *gurdwara* (Sikh temple). Religious persecution during the emperor Aurangzeb's long reign of intolerance drove the Sikhs to seek domination of the hill states. The situation was further complicated by the nascent Nepali power, the Gurkhas, expanding vigorously westwards. Their leader Amar Singh Thapa allied with the deposed Chamba and Kullu rulers against Kangra. To save himself, Sansar Chand had to call in the Sikhs, who halted the Gurkha invasion but now had a free hand to influence the power play in Himachal.

In 1966 Lahaul & Spiti, which had come under Punjab administration at Independence, became part of Himachal Pradesh (Land of the Snow Ranges), which attained full statehood in 1971.

Uttarakhand

The situation in Uttarakhand saw similar infighting between early fiefdoms but the rivalry was later confined to a Garhwal versus Kumaon matching of arms. From the 8th to the 14th century the Katyuri dynasty ruled from central Kumaon. It was succeeded by the Chand rajas whose first capital was at Champawat in the east, and later, more central, at Almora. Until the 14th century, Garhwal (Place of Forts) had 52 fortified fiefdoms, which were united under Raja Ajay Pal, whose first capital was at Chandpur. Later the capital was moved to Srinagar on the Ganges (not to be confused with the capital of Jammu & Kashmir state).

The Gurkhas overran both Kumaon and Garhwal and posed a threat to the British who sought to control the profitable shawl wool trade. After initial losses, by 1815 the British were able to confine the Gurkhas within the boundaries of Nepal. As the price of enlisting British help to evict the Gurkhas, the Garhwal maharaja ceded Pauri Garhwal east of the Ganges, including Srinagar, to the British. His new capital at Tehri gave the name to his truncated native state of Tehri Garhwal. The British also took over the administration of Kumaon.

The Uttarakhand hills of Garhwal and Kumaon (comprising the region between Himachal and the Nepal border) were merged in 1947 with the new and most populous Indian state of Uttar Pradesh.

Bangla (West Bengal) Hills & Sikkim

The eastern Himalaya remained isolated from the concerns of northern Indian rulers. Only in 1661 did a Mughal flotilla penetrate as far as the Brahmaputra Valley. Sikkim was originally inhabited by animist tribal Lepchas who were joined in the 15th century by Bhutias fleeing religious turmoil in Tibet.

A blood brotherhood was forged between the Lepchas and Bhutias that included marriage alliances and the adoption by the Lepchas of Nyingmapa (ancient) Buddhism, which was introduced by the Bhutias. Hereditary kingship under a Buddhist *chogyal* (king) was instituted in 1642.

The district of Kalimpong was lost to neighbouring Bhutan in the early 18th century and in 1780 more territory was lost to the Gurkha invaders from the west. British power forced the Gurkhas back to Nepal and returned Sikkimese territory in expectation of favour and influence. In 1835, the chogyal was forced to cede Darjeeling to the British as a convalescent station. Then, in 1861, to confirm their mastery, the British made Sikkim a protectorate. This infuriated the rulers in Tibet who considered Sikkim their cultural province. Lhasa mounted an expedition in 1886 that was thrown back. Two years later the British mounted their own expedition to Lhasa. Earlier, in 1864, similar territorial claims by Bhutan had caused the British to wrest by arms Kalimpong and the Duars.

The British encouraged emigration of Nepali labour to both Darjeeling and Sikkim. Gurkha families continue to be integral to Darjeeling's famous tea estates, once a lucrative revenue earner for the British that today remains the most important factor in the economy of the Bangla (West Bengal) hills.

In 1947 India took over the protectorate status of Sikkim. With their numerical majority the Nepali Hindu settlers were dissatisfied at the conservative policies of the chogyal and agitated for more representation. Widespread unrest resulted in 1975 in a referendum whereby the people of Sikkim voted for a democratic system. India annexed the state and replaced the chogyal with an elected legislature.

Arunachal Pradesh

Of all the states in the Indian Himalaya, Arunachal has one of the least documented histories. The Ahom dynasty in Assam – a Shan tribe from Myanmar (Burma), which had conquered neighbouring Assam in the 13th century – had a policy of not interfering with the hill tribes, except for retaliatory raids.

The British continued this policy and after declaring it off limits in 1873 ignored the area until the eve of WWII. After Independence, the tribes were gradually prepared for the impact of the modern world – village democracy was introduced, in preparation for a statewide legislature.

The region of Arunachal Pradesh has always acted as a buffer between empires on the plains and the Tibetan plateau, and in recent times between India and China. This strategic importance was underlined during the Chinese invasion of 1962 and the state has since seen an increase of troops and supply roads in an attempt to tie it to the rest of India militarily.

In 1972 Arunachal became a Union Territory, and in 1987 a state. The state's forests were increasingly overexploited, until a court ban on logging in 1997. Like many of the region's hill tribes, the Arunachalese are increasingly turning to Christianity to build social bonds as the tribal systems of mutual obligation break down in the modern cash economy. Since the ban on logging the state has been in a deep economic slump, which is partly why tourism is opening up.

GEOGRAPHY

In that most oft-quoted verse of the *Kumarsambhava*, by the renowned Sanskrit poet Kalidasa, the Himalaya is described as 'the King of mountains' and the 'measuring rod of the world'. These are apt appellations: the Himalaya Range extends in an arc some 2500km from Nanga Parbat (8125m) in Pakistan in the west, to the far-eastern Indian state of Arunachal Pradesh, with Namache Barwa (7755m) standing sentinel at the eastern perimeter inside Tibet. The world's premier range, it boasts some of its loftiest peaks, with 14 peaks over 8000m, including, of course, Everest, scraping the heavens in Nepal at a staggering 8848m.

The width of the range varies from some 200 to 300km and separates the Indian subcontinent from Chinese Central Asia and the Tibetan plateau to the north. Furthermore the Himalaya has a profound effect on the Indian monsoon and provides a biological barrier between India and the rest of northern Asia. The range encompasses three more or less parallel mountain zones, as described following.

Greater Himalaya

The main Himalayan range is also known as the Himadri. At its western end it divides Kashmir and Himachal Pradesh from Ladakh and Zanskar. From here the mountains sweep across to the Baralacha Range in Himachal Pradesh, before the main Himalayan range merges with the Parvati Range and continues across the Kinnaur Kailash Range. The highest peaks in this part of the western Himalaya are Nun (7135m) and Kun (7077m), in Zanskar, and Kinner Kailash (6050m) in Kinnaur. The range is crossed by the Zoji La, between Kashmir and Ladakh, the Shingo La, between Lahaul and Zanskar and the Pin Parvati Pass, between Kullu and Spiti. These western sections of the Himalaya have the largest glaciers in the range, partly because the mountains fall less steeply to the plains.

The Greater Himalaya continues into Uttarakhand, where rise the major tributaries of the Ganges and the source of the Yamuna.

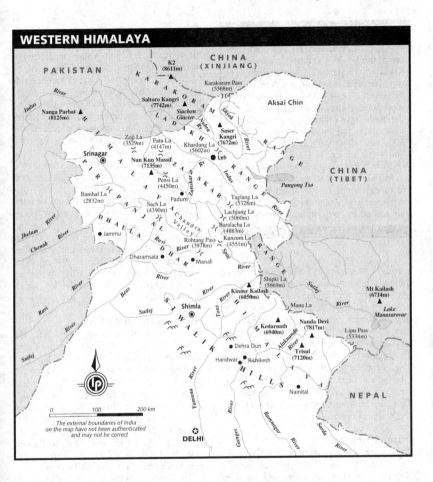

WESTERN HIMALAYA

The highest mountain here is beautiful Nanda Devi at 7817m. The range extends east into Nepal, to form the boundary between Nepal and Tibet.

At the far end of Nepal the Himalaya hits another high at Kanchenjunga (at 8598m the highest mountain in India) and embraces Sikkim, before projecting eastward into mountainous Bhutan and finally culminating in the Assam Himalaya at its far-eastern extremity, forming the mountainous region of Arunachal Pradesh.

Trans-Himalaya

Lying to the north of the Greater Himalaya at its western end are the Zanskar and Ladakh ranges. The regions of Ladakh, Zanskar, Spiti and upper Kinnaur, referred to as the Trans-Himalayan region, mark the transition zone between the Indian subcontinent and the Tibetan plateau.

The Zanskar and Ladakh ranges stand south and north of Leh respectively. The latter is crossed by the Khardung La (5602m) over the highest motorable road in the

The Highest Battlefield on Earth

Perhaps the most absurdly stubborn symbol of the troubles in Kashmir is India and Pakistan's 15 year military stalemate over the Siachen Glacier, dubbed 'the highest battlefield on earth'. Here at the northernmost point of Ladakh, not far from K2 and the border with China, Pakistani and Indian troops are dug in at altitudes between 6000 and 7000m, fighting over a 700 sq km chunk of ice, at the cost of around US$2 million a day, in temperatures as low as -40°C. The air is so thin that mortar trajectories cannot be estimated accurately, one reason why over 97% of all fatalities are caused by cold, altitude or avalanches.

world. The far north of Ladakh forms part of the eastern Karakoram Range, which separates India from Central Asia. The highest peak here is Saltoro Kangri (7742m) and the most important pass is the strategic Karakoram Pass (5568m), once the main trading link between Leh, Yarkand and Kashgar. The region is home to some of the longest glaciers on the planet, including the Siachen Glacier, site of the highest battlefield in the world (see the boxed text in this section). This entire northern region of Ladakh is currently out of bounds to foreigners.

Inner Himalaya

South of the Greater Himalaya lie the peaks and ridges of the Himanchal, or Middle Himalaya, with peaks averaging between 4000 and 5000m. This zone encompasses the Pir Panjal Range in the western Himalaya, which extends from Gulmarg in the southern Kashmir Valley to Kishtwar, from where it forms the divide between the Chandra (Lahaul) and Ravi (Chamba) valleys. Farther east it forms the natural divide between the Chandra and Kullu valleys. The Pir Panjal is breached only once – at Kishtwar – where the combined waters of the Warvan and Chandra rivers meet to form the Chenab, one of the main tributaries of the Indus. The most important pass over the Pir Panjal is the Rohtang Pass, which connects the Kullu Valley with Lahaul.

To the south of the Pir Panjal lies the Dhaula Dhar Range. It is most easily recognised as the snowcapped ridge behind Dharamsala, and it forms the divide between the Ravi (Chamba) and the Beas (Kangra) valleys. Farther west it provides the divide between the Chenab Valley below Kishtwar and the Tawi Valley, which twists south to Jammu.

Himalayan Foothills

At the bottom of the elevation profile is the Lower Himalaya, or Himalayan foothills. These are the first slopes reached by those heading north from the plains. In the west, they form the Siwalik Range, which extends from western Himachal Pradesh midway into northern Uttar Pradesh, and rises to elevations of between 1500 and 2000m. These are the hills seen around Shimla and between Dehra Dun and Almora. Farther east the foothills form the Terai region, which continues into Nepal.

The foothills of the eastern Himalaya are directly in the path of the monsoon and have

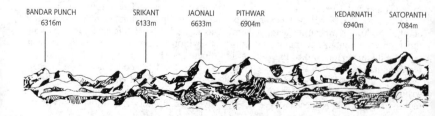

BANDAR PUNCH 6316m   SRIKANT 6133m   JAONALI 6633m   PITHWAR 6904m   KEDARNATH 6940m   SATOPANTH 7084m

been progressively buffeted and eroded over the ages to the point where they were completely levelled, and so this third and lower mountain fold is absent in this area.

Rivers

The Himalaya is embraced by two magnificent rivers, the Indus and Brahmaputra. Though the two rivers rise within 150km of each other, behind the mountains near Mt Kailash in Tibet, they head off in different directions for over 1500km and finally enter the Arabian Sea and Bay of Bengal, respectively, thus largely defining the subcontinent through their course.

The Indus threads its way westwards, then penetrates the mountains to enter India and proceeds through Ladakh into Pakistan. In the western Himalaya, the Indus and its tributaries provide the principal drainage system. The catchment area is extremely large and its tributaries drain the Hindu Kush to the west and the Karakoram to the north. On its long descent to the plains, the Indus is supplemented by the Jhelum, Chenab, Beas, Ravi and Sutlej rivers whose headwaters drain the entire western Himalaya. These five rivers, or *panj ab*, give the Punjab its name.

The Sutlej River also rises near Mt Kailash and flows into Kinnaur via the 5669m Shipki La. From here it crashes through the Himalaya in a series of gorges before finally joining the Beas and later the Indus in Pakistan.

Eastwards from the Sutlej River, river systems drain into the Ganges basin, with the mountains south of the Sangla Valley forming the watershed. First there is the Tons, which joins the Yamuna. The Ganges, as the Bhagirathi, rises at Gaumukh (Cow's Mouth) above Gangotri in northern Uttarakhand. It is joined by the Pindar, the Dhauliganga, the Nandakini, the Mandakini, and the Alaknanda, all of which rise in northern Uttarakhand, until finally the Ganges meets the Yamuna at Allahabad on the plains of Uttar Pradesh. According to Hindu mythology the mythical underground Saraswati River also flows south to join the Ganges at Allahabad. As the sacred Ganges continues its journey eastwards across north-east India, it is fed by all the main river systems of Nepal before reaching the Bay of Bengal.

From Mt Kailash the Brahmaputra courses eastwards 1000km through Tibet, passing around the back of the Himalaya. In eastern Tibet it makes a dramatic swing around Mt Namache Barwa and finally breaches the Himalaya through a dramatic series of gorges, passing into the Indian state of Arunachal Pradesh (where it is known as the Siang River). It curves through the north-eastern region in a south-westerly direction, before joining the Ganges.

GEOLOGY

The Himalaya is one of the youngest mountain ranges in the world. Its evolution can be traced to the Jurassic era (80 million years ago) when the world's land masses were split into two: Laurasia in the northern hemisphere, and Gondwanaland in the southern hemisphere. The land mass that is now India broke away from Gondwanaland and floated like a gigantic island 5000km across the earth's surface until it collided

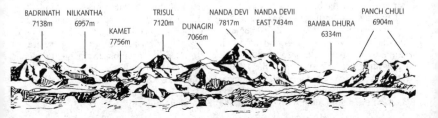

BADRINATH 7138m · NILKANTHA 6957m · KAMET 7756m · TRISUL 7120m · DUNAGIRI 7066m · NANDA DEVI 7817m · NANDA DEVII EAST 7434m · BAMBA DHURA 6334m · PANCH CHULI 6904m

with Asia. The hard volcanic rocks of India ploughed underneath the soft sedimentary crust of the Asian plate, compressing both plates, draining the ancient Tethys Sea, which lay between them, and eventually driving rocks up to a height of almost 9km. It was a collision that formed mountain ranges right across Asia, including the Karakoram, the Pamirs, the Hindu Kush, the Tian Shan and the Kunlun.

Geological samples retrieved from the summit of Mt Everest confirm that, millions of years ago, the Himalaya formed the ocean bed of the Tethys Sea. Once watery relics, left high and dry by the tectonic push, include marine fossils, which are easily found in Spiti at heights of 4500m, and the brackish lakes of Tso Moriri and Tso Pangong in Ladakh's Changtang region, which are all that's left of the Tethys.

As most Asian river systems were already in place before the big collision, these northern rivers rapidly cut through the relatively soft sedimentary uplift to create deep gorges through the high mountains. Dramatic examples include the Indus, Sutlej and the Kali Gandaki of Nepal.

Following this initial massive upward thrust, which took place over a period of some five to seven million years, the rate of impact slowed. The last major push took place around 600,000 years ago. The Himalaya at the front of this massive continental collision are still being formed, though, with the range continuing to rise up to 0.8cm annually.

CLIMATE
The weather will probably dictate when you travel to the Indian Himalaya. See the Best Times to Visit table in the Facts for the Visitor chapter for the best times to travel.

Climatically, the Indian Himalaya can be divided into three regions. The first contains the ridges and valleys to the south of the Pir Panjal Range, and the monsoonal hill states from Jammu to Uttarakhand, the Bangla (West Bengal) hills and the lower regions of Sikkim; the second includes the region south of the main Himalaya but beyond the

Pir Panjal – it encompasses the Kashmir Valley and the valleys of Lahaul & Spiti, and has a modified monsoon climate. The third region, that of Ladakh and its environs, lies beyond the Himalaya and has a high altitude desert climate.

Ladakh & Zanskar
Ladakh is isolated from most of the Indian climate patterns. It's one of the few places in India where humidity is always low. Rainfall is no more than a few centimetres each year, and can fall in the peak tourist summer months of July and August. Dramatic monsoons can drift over Zanskar in summer.

In winter, it is generally dry in Ladakh and Zanskar, but a lot windier and very cold. Temperatures rarely rise above 0°C from mid-November to early March.

Regular visitors to Ladakh have noticed a change in climatic patterns over the last decade or two and it seems that the region is becoming wetter, though studies are yet to confirm this.

Vale of Kashmir
Spring in the Kashmir Valley begins in mid-March and continues through to the end of May. At this time Kashmir experiences its heaviest rainfall, with storms breaking over the Pir Panjal. During July and August, the valley becomes hazy and humid, and temperatures often reach 30°C. Autumn is the most settled period. The months of September and October are typically clear with a minimum of rain. Winter is from December to March.

Jammu & Himachal Pradesh
In Jammu, the Kangra Valley, Chamba district, Kullu and Parvati valleys, Manali and Shimla, the rains last from about mid-June to mid-September. Winter, often accompanied by snow and subzero temperatures, is from early December to the end of March. The ideal time to visit is between September and November. Between March and April the weather can be clear and fine, although quite chilly.

The exceptions are Kinnaur and Lahaul & Spiti, which have a modified monsoon and a severe winter. Between June and October, the days are sunny and the evenings are cool. At other times of the year snow, and temperatures below -20°C, are responsible for blocking passes and isolating the regions.

Uttarakhand

The best weather is from mid-May to mid-July and mid-September to mid-November. The Char Dham (the four sacred shrines of Uttarakhand) are snowbound between November and April. Summer is from June to August and winter from December to February. At higher altitudes during the height of summer, it can be quite cool. During the

monsoon (July/August), expect delays due to landslides and road closures. At this time, too, the famed views of distant snowclad peaks are enshrouded in cloud. Rishikesh, Haridwar and the hill stations can be visited year-round, although it can get quite chilly in winter when temperatures drop to single figures.

Bangla (West Bengal) Hills

Down on the Bangla plains in the regions of Shiliguri and Jalpaiguri, it is very hot during the summer months of May and June, and quite cool between October and February. As you begin the ascent to Darjeeling, at 2134m, the temperature drops dramatically. Darjeeling has been described as having three seasons: cold, very cold, and very, very cold!

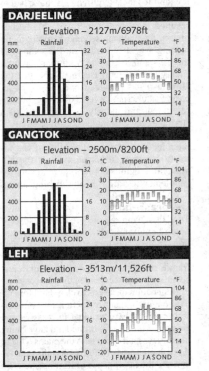

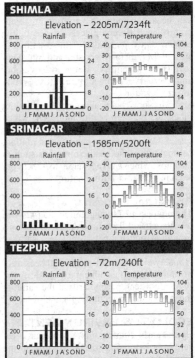

For mountain views from Darjeeling, the best time to visit is from mid-September to mid-December. Nights are pretty cold by December but the days remain clear and sunny, although Darjeeling has the occasional white Christmas.

The season resumes around mid-March and continues to mid-June, but as the haze builds up the views become less clear. During the monsoon months (June to September), clouds obscure the mountains and the rain is often so heavy that whole sections of the road from the plains are washed away, though the town is rarely cut off for more than a few days at a time.

Sikkim

Given the great variation in altitudes in Sikkim (from only a few hundred metres in the bottom of river valleys, to heights of over 6000m in the Greater Himalaya), there can be a considerable variation in temperature in different places. Places below 3000m enjoy particularly fine weather in spring (March to May) and autumn (September to November). Between November and February it can get quite chilly, even at lower elevations.

As the snowclad peaks of northern Sikkim block the passage of the monsoon, which sweeps across the state from June until August, Sikkim receives a phenomenal rainfall, particularly in the southern regions such as Gangtok, which can register up to 325cm per annum. It is drier farther north.

Arunachal Pradesh

The big pass to Tawang, the Se La (4249m) is often closed for a time during winter, although it doesn't get completely snowed over like the passes in other parts of the Himalaya. The rest of Arunachal sees a lot of rain (as much as 500cm a year along the Assam border), particularly in the summer months, so bring an umbrella.

ECOLOGY & ENVIRONMENT

By the early 20th century, population pressure was beginning to take its toll on the Himalayan regions, and the already limited resources were severely strained. While the density of population to land is much less than on the plains, the ratio between population and arable land is much higher, in some cases more than four times greater than down on the plains. To compound the problem, productivity of arable land is only a quarter of what it is on the plains, and with increasing population growth, ever more land is being sought for cultivation; plus wood consumption for domestic fuel is reaching dangerously high proportions. While the number of grazing animals has more than doubled in some instances since 1950, there is an ever-diminishing amount of grazing land available, and over-grazing has contributed to soil erosion.

Himalayan inhabitants, who previously depended almost solely on the bounty of the land for their requirements, have had to find alternative sources of income. This has resulted in a mass exodus of able-bodied men to the plains in search of employment, placing a greater burden on the women of the hills and disrupting traditional cultural lifestyles. An increase in tourism to the Himalaya has provided one means of securing an alternative form of living, but unrestricted and poorly managed tourism strategies have brought their own environmental and cultural problems (see Tourism later in this section). Poaching of the already besieged larger animals of the Himalayan regions is another means of supplementing an ever-diminishing living.

Deforestation

The Himalayan regions are acutely susceptible to environmental degradation. Precipitous slopes and torrential monsoon rains already place enormous pressure on the fragile ecosystem, and depletion of forest cover speedily accelerates this process.

Denudation of forests to clear land for cultivation, and timber extraction for commercial purposes have resulted in massive soil erosion, with the soil of the Himalaya being literally washed down onto the plains. Due to the vulnerability of the fragile hills ecosystem and the dependence of its inhabitants on the forests for fuel and fodder, a National Forest Policy now stipulates that at least 60% of forest cover should be preserved in the hills, as compared to around 30% on the plains. Recent satellite photographs have revealed that forest cover in the Himalayan regions is now below 11%.

The devastation caused by flooding in the Himalayan region and on the plains has increased exponentially over recent years. A current UN report estimates that over a 30 year period (1950-80) a staggering 40% of the Himalayan watershed was destroyed due to deforestation.

Hydroelectric Projects

A trend towards rapid industrialisation following the departure of the British in 1947 has resulted in the construction of enormous hydroelectricity projects to provide power for industry and irrigation on the plains. In 1963, the Bhakra Dam project, which harnessed the Sutlej River in present-day Himachal Pradesh, was completed, submerging some 371 villages and displacing 36,000 people. This project was followed by the construction of the Pong Dam on the Beas River, which displaced a further 150,000 people. Many of these people were promised land in the state of Rajasthan (the main beneficiary of the project), which wasn't fulfilled.

In Uttarakhand barrages have been built on the Yamuna, the Giri and the Ramaganga; barrages are also under construction on the Ganges and its tributary, the Alaknanda. Controversy is now rife regarding the Tehri Dam project on the Bhagirathi River in Uttarakhand, which was given the go-ahead in 1976. The 260m-high coffer dam is currently under construction. A leading environmentalist recently went on a 49 day hunger strike to protest at the dam's construction. This dam will result in the relocation of more than 85,000 people and the submerging of the ancient capital of Tehri.

The most worrying aspect of these schemes is the fact that the Himalaya is a seismically active area, possessing two major thrust faults, and a number of lesser faults. Periodically the Himalaya is shaken by major and minor earthquakes. In 1991, central Garhwal in Uttarakhand was devastated by a major earthquake: over 800 people were killed, thousands injured, and damages were estimated at US$130 million. The potential for a catastrophic disaster on a scale never before experienced is chilling, should any of these massive dam projects be damaged or destroyed in an earthquake.

The Chipko Movement

Not surprisingly, it is those who depend most intimately on the Himalaya's benevolence who have commenced the struggle to halt or reverse the environmental degradation. In the 1970s, the women of Uttarakhand embarked on a grassroots environmental movement to save the forests of the central Himalaya. Conforming to the Gandhian doctrine of ahimsa, or nonviolence, these Garhwali women founded the tree-hugging, or Chipko movement (chipko means 'to embrace').

These brave women, some of whom were prepared to die for their cause, literally clung to the trees that were marked for felling, held demonstrations against the auctioning of trees, or tied sacred threads around trees destined for the axe. The state government was finally compelled to issue an injunction suspending the felling of trees above altitudes of 1000m and on gradients of more than 30°.

The women of the Chipko movement recognised that the forests are neither the preserves of those who inhabit them, nor of those with the greatest economic ability to exploit them. The slogan of the movement was 'What do the forests bear? Soil, water and pure air. Soil, water and pure air are the basis of life'. There is a recognition that the forests belong to all people and all creatures, and that whatever threatens the forests threatens all life on earth.

Some analysts suggest that existing projects are not being managed or maintained as efficiently as they could be, with estimates of up to 30% underutilisation. They say that power output could be increased by upgrading these projects as opposed to building new plants.

The trend towards epic hydroelectric plants seems to be reversing, though. In Sikkim the state government recently put the brakes on the Rathong River project after environmentalists and local inhabitants fought against the proposed forced relocation of local tribal groups.

Other Threats to the Environment

Road building has further added to the already considerable strain on the environment. The British wasted no time building roads and laying railway tracks in the hills region. The trend was continued following Independence, motivated both by the intention to open the region to facilitate economic exploitation, and to provide access to the Himalaya's vast border areas for the deployment of troops. However, methods of road building have become more sophisticated – human labour has been supplemented with the introduction of explosives, which have weakened pre-existing fissures and resulted in a high increase in the numbers of landslides in the region. In August 1998 over 400 people were killed over 10 days in Uttarakhand when landslides wiped out 12 villages. A further 200 were killed near the Tibetan border on pilgrimage to holy Mt Kailash.

A further threat to the delicate ecological balance is the practice of monoculture (where one crop is planted repeatedly), generally to serve the economic interests of those on the plains. In addition to all of the above is the introduction of chemical fertilisers and pesticides.

Tourism

Contributing to the environmental and cultural degradation of the Himalaya is tourism. For centuries pilgrims have made the long arduous trek on foot to the holy sites of the mountains, causing little or no impact on the fragile ecosystem of the Himalayan zone. However, since roads have been blasted through the mountains, linking the holy sites with the plains, the situation has changed dramatically. The vast numbers of pilgrims to Badrinath are having diabolical impacts, not only ecologically, but also culturally. The *chattis* (simple wooden lodgings that once accommodated pilgrims en route to the shrines) have vanished, replaced by ugly tourist guesthouses and hotels.

The negative impacts of tourism are also felt in more secular destinations such as the hill stations of Mussoorie and Darjeeling. Up to 700,000 visitors converge on Mussoorie annually, and unrestricted development has left a legacy of ugly modern highrise hotels strung across the ridgetop and visible 34km distant from Dehra Dun. Critics also condemn the lack of foresight that saw the development of tourist amenities within the heart of Corbett Tiger Reserve, with no attempt to ensure that they blend into the environment. With tourism as a major revenue earner, it is difficult to envisage an end to the rapid development that is disfiguring the landscape and pushing resources to the limit.

The increase in trekking and mountaineering expeditions to the Himalaya following WWII has also taken its toll on this region. Some measures have been taken to preserve wilderness areas; for example, entry to the Nanda Devi Sanctuary is now prohibited.

In 1974, when Ladakh was officially opened to tourism, a group of seven Germans straggled into Leh and stayed at the only guesthouse. In about 20 years, over 100 guesthouses have been built in and near Leh, catering for the estimated 20,000 visitors each year. The political problems in Kashmir have also added considerably to the number of visitors who choose the safer areas of Ladakh and Zanskar. This continues to put enormous strains on the local environment and the infrastructure; there is now obvious pollution, ineffective sewerage, and unsafe drinking water. A similar situation can be found in McLeod Ganj.

Local environmental organisations have started to address these problems, however. The Ladakh Ecological Development Group (LEDeG) in Leh was set up in 1983 to foster appropriate eco-friendly technologies and sustainable development, and the Tibetan authorities in McLeod Ganj, Himachal Pradesh, have introduced a project to green the township. See those sections for details.

The almost 4000m-high Rohtang Pass, in Himachal Pradesh, is also suffering from the effects of pollution arising from the number of visitors to this region. The pass is littered with rubbish, which is carried by the high-velocity winds across the region, or finds its way into the Beas River, which has its source here. In 1998 the Himachal government banned the use of polythene bags in the state and anyone causing litter by throwing away plastic bags can now face a jail sentence of up to one month.

For more information on how to limit your impact in the Himalaya see the Responsible Tourism section in the Facts for the Visitor chapter.

FLORA & FAUNA
Flora
Himalayan flora is heavily influenced by the more ancient mountain flora of China. Over subsequent aeons, mutations, climatic changes and concomitant adaptation (and no doubt extinction in some cases), as well as

The dark forests of the temperate zone include deodars (*Cedrus deodara*).

glacial movement, has given rise to the present-day vegetational wealth of the Himalaya. It is interesting to note that glaciation had no impact on the lower reaches of the Himalaya, and the Himalayan foothills therefore remain repositories of flora that can be traced back beyond the Ice Age.

Western Himalaya The vegetation of the western and eastern Himalaya differs markedly. The lower humidity in the western zone means that the tree line is 1000m lower than in the east, and there is a higher representation of conifers.

Subtropical (200-1200m) The subtropical zone encompasses the region known as the Terai, which extends from Kashmir to Bhutan. Forests of the hardwood sal *(Shorea robusta)* are found at lower elevations. A rare type of palm *(Phoenix acaulis)*, two forms of ground orchid belonging to the genera *Zeuxine* and *Eulophia*, and swamp forests and grasslands (savanna) are also found in this zone. Other flora includes the Indian laburnum *(Cassia fistula)*, which bears vivid yellow flowers between April and June, the coral tree *(Erythrina suberosa)*, which bears scarlet flowers from March to May and the flame of the forest *(Butea monosperma)*, which bears distinctive orange flowers between February and May.

The easily identifiable hemp *(Cannabis sativa)* is often seen growing on the perimeters of cultivated land and road edges. Hemp has, of course, a myriad of uses other than the more obvious one, and is used in the making of rope and the weaving of cloth.

Temperate (1200-3500m) As you ascend above 1500m, the subtropical vegetation of the lower zones gives way to dark and dank forests of oak, birch, magnolia and laurel. Found between 1800 and 2400m are the **deodar** *(Cedrus deodara)* and blue pine *(Pinus wallichiana)*. Above 2400m is the spruce *(Picea smithiana)*, yew *(Taxus baccata)* and cypress *(Cupressus torulosa)*, and higher still, growing up to the tree line, is the Himalayan fir *(Abies spectabilis)*, found between 2850 and 3600m. The birch tree, known locally as *bhojpatra*, is particularly valued by many local communities, who have traditionally used its bark as paper.

Wildflowers include the fragrant white columbine *(Aquilegia fragrans)*, which grows profusely in Himachal Pradesh, and the wild strawberry *(Fragaria nubicola)*. The Himalayan mayapple *(Podophyllum hexandrum)*, found at high altitudes throughout the western Himalaya, has long been revered for its medicinal properties.

There are numerous species of rhododendron in this zone. Between March and May the hillsides are ablaze with the deep red flowers of the common tree **rhododendron**, or *Rhododendron arboreum*.

Alpine (3500m+)   As the snows begin to melt at the end of the long winter, the high altitude grazing grounds known as *bugyals*, and valleys, are carpeted with a multitude of wildflowers, which remain in bloom until early summer. With the onset of the monsoon, in July, a second and even more vibrant flowering occurs, which extends until the end of the monsoon, in late August or early September. Some of the varieties found at these higher elevations include anemones, forget-me-nots, dwarf irises, dwarf rhododendrons, primulas, delphiniums and ranunculus, among others. The beautiful but rare blue poppy *(Meconopsis aculeata)* flowers during the monsoon on the bugyals.

The best time to see rhododendrons blooming radiant red is between March and May.

Distributed throughout the Himalaya is the common *Primula denticulata*, with its distinctive tooth-edged leaves and pinkish or purplish blooms that grow in densely compacted heads. It can be found growing up to elevations of 4200m, and flowers between April and June.

Eastern Himalaya   The eastern Himalaya hosts an astonishing array of flora – over 4000 different species – some of which can be found in the western Himalaya, and some of which bear elements of Chinese and Malaysian influence. Sikkim alone supports ecosystems ranging from tropical to alpine. The region has over 30 species of rhododendron, including the *Rhododendron niveum* (the state tree of Sikkim) and more than 600 species of orchid.

Temperate rainforests are found between 1800 and 3500m, and include varieties of conifer (including India's only deciduous conifer, *Larix griffithiana*), magnolia, rhododendron, birch, maple and oak.

The subalpine zone extends from 3500 to 4500m, and supports varieties of rhododendron and ground flora such as primulas and anemones. Beyond the tree line and up to the snow line (5500m), tree species give way to low shrubs, lichens, mosses and alpine flowers such as the tiny *Rhododendron nivale*, edelweiss *(Leontopodium himalaynum)*, and varieties of primula, while the arid desertscapes found over 4500m support the hardy *androsace*.

Fauna

In the temperate regions of the eastern Himalaya, many animals bear distinct relationships with those of the countries extending to the east, such as Myanmar (Burma) and southern China, while others bear affinities with those that live in the moist, tropical regions of Asia, such as fruit bats and the oriental squirrel. This Oriental influence is negligible in the western Himalaya, where distinctive Indian species are found.

In the icy and desolate conditions that prevail in much of Ladakh, mammals have to survive in frequently freezing conditions, with scant vegetation and minimal rainfall. The largest mammal to be found in these icy areas is the yak (*Bos grunniens* or 'grunting ox'), braving out the elements at elevations of around 4200m to over 6000m and providing locals with everything from butter to shoes.

The brown bear *(Ursus arctos)*, found in the western Himalaya, may be seen above the tree line. It is distinguishable from its cousin the Himalayan black bear *(Selenarctos thibetanus)*, by its distinctive brown coat and heavier build. The black bear inhabits steep and densely forested hillsides. It may be found near the tree line in summer, but retreats well below the tree line in winter.

Below the tree line in the western Himalaya are various forms of deer, including the barking deer, or muntjac, and the sambar, the largest Indian deer with correspondingly imposing horns.

Monkeys include the common rhesus macaque, with its distinctive reddish fur on its loins and rump, the Assamese macaque, found in the Himalayan foothills extending eastwards from Mussoorie to Assam, and the common long-limbed black-faced langur, found throughout India. Arunachal Pradesh has communities of the monogamous Hoolock gibbon, India's only ape.

The lynx is found in the upper reaches of the Indus Valley and parts of Ladakh. Pallas' cat, with its distinctive low, broad head and low-set ears, about the size of your average domestic moggy, is found in Ladakh. Several varieties of civets, closely related to the cat family, are found throughout the Himalayan foothills.

Mammals found both in the lower reaches of the Himalaya and throughout the Indian peninsula include the Asiatic jackal, common red fox, Indian hare and Indian crested porcupine. Second to the marmot, the most commonly sighted animal in high altitude regions is the pika, a small mouse hare, which is the Himalaya's highest-dwelling mammal.

Sikkim alone has over 400 species of butterflies.

Goats & Antelopes The ibex is found in the western Himalaya above the tree line. The male stands about 1m, and has a great beard and a creamy, slightly brown-tinged coat in winter, which becomes darker brown in summer. In spring, ibex retreat below the snow line in search of fresh grass. Also belonging to the goat family is the Himalayan **tahr**, which is found across the Indian Himalaya at elevations of between 2500 and 4400m. The markhor is found below the snow line in Kashmir, though its absence of underwool restricts it from venturing to the icy regions farther north. Bucks stand to 1m and have a long flowing beard and mane, and enormous horns that bear distinct differences across this species, according to locality, from tight corkscrew forms to open spirals.

Other species include the bharal, or blue sheep, which shares characteristics of both sheep and goats. It is rarely found below 3660m in winter, and in summer, ascends as high as 4880m, its grey (not blue) coat making it almost indistinguishable from surrounding rocks and boulders. The Tibetan antelope, or chiru, is sometimes found in the northern and eastern regions of Ladakh.

Heavily built and majestic, tahrs have diminished in numbers recently.

The serow belongs to the goat-antelope family and can be found in both the eastern and western Himalaya. It is a thick-set animal whose coat comes in a variety of hues, from almost black, to red. It is usually found in temperate zones between 1850 and 3050m in heavily wooded gorges. Also belonging to this family is the smaller goral, with small, backward-tending horns. The grey goral is found in the western Himalaya, but the brown goral is found only in the eastern Himalaya and Assam.

Belonging to the same group is the heavy-set takin, found in limited numbers in the eastern Himalaya. It is found at temperate elevations and inhabits densely wooded regions.

The magnificent lammergier
has a wing span of 2.8m.

Birds The Himalaya is the home of a variety of endemic bird species, including broadbills, finfoots, honey guides and parrotbills. The chir pheasant and mountain quail, both belonging to the pheasant family, are found only in the Himalayan regions of India, as is the cardueline finch, which is found below the tree line in moist temperate forest conditions.

In the western Himalaya are 14 species that can be traced back *beyond* the period of extensive glaciation that occurred during the Pleistocene epoch. These include two species of bullfinch, the woodsnipe, Himalayan pied woodpecker, pied ground thrush, blackthroated jay and smoky leaf warbler.

Birds of prey include the enormous Himalayan golden eagle and the Himalayan bearded vulture, or **lammergier**, found at elevations above 1200m up to an extraordinary 7000m. The latter is notable for bearing aloft large bones, which are dropped mid-flight from heights of up to 50m, whereupon they are shattered on the rocks, exposing the marrow on which this bird feeds.

Various types of Himalayan pheasant, including the blood pheasant, an exotic bird with crimson-coloured blotches on its plumage and a crimson throat, are found in the eastern Himalaya. In the densely forested regions of the western Himalaya is found the Impeyan or Himalayan monal

pheasant, which is resplendent, in the males at least, with a beautifully coloured plumage of green, purple and blue.

Distributed across the lower regions of the Himalaya are various types of kaleej, also belonging to the Himalayan pheasant family, which feature a bright crimson head and a deep black plumage in the male, and russet-brown in the female. In the extreme north-eastern Himalaya is the eared pheasant, a large bird with a blue-grey plumage. In Sikkim, the peacock pheasant is found only at lower elevations in tropical jungle.

The red-billed blue magpie, found at lower elevations between Himachal Pradesh and farther east to eastern Sikkim, is frequently seen around hill stations. The tiny red-billed leiothrix has a distinctive yellow throat and breast, black wings trimmed with yellow and red and, as its name suggests, a bright red bill. It is often seen around tea plantations.

Migratory Birds Apart from its endemic species, the Himalaya also hosts a temporary population of some 300 transient species, which migrate from Central Asia to the Indian peninsula during the autumn and spring. For many years ornithologists doubted the ability of birds to cross over the top of the high Himalaya, theorising that birds penetrated the range through river valleys. However, it has now been discovered that not only large birds, but even some midsize to small species fly *over* the Himalaya on their annual migration. The return journey poses more difficult challenges, and many come to grief traversing the desolate and freezing glaciers of the upper realms of the Himalaya. These high altitude migrators include ducks, geese and cranes, most of whom arrive in the autumn. Even crows and finches have been observed above 7000m.

There are also many species that breed high up in the Himalaya, and descend to the foothills or the Indian peninsula in winter. Wall creepers generally don't venture far beyond the southern perimeters of the foothills, and the beautifully plumed grandala retreats only down to about 3000m in winter. Various types of flycatchers, thrush, woodcock and the blue chat migrate in winter to southern India. Some, such as the woodcock, fly virtually nonstop – a journey of some 2000km!

Endangered Species

Human encroachment is now taking its toll, in both direct and indirect ways, and the Himalaya now has the highest concentration of endangered mammals in India. The high rate of endemism makes protection of these species critical.

Poachers are the greatest threat to the larger wild inhabitants of the Himalaya. The record prices set for the pelts of some of these magnificent creatures in the world market due to ongoing demand has resulted in the hunting of many of the Himalaya's wild animals almost to the point of extinction.

Hunting of protected and/or endangered species for sport or meat continues unabated in the high Himalaya, and previously inaccessible regions are now within easy distance of roads. The border tensions between India and China have resulted in the dispatch of thousands of troops to these remote regions, and hunting is a popular recreational diversion from border patrol. The armed insurgencies in Kashmir have also taken their toll on wildlife populations. Local Buddhist populations live in relative harmony with wildlife as Buddhism prohibits the taking of any life.

Animals threatened due to illegal hunting include the markhor, ibex, tahr and rare hangul, or Kashmir stag, which has also suffered from human encroachment on its habitat. Populations of the hangul are estimated as low as 200 animals, down from an estimated 5000 in the 1920s. Populations of the urial, or shapu, which is found in Ladakh, the Tibetan antelope, or chiru, and rare Sikkim stag have all been decimated by military hunting. The heads of wild ass (kyang) are at risk of being more frequently seen adorning the space above mantelpieces than on the beast in question.

The musk deer is one of the most highly sought creatures in the Himalaya, with the lucrative trade in the musk gland, used in the preparation of perfume, affording a keen incentive for the slaying of this beast. Some measures have been taken to protect this creature, such as the establishment of the Kedarnath musk deer sanctuary in Uttarakhand. It is easily recognised by its external canines.

The beautiful red panda of Sikkim is highly sought after by illegal animal dealers. It is easily tamed, and sought by some keepers of private zoos around the world. This cute little nocturnal fellow spends its nights foraging for food and its days sleeping high up in the treetops. Its coat is a distinctive reddish chestnut, while its face is white, but has a reddish stripe on the forehead. Its tail is ringed with red bands.

Although the habitat of the beautiful snow leopard *(Panthera unica)* is vast, extending across the entire Himalaya Range and farther north into Tibet and Central Asia, it is rarely seen, as it inhabits one of the most desolate places on earth, some 3660 to 3965m above sea level. Only in the winter months, with the retreat of the mammals on which it preys to lower elevations, does the almost mythical snow leopard descend to elevations as low as 1850m. There are somewhere between 4000 and 7000 snow leopards left in the world, mainly in Siberia, Mongolia, Tibet, India and Afghanistan.

For the snow leopard and other animals, perhaps the only chance of survival may be breeding these animals in captivity. Unfortunately, success rates are very low (see the Fight for Survival boxed text in the Bangla Hills chapter), and even if successfully bred, there is no guarantee that these animals can be successfully returned to the wild.

Herds of wild Indian elephant can be seen at the Corbett National Park, as well as the Rajaji National Park. The low-lying savanna on the northern plains of Bangla (West Bengal) is one of the last homes of the Indian rhinoceros. The clouded leopard is found in the tropical east of Arunachal Pradesh.

The tiger is probably the region's most famous inhabitant. Current estimates figure that there are 52 tigers in the Namdapha Tiger Reserve in Arunachal Pradesh, 128 at Corbett Tiger Reserve and 31 at Buxa Tiger Reserve in Bangla (West Bengal). For more details see the Project Tiger boxed text in the Uttarakhand chapter.

Endangered species of birdlife include the western tragopan, a species of pheasant that is found in the western Himalaya and which is now a fully protected species. The Darjeeling zoo has announced plans to try to breed this bird in captivity. It's probably too late for the mountain quail, also a member of the pheasant family, which hasn't been spotted since the 1870s. It resides now only in a stuffed capacity in a few select museums in England and the USA. It was discovered in Uttarakhand.

The honey guide is another rare species of bird, notable for its ability to digest beeswax. Its curious name is derived from its usefulness in guiding animals and humans to honeycombs, flying before them and uttering distinctive calls, which lead honey seekers to the object of their search. After the honey has been extracted by these guests, the bird completes the meal, dining on the wax, remnants of honey and larvae.

Another rare visitor is the black-necked crane, which overwinters in the eastern Himalaya and the Changtang region of eastern Ladakh.

National Parks

National parks and wildlife sanctuaries are legion in the Indian Himalaya. Some, such as the Dachigam Wildlife Sanctuary in Kashmir, represent the last and only habitat of some of their inhabitants. Others, such as Corbett Tiger Reserve, have a well-developed infrastructure for visitors including a range of accommodation and safaris. Others were originally founded as game reserves, in the interests of hunters, not the protection of animals, and little has been done to enhance the preservation prospects of their inhabitants.

The establishment of wildlife reserves and sanctuaries has gone some way in stabilising animal numbers, but more reserves need to be created.

Buxa Tiger Reserve (Bangla) Accessible from either Jaldhapara or Shiliguri is the Buxa Tiger Reserve, covering 761 sq km. The reserve was recently adopted into Project Tiger, and forms part of the migration corridor for elephants between Bhutan and Assam. It is best visited from November to April.

Chitkul Sanctuary (Himachal Pradesh) In the remote Kinnaur district, this sanctuary encompasses an area of 140 sq km. Special permission is required to visit this sanctuary.

Corbett Tiger Reserve (Uttarakhand) The Corbett National Park and adjacent Sonanadi Wildlife Sanctuary are collectively known as the Corbett Tiger Reserve. Covering an area of 1318 sq km, it was established in 1936 as India's first national park. Corbett is most famous for its tigers, and boasts a population of one tiger per 5 sq km. Other mammals seen here include barking deer and sambar, and there is also abundant birdlife. The reserve has come under some criticism for permitting the construction of a hydroelectric project that submerged one-tenth of the park, severely disrupting the traditional migration route of herds of wild elephants. The tiger reserve is open 15 November to 15 June.

Dachigam Wildlife Sanctuary (Jammu & Kashmir) This sanctuary is in a very scenic valley with a large meandering river. The surrounding mountain slopes are possibly the last home of the rare Kashmir stag (hangul), as well as black and brown bears. There are also populations of musk deer. The instability in Kashmir in recent years has seriously endangered the wildlife of Dachigam.

The Yeti

A discussion of the animal life of the Himalaya would be incomplete without reference to its most enigmatic and mysterious inhabitant – the Yeti. *Yeti* is a Sherpa word, but yeti-like sightings range the entire Himalaya, from the Barmanu (Big Hairy One) in Pakistan's Hindukush to the Migoi (Strong Man) of Bhutan. Who or what is the yeti? Various theories have been proposed about the Himalaya's most infamous inhabitant. It has been suggested that the yeti, or Abominable Snowman, is a link between homosapiens and our primate ancestors. Sceptics have suggested it's a case of mistaken identity – the yeti is nothing more than an upright Himalayan Kodiak bear.

So how do you identify a yeti? Completely covered with hair, the yeti reputedly has feet spanning some 30cm long and 15cm wide, and is almost 2.5m tall. It is a malevolent creature possessing supernatural powers and is known for its blood-curdling call, although yetis have been known to provide sustenance to meditating hermits.

A little known fact about the yeti is its penchant for chocolate. According to Sonam Wangyal, a respected mountaineer and climber of Mt Everest, he and his climbing team witnessed a gigantic hairy creature of humanoid appearance stalking across the snow near their camp. After the creature had disappeared from sight, the stunned witnesses went to the spot where it had last been spotted. While no evidence of the creature remained (footprints had been concealed beneath a heavy snowfall), on their return to the camp site, they discovered to their amazement the inexplicable absence of a large box of chocolates! While this event took place in the Nanda Devi Sanctuary of Garhwal, most of the sightings of creatures conforming to yeti dimensions have been almost wholly restricted to the eastern Himalaya. Several (largely discredited) yeti scalps are stored in Tibetan monasteries in Nepal.

While it is only comparatively recently that the yeti has aroused the imagination of those of the west, finding its way into the distinguished pages of Britain's *Times* newspaper in 1931, the Tibetan Buddhist saint and poet, Milarepa, who lived in the 11th and 12th centuries, recounts in one of the songs of his *Mgur Abum* (the *Hundred Thousand Songs of Milarepa*) of a strange Himalayan-dwelling creature, which is referred to as *mitre*.

Can the legend of the yeti be easily discounted? The Himalaya encompasses some of the most desolate and inaccessible environs on the face of the earth. Of those creatures that science has, in its inimitable way, tracked down and recorded, there are vast gaps in our knowledge of their habits and habitats. It is not outside the realms of possibility that there are not just yetis, but other creatures living in remote and inaccessible regions of the Himalaya of which we have no knowledge.

While the yeti might easily be dismissed as simply the stuff of legend and lore, actual photographs of enormous footprints taken in 1951 by the respected and renowned mountaineer Eric Shipton will give sceptics food for thought. Photographs of unidentifiable large footprints and sightings of a large hairy beast by members of a mountaineering expedition to Annapurna in Nepal have further compounded the mystery.

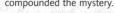

Fambonglho Wildlife Sanctuary (Sikkim) This sanctuary lies only 25km from Gangtok, and it is possible to visit it with a special permit issued by the District Forestry Officer (☎ 03592-23191) in Gangtok. The Himalayan black bear and red panda are found here, together with a wide variety of other animal and bird species. The sanctuary is open October to April.

Great Himalayan National Park (Himachal Pradesh) This park encompasses some 1700 sq km to the south-east of Kullu, and is known for its abundant birdlife. It also has a good representative population of animals found across the western Himalaya, including rare musk deer, Cheer pheasant and western tragopan. The best time to visit is between April and June, and September and October, outside the monsoon season.

Jaldhapara Wildlife Sanctuary (Bangla) Encompassing 116 sq km in Jalpaiguri district, 135km from Shiliguri, this sanctuary is home to around 35 endangered Indian rhinoceros *(Rhinoceros unicornis)*. It is possible to take elephant safaris from Hollong, within the sanctuary. The sanctuary is open 15 September to 15 June, but the best animal sightings are between March and April.

Kalatope Wildlife Sanctuary (Himachal Pradesh) This small sanctuary is in the Chamba Valley, only 8.5km from Dalhousie. It is home to a variety of species including the black bear and barking deer (muntjac), as well as an abundant variety of birdlife. The best time to visit is between May and June, and September and November.

Kanchenjunga National Park (Sikkim) Entrance into the heart of this magnificent alpine wilderness is prohibited to visitors, although treks along the Dzongri Trail from Yuksom enter the southern periphery. The park is bordered on the north by the Zemu Glacier; to the west rears the massive bulk of Kanchenjunga and the Nepal Peak. The southern boundary is formed by the Chhurong and Bokto rivers. Fauna found in the park include the beautiful snow leopard, the muntjac, or barking deer, the Himalayan black bear, and the red panda, among other species. Much of this pristine wilderness remains unexplored, and harbours a profuse variety of flora and bird species.

Kanji Game Reserve & Hemis High Altitude National Park (Ladakh & Zanskar) The Kanji Game Reserve is not far from Kargil; the Hemis National Park is accessible from Hemis. These are inhabited by some of the Himalaya's most rare and endangered species, such as the ibex, argali sheep and nine recorded snow leopards. These parks and others in this region are generally for the protection of animals and not for the pleasure of humans. There are proposals to add the Kharnak Valley to the park.

Kedarnath Sanctuary (Uttarakhand) Kedarnath Sanctuary covers an area of 957 sq km, and contains populations of musk deer, tahr, serow and leopard. It is in Chamoli district, in Garhwal.

Namdapha Tiger Reserve (Arunachal Pradesh) This is a remote and pristine park on the borders of Myanmar (Burma), which has been proposed as a biosphere reserve. Animals include over 150 wild elephants, gibbons, 43 tigers, 40 clouded leopards and red pandas. Many species of hitherto unknown fish, reptiles and butterflies have been found here.

Nanda Devi National Park (Uttarakhand) This beautiful park covers an area of 630 sq km in Chamoli district, in Garhwal, in the upper watershed of the Alaknanda River. It has been closed to visitors since 1982 due to the detrimental environmental impact of trekking and mountaineering expeditions. The sanctuary is inhabited by serow, musk deer, bharal and goral and has been proposed as a biosphere reserve.

Pin Valley National Park (Himachal Pradesh) This 675 sq km high altitude park in Spiti abuts the Great Himalayan National Park and Rupi Bahaba Sanctuary and forms one of the most important sanctuaries for snow leopard, bharal and ibex, who rut here in December and January. Contact the Assistant Commissioner for Forestry (Wildlife) in Kaza for details on visiting.

Rajaji National Park (Uttarakhand) Encompassing 820 sq km and easily accessible from Haridwar or Rishikesh, this park is known for its herds of wild elephants. Other mammals include the occasional tiger, as well as sloth bears, sambar, chital, barking deer and jungle fowl. The sanctuary is open 15 November to 15 June.

Valley of Flowers (Uttarakhand) The Valley of Flowers, known as the 'garden on top of the world' was designated as a 90 sq km national park in 1981. It is accessible from Govind Ghat, a small village on the main Joshimath to Badrinath road, and its profuse wildflowers are best seen during the monsoon, from July to early September, particularly between mid-July and mid-August.

Conservation Societies

Conservation societies worth contacting include:

Himalayan Environment Trust (☎ 011-621 5635, fax 686 2374), Legend Inn, E-4 East of

Kailash, New Delhi. This nonprofit trust was founded in 1988 and aims to raise public awareness about the increasing ecological threat to the Himalaya and its human and animal inhabitants, among other activities. It has published two volumes of its official journal, *The Himalayas: Ecology & Environment*, which seeks to focus world attention on the degradation of the Himalaya.

International Snow Leopard Trust (☎ 206-632 2421, fax 632 3967, email islt@serv.net), 4649 Sunnyside Ave N, Suite 325, Seattle, WA 98103, USA. Funds raised by the trust are used to help developing countries trying to establish parks for snow leopards, or help finance research and the education of the inhabitants of the Himalayan regions regarding conservation. Web site www.serv.net/islt/home2.html.

Wildlife Preservation Society of India, 7 Astley Hall, Dehra Dun, Garhwal, Uttar Pradesh. The society was founded in the 1970s to promote conservation awareness. Articles on conservation issues pertaining to Indian wildlife are published in its journal *Cheetal*.

Wildlife Protection Society of India (☎ 011-621 3864, fax 336 8729, email wpsi@nde.vsnl.net.in), Thapur House, 124 Janpath, New Delhi. Set up to prevent illegal trafficking in wildlife, in particular the tiger and musk deer.

World Wide Fund for Nature (WWF) (☎ 011-469 3744, fax 462 6837), 172-B Lodi Rd, PO Box 3058, New Delhi 110 003. There are also offices in Gangtok and Itanagar. Web site www.panda.org.

GOVERNMENT & POLITICS

India has a parliamentary system of government, with an upper house (the Rajya Sabha, or Council of States) and a lower house (the Lok Sabha, or House of the People). There are also state governments and there is a strict division between the activities handled by the states and by the national government. The police force, education, agriculture and industry are reserved for the state governments. Certain other areas are jointly administered by the two levels of government.

In the May 1996 national elections, the Congress (I) Party, which has ruled India for all but four years since Independence in 1947, lost its majority. Several coalition governments tottered before the Hindu nationalist Bharatiya Janata Party (BJP) and

its hastily assembled 13 political allies formed another coalition government after elections in March 1998. Votes from Ladakh and Manali were only counted two months after the result was announced due to bad weather in these remote districts.

The coalition BJP-led government of Atal Biharai Vajpayee again crumbled in 1999 when several key supporters withdrew their support. Shortly after, Sonia Gandhi, the Italian-born wife of assassinated Rajiv Gandhi, resigned her post as President of the Congress Party after a rebellion in her own party queried her 'Indianness' but she later resumed the post.

Ladakh & Zanskar

As a Buddhist enclave in a Muslim state in a Hindu country, Ladakhis effectively form a minority within a minority in India and resentments against discrimination have long simmered. Tensions first found expression in violent uprisings in 1969 and relations between the Buddhist and Muslim communities became particularly strained in 1989 when the majority Buddhists imposed a social boycott on the Muslims. In 1995, the Leh Autonomous Hill Development Council was formed according to the terms of a presidential order and tensions between the Buddhist and Muslim communities have eased, with members from both the Ladakh Buddhist Association and the Ladakh Muslim Association enjoying dual control. See the Buddhists, Muslims & Christians boxed text in the Ladakh & Zanskar chapter for more details.

There are also tenions in Zanskar, a Buddhist subdistrict under the administration of Muslim Kargil. In mid-1995, there was a local political protest in Zanskar, and in order to draw attention to their cause, foreign trekkers were discouraged from trekking in the region. Trekkers are now once again encouraged in the region but religious tensions remain hidden under the surface.

Kashmir

For information on the political troubles see The Kashmir Problem boxed text, later.

In the early 1990s at least 34 separate militant groups (or freedom fighters, depending on which side of the cease-fire line you stand) were operating in Kashmir, though the power of most had waned by the late 1990s. Some groups seek an independent Muslim republic of Kashmir, others a secular independent republic, others incorporation into Pakistan, and still others autonomy within India. Since 1996 even pro-India militia have appeared, reportedly funded by the Indian security services. Political violence occurs not only between rebels and the Indian authorities but also between the rebel groups themselves. The oldest of these groups is the Jammu & Kashmir Liberation Front (JKLF), which was founded in 1964. The JKLF has renounced violence and is now a political organisation based in Srinagar. The main groups today are the Lashkar-e-Toyeba, Harkat-al-Ansar and Hizb-ul-Mujahadeen. Many groups are

The Kashmir Problem

India and Pakistan's bitter dispute over the beautiful Vale of Kashmir has proved itself to be one of the world's most intractable problems. While negotiations in South Africa, northern Ireland and the Middle East show glimmers of light at the end of the tunnel, the tensions in Kashmir have stubbornly endured half a century and two major wars. Some doomsday analysts pinpoint the dispute as the most likely flash point for the world's first nuclear war. See the Warning boxed text in the Jammu & Kashmir chapter for an update.

Historical Background

Partition was never applied to India's 565 princely states and although most sided naturally with either Muslim Pakistan or Hindu India, at the time of Independence there were still three hold-outs. One was Kashmir, a predominantly Muslim state ruled by a Hindu maharaja, Hari Singh. In October 1947, while the maharaja was still toying with the idea of independence, a rag-tag Pathan (Pakistani) army crossed the border, intent on annexing Kashmir. The panicking maharaja appealed for Indian help, thus triggering the first India-Pakistan war.

The UN was eventually persuaded to step in and prise the two sides apart. In 1965 a second war was fought with Pakistan and to this day, India and Pakistan are divided in this region by a demarcation line known as the Line of Actual Control, yet neither side agrees that this constitutes the official border. Pakistan controls the western region known as the Northern Areas and Azad (Free) Jammu & Kashmir, which amounts to around 35%. India holds the bulk of Kashmir (65%) and China holds another chunk of disputed land equivalent to 20% of Kashmir in the disputed Aksai Chin, which it seized after a brief war with India in 1962.

The 1990s

The Kashmir issue again moved onto centre stage in 1989 when the Home Minister's daughter was kidnapped and armed insurgency erupted in Indian-held Kashmir. In 1990 the Indian army opened fire on a number of peaceful Kashmiri demonstrations. Later that year the J&K government was dissolved and the state was placed under direct Presidential rule from Delhi. Some 400,000 Indian troops were drafted into the region, the bulk of which remain there to this day.

India regularly accuses Pakistan of waging a low-cost proxy war in Kashmir. Islamabad has almost certainly been involved in encouraging, funding and supplying arms to the militants, though it hotly denies this. Afghan mujahadeen fighters have also crossed the border to bolster the Islamic *jihad* (holy war). Gross human rights violations by the Indian army (which represented by the All Party Hurriyat Conference, an umbrella organisation.

State elections in September 1996 were won by the National Conference Party (NCF – a pro-India, regional party), under the leadership of Farooq Abdullah, the son of the popular former chief minister Sheikh Abdullah. Kashmir has its own government, which is afforded special status in India and has control over most affairs except defence and foreign affairs. Political violence has abated to some degree in the wake of the election.

Himachal Pradesh

Himachal Pradesh came into being as a separate hills province only eight months after Independence. In 1956 the region was declared a Union Territory, and in 1966 the remote districts of Lahaul & Spiti, previously part of the Punjab, were incorporated into the new state of Himachal Pradesh. In 1996,

---

The Kashmir Problem

include torture and judicial killings in custody) have only served to further militarise the region.

In the decade since the outbreak of hostilities somewhere between 30,000 and 50,000 civilians have been killed, most caught in the crossfire. Shelling continues almost daily over the Line of Actual Control, which in places is less than 100m wide.

Foreign tourism in the region came to an abrupt halt in 1995 when five foreign tourists were kidnapped by militants. One was beheaded and the others are still missing, presumed dead. In 1996 a family of Indian tourists were murdered on their Dal Lake houseboat and in 1998 a French tourist was shot in Srinagar. Throughout the 1990s Srinagar has practically been a war zone, regularly paralysed by curfews, bomb blasts and demonstrations. Travel to the region is still inadvisable.

More recently, domestic violence has shifted away from the urban areas of the Kashmir Valley to southern Kashmir, upper Jammu and even the borders with Himachal Pradesh. Massacres of Kashmiri Hindus, known as Pundits, have escalated and in 1998 security forces even spread their sweeps into the Pir Panjal of Himachal Pradesh as far as Chamba. One thousand militants were killed in Kashmir in 1998 and there were over 300 kidnappings. Recently the struggle even reached cyberspace, when Muslim hackers hijacked the Indian army Web site on Kashmir and filled it with separatist slogans and four-letter words!

In June 1999 tensions were raised to a new high when several hundred Pakistani-inspired mujahadeen took advantage of early thaws to seize Tiger Hill, several kilometres inside Indian held territory, just above the Srinagar-Leh Hwy between Dras and Kargil. At the time of writing fighting was continuing in the most serious escalation of violence in 20 years in an attempt to dislodge the rebels, and most locals had been evacuated to neighbouring areas. Dras and large areas of Kargil were evacuated during the emergency and the Srinagar-Leh Hwy was closed. Check developments carefully before heading to Kargil.

Today the two countries remain as bitterly entrenched as ever. Pakistan demands international mediation and a plebiscite of Kashmir's eight million inhabitants (as promised by India in the 1950s) – but without the option of independence, while India insists on a bilateral solution, while maintaining that Kashmir is an inalienable part of India. The fratricidal dispute dominates almost every aspect of the two countries' dealings and is utterly ruinous to both economies. Tragically, few analysts expect the Kashmir problem to be solved within a generation.

For more information on the dangers and effects on tourism in the region see the Jammu & Kashmir chapter.

the Congress party was returned to power headed by Chief Minister Virbhadra Singh but in 1998 the state government fell to the Bharatiya Janata Party (BJP).

The massacres of 35 Hindu labourers in the Chamba district in August 1998 has led to fears that the violence in Kashmir might spill over in the remoter valleys of Himachal Pradesh.

Uttarakhand, Uttar Pradesh or Uttaranchal?

Many of the inhabitants of the hills regions of the Indian Himalaya feel isolated from mainstream central government politics and removed from the decision-making processes of the plains. Hills inhabitants are poorly represented in the corridors of power; the eight districts that comprise Uttarakhand, for example, have only 19 elected members in the Vidhan Sabha (Legislative Assembly), as compared to 14 members from the single district of Gorakhpur, on the Uttar Pradesh plains, although Uttarakhand's population is over five times greater.

In the early 1990s, the agitation for separate statehood was revived. Separatists cite the geographical, cultural and traditional distinctions of the hills as compared to the plains, and propose a separate state named Uttaranchal, comprising the two Uttarakhand districts of Garhwal and Kumaon. In 1998 a bill was passed proposing the creation of the new state, though several obstacles lie in its way.

One major sticking point is the district of Udham Singh Nagar. The wealthy district is comprised largely of Punjabi immigrants who fear that their large farms will be broken up by the new state and who have lobbied the Akali Dal party (a coalition partner of the ruling BJP) to oppose the bill. The ruling BJP itself is in favour of the new state (as it will almost certainly win the elections there) but it is still to be seen whether it has the power to push through the bill. It takes a two thirds majority in the Lok Sabha to create a state and at the time of research the motion had been frozen, even though the political Rubicon had been crossed. When the new 51,000 sq km state is eventually carved out from Uttar Pradesh it is expected that the capital will be Nainital, though some are pushing for Dehra Dun.

Bangla (West Bengal) Hills

Another simmering separatist movement centres around the Nepali Gurkhas of Darjeeling. In 1988, the Darjeeling Gorkha Hill Council was established in the hope that it would offer a solution to the widespread discontent of the majority Nepali-speaking community whose ancestors were brought to the district in the 1840s to clear land and work as labourers on the tea gardens. Friction was caused by the central and state government policy of only employing Bangali-speaking people for government positions, and this perceived discrimination resulted in widespread riots, the crippling of the administration and the loss of hundreds of lives. The Gurkhas were led by the Gurkha National Liberation Front (GNLF), with Subhash Ghising at the helm, who demanded a separate state to be known as Gurkhaland.

In December 1988, the GNLF gained 26 of the 28 seats in the hill council, with Ghising retaining the leadership as the chairperson of the council. Separate statehood aspirations were relinquished in return for greater autonomy for the Darjeeling district, which remains part of Bangla (West Bengal).

However, in mid-1995, and then again in 1998, widespread dissatisfaction with the council and its leader, Ghising, and accusations of financial mismanagement and even misappropriation of funds manifested in *bhands* (strikes) and demonstrations across the district, led by the revived Akhil Bharatiya Gorkha League (ABGL). Calls for statehood and even secession from India, still resound around the hills of Bangla.

Sikkim

The state of Sikkim, annexed by the Indian Union in 1975, is enjoying unprecedented economic prosperity and stability. Prior to its merger with India, Sikkim was in economic decline due to the closure of trade routes with Tibet.

Central government assistance in the form of tax concessions has enabled the growth of flourishing industries, and Sikkim proudly boasts new roads, bridges and (more controversially) hydroelectric plants. It has not, however, all been smooth sailing for India's 22nd state. Corruption charges are currently pending against former chief minister Nar Bahadur Bhandari, who remained at the helm almost continuously from 1979 when his Sikkim Sangram Parishad (SSP) party came to power, until early 1994, when a vote of no confidence was passed, and he was ousted. The Sikkim Democratic Front currently leads the state government and has earned the reputation as the most environmentally conscious government in India.

Arunachal Pradesh

Arunachal Pradesh was known as the North East Frontier Agency from 1954 to 1971, when it was named the union territory of Arunachal Pradesh. It became a state in 1987.

The remote region has so far been spared the separatist insurgencies that so dominate politics in the other north-eastern states. In 1999 the Chief Minister Gegong Apang was brought down by a rebellion in his Arunachal Congress party, after having served for 19 years, sparking fears that the state may be in for a period of political uncertainty. There are muted demands for a separate state among the far eastern districts.

ECONOMY

Despite the vagaries of the climate, the steep terrain, poor irrigation and the limited area available for cultivation, agriculture is still the mainstay of the Himalayan economy. In Himachal Pradesh over 90% of the working population is engaged in agriculture, though only about 10% of the land is cultivable. Cereals such as rice, wheat and maize are generally grown to meet subsistence requirements. Vegetables form important cash crops. In contrast to other regions in India, in the Himalayan region, most of those people engaged in agriculture are owner-cultivators. With the reduction in the size of land holdings, however, and the decreasing productivity of land due to soil erosion, men in many parts of the Himalaya have been increasingly compelled to seek employment on the plains, giving rise to a mail-order economy.

In 1975, the cultivation of hops was introduced into Lahaul on an experimental basis, and Lahaul is now the only area in which hops are grown in India. Other major bread earners of the Lahaul Valley are peas and potatoes, which line the roads when harvested in late October. The Dehra Dun district in Uttarakhand is renowned for its high-quality basmati rice. Saffron production is a major industry in Kashmir.

The Himalaya is also an important fruit-growing region. Apples are the most important fruit grown in Kullu, Kinnaur and Kashmir and this agricultural sector has grown considerably over recent years. In 1950-51, orchards in Himachal Pradesh covered an area of only 400 hectares. By 1981-82, that area had expanded to some 91,350 hectares. Other fruits grown here include apricots, peaches plums, lemons and oranges. Edible mushrooms are cultivated in Himachal Pradesh.

In the Darjeeling hills, tea cultivation forms the most important economic activity, with over 40,000 people employed on its 78 tea gardens, which produce almost a quarter of India's tea. Cardamom and oranges are the two main cash crops in Sikkim. Local agriculture here is often not sufficient to supply food requirements, and some staples, such as rice, are now imported from the plains.

In Kalimpong, an important economic activity is the cultivation of flowers, particularly orchids and gladioli; the orchards are almost exclusively owned by one family. Cut flowers are supplied to both the domestic and international markets. Revenue derived from forest extraction is another big earner, representing about one-third of the Himachal Pradesh state economy.

Animal husbandry is an important occupation in the Himalaya. The Gujar, Bakrawala and Gaddi tribes of the western

Himalaya are traditionally semipastoralist seminomadic herders of sheep, goats and buffalo, as are herders in Ladakh.

Prior to the closing of the borders between India and Tibet, trans-border trade formed a large component of economic activity in Sikkim, Kinnaur and Ladakh. Trade entrepots like Leh based their wealth entirely on trade, producing nothing itself. With the closure of the border, herds have been seriously depleted, as communities relied heavily on the grazing grounds in Tibet.

Cottage industries thrive throughout the Himalayan region. A network of cooperative stores in the major cities of India ensure a ready domestic market for many of the crafts and textiles of the Himalaya. Kashmir has a very old silk growing and weaving industry and shawl production is a major employer in the Kullu Valley.

Tourism is also a major money earner with large numbers of people deriving income from the associated industries of accommodation, food, guiding, porterage and entertainment. In Darjeeling, over half of the population is dependent on tourism. The disappearance of tourism in Kashmir has badly affected local entrepreneurs who have relocated en masse to set up shops and agencies in Ladakh, Delhi and Manali, often causing frustration among local communities.

The relative isolation and inaccessibility of the region has been seen as a barrier to effective exploitation of its vast resources. Rather than taking advantage of this perceived geographical hindrance to promote decentralised development, the focus of development has been on making the region more readily accessible to the plains. This priority is the predominant reason for the construction of roads in this region, mostly maintained by tar-soaked bands of migrant workers from Bihar. With the merger of Sikkim with India in 1975, extensive industrialisation has taken place, facilitated by generous central government subsidies in the form of tax concessions. Industrial development elsewhere has been minimal.

Since Independence, the government, in a massive drive for modernisation and industrialisation, has increasingly turned towards the Himalaya to exploit its hydroelectricity potential. See the Ecology & Environment section earlier for more information.

POPULATION

The Indian Himalaya supports a population of some 25 million people, most of whom live in the foothills. India's national population in 1999 was estimated at 984 million. With a national growth rate of around 1.7% (an additional 1.7 million souls per month!) the population is expected to exceed one billion and then streak past China in the early decades of the 21st century to become the world's most populous nation. The next scheduled nationwide census is due to be held over three weeks in February 2001, when two million bureaucrats will visit over 200 million households.

Population estimates for 2000 are:

state	population (2000 estimate)	growth rate %
J&K	9.67 million	2.54
HP	6.13 million	1.89
Uttarakhand	6.64 million	2.27
Sikkim	507,000	2.51
Bangla Hills	1.58 million	2.21
AP	1.14 million	3.14
Nationwide	984 million	1.70

Birth control is a perennial matter for concern in India. National campaigns gained notoriety in the 1970s when sterilisation squads roamed the countryside. Financial incentives are now given to men who have a vasectomy and there is widespread media promotion of the two child family. This has had a marginal effect in the hills, where children are largely seen as the key to financial security in old age.

The Himalaya are some of the least densely populated areas in India. Arunachal Pradesh is the least densely populated state with 10 people per sq km (compared to Bangla at 767 per sq km) and remote areas like Spiti are even emptier with a density of six people per sq km.

continued on page 49

PEOPLES OF THE HIMALAYA

There is evidence to suggest that the lower Himalayan region may have supported one of the earliest human habitations, dating from the middle Pleistocene period. The Himalaya later formed an ethnic bridge between southern and Central Asia, with entire population groups such as Tibetan Kirata and Aryan Khasa tribes crossing the many passes of the high Himalaya. This movement is reflected in the region's ethnic diversity. Traces of paleo-Mongoloid, Mongoloid, Mediterranean, Alpine and Nordic strains are all represented across the diverse human panorama, which encompasses three main ethnic groupings, Mongoloids, Negroids and Aryans. The eastern Himalaya has been influenced more by the neighbouring Mongoloid peoples of China, eastern Tibet and Burma, while the west has felt a much stronger Central Asian influence. India's caste system has, almost incidentally, prevented much racial blending.

The majority of the inhabitants of the Indian Himalaya dwell at elevations of between 1000 and 2500m. In the high altitude zone, there are very few settlements, with most of the inhabitants, who are generally of Mongoloid origin, engaged in a semipastoralist/seminomadic lifestyle.

Kashmiris & the People of Jammu

In the Kashmir Valley, the people are mainly Muslim and have a distinctly Central Asian appearance and Persian-influenced culture. The people of the Jammu region are predominantly Hindu and of Dogra origin. The **Bakrawalas** are goat herders, who reside during winter in the environs of Jammu, and from late April or early May proceed with their flocks to the high valleys in search of grazing grounds. The **Shi'ah Muslims** of Kargil and the Kashmir Valley are both owner-cultivators and waged agricultural labourers.

Ladakhis

Ladakh's diverse ethnic composition comprises four main groups. The **Mons**, who profess Buddhism, migrated from northern India. The **Baltis**, a predominantly Muslim people, settled in and around Kargil from somewhere in Central Asia. The **Dards** settled near Kargil, where they converted to Islam, and also in the Dha-Hanu region, where they are also known as Brokpas and remain mainly Buddhist. The largest ethnic group are the **Tibetans** (see also later), who migrated to Ladakh over the centuries. Other groups professing Buddhism include the **Bedas**, some of whom may also be Muslims, and the **Garas**.

The Mons and Bedas are traditionally musicians, while the Garas fulfil the role of blacksmiths in Ladakhi society. The Muslim Baltis and **Argons** are owner-cultivators, and the **Khampas**, who graze their yaks and goats on the high Ladakhi plains during the summer, are nomadic people. The wildernesses around Pangong Tso, Tso Moriri and on the high plateau

Vegetable seller, Manali.
Photo: Patrick Horton

CHRISTOPHER WOOD

sections of the Leh-Manali road are inhabited by these nomads, grazing their herds of yak, sheep and goats across the sparse pastures.

Ladakhi women wear woollen dresses called *nambus* and *phumets*, which are covered with silk or brocade by more affluent women. For more formal and festive occasions, they may wear a *perak*, a squarish hat made from lambskin and studded with turquoise jewellery. Men wear thick robes, often of red and maroon shades, called *gonchas*, which are tied at the waist with a *skerag*, or rope. Beneath the robe are worn coarse woollen leggings known as *kangphyings*. Worn by both sexes, but only formally, are woollen shoes called *papu*, which are made of brightly coloured yak hair and curled at the front.

Tibetans

Many of the peoples of the Himalaya have strong ethnic and cultural links with the Tibetan plateau. Some Tibetan wool traders and herders settled over the years in border areas such as Ladakh and Kalimpong. In 1951 China invaded (or as they say 'liberated') Tibet and in 1959 the Dalai Lama fled Lhasa, fearing for his life. In his wake 80,000 Tibetans came streaming over the passes.

Today there are over 100,000 Tibetan exiles in India, with 21,000 in Himachal Pradesh, 9000 in Uttar Pradesh, 14,000 in the Bangla (West Bengal) hills and Sikkim, 8000 in the North-East and 5600 in Ladakh. The vast majority are stateless and hold only Indian registration papers (but no passport).

Between 2000 and 3000 'pilgrim refugees' continue to brave 6000m passes and rapacious border guards each year to reach India or Nepal. The trek can take up to 25 days, normally at night to avoid Chinese border guards. Few refugees carry any supplies save for canvas shoes and all the dried yak meat and *tsampa* (barley flour) they can carry. Some flee political persecution, while others send their children to

Left: Festival time in Ladakh – a time when traditional dress is usually worn.

ensure a good education grounded in Tibetan and English. Refugees who do make it to Mustang, Namache Bazaar or Kathmandu (all in Nepal) are interviewed by the UN High Commission for Refugees (UNHCR) and then transferred to India. The Dalai Lama meets every new arrival personally, though most are urged to return to Tibet.

About half of India's resident Tibetan exiles are engaged in agriculture, though there is an unemployment rate of around 20%. Early refugees were often sent to work in road-building gangs and many succumbed to the new tropical diseases of the subcontinent. Handicraft production is an important employer today, with carpet weaving one of the most successful enterprises. Many Tibetans sell sweaters in the hill stations and plains during the winter. To date over 117 monasteries have been established in exile.

CRAIG PERSHOUSE

Right: Novice monk, one of the 120,000 Tibetans in exile.

Gujars

Originally from Gujarat, Gujars live in Jammu & Kashmir, Himachal Pradesh and some parts of Uttarakhand. What forced them to leave their homeland on the plains is not known, nor has the precise period of their permanent migration to the north been established. The Gujars converted to Islam from Hinduism during the reign of the emperor Aurangzeb. The initial migration originally brought the Gujars to Kashmir, but the paucity of grazing areas compelled some of them to migrate eastwards into the area now encompassed within the boundary of Himachal Pradesh, and there is a sizable community of Gujars in the Chamba district of this state. The Gujars traditionally reared buffaloes.

The Gujars are polygamous, with men sometimes taking more than one wife. During the summer they push their herds to high alpine pastures, covering distances of up to 20km each day along traditional trails, or, more recently, along roads, and camping en route. Temporary dwellings known as *deras* provide shelter on the grazing grounds, and these are either destroyed or abandoned when the Gujars complete the next stage of the migration.

Gaddis

The traditional home of the Gaddis is the village of Brahmaur, the ancient capital of the princely state of Chamba, in the upper Ravi Valley, although there are substantial populations around Dharamsala in the Kangra Valley. The Gaddis are Hindus, and are traditionally Shaivites (worshippers of the god Shiva).

In addition to their pastoralist activities, the Gaddis are also agriculturalists. During the annual summer migration the Gaddis generally sleep exposed to the elements among their flocks for warmth. A pillow is afforded by the multipurpose *dora*, a long length of black woollen rope traditionally worn around the waist by all Gaddis, including children. It also serves to tether sheep or goats together, or to secure items to the body. Essential items such as implements and grain supplies are carried, including the *hookah*, or tobacco water pipe, and a *lathi*, or wooden staff.

Gaddi men wear a *chola*, a loose grey or white coat with large pockets at the front in which are carried newborn lambs and kids, domestic utensils and foodstuffs. Beneath the chola they wear woollen trousers that are baggy to the knees, and tight at the shins and ankles. Gaddi women wear a cotton dress called a *luanchari*, which has a voluminous ankle-length cotton skirt, and a headdress known as a *chadru*.

Gaddis are generally monogamous. Following preparatory ceremonies in the village of the groom, the marriage party retires to the village of the bride, where the marriage ceremony is performed. The bride then returns to live in the groom's village. Naming ceremonies are performed six months after birth, and Gaddis cremate their dead. As with many inhabitants of the hills, Gaddis fear evil spirits. Held in particular dread are *autars*, the spirits of people who die childless. In order to placate autars, they are accorded the status of local deities and propitiated accordingly.

Lahulas

The inhabitants of Lahaul are known as Lahulas. Lahulas are primarily agriculturalists and pastoralists. The pastoralists, like the Gaddis and the Gujars, are compelled to adopt a seminomadic lifestyle; sheep and goats are pushed to the high altitude grazing grounds in the summer, and led across the Rohtang Pass to lower elevations in winter.

Like the Ladakhis, the Lahulas traditionally practised polyandry, with the household headed by the eldest male who is known as the *Yunda*. Lahuli society is divided by clans called *rhus*, and marriages are contracted across, but not within, clans. Unlike most regions of India, society is not stratified by caste divisions, and due to the relative isolation of the Lahaul Valley and its distinct ethnic and linguistic characteristics, marriage was rarely contracted outside the valley.

Kinnauris

In the remote Kinnaur Valley of Himachal Pradesh, the majority of the inhabitants are Kinnauris. The Kinnauri Rajputs, known as **Khosias**, profess either Hinduism or Buddhism, according to the region in which they dwell. Buddhism is more prevalent in those regions of Kinnaur that lie near the Tibetan border.

The Kinnauris are agriculturalists, other than in Puh district where, due to the short growing season, the limited livelihood afforded through agriculture is supplemented by animal husbandry. Possessing a position lower in the social hierarchy than the Khosias are the **Berus**, who comprise the artisan castes. Marriages within *khandans*, or clans, are forbidden.

Jaunsaris

Jaunsaris live in the Jaunsar-Bawar area of the Yamuna Valley in north-western Garhwal. The Jaunsaris claim that they are the ancestors of the Pandavas, the heroes of the *Mahabharata*. Sculptures retrieved from this area show a Greco-Roman influence leading to speculation that the origins of the inhabitants of this region can be traced to Kushan and Hun invaders.

The Jaunsaris practise polyandry. There are three castes forming the social hierarchy. At the bottom of the rung are the **Doms**, who were traditionally compelled to work as bonded labourers for the Rajputs and the Brahmans.

Most of the inhabitants are engaged in agriculture, and grain crops of barley, wheat, maize and rice are dependent on the monsoon rains.

Jadhs

These people, of Mongoloid origin, live in Uttarkashi district in the north-west region of Uttarakhand, to which they migrated from Tibet several centuries ago.

The Jadhs of the small settlements of Uttarkashi district derive their living primarily from animal husbandry, which entails a seminomadic existence requiring a retreat to the lower foothills region in the winter months. Trans-border trade also formed an important part of the local economy until it was terminated with the closure of the Indo-Tibetan border. Trade is still conducted between the Indian plains and the Janhvi Valley, with wool being exchanged for commodities such as salt, oil, and to a lesser degree, consumer goods.

Bhotias

Also of Tibeto-Mongoloid origin, Bhotias are found in the north-eastern part of Kumaon, in Uttarakhand, near India's frontiers with Tibet. There are several groups of Bhotias, which share a common ethnicity, but possess distinct cultural and linguistic characteristics.

They also share a common heritage (and name) with the Bhutias of the eastern Himalaya (see later). In the Johar Valley, in the Munsiyari area to the north of Pithoragarh, are the **Malla Johar Bhotias**, with the highest concentration living in the village of Milam. **Marchas**, an ethnically distinct group of Bhotias originally from Tibet and of Mongoloid origin, reside in the Vishnuganga Valley. Isolated from the Malla Johar Bhotias by the Panchchuli Range are the Bhotias of Dharchula, whose traditional lands border both Tibet and Nepal. This region supports three groups of Bhotias who reside in three separate valleys after which they are known: the **Darma**, **Vyas** and **Chandan** valleys.

Bhotias have traditionally supported their lifestyles through transborder trade. From June to October caravans of sheep and goats would carry grain, spices, sugar, cloth and hardware to be traded for Tibetan salt, wool, borax and gold dust. During trading expeditions, the families of the male Bhotia traders would accompany the men to the last village before the border, where they would remain until the men's return from Tibet.

The sealing of the Indo-Tibetan border in 1962 had a dramatic impact on the lives of the Bhotias of this region. Many of the higher Bhotia villages that flanked the trade routes are now abandoned, with Bhotias now residing for the most part in villages in the lower valleys, only returning to the higher tracts in the summer.

In 1992 the Lipu Pass to Tibet was reopened and limited trade and pilgrimages to Mt Kailash resumed through the border post of Taklakot/Purang. Salt is no longer traded and has been replaced with bricks of tea and Chinese-made goods. Trade is now also conducted with Uyghur Muslims from China's Xinjiang province, which shares a border with Pakistan but not India.

The drop in border trade has seen the increasing importance of transhumance and seminomadic pastoral activities. Many families move every spring to summer villages near high alpine meadows. Some income is also derived from the weaving of carpets, selling of valuable local herbs or supplying goods and services to the pilgrims en route to Badrinath.

Due to the paucity of arable land, populations of Bhotias in the northern regions of Uttarakhand remain small, and this population deficit has resulted in flexibility in cross-clan marriages, with some marriages even contracted with non-Bhotia immigrants.

During winter, the Darma, Vyas and Chandan Bhotias migrate to the lower reaches of Dharchula, during which time cultural, trade and social transactions take place, including marriage contracts.

Lepchas

The Lepcha people of Sikkim live in the area extending west to Bhutan, east to Nepal, and south to the Darjeeling hills. It is possible that the Lepchas may have migrated north from south-eastern Asia in the 5th-century CE (common era), although some scholars suggest their origins may lie in central Nepal or the far north-eastern states of India. The

Lepchas themselves believe they were created from two balls of snow taken from the summit of Kanchenjunga and fashioned into human form by the god Rom. The Lepchas' language differs in kind from most of the other indigenous languages of this region and is extremely ancient.

Prior to their conversion to Buddhism in the 17th century, the Lepchas practised a form of animism reflected in the worship of local spirits and deities. Even today, elements of this ancient worship can be discerned in contemporary religious practice in Sikkim. The main dichotomy is between the *rums*, which are benevolent spirits, and the more diabolical *mungs*, which have been known to possess human beings and work their malignant mischief, until dispatched by a *bongthing*, or exorcist.

Lepchas are traditionally agriculturalists, although many Lepchas now reside in the larger population centres of Sikkim where they are engaged in government service, business and commerce. Only in the Dzongu area of north and central Sikkim can Lepchas still be found engaged in their traditional lifestyles and relatively isolated from contemporary life.

Bhutias

The second important ethnic group in Sikkim are the Bhutias, who originated from Tibet in the 15th century, bringing Tibetan Buddhism in their wake. The word Bhutia is derived from Bod or Bhote, meaning Tibet. They share some ethnic similarities with the Bhutiyas of the western Himalaya. Isolation from Tibet has resulted in some regional differences in the Tibetan language, and the language spoken by those of Bhutia origin is now referred to as Sikkimese. In the high northern reaches of Sikkim are two groups of Bhutias known as the **Lachens** and **Lachungs**, their names derived from the valleys they inhabit.

The Bhutias are traditionally shepherds, although they have lost large tracts of grazing ground in Tibet following the closure of the border. Agriculture, and to a lesser degree, pastoralism, now constitute their primary occupations. Traditional dress includes a *bakhu* cloak for men and the *honju* gown for women.

Nepalis

Sikkim's population is 75% Nepali, who live predominantly in the eastern, western and southern regions of Sikkim. The vast majority of Nepalis were brought by the British to the Darjeeling hills to work on the tea gardens. Most of the Nepalis of the Bangla (West Bengal) hills and Sikkim profess Hinduism, although some have adopted Buddhism, and to a lesser degree, Christianity.

The **Gurkhas** originate from central Nepal. They are traditionally a warrior race whose main occupation is soldiering. The Gurkha divisions have played important roles in the armies of Britain, Nepal and India. A potent symbol of the Gurkhas' martial character is the curved *khukuri* knife.

Right: The *khukuri knife* – used by the famous Gurkha regiments.

Tribes of Arunachal Pradesh

The dense forests and rugged ranges of Arunachal Pradesh harbour an amazing diversity of peoples. The Anthropological Survey of India puts the number of communities at 66, though the 1971 census counted as many as 115 groups. They range from Hinduised groups living on the plains to spirit-worshipping animists practising slash-and-burn farming on the central plateau, and from the Thai-speaking Khampti to the east to the Tibetan Buddhist Monpas in the west.

The largest group are the **Adi** tribes, who live in the centre of the state in East and West Siang districts. Adi means Hill Men, and they live mostly in villages of bamboo huts raised on stilts. The institution of separate dormitories for boys and girls is fading, though the buildings are often still used as training centres. Bamboo weaving is highly developed, and rural Adi people often wear cane clothes such as hats and vests. Like most of the people of Arunachal, they have a distinctly South-East Asian appearance and speak a language classified in the Tibeto-Burman family.

East of the Adi lands, in Dibang and Lohit districts, the dominant tribes are **Mishmi**, who traditionally live in enormous bamboo and wood longhouses. Each Mishmi clan has its own distinctive dress, made from cotton, nettle fibre and wood.

One of the better known tribes of Arunachal is the **Apatani**. Unlike most of their neighbours, the Apatani don't practise slash-and-burn farming but cultivate a 26 sq km plateau centred on Ziro with paddy fields. Some women wear the traditional *yapinghules* (wooden nose plugs), a custom said to have started to make Apatani women unattractive enough to dissuade Nishi and Hill Miri tribesmen from kidnapping them.

At the eastern edges of the state there are Hinayana Buddhist tribes such as the **Singpho**, who emigrated from Myanmar and write in a Thai script. In the west, bordering Bhutan, the **Monpa** peoples follow Tibetan Buddhism and use a Tibetan script (India's biggest Buddhist monastery, Tawang, is in the Monpa heartland). Most of the other tribes were not literate until recently, and write their languages in the Roman or Devanagari (standard Hindi) scripts.

While Christianity has made big inroads in the last few decades, animism is still widely followed. Many of the Adi, Apatani, Mishmi and Tangsa peoples have brought their tribal faiths together under the umbrella of a new religion called Donyi Polo. *Donyi* means sun and *polo* means moon: the supreme entities. This new religion is without a scripture or idols, though it does have a wide array of deities, myths and hymns. The priests perform rituals to win the blessing of any god, goddess or spirit that the community wishes to cultivate. See the Donyi Polo boxed text in the Arunachal Pradesh chapter for more details.

continued from page 40

EDUCATION

Across the Himalaya, there is a sharp distinction in the degree of literacy between rural and urban areas. More surprising is the fact that female literacy in the Himalayan regions is in some cases well above the national average. Lower literacy levels are found in those areas where Buddhism predominates, including parts of Himachal Pradesh and Sikkim. However, in Hindu regions of Himachal Pradesh both male and female literacy is above the national averages. Hindu areas of Jammu & Kashmir have higher female literacy rates than Muslim areas.

India's national literacy rate stands at 52% (65.5% for men, 37.7% for women). Himachal Pradesh compares favourably at 64% but rates in Arunachal Pradesh are as low as 51% for men and 29% for women.

Under the Indian constitution, education is compulsory and free for all up to the age of 14. The hill stations, particularly Dalhousie, have some of the most famous private schools in India.

ARTS

Almost all Himalayan art is religious in both motivation and subject. Buddhist art in particular is deeply conservative and conventional with the result that little has changed in hundreds of years. Innovation and personal expression plays little part and can indeed be counter-productive to art's main purpose – religious devotion and instruction. Colour is decided by rigid symbolism and most artists remain anonymous. Hindu art follows looser constraints but remains devotional.

No art is truly static, though, and styles travelled both to and from the Himalaya. Artists fleeing tyranny and invasion in the plains would settle in the hills and portable art such as scrolls and statues would carry new styles along trade routes. In this way artistic styles travelled over the Karakoram Pass from Leh to the Central Asian Silk Road towns of Yarkand and Khotan and also over the Shipki La to the Guge kingdom of western Tibet. Thus it is possible to trace the threads of Kashmiri influence in the monastic artwork of Alchi (Ladakh), Tabo (Spiti) and Thöling (western Tibet). Cultural exchange also took place between Sikkim and Tibet through the Chumbi Valley. Both Hindu and Buddhist art was further influenced by the Gupta and Pala kingdoms of Bengal and Bihar to the south.

Dance & Drama

Ladakh & Zanskar Music and dance are an integral part of any gompa festival or family ceremony in Ladakh. Dances are often complicated series of steps, retelling Buddhist stories, accompanied by traditional trumpets *(thumpchen)* and drums. Mask dances, called *chaams* if performed by monks, are slow, intricate and mesmerising. Chaam dances often portray the slaying of Langdharma, the anti-Buddhist king of Tibet, or celebrate the victory of Buddhism over the preexisting Bön religion.

Dances also represent a battle between good and evil and are thought to help protect the valley and exorcise evil spirits. They can be seen at most festivals throughout Ladakh, including at Matho Gompa in Ladakh, where some monks go into a trance and inflict wounds on themselves that appear to miraculously and spontaneously heal. At the Hemis festival the oracle appears on the roof of the gompa during a dramatic trance.

Himachal Pradesh The most well-known dance of Himachal is the *natti*, in which an entire village can participate. Accompanied by musicians playing a variety of instruments including drums and cymbals, the dancers clasp each others' hands and form a circle, revolving slowly at first, but quickening their steps as the music increases its tempo.

Dancing forms an important role in the lives of the Gaddi shepherds of Himachal Pradesh, and this is particularly evident at wedding celebrations. Men and women always dance separately, the women exhibiting extraordinary poise and grace, while the men engage in apparently abandoned movements and gestures, threatening at every moment to topple earthwards, but maintaining a gravity-defying and impressive vertical equilibrium.

In the Bilaspur and Solan regions of Himachal Pradesh, a solo dance called a *gidha* is performed. Other solo dances of Himachal Pradesh include the *cherri*, *natarambah* and *prekshani*. Accompanied by singers and musicians, one or several men commence dancing, their places being taken by other performers as the music progresses.

At the Tibetan Institute of Performing Arts (TIPA) in McLeod Ganj, students are taught the traditional *lhamo* folk opera of Tibet. Accompanied by a chorus, the performers portray episodes from Buddhist scriptures and Tibetan history, while colourful costumes help the audience identify the various characters. Lhamo originally took place over many days, resembling more of a fair than an opera, but abridged versions of around two hours are now performed.

Spiti's Pin Valley holds a remarkable troop of minstrels known as the Buchan, who perform a mix of Tibetan opera and pagan dances in full costume and make-up. The minstrels work their fields in summer and wander the region in winter like a medieval circus, performing feats of strength and daring, like leaning on swords, having stones smashed on their chests and sticking pins in their cheeks.

Uttarakhand In Jaunsar, in western Uttarakhand, dances recreate scenes from the *Mahabharata*, particularly those episodes pertaining to the Pandavas, who are highly revered by the Jaunsaris. In the *mandavna* dance, villagers are possessed by the Pandavas, and the ensuing performance plays an important role in healing and divinatory rituals.

During the *khelwar*, performers comically mimic people who are known to the audience. The *barada nati* is also performed in this district on the eve of important religious festivals, with both boys and girls participating in the dance in traditional costume. In the Tehri Garhwal region of Uttarakhand, the *langvir nritya* is performed by men, who rotate on their stomachs on top of a long bamboo pole, accompanied by musicians. The distinctive *dhurang* and *dhuring* dances are performed by Bhotias at funeral ceremonies in order to release the spirit of the deceased from habitation in an animal.

Sikkim Music and dance take a similar form to their Ladakhi counterparts. Chaams are performed on auspicious dates according to the Tibetan lunar calendar at the gompas of Sikkim. In Sikkim, a chaam performed around Losong (Sikkimese New Year), known as the *kagyat* dance, involves the burning of effigies that represents the triumph of good over evil.

The Lepchas' close affinity with their environment has given rise to a wealth of unique dances, songs and folk tales, all of which rely on the natural world for their inspiration. They celebrate the harvest with the *limboo chyabrung* dance. During the Panghlapsol Festival, the warrior dance is performed by masked dancers. Kanchenjunga, the guardian deity of Sikkim, is portrayed by a dancer wearing a blood red mask featuring five human skulls, and his supreme commander, Yabdu, is depicted by a dancer in a black mask. Other dancers are adorned in traditional battle garb. The festival is dedicated to Kanchenjunga, the war god, and is believed to have been first performed to celebrate the brotherhood pact between the Lepchas and Bhutias.

Music
Apart from the ubiquitous Hindi musical earcandy and booming Bollywood soundtracks, you are most likely to come across local Himalayan music at festival time, when horns, pipes and drums are dusted off in celebration of a deity or the end of the harvest.

Musical instruments include the *shenai* (pipe), *sarangi* (like an upright violin but played with the fingernails), *karnal* (trum-

Musical Instruments

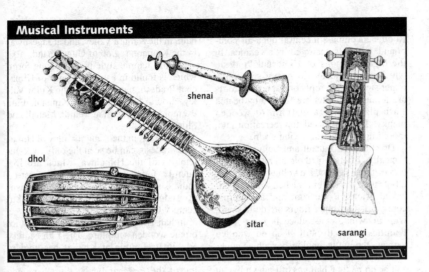

dhol

shenai

sitar

sarangi

pet), *bhana* (bronze disc) and various drums such as the *dhol*, *nagara*, *dhawn*, *tabla* and *dholak*. The tabla is actually two drums of different shape and sound and played with different parts of the hand. Tibetan monasteries normally have a large double-sided drum known as a *gna*, as well as a smaller double-sided hand drum (originally made out of human skulls) known as a *daru*.

McLeod Ganj has attracted many Tibetan musical exiles and several Tibetan musicians have been recorded there. Most are of the droning Tibetan chant variety. It's all pretty inaccessible stuff but if you fancy a try the following CDs are available in the west:

Chö, Choying Drolma & Steve Tibbets (Hannibal Music Label)
Dhama Suna, Tibetan Institute of Performing Arts (Detour)
Freedom Chants from the Roof of the World, The Gyuto Monks (Rykodisc)
Sacred Tibetan Chants from the Great Prayer Festival, Monks of Drepung Loseling Monastery (Music & Arts Programme of America)
The Gyuto Monks: Tibet Tantric Choir (Windham Hill)
Tibet Incarnations, The Meditative Sound of Buddhist Chants (Nascente)

Architecture

Domestic Dwellings Typical Himalayan domestic dwellings are of stone and wood. On the lower half, two parallel courses of beams are laid horizontally and the intervening space filled with stone. Above this is built a dwelling entirely of wood, which overhangs the lower storey, and is usually roofed with slate depending on local availability. The lower stone and wood storey traditionally not only afforded a strong foundation for the domestic quarters upstairs, but also provided a sturdy defence against adversaries and earthquakes. There are few, if any, windows in this lower storey. Livestock is kept in the ground floor, with grain stored on the next level, and above this is the wooden domestic dwelling, which contains the sleeping quarters and the hearth. There are no chimneys; smoke is released by the removal of a tile from the roof. A deep wooden veranda on the upper storey provides protection from the heavy monsoon rains. Staircases are sometimes little more than a series of steps cut in a log.

In the lower foothills of the western Himalaya, domestic dwellings are often made of compacted earth, or of brick, with roofs of galvanised iron, thatch or slate. Rooms encompass a central open-air compound, which is encircled by a veranda. In the higher regions of Himachal Pradesh, which are subjected to heavy snowfalls, either sloped slate roofs or flat terrace roofs are found. The latter are formed by beaten earth placed over a platform of wooden planks. They are used for recreation and, more importantly, for drying grain.

Dwellings in Lahaul and Spiti are more typically Tibetan in their architecture. Of two or three storeys, a dwelling would usually feature thick whitewashed walls of sun-baked bricks, a flat roof and an internal courtyard. The upper floors are quite small, with tiny windows to reduce the loss of heat. Families generally still sleep on woollen carpets, though technologies such as cookers and radios have reached most villages.

The nomadic Khampas of Ladakh live in large tents (called *rebos*) lined with yak wool, or in mud brick huts with minimal, if any, ventilation.

Hindu Temples Temple architecture in the hills conforms to various styles, with shrines ranging from tiny crude shelters of leaves and branches over the image of the deity to ornate temple complexes such as those seen at Chamba, Jageshwar and Brahmaur. Some of the most ancient temples can be seen at Brahmaur, such as the Lakhna Devi Temple, which was built in the 7th century CE.

Sikhara-style temples can be found in many areas of the western Himalaya. The *mandapa*, or holy inner sanctum, is surmounted by a large stone spire (the *Sikhara*), which is frequently topped by a fluted stone medallion-shaped disk called an *amalaka*. This forms the spiritual axis of the temple. The entranceway to the mandapa is often flanked by statues of the goddesses Yamuna and Ganga, who purify all those who pass through. The amalaka is often protected by an ornate square wooden edifice with a pyramidal roof, generally of wood or slate. The most notable examples of this style of temple can be found at Chamba and

Brahmaur, in the Chamba Valley, at Baijnath, in the Kangra Valley, and at Jageshwar in the Kumaon region of Uttarakhand.

A third temple style is the pagoda form, which is found in various regions of Himachal Pradesh, particularly in the Kullu Valley, around Shimla, and in Kinnaur. Fine examples are evident at Mandi, Manali and Shimla.

At Masrur, in the Kangra Valley of Himachal Pradesh, can be seen the only rock-cut temples of the Himalaya, which are frequently found in southern and western India, such as those at Ellora in Maharashtra state. The shrines date from the 8th century CE.

Indian Himalayan temples often feature ornate wooden sculpture. The 12th century Khajjinag Temple at Khajiar has ancient carvings featuring the Pandavas. The ceiling of the forechamber at the Chamunda Devi Temple in Chamba has intricate and ornate wooden carvings. Many wooden temples have a 'fringe' of wooden skittles lining the roof. There are often animal horns and brass bells among the wooden carvings, put there as offerings or thanks for a wish answered.

Gompas Himalayan Buddhist architecture draws its inspiration heavily from Tibet. The earliest monasteries, such as Tabo in Spiti and Alchi in Ladakh, were built on valley floors, often alongside trade routes, but after the 14th century gompas were more commonly sited on hilltops, reflecting their growing political and financial power. This relative isolation, lofty aspect and difficulty of access served several purposes. Merit could be derived from the difficult climb up to the gompa and the resident monks in their cloistered lofty perches were removed from the temptations of the flesh posed by the villages in their environs. The monasteries, which often held considerable wealth, were also better defended against marauders this way.

Gompas are generally oriented towards the east, although if this is restricted by geographical considerations, they can be found oriented towards the south-east or the south. The main prayer hall is known as the *dukhang*, and is surrounded by auxiliary buildings such as the monks' quarters and kitchen. The approach to the gompa is often flanked by rows of prayer flags, which in Sikkim are strung vertically on tall poles.

Dukhangs are usually two storeys high, with walls of whitewashed stone, fronted by a vibrantly painted facade. In the vestibule can be seen colourful frescoes featuring the four Guardian Kings and often a Wheel of Life mural (see the Tibetan Buddhist Symbols boxed text). The walls of the dukhang are completely covered in frescoes depicting various Buddhist deities and often the founder of the gompa or its order of Tibetan Buddhism.

The prayer hall consists of rows of low seats and tables, often strewn with cloaks, hats, ritual instruments, drums and horns. You may see the thunderbolt *(dorje)* and bell *(drilbu)* – ritual objects symbolising male and female aspects, which are used in Tantric rites. Other ritual implements include the *phurbu*, or dagger, used to drive Tantric invocations on their way, and a small double-sided hand drum, traditionally made from two halves of a human skull. *Torma* are small sculptured offerings made of yak butter and *tsampa* (barley flour) adorned with medallions of butter, often coloured.

The altar, known as the *chwa-shyam*, normally holds seven bowls of water alongside butter lamps and ewers of water. Behind the altar there are normally three enormous gilt statues. In Sikkim, these deities traditionally comprise Sakyamuni in the centre, flanked by Avalokiteshvara (Tibetan: Chenresig) to the right and Padmasambhava (Tibetan: Guru Rinpoche) to the left. In other monasteries the trinity often comprises Sakyamuni, Maitreya (Future Buddha) and Manjushri (the Bhodhisattva of wisdom). You may find a library of the Kangyur and Tangyur Buddhist texts near the altar.

Most gompas have side protector chapels, or *gönkhang* – dark gloomy places that house wrathful manifestations of Buddhist deities and are decorated with Tantric murals and masks used in chaam festivals. Paintings of skeletons are a common motif since they remind visitors of the transience of life. Foreign visitors, especially women, are often not allowed in protector chapels. Larger monasteries also have several subsidiary chapels, or *lhakhang*.

The outside wall of the dukhang is often encompassed by a series of prayer wheels *(manichorkor)*, which are spun by devotees

Chörtens

Chörtens, or stupas, were originally built to house the cremated relics of the historical Buddha Sakyamuni and as such have become a powerful symbol of Buddha and his teachings. In the early stages of Buddhism there were no images of Buddha and chörtens became the major symbol of the new faith.

The square base represents earth, the dome symbolises water, the spire is fire and the top moon and sun, or air and space (or ether). The 13 discs of the ceremonial umbrella can represent the branches of the tree of life or the 10 powers and three mindfulnesses of Buddha. The top seed pinnacle symbolises enlightenment and the chörten as a whole can be interpreted as a representation of the path to enlightenment. The construction can also physically represent Buddha, with the base as his seat and the dome as his body.

Symbolic chörten, Leh.

CHRISTOPHER WOOD

when circumambulating the building. You will often find a honeycomb of meditation caves high in the hills above the gompa.

Painting

Buddhist Painting Early Buddhist art was purely symbolic. The first image of Buddha was only produced around the 1st century CE at Mathura and developed in the Gandhara region of present-day Pakistan. As Buddha underwent a process of deification so images of him became stylised and diversified.

Most Himalayan painting is seen in gompas and is purely devotional in nature. Images are marked out on a grid according to mathematical rules, which strictly govern proportion and colour. Images include a wide range of buddhas, *dharmapalas* (protector deities), founding lamas, three-dimensional mandalas and sometimes *jataka* scenes, depicting events in the life of Buddha. Many icons are depicted with dreamy, half-closed eyes to symbolise meditation and introspection.

A **mandala** (literally 'circle' in Sanskrit) is a bit like a 3D picture. What on the surface appears a plain two-dimensional design, with the right visual approach, emerges as a three-dimensional picture. A typical mandala will figure a central deity surrounded by four or eight other deities who are aspects of the central figure. The ultimate aim of mandala visualisation is to enter the three-dimensional world of the mandala through imaginative concentration and to merge with the deity at the centre of that world.

While most mandalas are painted, extraordinarily fine sand mandalas are made in McLeod Ganj. A complete mandala can take up to a week, with seven or eight monks working in relays. First, coarse stones are crushed into a fine powder, which is then coloured. The sand is poured into a ridged metal pipe, which is tapped with a metal implement permitting the flow of a few grains of sand at a time onto a board on which the mandala design has been drawn. It is an extraordinarily painstaking and precise process, and monks take many years to learn their craft.

Thangkas are Buddhist religious paintings executed on cloth with vegetable dyes, and often surrounded by fine silk brocade. The cloth is pre-stiffened with starch or clay (and traditionally coated with lime and yak-skin glue) before it is stretched on a wooden frame. The religious motifs are drawn with charcoal and then filled in using coloured dyes. A range of motifs can be employed on thangkas, but generally there is a large central image of a Buddhist deity surrounded by four smaller images.

The design may encompass a narrative, with the edges of the thangka depicting episodes from the life of Buddha or of Buddhist saints. Thangkas can range in size from less than 40 sq cm to enormous thangkas that cover entire gompa walls. They can be used as instructive tools or meditational prompts, and some are believed to possess occult powers. Since they can be rolled up and are eminently portable, you will sometimes see itinerant preachers, minstrels and doctors using them to illustrate their discourses.

Pahari Miniatures The Chamba and Kangra valleys of Himachal Pradesh are renowned for their miniature paintings, often referred to as Pahari paintings. In the mid-18th century following the invasion of Delhi by the Persian emperor Nadir Shah, many artists fled to the western Himalaya where they found employment under the patronage of local rajas. Paintings were also produced for the courts by local craftspeople who were descended from families of artisans.

Unlike in the west, paintings were not seen as expressions of individual artists, but were produced anonymously by artists who took their inspiration from the sacred scriptures and infused their paintings with the purples and greens of the hills environment in which they found themselves. Unlike Mughal miniatures, which depicted the exploits of the Mughal emperors and glorified their subjects, Pahari miniatures revolved predominantly around the god Krishna, an incarnation of Vishnu, and his wife Radha. To reflect the great reverence in which the deities were held, artists aspired to technical excellence in their representations. Exposure of the local Rajput rulers to the Mughal courts also influenced the quality of the paintings and their expectations of the artists who produced them.

The raja of Guler, in Kangra, Goverdhan Singh (1744-73) was a keen patron of the arts, and provided commissions for a number of artists at his court, as did Maharaja Sansar Chand of Kangra (1775-1823). Finely executed works commissioned by these rulers soon adorned their palaces, with Sansar Chand's fort at Kangra attracting lovers of art from far and wide. Later he shifted his capital to Nadaun, near Jawalamukhi, which soon became a thriving cultural capital for the production of finely executed works of Kangra art. The capital

Tibetan Buddhist Symbols

Prayer Flags These are strips of coloured cloth printed with Buddhist sutras, strung up at the top of passes, streams and houses to purify the air and pacify the gods. When the flags flutter, prayers are thought to be released to the heavens. Travellers place them along traditional trading routes to ensure a safe passage on their long journeys. The colours of prayer flags are symbolic – red stands for fire, blue for water, white for iron, green for wood and yellow for earth. The Windhorse is the main symbol found on prayer flags. It carries the Three Jewels of Buddhism (Buddha, Dharma and Sangha) on its back and carries prayers to the heavens.

Prayer Wheels Containing up to a mile of prayers inside, prayer wheels are turned manually by pilgrims to gain merit. They can be the size of a fist or a small building and are powered by hand, water, wind and even hot air (a paper cylinder suspended over a hot flame).

Mani Walls Mani stones are carved with sutras as an act of merit and placed in walls often hundreds of metres long at holy sites. *Om Mani Padme Hum* is the most common mantra carved on mani stones. Its six syllables mean 'Hail to the Jewel in the Lotus' and form the mantra of Avalokiteshvara (Tibetan: Chenresig), the Bhodhisattva of compassion.

Swastikas An ancient symbol of Buddhism, swastikas are often found painted on houses to bring good luck. Swastikas that point clockwise are Buddhist, while those pointing anticlockwise are Bön. Another popular protective motif is the sun and moon, symbolising complementary opposites in the form of wisdom and compassion.

Dharma Wheel This is the eight-spoked Wheel of Law, symbolising the Eightfold Path of Buddhism. It is often flanked by two deer (which symbolise Buddha's first sermon at the deer park at Sarnath) and is seen on the roof of a gompa.

Rosary Beads This is a string of beads (traditionally 108) made from dried seeds. Prayers are marked off by each bead, with a second string to mark off higher multiples. British spies, or pundits, used adapted rosaries to keep record of distances as they secretly mapped trade routes through the Himalaya to Tibet during the 19th century.

Wheel of Life Symbolising the earthly cycle of death and rebirth, the wheel of life is held in the mouth of Yamantaka, the God of the Dead. The six sections of the circle are the six realms of rebirth, ruled over by gods, titans, hungry ghosts, hell, animals and humans. Around this are the 12 experiences of earthly existence, including love, desire and death (a man carrying a corpse up to a sky burial). Inside the wheel you can see a cockerel (greed and desire) biting a snake (hatred and aversion) biting a pig (delusion and ignorance).

was again shifted, this time to Sujanpurtira, on the banks of the Beas River, and Pahari miniatures reached their apotheosis here. The demise of Sansar Chand in 1823 heralded the decline of the Kangra school of painting. Unfortunately, many of the thousands of paintings and murals that adorned the temples here were destroyed in the 1905 earthquake. Today, the finest examples of Pahari art can be seen in the museum at Chamba, and there is also a small collection in the museum at Dharamsala.

During the 18th century, miniature painting also flourished in Garhwal, where it was introduced by the master painter Maularam Tomar from the region to the west of present-day Uttarakhand, beyond the Sutlej River.

Sculpture

As with other arts, sculpture is almost exclusively used for religious aims and is mostly seen in temples or monasteries. One of the most remarkable examples of sculpture is the rock-carved Maitreya Buddha at Mulbekh in Ladakh.

Cast bronze statues are important to both Buddhism and Hinduism. The most popular way of casting is the lost wax method, which involves making a model in wax, covering it in clay and firing it so that the wax melts and leaves a mold, into which can be poured molten metal.

Mohras are metal masks that are displayed in temples and during festival processions to represent Hindu deities. They are fashioned out of an alloy of eight metals and are made using the repoussé method of beating raised metal.

Woodcarving is another important art in both temple and domestic architecture. Walnut, deodar and shisham wood are all used.

Folk Art

The Himalaya has a rich tradition of folk art, much of which has its origins in protective symbols to prevent the influence of evil spirits.

Embroidery is practised throughout the Himalaya and has its roots in miniature painting. *Rumals*, literally handkerchiefs, are reversible embroidered squares of cloth, which are common in Himachal Pradesh (particularly Chamba). Originally used as coverings for deities, today they are most commonly presented at weddings.

Alpanas are geometric and auspicious symbols painted in white by rural women on the floors and walls of homes during auspicious occasions.

SOCIETY & CONDUCT
Traditional Culture

Most traditional communities in the Himalaya are immersed in agriculture and the upkeep of fragile irrigation schemes. Families supplement their income by raising livestock and women in particular fill whatever spare time they have making crafts. Two common sights in the Himalaya are the herdsman spinning yarn on a portable spindle and women weaving shawls and hangings.

The village year is defined by sowing and harvest times, the auspicious dates of which are normally fixed by astrologers or lamas. The social calendar is structured around a series of local festivals, some religious, others agricultural or mercantile in nature, all of which provide relief from the rigours of work and also a chance to trade and even find a husband or wife. Weddings are generally arranged in the winter time when time is more freely available. Entertainment generally takes the form of folk tales, epic ballads, religious stories and oral histories.

In Buddhist communities women generally enjoy a high status but have a hard life, often working in both the home and the fields (though never the ploughing, which is exclusively a male profession). Jewellery is an important means of storing and displaying a woman's wealth and provides the only form of financial independence (a woman's dowry often consists of jewellery). Typical items include the *balu* (nose stud), *nath* (nose ring), and various anklets and brooches. Tibetan-influenced areas particularly value turquoise, coral and amber. Children throughout the Himalaya wear silver amulets to protect against evil spirits. Many Tibetan Buddhists carry a *gau* or amulet, as a talisman.

Widows generally have a hard lot in India. They lose status and even many of their worldly goods after the death of their husbands. If a widow has no sons to support her and is too old to work she is often in dire need. Marriages are still commonly arranged. Though outlawed in 1961, dowries are still widely demanded and daughters are commonly seen as a financial burden.

Mountain and particularly Buddhist communities have less emphasis on caste and are informally divided according to their profession. Blacksmiths, weavers, potters, woodcarvers, leather workers and other craftsmen often form distinct communities, which act as trade guilds or unions. An aristocracy does exist, and local headmen, known as *nonos* in Spiti, *wazirs* in Kashmir and *thakurs* in Lahaul, often exert great influence and political power.

In Buddhist areas the local monastery plays a particularly important role in daily life. Monks are brought in for marriages, deaths, to bless the harvest, change prayer flags or consecrate a new chörten or shrine.

The life of a Hindu is defined by 16 *sanskars*, or rites. These include a baby's first haircut, first solid food, the naming of the child, the formal initiation into Hinduism, marriage and death rites. An ideal Hindu's life is also divided into four stages called *ashrama*. These include childhood, the householder, the recluse, who retreats from the material world, and finally the ascetic, who prepares himself for death.

Hindus are generally cremated. The dead body is washed, laid on a bier and covered with a shroud. The chief mourner (usually the deceased's eldest son) takes a ritual bath and then the body is carried to the pyre. The third day after cremation the family collect

Life on the Move

Many of the Himalayan peoples, such as the Gujars, Gaddis and Jadhs, are seminomadic and practise transhumance – the annual migration from winter villages to high summer pastures, or *bugyals*. While some shepherds are truly nomadic, villagers who practise transhumance have homes in both winter and summer pastures and only live in tents during the actual migration.

During the summer they push their herds and flocks to high alpine pastures, covering distances of up to 20km each day along traditional trails or, more recently, along roads, and camping en route. The entire family is involved in this cycle of migration, with women sharing in the burden of carrying utensils and infants, and even giving birth during the annual migration. Dogs also make the migration, serving the dual function of keeping wild animals at bay and containing the flock. Fresh milk is traded at the villages along the migration routes, or butter and ghee are produced, which is sold farther afield.

Temporary dwellings known to the Gujars as *deras*, provide shelter on the grazing grounds, and these are either destroyed or abandoned when the herders complete the next stage of the migration.

In some cases the women and children remain in the village with one male member of the family in order to undertake the onerous task of tending the fields during the annual summer migration. Livelihood is thus derived both from agriculture and trade in milk and animal products, though the timing of the move then becomes vital.

The long descent commences in early autumn, and during winter livestock graze on the plains at the foot of the lower Himalayan slopes. With the increasing development of the Himalayan foothills, herders are finding it harder to find adequate grazing during winter and are increasingly coming into conflict with local settlers.

the deceased's ashes, which are then ideally scattered in the Ganges. On the 10th day after cremation the entire family bathes and the house is ritually purified.

In Tibetan Buddhism the dead have traditionally been disposed of by sky burial, partly because of the scarcity of wood for cremation and spare land for burial. For more information see the Life and Death in Ladakh boxed text in the Ladakh & Zanskar chapter.

For more information on traditional culture see the following Popular Religion section, the Peoples of the Himalaya special section earlier and relevant regional chapters.

Dos & Don'ts

See also the Responsible Tourism section in the Facts for the Visitor chapter.

Visiting a Home Never throw food into a fire whether at a camp site or in a home. It is also expedient not to touch food or cooking utensils that local people will use, particularly in Hindu regions. If drinking out of a communal water container make sure it doesn't touch your lips when you take a swig. Use your right hand for all social interactions, whether passing money or food or any other item. The hearth is the sacred centre of the home, so never approach it unless you have been invited to do so.

Religious Etiquette Always take off your shoes and all leather goods, including belts, when visiting Hindu shrines (there is normally a safe place to store them). If the *pujari* offers you *prasaad* (food offerings), it is respectful to at least taste it.

At Sikh temples take off your shoes, wash your feet and cover your head (there is normally a place where you can borrow a scarf or cap).

For religious reasons, do not touch local people on the head and similarly never direct the soles of your feet at a person, religious shrine, or image of a deity, as this may cause offence. It's better not to point with your finger but with your palm facing upwards. Never touch a deity and always ask

before taking a photograph. Always walk around a Buddhist monument (such as a gompa or chörten) in a clockwise direction.

Washing Nudity is completely unacceptable and a swimsuit must be worn even when bathing in a remote locality.

RELIGION

The Himalaya has been revered for millennia as *Dhev-bumi*, the home of the gods, and it is a place where myth and reality blend seamlessly. Many of the great Hindu scriptures draw upon the Himalaya for their inspiration, or weave their narratives around the exploits of the gods in the lofty Himalayan realm. It was here that Shiva, widely revered in the hills regions, married Parvati, and here that he led the heroes of the *Mahabharata*, the Pandavas, on a merry dance as they sought his atonement for slaying their kinsfolk, the Kauravas. Two of the great battles recorded in the *Rigveda*, the Shambar Yuddha and the Dasarajna Yuddha, are believed to have been fought in the Himalaya.

Buddhism made great inroads in the Himalayan region, both with Buddhists crossing the high Himalaya from Tibet and spreading the tenets of the religion throughout the Indian Himalaya, and due to the endeavours of Buddhism's greatest convert, the emperor Ashoka, who lived in the 3rd century BCE (before common era) and left a legacy of rock-carved edicts throughout his empire, at least one of which was installed in the Himalaya.

There are also sizeable Muslim communities, particularly in the state of Jammu & Kashmir, and Sikhism and Christianity are also professed by some inhabitants.

Popular Religion

Few areas of the Himalaya can be neatly pigeon-holed as simply 'Buddhist' or 'Hindu'. The reality is far more complex, with ancient traditions, beliefs and superstitions merging with recent imported belief systems. Many parts of Lahaul and Kinnaur effortlessly draw together both Hindu and

Buddhist deities into the same village and even the same temple.

Surrounded by the destructive and uncontrollable natural forces of the Himalaya and the constant threat of earthquakes, landslides or floods it is perhaps not surprising that mountain people generated a fearsome pantheon of evil spirits and then a series of rituals and mediums to appease them. Animist beliefs and a reliance on shamans and sacrifices remains to this day the dominant religion among the tribes of Arunachal Pradesh.

Animism was echoed in the western Himalaya by the pre-Buddhist religion of Bön, which had its heartland in neighbouring western Tibet. Bön incorporated elements of nature worship and a belief in earth and sky spirits and developed elements of magic and ritual to summon up a vast number of protective deities. Protective symbols such as the scorpion, which are used today to ward off the evil eye, have their origins deep in Bön.

Hinduism and Buddhism were superimposed on top of these ancient beliefs and have both absorbed and been transformed by them. Ancient animist and Vedic beliefs are echoed in Hindu deities like Surya, the sun god and Indra, the god of the sky, and many Buddhist practices such as the hanging of prayer flags have their origins in Bön. The very remoteness of the Himalaya has kept alive traces of ancient beliefs that have long since disappeared from their place of origin.

A peculiar phenomenon in the western Himalaya is the institution of village and household gods, many of whom are manifestations of Shiva, Parvati and Vishnu, as well as *nagas*, or snake-spirits, which are worshipped in various forms in thousands of villages. Worship of the five Pandava brothers is also common in the hills regions. Worship of household gods is motivated more by fear than by abject devotion, as household gods are believed to wreak havoc on the families to which they belong if they are not afforded due respect and placated with appropriate reverence and worship. In the

case of trouble or misfortune, a shaman is consulted who advises how it can be averted, and how the household god can be appropriately appeased. Holy men still forecast weather, and protect against crops and disease. In cases of illness most Buddhists still visit the lama as a first port of call.

Village gods, in contrast to household gods, are worshipped collectively by entire villagers in a village temple, with worship conducted by a Brahman. They are less universally feared than household gods, although as with household gods, they are worshipped according to the degree of trouble they are capable of inflicting upon the village. Village gods speak through a *gur*, or oracle, who is possessed by the god, generally at festivals held in its honour, causing the object of their possession to dance and speak with the god's voice. They are an integral part of the cultural life of the village, directing marriage and death rituals and controlling the destinies of the villagers. Local Himalayan deities such as Gyepang (Lahaul), Purgyal (Kinnaur), Nanda Devi (Garhwal) and Kanchenjunga (Sikkim) directly personify the natural forces of the mountains and are always appeased before setting off on a trip or blessing the year's harvest.

Other supernatural phenomena that play important roles in the lives of the hills inhabitants are ancestor spirits and ghosts. Ancestor spirits may demand worship according to various conditions. A common reason for ancestor worship is to appease a deceased person who returns in spirit form if it feels it did not receive appropriate burial rites, or who has returned to torment family members for indiscretions during its lifetime. A shaman diagnoses the source of the affliction for the family members, and the ancestors are worshipped as household gods.

Ghosts, or *bhuts* (who can also be the spirits of deceased people) are thought to roam at night and are held responsible for inexplicable occurrences such as strange noises, rockslides and the like. They have also been thought to possess hapless victims, thus causing disability, illness, insanity, and even death, and are sometimes considered responsible for the inability of women to bear children, or still-births. Unlike household gods, ghosts can strike randomly, and their malevolent machinations are not necessarily punishments for perceived slights or indiscretions. Charms and incantations can keep them at bay, and ghosts who possess people can be driven out with the aid of an exorcist.

Sprites, or *matris*, are invisible beings who do not deliberately attack their victims; victims are simply afflicted from having inadvertently wandered across their path. They cannot be avoided or appeased with worship, and the maladies with which they strike their unfortunate victims frequently cannot be cured or dislodged by a shaman. Sprites do not possess people, but they can cause illness, disability or insanity. Fractures resulting from tripping over a branch or similar obstruction could be attributed to the playful but not malicious machinations of sprites.

Hinduism

Hinduism is the dominant religion of the Himalayan region, particularly in Himachal Pradesh, where over 87% of the inhabitants profess this religion, and in Uttarakhand. About 60% of the population of Sikkim and the Bangla (West Bengal) hills are Hindu.

Hinduism is one of the oldest extant religions, with firm roots extending back to beyond 1000 BCE. The word *Hindu* is an Arabic word that means 'beyond the Indus'. Indians traditionally refer to Hinduism as the Santana Dharma, or Eternal Way of Truth.

The Indus Valley civilisation developed a religion as early as the 3rd millennia BCE that shows many similarities to Hinduism and features a horned figure described as a proto-Shiva. Hinduism probably got concepts of ritual bathing, fertility ritual and sacrifice from this early religion. The roots of Hindu ritual and literature can also be traced to the later Dravidians of the south and the Aryan invaders who arrived in the north of India around 1500 BCE. Around 1000 BCE, the Vedic scriptures were introduced and gave the first loose framework to the religion.

Hinduism today has a number of holy books, the most important being the four *Vedas* (Divine Knowledge), which are the foundation of Hindu philosophy. The *Upanishads* are contained within the *Vedas* and delve into the metaphysical nature of the universe and the soul. The *Mahabharata* (Great War of the Bharatas) is an epic poem containing over 220,000 lines. It describes the battles between the Kauravas and Pandavas, who were descendants of the Lunar race. In it is the story of Rama, and it is probable that the most famous Hindu epic, the *Ramayana*, was based on this. The *Ramayana* is highly revered by Hindus. The *Bhagavad Gita* is a famous episode of the *Mahabharata* where Krishna relates his philosophies to Arjuna.

Basically, Hinduism postulates that we will all go through a series of rebirths or reincarnations that eventually lead to moksha, the spiritual salvation that frees one from the cycle of rebirths. With each rebirth you can move closer to or farther from eventual moksha; the deciding factor is your karma, which is literally a law of cause and effect. Bad actions during your life result in bad karma, which ends in a lower reincarnation. Conversely, if your deeds and actions have been good you will reincarnate on a higher level and be a step closer to eventual freedom from rebirth.

Lingam & Yoni

Apart from being a potentially great name for an Indian crime-fighting duo, the *lingam* and *yoni* are probably the two most common religious symbols in India. The phallic lingam represents male energy, and Shiva in particular, while the vaginal yoni symbolises Parvati and female energy in general. Together they symbolise light and dark, spirit and matter, as well as the union of the male and female, and the totality of existence.

The Hindu Gods

There are many Hindu gods, and related auspicious beings. You can look upon all these different gods simply as pictorial representations of the many attributes of a god. The multiple arms of the various gods symbolise the gods' greater capability and their multiple heads show their greater vision and wisdom. The one omnipresent god usually has three physical representations: Brahma is the creator, Vishnu is the preserver and Shiva is the destroyer and reproducer.

There are subtle differences between an incarnation, a manifestation and an aspect. Vishnu has incarnations, 10 of them in all. Shiva, on the other hand, may be the god of 1000 names but these are manifestations – what he shows himself as – not incarnations.

Each of the gods is associated with a particular animal, which can either be an attendant or a vehicle on which the god may ride. These creatures are a clue to identifying a god. Ganesh's vehicle, for example, is the rat or shrew; a statue of a rat will indicate that you are in a Ganesh shrine.

Shiva

Shiva is creator and destroyer – so it's important to keep on his good side! Shiva is often represented by the phallic lingam, symbolic of his creative role and his symbol is the trident (the three prongs representing past, present and future). Shiva rides on the bull Nandi and his matted hair is said to have Ganga, the goddess of the river Ganges, in it. He has a blue throat from drinking poison in order to save the world.

Shiva is also known as Nataraja, the cosmic dancer whose dance shook the cosmos and created the world. In his upper right hand Nataraja holds a drum to show the rhythm of creation; in his upper left hand he holds the flame of destruction; and beneath his foot he tramples on the dwarf of ignorance and evil. Shiva's home is Mt Kailash in the Tibetan Himalaya. He has various manifestations including Mahakala, 'Transcendent Time', peaceful Pashupati and destructive Bhairava, who haunts cemeteries and funeral pyres. Usually his fearsome side is handled by Shakti.

Shakti

While Shakti the goddess is Shiva's consort, *shakti* is the creative/reproductive energy of the gods, which often manifests in their consorts. A Hindu god's consort is also known as his shakti, as she is far more than just a companion. A shakti often symbolises certain parts of a god's personality, so while Shiva is the god of both creation and destruction, it is often his shakti, Parvati, manifesting as Kali or Durga, who handles the destructive business and demands the blood sacrifices. She is also the energetic and dominant partner in their sexual relationship, and shakti has come to mean any goddess in her energetic and dynamic mode.

Parvati

Shiva's shakti is Parvati the beautiful and she is the dynamic element in their relationship. Just as Shiva is also known as Mahadev, the Great God, so she is Mahadevi, the Great Goddess. Just as Shiva is often symbolised by the phallic lingam, so Parvati's symbol is the *yoni*, representing the female sex organ. Their relationship is a sexual one and it is often Parvati who is the energetic and dominant partner.

Parvati has as many forms as the Great God himself. She may be the peaceful Parvati but she may also be fearsome and destructive Kali, the black goddess, or Durga, the terrible. In these terrific forms she holds a variety of weapons in her hands, struggles with demons and rides a lion. As Kali, the fiercest of the gods and goddesses, she demands sacrifices and wears a garland of skulls.

The Hindu Gods

Ganesh

With his elephant head, Ganesh is probably the most easily recognised of the gods and also the most popular. Ganesh is the god of prosperity and wisdom and is known as the remover of obstacles. He has the limbs of a child, a snake around his waist and a broken tusk (the missing section of which Ganesh used to write down the *Mahabharata* after his pen broke). He is worshipped at the beginning of a journey or new undertaking, especially weddings (and even school exams).

Ganesh

Ganesh's parents are Shiva and Parvati and he obtained his elephant head due to his father's notorious temper. Coming back from a long trip, Shiva discovered Parvati in bed with a young man. Not pausing to think that their son might have grown up a little during his absence, Shiva lopped his head off! Shiva was then forced by Parvati to bring his son back to life but could only do so by giving him the head of the first living thing he saw – which happened to be an elephant.

Vishnu

Vishnu is the preserver and also plays a role in the original creation of the universe. Narayan is the reclining Vishnu, sleeping on the cosmic ocean, and from his navel appears Brahma, who creates the universe.

Vishnu has four arms for the four directions and can often be identified by the symbols he holds – the conch shell or *sankha*, the disc-like weapon known as a *chakra*, the stick-like weapon known as a *gada* and a lotus flower or *padma*.

Vishnu has 10 incarnations starting with Matsya, the fish. Then he appeared as Kurma, the tortoise on which the universe is built. Number three was his boar incarnation as Varaha, who destroyed a demon who would have drowned the world. Vishnu was again in a demon-destroying mood in incarnation four as Narsingha, half-man and half-lion. Still facing difficulties from demons, Vishnu's next incarnation was Vamana, the dwarf who reclaimed the world from the demon-king Bali. In his sixth incarnation Vishnu appeared as Parasurama, a warlike Brahman. Incarnation seven was as Rama, the personification of the ideal man (obedient son, conscientious ruler, loving husband and heroic warrior) and the hero of the *Ramayana* who, with help from Hanuman the monkey god, rescued his beautiful wife Sita

The Hindu Gods

from the clutches of Ravana, evil king of Lanka. Incarnation eight was a gentle and much-loved one when Vishnu appeared as Krishna, the fun-loving cowherd, who dallied with the *gopis* (milkmaids), danced, played his flute and still managed to remain devoted to his wife Radha. Krishna is often blue in colour. For number nine Vishnu appeared as the teacher, the Buddha. Of course the Buddhists don't agree that Buddha was just an incarnation of some other religion's god.

Incarnation 10? Well we haven't seen that one yet but it will be as Kalki, a white horse, when Vishnu wields the sword that will destroy the world at the end of the Kali Yurga, the age that we are currently in.

When Vishnu appears as Vishnu, rather than one of his incarnations, he sits on a couch made from the coils of a serpent and in his hands he holds two symbols, the conch shell and the discus. Vishnu's vehicle is the half-man half-eagle known as the Garuda.

Krishna

Lakshmi
Also known as Lakshmi-Naryan, this beautiful goddess is the shakti of Vishnu. She is also the goddess of wealth and prosperity and is celebrated during the Diwali festival, particularly by businessmen.

Garuda
The Garuda is a firm do-gooder and has a deep dislike of snakes. A winged Garuda statue will often be found kneeling reverentially in front of a Vishnu temple. The Garuda has been adopted as the symbol of Indonesia's state airline.

Brahma
Brahma, despite his supreme position, appears much less often than Shiva or Vishnu. Like those gods, he has four arms but Brahma also has four heads, to represent his all-seeing presence. The four *Vedas* are supposed to have emanated from his mouths.

Saraswati
The goddess of learning and consort of Brahma is the favourite deity of students. She is the mother of poetry and is said to have revealed language and writing to humankind. She rides upon a white swan and holds the stringed musical instrument known as a *veena*.

Hanuman
Hanuman is the monkey god, the important character from the *Ramayana* who came to the aid of Rama and helped to defeat the evil Ravana and release Sita from his grasp. Hanuman's characteristics are trustworthiness and alertness.

Sadhus

Sadhus are an easily recognised group, usually wandering around half-naked, smeared in dust with their hair and beard matted. A sadhu is often someone who has decided that his business and family life have reached their natural conclusions and that it is time to throw everything aside and go out on a spiritual search. He may previously have been the village postman, or a businessman. There are around five million sadhus in India, of which maybe 10% are women. Even Alexander the Great discussed philosophy with naked sadhus at the end of his trip to India.

Sadhus are divided into many groups. Those who follow Shiva normally carry his symbol, the trident, as well as a water pot, tongs and a lingam. Followers of Vishnu carry a conch and discus. Vaishnavites often have three vertical lines painted on their face while Shaivites have three horizontal lines or two lines either side of a dot. Most sadhus are affiliated to one of 10 orders, known as the *dasnamis*. The *naga babas* are the most easily recognised group as they are naked.

Sadhus perform various feats of self mortification and wander all over India, occasionally coming together in great pilgrimages and other religious gatherings, like the great Kumbh Mela. Many sadhus are completely genuine in their search, but others are simply beggars following a more sophisticated approach to gathering in the rupees.

Dharma, or the natural law, defines the total social, ethical and spiritual harmony of your life. There are three categories of dharma, the first being the eternal harmony, which involves the whole universe. The second category is the dharma that controls castes, the relations between castes, and behaviour appropriate to individuals within castes. The third dharma is the moral code that an individual should follow.

The Hindu religion has three basic practices. They are *puja*, or worship, the cremation of the dead, and the rules and regulations of the caste system. There are four main castes: the Brahman, or priest caste; the Kshatriyas, or soldiers and governors; the Vaisyas, or tradespeople and farmers; and the Sudras, or menial workers and artisans. These basic castes are then subdivided into a great number of lesser divisions. Beneath all the castes are the Dalits (formerly known as Harijans), or Untouchables, the lowest casteless class for whom all the most menial and degrading tasks are reserved.

In traditional Hindu belief, time is divided into four *yurgas*, ranging from the Krita Yurga, or Golden Age, to the current Kali Yurga, when morality is at its lowest point. Together the four yurgas form a *mahayurga* of 4,320,000 years. Two hundred mahayurgas constitute a single day in the life of Brahma.

Westerners may have trouble understanding Hinduism principally because of its vast hierarchy of gods (there are traditionally 333 million gods). See The Hindu Gods boxed earlier text in this chapter for more information on the most interesting and frequently encountered gods. The various deities are seen by many as symbols of the various forces alive in humanity's collective consciousness. Deities may be given a gender, character and even a husband or wife to render them more easily comprehensible but these again are essentially only personified aspects or powers of a genderless divine power.

A variety of lesser gods and goddesses also contribute to the Hindu pantheon. Most temples are dedicated to one or other of the gods, but curiously there are very few Brahma temples – perhaps just two or three in all of India. Most Hindus profess to be either Vaishnavites (followers of Vishnu) or Shaivites (followers of Shiva). The cow is, of course, the holy animal of Hinduism and its products, such as milk, curd, ghee, dung and urine, are thought to be particularly purifying.

Hinduism is not a proselytising religion, since you cannot be converted. You're either born a Hindu or you are not; you can never become one. Similarly, once you are a Hindu you cannot change your caste – you're born into it and are stuck with it for the rest of that lifetime. Nevertheless, Hinduism has a great attraction to many westerners and India's 'export gurus' are many and successful.

A guru is not so much a teacher as a spiritual guide, somebody who by example or simply by their presence indicates what path you should follow. In a spiritual search, one always needs a guru. A sadhu is an individual on a spiritual search. A swami is a spiritual teacher who is also an ascetic. Ashrams (literally 'place of striving') are spiritual centres that form around a guru. Disciples make donations, buy land and often build quite extensive and beautiful complexes.

The Sacred Landscape of the Himalaya

To Hindus the Himalaya is a network of tirthas (literally a 'crossing point' or ford) – sacred nodes where the mundane world meets the spiritual. Tirthas can be a mountain, river confluence *(prayag)*, river source, birthplace of a saint or even the saint himself, but all are worthy of pilgrimage.

The Himalaya is the mythical home of Shiva, who resides in several mountains including Kinner Kailash, Manimahesh and Mt Kailash in Tibet. The sacred Ganges falls from the dreadlocks of Shiva's hair to emerge at Gangotri, a particularly pure and sacred spot. The source of the Yamuna, India's second holiest river, at Yamunotri, is another particularly pure tirtha.

There are many other holy sites, which form a Himalayan pilgrim circuit. There are 12 jyothirlinga, or lings of light, which are sacred to Shaivites. In the Himalaya these include Baijnath in Himachal Pradesh and Jageshwar in Kumaon. According to Hindu texts there are also 51 shakti-pirthas, or seats of the goddess, where various parts of Sati's body fell after her charred body was dismembered by Vishnu. Sati's tongue fell to earth at Jawalamukhi in Kangra, her right temple fell along the Indus River in Ladakh, her eye formed Nainital and her right palm landed at Lake Mansarovar in Tibet.

The Panch Kedar in Uttarakhand mark the five sites where parts of Shiva's body emerged from the earth in the form of a bull after he plunged into the earth to escape the Pandavas. His hump appeared at Kedarnath, his hand at Tunganath, his face at Rudranath, his middle at Madmaheshwar and his hair at Kalpeshwar, and together these form a powerful pilgrim circuit.

Hindus also describe seven sacred cities (of which Haridwar is one), seven sacred rivers (which include the Ganga, Yamuna, Saraswati and Indus) and four cardinal points, of which Badrinath is the north. Badrinath also forms one of the Char Dham (together with Yamunotri, Kedarnath and Gangotri), which are considered the foremost Hindu pilgrimage sites in the Himalaya.

Yoga (literally 'union with god') is a holistic system of spiritual growth that is several thousand years old. The more specific regime of exercises that most foreigners regard as yoga is properly known as *hatha yoga*. This uses various *asanas*, or postures, to 'settle the mind into silence and open the body to the divine within'. Linked to this is *pranayama*, a system of breath control that is used to activate the various *pranas* (life currents) and *chakras* (energy systems) of the body. A *yogi* is simply a master of yoga.

Temples & Puja Temples are set up to commemorate a divine act or person or to invite the divine onto earth. They are a place where the mundane and spiritual worlds can meet. The most important reason for visiting a temple is to show *bhakti*, or devotion, to conduct a puja, or religious ritual, and to gain *darshan*, a word that means viewing a deity but which also carries connotations of being viewed by a deity. As devotees pass through the various courtyards they move from the profane into the sacred, until they reach the inner sanctum, which resembles a cave or, as some suggest, a womb.

Once consecrated, a temple's statue of a deity temporarily becomes that deity. The

Important Figures of Tibetan Buddhism

The following is a brief guide to some of the gods and goddesses of the Tibetan Buddhist pantheon. It is neither exhaustive nor scholarly, but it may help you to recognise a few of the statues you encounter in the many gompas of the Indian Himalaya.

Padmasambhava (Tibetan: Guru Rinpoche) – the Lotus-Born – 8th century Tantric master from modern-day Swat in Pakistan. He helped establish Buddhism in Tibet by subduing its evil spirits. He is regarded by followers of Nyingmapa Buddhism as the second Buddha. He holds a thunderbolt in his right hand, a skull cup in his left and a *khatvanga* staff topped with three heads in the crook of his arm.

Avalokiteshvara (Tibetan: Chenresig) – Glorious Gentle One. He is the Bhodhisattva of compassion and is either pictured with 11 heads and 1000 pairs of arms, or in a white, four-armed manifestation. The Dalai Lama is considered an incarnation of Avalokiteshvara.

Manjushri (Tibetan: Jampelyang) – Princely Lord of Wisdom. He is regarded as the first divine teacher of Buddhist doctrine. His right hand holds the flaming sword of awareness, which cuts through ignorance. His left arm cradles a scripture in a half-opened lotus blossom and his left hand is in the teaching *mudra* (hand position). Manjushri is often yellow.

Vajrapani (Tibetan: Channa Dorje) – thunderbolt in hand. Vajrapani is the wrathful Bhodhisattva of energy. The thunderbolt represents indestructibility and is a fundamental symbol of Tantric faith. It is called a *dorje* in Tibetan and a *vajra* in Sanskrit.

Sakyamuni (Tibetan: Sakya Thukpa) – the historical Buddha. Born in Lumbini in the 5th century BCE (before common era) in what is now southern Nepal, he attained enlightenment under a *bo* (peepul) tree and his teachings set in motion the Buddhist faith. In Tibetan-style representations he is always pictured sitting cross-legged on a lotus flower throne. Buddha is recognised by 32 marks on his body, including a dot between the eyes and a bump on the top of his head. His right hand touches the earth in the 'witness' mudra.

nurti, or image, is treated like a royal guest; he or she is awakened, washed, dressed, fed, given water and later put to bed, during ceremonies conducted by the *pujari*, or priest. The deity is offered food known as *prasaad* (literally 'God's grace') by pilgrims who receive prasaad back in return, normally in the form of sweetmeats. Stalls lining the road to most temples overflow with coconuts, camphor oil, postcards, plastic flowers, garlands of marigolds, milk, vermilion powder, oils, incense and sandalwood paste with which to anoint the main statue.

In the Himalaya most Hindu gods are represented by *mohra* masks fashioned out of plates of metal and housed on a *rath* (ceremonial palanquin) or under a *chaatra* (silver umbrella). All the local gods have their own oral history known as a *chironag*.

Buddhism

There are only about five million Buddhists in India, but the religion is of great importance and there are many reminders of its historic role. Strictly speaking Buddhism is not a religion, since it is not centred on a god, but rather a system of philosophy and a code of morality.

Buddhism was founded in northern India about 500 BCE when Siddhartha Gautama,

Important Figures of Tibetan Buddhism

Maitreya (Tibetan: Jampa) – the Future Buddha. He is passing the life of a Bhodhisattva and will return to earth in human form 4000 years after the disappearance of Sakyamuni Buddha. He is normally seated with his hands by his chest in the mudra of 'turning the Wheel of Law'.

Milarepa A great Tibetan magician and poet and leading figure of the Kagyupa order who is believed to have attained the supreme enlightenment of buddhahood in the course of one life. He lived in the 11th century and travelled extensively throughout the Himalayan borderlands. Most images of Milarepa picture him smiling, holding his hand to his ear as he sings. He is often depicted in green because he lived in a cave for many years on a diet of nettles.

Tara (Devi) (Tibetan: Drölma) – the Saviouress. Tara has 21 different manifestations. She symbolises purity and fertility and is believed to be able to fulfil wishes. Tara was born from a tear of compassion that fell from Avalokiteshvara's eyes. Statues of Tara usually represent Green Tara, who is associated with night, or White Tara, who is associated with day.

White Tara

born a prince near the modern Nepal border, achieved enlightenment at Bodhgaya. Gautama (also known as Sakyamuni) Buddha was not the first buddha but the fourth, and is not expected to be the last enlightened one (Maitreya is the Future Buddha). Buddhists believe that the achievement of enlightenment is the goal of every being, so eventually we will all reach buddhahood.

In India, Buddhism developed rapidly when it was embraced by the great emperor Ashoka in the 3rd century BCE, whose empire extended over much of India. He also sent out missions to other lands to preach Buddha's word, and his own son is said to have carried Buddhism to Sri Lanka. Later, however, Buddhism began to contract in India because it had never really taken a hold on the great mass of people. With the revival of Hinduism in the 9th century Buddhism in India was gradually reabsorbed into the older religion.

Although Buddhism was to gain favour after the kings of Tibet invaded Ladakh in the 8th and 9th centuries, it took many generations for the Buddhist teachings to capture the local imagination. The sage Naropa is said to have founded one of the earliest gompas at Lamayuru high above the Indus. Legend has it that the Lamayuru Valley was once filled by a lake that was drained by Naropa to found the gompa. The original building, situated below the main gompa, was built in the 10th century. The gompa at Sani, close to Padum in the Zanskar Valley, also dates from this period, with its origins again attributed to the miraculous deeds of Naropa. In Kinnaur and Spiti dozens of gompas are attributed to the Great Translator Ringchen Zangpo.

During the 11th century, Buddhist monks began migrating over the Himalaya in search of patronage. The artistic designs in gompas such as Alchi, dating from the 11th century, still provide some of the best surviving examples of Buddhist art of this period. From now on the movement and inspiration of Buddhist thought would be initiated from the far side of the Himalaya.

One of the greatest influences came from Tibet in the 14th century when the saint Tsongkhapa founded the Gelukpa order (see following). In Ladakh, the gompas of Tikse Likir and Stakna were founded by this order in the early half of the 15th century. It was headed by the Dalai Lama, and even today the 14th Dalai Lama undertakes regular visits to the gompas in Ladakh and Zanskar.

The teachings of the Tantric sages, too, were revised in the 16th century. A new gompa at Hemis was founded with the patronage of the Ladakhi royal family. Affiliated gompas at Stakna and in the King's palace at Leh also date from this period. The traditions of Padmasambhava were revered, and today the annual festival at Hemis during the time of the June/July full moon is held in his honour.

Buddhism was introduced into Sikkim by three Tibetan lamas, Lhatsun Chempo, Kathok Rikzin Chempo and Ngadak Sempa Chempo, in the 17th century, who belonged to the Nyingmapa order. The lamas left Tibet following the schism between the various orders, in which the Gelukpa was beginning to emerge as the dominant order. The establishment of Buddhism in the former kingdom was believed to have been foretold by Padmasambhava when he travelled through the region en route to Tibet. The three lamas consecrated Sikkim's first king, or *chogyal* Phuntsog Namgyal, in 1642.

Schools of Buddhism Buddha never wrote down his dharma (teachings), and a schism later developed, so today there are two major Buddhist schools. Theravada Buddhism (Doctrine of the Elders), or Hinayana, holds that the path to *nirvana*, the eventual aim of all Buddhists, is an individual pursuit. In contrast, the Mahayana school holds that the combined belief of its followers will eventually be great enough to encompass all of humanity and bear it to salvation. Today Mahayana is chiefly practised in Vietnam, Japan and China, while the Hinayana school is followed in Sri Lanka, Myanmar (Burma), Cambodia and Thailand.

A further development of Mahayana Buddhism of particular relevance to Tibet, Ladakh and Sikkim is Vajrayana, or Tantrism

Guru Rinpoche – The Precious Sage

The sage Padmasambhava (750-800 CE – common era), known as Guru Rinpoche in Tibetan, is revered as one of the foremost Tantric masters and the founder of Buddhism in Tibet. To followers of the Nyingmapa order he is regarded as the 'second buddha'.

According to tradition, he was summoned to Tibet by King Trisong Detsen, the Tibetan son of a Chinese Buddhist princess. The king wanted to build a gompa at Samye and install Buddhism as the state religion in Tibet but was plagued by a succession of earthquakes caused by local demons (symbolising the dominant Bön clergy in Tibet). In order to eliminate these demons, the king dispatched a messenger to the great Indian university of Nalanda to fetch Padmasambhava, who set out on the long journey from Rewalsar in modern day Himachal Pradesh. Some of the Himalaya's best loved legends describe how the guru, armed with his *dorje* (thunderbolt) and Tantric magic, speedily subdued the demons and Bön magicians with his incredible powers. With the help of the Indian monks Santarakshita and Tamalashila, he then completed the construction of Tibet's first Buddhist monastery.

To cool-headed historians Padmasambhava is indeed a historical figure, born in Swat in modern day Pakistan, whose missionary work went a long way in popularising mystical Tantricism. His greatest success was that of overcoming court resistance to Buddhism and blending Tibet's Bön animism and pantheon of local gods into mainstream Buddhism.

The Indian Himalaya holds many relics of Padmasambhava. He travelled to Tibet several times up the Sutlej Valley, where his footprints are said to have been cast in stone at Nako. He also set up many shrines in the eastern Himalaya, especially in Bhutan and the Tawang area of Arunachal Pradesh, where there are 16 places associated with the guru. His celestial abode is known as Zangdok Palri, which takes the form of a three-roofed pagoda surrounded by the four guardian Kings, as seen in Zang Dog Palri Fo-Brang Gompa near Kalimpong.

Padmasambhava

(also known as Lamaism or Tibetan Buddhism), a form of Buddhism overlaid with mystical and occult elements. Tantric adepts claimed that they could jolt themselves towards enlightenment, shortening the long road to bhodhisattvahood. Tantric practice involves recitation of mantras, yogic techniques and meditation. Most of the ritual objects found in Himalayan monasteries are Tantric in nature. Tantric techniques are rarely written down but are passed down verbally from tutor to student.

Tibetan Buddhism divided into various schools or orders, of which the main ones are:

Nyingmapa This is the oldest order, also known as the Old or Unreformed School. It has its origins in the teachings of Padmasambhava (Guru Rinpoche), who is known by Nyingmapas as the 'second Buddha'. The order is commonly known as the Red Hat, though this is not a helpful distinction as the Sakyapa order also wears red hats. Nyingmapa monasteries are most commonly found in Sikkim and include Enchey, Pemayangtse and Tashiding gompas.

Gelukpa Literally 'Virtuous School', this order was reformed by the Tibetan monk Tsongkhapa in the 14th century in a return to doctrinal purity and monastic discipline. The Dalai Lama is the head of the Gelukpa order. The order is strong in Ladakh, Zanskar and Spiti, where Gelukpa monasteries include Alchi, Thikse, Likir and Rizong in Ladakh, and Ki, Tabo and Dhankar in Spiti.

Kagyupa The 'Whispered Lineage' order traces its lineage back to early Indian teachers and the Tibetan yogi Marpa and his disciple Milarepa. The order is sub-divided into the Karmapa (headquartered at Rumtek in Sikkim), Drukpa, Drigungpa and Kadampa sects. Drukpa monasteries include Khardung in Lahaul, Sani in Zanskar and Chemre, and Hemis and Stakna in Ladakh. Drigungpa monasteries include Phyang and Lamayuru in Ladakh.

Sakyapa This order was founded by the Tibetan scholar Sakya Pandita in the 11th century and grew up around the Sakya monastery in central Tibet. Sakyapa monasteries are not all that common in the Indian Himalaya but include Matho in Ladakh.

Beliefs Buddha renounced his material life to search for enlightenment but, unlike other prophets, found that starvation did not lead to discovery. Therefore, he developed his rule of the Middle Way – moderation in everything. Buddha taught the Four Holy Truths – essentially that all life is suffering but that suffering comes from our sensual desires and the illusion that they are important. By following the Eight-Fold Path these desires will be extinguished and a state of nirvana, where we are free from their delusions, will be reached.

Following this process requires going through a series of rebirths until the goal is eventually reached and no more rebirths into the world of suffering are necessary. The path that takes you through this cycle of births is karma, but this is not simply fate. Karma is a law of cause and effect; your actions in one life determine the role you will play and what you will have to go through in your next life.

Like the Jain religion early Buddhism was an offshoot of Hinduism and many of that religion's core doctrines are shared by Buddhism. Many of Buddhism's deities are based on early Hindu iconography. The god Avalokiteshvara (Tibetan: Chenresig) is thought to have its roots in the Hindu god Shiva and Manjushri has similarities with Brahma. The protector Mahakala is the Tibetan equivalent of Mahakali and the concept of *yab-yum* (sexual Tantric depictions of Tibetan deities with their consorts) has its root in the Hindu concept of shakti. Hindus even regard Buddha as a reincarnation of Vishnu.

Islam

Muslims, followers of the Islamic religion, are India's largest religious minority. They number about 75 million in all, over 10% of the country's population. This makes India one of the largest Islamic nations in the world.

In the Himalayan region, Muslims only predominate in the Kashmir Valley. Some 92% of the valley's population is Muslim, the majority of whom are Sunnites. To the east of the Kashmir Valley, in the upper valleys of the Drass, Suru and Bodhkarbu, there are pockets of Shi'ah Muslims who were linked with Baltistan prior to Partition in 1947. For information on Shi'ahs, see The Shi'ahs of Ladakh boxed text in the Ladakh & Zanskar chapter. There is also a sizeable Muslim community in Leh, and a small community of Muslims in Padum.

The religion's founder, the prophet Mohammed, was born in 570 CE at Mecca, now part of Saudi Arabia. He had his first revelation from Allah (God) in 610 CE and this and later visions were compiled into the Muslim holy book, the *Quran*. Muslims are strictly monotheistic and believe that to search for God through images is a sin. Muslim teachings correspond closely with the Old Testament of the Bible, and Moses and Jesus are both accepted as Muslim prophets (Musa and Isa), although Jesus is not seen as the son of God.

The Muslim faith was more than a religion; it called on its followers to spread the word – if necessary by the sword. Islam only travelled west for 100 years before being pushed back at Poitiers, France, in 732 CE, but it continued east for centuries. In 711 CE, the same year the Arabs landed in Spain, they sent dhows up the Indus River to India. This was more a casual raid than a full-scale invasion, but in the 12th century all of northern India fell into Muslim hands. Eventually the Mughal empire controlled most of the subcontinent. From here Islam was spread by Indian traders into South-East Asia.

At an early stage Islam suffered a fundamental split that remains to this day. The third caliph, successor to Mohammed, was murdered and followed by Ali, the Prophet's son-in-law, in 656 CE. Ali was assassinated in 661 CE by the governor of Syria, who set himself up as caliph in preference to the descendants of Ali. Most Muslims today are Sunnites, followers of the succession from the caliph, while the others are Shias, or Shi'ites, who follow the descendants of Ali.

An important branch of Islam is Sufism, which has a strong base in Kashmir. Sufism is the mystical side of Islam, which lays particular stress on music, dance and poetry as a medium to get closer to God. Many of Islam's early missionaries were Sufis and the cult of Sufi *pirs* (holy men) is still strong in Kashmir.

Although it did not make great numbers of converts, the visible effects of Muslim influence in India are strong in architecture, art and food. The *azan*, or call to prayer, is a particularly evocative mark of Islam. Friday is the Muslim holy day and the main mosque in each town is known as the Jama Masjid or Friday Mosque. Muslims do not eat pork or drink alcohol.

The five pillars of Islam are:

The Profession of Faith To become a Muslim one need only profess (with conviction) 'There is only one God and Mohammed is his messenger'.

Prayer Muslims pray five times a day, in the direction of the Kaaba stone of Mecca.

Charity Muslims give a proportion of their income to help the poor.

Fasting Muslims fast from sunrise to sunset during the month of Ramadan to mark Mohammed's first revelation.

Pilgrimage It is the aim of every Muslim to make the pilgrimage *(hajj)* to Mecca and become a *hajji* (a Muslim who has made the pilgrimage).

Sikhism

The Sikhs in India number 13 million and are predominantly located in the Punjab, although they are found all over India. Sikhs are the most visible of the Indian religious groups because of the five symbols introduced by Guru Govind Singh so that Sikh men could easily recognise each other. They are known as the five *kakkars* and are: *kesh* (uncut hair), *kangha* (the wooden comb), *kachha* (shorts), *kara* (the steel bracelet), and *kirpan* (the sword). Because of their kesha, Sikh men wear their hair tied up in a bun and hidden by a long turban. Wearing kachha and carrying a kirpan came about because of the Sikhs' military tradition – they didn't want to be tripping over a long dhoti or be caught without a weapon. Normally the sword is simply represented by a tiny image set in the comb.

The Sikh religion was founded by Guru Nanak, who was born in 1469. It was originally intended to bring together the best of the Hindu and Islamic religions. Its basic tenets are similar to those of Hinduism with the important modification that the Sikhs are opposed to caste distinctions and pilgrimage to rivers. They are not, however, opposed to pilgrimages to holy sites.

They worship at temples known as *gurdwaras*, baptise their children (when they are old enough to understand the religion) in a ceremony known as *pahul*, and cremate their dead. The holy book of the Sikhs is the *Granth Sahib*, which contains the works of the 10 Sikh gurus together with Hindu and Muslim writings. The last guru died in 1708.

In the 16th century, Guru Govind Singh introduced military overtones into the religion in an attempt to halt the persecution the Sikhs were then suffering. A brotherhood, known as the *khalsa* was formed, and entry into it was conditional on a person undergoing baptism *(amrit)*. From that time the majority of Sikhs have borne the surname Singh, which means Lion (although just because a person has the surname Singh doesn't mean they are necessarily a Sikh; many Rajputs also have this surname). The tricentennial of the formation of the khalsa was celebrated by hundreds of thousands of Sikhs on 13 April 1999.

Sikhs believe in one god and are opposed to idol worship. They practise tolerance and love of others; their belief in hospitality extends to offering shelter to anyone who comes to their gurdwaras. Because of their get-on-with-it attitude they are one of the better-off groups in Indian society. They have a well-known reputation for mechanical aptitude and can handle machinery of every type, from auto-rickshaws to jumbo jets.

The most sacred site in the Himalayan region for Sikhs is the lake of Hem Kund, in Uttarakhand, near the Valley of Flowers National Park. In the *Granth Sahib*, Govind Singh recounts that he meditated on the shores of a lake that was surrounded by seven snowcapped mountains; in the 20th century this lake was identified as Hem Kund. Other Sikh Himalayan pilgrimage spots include Manikaran (Parvati Valley) and Rewalsar Lake, both in Himachal Pradesh.

Facts for the Visitor

SUGGESTED ITINERARIES

The Indian Himalaya is a vast region; you could spend months here exploring tiny mountain villages, ancient *gompas* (monasteries) and pilgrimage sites. There is a danger in prescribing suggested itineraries, as one of the inherent joys of travel is the element of surprise. Nevertheless, if your time is limited, the following outlines might give you a place to start. The idea is to use these as a guideline only. Deviating from the main tourist centres is always to be recommended. Except for Arunachal Pradesh, most of the following itineraries will take about three weeks.

Himachal Pradesh & Ladakh
Delhi-McLeod Ganj-Kullu-Parvati Valley-Kullu-Naggar-Manali-Leh-Delhi

First port of call is McLeod Ganj, home to thousands of Tibetan refugees, and headquarters of the Tibetan Government in Exile. From Delhi you can take the train to Pathankot or get a direct overnight bus. You can spend days here, visiting Tsuglagkhang, the Dalai Lama's temple, attending meditation classes, tucking into the best food you'll find just about anywhere as well as shopping for Tibetan artefacts in the town centre.

Next stop is Kullu, from where you can head out along the Parvati Valley to the laid-back village of Manikaran, renowned for its hot springs and fine Hindu and Sikh shrines. Then it's back to Kullu and on to Manali, stopping off at beautiful Naggar, ancient capital of the Kullu Valley, where you can visit temples built during the reign of the *rajas* (kings).

Manali has been a centre for travellers in search of the cosmic since the 1970s. It's still a good place to spend a few days, with fine old guesthouses and some interesting temples. After you're well rested, it's time to embark on one of the classic trips in India

– the two day haul by bus to the capital of Ladakh, Leh. In the town of Leh and environs are some spectacular and colourful gompas – rich repositories of Buddhist art. You can also study aspects of Buddhist philosophy here. From Leh you can reduce the long journey back to the capital to a couple of hours by flying back to Delhi, though make sure you have a reservation before you set off if time is tight, as this is a popular route.

Himachal Pradesh Hill Stations
Delhi-Pathankot-Dalhousie-Khajiar-Chamba-McLeod Ganj-Mandi-Shimla-Delhi

Take the overnight train to Pathankot from the capital, from where it's a 3½ hour trip by bus to the old British hill station of Dalhousie. There are some fine walks in the town's environs, and you can walk in a day to the grassy meadow of Khajiar, spend the night in a guesthouse here and catch the afternoon bus the following day to Chamba, renowned for its extraordinary and ancient temple complexes.

It's then a long 10 hour haul to McLeod Ganj, where you can easily spend four or five days. If you have the time and inclination, it's possible to trek from the Chamba Valley to McLeod Ganj over the high Indrahar Pass across the Dhaula Dhar Range. Alternatively, you could continue down the Chamba Valley to the end of the road at ancient Brahmaur, which also has a beautiful group of ancient temples.

From McLeod Ganj, it's on to Mandi, the gateway of the Kullu Valley, with the fine 16th century Bhutnath Temple, among others, before proceeding to the pleasant hill station of Shimla, which still retains fine old colonial buildings, as well as two interesting bazaars. There's enough to keep you busy here for days. From Shimla, you can catch the toy train to Kalka, and then proceed from there to Delhi.

Highlights of the Indian Himalaya

Hindu Pilgrimage Sites

- **Haridwar (Uttarakhand)** Watch dusty pilgrims bathe their sins away at the *ghats* (steps) of the holy Ganga, or observe the evening Ganga Aarti (river worship) ceremony, performed by priests who set floating lamps adrift on the current.
- **Rishikesh (Uttarakhand)** The Yoga capital of India, with the highest concentration of ashrams in the world. A walk through the blissfully traffic-free Swarg Ashram area reveals dozens of beautiful ashrams, *dharamsalas* (pilgrim's lodging) and temples, many featuring technicolour statues of Shiva.
- **Char Dham (Uttarakhand)** The four holy pilgrimage sites of Yamunotri, Gangotri, Kedarnath and Badrinath are the most revered destinations of all Indian pilgrims. At Gangotri and Badrinath, buses will drop you at their respective sacred shrines. To reach Yamunotri and Kedarnath a 14km trek on foot or horseback is required.

Ancient Temple Complexes

- **Chamba (Himachal Pradesh)** Legacy of the Varman dynasty, the towns of Chamba and Brahmaur have some fine temple groups, including the Lakshmi Narayan.
- **Jageshwar (Kumaon, Uttarakhand)** Fifty-four small temples in a peaceful location. The main temple enshrines a *jyothirlingam,* one of the 12 'lingams of light' in India.

Buddhist Gompas

- **Hemis Gompa (Ladakh)** Fine, well-preserved wall paintings and ornate images of the deities.
- **Matho Gompa (Ladakh)** Hosts extraordinary oracle festivals around Losar.
- **Tikse Gompa (Ladakh)** A good place to witness a *puja* (worship).
- **Alchi Gompa (Ladakh)** The best preserved Indo-Kashmiri art in the world and a beautiful location on the banks of the Indus River.
- **Ki Gompa (Spiti, Himachal Pradesh)** Heaped up on the cliff side like a giant mound of rice, this monastery has a dramatic location.
- **Tabo Gompa (Spiti, Himachal Pradesh)** Along with Alchi, more excellent examples of early Buddhist art. There's a great library where you can learn more about Buddhism.
- **Rumtek (Sikkim)** Headquarters of the Kagyupa order of Tibetan Buddhism.
- **Sangachoeling Gompa (Sikkim)** One of the oldest gompas in Sikkim, it has a sublimely peaceful atmosphere with the murmurs of village life drifting up from the valleys below.
- **Zong Dog Palri Fo-Brang Gompa (Gangtok)** Extraordinary wall paintings and a three-dimensional *mandala* (circular symbol of the universe), one of only three in the world.
- **Tawang Gompa (Arunachal Pradesh)** Founded by the sixth Dalai Lama, this 17th-century monastery on the border of Bhutan is the most important in the north-east. It has a fine collection of *thangkas* (rectangular Tibetan paintings on cloth) and a beautiful gilded statue of Sakyamuni (the historical Buddha) in the massive main prayer hall.

Hill Stations of the Raj

- **Shimla (Himachal Pradesh)** Summer capital of British Indian *sahibs* (lords) and *memsahibs* (ladies). Walks around Shimla are the best way to see its colonial vestiges.
- **Mussoorie (Uttarakhand)** Fine mountain vistas and a pleasant climate.
- **Nainital (Uttarakhand)** Take a boat out onto the lake and then grab a pot of tea at the Nainital Boat Club, an old British club with a lakeside ballroom.

Highlights of the Indian Himalaya

- **Darjeeling (West Bengal Hills)** The queen of the hill stations. Take afternoon tea at Glenary's Tea Rooms and later retire for a cocktail in front of the open fire. There are also some fine Buddhist gompas, pleasant walks, several museums, a zoo, and nearby tea gardens.

Travellers' Hang-Outs
- **Manikaran (Parvati Valley, Himachal Pradesh)** A laid-back mix of hot springs, temples, trekking and *charas* (marijuana).
- **McLeod Ganj (Himachal Pradesh)** New home to the Dalai Lama and a thriving community of Tibetan refugees. It is also an excellent place to spend some time, particularly if you're interested in studying Buddhist philosophy.

National Parks & Wildlife Sanctuaries
- **Corbett Tiger Reserve (Uttarakhand)** India's oldest national park provides the opportunity to take a trip on elephant-back to spot the elusive Bengal tiger in its natural habitat.
- **Rajaji National Park (Uttarakhand)** Known for its herds of wild elephants.
- **Jaldhapara Wildlife Sanctuary (West Bengal Hills)** One of the last homes of the endangered one-horned rhino *(Rhinoceros unicornis)*.
- **Fambonglho Wildlife Sanctuary (Sikkim)** Small populations of Himalayan black bear, red panda and other mammals.
- **Namdapha National Park (Arunachal Pradesh)** A remote and little-visited 1850 sq km forested reserve, rising from the plains up to 4500m. Unique in being home to four big cats: tiger, leopard, clouded leopard and snow leopard.

Himalayan Views
- **Kausani (Uttarakhand)** Stunning sunsets over Nanda Devi, Trisul and the Panchchuli massif, and you don't even have to get out of bed.
- **Kalpa (Kinnaur, Himachal Pradesh)** Fine views of Kinner Kailash, and you still don't have to get out of bed.
- **Lago La (Suru Valley, Zanskar)** A short but hard climb from the road to the Lago La near Panikhar gives an unforgettable view of the Nun Kun massif.

Great Journeys
- **Kalpa to Kaza and Manali (Kinnaur, Spiti & Kullu)** Scenically majestic and culturally fascinating 10 day trip, up the dramatic Sutlej Valley, into the Trans-Himalayan zone of Spiti. Then over the 4551m Kunzum La into Lahaul and finally the historic Rohtang Pass to Manali. Only possible July to October.
- **Manali to Leh (Himachal Pradesh to Ladakh)** Two day bus ride with an overnight camp stop. Crosses two passes over 4800m high
- **Leh to Nubra (Ladakh)** A remote ride over the highest motorable road in the world at 5602m, from the Indus to the Shyok valleys.
- **Kargil to Padum (Ladakh to Zanskar)** Skirts glaciers and traditional villages, following the beautiful Suru Valley upstream to Pensi La and then down into the heartland of Zanskar.
- **Ziro to Pasighat (Arunachal Pradesh)** Takes in virgin forest, tribal longhouses and the fascinating Apatani plateau.

Little Tibet
Shimla-Kalpa-Kaza-Keylong-Leh-Delhi

This is a tougher trip reaching altitudes of over 5000m. From Shimla you can head up the Sutlej Valley into Kinnaur, stopping off at the Bhimakali Temple in Sarahan. Kalpa is a lovely place to stay and you can make a visit to the pretty Sangla Valley. You need to get an inner line permit in Kalpa before continuing up into barren but beautiful Spiti, stopping to visit the stunning gompas at Tabo, Ki and Dhankar. From here catch a bus over the stunning Kunzum La into the Lahaul Valley. From here pay a visit to Keylong or head straight over the Rohtang Pass to Manali. Alternatively, continue over the high passes to Ladakh. You could spend weeks just here, before flying back to Delhi.

Uttar Pradesh Hill Stations
Delhi-Haridwar-Rishikesh-Mussoorie-Haridwar-Nainital-Ranikhet-Kausani-Almora-Delhi

Catch the overnight train to Haridwar, with its hundreds of ashrams and modern temples, and take a day trip out to the Rajaji National Park (open mid-November to mid-June) and then continue to Rishikesh, where serious students of Hindu philosophy can study at the feet of the masters. From Rishikesh it takes little over an hour to Dehra Dun, from where there are numerous buses up to the nearby hill station of Mussoorie. Catch the cable car up to Gun Hill for fine Himalayan panoramas and have your fortune told by astrologers back down on The Mall.

Next it's a long day's journey to Nainital via Haridwar, where you can row around the beautiful lake and visit scenic viewpoints on horseback. Between mid-November and mid-June, take a day trip out to the Corbett Tiger Reserve for an elephant-back tiger-spotting safari. A couple of days at either Ranikhet, Kausani or Almora (or all of them) will have you relaxed and ready to face the chaos back down on the plains.

From Kausani, it's only a short bus ride north to the ancient temple group at Baij-nath, and from Almora, you can visit the beautiful village of Jageshwar, which has fine walks and a stunning group of ancient stone temples.

Char Dham
Delhi-Mussoorie-Rishikesh/Haridwar-Yamunotri-Gangotri-Kedarnath-Badrinath-Rishikesh-Delhi

If you're really pressed for time, you could take the 13 day *yatra* (pilgrimage) run by UP Tourism to the four shrines of Yamunotri, Gangotri, Kedarnath and Badrinath. However, you'd do better to make your own leisurely way around this region. Ideally, the best way to visit these remote shrines is by taxi; you can complete the yatra by public bus, but they tend to leave the sacred spots at ungodly hours of the morning.

After visiting the hill station of Mussoorie head for Rishikesh and Haridwar on the holy Ganges, before proceeding to the holy shrines farther north. It's a long and nerve-shattering trip to Hanumanchatti, road head for the 14km trek to Yamunotri. If you're really keen, you'll make it to Yamunotri in a day's trek; the less energetic can stop overnight at Jankibaichatti, and if the thought of the remaining 5km *uphill* trek to the holy site still doesn't thrill after a good night's sleep, you can complete the last leg on a mountain pony.

It's a long haul to Gangotri, via the pleasant town of Uttarkashi, but at least the bus will drop you practically at the door of the sacred shrine. From Gangotri you can trek in two days to the source of the Ganges (technically the Bhagirathi), at the Gangotri Glacier. The next stage of the yatra, to Kedarnath, will require an overnight halt en route – probably at Srinagar.

On arrival at Gaurikund, road head for the 14km trek to the holy shrine, you'll be assailed by pony owners vying for your custom. In fact, it's not such a bad way to traverse the steep trail to Kedarnath, but if you'd prefer to walk, you can stay overnight at the village of Rambara, halfway up the trail, or plough on upwards to reach Kedarnath at dusk.

It's possible to reach Gangotri in a day from Gaurikund, but the bus leaves at an obscenely early hour. After 12 long, dusty hours it will drop you in the large village of Badrinath where you can pay homage to Vishnu the following morning at the temple, and walk to the tribal village of Mana, 3km distant.

How you make your way back to Delhi is up to you. You might like to stop at Govind Ghat, between Badrinath and Joshimath, and trek (or take a pony) out to Ghangaria, from where you can take day trips into the beautiful Valley of Flowers National Park. At Joshimath you can arrange a guide to take you on some of the fine treks in this region. If you're not a trekker, head down to the Kumaon region with its renowned hill stations, or backtrack to Rishikesh.

Bangla (West Bengal) Hills & Sikkim
Kolkata (Calcutta) or Delhi-Shiliguri-Darjeeling-Gangtok-West Sikkim-Kalimpong-Shiliguri-Kolkata (or Delhi)

Find your way to Shiliguri on the northern Bangla (West Bengal) plains, then check to see if the toy train is running for the nine hour journey to the queen of the hill stations – Darjeeling. If it's not then consider breaking the journey at Kurseong, a delightful town with the ambience of a hill station but without the tourist paraphernalia.

In Darjeeling, check out the snow leopards at India's only snow leopard breeding program, imbibe the beverage for which Darjeeling is famous (and visit the tea plantations), have a spot of badminton at the Gymkhana Club, then proceed to Gangtok, capital of Sikkim (with your easily obtained tourist permit, of course).

Tee up your trekking permit for west Sikkim at a reputable travel agent, then head off under your own steam to the beautiful Phodang and Labrang gompas in North Sikkim. During your stay in Gangtok, take a day trip to Rumtek Gompa, headquarters of the Kagyupa order. Then set forth for Yuksom in west Sikkim, road head for the Dzongri trail (on your organised trek).

Afterwards visit the beautiful Tashiding Gompa and head for Pelling, taking in the stunning gompas at Pemayangtse and Sangachoeling and a wander through the ruins of the Rabdentse Palace.

Fifteen-day permits are available for Sikkim, and the regulations are expected to ease in the near future. The above itinerary will only allow four or five days for trekking in the Dzongri region. At present, if you're a keen trekker and would prefer a longer trek, you might have to forego a visit to east and north Sikkim.

After visiting Sikkim set off for Jorethang and proceed to Kalimpong, back in Bangla (West Bengal), where you can visit the ornate Zong Dog Palri Fo-Brang Gompa, and then return to Shiliguri and back to Kolkata (Calcutta) or Delhi.

Arunachal Pradesh
Kolkata (Calcutta) or Shiliguri-Gauhati-Tezpur-Tawang-Tezpur-Ziro-Pasighat

Take the train from either Kolkata (Calcutta) or Shiliguri to Gauhati, the biggest city in the north-east. Presuming you have your permit and have paid the US$50 per day to visit Arunachal (most foreigners take guided tours costing US$150 per day), you can proceed to the Assamese town of Tezpur on the north bank of the Bhramaputra. From here it's a few hours to the border at Bhalukpong. Just across the border in Arunachal lies the Orchid Research Centre Sanctuary at Tipi on the forested banks of the beautiful Bharali River. Its a long, slow drive north into the Buddhist Sherdrukpen area of Bomdila and Dirang Dzong, where there are several gompas. After an overnight stay it's uphill again to the dramatic Se La at 4249m, and a winding drive into the Buddhist Monpa heartland of Tawang. Here you can visit the enormous Tawang Gompa, said to be the biggest in India, and perhaps visit some of the high-altitude lake areas above Tawang town. Then it's a long drive back to Tezpur.

From Tezpur you head for Ziro in central Arunachal, the centre of the Apatani tribe.

Another long day's drive takes you to Daporijo on the Subansiri River, a market town home to Tagin and Hill Miri tribespeople. The road continues into the Adi tribal homeland around Along on the mighty Siang River (known as the Brahmaputra in Assam) and down to the plains at Pasighat. From Pasighat it's a long journey back to North Lakhimpur in Assam, where there are trains connecting back to Gauhati.

PLANNING
When to Go

The weather will probably be your most important consideration in determining when you plan to visit the Indian Himalaya – see the Climate section in the Facts about the Region chapter. It's a good idea to give all of the hill stations a miss during school holidays, Christmas and the Dussehra and Diwali festivals (September and October), when it can be difficult to find accommodation, and prices increase threefold. An exception is Kullu, which is a great place to visit during Dussehra. It hosts one of the most colourful celebrations of this festival that you'll see anywhere in India. Another exception is Darjeeling, which is delightful at Christmas, with Christmas trees, log fires and bands of carol singers.

Himalaya 2000 The new millennium sees a year-long program of cultural and religious festivals in the eastern Indian Himalaya, mainly in Sikkim. For a program of events contact the local tourist office (see the regional chapters).

What Kind of Trip?

In most parts of the Himalaya it is possible to travel around independently, and in many regions reputable trekking agents can tailor treks to individual requirements. If you'd prefer to join a tour, the state government tourist authorities in Delhi and Kolkata (Calcutta) have a range of tour options, including pilgrimage tours, river rafting, trekking, skiing and other activities. A list of reputable adventure tour operators in Delhi can be found in the Gateway Cities chapter.

Arunachal Pradesh and Sikkim restrict visits to a maximum of 10 and 15 days respectively so you will have to get your skates on when travelling there. Other restricted areas such as the Nubra Valley in Ladakh also limit the time you can spend there (seven days) and require you to travel in a group of four so this may also affect how you travel in these areas. See the Travel Permits section for more details.

Maps

Abroad Lonely Planet's *India travel atlas* breaks the entire country down into over 100 pages of maps. It is fully indexed and the book format means it is easy to refer to.

Nelles Verlag publishes a good *Himalaya* map, which gives an overview of the whole range at a scale of 1:1,500,000. It also produces a *Northern India* map at the same scale covering Himachal Pradesh with a 1:650,000 insert covering Ladakh. A third choice is its *North-Eastern Indian and Bangladesh* map.

Valleys & Passes

pass	height (metres)	valleys it divides	open
Baralacha La	4883	Lahaul to Ladakh	early Jun to mid-Oct
Khardung La	5602	Leh (Indus) to Nubra	Jun to Sept
Kunzum La	4551	Lahaul to Spiti	mid-Jul to mid-Oct
Pensi La	4450	Kargil (Suru) to Zanskar	early Jul to early Oct
Rohtang Pass	3978	Kullu to Lahaul	mid-Jun to mid-Nov
Zoji La	3529	Kashmir to Ladakh	Jun to mid-Oct

Best Times to Visit the Indian Himalaya

region	best time to go	comments
Arunachal Pradesh	early Oct to mid-Mar (*except mid-May to Sept)	Tawang Gompa (Oct/Nov, Mar/Apr)
Bangla Hills (West Bengal)	Mar to mid-April & mid-Sept to mid-Dec (*except Jun to Sept)	Best Himalayan views after monsoon Jaldhapara Wildlife Sanctuary (Mar/Apr)
Himachal Pradesh	mid-Apr to end Nov (*except mid-Jun to mid-Sept)	Jul/Aug is also a popular time to visit the Kullu Valley
Kashmir	early Jun to end Nov	Travel not recommended at present
Ladakh & Zanskar	early Jun to end Oct	Ladakh reached by plane in winter
Lahaul & Spiti	early Jul to end Oct	Lahaul totally isolated from Nov-Jun
Sikkim	early Mar to end Nov (*except Jun to mid-Aug)	Orchids (end Sept) Rhododendrons (May)
Uttarakhand	mid-May to mid-Nov (*except mid-Jul to mid-Sept)	Corbett Tiger Reserve (Nov to June) Valley of Flowers (Jul to Aug)

*monsoon

The *Ladakh Zanskar Trekking Map* by Editions Olizane and Artou Guides is a good 1:350,000 map but it can be hard to find.

Geocenter produces a 1:2,000,000 map of *India – North-Eastern Region*. It covers everything from Delhi to Arunachal Pradesh so it's not all that detailed on the Himalayan states.

The best topographic map to Sikkim is the *Sikkim Himalaya* by the Swiss Foundation for Alpine Research (1997) at a scale of 1:150,000.

Leomann produces a series of excellent trekking maps at a scale of 1:200,000 including the following:

Sheet 1 Srinagar, Kolohoi Glacier, Kishtwar
Sheet 2 Kargil, Zanskar, Nun Kun area
Sheet 3 Leh, Zanskar, Nubra Valley
Sheet 4 Chamba, Dhaula Dhar passes, Pangi Valley, western Lahaul
Sheet 5 Kullu Valley, Parvati Valley, central Lahaul
Sheet 6 Kalpa-Kinnaur, Spiti, Shimla area
Sheet 7 Gangotri, Har ki Dun, Mussoorie area
Sheet 8 Pindari Glacier, Badrinath, Nanda Devi

In the UK, Edward Stanford Ltd (☎ 020-7836 1321), 12-14 Long Acre, Covent Garden, London WC2E 9LP stocks several Indian-made maps and guides and publishes a free catalogue of available maps of the Himalaya region.

In India The Government Map Office (Survey of India) produces a series of maps covering India. The headquarters of the Survey of India, which was established in 1767, is in Dehra Dun and there's a showroom in Delhi. The maps are generally not all that useful since the government will not allow production of anything at a reasonable scale which shows India's sea or land borders, and many of them date back to the 1970s. They do, however, have some good city maps. It is illegal to take any Survey of India map of a scale larger than 1:250,000 out of the country.

The survey's colour Trekking Map Series (1:250,000) includes *Badari-Kedar*, covering the northern Garhwal region and *Kumaun Hills*, covering everything north of Almora. The following series of *Trekking Route Maps of Himachal Pradesh*, at a scale of 1:250,000, aren't bad but don't have enough detail to be of much use:

Sheet 1 Dhaula Dhar Range, Dharamsala, Brahmaur, Chandra Valley
Sheet 2 Kullu Valley, western Lahaul, Spiti
Sheet 3 Shimla, Kinnaur, Sangla Valley

The survey's *Sikkim* is a fine state map, with a scale of 1:150,000, but it's difficult to procure. It also produces a map of *Assam, Arunachal Pradesh, Manipur, Meghalaya, Mizoram, Nagaland & Tripura*. The Discover India Series has road guides to *Sikkim, Himachal Pradesh* and *Jammu & Kashmir*.

Nest & Wings publishes a good series of books and maps, including both trekking and touring maps. Trekking maps include *Ladakh, Jammu & Kashmir* (Rs 150); *Himachal Pradesh*, including Lahaul and Spiti; and *Zanskar, Ladakh & Nubra Valley, Tso Moriri & Pangong Tso* (Rs 200). *Darjeeling Area, Sikkim & Bhutan* (Rs 60) is a road and trekking map. Its tourist maps include *Himachal Pradesh* (Rs 50) and the *Garhwal & Kumaon Himalayas* (Rs 40), but neither are to scale.

The Government of India tourist offices have a number of excellent giveaway city maps and also a reasonable all-India map. State tourist offices do not have much in the way of maps.

What to Bring

The usual traveller's rule applies – bring as little as possible. It's much better to have to buy something you've left behind than find you have too much and need to get rid of it.

Clothes In the Himalayan regions, it can be quite cool in the evenings, even in summer, and farther north it will get down to freezing at night, so you will need at least some cold-weather gear whatever time of year you plan to go. If you are travelling between October and March you will probably need a fleece and a down jacket, especially if you are headed for higher altitudes. For colder climates, the 'layers theory' is your best bet.

If you're travelling to Ladakh or Spiti, be prepared for dramatic temperature changes and for the extreme burning power of the sun in the thin air. A cloud across the sun can change the air temperature from T-shirt to sweater level in seconds.

A reasonable clothes list might include:

- one pair of cotton trousers (for summer and lower elevations)
- one pair of warmer and more durable trousers (for winter and higher elevations)
- one long cotton skirt (women)
- a few T-shirts or short-sleeved cotton shirts
- one fleece, thick sweater or woollen shirt (for high elevations and cold nights)
- one pair of sneakers or shoes, plus socks; good, comfortable walking boots with ankle support if you're planning to trek
- sandals or thongs (flipflops; handy when showering in common bathrooms)
- lightweight jacket or raincoat (during the monsoon) or a more heavyweight jacket of high-quality fabric, such as a Gore-Tex (for higher elevations)
- gloves and balaclava for winter (both items can be purchased locally; a balaclava is particularly important at higher elevations, as considerable body heat is lost through the head)
- sun hat or cap
- set of 'dress up' clothes (for dining in Raj-era hotels!)

Bedding A sleeping bag can be a hassle to carry, but can serve as something to sleep in (and avoid unsavoury-looking hotel bedding), a cushion on hard train seats, a pillow on long bus journeys or a bed-top cover (since cheaper hotels rarely give you one). They are particularly useful in places like Ladakh and Spiti where the nights can get very cold. Visiting many of the remote gompas by public transport will require an overnight stop, often in basic guesthouses. If you're trekking then a sleeping bag will be an absolute necessity.

A sheet sleeping bag can be very useful, particularly on overnight train trips or if you don't trust the hotel's sheets. They can also be used as liners if you hire a sleeping bag.

Some travellers find that a plastic sheet is useful for a number of reasons, including to bedbug-proof unhealthy-looking beds.

Others have recommended an inflatable pillow as a useful accessory. These are widely available in India (Rs 60).

Equipment Rental Sleeping bags, tents and sleeping mats can be rented in places like Leh, McLeod Ganj, Uttarkashi, Gangtok and Darjeeling, but are not of very high quality and often require a large security deposit of several thousand rupees. You are better off bringing your own sleeping bag, though renting a tent can be handy if you are just planning one small trek or an overnight trip.

Toiletries Western brands of soap, toothpaste and other toiletries are readily available (often in handy sachets so you don't have to carry around a whole bottle of the stuff).

Monsoon Essentials

If you're planning to travel to the Himalayan region during the monsoon, don't underestimate its ability to turn your trip into a waterlogged misery, if you're not properly prepared. Monsoon essentials include:

- sturdy umbrella (available just about everywhere)
- raincoat
- full set of wet-weather gear, including overpants with elasticised ankles
- waterproofing spray for boots and packs
- plastic cover for your pack
- gumboots/Wellingtons (readily available in the hill stations, but if you have large feet, you'll need to bring a pair with you)
- plastic envelopes (for important documents)
- good, sturdy plastic bags (to keep sodden clothes separate from dry clothes in your pack)
- waterproof cover for your camera (which enables you to take pictures without having to juggle the camera *and* an umbrella)

Hair conditioner usually comes in the 'shampoo and conditioner in one' format, so if you don't use this, bring your own. Astringent is useful for cleaning away the grime at the end of the day – bring cotton balls for application. Tampons are not readily available in the Himalayan regions – bring a supply. Sanitary pads are widely available in the hill stations, but not in the more remote regions.

Men can safely leave their shaving gear at home. One of the pleasures of Indian travel is a shave in a barber shop every few days. With AIDS becoming more widespread in India, however, choose a barber shop that looks clean, and make sure that a fresh blade is used. For around Rs 10 you'll get the full treatment – lathering, followed by a shave, then the process is repeated, and finally there's the hot, damp towel and buckets of cheap cologne. If you're not quick you'll find that before you know it you're also in for a scalp massage.

Always keep an emergency stash of toilet paper with you in case of emergencies. Bring your own deodorant. See the Health section later in this chapter for details about medical supplies.

Miscellaneous Items For budget travellers, a padlock is a virtual necessity. Most cheap hotels and a number of mid-range places have doors locked by a flimsy latch and padlock. A reasonably heavy duty chain will secure your pack to the luggage racks of trains and buses. It's worth having several sizes, for say a daypack and also a hotel door. You can buy a reasonable lock in India for Rs 25 to Rs 50. Some women carry a high-pitched whistle that may act as a deterrent to would-be assailants.

Some travellers rhapsodise about the usefulness of a miniature electric element to boil water in a cup, widely available in India for as little as Rs 30. You can get jars of instant coffee in major centres but bring a few sachets of hot chocolate or whatever you crave, for when you need a moment of luxury. A sarong is a handy item. It can be used as a bed sheet, an item of clothing, an emergency towel, and a pillow on trains!

Insect repellent can be extremely useful in lower altitudes. Pick up an electric mosquito zapper (Rs 70) in Delhi or Kolkata (Calcutta) before heading north. A lightweight mosquito net can be very useful on the plains and en route to the hills (at Shiliguri, in Bangla, for example), as well as in mosquito-prone areas such as Gangtok. Power cuts are common in the Indian Himalaya ('load shedding' as it is euphemistically known) and there's little street lighting at night so a torch (flashlight), candles and matches are essential. A small alarm clock is useful for catching those 5 am buses and trains.

For high-altitude zones like Ladakh and Spiti, a sun hat, sunglasses, lip balm (or Blistex) and high-factor sunscreen are essential. Sunscreen is available in most cities on the plains but is expensive. A water bottle should always be by your side; and also water purification tablets (which also reduce the quantity of waste plastic bottles). Earplugs are absolutely essential to shut out India's 24 hour noise.

If you are travelling in winter you can buy small heaters for around Rs 100 to Rs 300, though the hotel may charge a little extra for electricity.

Other miscellaneous items worth considering are:

calamine lotion or an anti-itch preparation (for mosquito bites), umbrella (available cheaply in India), sewing kit, dental floss, vitamins, Lomotil (for diarrhoea), condoms, contraceptives, special medication, short-wave radio, scrubbing brush (for laundry), photocopies of passport and air ticket, spare set of spectacles (and spectacle prescription), small rubber wedge door stop (to keep doors closed), visa photos, copy of your address book, universal sink plug, knife (preferably Swiss Army), extra camera battery, clothesline and pegs (elastic 'pegless' clotheslines are better), string, tape, zip-shut bags and plastic containers (for carrying snacks, opened packets of laundry powder etc).

How to Carry It Where to put all this gear? Well, for budget travellers the backpack is still the best carrying bag. Many packs these days are lockable, otherwise you can make it a bit more thief-proof by sewing on tabs so you can padlock it shut. It's worth paying the money for a strong, good quality pack, as it's much more likely to withstand the rigours of Indian travel. The best makes have a lifetime guarantee. If you like to travel light consider taking two smaller packs, leaving one in a hotel store while you scoot around for a week or so with a mini-pack.

An alternative is a large, soft, zip bag with a wide shoulder strap. This is obviously not an option if you plan to do any trekking. Suitcases are only for jet-setters on a group tour.

See the Monsoon Essentials boxed text earlier in this chapter for advice about keeping your things dry.

RESPONSIBLE TOURISM
Despite its epic grandeur, the Himalaya and its network of isolated communities is surprisingly fragile. As ancient traditions come into contact with the modern world local traditions are increasingly at risk. The pace of cultural and environmental change has never been greater.

Travellers can lessen their impact on the culture and the environment by observing the points outlined below. Other cultural tips are covered in the Dos & Don'ts section of the Facts about the Region chapter. Please be particularly sensitive in remote areas such as Spiti, Ladakh and Arunachal Pradesh. See the Responsible Trekking boxed text later in this chapter if you are heading off into wilderness areas.

- Avoid buying anything in plastic bags and bottles. Don't throw them away; keep them and reuse them. Try water purification tablets rather than buying water in plastic bottles. Always hike out your rubbish.
- Modesty rates highly in India, as in most Asian countries. In the hill stations, you can get away with wearing shorts (of a decent length) as a western eccentricity, but in the more remote regions of the Himalaya, you should be more conservatively dressed. Wearing shorts or a T-shirt in a more formal situation, in a remote village, or in any sacred place such as a temple, mosque or gompa, is definitely disrespectful. Public hand holding or kissing is disapproved of.

- Always be fair in a bargaining situation and always keep your word. For example, if you have promised to pay a porter for six stages which you discover later you could complete in two, so be it. The porters must be paid the agreed amount. The same applies to staff and horsemen.
- Try to patronise local business, hotels, tour agencies and guides as much as possible, particularly in places like Ladakh and Zanskar, so that money stays in the community.
- Never offer money for photographs unless there is a particular sign in a gompa requesting a donation. Some gompas prohibit photography in the *dukhang*, or main prayer hall. Respect people's privacy, especially women, and obtain permission before whipping your camera out. Never let your photography interfere with a religious festival and make sure you don't block the view of the local spectators.
- If you agree to post someone a copy of the photograph please follow through on this.

- Don't hand out sweets, pens or money to children since it encourages begging. A donation to a project, health centre or school is a more constructive way to help.
- Try to give mountain people a balanced perspective of life in the west. Point out that you are only temporarily 'rich' in India and that income and costs balance out in London like they do in Leh. Try also to point out the strong points of the local culture – strong family ties, low crime, a lack of pollution etc.

TOURIST OFFICES
Local Tourist Offices
Within India the tourist office story is somewhat blurred by the overlap between the national and state tourist offices. Some states, such as Uttar Pradesh, even have divisional offices for separate districts, such as Garhwal and Kumaon in Uttarakhand.

Visiting Gompas

Most gompas extend a warm welcome to foreign guests. You can maintain this good faith by observing the following courtesies:

- Always circumambulate gompas, chapels and chörtens in a clockwise direction, keeping shrines and chörtens to your right.
- Some gompas, including many in Ladakh, require an entrance fee. This money is used for the maintenance of gompas, so don't begrudge the small amount asked. All visitors, not just foreigners, give donations. It is customary to also leave a few rupees at the altar.
- Do not use flash photography in the prayer rooms. It will destroy ancient murals. (A torch or flashlight is handy for examining murals.) Some chapels forbid photography.
- Do not touch or remove any object in a gompa, or prayer flags outside.
- Remove your shoes when you enter a prayer hall. (You can leave your socks on, which is a good idea because the floors can sometimes be dirty or cold.) You are allowed to wear shoes within the general gompa compound.
- Don't wear shorts or short skirts and remove your hat when entering a chapel. Don't smoke inside the monastery.
- If you hire a guide to show you around the gompa, make sure they are authorised, knowledgeable and preferably from the local area.
- Do not insist on accommodation in gompas. Some places do offer small rooms, but they are usually for the benefit of genuine Buddhist students. If you are allowed to stay then bring your own food as the monks often don't have enough to share (though they will probably offer anyway).
- Do not disturb any monks while they are praying. Ask if you want to attend prayers.

In many Himalayan states the state tourism ministry also runs a chain of tourist bungalows and large, sometimes ex-colonial, hotels, which generally offer good accommodation at reasonable prices. They also have good tourist bus services, sightseeing tours, and skiing packages, as well as other travel services. State tourist offices will usually be in the tourist bungalows (where there is one). State tourist offices are listed at the beginning of each regional chapter. See the Gateway Cities chapter for tourist offices in Delhi and Kolkata.

Tourist Offices Abroad

The Government of India Department of Tourism maintains a string of tourist offices in other countries where you can get some good brochures, leaflets and other information about India. Some of the foreign offices are not always as useful for obtaining information as those within India. There are also smaller 'promotion offices' in Osaka (Japan) and in Dallas, Miami, San Francisco and Washington DC (USA). You can find the useful Department of Tourism Web site at www.tourindia.com/.

Australia
  (☎ 02-9264 4855, fax 9223 3003,
  email info@india.com.au)
  Level 2, Piccadilly, 210 Pitt St,
  Sydney NSW 2000
Canada
  (☎ 416-962 3787, fax 962 6279)
  60 Bloor St West, Suite No 1003,
  Toronto Ontario M4W 3B8
France
  (☎ 01 45 23 30 45, fax 45 23 33 45,
  email info.fr@India-Tourism)
  13 Blvd Haussmann, 75008 Paris
Germany
  (☎ 069-242 9490, fax 242 9497)
  Basler Strasse 48 D60329,
  Frankfurt-am-Main-1
Japan
  (☎ 03-571 5062, fax 571 5235)
  Pearl Bldg, 9-18 Ginza, 7-Chome, Chuo Ku,
  Tokyo 104
Malaysia
  (☎ 03-242 5285, fax 242 5301)
  Wisma HLA, Lot 203 Jalan Raja Chulan,
  50200 Kuala Lumpur

The Netherlands
  (☎ 020-620 8991, fax 638 3059)
  Rokin 9-15, 1012 KK Amsterdam
  Web site www.qqq.com/india/
Singapore
  (☎ 286-235 3800, fax 235 8677)
  United House, 20 Kramat Lane,
  Singapore 0922
Thailand
  (☎ 02-235 2585, fax 236 8411)
  Kentucky Fried Chicken Bldg, 3rd floor,
  62/5 Thaniya Rd (Silom), Bangkok 10500
UK
  (☎ 020-7437 3677, fax 7494 1048,
  24 hour brochure line ☎ 01233-211999)
  7 Cork St, London W1X 2AB
USA
  (☎ 212-586 4901, fax 582 3274)
  1270 Avenue of Americas, Suite 1808
  (18th floor), New York NY 10020
  (☎ 213-380 8855, fax 380 6111)
  3550 Wilshire Blvd, Suite 204,
  Los Angeles CA 90010

VISAS & DOCUMENTS
Passport

You must have a passport with you all the time; it's the most basic travel document. Ensure that your passport will be valid for at least six months beyond your expected return. If your passport is lost or stolen, immediately contact your country's embassy or consulate in Delhi or Kolkata.

Indian Visas

Virtually everybody needs a visa to visit India. The application is generally straightforward and visas are usually issued with a minimum of fuss. A few Indian embassies and consulates will not issue a visa to enter India unless you are holding an onward or return ticket.

Embassies now issue six-month multiple-entry tourist visas as standard. This visa is valid from the date of issue of the visa, *not the date you enter India*. This means that if you enter India five months after the visa was issued, it will be valid only for one month, not the full six months. If you enter India the day after it was issued, you can stay for the full six months. We get many letters from travellers who get caught out, thinking a six month visa gives them a six month stay in India. Note that if you do for some reason get a three month visa, your entry to India must be within a fixed period (normally either 30 days or three months) from the date of issue of the visa.

The cost of the visa varies depending on your nationality. At the time of research, six month visas cost US$50 in the US, UK£26 in Britain, 200FF in France and A$55 in Australia. Transit visas are cheaper and normally valid for seven days.

Nepal Fifteen-day to six-month visas are available (multiple entry is possible); the cost varies according to your nationality. According to a recent report from travellers, it is no longer possible to get a new Indian visa in Kathmandu if you already have a six month visa in your passport. Some travellers have managed to get a short visa extension, however, by having their current visas changed to three or six months from date of entry instead of from date of issue. The Indian embassy in Kathmandu is open Monday to Friday 9 am to 1 pm and 1.30 to 5.30 pm; visa applications are accepted Monday to Friday 9.30 am to 12.30 pm and visas are available for collection between 4.45 and 5.30 pm – allow at least seven days for processing.

Pakistan The high commission in Islamabad is fantastically busy but quite efficient; foreigners can go straight through into the visa office so wave your passport at the harassed guards outside the front gates. Most nationalities can get a six month visa the same day for Pak Rs 760, though US citizens may need to pay an extra Pak Rs 760 'computer' fee and wait three days while the embassy faxes home to check that you are not wanted by the police or in some other way 'undesirable'.

Visa Extensions Most visas are marked whether they are extendable or not. Most six month visas are stamped 'non-extendable'. It is normally possible to extend a one or three month visa up to a maximum of six months. Applications can be made at Foreigners' Registration Offices (see the Gateway Cities chapter for their locations), and in all state and district capitals at the office of the Superintendent of Police. A three month extension costs Rs 850 and an extension of up to six months costs Rs 1700. Bring a couple of passport photos and, to be safe, several photocopies of your passport.

If your six month visa is up (whether you've actually been in the country all this time or not), then the Foreigners' Registration Office in Delhi will normally give you up to two weeks extension free of charge. After this you need clearance from the Home Ministry in Delhi, which is only given in extenuating circumstances.

If you stay beyond four months you are also supposed to get an income tax clearance before you leave. See the Tax Clearance Certificates section later in this chapter for details.

Visas for Neighbouring Areas & Countries

If you're heading to other places near the Indian Himalayan region, the visa situation is as follows.

North-Eastern Region No permits are needed for Assam, Meghalaya or Tripura. Permits for the other states must be approved by the Ministry of Home Affairs in Delhi, which can take forever if you don't have a travel agent, the state office or someone with good connections on your side. It usually takes three weeks to a month for a permit to be issued, though it can take longer. Permits allow for a maximum 10 day stay in each state.

Permits to Mizoram are granted to groups of four or more people fairly readily; the best places to apply are through the state representatives in Delhi and Kolkata.

Manipur and Nagaland are the most difficult states to acquire permits for. Currently foreigners are only allowed to enter Manipur by air on a tour arranged by the state tourism authority or a travel agent (in a group of at least four). Nagaland can be entered by land but again you need to arrange travel for a group of at least four through a travel agent. The state representatives and emporia in Delhi and Kolkata are the best places to organise a permit.

Manipur
(☎ 011-301 3009) Manipur Bhawan,
2 Sardar Patel Marg, Chanakyapuri,
New Delhi
(☎ 033-350 4412) Manipur Bhawan,
25 Ashutosh Shastri Rd, Kolkata
Mizoram
(☎ 011-301 5951) Mizoram Bhawan,
Circular Rd, Chanakyapuri, New Delhi
(☎ 033-247 7034) Mizoram House,
4 Old Ballygunge Rd, Kolkata
Nagaland
(☎ 011-379 3019) Nagaland House,
29 Aurangzeb Rd, New Delhi
(☎ 033-242 5247) Nagaland House,
13 Shakespeare Sarani, Kolkata

Myanmar (Burma) The embassy in Delhi is fast and efficient and issues four-week visas.

Nepal The Nepali Embassy in Delhi is on Barakhamba Rd close to Connaught Place, not out at Chanakyapuri like most other embassies. It is open 9 am to noon Monday to Thursday, and 9 to 11 am Friday. Single entry, 15/30-day visas cost Rs 630/1050. A double entry, 30 day visa costs Rs 1680 and a 60 day multiple entry costs Rs 2520. You need to supply one passport photo. Passports are ready the next day, unless you apply on a Friday, in which case you can pick up your passport the same day between 2.30 and 3 pm.

The consulate in Kolkata is open 10 am to 1 pm and 2 to 4 pm. Visas are issued while you wait.

A 30 day visa is available on arrival in Nepal for US$25 (in cash), and can be extended, but doing so involves rather a lot of form filling and queuing – it's better to have a visa in advance if possible.

Bhutan Applications to visit Bhutan must be made through a Bhutanese tour operator, who will arrange an organised tour costing around US$200 per day. Your visa is then issued when you arrive at Paro Airot or Phuentsholing, the only land crossing with India. For more information you could contact the Royal Bhutanese Embassy in Delhi or Bhutan Travel Service (☎ 212-838 6382, fax 750 1269, email 5195426@mcimail.com), 120 East 56th St, Suite 1130, New York, NY 10022. Otherwise, you could take a look at Lonely Planet's *Bhutan*.

Travel Permits
Even with a visa you are not allowed everywhere in the Indian Himalaya. Certain sensitive border areas require special additional permits. These are covered in the appropriate sections in the relevant chapters, but briefly they are:

Ladakh While you don't require a special permit to visit Leh, or to travel along the Manali-Leh and Srinagar-Leh highways, permits are required for the four regions in Ladakh which have been opened comparatively recently to foreign visitors. These are the Nubra Valley, Pangong Tso, Tso Moriri and the Dha-Hanu region. At the time of research, permits were only valid for groups of four people for seven days and were most easily arranged through a travel agency in Leh. Although four people must *apply* for a permit together, checkpoints do not require that you actually need to *travel* together. See the Ladakh & Zanskar chapter for more details.

Kinnaur & Spiti An inner line permit is required to travel between Kinnaur and Spiti in the remote north-eastern region of Himachal Pradesh near Tibet. They can be easily obtained from the District and Sub-District Magistrates in Kaza (Spiti) and Rekong Peo (Kinnaur). See the Inner Line Permits boxed text in the Kinnaur section of the Himachal Pradesh chapter for details.

Sikkim Fifteen-day permits are issued at various different offices in Delhi, Kolkata, Shiliguri and Darjeeling, either while you wait or within two or three hours. Officials claim that permit restrictions will be eased within the next year or two. Until then extra permits are required for a few destinations in Sikkim and are issued to parties of four at the permit office in Gangtok. Trekking permits are extra and best arranged through a trekking agency in Gangtok. See the Sikkim chapter for full details.

Arunachal Pradesh The state government charges US$50 per day just to be in this state. To get a permit, foreigners must travel in a group of four and apply at least three weeks in advance to permit offices in the Arunachal Bhawan offices in Delhi, Kolkata or Gauhati. Once approval is granted you then pay the total fees for your visit up front to the *bhawans* (simply, 'offices'). Permits can theoretically also be arranged through the Foreigners' Registration Offices in Delhi and Kolkata. Permits for foreigners are valid for 10 days and only allow you to visit certain towns and routes. See the Arunachal Pradesh chapter for more details.

Travel Insurance
A travel insurance policy to cover theft, loss and medical problems is a wise idea. The international student travel policies handled by STA Travel, Council Travel and other student travel organisations are usually good value. Check the small print for the following:

- Some policies specifically exclude 'dangerous activities' which can include motorcycling and even trekking. If such activities are on your agenda you don't want that sort of policy. A locally acquired motorcycle licence may not be valid under your policy.
- You may prefer a policy that pays doctors or hospitals directly rather than you having to pay on the spot and claim later. If you have to claim later make sure you keep all documentation and receipts. Some policies ask you to call back (reverse charges) to a centre in your home country where an immediate assessment of your problem is made.
- Check whether the policy covers ambulances, an emergency helicopter airlift out of a remote region (especially if trekking), or an emergency flight home.
- Some companies offer a cheaper policy, which covers only medical cover and not baggage

loss. This can be worthwhile if you're not carrying any valuables in your grotty 10-year-old backpack. Many policies require you to pay the first US$100 or so of a claim and only cover valuables to a set limit (thus if you lose your camera you may find yourself only covered for US$300 and paying the first US$100 yourself!). In case of theft you will almost certainly need a police report to show the insurance company.
- Insurance policies can normally be extended while on the road but bear in mind you will have to do this *before* it expires, otherwise you will have to pay a considerably higher premium.
- Paying for your airline ticket with a credit card often provides some limited insurance cover, at least to loss of the ticket. Check the fine print to see what is actually covered by your card.

Driving Licence & Permits
If you are planning to drive in India, get an International Driving Permit from your local national motoring organisation. In some centres, such as Delhi and Mussoorie (the latter during the high season only) it's possible to hire motorcycles.

Other Documents
A health certificate, while not necessary in India, may well be required for onward travel. Student cards such as ISIC (Web site www.istc.org) won't help much with cheap fares these days but offer services like 24 hour help lines. Similarly, a Youth Hostel (Hostelling International – HI) card is not generally required for India's many hostels, but you do pay slightly less at official youth hostels if you have one.

It's worth having a batch of passport photos for visa applications and for obtaining permits to remote regions. If you run out, Indian photo studios will do excellent portraits at pleasantly low prices.

Photocopies
It's a good idea to carry photocopies of your important travel documents, which obviously should be kept separately from the originals in the event that these are lost or stolen.

Take a photocopy of the first page of your passport (ie with your personal details and photograph), as well as a copy of the page with your Indian visa and any additional permits, such as that for Sikkim. A photocopy of your airline ticket, credit card and travel insurance policy could be handy. Keep a record of the travellers cheques you have exchanged, where they were encashed, the amount and serial number. Encashment receipts should also be kept separate from your travellers cheques. It's not a bad idea to leave photocopies of your important travel documents with a friend or relative at home.

EMBASSIES & CONSULATES
Indian Embassies Abroad

India's embassies, consulates and high commissions abroad are listed below (unless stated otherwise the addresses are for embassies):

Australia
    High Commission:
    (☎ 02-6273 3999, fax 6273 3328,
    email hicanb@ozemail.com.au)
    3-5 Moonah Place, Yarralumla, ACT 2600
    Consulate General:
    (☎ 02-9223 9500, fax 9223 9246,
    email indianc@enternet.com.au)
    Level 27, 25 Bligh St, Sydney, NSW 2000
    Honorary Consulates:
    (☎ 03-9384 0141)
    15 Munro St, Coburg, Melbourne, VIC 3058
    (☎ 08-9221 1485, fax 9221 1206,
    email india@vianet.net.au)
    49 Bennett St, Perth, WA 6004
Bangladesh
    High Commission:
    (☎ 02-503606, fax 863662,
    email hcindia@bangla.net)
    120 Road 2, Dhanmondi, Residential Area,
    Dhaka
    Assistant High Commission:
    (☎ 031-654201, fax 654147,
    email ahcindia@spnetctg.com)
    Bungalow 2, B-2, Road No 1, Kulsi,
    Chittagong
Belgium
    (☎ 02-640 9802, fax 648 9638,
    email eoibru@skynet.be)
    217 Chaussee de Vleurgat, 1050 Brussels
Bhutan
    (☎ 09752-22162, fax 23195)
    India House Estate, Thimpu

Canada
    High Commission:
    (☎ 613-744 3751, fax 744 0913,
    email hicomind@ottawa.net)
    10 Springfield Rd, Ottawa,
    Ontario K1M 1C9
    Consulates General:
    (☎ 416-960 4831, fax 960 9812,
    email cgindia@pathcom.com)
    Suite No 500, 2 Bloor St West,
    Toronto, Ontario M4W 3E2
    (☎ 604-662 8811, fax 682 2471,
    email indiaadm@axionet.com)
    325 How St, 2F, Vancouver, BC V6C 1Z7
China
    (☎ 01-532 1908, fax 532 4684,
    email indembch@public3.bta.net.cn)
    1 Ri Tan Dong Lu, Beijing 100 600
    Consulate General:
    (☎ 21-275 8885, fax 275 8881,
    email cgisha@public.sta.net.cn)
    1008 Shanghai International Trade Centre,
    2200 Yan An (West) Rd, Shanghai 200335
    Web site www.shanghai-ed.com/india/
France
    (☎ 01 40 50 70 70, fax 01 40 50 09 96,
    email culture@indembparis.zee.net)
    15 rue Alfred Dehodencq, 75016 Paris
Germany
    (☎ 228-54050, fax 540 5153,
    email info-indembassy@csm.de)
    Adenauerallee 262-264, 53113 Bonn 1 & 11
    (☎ 30-4853002, fax 4853000,
    email Berlindinfo@compuserve.com)
    Majakowskiring 55, 13156 Berlin
    Consulate General:
    (☎ 069-153 0050, fax 554 4125,
    email 100573.1322@compuserve.com)
    Mittelweg 49, 60318 Frankfurt
Ireland
    (☎ 01-497 0483, fax 497 8074,
    email eoidublin@indigo.ie)
    6 Leeson Park, Dublin 6
Israel
    (☎ 03-510 1431, fax 510 1434,
    email indembtel@netvision.net.il)
    4 Kaufman St, Sharbat House,
    Tel Aviv 68012
Japan
    (☎ 03-3262 2391, fax 3234 4866,
    email indembjp@gol.com)
    2-2-11 Kudan Minami, Chiyoda-ku,
    Tokyo 102
Myanmar (Burma)
    (☎ 01-282550, fax 289562,
    email amb.indembygn@mtpt400.stems.com)
    545-547 Merchant St, Yangon (Rangoon)

Nepal
(☎ 071-410900, fax 413132,
email indemb@mos.com.np)
Lain Chaur, PO Box 92, Kathmandu
Netherlands
(☎ 070-346 9771, fax 361 7072,
email fscom@indemb.nl)
Buitenrustweg 2, 2517 KD, The Hague
New Zealand
High Commission:
(☎ 04-473 6390, fax 499 0665,
email hicomind@globe.co.nz)
180 Molesworth St, Wellington
Pakistan
High Commission:
(☎ 051-814371, fax 820742,
email hicomind@isb.compol.com)
G5 Diplomatic Enclave, Islamabad
Singapore
(☎ 286-737 6777, fax 732 6909)
India House, 31 Grange Rd, Tenglin
Sri Lanka
High Commission:
(☎ 01-421605, fax 446403,
email hicomind@ sri.lanka.net)
36-38 Galle Rd, Colombo 3
Assistant High Commission:
(☎ 08-24563, fax 32479)
31 Rajapihilla Mawatha, Kandy
Thailand
(☎ 02-258 0300, fax 258 4627,
email indiaemb@mozart.inet.co.th)
46 Soi 23 (Prasarnmitr), Sukhumvit Rd,
Bangkok
Consulate:
(☎ 053-242491, fax 247879)
113 Bumruangrat Rd, Chiang Mai 50000
UK
High Commission:
(☎ 020-7836 8484, fax 7836 4331)
India House, Aldwych, London WC2B 4NA
Consulate General:
(☎ 021-212 2782, fax 212 2786,
email cgi@congend.demon.co.uk)
20 Augusta St, Jewellery Quarters, Hockley,
Birmingham B18 6JL
USA
(☎ 202-939 7000, fax 939 7027,
email indembwash@indiagov.org)
2107 Massachusetts Ave NW, Washington,
DC 20008
Web site www.indianconsulate-sf.org
Consulates General:
(☎ 212-774 0699, fax 861 3788,
email indiacgny@aol.com)
3 East 64th St, Manhattan, New York, NY
10021-7097

(☎ 415-668 0662, fax 668 9764,
email indiancon@best.com)
540 Arguello Blvd, San Francisco, CA 94118
(☎ 312-595 0405, inquiries hotline ☎ 595 0417,
fax 595 0416, email congendia@aol.com)
NBC Tower, 455 North Cityfront Plaza
Drive, Suite No 850, Chicago, IL 60611

Foreign Embassies & High Commissions in India

Most foreign diplomatic missions are in the nation's capital, Delhi, but there are also quite a few consulates in the other major cities of Mumbai (Bombay), Kolkata (Calcutta) and Chennai (Madras).

As a tourist, it's important to realise what your own embassy – the embassy of the country of which you are a citizen – can and can't do. Embassies may have copies of home newspapers. for you to read.

Generally speaking, it won't be much help in emergencies if the trouble you're in is remotely your own fault. Remember that you are bound by the laws of the country you are in. Your embassy will not be sympathetic if you end up in jail after committing a crime locally, even if such actions are legal in your own country.

In genuine emergencies you might get some assistance, but only if other channels have been exhausted. For example if you need to get home urgently, a free ticket home is exceedingly unlikely – the embassy would expect you to have insurance. If you have all your money and documents stolen, it might assist with getting a new passport, but a loan for onward travel is out of the question.

Embassies and consulates in Delhi (most concentrated around Chanakyapuri) and Kolkata are as follows (telephone area codes are ☎ 011 for Delhi and ☎ 033 for Kolkata):

Australia
(☎ 688 8223, fax 687 4126)
1/50-G Shantipath, Chanakyapuri, Delhi
Bangladesh
(☎ 683 4668, fax 683 9237)
56 Ring Rd, Lajpat Nagar III, Delhi
(☎ 247 5208)
9 Circus Ave, Kolkata

Bhutan
    (☎ 688 9807, fax 687 6710)
    Chandragupta Marg, Chanakyapuri, Delhi
    (☎ 241301)
    48 Tivoli Court, Pramothesh Barua Sarani,
    Kolkata
Canada
    (☎ 687 6500, fax 687 6579)
    7/8 Shantipath, Chanakyapuri, Delhi
China
    (☎ 687 1585, fax 688 5486)
    50-D Shantipath, Chanakyapuri, Delhi
France
    (☎ 611 8790, fax 687 2305)
    2/50-E Shantipath, Chanakyapuri, Delhi
    (☎ 229 2314, emergency 245 7300)
    26 Park St (inside the courtyard on the right-
    hand side of Alliance Française), Kolkata
Germany
    (☎ 687 1831, fax 687 3117)
    6/50-G Shantipath, Chanakyapuri, Delhi
    (☎ 479 1141, fax 479 3028)
    1 Hastings Park Rd, Kolkata
Ireland
    (☎ 462 6733, fax 469 7053)
    13 Jor Bagh Rd, Delhi
Israel
    (☎ 301 3238, fax 301 4298)
    3 Aurangzeb Rd, Delhi
Japan
    (☎ 687 6581, fax 688 5587)
    4-5/50-G Shantipath, Chanakyapuri, Delhi
    (☎ 282 2241)
    12 Pretoria St, Kolkata
Maldives
    (☎ 248 5102)
    7C Kiron Shankar Roy Rd, Kolkata
Myanmar (Burma)
    (☎ 688 9007, fax 687 7942)
    3/50-F Nyaya Marg, Chanakyapuri, Delhi
Nepal
    (☎ 332 9969, fax 332 6857)
    Barakhamba Rd, Delhi
    (☎ 479 1117/1224, fax 479 1410)
    1 National Library Ave, Kolkata
Netherlands
    (☎ 688 4951, fax 688 4956)
    6/50-F Shantipath, Chanakyapuri, Delhi
New Zealand
    (☎ 688 3170, fax 687 2317)
    50-N Nyaya Marg, Chanakyapuri, Delhi
Pakistan
    (☎ 467 6004, fax 637 2339)
    2/50-G Shantipath, Chanakyapuri, Delhi
Sri Lanka
    (☎ 248 5102)
    Nicco House, 2 Hare St, Kolkata

UK
    (☎ 687 2161, fax 687 2882)
    50 Shantipath, Chanakyapuri, Delhi
    (☎ 282 5171/75, 24 hour line 282 5172)
    1 Ho Chi Minh Sarani, Kolkata
USA
    (☎ 688 9033) Shantipath, Chanakyapuri,
    Delhi
    (☎ 282 3611, fax 282 2335)
    5/1 Ho Chi Minh Sarani, Kolkata

CUSTOMS

The usual duty-free regulations apply for India, that is, one bottle of alcohol and 200 cigarettes.

You're allowed to bring in all sorts of western technological wonders, but big items, such as video cameras, are likely to be entered on a 'Tourist Baggage Re-Export' form to ensure you take them out with you when you go. This also used to be the case with laptop computers, but some travellers have reported that it is no longer necessary. It's not necessary to declare still cameras, even if you have more than one.

Note that if you are entering India from Nepal you are not entitled to import anything free of duty.

MONEY
Currency

The Indian rupee (Rs) is divided into 100 paise (p). There are coins of 5, 10, 20, 25 and 50 paise, Rs 1, 2 and 5 (though they're rare), and notes of Rs 1, 2, 5, 10, 20, 50, 100 and 500. There are plans to phase out the Rs one, two and five notes and introduce a Rs 1000 bill.

You are not allowed to carry Indian currency into or out of the country. You are allowed to bring in unlimited amounts of foreign currency or travellers cheques, but you are supposed to declare anything over US$10,000 on arrival.

It's a good idea to bring at least some US dollars cash or travellers cheques with you as it is impossible to buy dollars legally in India. For example, flights to Kathmandu from just across the border in Bangla (West Bengal) can only be bought in US dollars but there is nowhere in Darjeeling to buy US dollars.

One of the most annoying things about India is that no one ever seems to have *any* change, and you'll find on numerous occasions you'll be left waiting for five minutes while a shopkeeper hawks your Rs 100 note around five other shops to rustle up enough notes. In corner stores you will often find yourself receiving handfuls of sweets in lieu of a few rupees change.

Exchange Rates

To check current exchange rates on the Internet follow the links from Lonely Planet's subWWWay page: www.lonelyplanet.com/weblinks/weblinks.htm.

country	unit		rupees
Australia	A$1	=	Rs 29
Canada	C$1	=	Rs 29
euro	€1	=	Rs 45
France	10FF	=	Rs 70
Germany	DM1	=	Rs 23
Japan	¥100	=	Rs 36
Nepal	Nep Rs 100	=	Rs 63
New Zealand	NZ$1	=	Rs 23
Pakistan	Pak Rs 100	=	Rs 84
UK	UK£1	=	Rs 69
USA	US$1	=	Rs 43

Dirty Money

Be careful when accepting particularly tatty or folded banknotes. Staple holes in the middle of the notes are fine but you'll have real troubles getting rid of anything with a tear, especially on the crease line. Some notes are just holding on by the skin of their teeth and a bit of sticking tape. You can exchange torn notes at any bank but it's easier to refuse them in the first place.

Another thing to watch out for is that Rs 10 and Rs 50 notes are a very similar colour, as are the Rs 100 and Rs 500 notes. When changing money don't just count the notes but check they are the right denomination too.

Exchanging Money

In Delhi and Kolkata you can change most foreign currencies or travellers cheques – Australian dollars, Deutschmarks, yen or whatever – but up in the hills it's best to stick to US dollars or pounds sterling. Thomas Cook and American Express are both popular brands of travellers cheques, and can be exchanged readily in most major tourist centres, such as the hill stations.

Outside the main cities, the State Bank of India is usually the place to change money, although occasionally they'll direct you to another bank, such as the Punjab National Bank or the Bank of Baroda. In the more remote regions, few (if any) banks offer exchange facilities, so change money in the hill stations before heading farther north.

There are decent exchange facilities in popular tourist centres like Shimla and Dharamsala but nothing farther north of Rishikesh in Uttarakhand, in Lahaul and Spiti, and Kinnaur in Himachal Pradesh, as well as outside Gangtok in Sikkim. In Ladakh you can only change money in Kargil and Leh. There's nowhere to change money in Arunachal Pradesh – change in Gauhati or before you head to the north-east.

Some banks charge an encashment fee (often to issue an encashment certificate) which may be levied for the entire transaction or on each cheque. Check the fee before you sign your cheques.

Many people make the mistake of bringing too many small-denomination cheques. Unless you are moving rapidly from country to country you only need a handful of small denominations for end-of-stay conversions. In between, change as much as you feel happy carrying. This applies particularly in India where changing money can take time – especially in the smaller towns. The answer is to change money as infrequently as possible and to change it only in big banks in big cities or at the hill stations.

Travellers Cheques Although it's usually not a problem to change travellers cheques, it's best to stick to the well known brands – American Express and Thomas Cook – as more obscure ones may cause problems. It also happens occasionally that a bank won't accept a certain type of cheque – Citicorps in particular – and for this reason it's worth carrying more than one flavour. At the time of research, it was difficult to exchange anything other than Visa and American Express cheques in Himachal Pradesh whereas Visa cheques were hard to change in Uttarakhand, Bangla (West Bengal) hills and Sikkim.

A few simple measures should be taken to facilitate the replacement of stolen travellers cheques; see Stolen Travellers Cheques in the Dangers & Annoyances section later in this chapter.

Credit Cards Credit cards are widely accepted at the curio shops and top-end hotels in the hill stations, but outside these areas, forget it. If you do see a credit card sign check that they accept foreign cards not just Indian versions.

With American Express, MasterCard or Visa cards you can use your card to obtain rupees in Delhi and Kolkata, as well as at some of the larger hill stations, including Dharamsala, Darjeeling and Shimla.

Almost any Bank of Baroda will give a cash advance on a Visa card. There is normally a charge of around 1% and possibly a Rs 100 communication fee to check your

Baksheesh & Beggars

In most Asian countries tipping is virtually unknown, but the Indian subcontinent is an exception to that rule – although tipping has a rather different role in India than in the west. The term *baksheesh* encompasses tipping and a lot more besides. You 'tip' not so much for good service, but to get things done.

Judicious baksheesh will open closed doors, find missing letters and perform other small miracles. Tipping is not necessary for taxis nor for cheaper restaurants, but if you're going to be using something repeatedly, an initial tip will ensure the standards are kept up. Keep things in perspective though. Demands for baksheesh can quickly become never-ending. Ask yourself if it's really necessary or desirable before shelling out.

In tourist restaurants or hotels, where service is usually tacked on in any case, the normal 10% figure usually applies. In smaller places, where tipping is optional, you need only tip a few rupees, not a percentage of the bill. Hotel porters usually get about Rs 1 per bag; other possible tipping levels are Rs 1 to Rs 2 for bike-watching, Rs 10 for train conductors or station porters performing miracles for you, and Rs 5 to Rs 15 for extra services from hotel staff.

Although most people think of baksheesh in terms of tipping, it also means giving alms to beggars. Wherever you turn in India you'll be confronted by beggars – many of them (often handicapped or hideously disfigured) genuinely in dire need, others, such as kids hassling for a rupee or a pen, obviously not.

All sorts of stories about beggars do the rounds of the travellers' hang-outs, many of them with little basis in fact. Stories such as rupee millionaire beggars, people (usually kids) being deliberately mutilated by their parents so they can beg, and a beggars' Mafia are all common.

It's a matter of personal choice how you approach the issue of beggars and baksheesh. Some people feel it is best to give nothing to any beggar, believing it 'only encourages them' and preferring to contribute in a voluntary capacity; others give away loose change when they have it. Some benevolent souls have even been known to exchange large notes for handfuls of Rs 1 notes, so that they always have change on hand specifically for this purpose. Others insulate themselves entirely and give nothing in any way. If you decide you want to donate money to a charity working in India see the Donations boxed text later in this chapter for suggestions.

account details with the mother ship in Delhi. Grindlays ANZ offers a similar service at branches in Shimla and Darjeeling. Some banks in Darjeeling will charge extra to issue funds the same day so check this.

For details of getting cash from ATMs, branches of American Express and other foreign banks see the Delhi and Kolkata sections of the Gateway Cities chapter.

International Transfers Don't run out of money in the India Himalaya unless you have a credit card against which you can draw cash. If you need to have money transferred from abroad you will most likely have to return to Delhi or Kolkata.

In Delhi you can have money transferred easily though Western Union (via Sita Travels or DHL branches) or Thomas Cook's Moneygram system. Western Union produces a directory that tells you which offices of which companies in your home country can arrange a transfer. Money can be wired almost instantaneously. You will need to bring your passport to collect the money and a maximum of Rs 20,000 (US$500) can be given in cash, in rupees only. Charges are around 5% of the total sum. Western Union is a little cheaper than Thomas Cook if transferring sums of less than US$1000.

Black Market The rupee is a fully convertible currency, so the rate is set by the market not the government. For this reason there's not much of a black market, although you can get a couple of rupees more for your dollars or pounds cash. In the major tourist centres you will have constant offers to change money. There's little risk involved but it is officially illegal; the major advantage is it's much quicker than changing at a bank. If you do decide to change on the black market, do it off the street rather than in the open. US$100 bills in good condition (with no rips or tears) fetch the best rates. Always check the quality of the notes you receive during any transaction; the slightest tear can render a note worthless.

Encashment Certificates All money is supposed to be changed at official banks or moneychangers, and you are supposed to be given an encashment certificate for each transaction. In practice, some people surreptitiously bring rupees into the country with them – they can be bought at a discount price in places such as Singapore, Bangkok and Kathmandu.

Banks will usually give you an encashment certificate, but occasionally they don't bother. It is worth getting them, especially if you want to re-exchange excess rupees for hard currency when you depart India.

The other reason why it's a good idea to save encashment certificates is that if you stay in India longer than four months, you have to get an income tax clearance. See Tax Clearance Certificates section later in this chapter for more information.

Security
A money belt worn around your waist beneath your clothes is probably one of the safest ways to carry important documents such as your passport and travellers cheques on your person. It's not a bad idea to place these documents inside a plastic bag in the money belt to protect them from rain and sweat. 'Bum bags' – pouches which are worn around your waist *outside* your clothes – are popular and more readily accessible, but extremely conspicuous. Some travellers prefer a pouch attached to a string, which is worn around the neck and concealed beneath a shirt or pullover. It is now possible to purchase innocuous looking leather belts from travel goods suppliers which a have a secret compartment in which you could hide your 'emergency stash'.

Other golden rules include: never leave money in a hotel room, keep your travellers cheque receipts separate from the actual cheques, and always keep an emergency supply of US$50 or US$100 separate from your money belt.

Costs
Whatever budget you decide to travel on, you can be assured that you'll be getting a

whole lot more for your money than in most other countries – it's fantastic value.

If you stay in luxury hotels, fly to the hills regions and see a lot of the Himalaya in a hired car, you can easily spend a lot of money. At the other extreme, if you scrimp and save, stay in dormitories or the cheapest hotels, always travel in ordinary public buses, and learn to exist on *dhal* (curried lentil gravy) and rice, you can see the Indian Himalaya on less than US$7 a day.

Most travellers will probably be looking for something between these extremes. If so, for US$15 to US$20 a day on average, you'll stay in reasonable hotels, eat in regular restaurants but occasionally splash out on a fancy meal, and take auto-rickshaws rather than a bus.

A fully inclusive trek including transport, meals, guides, porters, cook, tent and sleeping mat could cost upwards of US$30 per day, depending on the number of trekkers.

As a rule of thumb, the higher up you get in the Himalaya, the cheaper it gets – there's just less to spend your money on.

Tax Clearance Certificates

If you stay in India for more than 120 days you need a 'tax clearance certificate' to leave the country. This supposedly proves that your time in India was financed with your own money, not by working in India or by selling things or playing the black market.

Basically all you have to do is find the Foreign Section of the Income Tax Department in Delhi, Kolkata, Chennai (Madras) or Mumbai (Bombay) and turn up with your passport, visa extension form (if applicable) and a handful of bank exchange receipts (to show you really have been changing foreign currency into rupees officially). You fill in a form and should get the certificate on the spot. We've never yet heard from anyone who has actually been asked for this document on departure.

POST & COMMUNICATIONS
Post

The Indian postal and poste restante services are generally excellent. Expected letters almost always are there, and letters you send almost invariably reach their destination, although they take up to three weeks. If you want to avoid queuing in crowded post offices, you can often buy stamps at good hotels.

Postal Rates Airmail letters cost Rs 11 and postcards Rs 6 to anywhere in the world. International aerograms cost Rs 6.50. Airmail parcels of 250g/1kg cost Rs 570/879 to the US, Rs 698/962 to Australia and Rs 707/878 to Europe. Sea mail costs Rs 102/195/363 for 500g/1kg/2kg. Speed post is another option and this costs Rs 200 for a minimum 200g and Rs 60 for each additional 200g.

Posting Parcels Most people discover how to do this the hard way, in which case it'll take half a day. Go about it as described below, though it can still take up to an hour:

* Take the parcel to a tailor and tell him you'd like it stitched up in cheap linen for a few rupees. Negotiate the price first.
* Go to the post office with your parcel and ask for the necessary customs declaration forms. Fill them in and glue one to the parcel. The other will be stitched onto it. To avoid excise duty at the delivery end it's best to specify that the contents are a 'gift'. Be careful with how much you declare the contents to be worth. If you specify over Rs 1000, your parcel will not be accepted without a bank clearance certificate. You can imagine the hassles involved in getting one of these so always state the value as less than Rs 1000.
* Have the parcel weighed and franked at the parcel counter.

If you are just sending books or printed matter, these can go by bookpost, which is considerably cheaper than parcel post. You must make sure that the package can either be opened for inspection along the way, or that it is just wrapped in brown paper or cardboard and tied with string, with the two ends exposed so that the contents are visible. To protect the books, it might be worthwhile first wrapping them in clear plastic. No customs declaration form is necessary for such parcels but there is a maximum weight of 5kg (which costs about Rs 1000 airmail or Rs 175 seamail). Entrepreneurs in places like McLeod Ganj will wrap and help post parcels for between Rs 20 and Rs 40. The maximum length for parcels is 1.8m.

Be very cautious about any shop which offers to mail things to your home address after you have bought them. No matter how many travellers' testimonies you are shown guaranteeing that parcels arrived at their destinations, it pays to take the parcel to the post office yourself. Government emporiums are usually OK.

Receiving Mail American Express, in Delhi and Kolkata, will hold mail for account or travellers cheques' holders, offering an alternative to the poste restante system.

Have letters addressed to you with your surname in capitals and underlined, followed by the poste restante, GPO, and the city or town in question. Many 'lost' letters are simply misfiled under given (Christian) names, so always check under both your names (and even M for Mr, Miss etc). Letters sent via poste restante are generally held for one month only, after which they are returned to sender. The most reliable poste restantes seem to be Shimla, McLeod Ganj, Manali, Rishikesh and Gangtok.

Sending parcels to you in India is an extremely hit-and-miss affair. Don't count on anything bigger than a letter getting to you. And don't count on a letter getting to you if there's anything worthwhile inside it.

Telephone
India's international country code: ☎ 91
See regional chapters for area codes.

The telephone system in India is generally very good. Everywhere you'll come across private 'STD/ISD' call booths with direct local, interstate and international dialling. A digital meter lets you keep an eye on what the call is costing, and gives you a printout at the end. You then just pay the shop owner – quick, painless and a far cry from the not so distant past when a night spent at a tele-graph office waiting for a line was not unusual. Government-run Central Telegraph Offices in major towns are also reasonably efficient and some are open 24 hours.

Direct international calls from Public Call Offices (PCOs) cost around Rs 80 per minute, depending on the country you are calling, which is about Rs 10 more than the Central Telegraph Offices. Direct international calls from these phones cost around Rs 80 per minute, depending on the country you are calling, which is about Rs 10 more than the government-run Central Telegraph Offices. Charges are cheaper between 7 pm and 8 am. To make an international call in India, you will need to dial the following:

☎ 00 (international access code from India) + country code (of the country you are calling) + area code (minus the first zero) + local number

In some centres, STD/ISD booths may offer a 'call back' service – you ring your folks or friends, give them the number of the booth and wait for them to call you back. The booth operator will charge about Rs 3 to Rs 5 per minute for this service, in addition to the cost of the preliminary call. Advise your callers how long you intend to wait at the booth in the event that they have trouble getting back to you. You can do the same thing at most hotels if you give your callers the room number. Most hotels don't charge to receive calls, though you should check this at reception. To call India from abroad, dial the following:

☎ (caller's country international access code) + 91 (international country code for India) + area code (minus the first zero) + local number

Also available is the Home Country Direct service, which gives you access to the international operator in your home country. You can then make reverse charge (collect) or credit card calls, although this is not always easy, and beware in hotels of exorbitant connection charges on these sorts of calls. You may also have trouble convincing the owner of the telephone you are using that they are not going to get charged for the call. The countries and numbers to dial are listed below:

country	number
Australia	☎ 0006117
Canada	☎ 000167
Germany	☎ 0004917
Japan	☎ 0008117
The Netherlands	☎ 0003117
New Zealand	☎ 0006417
UK	☎ 0004417
USA	☎ 000117

Fax

Most of the government-run Central Telegraph Offices offer a public fax service. Charges are standard; a one page fax costs Rs 100 to the UK, Rs 116 to the US and Rs 63 to neighbouring South Asian Association for Regional Cooperation (SAARC) countries (Nepal, Pakistan etc). Make sure you receive a confirmation printout that the fax went through 'OK'.

To receive a fax costs Rs 10 for the first three pages and Rs 3 per page thereafter. One potential snag is that some telegraph offices turn off their fax machine at night and weekends, just when most international faxes will arrive!

Private STD/ISD booths often have a fax machine for public use, normally at slightly higher rates.

Email & Internet Access

You may want to open a free Web-based email account such as Lonely Planet's eKno (www.ekno.lonelyplanet.com), Hot-Mail (www.hotmail.com) or Yahoo! Mail (mail.yahoo.com). You can then access your mail from anywhere in the world using any net-connected computer.

It is possible to send and receive email messages, and access an eKno-type account, at McLeod Ganj, Leh, Rishikesh, Darjeeling, Kalimpong and Kurseong, as well as Delhi and Kolkata.

Email messages cost around Rs 40 per page to send, Rs 10 to receive. An hour's Internet time costs between Rs 100 to Rs 150 and is getting cheaper all the time as private service providers challenge the government monopoly. Local servers have already popped up in Shimla and Shiliguri, further reducing prices.

INTERNET RESOURCES

The World Wide Web is a rich resource for travellers. You can research your trip, check flight schedules and festival dates and chat with other travellers about the best places to visit (or avoid).

There's no better place to start your Web research than the Lonely Planet Web site (www.lonelyplanet.com). Here you'll find succinct summaries of places in India, postcards from other travellers and the Thorn Tree bulletin board, where you can ask questions before you go or dispense advice when you get back. You can also find updates to our guides to India and the sub-WWWay section, which links you to useful travel resources elsewhere on the Web.

This list is by no means an exhaustive selection of general sites on India:

All India Site
    www.gadnet.com/india.html
    Lots of links to tour and travel companies in India, plus film, music and current affairs
Himachal Pradesh Home Page
    http://metalab.unc.edu/himachal/
    General information on the state
India Info
    www.mahesh.com
    Excellent first stop site which has information or links to almost anything you might want
Kashmir Virtual Library WWW
    www.clas.ufl.edu/users/gthursby/kashmir/
    Excellent links to Kashmir-related information
Ministry of External Affairs
    www.indiagov.org/
    Has embassy addresses and the Discover India magazine
National Informatics Centre
    www.nic.in
    A wide range of links to government offices and agencies, including Indian Airlines and general information on Sikkim
Office of the Dalai Lama
    www.tibet.com
    Information on Tibet, the government exile and a mini-guide to Dharamsala

Rediff India
www.rediff.com
Another excellent general Web site with current affairs, music and travel news, including airline schedules and hotel information

Services International
www.india-travel.com
General travel Web site maintained by a travel agent

Shangri La
http://aleph0.clarku.edu/rajs/Shangri_La.html
Interesting personal Web site on the Himalayan region

BOOKS

India is one of the world's largest publishers of books in English. You'll find a great number of interesting books on India by Indian publishers (some listed below), which are generally not available in the west.

Indian publishers also do cheap reprints of popular western novels and India-related books at prices far below western levels. Unless there's a specific book you want you're probably better off buying your reading material in Delhi or Kolkata, or at the second-hand booksellers in popular travellers centres. Indian publishers have reprinted many classic Raj-era accounts of forays into the Himalayan regions during the British Raj era originally published in the mid to late 1900s.

Foreign-language titles are harder to come by, but you'll often find second-hand copies of French, German and Japanese editions in places like Leh, McLeod Ganj and Darjeeling.

Titles which are hard, if not impossible, to find outside India are marked with a '*'.

Lonely Planet

When it comes to the Indian subcontinent Lonely Planet has the place covered. Lonely Planet's award-winning *India* is now in its 8th edition. One of our most successful and popular titles, this is the most comprehensive guide you'll find.

Lonely Planet's *Trekking in the Indian Himalaya*, by Garry Weare, and this *Indian Himalaya* regional guide have been written to complement each other. Garry has spent years discovering the best trekking routes in

the Himalayan region, and his guide is full of practical descriptions and excellent maps. Lonely Planet's city guide *Delhi* has all the information you need to find your way around this often chaotic city.

Read This First: Asia & India is essential reading for those tackling India for the first time – even those on a second, third or forth trip will find it informative and detailed for planning itineraries, advice on budgeting and many more aspects of travel.

In 1999, Lonely Planet published *Sacred India*, another full-colour book with stunning images of India's diverse religious culture written by Lonely Planet staff and authors.

Other Lonely Planet guides to the Indian subcontinent include: *Nepal, Trekking in the Nepal Himalaya, Tibet, Pakistan, Karakoram Highway, Trekking in the Karakoram & Hindukush, Rajasthan, Mumbai (Bombay), South India, Goa, Kerala, Bangladesh* and *Sri Lanka*.

Guidebooks

Exploring Kinnaur & Spiti in the Trans-Himalaya*, Deepak Sanan & Dhanu Swadi, 1998. This superbly detailed guide is essential reading for anyone with a detailed interest in Kinnaur or Spiti. It also has good maps and detailed trek descriptions.

From Here to Nirvana, Anne Cushman & Jerry Jones. An excellent guide to India's many and varied ashrams and gurus. It provides useful practical information that will help you figure out which place suits your particular needs and aspirations. It also provides useful tips on how to spot dodgy operators.

Hill Stations of India, Gillian Wright, Odyssey 1998. Second edition of well-produced guide with an historical slant. Around half the book covers the Himalaya.

The Himalayas: Playground of the Gods*, Capt MS Kohli. This is primarily a trekking book, short on cultural notes (and good maps!), and is now slightly out of date.

India's Western Himalaya, Insight Guides 1992. While it's a great souvenir to read before your trip, this book is now hard to find, a bit short on practical travel information and deals only with the states of Jammu & Kashmir and Himachal Pradesh.

Leh and Trekking in Ladakh, Charlie Loram, Trailblazer 1996. A detailed trekking guide that covers several of Ladakh's most popular treks. It's normally available in Leh.

Sikkim, Insight Pocket Guides, 1998.

Travel

Valley of Flowers, Frank Smythe, 1938. This classic travelogue is fascinating reading for anyone interested in the western Himalaya and its prolific flora.

Himalayan Circuit: A Journey in the Inner Himalaya*, GD Khosla. Recounts the author's travels as part of an official tour through the remote tribal regions of Lahaul and Spiti in the 1950s. The author writes evocatively of the magnificent landscapes and their isolated inhabitants.

Account of Koonawaur in the Himalaya, Capt Alexander Gerard. An old British stiff upper-lip account of the 'discovery' of the Kinnaur region.

Across the Top, Sorrel Wilby. An account of the author's traverse of the entire length of the Himalaya from Pakistan to Arunachal Pradesh accompanied by her husband, Chris Ciantar. It makes compelling reading, and includes some of Sorrel's fine colour photographs.

Slowly Down the Ganges, Eric Newby. Newby is one of the finest travel writers. This trip takes him downstream from Haridwar. It borders at times on sheer masochism!

Kulu: The End of the Habitable World, Penelope Chetwoode. An entertaining story of a woman's travel on horseback through the region.

The Ochre Border, Justine Hardy. Subtitled 'A Journey through the Tibetan Borderlands', this slightly naive travelogue describes a 1992 trek over the Pin Parvati Pass into Spiti.

Western Himalayas & Tibet*, Thomas Thomson. Details the author's travels through the Indian Himalaya in the mid-1800s. It includes some fine old black-and-white plates.

Wonders of the Himalaya*, Francis Younghusband (reprinted in 1993). Classic account of the Himalaya by the British Great Game adventurer.

Are You Experienced?, William Sutcliffe. Hip and funny modern look at the backpacker culture in India, following a first-time backpacker who accompanies his best friend's girlfriend to India in an attempt to seduce her. Recommended by many travellers.

History & General Interest

A History of India, Romila Thapar & Percival Spear. This Pelican two-volume tome offers a thorough introduction to Indian history. Volume 1 follows Indian history from 1000 CE (commn era) to the coming of the Mughals in the 16th century. Volume 2 follows the rise and fall of the Mughals, through to India since Independence.

Oxford History of India, Vincent Smith. A cumbersome but very detailed 900 page paperback.

Himalayan Environment & Culture, NK Rustomji & Charles Ramble. A collection of scholarly essays on subjects ranging from ecological issues (including the effects of tourism on the Indian Himalaya) to the artistic and literary heritage of the Himalayan region, including chapters on the architecture of the western Himalaya and miniature painting of the Kangra Valley.

The Himalaya: Aspects of Change, JS Lall (ed). Probably the best contemporary collection of essays on the Himalaya, this paperback volume includes essays by various scholars on Himalayan flora and fauna, art, population and society, and the effects of development.

An Introduction to the Hill Stations of India, Graeme D Westlake. Probably the most comprehensive history of the former British hill stations you'll find anywhere. This book is widely available in northern India, including good bookstores in Delhi and Kolkata.

Plain Tales from the Raj, Charles Allen. Consists of interviews with people who took part in British India on both sides of the table. It's extremely readable and full of fascinating little insights into life during the British Raj.

Kashmir

Kashmir – Garden of the Himalaya, Rughubir Singh. The best illustrated photo book on the Kashmir Valley.

Kashmir, Francis Brunel. Another good one.

This is Kashmir, Pearce Gervis. A storehouse of historical information on the valley.

Travels in Kashmir, Bridgid Keenan. A highly readable account of the history and handicrafts of the Kashmir Valley.

Ladakh

Many of these books may be difficult to find outside India, or even outside Leh.

Ladakh Through the Ages*, Shridhaul Kaul & HN Kaul. A good study of regional history and culture.

Ladakh: Nubra, the Forbidden Valley*, Major HPS Ahluwalia. A moderately priced coffee-table book, with plenty of good photos and essays on historical and contemporary themes pertaining to Ladakh. There's a particular emphasis on the Nubra Valley.

Ladakh*, Neetu & DJ Singh. A wonderful collection of information on Ladakhi history and culture, with great photos of the area.

Ladakh, Janet Rizvi, written in 1983 and revised in 1996. Excellent introduction to Ladakh, past and present, especially the economic and social changes that have occurred since the region opened up in 1974.

The Cultural History of Ladakh, David & Skorupski Snellgrove. This provides the most comprehensive cultural background on Ladakh.

Ancient Futures: Learning from Ladakh, Helena Norberg-Hodge. An enjoyable contemporary study of Ladakh, and an analysis of what the future holds.

Zanskar: the Hidden Kingdom, Michael Peissel. One of the very few good books on Zanskar.

A Journey in Ladakh, Andrew Harvey. Erudite, almost poetic Buddhist travelogue through Ladakh.

Himachal Pradesh

Simla: Summer Capital of British India*, Raja Bhasin. A great account of the colonial history of this hill station.

Imperial Shimla, Pamela Kanwar. Includes some lovely old photos of the colonial era.

Simla: A Hill Station in British India, Pat Barr & Ray Desmond. Another readable book on Shimla.

Kinnaur: A Restricted Land in the Himalaya* and *Lahaul-Spiti: A Forbidden Land in the Himalayas**, SC Bajpai. Mines of information about the local customs, language, lifestyle and history.

Exploring Pangi Himalaya*, Minakshi Chaudhry. A detailed two-volume look at this little-visited valley, with some trekking information.

Living Tibet – the Dalai Lama in Dharamsala, Bill Warren (photos) & Nancy Hoetzlein (text). Glossy introduction to the Tibetan community and its various religious institutions.

Sikkim

Sikkim, Earl Kowall (text) & Nazima Kowall (photos), 1994. This good coffee-table souvenir is short on text, but the beautiful photographs are well captioned.

Gazetteer of Sikkim*. First published in 1894, and reprinted in 1989 by the Sikkim Nature Conservation Foundation, this is the definitive volume on the former kingdom of Sikkim. For readers interested in Tibetan Buddhism, the chapters dealing with its manifestation in Sikkim are astonishing and detailed. It's not cheap at Rs 400, but is truly a collector's item. There is a cheaper edition for Rs 200, printed on poor quality paper. It's normally only available in Gangtok.

Sikkim: Among the Himalayas*, Austine Waddell. Out of print for nearly 100 years, this account of the former independent and isolated kingdom is complemented by original illustrations and maps.

Travels in Nepal & Sikkim: 1875-76*, Sir Richard Temple. This fine old hardcover edition includes contemporary black-and-white illustrations and several maps.

Kumaon & Garhwal

Garhwal Himalayas: Ramparts of Heaven*, Pushpesh Pant. This weighty tome has a foreword by Sir Edmund Hillary and magnificent colour photographs by Ashok Dilwali.

Mountain Delight, Bill Aitken. A collection of published articles by this prolific writer and mountain lover who has resided in Garhwal for over 30 years. This collection includes little-known facts about the British presence in the Garhwal Himalaya, as well as essays on contemporary issues. He also writes evocatively of the lakes and mountains of Garhwal and Kumaon.

Man-Eaters of Kumaon, Jim Corbett. An immensely readable account of the great white hunter-turned-conservationist's experiences dispatching tigers in Uttarakhand early this century. This book was first published in 1944, but has been reprinted numerous times over the years.

Temple Tiger, Jim Corbett. His second book, first published in 1954, continues the tradition with a further five hunting tales.

The Himalayan Districts of the North-Western Provinces of India*, ET Atkinson. Published in 1882 in three volumes, this is one of the best references on Uttarakhand.

Statistical Sketch of Kamaon*, GW Traill. Published in 1828, this is a similar reference on the Kumaon region of Uttarakhand.

Arunachal Pradesh

Strangers of the Mist, Sanjoy Hazarika. A first-rate account of the troubles of the north-east.

The Tribal World of Verrier Elwin*, Verrier Elwin. This English anthropologist was crucial in establishing tribal policies for Arunachal Pradesh in the 1950s and 1960s and this has some good chapters on his travels in Arunachal in the course of his research. Elwin also wrote *Philosophy for NEFA* (Arunachal used to be called the North East Frontier Agency) and *Democracy for NEFA*, which you can find with some difficulty in Gauhati, Itanagar and Kolkata. These outline his ideas on how to develop the state without destroying tribal self-esteem.

Anthropological Survey of India. Volume 23 on Arunachal Pradesh is the best thing around on the tribes of the state, although it's very detailed (lots of stuff on physiology and genomes).

Tibet

Tears of Blood, Mary Craig. A moving and evocative commentary on the Chinese occupation of Tibet and the Tibetan's struggle for independence.

Freedom in Exile. An account by His Holiness, the Dalai Lama, of the Chinese occupation of his country and his subsequent exile and endeavours to preserve the culture and traditions of the Tibetan people in exile.

Heirs to Tibet, Andrew Powell. Companionable, though not all that enlightening, portrayal of the Tibetan exile community in India.

In Exile from the Land of Snows, John Avedon. Definitive history of Tibetan modern history.

Art

Unfortunately there is not a great selection of titles dealing with the rich artistic heritage of the Indian Himalaya.

Himalayan Art, JC French. First published in 1931 and reprinted in 1983, this focuses mainly on Kangra miniatures, with detailed descriptions of the paintings in the Kangra and Chamba museums.

Himalayan Art, Madajeet Singh. An excellent guide to the various art styles that have evolved in the Himalaya.

Travels in the Western Himalayas, MS Randhawa. Again, this deals predominantly with Kangra miniatures, but also discusses cultural aspects of the Chamba and Kangra valleys.

Woodcut Prints of Nineteenth Century Kolkata, Ashit Paul. A collection of woodcut prints from 1816 to the early years of the 20th century. Four essays focus on different aspects of this short-lived but intensely vital, popular urban art form, and its synthesis of western and eastern cultures.

People & Culture

Hindus of the Himalaya, Gerald D Berreman. A brilliant but scholarly discussion of the lifestyles and customs of the inhabitants of Garhwal. It was first published in 1963, and the current edition, reprinted in 1993, includes a prologue on the village a decade after the initial study.

The Gaddi Tribe of Himachal Pradesh, SS Shashi. A similar ethnographic exposition of this seminomadic tribal group.

Over the High Passes: A Year in the Himalaya, Christina Noble. Details the author's travels with the Gaddis as they traverse their traditional migration routes in Himachal Pradesh.

At Home in the Himalayas, Christina Noble. In this later book, Noble writes with great insight and affection of the hill people of Himachal Pradesh.

Folk Tales from the Himalayas, Alice Elizabeth Dracott. The author spent years early this century faithfully recording the folktales of the inhabitants of the Himalaya. Her work was first published in 1906 as *Simla Village Tales*, and is now available in a limited edition published in 1992.

The Nanda Devi Affair, Bill Aitken. An account of the history and lore of Nanda Devi, the patron goddess of Garhwal and Kumaon, who is worshipped in the form of the beautiful Nanda Devi mountain.

The Crisis of India, Ronald Segal. Written by a South African Indian, this book explores the theme that spirituality is not always more important than a full stomach.

Unveiling India, Anees Jung. A contemporary documentary on women in India.

May You Be the Mother of One Hundred Sons, Elizabeth Bumiller. This book offers some excellent insights into the plight of women in India, with an emphasis on rural women.

Tribes of India – the Struggle for Survival, Christof Von Fürer-Haimendorf. A scholarly book, written in 1982, which highlights the continuing and often shocking and sad story of India's tribal people.

Karma Cola, Gita Mehta. Amusing and cynical take on India's quest for western technology and modernity and the west's search for wisdom and enlightenment in India.

Flora & Fauna

100 Himalayan Flowers, Professor PV Bole & Ashvin Mehta (photos). A handy field guide to the prolific flora of the Himalaya, with 150 colour photos.

Sikkim Himalayan Rhododendrons, UC Pradhan & ST Lachungpa. Another useful guide for those visiting the eastern Himalaya, with colour photos and black-and-white illustrations.

Flowers of the Western Himalayas, Rupin Dang. A practical guide to the flora of Kashmir, Himachal Pradesh and Uttarakhand. Field notes are complemented with colour photos.

Flowers of the Himalaya, Oleg Polunin & Adam Stainton. Classic (but heavy) guide to the entire region, reprinted in 1984.

Indian Hill Birds, Sálim Ali. First published in 1949 (current edition 1994), it is the definitive guide to the birdlife of the Himalaya.

The Birds of Sikkim, Sálim Ali. A more specialised guide by this author.

The Book of Indian Animals, SH Prater. The best guide to India's fauna. First published in 1948 (current edition 1993).

A Photographic Guide to the Birds of the Himalaya, Bikram Grewal & Otto Pfister. This handy-sized guide's photos of each bird listed make it a good guide to take with you.

Indian Wildlife, Insight Guides. Another excellent guide to India's wildlife, with a very good chapter on the wildlife of the Indian Himalaya.

Birds and Trees of Tolly, Kushal Mookherjee. A beautiful and informative book to have by your side if you are visiting or staying at the Tollygunge Club in Kolkata. Written in collaboration with Anne and Robert Wright who ran the Tolly for several decades, it is available from the club.

Religion

If you want a better understanding of India's religions there are plenty of books available in India. The English series of Penguin paperbacks are among the best and are generally available in India. Many of the Hindu holy books are available in translation, including *The Upanishads* and *The Bhagavad Gita*.

Hinduism, KM Sen. Brief and to the point.

Hindu Mythology, Wendy O'Flaherty (ed). An interesting annotated collection of extracts from the Hindu holy books.

A Classical Dictionary of Hindu Mythology & Religion, John Dowson. An Indian paperback reprint of an old English hardback. In dictionary form it is one of the best sources for unravelling who's who in Hinduism.

Handbook of Living Religions, John R Hinnewls. Provides a succinct and readable summary of all the religions you will find in India.

Guru – the Search for Enlightenment, John Mitchiner. Excellent for anyone interested in the relevance and contribution of Indian gurus to contemporary thought and experience.

Sadhus: Holy Men of India, Dorf Hartsuiker. A fine paperback volume that examines the compulsions and lifestyles of India's wandering ascetics.

The Heart of Buddhism, Guy Claxton. A good starting point if you are interested in Buddhism.

The Power of Compassion, His Holiness the Dalai Lama. A collection of essays, available in bookshops in McLeod Ganj and other parts of Himachal Pradesh, as well as in Delhi.

The Way to Freedom, His Holiness the Dalai Lama, Snow Lion, 1994. Outlines the essence of Tibetan Buddhism in an accessible form.

The Tibetan Book of Living & Dying, Soygal Rinpoche. A lucid and erudite discussion of the principles of Tibetan Buddhism. It should not be confused with the original *Tibetan Book of the Dead*, or *Bardo Thödol*, translated by WY Evans-Wentz, a complex religious text that deals with the experience of death and the nature of existence after death.

Travels Through Sacred India, Roger Housden. Provides a very readable account of popular and classical traditions and contains a gazetteer of sacred places plus a roundup of ashrams and retreats.

Cooking Back Home

There are all sorts of books about Indian cooking should you want to pursue this after you leave India. Premila Lal is one of the country's leading cookery writers, and her books are widely available. The problem is that ingredients are only given in their local name, which makes many of the recipes impractical or impossible if you don't know exactly what is being called for.

Indian Cookery, Dharamjit Singh. A useful paperback introduction to the art.

Asian Cookbook, Charmaine Solomon. An excellent source, and includes Indian and other Asian cuisine.

Himalayan Recipes, Inner Wheel Club of Darjeeling (Rs 100). Proceeds of this little booklet are directed towards the establishment of a rehabilitation centre for alcoholics and drug addicts of the Darjeeling district. Recipes include both traditional Tibetan and Nepali dishes such as *momos* (stuffed dumplings), *thukpa* (Tibetan noodle dish) and *quasi* (Tibetan cookies).

Ecological Issues

Himalaya: A Regional Perspective: Resources, Environment & Development, MSS Rawat. Considers the ramifications of development for the fragile ecosystem of the Himalaya and its effects on the traditional cultural practices of its inhabitants.

Novels

Kim, Rudyard Kipling. Partly set in the Himalaya, this classic novel recounts the tale of a young streetwise Anglo-Indian boy who devotes himself to a Tibetan lama who is searching for the river of immortality. In the process, recruited by the British secret service, Kim finds himself immersed in the political intrigue of the Great Game.

Plain Tales from the Hills, Rudyard Kipling. In this, and other books, Kipling, who lived and worked in Shimla for many years, proves himself as the Victorian English interpreter of India *par excellence*.

Quest for Kim, Peter Hopkirk. Required reading for certified Kipling fans, this literary detective travelogue tries to match real places and Great Game history to Kipling's not-always-so-fictional characters. Hopkirk visits Shimla, Mussoorie and Dehra Dun in the course of his investigations.

Himalayan Exploration

Where Men and Mountains Meet and *The Gilgit Game*, John Keay. Two indispensable books on the history of exploration in the western Himalaya during the 19th century.

Abode of the Snows, Kenneth Mason. A classic on Himalayan exploration and climbs.

Mountain Travel and *The Mountaineers*, Eric Shipton and HW Tilman. Both are highly recommended for reading on exploration in the Indian Himalaya and beyond.

Spy on the Roof of the World, Sydney Wignall. The story of Wignall's 1950s climbing expedition, which turned into an extraordinary and life-threatening adventure that would involve the Indian and Chinese governments at the highest level.

Phrasebooks

Lonely Planet has the subcontinent well covered, with phrasebooks for Hindi/Urdu, Bangali and Tibetan. Helen Norberg-Hodge co-publishes a largish Ladakhi-English dictionary. *Getting Started in Ladakhi* by Rebecca Norman is useful pocket-sized phrasebook available in Leh for Rs 75.

Journals

Himal, published bi-monthly in Nepal and distributed internationally, contains good essays on cultural and ecological issues pertaining to the Himalaya. It is available by subscription. Distributors can be found in Japan, Australia, the USA, UK, the Netherlands, Switzerland, Germany and India. For their addresses contact Himal Magazine, GPO PO Box 7251, Kathmandu Nepal (☎ 977-1-543333, fax 521013, email info@himalmag.com) or check out the Web site www.himalmag.com.

The Tibetan Government in Exile produces a range of journals, some of which are available on subscription. See the McLeod Ganj section in the Himachal Pradesh chapter for more details.

FILMS

The Indian film industry is the largest in the world in terms of volume and boasts an enormous following – there are many thousands of cinemas. While the vast proportion of what is produced are Bollywood 'masala movies', few cover the Himalaya.

A number of foreign films, however, have been made about the region over the years. The Australian ABC TV has produced an excellent documentary series titled *Journey into the Himalayas*. Worth seeing if you get a chance.

If you are interested in the plight of Tibet Martin Scorcese's *Kundun* features an all Tibetan and Chinese cast, many of them descendants of the original figures they are portraying (the Dalai Lama's mother is played by the Dalai Lama's real life niece). The cinematography of the film in particular is gorgeous.

CD ROMS

Magic Software (Web site www.magi.csw .com) produces several multimedia CD ROMs about India, including *India Mystica, India Festiva, Hindi Guru, Yoga and Meditation* and *The Mahabharata. The Pleasure of Indian Cooking*, produced by Ascent Interactive Multimedia Services has over 600 recipes. *Indian Classical Dance* (Rizvie

Software Consultancy) gives a rundown on major classical dance forms. *Magic of India* is a general introduction to the country by Anchalsoft (www.anchalsoft.com).

These are all available at Delhi and cost around Rs 1500 each. Try BPB Publications (☎ 011-332 5760), B-14 Connaught Circus, Delhi.

In the US, Synforest (www.synforest .com) produces a CD ROM to the Himalaya entitled *Himalayas – The Mountains Where God Lives*, priced at US$28.

NEWSPAPERS & MAGAZINES

English-language dailies include the *Times of India*, the *Hindustan Times*, the *Indian Express* and the *Statesman*; many feel the *Express* is the best of the bunch. The *Independent*, which is published in Mumbai, is an excellent broadsheet. The *Times of India* (Web site www.timesofindia.com/) is the largest-selling English daily, with a circulation of over one million.

International coverage is generally pretty good. However, when it comes to national news, the copy is invariably strewn with a plethora of acronyms and Indian words, the majority of which mean nothing to the uninitiated. One exception is the *Independent*.

In the hill stations, English-language dailies generally arrive after 11.30 am. In larger centres farther north, you'll be able to get hold of day-old English-language papers after noon.

There's an excellent variety of weekly magazines, which include *Frontline* (possibly the best of the lot), *India Today* (www .india-today.com) and the *Illustrated Weekly of India*. They're all available from bookshops, especially those at major train stations, and are interesting for the different slant they give to political and social issues of worldwide concern.

RADIO & TV

The revolution in the TV network has been the introduction of cable TV. It's amazing to see satellite dishes, even in the remotest villages. The result is that viewers can tune in to the BBC, and, broadcasting from Hong Kong, Murdoch's Star TV, Prime Sports and V (an MTV-type Hindi music channel). ZTV is a local Hindi cable channel.

The national broadcaster, Doordarshan, which prior to the coming of satellite TV used to plod along with dry, dull and generally dreadful programs, has lifted its game and now offers some refreshingly good viewing.

Most mid-range and all top-end hotels have a TV in every room with a choice of satellite or Doordarshan.

PHOTOGRAPHY & VIDEO
Film & Equipment

Colour print film processing facilities are readily available in the hill stations and popular tourist centres such as Manali and Leh. Film is relatively cheap and the quality is usually good, though you should always check the use-by date. The humidity during the monsoon can play havoc with film, even if the use-by date hasn't passed. Kodak 100/400 ASA colour print film costs around Rs 90/125 for 36 exposures. Developing costs for 36 prints are between Rs 120 and Rs 200 depending on the print size.

If you're taking slides, bring film with you. Colour slide film such as Fuji Sensia (Rs 200) is only available in major cities. Colour slides can be developed only in Delhi, and quality is not guaranteed. A better bet is to carry your film home with you. Kodachrome and 'includes developing' film will have to be sent overseas.

Carrying a tripod means extra bulk, but may be the only way you'll be able to take reasonable photos in dimly lit interiors, such as gompas (those where photography is permitted). A UV filter permanently fitted to your lens will not only cut down ultraviolet light, but will protect your lens. Spare batteries should also be carried at all times.

Serious photographers will consider bringing a macro lens for shots of wildflowers, a telephoto lens for dramatic mountain shots, and a wide-angle lens for gompa interiors, mountain panoramas and village profiles.

Technical Tips

Film manufacturers warn that once exposed, film should be developed as quickly as possible; in practice the film seems to last, even in India's summer heat, without deterioration for months. If you're going to be carrying exposed film for long, consult a specialist photography handbook about ways to enhance preservation. Try to keep your film cool, and protect it in water and air-proof containers if you're travelling during the monsoon. Silicone sachets distributed around your gear will help to absorb moisture.

In the mountains you should allow for the extreme light intensity, and take care not to overexpose your shots. In general, photography has the best results when shots are taken in the early morning and late afternoon. Some fast film, up to 400 ASA, is useful if you're using a zoom or telephoto lens in low light conditions. A polarising filter produces unearthly blues in high-altitude spots like Ladakh ad Spiti.

In Delhi and Kolkata there are plenty of camera shops that should be able to make minor repairs should you have any mechanical problems, but up in the hills you're in trouble if you break or damage your camera. It's worthwhile having your camera serviced by a reputable outfit before you leave home. Places such as Shimla, Manali, Darjeeling and Dharamsala sell small basic cameras. Canon's authorised dealer in Delhi is Mahatta & Co (☎ 011-332 9769), 59 M-block, Connaught Place.

Video

Properly used, a video camera can create a fascinating record of your holiday. As well as videoing the obvious things – sunsets and spectacular views – remember to record some of the ordinary everyday details of life in the country. Remember too that, unlike still photography, video 'flows' – so, for example, you can shoot scenes of countryside rolling past the train window, to give an overall impression that isn't possible with ordinary photos.

Video cameras these days have amazingly sensitive microphones, which can be a problem when filming by the side of a busy road (or almost anywhere in India!). One good rule to follow for beginners is to try to film in long takes, and don't move the camera around too much. Otherwise, your video could well make your viewers seasick! If your camera has a stabiliser, you can use it to obtain good footage while travelling on various means of transport, even on bumpy roads. And remember, you're on holiday – don't let the video take over your life and turn your trip into a Cecil B De Mille production.

Video in India uses the VHS format, although it is possible to convert to and from PAL and NTSC in the larger cities. You can readily get VHS, CVHS, Hi8, Betacam and Umatic (high and low) tapes in Delhi and Kolkata. Make sure you keep the batteries charged and have the necessary charger, plugs and transformer. Unreliable electrical supplies in the Himalaya can make recharging your batteries tricky. Top them up whenever you get to a large town and perhaps bring one more than you would normally need.

Finally, remember to follow the same rules regarding people's sensitivities as for still photography – having a video camera shoved in one's face is probably even more annoying and offensive than a still camera. Always ask permission first.

Restrictions & Photographing People

India is touchy about places of military importance – this can include train stations, bridges, airports, military installations and sensitive border regions. Some gompas prohibit photography in the main prayer chambers, while others charge. If in doubt, ask.

In general most people are happy to be photographed, but care should be taken in pointing cameras at Muslim women. Again, if in doubt, ask. A zoom is a less intrusive means of taking portraits – even when you've obtained permission to take a portrait, shoving a lens in your subject's face can be disconcerting. A reasonable distance between you and your subject will help to reduce your subject's discomfiture, and will result in more natural shots.

Airport Security

It's worthwhile investing in a lead-lined (x-ray proof) bag, as repeated exposure to x-ray (even so-called 'film proof' x-ray) can damage film. Most airport officials will let you pass your film to them and will hand it back when you have cleared the x-rays. It's a good idea to take your films out of their canisters and arrange them in a plastic bag or box so that they are clearly visible. *Never* put your unprocessed film in check-in baggage, which will be placed in the cargo holds of aeroplanes. It will probably be subjected to large doses of x-ray which will spoil or completely ruin it.

TIME

Indian Standard Time is 5½ hours ahead of GMT/UTC. When it's noon in India, the time in other cities around the world is:

city	local time
Auckland	6.30 pm
Hong Kong	2.30 pm
Islamabad	11.30 am
Kathmandu	12.30 pm
London	6.30 am
Los Angeles	10.30 pm (previous day)
New York	1.30 am
Paris	7.30 am
Sydney	4.30 pm
Tel Aviv	8.30 am

ELECTRICITY
Voltages & Cycles

The electric current is 230-240V AC, 50 cycles. Electricity is widely available in the lower regions of the Indian Himalaya, but in the more remote regions, such as Yamunotri and Gangotri in Uttarakhand, the electricity supply is either nonexistent or connected to only a few establishments. In parts of Lahaul and Spiti, and most of Ladakh, blackouts ('load shedding') regularly occur at dusk, generally lasting until everyone is well asleep.

Darjeeling is notorious for being plunged into darkness regularly between 6 and 8 pm.

Many mid-range and top-end hotels have their own (noisy) backup generators in the event of power failure. Make sure your room isn't next to one of them! If you are using a laptop or other sensitive electrical equipment, bring a voltage stabiliser/surge protector to prevent your expensive toys getting fried.

Plugs & Sockets

Sockets are of a three round-pin variety, similar (but not identical) to European sockets. European round-pin plugs will go into the sockets, but as the pins on Indian plugs are somewhat thicker, the fit is loose and connection is not always guaranteed.

WEIGHTS & MEASURES

Although India officially uses the metric system, imperial weights and measures are a colonial hangover and are still used in some areas of commerce. If you are hiking check whether distances given are in miles or kilometres. A weights and measures conversion chart has been included on the inside back cover of this book.

LAUNDRY

Getting your laundry done in the main hill stations is usually no problem. At private laundries and even the smallest hotel you'll be able to hand in your dirty clothes in the morning and have them back freshly laundered and pressed in the evening. The secret lies in the *dhobi-wallahs*, the people who still do this enormous task by hand. The charge is around Rs 5 for underwear, Rs 10 for a T-shirt and Rs 15 for a pair of trousers. Most hotel bathrooms come equipped with a bucket if you are doing your own laundry, though some hotels have signs which expressly forbid this.

TOILETS

'Western' hotels have a sit-up-style toilet. Cheaper ones usually (but not always) have the traditional Asian squat style, which is a toilet bowl recessed into the floor with footpads on the edge of the bowl. One strange hybrid is a sit toilet with foot platforms on either side for squatters. If you can't adapt to the Indian method of a jug of water and your left hand, toilet paper is widely available in the hill stations; it is less readily available farther north in the more remote regions. If a receptacle is provided for used toilet paper you'd better use it as the plumbing might not be able to cope with the paper.

HEALTH

Travel health depends on your predeparture preparations, your daily health care while travelling and how you handle any medical problem that does develop. While the potential dangers can seem quite frightening, in reality few travellers experience anything more than an upset stomach.

Predeparture Planning

Immunisations Plan ahead for getting your vaccinations: some of them require more than one injection, while some vaccinations should not be given together. Note that some vaccinations should not be given during pregnancy or in people with allergies – discuss with your doctor.

It is recommended you seek medical advice at least six weeks before travel. Be aware that there is often a greater risk of disease with children and during pregnancy.

Discuss your requirements with your doctor, but vaccinations you should consider for this trip include the following (for more details about the diseases themselves, see the individual disease entries later in this section). Carry proof of your vaccinations, especially yellow fever, as this is sometimes needed to enter some countries.

Diphtheria & Tetanus Vaccinations are usually combined and are required for everyone. After an initial course of three injections, boosters are given every 10 years.

Polio Everyone should keep up to date with this vaccination, which is normally given in childhood. A booster every 10 years maintains immunity.

Hepatitis A Hepatitis A vaccine (eg Avaxim, Havrix 1440 or VAQTA) provides long-term immunity (possibly more than 10 years) after an initial injection and a booster at six to 12 months. Alternatively, an injection of gamma globulin can provide short-term protection against hepatitis A – two to six months, depending on the dose given. It is not a vaccine, but is ready-made antibody collected from blood donations. It is reasonably effective and, unlike the vaccine, it is protective immediately, but because it is a blood product, there are current concerns about its long-term safety.

Hepatitis A vaccine is also available in a combined form, Twinrix, with hepatitis B vaccine. Three injections over a six-month period are required, the first two providing substantial protection against hepatitis A.

Typhoid Vaccination against typhoid may be required if you are travelling for more than a couple of weeks in India. It is now available either as an injection or as capsules to be taken orally.

Cholera The current injectable vaccine against cholera is poorly protective and has many side effects, so it is not generally recommended for travellers. However, in some situations it may be necessary to have a certificate as travellers are very occasionally asked by immigration officials to present one, even though all countries and the WHO have dropped cholera immunisation as a health requirement for entry.

Meningococcal Meningitis Vaccination is recommended for travellers to northern India (north of Delhi) and Nepal. A single injection gives good protection against the major epidemic forms of the disease for three years. Protection may be less effective in children under two years.

Hepatitis B Travellers who should consider vaccination against hepatitis B include those on a long trip, as well as those visiting countries where there are high levels of hepatitis B infection, where blood transfusions may not be adequately screened or where sexual contact or needle sharing could be a possibility. Vaccination involves three injections, with a booster at 12 months. More rapid courses are available if necessary.

Rabies Vaccination should be considered by those who will spend a month or longer in a country where rabies is common, especially if they are cycling, handling animals, caving or travelling to remote areas, and for children (who may not report a bite). Pretravel rabies vaccination involves having three injections over 21 to 28 days. If someone who has been vaccinated is bitten or scratched by an animal, they will require two booster injections of vaccine; those not vaccinated will require more.

Japanese B Encephalitis Consider vaccination if spending a month or longer in rural areas in northern India during July to November, making repeated trips to a risk area or visiting during an epidemic. It involves three injections over 30 days. Cases have been reported in Uttar Pradesh, Assam and Bangla but not Himachal Pradesh, Arunachal Pradesh, Kashmir or Sikkim.

Tuberculosis The risk of TB to travellers is usually very low, unless you will be living with or closely associated with local people. Vaccination against TB (BCG) is recommended for children and young adults living in these areas for six months or more.

Malaria Medication The mosquitoes that carry malaria are not prevalent in the Indian Himalaya but you may need to consider prophylactic medication if you are coming from or visiting other areas of India.

Antimalarial drugs do not prevent you from being infected but kill the malaria parasites during a stage in their development and significantly reduce the risk of becoming very ill or dying. Expert advice on medication should be sought, as there are many factors to consider, including the area to be visited, the risk of exposure to malaria-carrying mosquitoes, the side effects of medication, your medical history and whether you are a child or an adult or pregnant.

Travellers to isolated areas in high risk countries may like to carry a treatment dose of medication for use if symptoms occur.

Health Insurance

It is important to make sure that you have adequate health insurance. See Travel Insurance under the Visas & Documents section earlier in this chapter for details.

Travel Health Guides

If you are planning to be away or travelling in remote areas for an extensive period of time, you may like to consider taking a more detailed health guide.

Healthy Travel Asia & India, Dr Isabelle Young, Lonely Planet Publications, 2000. Covers it all from how to treat a nose bleed in Delhi to finding a doctor in Mumbai.

Travel with Children, Maureen Wheeler, Lonely Planet Publications, 1995. Includes advice on travel health for younger children.

CDC's Complete Guide to Healthy Travel, Open Road Publishing, 1997. The US Centers for Disease Control & Prevention recommendations for international travel.

Staying Healthy in Asia, Africa & Latin America, Dirk Schroeder, Moon Publications, 1994. An all-round guide; it's detailed and well organised.

Travellers' Health, Dr Richard Dawood, Oxford University Press, 1995. Comprehensive, easy to read, authoritative and highly recommended, although it's rather large to lug around.

Where There Is No Doctor, David Werner, Macmillan, 1994. A very detailed guide intended for someone, such as a long-term volunteer worker, going to work in a developing country.

Other Travel Advice Medical Advisory Services for Travellers Abroad (MASTA), a private group associated with the London School of Hygiene & Tropical Medicine, has a travellers' health line (☎ 0891-224100) where you can order a 'health brief' with information on immunisations, malaria, Foreign Office advisories and health news, for the cost of the (premium-rate) call. It also offers more detailed briefs for long or complex trips, plus mail-order health supplies. In the UK, the Malaria Reference Laboratory has a 24 hour premium-rate help line at ☎ 0891-600350.

MASTA in Australia (☎ 02-971 1499, fax 971 0239), associated with the Tropical Health Program of the University of Queensland, offers similar services. Alternatively, call the Australian Government Health Service (part of the Commonwealth Department of Human Services & Health) or a clinic like the Travellers' Medical & Vaccination Centre (☎ 03-9670 3969) in Melbourne, Victoria.

In the USA the Center for Disease Control & Prevention has a travellers' hotline (☎ 404-332 4555 or 332 4559) and a free fax-back service within the USA (fax 404-332 4565). You can also call the International Medicine Program at Cornell University Medical Center in New York (☎ 212-746 5454). Another resource is the International Association for Medical Assistance to Travellers (☎ 716-754 4883), 417 Center St, Lewiston, NY 14092.

Medical Kit Check List

Following is a list of items you should consider including in your medical kit – consult your pharmacist for brands available in your country.

☐ **Aspirin** or **paracetamol** (acetaminophen in the USA) – for pain or fever
☐ **Antihistamine** – for allergies, eg hay fever; to ease the itch from insect bites or stings; and to prevent motion sickness
☐ **Antibiotics** – consider including these if you're travelling well off the beaten track; see your doctor, as they must be prescribed, and carry the prescription with you
☐ **Loperamide** or **diphenoxylate** –'blockers' for diarrhoea; **prochlorperazine** or **metaclopramide** for nausea and vomiting
☐ **Rehydration mixture** – to prevent dehydration, eg due to severe diarrhoea; particularly important when travelling with children
☐ **Insect repellent**, **sunscreen**, **lip balm** and **eye drops**
☐ **Calamine lotion**, **sting relief spray** or **aloe vera** – to ease irritation from sunburn and insect bites or stings
☐ **Antifungal cream** or **powder** – for fungal skin infections and thrush
☐ **Antiseptic** (such as povidone-iodine) – for cuts and grazes
☐ **Bandages**, **Band-Aids (plasters)** and other wound dressings
☐ **Water purification tablets** or **iodine**
☐ **Scissors**, **tweezers** and a **thermometer** (note that mercury thermometers are prohibited by airlines)
☐ **Syringes** and **needles** – in case you need injections in a country with medical hygiene problems. Ask your doctor for a note explaining why you have them.
☐ **Cold** and **flu tablets**, **throat lozenges** and **nasal decongestant**
☐ **Multivitamins** – consider for long trips, when dietary vitamin intake may be inadequate

There are also a number of excellent travel health sites on the Internet. From the Lonely Planet home page there are links at www.lonelyplanet.com/weblinks/weblinks.htm to the World Health Organization (www.who.int) and the US Centers for Disease Control & Prevention (www.cdc.gov/travel/travel.html).

Other Preparations Make sure you're healthy before you start travelling. If you are going on a long trip make sure your teeth are OK. If you wear glasses take a spare pair and your prescription.

If you require a particular medication take an adequate supply, as it may not be available locally. Take part of the packaging showing the generic name rather than the brand, which will make getting replacements easier. It's a good idea to have a legible prescription or letter from your doctor to show that you legally use the medication to avoid any problems.

Basic Rules

Food There is an old colonial adage that says: 'If you can cook it, boil it or peel it you can eat it ... otherwise forget it'. Vegetables and fruit should be washed with purified water or peeled where possible. Beware of ice cream that is sold in the street or anywhere it might have been melted and refrozen; if there's any doubt (eg a power cut in the last day or two), steer well clear. Popular brands such as Kwality are generally OK. Undercooked meat, particularly in the form of mince should be avoided.

If a place looks clean and well run and the vendor also looks clean and healthy, then the food is probably safe. In general, places that are packed with travellers or locals will be fine, while empty restaurants are questionable. The food in busy restaurants is cooked and eaten quite quickly with little standing around and is probably not reheated.

Paranoia about food in India can spoil what is otherwise an enjoyable culinary and cultural experience. Some of the gloomy *dhabas* (basic restaurants) might look pretty grim but unless the food has been pre-

Nutrition

If your diet is poor or limited in variety, if you're travelling hard and fast and therefore missing meals or if you simply lose your appetite, you can soon start to lose weight and place your health at risk.

Make sure your diet is well balanced. Cooked eggs, tofu, beans, lentils (dhal in India) and nuts are all safe ways to get protein. Fruit you can peel (bananas, oranges or mandarins for example) is usually safe (melons can harbour bacteria in their flesh and are best avoided) and a good source of vitamins. Try to eat plenty of grains (including rice) and bread. Remember that although food is generally safer if it is cooked well, overcooked food loses much of its nutritional value. If your diet isn't well balanced or if your food intake is insufficient, it's a good idea to take vitamin and iron pills.

In hot climates make sure you drink enough – don't rely on feeling thirsty to indicate when you should drink. Not needing to urinate or small amounts of very dark yellow urine is a danger sign. Always carry a water bottle with you on long trips. Excessive sweating can lead to loss of salt and therefore muscle cramping. Salt tablets are not a good idea as a preventative, but in places where salt is not used much, adding salt to food can help.

---

cooked and left to stand in the heat, you probably won't encounter too many problems. Keep in mind that food that is cooked in front of you is the best.

Water The number one rule is *be careful of the water* and especially ice. If you don't know for certain that the water is safe, assume the worst. Reputable brands of bottled water or soft drinks are generally fine, although in some places bottles may be refilled with tap water. Only use water from containers with a serrated seal – not tops or corks. Take care with fruit juice, particularly if water may have been added. Milk should be treated with suspicion as it is often unpasteurised, though boiled milk is fine if it is kept hygienically. Tea or coffee should also be OK, since the water should have been boiled.

Water Purification The simplest way of purifying water is to boil it thoroughly. Vigorous boiling should be satisfactory; however, at high altitude water boils at a lower temperature, so germs are less likely to be killed. Boil it for longer in these environments.

Consider purchasing a water filter for a long trip. There are two main kinds of filter.

Total filters take out all parasites, bacteria and viruses and make water safe to drink. They are often expensive, but they can be more cost effective than buying bottled water. Simple filters (which can even be a nylon mesh bag) take out dirt and larger foreign bodies from the water so that chemical solutions work much more effectively; if water is dirty, chemical solutions may not work at all. It's very important when buying a filter to read the specifications, so that you know exactly what it removes from the water and what it doesn't. Simple filtering will not remove all dangerous organisms, so if you cannot boil water it should be treated chemically. Chlorine tablets (generally not available in India) will kill many pathogens, but not some parasites like giardia and amoebic cysts. Iodine is more effective in purifying water and is available in tablet form. Follow the directions carefully and remember that too much iodine can be harmful.

Medical Problems & Treatment

Self-diagnosis and treatment can be risky, so you should always seek medical help. An embassy, consulate or five star hotel can usually recommend a local doctor or clinic. Although we do give drug dosages in this

Everyday Health

Normal body temperature is up to 37°C (98.6°F); more than 2°C (4°F) higher indicates a high fever. The normal adult pulse rate is 60 to 100 per minute (children 80 to 100, babies 100 to 140). As a general rule the pulse increases about 20 beats per minute for each 1°C (2°F) rise in fever.

Respiration (breathing) rate is also an indicator of illness. Count the number of breaths per minute: between 12 and 20 is normal for adults and older children (up to 30 for younger children, 40 for babies). People with a high fever or serious respiratory illness breathe more quickly than normal. More than 40 shallow breaths a minute may indicate pneumonia.

section, they are for emergency use only. Correct diagnosis is vital. In this section we have used the generic names for medications – check with a pharmacist for brands available locally.

In India and many other developing countries, if a medicine is available at all it will generally be available over the counter and the price will be much cheaper than the west. However, be careful if buying medicines in these places, particularly where the expiry date may have passed or correct storage conditions may not have been followed. Bogus drugs are common and it's possible that medicines which are no longer recommended, or even have been banned, in the west are still being dispensed in India.

Note that antibiotics should ideally be administered only under medical supervision. Take only the recommended dose at the prescribed intervals and use the whole course, even if the illness seems to be cured earlier. Stop immediately if there are any serious reactions and don't use the antibiotic at all if you are unsure that you have the correct one. Some people are allergic to commonly prescribed antibiotics such as penicillin; carry this information (eg on a bracelet) when travelling.

Hospitals Although India does have a few excellent hospitals such as the All India Institute of Medical Sciences in Delhi, most Indian cities do not have the quality of medical care available in the west. Usually, hospitals run by western missionaries have better facilities than government hospitals where long waiting lines are common. Unless you have something very unusual, these Christian-run hospitals are the best places to head for in an emergency. In remote areas, medical services are less than adequate and some nonexistent, and if you require hospitalisation, evacuation to Delhi or Kolkata should be considered.

India also has many qualified doctors with their own private clinics that can be quite good and, in some cases, as good as anything available anywhere in the world. The usual fee for a clinic visit is about Rs 100; Rs 250 for a specialist. Home calls usually cost about Rs 150.

In centres where there is a large Tibetan population, such as McLeod Ganj or Darjeeling, you may be able to avail yourself of traditional Tibetan medicine. Some travellers swear by some Tibetan herbal remedies for minor stomach complaints, but check your symptoms against those listed under the more serious gastric disorders in this health section. For more information on traditional Tibetan medicine, see under McLeod Ganj in the Himachal Pradesh chapter.

Environmental Hazards

Altitude Sickness Acute Mountain Sickness (AMS) is a particular problem in the Indian Himalaya and with buses climbing up to 5600m it's a problem not just restricted to trekkers. Lack of oxygen at high altitudes (over 2500m) affects most people to some extent. The effect may be mild or severe and occurs because less oxygen reaches the muscles and the brain at high altitude, requiring the heart and lungs to compensate by working harder. Where possible, altitudes of the towns have been given at the beginning of the entry (see regional chapters) to help you plan your acclimatisation.

Acclimatisation AMS is linked to low atmospheric pressure. With an increase in altitude the human body needs time to develop physiological mechanisms to cope with the decreased oxygen. This process of acclimatisation is still not fully understood but is known to involve modifications in breathing patterns and heart rate induced by the autonomic nervous system, and an increase in the blood's oxygen-carrying capabilities. These compensatory mechanisms usually take about one to three days to develop at a particular altitude. Once you are acclimatised to a given height you are unlikely to get AMS at that height, but you can still get ill when you travel higher. If the ascent is too high and too fast, these compensatory reactions may not kick into gear fast enough.

Symptoms Mild symptoms of AMS are very common in travellers to high altitudes, and usually develop during the first 24 hours at altitude. Symptoms tend to be worse at night and include headache, dizziness, lethargy, loss of appetite, nausea, breathlessness and irritability. Difficulty sleeping is another common symptom.

AMS may become more serious without warning and can be fatal. Symptoms are caused by the accumulation of fluid in the lungs and brain, and include breathlessness at rest, a dry irritative cough (which may progress to the production of pink, frothy sputum), severe headache, lack of coordination (typically leading to a 'drunken walk'), confusion, irrational behaviour, vomiting and eventually unconsciousness.

These signs should be taken very seriously; travellers to the Indian Himalaya should keep an eye on each other as those experiencing symptoms, especially severe symptoms, may not be in a position to recognise them. One thing to note is that while the symptoms of mild AMS often precede those of severe AMS, this is not always the case. Severe AMS can strike with little or no warning.

Prevention The best prevention of AMS is to avoid rapid ascents to high altitudes.

After your arrival, take it easy for at least three days – for most travellers this is enough to get over any initial ill-effects.

To prevent acute mountain sickness:

- Ascend slowly – have frequent rest days, spending two to three nights at each rise of 1000m. If you reach a high altitude by trekking, acclimatisation takes place gradually and you are less likely to be affected than if you fly directly to high altitude.
- It is always wise to sleep at a lower altitude than the greatest height reached during the day. Also, once above 3000m, care should be taken not to increase the sleeping altitude by more than 300m per day.
- Drink extra fluids. The mountain air is dry and cold and moisture is lost as you breathe. Evaporation of sweat may occur unnoticed and result in dehydration.
- Eat light, high-carbohydrate meals for more energy.
- Avoid alcohol as it may increase the risk of dehydration.
- Avoid sedatives.

The symptoms of AMS, however mild, are a warning – take them seriously!

Treatment Treat mild symptoms by resting at the same altitude until recovery, usually a day or two. Take paracetamol or aspirin for headaches. If symptoms persist or become worse, however, *immediate descent is necessary*; every 500m can help.

The most effective treatment for severe AMS is to get down to a lower altitude as quickly as possible. In less severe cases the victim will be able to stagger down with some support; however sufferers may need to be carried down. Whatever the case, do not delay, as any delay could be fatal.

The drugs acetazolamide (Diamox) and dexamethasone are recommended by some doctors for the prevention of AMS, but their use is controversial. They can reduce the symptoms, but they may also mask warning signs; severe and fatal AMS has occurred in people taking these drugs. Drug treatments should never be used to avoid descent or to enable further ascent. In general we do not recommend them for travellers.

Heat Exhaustion Dehydration and salt deficiency can cause heat exhaustion. Take time to acclimatise to high temperatures, drink sufficient liquids and do not do anything too physically demanding.

Salt deficiency is characterised by fatigue, lethargy, headaches, giddiness and muscle cramps; salt tablets may help, but adding extra salt to your food is better.

Heatstroke This serious, occasionally fatal, condition can occur if the body's heat-regulating mechanism breaks down and the body temperature rises to dangerous levels. Long, continuous periods of exposure to high temperatures and insufficient fluids can leave you vulnerable to heatstroke.

The symptoms are feeling unwell, not sweating very much (or at all) and a high body temperature (39° to 41°C or 102° to 106°F). Where sweating has ceased, the skin becomes flushed and red. Severe, throbbing headaches and lack of coordination will also occur, and the sufferer may be confused or aggressive. Eventually the victim will become delirious or convulse. Hospitalisation is essential, but in the interim get victims out of the sun, remove their clothing, cover them with a wet sheet or towel and then fan continually. Give fluids if they are conscious.

Hypothermia Too much cold can be just as dangerous as too much heat. If you are trekking at high altitudes or simply taking a long bus trip over mountains, particularly at night, be prepared. In areas like Ladakh or Spiti you should always be prepared for cold, wet or windy conditions even if you're just out walking or hitching.

Hypothermia occurs when the body loses heat faster than it can produce it and the core temperature of the body falls. It is surprisingly easy to progress from very cold to dangerously cold due to a combination of wind, wet clothing, fatigue and hunger, even if the air temperature is above freezing. It is best to dress in layers; silk, wool and some of the new artificial fibres are all good insulating materials. A hat is important, as a lot of heat is lost through the head.

A strong, waterproof outer layer (and a 'space' blanket for emergencies) is essential. Carry basic supplies, including food containing simple sugars to generate heat quickly, and fluid to drink.

Symptoms of hypothermia are exhaustion, numb skin (particularly toes and fingers), shivering, slurred speech, irrational or violent behaviour, lethargy, stumbling, dizzy spells, muscle cramps and violent bursts of energy. Irrationality may take the form of sufferers claiming they are warm and trying to take off their clothes.

To treat mild hypothermia, first get the person out of the wind and/or rain, remove their clothing if it's wet and replace it with dry, warm clothing. Give them hot liquids – not alcohol – and some high-kilojoule, easily digestible food. Do not rub victims: instead, allow them to slowly warm themselves. This should be enough to treat the early stages of hypothermia. The early recognition and treatment of mild hypothermia is the only way to prevent severe hypothermia, which is a critical condition.

Jet Lag Jet lag is experienced when a person travels by air across more than three time zones (each time zone usually represents a one-hour time difference). It occurs because many of the functions of the human body (such as temperature, pulse rate and emptying of the bladder and bowels) are regulated by internal 24 hour cycles. When we travel long distances rapidly, our bodies take time to adjust to the 'new time' of our destination, and we may experience fatigue, disorientation, insomnia, anxiety, impaired concentration and loss of appetite. These effects will usually go within three days of arrival, but to minimise the impact of jet lag:

- Ensure that you rest for a couple of days prior to departure.
- Try to select flight schedules that minimise sleep deprivation; arriving late in the day means you can go to sleep soon after you arrive. For very long flights, try to organise a stopover.
- Avoid excessive eating (which bloats the stomach) and alcohol (which causes dehydration) during the flight. Instead, drink plenty of

noncarbonated, nonalcoholic drinks such as fruit juice or water.

- Avoid smoking.
- Make yourself comfortable by wearing loose-fitting clothes and perhaps bringing an eye mask and ear plugs to help you sleep.
- Try to sleep at the appropriate time for the time zone you are travelling to.

Motion Sickness Eating lightly before and during a trip will reduce the chances of motion sickness. If you are prone to motion sickness try to find a place that minimises movement – near the wing on aircraft, close to midships on boats, near the centre on buses. Fresh air usually helps; reading and cigarette smoke don't. Commercial motion-sickness preparations, which can cause drowsiness, have to be taken before the trip. Ginger (available in capsule form) and peppermint (including mint-flavoured sweets) are natural preventatives.

Prickly Heat Prickly heat is an itchy, and sometimes blister-like, rash caused by excessive perspiration trapped under the skin. It usually strikes people who have just arrived in a hot climate. Keeping cool, bathing often, drying the skin and using a mild talcum or prickly heat powder or resorting to air-conditioning may help.

Sunburn In high altitude areas like Ladakh, Zanskar and Spiti you can get sunburnt surprisingly quickly, even through cloud. Use a sunscreen, a hat, and a barrier cream for your nose and lips. Calamine lotion or a commercial after-sun preparation are good for mild sunburn. Protect your eyes with good quality UV protective sunglasses, particularly if you will be near water, sand or snow.

Infectious Diseases

Diarrhoea Simple things like a change of water, food or climate can all cause a mild bout of diarrhoea, but a few rushed toilet trips with no other symptoms is not indicative of a major problem.

Dehydration is the main danger with any diarrhoea, particularly in children or the elderly as dehydration can occur quite quickly. Under all circumstances *fluid replacement* (at least equal to the volume being lost) is the most important thing to remember. Weak black tea with a little sugar, soda water, or soft drinks allowed to go flat and diluted 50% with clean water are all good. With severe diarrhoea a rehydrating solution is preferable to replace minerals and salts lost. Commercially available oral rehydration salts (ORS) are very useful; add them to boiled or bottled water. In an emergency you can make up a solution of six teaspoons of sugar and a half teaspoon of salt to a litre of boiled or bottled water. You need to drink at least the same volume of fluid that you are losing in bowel movements and vomiting. Urine is the best guide to the adequacy of replacement – if you have small amounts of concentrated urine, you need to drink more. Keep drinking small amounts often. Stick to a bland diet as you recover.

Gut-paralysing drugs such as loperamide or diphenoxylate can be used to bring relief from the symptoms, although they do not actually cure the problem. Only use these drugs if you do not have access to toilets, eg if you *must* travel. Note that these drugs are not recommended for children under 12 years.

In certain situations antibiotics may be required: diarrhoea with blood or mucus (dysentery), any diarrhoea with fever, profuse watery diarrhoea, persistent diarrhoea not improving after 48 hours and severe diarrhoea. These suggest a more serious cause of diarrhoea and in these situations gut-paralysing drugs should be avoided.

In these situations, a stool test may be necessary to diagnose what bug is causing your diarrhoea, so you should seek medical help urgently. Where this is not possible the recommended drugs for bacterial diarrhoea (the most likely cause of severe diarrhoea in travellers) are norfloxacin 400mg twice daily for three days or ciprofloxacin 500mg twice daily for five days. These drugs are not recommended for children or pregnant women. The drug of choice for children would be co-trimoxazole with dosage dependent on weight. A five day course is given. Ampicillin or amoxycillin may be given to pregnant women, but medical care is necessary.

Two other causes of persistent diarrhoea in travellers are giardiasis and amoebic dysentery.

Giardiasis is caused by a common parasite, *Giardia lamblia*. Symptoms include stomach cramps, nausea, a bloated stomach, watery, foul-smelling diarrhoea and frequent gas. Giardiasis can appear several weeks after you have been exposed to the parasite. The symptoms may disappear for a few days and then return; this can go on for several weeks.

Amoebic dysentery, caused by the protozoan *Entamoeba histolytica*, is characterised by a gradual onset of low-grade diarrhoea, often with blood and mucus. Cramping abdominal pain and vomiting are less likely than in other types of diarrhoea, and fever may not be present. It will persist until treated and can recur and cause other health problems.

You should seek medical advice if you think you have giardiasis or amoebic dysentery, but where this is not possible, tinidazole or metronidazole are the recommended drugs. Treatment is a 2g single dose of tinidazole or 250mg of metronidazole three times daily for five to 10 days.

Fungal Infections Fungal infections occur more commonly in hot weather and are usually found on the scalp, between the toes (athlete's foot) or fingers, in the groin and on the body (ringworm). You get ringworm (which is a fungal infection, not a worm) from infected animals or other people. Moisture encourages these infections.

To prevent fungal infections wear loose, comfortable clothes, avoid artificial fibres, wash frequently and dry yourself carefully. If you do get an infection, wash the infected area at least daily with a disinfectant or medicated soap and water, and rinse and dry well. Apply an antifungal cream or powder like tolnaftate. Try to expose the infected area to air or sunlight as much as

possible and wash all towels and underwear in hot water, change them often and let them dry in the sun.

Hepatitis Hepatitis is a general term for inflammation of the liver. It is a common disease worldwide. There are several different viruses that cause hepatitis, and they differ in the way that they are transmitted. The symptoms are similar in all forms of the illness, and include fever, chills, headache, fatigue, feelings of weakness and aches and pains, followed by loss of appetite, nausea, vomiting, abdominal pain, dark urine, light-coloured faeces, jaundiced (yellow) skin and yellowing of the whites of the eyes. People who have had hepatitis should avoid alcohol for some time after the illness, as the liver needs time to recover.

Hepatitis A is transmitted by contaminated food and drinking water. You should seek medical advice, but there is not much you can do apart from resting, drinking lots of fluids, eating lightly and avoiding fatty foods. Hepatitis E is transmitted in the same way as hepatitis A; it can be particularly serious in pregnant women.

There are almost 300 million chronic carriers of **hepatitis B** in the world. It is spread through contact with infected blood, blood products or body fluids, for example through sexual contact, unsterilised needles and blood transfusions, or contact with blood via small breaks in the skin. Other risk situations include having a shave, tattoo or body piercing with contaminated equipment. The symptoms of hepatitis B may be more severe than type A and the disease can lead to long term problems such as chronic liver damage, liver cancer or a long term carrier state. Hepatitis C and D are spread in the same way as hepatitis B and can also lead to long term complications.

There are vaccines against hepatitis A and B, but there are currently no vaccines against the other types of hepatitis. Following the basic rules about food and water (hepatitis A and E) and avoiding risk situations (hepatitis B, C and D) are important preventative measures.

HIV & AIDS Infection with the human immunodeficiency virus (HIV) may lead to acquired immune deficiency syndrome (AIDS), which is a fatal disease. Any exposure to blood, blood products or body fluids may put the individual at risk. The disease is often transmitted through sexual contact or dirty needles – vaccinations, acupuncture, tattooing and body piercing can be potentially as dangerous as intravenous drug use. HIV/AIDS can also be spread through infected blood transfusions; some developing countries cannot afford to screen blood used for transfusions.

If you do need an injection, ask to see the syringe unwrapped in front of you, or take a needle and syringe pack with you. Fear of HIV infection should never preclude treatment for serious medical conditions.

Intestinal Worms These parasites are most common in rural, tropical areas. The different worms have different ways of infecting people. Some may be ingested on food such as undercooked meat (eg tapeworms) and some enter through your skin (eg hookworms). Infestations may not show up for some time, and although they are generally not serious, if left untreated some can cause severe health problems later. Consider having a stool test when you return home to check for these and determine the appropriate treatment.

Meningococcal Meningitis This serious disease is a risk in northern India and can be fatal. A fever, severe headache, sensitivity to light and neck stiffness which prevents forward bending of the head are the first symptoms. There may also be purple patches on the skin. Death can occur within a few hours, so urgent medical treatment is required.

Treatment is large doses of penicillin given intravenously, or chloramphenicol injections.

Sexually Transmitted Diseases HIV/AIDS and hepatitis B can be transmitted through sexual contact – see the relevant sections earlier for more details. Other STDs include gonorrhoea, herpes and syphilis; sores, blisters or rashes around the genitals and discharges or pain when urinating are common symptoms. In some STDs, such as wart virus or chlamydia, symptoms may be less marked or not observed at all, especially in women. Chlamydia infection can cause infertility in men and women before any symptoms have been noticed. Syphilis symptoms eventually disappear completely but the disease continues and can cause severe problems in later years. While abstinence from sexual contact is the only 100% effective prevention, using condoms is also effective. The treatment of gonorrhoea and syphilis is with antibiotics. The different sexually transmitted diseases each require specific antibiotics.

Typhoid Typhoid fever is a dangerous gut infection caused by contaminated water and food. Medical help must be sought.

In the second week the high fever and slow pulse continue and a few pink spots may appear on the body; trembling, delirium, weakness, weight loss and dehydration may occur. Complications such as pneumonia, perforated bowel or meningitis may occur.

Insect-Borne Diseases

Malaria This serious and potentially fatal disease is spread by mosquito bites. If you are travelling in endemic areas it is extremely important to avoid mosquito bites and to take tablets to prevent this disease. Symptoms range from fever, chills and sweating, headache, diarrhoea and abdominal pains to a vague feeling of ill-health. Seek medical help immediately if malaria is suspected. Without treatment malaria can rapidly become more serious and can be fatal.

If medical care is not available, malaria tablets can be used for treatment. You need to use a malaria tablet which is different from the one you were taking when you contracted malaria. The standard treatment dose of mefloquine is two 250mg tablets and a further two six hours later. For Fansidar, it's a single dose of three tablets. If you were previously taking mefloquine and cannot obtain Fansidar, then other alternatives are Malarone (atovaquone-proguanil; four tablets once daily for three days), halofantrine (three doses of two 250mg tablets every six hours) or quinine sulphate (600mg every six hours). There is a greater risk of side effects with these dosages than in normal use if used with mefloquine, so medical advice is preferable. Be aware also that halofantrine is no longer recommended by the WHO as emergency standby treatment, because of side effects, and should only be used if no other drugs are available.

Travellers should prevent mosquito bites at all times. The mosquitoes that transmit malaria bite from dusk to dawn, and during this period travellers are advised to:

- Wear light-coloured clothing.
- Wear long trousers and long-sleeved shirts.
- Use mosquito repellents containing the compound DEET on exposed areas (prolonged overuse of DEET may be harmful, especially to children, but its use is considered preferable to being bitten by disease-transmitting mosquitoes).
- Avoid perfumes or aftershave.
- Use a mosquito net impregnated with mosquito repellent (permethrin) – it may be worth taking your own.
- Impregnating clothes with permethrin effectively deters mosquitoes and other insects.

Dengue Fever This viral disease is transmitted by mosquitoes and is fast becoming one of the top public health problems in the tropical world. Unlike the malaria mosquito, the *Aedes aegypti* mosquito, which transmits the dengue virus, is most active during the day, and is found mainly in urban areas, in and around human dwellings. There have been outbreaks of dengue fever in Delhi in the past few years.

Signs and symptoms of dengue fever include a sudden onset of high fever, headache, joint and muscle pains (hence its old name, 'breakbone fever') and nausea and vomiting. A rash of small red spots sometimes appears three to four days after the onset of fever. In the early phase of illness, dengue may be mistaken for other infectious diseases, including malaria and influenza. Minor bleeding such as nose bleeds may occur in the course of the illness, but this does not necessarily mean that you have progressed to the potentially fatal dengue haemorrhagic fever (DHF). This is a severe illness, characterised by heavy bleeding, which is thought to be a result of second infection due to a different strain (there are four major strains) and usually affects residents rather than travellers. Recovery even from simple dengue fever may be prolonged, with tiredness lasting weeks.

You should seek medical attention as soon as possible if you think you may be infected. A blood test can exclude malaria and indicate the possibility of dengue fever. There is no specific treatment for dengue. Aspirin should be avoided, as it increases the risk of haemorrhaging. There is no vaccine against dengue fever. The best prevention is to avoid mosquito bites at all times by covering up, using insect repellents containing the compound DEET and mosquito nets – see the Malaria section earlier for more advice on avoiding mosquito bites.

Japanese B Encephalitis This viral infection of the brain is transmitted by mosquitoes. Most cases occur in rural areas as the virus exists in pigs and wading birds. Symptoms include fever, headache and alteration in consciousness. Hospitalisation is needed for correct diagnosis and treatment. There is a high mortality rate among those who have symptoms; of those who survive many are intellectually disabled.

Cuts, Bites & Stings
See Less Common Diseases for details of rabies, which is passed through animal bites.

Cuts & Scratches Wash well and treat any cut with an antiseptic such as povidone-iodine. Where possible avoid bandages and sticking plasters, which keep wounds wet.

Bedbugs & Lice Bedbugs live in various places, but particularly in dirty mattresses and bedding, evidenced by spots of blood on bedclothes or on the wall. Bedbugs leave itchy bites in neat rows. Calamine lotion or a sting relief spray may help.

All lice cause itching and discomfort. They make themselves at home in your hair (head lice), your clothing (body lice) or in your pubic hair (crabs). You catch lice through direct contact with infected people or by sharing combs, clothing and the like. Powder or shampoo treatment will kill the lice and infected clothing should then be washed in very hot, soapy water and left in the sun to dry.

Bites & Stings Bee and wasp stings are usually painful rather than dangerous. However, in people who are allergic to them severe breathing difficulties may occur and require urgent medical care. Calamine lotion or a sting relief spray will give relief and ice packs will reduce the pain and swelling. There are some spiders with dangerous bites but antivenins are usually available.

Leeches & Ticks Leeches are a particular problem in the eastern Himalaya (especially west Sikkim) and are particularly prevalent during the monsoon. They attach themselves to your skin to suck your blood; trekkers often get them on their legs or in their boots. Salt or a lighted cigarette end will make them fall off. Do not pull them off, as the bite is then more likely to become infected. Clean and apply pressure if the point of attachment is bleeding. An insect repellent may keep them away.

You should always check all over your body if you have been walking through a potentially tick-infested area as ticks can cause skin infections and other more serious diseases. If a tick is found attached, press down around the tick's head with tweezers, grab the head and gently pull upwards. Avoid pulling the rear of the body as this may squeeze the tick's gut contents through the attached mouth parts into the skin, increasing the risk of infection and disease. Smearing chemicals on the tick will not make it let go and is not recommended.

Snakes To minimise your chances of being bitten always wear boots, socks and long trousers when walking through undergrowth where snakes may be present. Don't put your hands into holes and crevices, and be careful when collecting firewood.

Snake bites do not cause instantaneous death and antivenins are usually available. Immediately wrap the bitten limb tightly, as you would for a sprained ankle, and then attach a splint to immobilise it. Keep the victim still and seek medical help, if possible with the dead snake for identification. Don't attempt to catch the snake if there is a possibility of being bitten again. Tourniquets and sucking out the poison are now comprehensively discredited.

Women's Health

Gynaecological Problems Antibiotic use, synthetic underwear, sweating and contraceptive pills can lead to fungal vaginal infections, especially when travelling in hot climates. Fungal infections are characterised by a rash, itch and discharge and can be treated with a vinegar or lemon-juice douche, or with yoghurt. Nystatin, miconazole or clotrimazole pessaries or vaginal cream are the usual treatment. Maintaining good personal hygiene and wearing loose-fitting clothes and cotton underwear may help prevent these infections.

Sexually transmitted diseases are a major cause of vaginal problems. Symptoms include a smelly discharge, painful intercourse and sometimes a burning sensation when urinating. Medical attention should be sought and sexual partners must also be treated. For more details see Sexually Transmitted Diseases earlier. Besides abstinence, the best thing is to use condoms.

Pregnancy It is not advisable to travel to some places while pregnant as some vaccinations normally used to prevent serious diseases are not advisable during pregnancy (eg yellow fever). In addition, some diseases are much more serious for the mother (and may increase the risk of a stillborn child) in pregnancy (eg malaria).

Most miscarriages occur during the first three months of pregnancy. Miscarriage is not uncommon and can occasionally lead to severe bleeding. The last three months should also be spent within reasonable distance of good medical care. A baby born as early as 24 weeks stands a chance of survival, but only in a good modern hospital. Pregnant women should avoid all unnecessary medication, although vaccinations and malarial prophylactics should still be taken where needed. Additional care should be taken to prevent illness and particular attention should be paid to diet and nutrition. Alcohol and nicotine, for example, should be avoided.

Less Common Diseases

The following diseases pose a small risk to travellers, and so are only mentioned in passing. You are advised to seek medical advice if you think you may have any of these diseases.

Cholera This is the worst of the watery diarrhoeas and medical help should be sought. Outbreaks of cholera are generally widely reported, so you can avoid such problem areas. *Fluid replacement is the most vital treatment* – the risk of dehydration is severe as you may lose up to 20L a day. If there is a delay in getting to hospital, then begin taking tetracycline. The adult dose is 250mg four times daily. It is not recommended for children under nine years nor for pregnant women. Tetracycline may help shorten the illness, but adequate fluids are required to save lives.

Filariasis This is a mosquito-transmitted parasitic infection found in India. Possible symptoms include fever, pain and swelling of the lymph glands; inflammation of lymph drainage areas; swelling of a limb or the scrotum; skin rashes; and blindness. Treatment is available to eliminate the parasites from the body, but some of the damage already caused may not be reversible. Medical advice should be obtained promptly if the infection is suspected.

Rabies This fatal viral infection is found in many countries. Many animals can be infected (such as dogs, cats, bats and monkeys) and it is their saliva which is infectious. Any bite, scratch or even lick from an animal should be cleaned immediately and thoroughly. Scrub with soap and running water, and then apply alcohol or iodine solution. Medical help should be sought promptly to receive a course of injections to prevent the onset of symptoms and death.

Tetanus This disease is caused by a germ that lives in soil and in the faeces of horses and other animals. It enters the body via breaks in the skin. The first symptom may be discomfort in swallowing, or stiffening of the jaw and neck; this is followed by painful convulsions of the jaw and whole body. The disease can be fatal. It can be prevented by vaccination.

Tuberculosis (TB) TB is a bacterial infection usually transmitted from person to person by coughing but which may be transmitted through consumption of unpasteurised milk. Milk that has been boiled is safe to drink, and the souring of milk to make yoghurt or cheese also kills the bacilli. Travellers are usually not at great risk as close household contact with the infected person is usually required before the disease is passed on. You may need to have a TB test before you travel as this can help diagnose the disease later if you become ill.

Typhus This disease is spread by ticks, mites or lice. It begins with fever, chills, headache and muscle pains followed a few days later by a body rash. There is often a large painful sore at the site of the bite and nearby lymph nodes are swollen and painful. Typhus can be treated under medical supervision. Seek local advice on areas where ticks pose a danger and always check your skin carefully for ticks after walking in a danger area such as a tropical forest. An insect repellent can help, and walkers in tick-infested areas should consider having their boots and trousers impregnated with benzyl benzoate and dibutylphthalate.

WOMEN TRAVELLERS

Foreign women travelling in India are frequently viewed by Indian men as free and easy, based largely on what they believed to be true from watching B grade western soap operas. Women can expect to be stared at and hassled and, in some extreme cases, groped or spied on in hotel rooms, although these situations are rarely threatening.

Many western women have observed that the untoward attentions of Indian males decreases rapidly once they hit the hills. While women travelling alone in the Indian Himalaya are still disconcertingly stared at constantly, the attention is usually due to sheer curiosity rather than any lecherous or sinister motives.

Close attention to standards of dress will go a long way to minimising problems for female travellers. The light cotton drawstring skirts that many foreign women pick up in India are really sari petticoats and to wear them in the street is rather like going out half dressed. Ways of blending into the Indian background include avoiding sleeveless blouses, skirts that are too short and, of course, the braless look.

Getting stared at is something you'll have to get used to. Don't return male stares, as this will be considered a come-on; just ignore them. Some women procure a fake wedding ring and refer to their travelling companions as 'my husband', which seems to help. Sunglasses can help avoid eye contact. Also, try to walk confidently, even when you're feeling a little confused or lost.

Getting involved in inane conversations with men is also considered a come-on. Keep discussions down to a necessary minimum unless you're interested in getting hassled. If you get the uncomfortable feeling he's encroaching on your space, the chances are that he is. A firm request to keep away is usually enough. Firmly return any errant limbs, put some item of luggage between you and if all else fails, find a new spot. You're also within your rights to tell

him to shove off! There is often a special ladies' queue for train tickets or even a ladies' quota and ladies' compartments. One woman wrote that these ladies' carriages were often nearly empty, another said they were full of screaming children.

GAY & LESBIAN TRAVELLERS

While overt displays of affection between members of the opposite sex, such as cuddling and hand-holding, are frowned upon in India, it is not unusual to see Indian men holding hands with each other or engaged in other close affectionate behaviour. This does not necessarily suggest that they are gay. The gay movement in India is confined almost exclusively to larger cities such as Delhi and Mumbai (Bombay). As with relations between heterosexual western couples travelling in India – both married and unmarried – gay and lesbian travellers should exercise discretion and refrain from displaying overt affection towards each other in public.

Keep in mind that homosexual relations for men are illegal in India. The penalties for transgression can be up to life imprisonment. Because of this, gay travellers could be the subject of blackmail – take care. There is no law against lesbian relations.

DISABLED TRAVELLERS

Travelling in the Indian Himalaya can entail some fairly rigorous challenges, even for the able-bodied traveller – long bus trips in crowded vehicles along rough, unsealed mountain roads can test even the hardiest traveller. For the mobility impaired traveller, these challenges are increased manyfold. Few, if any, buildings in the Indian Himalaya have ramps or lifts (elevators); toilets have certainly not been designed to accommodate wheelchairs; footpaths, where they exist (only in larger towns), are generally riddled with potholes and crevices.

If, despite these impediments, you are determined to travel to the Indian Himalaya, if your mobility is restricted, you will require an able-bodied companion to accompany you, and you should definitely consider hiring a private vehicle and driver.

The following organisations offer general travel advice and links to travel agencies and other resources, but have little specific information on the Indian Himalaya.

Australia
NICAN
(☎ 02-6285 3713, fax 6285 3714)
PO Box 407, Curtin, ACT 2605

UK
Holiday Care Service
(☎ 01293-774535, fax 784647)
Imperial Buildings, Victoria Rd,
Horley, Surrey RH6 7PZ
Royal Association for Disability & Rehabilitation
(RADAR, ☎ 020-7250 3222, fax 7250 0212,
email radar@radar.org.uk)
12 City Forum, 250 City Rd, London EC1V 8AF,
Web site www.radar.org.uk. Produces three
holiday fact packs for disabled travellers.
Travelcare
(☎ 020-8295 1797, fax 8467 2467)
35A High St, Chislehurst, Kent BR7 QAE.
Specialises in travel insurance for the disabled.

USA
Access – The Foundation for Accessibility by the Disabled
(☎ 516-887 5798) PO Box 356, Malverne, NY 11565.
Mobility International USA
(☎ 541-343 1284 email info@miusa.org)
PO Box 10767, Eugene, OR 97440.
Society for the Advancement of Travel for the Handicapped (SATH)
(☎ 212-447 7284) 347 Fifth Ave No 610, New York, NY 10016.

For general travel advice, bulletin boards and searchable databases on the Internet try looking at the following Web sites: www.travelhealth.com/disab.htm, www.newmobility.com, www.access-able.com.

SENIOR TRAVELLERS
Unless your mobility is impaired (see Disabled Travellers earlier in this chapter), or you are vision impaired or in any other way incapacitated, and are in reasonable health, there is no reason why the senior traveller should avoid the Himalaya as a potential holiday destination. Octogenarian Indian travellers heading for the high Himalaya are not an uncommon sight on pilgrim-packed buses throughout the hills. It may be helpful to discuss your proposed trip with your local doctor.

TRAVEL WITH CHILDREN
The numbers of intrepid souls travelling around India accompanied by one, or even two, young children, seems to be on the increase. Children can often enhance your encounters with local people, often possessing little of the self-consciousness and sense of the cultural differences that can inhibit interaction between adults. Many hotels offer family rooms with three beds and often a separate sleeping area.

Nevertheless, travelling with children can be hard work, and the rigours of travel in the Himalaya can be tiring at the best of times. Your child needs to be prepared in advance for shocks like beggars. Ideally the burden needs to be shared between two adults. For more information, see the Health section earlier in this chapter, and get hold of a copy of Lonely Planet's *Travel with Children* (1995), by Maureen Wheeler.

USEFUL ORGANISATIONS
The Tibetan Government in Exile has offices around the world and is a good contact point for information regarding various government offices in Dharamsala, Tibetan communities across the region and voluntary work. The Tibetan government has a good Web site at www.tibet.com. Offices abroad include:

Australia
(☎ 02-6285 4046, fax 6282 4301,
email offtibet@onaustralia.com.au)
Tibet Information Office, 14 Napier Close,
Deakin, ACT 2600
France
(☎ 01-46 56 54 53, fax 46 56 08 18,
email tibetparis@hol.fr)
Bureau du Tibet, 84 BD Adophe Pinard,
Paris 75014
Nepal
(☎ 1-419240, fax 411660,
email tiboff@tibetnet.mos.com.np)

Gadhen Kangsar, PO Box 310, Lazimpat Kathmandu

UK
(☎ 020-7722 5378, fax 7722 0362,
email tibetlondon@gn.apc.org)
Tibet House, 1 Culworth St, London NW8 7AF

USA
(☎ 212-213 5010, fax 779 9245,
email otny@igc.apc.org)
The Office of Tibet, 241 East 32nd St,
New York

DANGERS & ANNOYANCES
Theft
Having things stolen is a problem in India, not because it's a thief-ridden country (it isn't) but because it's a hassle getting the items replaced. If your passport is stolen it may be a long trip back to an embassy to replace it. Likewise, you may be able to replace stolen travellers cheques only in major cities. Always lock your room, preferably with your own padlock in cheaper hotels. Lock it at night, as well; people have had things stolen from their rooms when they've been inside. Never leave valuables in your room when you are out exploring the town. Remember also irreplaceable things like films (and research notes!) which, though of little or no value to a thief, would cause endless heartbreak to you if lost.

Carry valuables (passport, tickets, health certificates, money, travellers cheques) with you at all times. Either have a stout leather passport wallet on your belt, or a passport pouch under your shirt, or extra internal pockets in your clothing. On trains at night keep your gear near you, ideally padlocked to a luggage rack. Never walk around with valuables casually slung over your shoulder. Take extra care in crowds.

Train and bus departure times, when the confusion and crowds are at their worst, is the time to be most careful. Just as the train or bus is about to leave, you may be distracted by someone, while his or her accomplice is stealing your bag from by your feet. Airports are another place to be careful, especially when international arrivals take place in the middle of the night, when you are unlikely to be at your most alert.

Government Travel Advice

The US State Department's Bureau of Consular Affairs issues periodically updated bulletins for travellers. Consular Information Sheets include data such as entry and permit requirements, medical facilities, the crime situation, and areas of general instability (such as Kashmir).

Residents of the USA can receive copies of these by sending a stamped, self-addressed envelope to Overseas Citizens Services, Room 4800, Department of State, Washington DC 20520-4818. You'll also find them on the Web (http://travel.state.gov/travel_warnings.html). You can listen to 24 hour travel warnings at ☎ 202-647 5225 on a touch-tone phone, or get information via automated fax by dialling ☎ 202-647 3000 from a fax machine. US embassies and consulates in India offer a booklet called 'Guidelines for American Travelers in India'.

British Foreign Office travel advisories are available from the Travel Advice Unit, Consular Division, Foreign and Commonwealth Office (☎ 020-7238 4503, fax 7238 4545), 1 Palace St, London SW1E 5EH, UK and on BBC2 Ceefax, pp 470ff. It also has a regularly updated recorded travel advice line at ☎ 0374-500900. Check out their Web site www.fco.gov.uk/.

Australians can contact the Department of Foreign Affairs advice line in Canberra on ☎ 06-6261 3305 or visit its Web site www.dfat.gov.au/consular/advice/.

Canadians can get Department of Foreign Affairs travel advice by calling ☎ 1-800-267 6788, fax 1-800-575 2500 or its Web site www.dfaimaeci.gc.ca.

Chaining your backpack to the roof racks on buses is a good idea, or better still, insist that the bag be carried on board with you.

From time to time there are also drugging episodes, which often seem to take the following form: A traveller meets somebody on a train or bus or in a town, starts talking and is then offered a cup of tea or something similar. Hours later they wake up with a headache and all their gear gone, the tea having been full of sleeping pills. Don't accept drinks or food from strangers no matter how friendly they seem, particularly if you're on your own.

Beware also of some of your fellow travellers who make their money go further by helping themselves to other people's. Remember that backpacks are very easy to rifle through. Don't leave valuables in them, especially during flights. Finally, a good travel insurance policy helps ease the pain on the pocket.

If you do have something stolen, you're going to have to report it to the police. You'll also need a statement proving you have done so, if you want to claim on insurance. Most policies insist that the stolen item must be reported within a limited amount of time, which can pose problems if you're in a remote region days away from the nearest police post. Unfortunately the police are generally less than helpful, and at times are downright unhelpful, unsympathetic and even disbelieving, implying that you are making a false claim in order to defraud your insurance company.

Insurance companies, despite their rosy promises of full protection and speedy settlement of claims, are just as disbelieving as the Indian police and will often attempt every trick in the book to avoid paying out on a baggage claim.

Stolen Travellers Cheques If you're unlucky enough to have things stolen, some precautions can ease the pain. All travellers cheques are replaceable but this does you little immediate good if you have to go home and apply to your bank to get them. What you want is instant replacement. Furthermore, what do you do if you lose your cheques and money and have a day or more to travel to the replacement office? The answer is to keep an emergency cash-stash in a totally separate place. In that same place you should keep a record of the cheque serial numbers, proof of purchase slips and your passport number.

American Express makes considerable noise about 'instant replacement' of their cheques but a lot of people find out, to their cost, that without a number of precautions 'instantly' can take longer than you think. If you don't have the receipt you were given when you bought the cheques, rapid replacement will be difficult. Obviously the receipt should be kept separate from the cheques, and a photocopy in yet another location doesn't hurt. Chances are you'll be able to get a limited amount of funds on the spot, and the rest will be available when the bank has verified your initial purchase of the cheques. American Express has a 24 hour number in Delhi (☎ 011-687 5050) which you must ring within 24 hours of the theft.

One traveller wrote that his travellers cheques were stolen and he didn't discover the loss for a month. They had been left in his hotel room and the thief (presumably from the hotel) had neatly removed a few cheques from the centre of the cheque pouch. Explaining that sort of theft is really difficult and, of course, the thief has had plenty of time to dispose of them.

Other Dangers

Himalayan roads are some of the most scenic, and dangerous, in the world. Be particularly careful about travelling at night and on the roof of the bus (see the warning in the Getting Around chapter).

Never burn charcoal in poorly ventilated hotel rooms. Ask the proprietor for more blankets if you are cold. Under no circumstances should you burn charcoal or other fuels that give off toxic fumes.

There are a few specific places to avoid. Lonely Planet doesn't recommend travel to Kashmir at present (see the warning in the Jammu & Kashmir chapter). Travel anywhere near the cease fire line entails potential dangers. In 1998 most government officers were evacuated from the town of Kargil when several Pakistani shells landed in the town and in 1999 the highway was temporarily closed due to fighting with Pakistan.

Any place where drugs are relatively prevalent has a small risk. Over 30 foreign tourists have disappeared from the Kullu Valley in the last three years (see the warning in the Kullu Valley section of the Himachal Pradesh chapter).

Annoyances

The Himalayan regions are generally free of the hassle regularly encountered by travellers down on the plains but there will undoubtedly be times when you become frustrated and defensive in the face of unwanted attention. Hawkers, rickshaw-wallahs and guides can all sometimes be a little pushy in soliciting your custom but you'll gain nothing by getting angry. Perhaps the best tactic is to joke and establish some human contact with the people who are harassing you, while continuing to show absolutely no interest in whatever they wish to sell.

LEGAL MATTERS

If you find yourself in a sticky legal predicament, contact your embassy. You should carry your passport with you at all times.

In the Indian justice system it seems the burden of proof is on the accused, and proving one's innocence is virtually impossible. The police forces are often corrupt and will pay 'witnesses' to give evidence.

Drugs

For a long time India was a place where you could indulge in all sorts of illegal drugs (mostly grass and hashish) with relative ease – they were cheap, readily available and the risks were minimal. These days things have changed. Although dope is still widely available, the risks have certainly increased.

Penalties for possession, use, or trafficking in illegal drugs are strictly enforced. The minimum sentence for anything the judge believes is not personal use is a *minimum* of 10 years, even for minor offences, and there is no remission or parole.

BUSINESS HOURS

Indian shops, offices and post offices are not early starters and nothing much happens before 10 am. While many government offices are open 9 am to 5 pm you should never expect bureaucracy to kick in before 11 am, after 4.30 pm or any time which could be construed as lunch time or an hour either side of that.

Post offices are generally open Monday to Friday, 10 am to 5 pm, and on Saturday morning. Main city offices may be open longer hours, such as 8 am to 6 pm in Delhi. Banks are open for business Monday to Friday 10 am to 2 pm and on Saturday morning. Travellers cheque transactions usually cease 30 minutes before the official bank closing time.

Many government offices are closed on the second Saturday of the month. Museums are often shut on Monday. Shops and offices are usually closed on Sunday, public holidays and most festivals.

PUBLIC HOLIDAYS & SPECIAL EVENTS

With its populations of Tibetan refugees and tribal groups, and the special reverence in which the Indian Himalaya is held as the abode of the gods, it is not surprising that some of India's most colourful and interesting festivals are held in this region. The important gompas of Ladakh and Sikkim have their own special celebrations, and in other areas of the Himalaya, the change of seasons, the sowing or reaping of crops, or devotion to a local presiding deity can all be the impetus for a colourful local festival. Muslim festivals are celebrated mainly in Jammu & Kashmir. The dates are not fixed; they fall about 11 days earlier each year.

The festival calendar following includes those which are celebrated either nationally or throughout northern India. Dates are often fixed only a year ahead; you can find out precise dates nearer the time from tourist information offices and Web sites. At the beginning of each regional chapter is a list of local and village festivals which are either unique to that region, or are renowned for the exuberant or colourful celebration of a nationwide festival.

December-January

Id-ul-Fitr This Muslim festival celebrates the end of Ramadan, the Muslim month of fasting which generally falls between December and January (8 January 2000, 27th December 2000, 16 December 2001 and 6 December 2002).

Christmas Day A public holiday in India.

Republic Day This public holiday, on 26 January, celebrates the anniversary of India's establishment as a republic in 1950.

February-March

Shivratri This day of fasting is dedicated to Lord Shiva; his followers believe that it was on this day he danced the *tandava* (the Dance of Destruction). Processions to the temples are followed by the chanting of mantras and anointing of lingams. Mandi, gateway for the Kullu Valley, or Baijnath, in the Kangra Valley, are the two places to be for Shivratri if you're in Himachal Pradesh at this time. Devotees make special pilgrimages to these places, at which there are week long devotions and celebrations.

Holi This is one of the most exuberant Hindu festivals, with people marking the end of winter by throwing coloured water and red powder at one another. On the night before Holi, bonfires are built to symbolise the destruction of the evil demon Holika.

Losar Tibetan New Year falls in either February or March according to the Tibetan lunar calendar. Colourful local festivals celebrate the commencement of the new year, and it's a good time to be in a Tibetan centre.

Id-ul-Azha This Muslim festival commemorates Abraham's attempt to sacrifice his son. It is celebrated with prayers and feasts (8 March 2000, 25 February 2001, and 14 February 2002).

March-April

Ramanavami In temples all over India the birth of Rama, an incarnation of Vishnu, is celebrated on this day. In the week leading up to Ramanavami, the *Ramayana* is widely read and performed.

Baisakhi This Sikh festival commemorates the day that Guru Govind Singh founded the Khalsa, the Sikh brotherhood, which adopted the five *kakkars* (means by which Sikh men recognise each other), as part of their code of behaviour. The *Granth Sahib*, the Sikh holy book, is read through at *gurdwaras* (Sikh temples). Normally falls around 13 or 14 April.

Muharram This is a 10 day Muslim festival commemorating the martyrdom of Mohammed's grandson, Imam Hussain.

May-June

Buddha Jayanti Buddha's birth, enlightenment and attainment of *nirvana* (final release from the cycle of existence), are all commemorated on this day. Buddha experienced each of these on the same day but in different years. The festival falls on the full moon on the fourth lunar month and is known as Saga Darwa in Tibetan.

Milad-un-Nabi This Muslim festival celebrates the birth of Mohammed (15 June 2000, 4 June 2001 and 25 May 2002).

July-August

Naag Panchami This festival is dedicated to Ananta, the serpent upon whose coils Vishnu rested between creating universes. Offerings are made to snake images, and snake charmers do a roaring trade. Snakes are supposed to have power over the monsoon rainfall and keep evil from homes.

Raksha Bandhan (Narial Purnima) On the full-moon day of the Hindu month of Sravana, girls fix amulets known as *rakhis* to their brothers' wrists to protect them in the coming year. The brothers give their sisters gifts.

Independence Day This public holiday on 15 August celebrates the anniversary of India's independence from Britain in 1947. The prime minister delivers an address from the ramparts of Delhi's Red Fort.

August-September

Janmashtami The anniversary of Krishna's birth is celebrated with happy abandon in tune with Krishna's own mischievous moods.

Ganesh Chaturthi This festival, held on the fourth day of the Hindu month Bhadra, is dedicated to Ganesh, the god of wisdom and prosperity. It is considered to be the most auspicious day of the year, and to look at the moon on this day is considered unlucky.

Shravan Purnima After a day-long fast, high-caste Hindus replace the sacred thread which they always wear looped over their left shoulder.

September-October

Dussehra Dussehra is celebrated by Hindus all over India in the month of Asvina, but a particularly colourful week-long festival is held at Kullu, in Himachal Pradesh. Dussehra celebrates the victory of Rama over the demon king of Lanka, Ravana.

Gandhi Jayanti This public holiday is a solemn celebration of Gandhi's birthday on 2 October.

October-November

Diwali (Deepavali) This is the happiest festival of the Hindu calendar, celebrated on the 15th day of Kartika. At night countless oil lamps are lit to show Rama the way home from his period of exile. The festival runs over five days. On the first day, houses are thoroughly cleaned and doorsteps are decorated with intricate *rangolis* (chalk designs). Day two is dedicated to Krishna's victory over Narakasura, a legendary tyrant. Day three is spent in worshipping Lakshmi, the goddess of fortune. Traditionally, this is the beginning of the new financial year for companies. Day four commemorates the visit of the friendly (but uppity) demon Bali whom Vishnu put in his place. On the fifth day men visit their sisters to have a *tikka* placed on their forehead.

Ramadan The most important Muslim festival is a 30 day dawn-to-dusk fast. It was during this month that the prophet Mohammed had the *Quran* revealed to him in Mecca. Ramadan starts on 10 December, 1999, 30 November, 2000, 20 November 2001, 10 November, 2002.

Govardhana Puja This is a Hindu festival dedicated to that holiest of animals, the cow.

Nanak Jayanti The birthday of Guru Nanak, the founder of the Sikh religion, is celebrated with prayer readings and processions.

ACTIVITIES
Cycling

A cycling tour of the Indian Himalaya is not an unrealistic proposition, but if you've never done long-distance touring before, this is probably not a good region to begin! In some of the larger hill stations, mountain bicycles are available for hire, and some local travel agencies offer mountain-bike day tours. A few western travel agencies offer mountain bike tours from Manali to Leh (see Organised Tours in the Getting There & Away chapter).

You can hire rattly old push-bikes in Leh, which are handy for exploring nearby gompas, and at Haridwar, on the northern plains in Uttar Pradesh. The even terrain in the environs here makes this ideal for day trips by bicycle, particularly out to the Rajaji National Park. Gurudongma Travels in Kalimpong offers extended mountain-bike tours; see the Bangla (West Bengal) Hills chapter for information.

More information on preparing for a cycling trip and other details for cyclists is included in the Getting There & Away and Getting Around chapters.

Skiing

With the political problems and unrest in Jammu & Kashmir, the ski resort of Gulmarg is closed indefinitely, and other ski centres are being developed in the Himalayan region.

India's premier ski resort is at Auli, near Joshimath in Uttarakhand. UP Tourism offers very competitive ski packages, which include ski hire, tows, lessons and accommodation. The ski season at Auli extends from the beginning of January to the end of March. See the Uttarakhand chapter for details.

There are also less developed resorts in Himachal Pradesh, at Solang Nullah, north of Manali, and Narkanda, near Shimla. The Himachal Pradesh Tourist Development Corporation (HPTDC) organises courses at Solang Nullah and Narkanda. Complaints of poor equipment, tuition and facilities are common.

The Mountaineering Institute & Allied Sports at Manali (see the Mountaineering & Rock Climbing section below) also runs ski courses. At Solang, the season extends from

> ### Trekking Disclaimer
>
> Although the authors and publisher have done their utmost to ensure the accuracy of all information in this guide, they cannot accept any responsibility for any loss, injury or inconvenience sustained by people using this book. They cannot guarantee that the tracks and routes described in the regional chapters have not become impassable for any reason in the interval between research and publication.
>
> The fact that a trip or area is described in this guidebook does not mean that it is safe for you and your trekking party. You are ultimately responsible for judging your own capabilities in the light of the conditions you encounter.

December to March, and at Narkanda, from December to April. See the Himachal Pradesh chapter for details.

Trekking

The Ladakh and Zanskar regions boast the fine 10 day Manali to Padum trek. In Himachal Pradesh the trek across the Indrahar Pass from McLeod Ganj (Kangra Valley) to Machhetar (Chamba Valley) is difficult but rewarding. From Brahmaur, at the eastern end of the Chamba Valley, you can trek to sacred Manimahesh Lake or over the Pir Panjal Range to the Lahaul and Chandra valleys. There are some rewarding treks in the Palampur region of the Kangra Valley. In Kinnaur, a network of mountain trails affords some wonderful trekking possibilities, as does the remote region of Lahaul and Spiti, while there are numerous worthwhile treks around Manali in the Kullu Valley.

Uttarakhand has some fantastic short and long treks, including those to the remote Har ki Dun Valley in Garhwal; treks to the Milam, Pindari and Khatling glaciers; as well as a short trek to the magnificent Valley of Flowers, above Joshimath, among others.

The environs of Darjeeling have been a popular trekking destination for years, and this is one of the few regions where a network of rustic lodges and tea houses means that you don't need to carry a tent. West Sikkim affords some fine trekking possibilities from Yuksom along the Dzongri trail. For more trekking details, get hold of a

copy of Lonely Planet's *Trekking in the Indian Himalaya* by Garry Weare.

Mountaineering & Rock Climbing

The Himalayan Mountaineering Institute is based at Darjeeling, and for many years Sherpa Tenzing Norgay was the director here. There are two excellent museums here for those interested in the history of mountaineering in the Himalaya: the Everest Museum and the adjacent Mountaineering Museum.

Indian Mountaineering Foundation (IMF)
(☎ 011-671211, fax 688 3412)
Benito Juarez Rd, Anand Niketan, Delhi, 110021. Mountaineering expeditions interested in climbing peaks over 6000m need to obtain clearance from IMF.

Mountaineering Institute & Allied Sports
(☎ 01901-52342) Manali, Himachal Pradesh. Runs beginners and advanced courses in mountaineering and other adventure activities, but a large group is required for classes (from 20 to 30 students). See under Manali in the Himachal Pradesh chapter for details on the institute. The institute in Manali and its sub-branch at Brahmaur in the Chamba Valley can arrange guides and porters and give advice about trekking and mountaineering in this region, though both cater mainly to Indian youth groups.

Mount Support
(☎ 01374-2419, fax 2459)
PO Box 2, BD Nautial Bhawan, Bhatwari Rd, Uttarkashi, Garhwal, Uttar Pradesh. Mountain guides (graduates from the prestigious Nehru Institute of Mountaineering) can be organised here.

Nanda Devi Mountain Travel
(☎ 01389-22170) Hotel Nanda Devi, Joshimath, Garhwal, Uttar Pradesh. Also arranges graduates from the Nehru institute for guided tours.

Trekking & Mountaineering Division
(☎ 0135-430799, fax 430372,
email gmvm@nda.vsnl.net.in)
GMVN, Muni-ki-Reti, Rishikesh, Uttar Pradesh. Has information on mountaineering expeditions to less lofty heights in Uttarakhand and hires trekking and mountaineering equipment.

Kayaking & River Rafting

The Mountaineering Institute & Allied Sports in Manali can arrange two-week kayaking trips on the Beas River in October

---

Warning

! With the escalation of the troubles in Jammu & Kashmir, and the kidnapping of western trekkers (including the murder of a Norwegian man) in 1995, Lonely Planet still strongly recommends that travellers do not trek in these regions. Instead, consider some of the Indian Himalaya's other fine trekking possibilities.

Responsible Trekking

Rubbish Carry out your rubbish. If you've carried it in you can carry it out. Make an effort to carry out rubbish left by others. Take reusable containers. Never bury your rubbish; digging disturbs ground cover and encourages erosion. Buried rubbish will more than likely be dug up by animals. It may take years to decompose, especially at high altitudes.

Water Contamination Contamination of water sources by human faeces can lead to the transmission of hepatitis, typhoid and intestinal parasites such as *Giardia*. Where there is a toilet please use it. Elsewhere, below the tree line, bury your waste. In uninhabited areas above the tree line spread faeces out thinly on the rocks where the suns UV rays can kill some microorganisms. In inhabited areas ask locals if they have any concerns about your chosen toilet site. In snow dig down to the soil; otherwise your waste will be exposed when the snow melts. Relieve yourself at least 50m from any open water source.

Washing Don't use detergents or toothpaste within 50m of a watercourse. Wash pots and yourself a similar distance away, use biodegradable soap and spread the waste water as widely as possible to allow the soil to filter it before it makes it back to the watercourse.

Erosion The steepness of the Himalaya makes it particularly vulnerable to erosion. Arable land is scarce so take care not to damage fields. Stick to existing tracks and avoid short-cuts. Do not cut trees for firewood. Rely on a kerosene, alcohol or white gas, supply stoves for your porters and guides and make sure that they follow the same guidelines.

Economy Give business to locally owned and operated trekking companies with an environmentally friendly policy. Hire local porters and guides to keep money in the community. Be aware of current wages and local rates; paying too much contributes to local inflation, while paying too little denies a fair return. Avoid giving inappropriate tips.

Wildlife Conservation Don't assume animals in huts to be nonindigenous vermin and attempt to exterminate them. In wild places they are likely to be protected native animals. Do not feed the wildlife or leave food scraps as this can lead to animals becoming dependent on hand-outs, to unbalanced populations and to diseases such as 'lumpy jaw'. Place gear out of reach.

See also the Responsible Tourism section earlier in this chapter.

and November for US$189. Private agencies offer shorter day trips. See the Outdoor Sports in Manali boxed text under Manali in the Himachal Pradesh chapter for details.

River rafting expeditions are also possible on the Ganges and its tributaries from Rishikesh, on the Indus and Zanskar rivers in Ladakh and Zanskar, and on the Teesta River in Sikkim and the Bangla (West Bengal) hills. See the Leh, Rishikesh, Kalimpong and Gangtok entries in the relevant chapters for details.

Horse Riding

At many hill stations it's possible to hire horses for rides around the environs, including Shimla, McLeod Ganj, Mussoorie, Nainital and Darjeeling, as well as at Kufri, near Shimla, and Solang Nullah, above Manali. Hiring a mountain pony is a fine way to head up to the sacred shrines of Yamunotri and Kedarnath in Uttarakhand, or out to Ghangaria from Govind Ghat to visit the beautiful Valley of Flowers. There are no established agencies for hiring horses and mountain ponies in Ladakh, but it's possible to hire local horses to ride out along some of the trekking routes in this region. See the Ladakh & Zanskar and Himachal Pradesh chapters for more details.

Other Activities

See the relevant chapters for details about these activities.

There's a nine hole **golf** course near Ranikhet in the Kumaon region of Uttarakhand, and a spectacular nine hole course at Naldehra, just to the north of Shimla. There's also a lovely 18 hole course at Nainital. Green fees are generally around Rs 400 for foreigners, with club hire about Rs 100.

Fishing for the mahseer *(Tor putitora)* is the main attraction for anglers in Uttarakhand and the Bangla (West Bengal) hills. In Himachal Pradesh, Katrain, along the Beas River, Larji on the Tirthan River, and Rohru on the Pabar River are places that afford good fishing, mainly for trout. Licences are required for all fishing, but are easily obtained from local fisheries offices and some tourist information offices.

Elephant-back **safaris** are possibilities at Rajaji National Park and Corbett Tiger Reserve in the lower reaches of Uttarakhand, and the Jaldhapara Wildlife Sanctuary on the northern Bangla plains.

During summer, it's possible to go **paragliding** at Solang Nullah, north of Manali. See the Himachal Pradesh chapter for details.

Hang-gliding is being developed in Himachal Pradesh at Billing in the Kangra Valley but is still in its very early stages.

COURSES
Language

The Landour Language School, near Mussoorie in Uttarakhand, offers private and group beginners' and advanced courses in Hindi for the equivalent of around US$1 or US$2 an hour. At McLeod Ganj it's possible to learn Tibetan either at the Library of Tibetan Works & Archives or from private teachers. In Darjeeling, three month beginners' courses in Tibetan are available at the Manjushree Centre of Tibetan Culture. For all these courses, see the relevant chapters for details.

Buddhist Philosophy

Courses in aspects of Tibetan Buddhism and culture are offered in McLeod Ganj, Darjeeling, Choglamsar (near Leh) and Leh. Indian Hinayana Buddhism can also be studied in McLeod Ganj. See the relevant chapters for details of these courses.

Hindu Philosophy, Yoga & Meditation

Rishikesh is the place to head if you're interested in staying at an ashram and learning about aspects of Hindu philosophy, yoga and meditation, though caution is advised as some travellers have complained of unqualified and unscrupulous teachers in some centres. See Meditation & Yoga Courses under Rishikesh in the Uttarakhand chapter.

The Ananda Puri Ashram near Ranikhet is a beautiful, peaceful place, and westerners are welcome to stay here. See the Ranikhet section in the Uttarakhand chapter for details.

Traditional Dance

The Tibetan Institute of Performing Arts (TIPA) at McLeod Ganj offers private tuition from teachers in traditional Tibetan dance and drama. See the Himachal Pradesh chapter for details.

The Omkarananda Ashram (Durga Mandir) at Rishikesh offers instruction in various forms of Indian classical dance. See Meditation & Yoga Courses under Rishikesh in the Uttarakhand chapter for details.

Woodcarving

With advance notice it's possible to learn traditional Tibetan woodcarving at the Tibetan Refugee Self-Help Centre in Darjeeling. See the Bangla Hills chapter for details.

VOLUNTEER WORK

Numerous development organisations and international aid agencies have branches in India and, although they're mostly staffed

CRAIG PERSHOUSE

RICHARD I'ANSON

CRAIG PERSHOUSE

CRAIG PERSHOUSE

Bridging Central and South-East Asia, the Himalayan region is home to a wide variety of ethnic groups. The majority of the 50 million inhabitants live at elevations between 1000m and 2500m.

CRAIG PERSHOUSE

CRAIG PERSHOUSE

KERRY LORIMER

RICHARD I'ANSON

Top left: Two Muslim men praying in the open fields, Kashmir. **Top right:** Beaming vegetable seller, Leh. **Bottom left:** Gaddi shepherd wearing a traditional *chola* – the large pockets carry foodstuffs and utensils, as well as newborn kids. **Bottom right:** Children – happy to have their photo taken.

by locals, there are some opportunities for foreigners. Though it may be possible to find temporary volunteer work when you are in India, you'll probably be of more use to the organisation concerned if you write in advance and, if they need you, stay for long enough to be of help. A week in a hospital ward may go a little way towards salving your own conscience, but you may actually do no more than get in the way of the people who work there long term.

For information on international aid organisations in the Indian Himalaya, contact the main branches in your own country. The following organisations often accept volunteers (see entries in individual chapters for details):

Dr Graham's Homes
(☎ 033-297211) Berkmyre Hostel, 4 Middleton Rd, Kolkata 700071. Volunteers are needed in the fields of teaching, nursing, childcare, carpentry, engineering and mechanical and agricultural skills for this school and hospital at Kalimpong. There is a six month minimum placement but board and lodging is provided. Gap year students are accepted.

Hayden Hall
(email hayden@cal.vsnl.net.in) 42 Laden La Rd, Darjeeling 734101, Bangla. Christian organisation that works on grass roots level integrated development projects. Specific projects include paramedic training, mother and child clinics, production of saleable handicrafts, adult and pre-school education and nutritional programs. Volunteers (for a minimum placement of six months) are needed with the following backgrounds: doctors, nurses, paramedics, teachers, handicraft workers and those with counselling and motivational skills. Contact Father EP Burns or Noreen Dunne.

International Society for Ecology and Culture (ISEC)
(☎ 01803-868650, fax 868651, email isec@gn.apc.org)
Apple Barn, Week, Totnes, Devon TQ9 6JP UK. Web site www.isec.org.uk
(☎ 510-548 4915, fax 548 4916) PO Box 9475, Berkeley, CA 94709, USA. Arranges for foreign volunteers to live and work on a traditional Ladakhi homestead for a minimum of one month between June and October. Volunteers are responsible for their own airfare and pay UK£250 placement fee, which includes one month's board and lodging. In Leh contact the Ladakh Ecological Development Group (LEDeG).

Donations

Many travellers return from India with a desire to contribute to organisations working in the areas they have visited.

American Himalayan Foundation
(☎ 415-288 7425, fax 434 3130) 909 Montgomery St, Suite 400, San Francisco, California 94133. Funds educational projects in India, Nepal and Tibet, including scholarships and text books for Tibetan refugees and support for the Tibetan Children's Village in Dharamsala.

Appropriate Technology for Tibetans
(☎ 1020-8450 8090, fax 8450 4705) 2nd Floor, 117 Cricklewood Broadway, London NW2 3JG, UK, Web site www.aptibet.org/flash.htm. Works at grass roots levels with Tibetan refugees in India in emergency aid (for example when early winters decimated herds in Ladakh in 1998) and also bringing appropriate technology to build a sustainable future.

Central Tibetan Relief Committee
Donations can be made through the Tibet Fund 107 E 31st St New York, NY 10016, USA. Part of Central Tibetan Secretariat in Dharamsala, the committee runs a scheme where you can sponsor an elderly Tibetan exile. Annual sums or donations for emergency help are required, in exchange for a card every year and a case history.

CRY (Child Relief and You)
28 Terrapin Lane, Mercerville, NL 08619, USA, Web site www.wnx.com/~cry/. Indian based charity concentrating on rights of child in India.

See also Volunteer Work in this chapter.

Mahabodhi Meditation Centre
(☎ 0812-260684, fax 260292) 14 Kalidas Rd, Gandhinagar, Bangalore, 560 009; PO Box 22, Leh, Ladakh, 194101 J&K.

Operates a residential school for poor children, requires volunteers to assist with teaching and secretarial work.

The Nepali Girls' Social Service Centre
(☎ 0354-2985) Gandhi Rd, Darjeeling, Bangla. May be able to offer voluntary work on an informal basis to travellers interested in teaching English, art or musical instruments.

St Alphonsus Social & Agricultural Centre (SASAC)
(☎ 0354-42059) Post Office Tung, Darjeeling District, Bangla. Self-help organisation run by a Canadian Jesuit priest, Father Abraham. Projects include a model teaching farm, a cooperative savings scheme, introduction of gas stoves to cut down on wood usage, reforestation schemes and environmental management. Anyone wishing to volunteer, make a donation or purchase a tree for the plantation can contact Father Abraham.

Student's Educational & Cultural Movement of Ladakh (SECMOL)
(☎ 52421) PO Box 4, Leh, Ladakh, 194101, Jammu & Kashmir. Volunteers interested in conducting English conversation classes at summer camps near Phyang should contact this office. See the Ladakh & Zanskar chapter for more details.

Long-term visitors at McLeod Ganj are always welcome to teach English or computer skills to newly arrived Tibetan refugees. Check at the noticeboard of the Library of Tibetan Works & Archives in Gangchen Kyishong, near McLeod Ganj or *Contact* magazine. In Darjeeling contact the Tibetan Refugee Self-Help Centre.

Volunteer Agencies Abroad

For long-term work, the following organisations may be able to help or offer advice and further contacts:

Australian Volunteers International
(☎ 03-9279 1788, fax 9419 4280, email ozvol@ozvol.org.au)
PO Box 350, Fitzroy Vic 3065, Australia
Web site www.ozvol.org.au

Co-ordinating Committee for International Voluntary Service
(☎ 01 45 68 27 31) c/o UNESCO, 1 rue Miollis, F-75015 Paris, France

International Voluntary Service (IVS)
(☎ 0131-226 6722, fax 226 6723)
7 Upper Bo, Edinburgh EH1 2JN, UK

Peace Corps of the USA
(☎ 1-800 424 8580, fax 202-692 2201, email webmaster@peacecorps.gov)
1111 20thSt NW, Washington DC 20526, USA
Web site www.peacecorps.gov

Voluntary Service Overseas (VSO)
(☎ 020-8780 7200, fax 8780 7300)
317 Putney Bridge Rd, London SW15 2PN, UK
Web site www.oneworld.org/vso

ACCOMMODATION
Youth Hostels

There are youth hostels in Dalhousie, Nainital and Darjeeling and prices are similar for members and nonmembers (normally Rs 40 for a dorm bed). Some like the Tenzing Norgay Youth Hostel in Darjeeling offer excellent value, and others are downright shabby and should be given a miss.

Government Accommodation

Back in the days of the British Raj, a whole string of government-run accommodation units were set up with names such as Dak Bungalows, Circuit Houses, PWD (Public Works Department) Bungalows, Forest Rest Houses and so on. Today most of these are reserved for government officials, although in some places they may still be available for tourists, if there is room and you have booked in advance. In remote areas they are often the only accommodation available.

The problem is that they all have separate booking offices which makes booking very inconvenient. In remote villages there's a good chance that a room will be available and you can book on the spot with the *chowkidar* (caretaker). Most places cost between Rs 100 and Rs 200 for a decent room with attached bathroom.

Tourist Bungalows

Usually run by the state government tourist authority, tourist bungalows often serve as replacements for the older government-run accommodation units. Tourist bungalows are generally excellent value, although they vary enormously in facilities and level of service offered.

They often have dorm beds, as well as rooms; typical prices are around Rs 50 for dorm bed, and Rs 200 to Rs 400 for a double room. Generally there's a restaurant and often a bar. In Uttarakhand, tourist bungalows are operated by the two hills divisions of UP Tourism: Garhwal Mandal Vikas Nigam (GMVN) and Kumaon Mandal Vikas Nigam (KMVN). The Himachal Pradesh Tourist Development Corporation (HPTDC) offers a wide selection of interesting accommodation including that in castles, log huts and tent sites. Refer to the Himachal Pradesh chapter for details. Mid-season and low-season discounts are normally available.

Railway Retiring Rooms

These are just like regular hotels or dormitories except they are at the train stations. To stay here you are generally supposed to have a railway ticket or Indrail Pass. The rooms are convenient if you have an early train departure, although they can be noisy, hard to book and generally more trouble than they are worth.

Ashrams, Gompas & Gurdwaras

Ashrams should not be treated as guesthouses – while western visitors are welcome at many ashrams, particularly in Rishikesh, they are generally for those seriously interested in learning about Hindu philosophy, and have strict rules governing visitors' stays. See under Rishikesh in the Uttarakhand chapter for more details. Visitors are also welcome at several ashrams and *haramsalas* (pilgrims' lodgings) at the Char Dham temples of Yamunotri, Gangotri, Kedarnath and Badrinath in Uttarakhand.

In Himachal Pradesh, several gompas (eg Tabo, Ki, Tashijong) also provide guesthouse-style accommodation for travellers. While you don't have to be a Buddhist student to stay at these, it should be remembered that they are holy places, and appropriate respect and decorum should be observed.

Free accommodation is available at some Sikh temples *(gurdwaras)* where there is a tradition of hospitality to visitors. It can be interesting to try one, but please don't abuse this hospitality and spoil it for other travellers.

Chai Stalls & House Rentals

In some little-visited centres or along trekking routes, there are no guesthouses as such, but visitors may be afforded accommodation in very rustic lodgings or chai stalls. To avoid embarrassment later, establish at the outset whether payment is solicited or expected. Where you are offered free hospitality, a small gift, while not solicited, is appropriate.

In popular travellers centres, such as the villages around McLeod Ganj, in Manikaran and Manali in Himachal Pradesh, and in the environs of Almora, in the Kumaon region of Uttarakhand, many long-term visitors rent rooms in village homes, or even rent entire houses. Visitors intent on self-catering will need some form of cooking device. Gas cylinders are rare commodities in Himachal Pradesh, with waiting lists of sometimes up to a year. In the low season, you may be able to procure a gas cylinder from a cafe that is closing over the winter season. Otherwise, it is possible to purchase electric hot plates in larger bazaars, or kerosene burners for cooking.

Hotels

There are cheap hotels all over the Indian Himalaya – in larger centres, you'll find them clustered around the bus station. They can range from filthy, uninhabitable dives (but with rock bottom prices) up to quite reasonable places in both standards and prices. Ceiling fans, private toilets and bathrooms are all possibilities even in rooms for Rs 120 or less per night for a double.

Although prices are generally quoted in this book for singles/doubles, most hotels will put an extra bed in a room to make a triple for about an extra 25%. A 'family room' has three to five beds and is good value for a small group.

Many places offer hot water in geysers, which are boilers you must switch on 20 minutes before you want the hot water. In this case, water normally comes out of taps so you are restricted to a bucket wash not a proper shower.

Carbon Monoxide Poisoning

Tragically a number of people have died of carbon-monoxide poisoning due to burning charcoal in their poorly ventilated hotel rooms. Avoid lighting charcoal-fuelled fires: ask the proprietor for more blankets if you are cold. If you do wish to light a fire, ensure that the room is well ventilated. Under no circumstances should you allow the use of burning charcoal or other fuels that give off toxic fumes.

It's important to be aware that the hotel prices quoted in this book are a guideline only. Room rates in popular tourist haunts such as Shimla, Manali and Darjeeling swing wildly according to the season, the number of tourists in town and your bargaining skills. Inflation and renovation will also affect prices, so treat prices as a comparison as much as anything and don't badger hotel owners to accept the prices in this book. Prices listed in this book are for high season, unless otherwise noted; in the low season you'll get offered a discount of up to 60% anyway – a good way to save quite a few rupees. It's also worth looking at more than one room.

Expensive Hotels

You won't find many five-star hotels in the Indian Himalaya, although in the larger hill stations, there is always a range of top-end hotels, generally with rates for double rooms ranging from Rs 1000 to Rs 3000. Quite frankly, your rupee doesn't go as far up in the hills as it does on the plains, and even some of the most expensive places can be quite shabby and showing signs of wear and tear. Always ask for a discount in the low season – prices can be reduced by up to 60% or more during the winter (but not over Christmas) or monsoon in the hill stations.

Something Special

It's worth spending at least one or two nights in some of the Indian Himalaya's famous (or infamous!) grand hotels, usually old Raj relics or former maharaja's palaces. A stay in one of these could be a highlight of your trip. Most are stuffed to the ceiling with period furniture, tiger skins, fine old photos and even the odd ghost. A brief list of some of these special places follows. The best have been marked as Heritage Hotels by the Indian tourist authorities. For more details, see the relevant chapters.

Himachal Pradesh Woodville Palace Resort, Shimla; Palace Hotel, Chail; Castle Hotel, Naggar; Taragarh Palace Hotel, Kangra Valley; Raj Mahal, Mandi

Uttarakhand Hakman's Grand Hotel, Hotel Prince, Hotel Padmini Niwas, Savoy Hotel, Hotel Kasmanda and Hotel Carlton Plaisance, Mussoorie; Sagar Ganga Resort, Haridwar; Fairhavens and Belvedere Hotel, Nainital

Bangla Hills Windamere Hotel, Darjeeling; The Himalayan Hotel, Kalimpong

Sikkim Hotel Norkhill, Gangtok

Taxes & Service Charges

Most state governments impose a variety of taxes on hotel accommodation (and restaurants). At most rock-bottom hotels you shouldn't have to pay any taxes. Once you get into the top end of budget places, and certainly for mid-range accommodation, you will have to pay something. Room taxes vary between states, from 10% in Himachal Pradesh, to 5% in Uttarakhand. Check how much tax you'll be paying in low season even if you negotiate a discount you may well still have to pay tax on the full room rate!

Another common tax, which is additional to the above, is a service charge, which is around 8% to 10%. In some hotels, this is only levied on food, room service and use of telephones, not on the accommodation costs. At others, it's levied on the total bill. If you're trying to keep costs down and you know that the service charge is levied on the total bill, don't sign up meals or room service to your room bill and keep telephone use to a minimum.

Rates quoted in this book are the basic high-season rate only, unless otherwise indicated. Taxes and service charges are extra.

FOOD

Despite the very fine meals that can be prepared in India, you'll often find food a great disappointment. In many smaller centres there is not a wide choice and you'll soon get bored with *chaval* (rice), *sabzi* (mushy vegetables) and dhal (curried lentil gravy). Even if you are a big Friday-night-curry-and-lager fan back home you'll find few similarities between the food served in curry houses abroad (Indian food is now the most popular cuisine in the UK) and that served in India.

Contrary to popular belief, not all Hindus are officially vegetarians. Strict vegetarianism is confined more to the south, which has not had the meat-eating influence of the Aryan and later Muslim invasions, and also to the Gujarati community. For those who do eat meat (known on most menus as 'nonveg'), it is not always a pleasure to do so in India – the quality tends to be low (most chickens give the impression that they died from starvation) and the hygiene is not all that it might be. Beef, from the holy cow, is strictly taboo of course – and leads to interesting Indian dishes like the mutton burger and buffalo steak. Pork is equally taboo to Muslims and is generally only available among the Tibetans in Himachal Pradesh and Sikkim. If you're a nonvegetarian you'll end up eating a lot more vegetarian food in India. In some of the Indian Himalaya's particularly holy places, such as Haridwar, in Uttarakhand, consuming any form of meat is forbidden by law! 'Pure veg' places don't serve eggs.

Although you could travel throughout the Indian Himalaya and not eat a single curry, Indian interpretations of western cuisine can be pretty horrific; in smaller places it's usually best to stick to Indian food. The one exception is Chinese food, various approximations of which are available in most towns and is generally pretty good.

If, after some time in India, you do find the food is getting you down physically or psychologically, there are a couple of escapes. It is very easy for budget travellers to lose weight in India and feel lethargic and drained of energy. The answer is to increase your protein intake – eat more eggs, which are readily available. It also helps to eat more fruit and nuts, so buy bananas, mandarins, oranges or peanuts, all easily found at bus stations or in the markets. Many travellers carry multivitamins with them. Another answer, if you're travelling on a budget, is to occasionally splash out on a meal in a fancy hotel or restaurant. Be particularly careful with buffets in mid-range hotels as these are notorious breeding grounds for bugs, kept nice and warm for hours over an ineffectual flame.

Some travellers thrive on Indian food, but crave western breakfasts – it's hard to get excited about a plate of dhal and rice first thing in the morning. Many of the flashier hotels in the hill stations offer continental breakfast buffets, which are a great indulgence. Other hangouts, like Manali, and the Kullu and Parvati valleys, have little cafes serving great omelettes, porridge and toast.

The dominant cuisine in northern India is 'Mughal style' (often spelt 'Mughlai'), which bears a closer relationship to food of the Middle East and Central Asia. The emphasis is more on spices and less on chilli and grains, and breads are eaten far more than rice.

In the larger centres of the Indian Himalaya, some restaurants will offer south Indian cuisine, including the ubiquitous *dosa* (see snacks, later). Gujarati cuisine can also be found in most of the popular hill stations.

In the most basic Indian restaurants and eating places, known as *dhabas*, the cooking is usually done right out the front so you can see exactly what is going on and how it is done. Vegetables will be on the simmer all day and tend to be overcooked and mushy to western tastes. In these basic places you can get a vegetable dish, dhal and a few *chapatis* for around Rs 20. If you order half-plates of the various dishes brewing out the front you get half the quantity at half the price and get a little more variety. With chutneys and a small plate of onions, which come free, you can put together a reasonable vegetarian meal for Rs 30, or nonvegetarian for Rs 40.

At the other end of the price scale there are many restaurants in the Indian Himalaya's top-end hotels that border on the luxurious and by western standards are absurdly cheap. Paying US$10 to US$15 for a meal in India seems exorbitant after you've been there for a while, but check what a meal in your friendly local Hilton would cost you.

The majority of places lie somewhere in the middle. Most have waiter service and English menus. In most Tibetan restaurants in places like McLeod Ganj and Leh you are supposed to write your order down on a slip of paper.

Finally, a couple of hints on how to cope with curry. After a while in India you'll get used to even the fiercest curries and will find western food surprisingly bland. If, however, you do find your mouth is on fire, don't reach for water; in emergencies, that hardly helps at all. *Dahin* (curd or yoghurt) or fruit does the job much more efficiently.

Curry & Spice

Believe it or not, there is no such thing as 'curry' in India. It's an English invention, an all-purpose term to cover the whole range of Indian food spicing. *Carhi*, incidentally, is a Gujarati dish, but never ask for it in Kumaon where it's a very rude word!

Although all Indian food is certainly not curry, this is the basis of Indian cuisine. Curry doesn't have to be hot enough to blow your head off. Indian cooks have about 25 spices on their regular list and it is from these that they produce the curry flavour. Normally the spices are freshly ground in a mortar and pestle known as a *sil-vatta*. Spices are usually blended in certain combinations to produce *masalas* (mixes), eg *garam masala* (hot mix) is a combination of cloves, cinnamon, cardamom, coriander, cumin and peppercorns.

Popular spices include saffron *(kesar)*, an expensive flavouring produced from the stamens of certain crocus flowers. This is used to give rice that yellow colouring and delicate fragrance. Saffron is produced in Kashmir and is an excellent buy in India, where a 1g packet costs around Rs 35 –

you'll pay about 10 times more at home. Turmeric also has a colouring property, acts as a preservative and has a distinctive smell and taste. Chillies are ground, dried or added whole to supply the heat. They come in red and green varieties but the green ones are the hottest. Ginger is supposed to be good for digestion (and flatulence), while many masalas contain coriander because it is said to cool the body. Strong and sweet cardamom are used in many desserts and in rich meat dishes. Other popular spices and flavourings include nutmeg, poppy seeds, caraway seeds, fenugreek *(methi)*, mace, garlic, cloves, bay leaves and curry leaves.

Jarice is a digestive aid which is normally served at the end of the meal (with the bill) and helps neutralise the effect of the spices. It is made up of ground coconut, cardamom, aniseed and rock sugar.

Breads & Grains

The best Indian rice, it is generally agreed, is found in the north where Basmati rice grows in the Dehra Dun Valley. It has long grains, is yellowish and has a slightly sweetish or '*bas*' smell.

Indian breads are varied but always delicious. Simplest is the chapati/roti, which is a mixture of flour and water (no yeast) cooked on a hotplate griddle known as a *tawa*. Direct heat blows them up but how well that works depends on the gluten content of the wheat. In restaurants featuring Punjabi cuisine, a roti is called *phulka/fulka*. A *paratha* (or parantha) is also cooked on the hotplate but ghee (clarified butter) is used and the bread is rolled in a different way. There are also parathas that have been stuffed with peas or potato. Deep-fried bread which puffs up is known as a *puri*. Bake the bread in a clay (tandoori) oven and you have naan, usually thicker and more filling than a chapati. It's fascinating to watch the bakers in the dhabas and bakeries, especially early in the morning – the best time to buy your Indian bread.

Breads also double as cutlery and are used to mop or scoop up your curry. Western-style white sliced bread is widely available, and it's generally pretty good.

Dishes

Curries can be vegetable, meat (usually chicken or lamb) or fish, but they are always fried in ghee (clarified butter) or vegetable oil. They are normally eaten with rice or bread. See the Indian Dishes boxed text for a run down on the most common dishes.

Tandoori food is a northern speciality and refers to the clay oven in which the food is cooked after first being marinated in a complex mix of herbs and yoghurt. Tandoori chicken is a favourite. This food is not as hot as curry dishes and usually tastes terrific. The humble tandoori took on a more sinister light recently, when the chopped up remains of the wife of a prominent politician were found stuffed in one!

Thalis

A *thali* is the all-purpose blue collar Indian meal. The name 'thali' is taken from the dish in which the meal is served. This consists of a metal plate with a number of small metal bowls known as *katoris* on it. Sometimes the small bowls will be replaced by simple indentations in the plate. A thali consists of a variety of curry vegetable dishes, relishes, a couple of *pappadams*, puris or chapatis and a mountain of rice. A fancy thali may have a *pataa*, a rolled leaf stuffed with fruit and nuts. There'll probably be a bowl of curd and possibly even a small dessert or *paan* (see Paan, later). Gujarati thalis are particularly sumptuous and sweet.

Thalis are consistently tasty and good food value, but they have two other unbeatable advantages for the budget traveller – they're cheap and they're usually 100% filling. Thalis can be as little as Rs 15 and will rarely cost more than Rs 30. Most are totally satisfying because they're normally 'all you can eat'. When your plate starts to look empty the waiter comes round, adds another mountain of rice and refills the katoris. Thalis are eaten with fingers, although you may get a spoon for the curd or dhal. Always wash your hands before you eat one – a sink or other place is provided in a thali restaurant.

Snacks

Samosas are curried vegetables fried in a pastry triangle. They are very tasty and are found all over India. *Bhujias* or *pakhoras* are bite-size pieces of vegetable dipped in chickpea flour batter and deep-fried. Along with samosas they're the most popular snack food in the country.

Bhelpuri is a popular Mumbai (Bombay) snack peddled across the city, and always found in holiday resort towns around the country. *Channa* is spiced chickpeas (garbanzo beans) served with small puris or *bhatura* (fried bread). *Sambhar* is a soup-like lentil and vegetable dish with a sour tamarind flavour. *Chaat* is the general term for snacks, while *namkin* is the name for the various spiced nibbles that are sold prepackaged.

That peculiar Raj-era term for a midmorning snack still lives – *tiffin*. Today tiffin means any sort of light meal or snack. One western dish which Indians seem to have come 100% to terms with is chips (french fries) – sometimes curried, and delicious! Unfortunately, ordering chips is very much a hit and miss affair – sometimes they're excellent, and at other times truly dreadful. Some Indian cooks call potato chips 'Chinese potatoes', and 'finger chips' is also quite common.

Found all over India, but originating from the south, are *dosas*, which you'll find in restaurants featuring south Indian cuisine. These are basically paper-thin pancakes made from lentil and rice flour. Curried vegetables wrapped inside a dosa makes it a *masala dosa* – a terrific snack meal. An *idli* is a kind of south Indian rice dumpling, often served with a spicy curd sauce *(dahin idli)* or with spiced lentils and chutney. Pappadams (or papad) are crispy deep-fried lentil-flour wafers often served with thalis or other meals. An *uttapam* is a south Indian dish like a dosa.

Himalayan Specialities

Rogan josh is lamb curry, always popular in the north and in Kashmir where it originated. *Gushtaba*, pounded and spiced meatballs cooked in a yoghurt sauce, is another Kashmiri speciality.

An indication of the influence of central Asian cooking styles on north Indian food is the popularity of *kababs*. You'll find them all across north India with a number of local variations and specialities, but they're usually made with mutton. The two basic forms are *seekh* (skewered) or *shami* (wrapped).

There are some local specialities which you will only find in a particular region. The staple diet in Ladakh, Garhwal and Kumaon is *dhal bhat* (dhal and rice), but other local dishes from the Kumaon region of Uttarakhand include *alu ke gutke* (fried potato with masala), *badeel* (chickpea paste with masala, deep fried and served in wedges with chutney/relish), and *raita* (curd with cucumber).

In the Chamba Valley of Himachal, Pradesh are several local dishes. *Madhra* is kidney beans with curd and ghee. The curd is fried with the ghee until dark brown, then mixed with the kidney beans along with spices including cloves and cardamom.

Khamod is the nonvegetarian form of madhra. It consists of ground mutton, curd and ghee. Also in Chamba you'll find *chukh*, a chilli sauce of red and green peppers, lemon juice, mustard oil and salt.

Sweet dishes from Kumaon include *sai*, a dish consisting of semolina, curd and sugar, cooked in oil then sprinkled with shredded coconut, raisins and cashew nuts. *Sooji ke pue* is semolina, curd and sugar, rolled into balls and deep fried. *Singal* is usually made for Diwali; it consists of the same base as sooji ke pue, but the contents are forced through a bag into swirl shapes and fried.

Other sweets include *bal mithai*, a form of brown *barfi* (milk-based sweet) covered in tiny white sugar balls. It's found in the foothills of Kumaon, especially Almora, but also in other areas. Also famous is *singauri*. Found only in Kumaon district, especially Almora, this milk-based sweet comes in two forms, the soft off-white version, and the tastier brown variety.

Desserts & Sweets

Indians have quite a sweet tooth and an amazing selection of desserts and sweets to satisfy it. Desserts are usually rice-based

Indian Dishes

Meat (Nonveg) Dishes
chicken tikka – tasty cubes of chicken cooked on a skewer
dahiwala – braised with yoghurt
dopiaza – literally means 'two onions' and is a type of korma that uses onions at two stages in its preparation
gosht – mutton
handi – cooked over a griddle
kaleji – liver
karahi/kadahi – cooked in a wok-type pan (karahi), normally with tomatoes
keema – minced meat
korma – rich, creamy dish prepared by braising
makhani – meat dish, often chicken, made with butter
murgh – chicken
saagwala – with spinach

Vegetable (Sabzi) Dishes
alu/aloo – potato
alu ghobi – potatoes and cauliflower
alu jeera – fried potatoes and cumin
alu mutter – potato and peas
baigan bhata – pureed aubergine
bhindi – okra or ladies finger
brinjal – aubergine
channa – chickpeas
cheese tomato – chunks of soft cheese (paneer/panir) in a rich tomato sauce
chole – chickpeas
dhal/dal – lentils
dhal bhat – the staple of hill folk
dhal tarka – tasty fried lentil paste
dum alu – pot-roasted (dum) potato
malai kofta – rich dish of meatballs (kofta) in a creamy (malai) sauce
mirch – green pepper
mutter paneer – peas and cheese in gravy
navratan korma – sweet dish with nuts and fruit
palak – spinach (also known as sag)
palak paneer – spinach and cheese
shahi paneer – 'Royal' cheese

Indian Dishes

Rice

biryani – meat (often chicken) mixed with a deliciously flavoured, orange-coloured rice which is sometimes spiced with nuts or dried fruit; a *Kashmiri biryani* is basically fruit with rice

pulao – flavoured rice, often containing pulses, and can be with or without meat; a *Kashmiri pulao* is quite sweet with raisins, nuts and fruit

Others

dahin – yoghurt

mulligatawny – peppery *(mullaga)* broth *(tanni)*

raita – yoghurt and vegetables (usually cucumber)

Desserts

barfi – sweet and with a fudge-like consistency, can also be made from khoya and is available in flavours such as coconut, pistachio *(pista)*, chocolate or almond *(badam)*

gajar ka halwa – translucent, vividly coloured sweet made from carrot *(gajar)*, sweet spices and milk

gulaab jamun – fried and made from thickened boiled-down milk (known as *khoya*) and flavoured with cardamom and rose water *(gulaab pani)*

jalebi – fun orange-coloured squiggles that have syrup inside; they are made of flour and are coloured and flavoured with saffron

kulfi – a delicious pistachio flavoured sweet similar to ice cream widely available

ladu – yellow coloured balls made from chickpea flour

mitha chaval – special sweet prepared on festive occasions, with rice, sugar, coconut, dried fruit and ghee

ras gulla – sweet little balls of cream cheese that are flavoured and scented with rose water

or milk-based, and consist of various interesting things in sweet syrup or else sweet pastries. Most are horrendously sweet. You can, of course, also get western style ice cream all over India. The major brands, such as Kwality and Havmor, are safe and very good.

Many of the Indian sweets are covered in a thin layer of silver, as are some of the desserts. It's just that, silver beaten paper-thin. Don't peel it off, it's quite edible. There are countless sweet shops with their goodies all lined up in glass showcases. Prices vary from Rs 40 to Rs 60 for a kilogram but you can order 50 or 100g at a time or simply ask for a couple of pieces. Most places will sell you a variety of things by weight if you just ask to try everything. These shops often sell curd, as well as sweet curd which makes a very pleasant dessert.

There are plenty of tasty western style bakeries in Shimla, and you'll also find freshly baked western cakes and breads in McLeod Ganj and Darjeeling.

Fruit

If you don't have a super sweet tooth, you'll be able to fall back on India's wide variety of fruit. Apricots and other temperate-region fruits can be found in the Himalayan region. Some local specialities include cherries and strawberries in Kashmir and apricots in Ladakh and Himachal Pradesh. Apples are found all over this north-western region but particularly in the Kullu Valley and Kinnaur regions of Himachal Pradesh and the higher reaches of Garhwal in Uttarakhand.

Paan

An Indian meal should properly be finished with *paan* – the name given to the collection of spices and condiments chewed with betel nut. Found throughout eastern Asia, betel is a mildly intoxicating and addictive nut, but by itself it is quite inedible. After a meal paan is chewed as a mild digestive.

Paan sellers have a whole collection of little trays, boxes and containers in which they mix either *saadha* (plain) or *mitha*

Tibetan Cuisine

With its high concentration of Tibetan refugees and proximity to Tibet, you'll find Tibetan cuisine on many menus in the Himalayan region. While Buddhists generally espouse the virtues of vegetarian cuisine, the arid Tibetan plateau is not conducive to the cultivation of many forms of vegetable, and the Tibetan diet is frequently supplemented with meat. The food found in McLeod Ganj is far better than anything produced in Tibet.

Staples found in McLeod Ganj, and nearby regions such as Ladakh, Lahaul & Spiti and Kinnaur, include:

chura – yak cheese
detuk – rice thukpa; good if you're suffering from diarrhoea
fingsha – fried noodles and soy sauce
kothey – half-steamed, half-fried momos
momo – you'll find the ubiquitous momo wherever there is a sizable Tibetan population, and in Ladakh and the remote eastern regions of Himachal Pradesh. It consists of small dough parcels containing meat or vegetables, which are fried or steamed.
pish – small triangular noodles in a soup
sanghan baklep – large momos with the edges crimped and then deep fried
sha – meat
sha khampo – dried yak meat
thukpa – Tibetan noodle soup with vegetables or meat. There are various types of noodles in thukpa: *ghaytuk* (long round noodles), *thantuk* (flat square noodles), and *chitse* (long flat noodles).
tsampa – roasted barley flour. This is a staple in Tibet; it's mixed with tea, butter or *chang* (Tibetan barley beer), and rolled in the hand into a ball. Also known as *ngamphe* in Ladakh.

(sweet) paans. The ingredients may include, apart from the betel nut itself, lime paste (the ash not the fruit), the powder known as *catachu*, various spices and even a dash of opium in a pricey paan. The whole concoction is folded up in a piece of edible leaf which you pop in your mouth and chew. When finished you spit the leftovers out and add another red blotch to the pavement. Over a long period of time, indulgence in paan will turn your teeth red-black and even addict you to the betel nut. Trying one probably won't do you any harm.

DRINKS
Nonalcoholic Drinks
Tea & Coffee The Indians, for all the tea they grow, make some of the most hideously over-sweetened, murkily milky excuses for this fine beverage that you'll ever see. Nevertheless, it's cheap, at Rs 2 or Rs 3 for a cup of *chai* (Rs 5 in a restaurant), and filling. It's drunk in vast quantities in poorer regions where it serves to take away the pangs of hunger.

Better tea can be obtained if you ask for 'tray tea', which gives you the tea, the milk and the sugar separately and allows you to combine them as you see fit. Unless you specify otherwise, tea is 'mixed tea' or 'milk tea', which means it has been made by putting cold water, milk, sugar and tea into one pot and bringing the whole concoction to the boil, then letting it stew for a long time.

In Tibetan and Tibetan-influenced areas such as Ladakh, the gastronomically intrepid can try *gur-gur*, or butter tea. It's traditionally made with rancid yak butter mixed with salt, milk, green leaf tea and hot water. Drink it quick – the only thing worse than hot yak butter tea is cold yak butter tea. Kashmiri tea, on the other hand, is fragrant and delicious. In Ladakh you will also find hot lemon water and delicious ginger chai, perfect during cold weather.

Coffee is not as popular in the Himalayan region as in the south of the country, and it's difficult to get a decent cuppa anywhere in the hills. The branches of the Indian Coffee House are some of the few places with half-decent coffee. It's possible to buy a cheap element and a jar of Nescafe and make your own.

Water In the big cities, the water is chlorinated and safe to drink, although if you've just arrived in India, the change from what you are used to drinking is enough to bring on a mild dose of diarrhoea.

Outside the cities you're on your own. Some travellers drink the water everywhere and never get sick, others are more careful and still get hit with a bug. Basically, you should not drink the water in small towns unless you know it has been boiled, and definitely avoid the street vendors' carts everywhere. Even in the better class of hotel and restaurant, the water is usually only filtered and not boiled. The local water filters remove solids and do nothing towards removing any bacteria. Water is generally safer in the dry season than in the monsoon when it really can be dangerous. See the Health section for further information.

Mineral Water Most travellers to India avoid tap water altogether and stick to bottled mineral water. It is available virtually everywhere along the hill station belt, although it's more difficult to find farther north, and impossible to procure in Ladakh outside Leh, and in the remote regions of eastern Himachal Pradesh. The price ranges from Rs 12 to Rs 30, with Rs 15 being about the average. Brand names include Bisleri, Baileys, Honeydew and Aqua Safe, though Yes is probably the best. You should always check that the seal hasn't been broken.

Making Momos

If you wonder how you'll ever cope when you get back home, denied traditional Tibetan momos, or stuffed dumplings, following is a recipe supplied by the chef at the Dreamland Restaurant in McLeod Ganj:

3 cups white flour
2 onions
4-5 cloves garlic
500g minced steak (with fat)
2 tsp salt
2 tsp garam masala

Finely chop the meat, onion and garlic, and combine with the salt and masala. Mix the flour and water to a dough with a consistency that enables it to be kneaded. Roll it flat and cut into round shapes (thicker in the centre than around the edges). Place the mixed ingredients in the centre and fold, then trim sides.

Bring the water in the *mok-tsang* (steamer) base to the boil, adding a little oil. Place momos one by one into the top section of the steamer, leaving a 2cm gap between each one and steam for 15 to 20 minutes. Serves four people.

Another bad sign is if you squeeze the bottle and water comes out of the top.

Virtually all the so-called mineral water available is actually treated tap water. A recent reliable survey found that 65% of the available mineral waters were less than totally pure, and in some cases were worse than what comes out of the tap! Generally, though, if you stick to bottled water, any gut problems you might have will be from other sources – food, dirty utensils, dirty hands etc.

Soft Drinks Soft drinks are a safe substitute for water although they tend to have a high sugar content. Coca-Cola got the boot from India a number of years back for not cooperating with the government, but both they and Pepsi Cola are back with a

vengeance. There are many similar indigenous brands with names like Campa Cola,
Thums Up, Limca, Gold Spot or Double
Seven. They are reasonably priced at
around Rs 10 for a 250ml bottle (more in
restaurants).

Juices & Other Drinks   One very pleasant escape from soft drinks is apple juice,
sold by the glass from the Himachal fruit
stands found at many train stations. Also
good are the small cardboard boxes of various fruit juices like Frooti and Jumpin.

Soda water – Bisleri, Spencer's and other
brands – are widely available and cheaper
than soft drinks, at around Rs 7. Add a slice
of lemon and you get excellent, and safe,
lemon sodas.

Falooda is a popular drink made with
milk, nuts, cream and vermicelli strands.
Also popular in Himachal Pradesh are delicious bottles of cardamom-flavoured milk
known by the brand name *Abhi*.

Finally there's *lassi*, that oh-so-cool, refreshing and delicious curd/yoghurt drink.
As water is usually added to lassis, ask for
a lassi without water (and ice). Sweet lassis
have sugar added, otherwise they are
known as salt lassis.

Alcoholic Drinks

Alcohol is relatively expensive – a bottle of
Indian beer can cost anything from Rs 40 up
to Rs 160 in a flash hotel; Rs 60 is the average. In Sikkim it is quite cheap (Rs 40), but
in other Himalayan regions it can be up to Rs
125. Avoid over-indulgence or you'll wake
up late in the morning feeling thoroughly
disoriented with a thumping headache to
boot (perhaps that's where the name of the
popular Thunderbolt and Turbo brands were
derived!). Preservatives (sulphur dioxide is
the main one) are lavishly used to combat the
effects of climate on 'quality'.

Beer and other Indian interpretations of
western alcoholic drinks are known as
IMFL – Indian Made Foreign Liquor. They
include imitations of Scotch and brandy
under a plethora of different brand names.
The taste varies from hospital disinfectant

to passable imitation Scotch. Always buy
the best brand. In Himachal Pradesh, an
'English Wine Shop' is often found in each
village. They are not remotely 'English',
and rarely sell wine, but you can obtain
cheap IMFL and beer at these places.

With the continuing freeing up of the
economy, it is likely that in the near future
well known foreign brands of beer and spirits will be available. Fosters is a recent addition to the scene.

Local drinks are known as Country
Liquor and include *toddy*, a mildly alcoholic extract from the coconut palm flower,
and *feni*, a distilled liquor produced from
fermented cashew nuts or from coconuts.
The two varieties taste quite different.

Arrack is what alcoholics (and bus drivers' best boys) drink to get blotto. It's a
clear, distilled rice or barley liquor and it
creeps up on you without warning. Treat
with caution and only ever drink it from a
bottle produced in a government-controlled
distillery. *Never, ever* drink it otherwise –
hundreds of people die or are blinded every
year in India as a result of drinking arrack
produced in illicit stills. You can assume it
contains methyl alcohol (wood alcohol). In
remote regions of Himachal Pradesh, *angoori* (grape) wine is traditionally drunk,
especially during the long, cold winters.
The tribes of central Arunachal Pradesh
brew some fierce rice beers, known as
apang or *opong*.

Chang is Tibetan barley beer; the barley
is boiled until a little soft, then placed outside until lukewarm. Yeast is added, then it
is covered and left to ferment for a couple
of months. The eastern Himalaya has a similar version made from millet called *tongba*.
See the Tongba – Nectar of the Gods boxed
text in the Bangla Hills chapter for details.

ENTERTAINMENT

There's not much to do in the Himalaya
after dark but then you probably didn't
come all the way here to go clubbing. Bars
are generally dark and dingy places unless
they are in the top-end hotels. Videos are
shown in McLeod Ganj. Impromptu parties

and even raves are occasionally held in Manali. Possibly the best form of local entertainment is to go to one of the larger cinemas to see a no-holds-barred Hindi movie extravaganza. You might not be able to sit all the way through it but the experience is well worth tasting.

SPECTATOR SPORTS

India's national sport (obsession almost) is cricket. There's something about a game with as many idiosyncrasies and peculiarities as cricket which simply has to appeal to the Indian temperament. During the cricket season, if an international side is touring India and there is a test match on, you'll see crowds outside the many shops that have a TV, and people walking down the street with a pocket radio pressed to their ear. Test matches with Pakistan have a particularly strong following as the rivalry is intense. One thing you can count on is that most Indians will know the names of your country's entire team and if you don't even know their names, they may well think there's something wrong with you. On the other hand, if you do have an interest in cricket, it can be a great way to start conversations.

Soccer has a growing following throughout India. Sikkim's Bhaichung Bhutia recently signed to Britain's Aston Villa and is the first Indian to play in the Premiership. The national side needs all the help it can get, though – it is currently ranked 116th in the world.

India's latest international sporting stars are tennis players Leander Paes and Mahesh Bhupathi. They won the men's doubles title at Wimbledon in 1999 after entering the tournament as top seeds.

SHOPPING

The Indian Himalaya is packed with beautiful handicrafts. The cardinal rule when purchasing is to bargain and bargain hard. You can get a good idea of what is reasonable in quality and price by visiting the various state emporiums, particularly in Delhi, and the Central Cottage Industries Emporiums in Delhi and Kolkata (see the Gateway

Cities chapter). You can inspect items at these places from all over the country. Because prices are fixed, you will get an idea of how hard to bargain when you purchase similar items from regular dealers.

As with handicrafts in any country, don't buy until you have developed a little understanding and appreciation. Rushing in and buying the first thing you see will inevitably lead to later disappointment and a considerably reduced stash of travellers cheques.

Be careful when buying items that include delivery to your home country. You may well be given assurances that the price includes home delivery and all customs and handling charges. Inevitably this is not the case, and you may find yourself having to collect the item yourself from your country's main port or airport, pay customs charges (which could be as much as 20% of the item's value) and handling charges levied by the airline or shipping company (up to 10% of the value). If you can't collect the item promptly, or get someone to do it on your behalf, exorbitant storage charges may also be charged.

Be careful also if a storeholder disappears out into the back to wrap your purchase – you may find it has been swapped for an inferior product when you open it up. Similarly keep an eye on your credit card at all times and check that the transaction slip has no empty spaces where a salesman can slip in an extra charge.

Many handicraft and carpet sellers in the Himalaya, especially Leh, are Kashmiris who have relocated since the troubles there.

Carpets

India produces and exports more handcrafted carpets than Iran, and some of them are of virtually equal quality. In Kashmir, where India's best carpets are produced, the carpet-making techniques and styles were brought from Persia even before the Mughal era. The art flourished under the Mughals and today Kashmir is packed with small carpet producers. Persian motifs have been much embellished on Kashmiri carpets, which come in a variety of sizes. They

Child Labour & the 'Smiling Carpet'

In India hundreds of thousands of children, mostly poor and virtually all uneducated, work in factories across the country. This is despite the Child Labour Prohibition & Regulation Act of 1986, which prohibits the employment of children below the age of 14 in hazardous industries.

The carpet-weaving industry employs an estimated 300,000 children, mostly in Uttar Pradesh. The children are in demand because their small, nimble fingers are ideal for intricate weaving work, and, of course, being young, they get minimal wages. The conditions the children work under are generally atrocious – up to 16 hour working days, poor lighting and dangerous workplaces are all common.

In an effort to combat this exploitation of children, in 1992 the UN children's fund (UNICEF), the Indo-German Export Promotion Council (IGEP) and a group of nongovernment organisations came up with the 'Smiling Carpet' label – a label that was to be attached to any carpet produced without child labour. Also throwing its weight behind the project was the South Asian Coalition Against Child Servitude (SACACS). These bodies lobbied to ban the export of Indian child-made carpets.

Predictably, there has been opposition to the new label from the carpet manufacturers and exporters and the government, which say there are insufficient controls within the industry to allow for detailed inspection and therefore legitimate labels. But despite the opposition, the scheme is gaining credibility and increasing numbers of manufacturers are getting involved. While it is obviously not going to put an end to child labour, the 'Smiling Carpet' label is a major achievement.

are either made of pure wool, wool with a small percentage of silk to give a sheen (known as silk touch) or pure silk. The latter are more for decoration than hard wear. Expect to pay from Rs 7000 for a good quality 120 x 180cm carpet and don't be surprised if the vendor's initial price is more than twice as high.

Also made in Kashmir, coarsely woven woollen *numdas* and *gabbas* are appliqué-like rugs. These are more primitive and folksy than the fine carpets. *Dhurries*, flat-weave cotton warp-and-weft rugs are also found in the Himalayan regions. The many Tibetan refugees in India have brought their craft of making superbly colourful Tibetan rugs with them. A 90 x 150cm Tibetan rug will be less than Rs 1500. Two of the best places to buy them are Darjeeling and Gangtok. Check whether the carpet is pure wool or a woollen blend. Fine New Zealand wool carpets are more expensive than those which use Indian wool. Leh has a good selection of Tibetan and Kashmiri carpets.

Unless you're an expert it is best to have expert advice or buy from a reputable dealer if you're spending large amounts of money on carpets. Check prices back home, too; many western carpet dealers sell at prices comparable with those at the source.

Papier Mâché

Papier mâché is probably the most characteristic Kashmiri craft. The basic papier-mâché article is made in a mould, then painted and polished in successive layers until the final intricate design is produced. Prices depend upon the complexity and quality of the painted design and the amount of gold leaf used. Items include bowls, cups, containers, jewel boxes, letter holders, tables, lamps, coasters, trays and so on. A cheap bowl might cost only Rs 25, a large, well-made item might approach Rs 1000.

Jewellery

Many Indian women put most of their wealth into jewellery, so it is no wonder that so much of it is available. In the Himalayan regions you'll find chunky Tibetan jewellery, which often incorporates coral, turquoise and seed pearls. In the Muslim dominated areas of Jammu & Kashmir, silversmiths produce plain silver jewellery drawing their inspiration from Baltistan.

Leatherwork
Indian leatherwork is not made from cowhide but from buffalo-hide, camel, goat or some other substitute. *Chappals*, those basic sandals found all over India, are the most popular purchase. Chamba, in Himachal Pradesh, is renowned as *the* chappal-producing region. In Dharamsala, men can have a pair of leather shoes made to order and Kashmiri leather shoes and boots, often of quite good quality, are widely found, along with coats and jackets of often low quality.

Thangkas
A thangka is Tibetan religious art produced on cloth with vegetable dyes; some thangkas are embroidered in silk. Often Tibetan Buddhist deities or compositions are represented and used as meditation aids. Unfortunately, the quality of thangkas is nowhere near what it was 10 years ago.

Textiles
The textiles industry is still India's major industry and 40% of the total production is at the village level where it is known as *khadi*. There are government khadi emporiums (known as Khadi Gramodyog) around the country, and these are good places to buy handmade items of homespun cloth, such as the popular 'Nehru jackets' and the *kurta pajama*, bedspreads, tablecloths, cushion covers or material for clothes. Khadi emporiums often offer discounts around the time of Gandhi's birthday (2 October). Almora, in the Kumaon region of Uttarakhand, is renowned for its khadi products, and you can also purchase woollen items here.

In Kashmir, embroidered materials are made into shirts and dresses. Fine shawls and scarves of pashmina goats' wool are popular purchases in the Kullu Valley. Kullu shawls are known as *pattoos*, and are fastened with a *gachi*. Shawls from Kinnaur feature borders of bold designs that are more colourful than the muted hues prominent in Kullu shawls.

Ranikhet in Kumaon is known for its tweed. You can purchase lengths of fine tweed here, or plain gents' shawls known as *pankhis*. In Leh, traditional Ladakhi clothes, hats and shoes are available, if not a little impractical when you get back home!

In Tibetan centres such as McLeod Ganj, Darjeeling and Gangtok, women can have the traditional Tibetan dress, or *chuba* (known in Sikkim as the *bakhu*), made to order.

The Kullu Valley is the place to find traditional Kullu jackets, shawls and *topis*, or caps. Chamba is reputed for its finely embroidered *rumals* – small muslin cloths featuring depictions of local people or religious themes that are embroidered in satin stitch by the women of Chamba, according to a tradition dating back over 1000 years. Rumals were traditionally used for covering religious texts, but today the craft is being revived to cater for the tourist market.

Hats
The Himalaya has a fantastic range of hats. Pick from multicoloured *topis* from Kullu, wool and felt *thepangs* from Kinnaur, fantastic top hats from Ladakh, fur-lined Tibetan hats with gold brocade, Lepcha hats covered in black felt with a colourful brim, Sikkimese hats, Kashmiri skullcaps and even the odd red or yellow lama's hats. Most of the hats you will find are quite cheap at under US$10.

Bronze Figures
Bronze figures of the pantheon of Hindu (and Buddhist) deities can be found in all the major tourist centres of the Indian Himalaya. Figures of Shiva as dancing Nataraj are among the most popular, as are those of the Buddha adopting various *mudras* (postures). There are five main mudras.

Woodcarving

In Kashmir, intricately carved wooden screens, tables, jewellery boxes, trays and the like are carved from Indian walnut. They follow a similar pattern to that seen on the decorative trim of houseboats. Old temple carvings can be delightful.

Traditional Tibetan woodcarvings can be purchased in McLeod Ganj and Darjeeling. Woodcarving has traditionally been employed as ornamentation on homes in Himachal Pradesh, with artisans achieving high levels of skill in the carving of walnut, deodar and shisham into floral and animal motifs, representations of the deities and domestic scenes. Hand-carved wooden masks used in religious rituals are also found in the lower hills region of Himachal Pradesh. In Mussoorie you can pick up finely carved wooden walking sticks.

Pottery

Red and black pottery can be found in the Kangra Valley of Himachal Pradesh, produced by local *kumbhars*, or village potters. It is decorated with motifs in black and brown, and then fired. Most regions of the Himalaya produce their own domestic utensils such as pots, pans and water pitchers that are readily available in bazaars.

Other Himalayan Buys

In curio shops in the hill stations you might be able to pick up a *khukuri* – the traditional Gurkha knife. They come in ornamented tourist models, or the more sinister-looking, and more authentic, plain model. Particularly vicious looking items might not make it through your country's customs when you return home.

Darjeeling is the place to buy high quality tea. It can range in price from Rs 150 to Rs 3000 per kg! Worth trying is the unique honey available in and around Shimla. The Kangra Valley is also famous for its tea. Traditional ayurvedic medicines are a good buy in Rishikesh, as are *rudraksh melas*, puja beads made from the nuts of the rudraksh tree.

In all Tibetan centres, you can pick up a set of colourful Tibetan prayer flags for about Rs 20. Hand-held Tibetan prayer wheels can be found in hill stations where there are Tibetans, such as McLeod Ganj and other regions of Himachal Pradesh, as well as Darjeeling and Sikkim. The prayer wheels consist of a small drum containing the sacred mantra *Om Mani Padme Hum* (Hail to the Jewel in the Lotus) written thousands of times. The drum is rotated by means of a small chain with a weight at the end, and each rotation is equivalent to the recital of thousands of prayers!

From the abundance of apple, apricot and almond trees, especially around the Kullu Valley and Manali, there is a burgeoning local industry making delicious jams and pickles, as well as oils and shampoos made from other local fruits and nuts.

If you're keen to whip up a cuppa of yak butter tea when you get home, pick up a copper kettle and wooden tea churner, available in all Tibetan centres. (You might have trouble getting the yak through customs, though.)

Antiques

Articles over 100 years old are not allowed to be bought, sold, or exported from India without an export clearance certificate. If you have doubts about any item and think it could be defined as an antique, you can check with:

Kolkata (Calcutta)
    Superintending Archaeologist, Eastern Circle, Archaeological Survey of India, Narayani Bldg, Brabourne Rd
Chennai (Madras)
    Superintending Archaeologist, Southern Circle, Archaeological Survey of India, Fort St George
Delhi
    Director, Antiquities, Archaeological Survey of India, Janpath
Mumbai (Bombay)
    Superintending Archaeologist, Antiquities, Archaeological Survey of India, Sion Fort
Srinagar
    Superintending Archaeologist, Frontier Circle, Archaeological Survey of India, Minto Bridge

Getting There & Away

No international airlines fly directly to the Indian Himalaya, so getting there is a two part journey. This chapter deals with travel from international destinations to India. For specifics on getting to the hills from Delhi and Kolkata (Calcutta) see the Gateway Cities chapter and also Getting Around for more general information.

AIR
Airports & Airlines

As India's capital and major international gateway, Delhi is the country's most common international destination. It's also the closest international airport to the western Indian Himalaya. Many flights between Europe and South-East Asia/Australia or to/from East Africa pass through Mumbai (Bombay), though you are much farther from the mountains here. Kolkata is another major air hub and the closest international airport to Sikkim, Arunachal Pradesh and northern Bangla (West Bengal).

Air India is the nation's international carrier, with a few domestic flights. Indian Airlines on the other hand is a domestic airline, which also runs a few regional flights. You can't normally book Indian Airlines flights at Air India offices abroad.

It can be difficult booking a domestic air ticket abroad, so you will probably have to spend one or two days in either Delhi or Kolkata, even if you are headed straight for the hills. See the Gateway Cities chapter for Places to Stay & Eat in those cities. If you do want to arrange a domestic flight in advance then a specialist Indian-run travel agency in your country is probably your best bet; otherwise stay at the airport (change from the international to domestic terminals) and try to get a seat on the next flight.

Buying Tickets

Your plane ticket will probably be the single most expensive item in your budget, and buying it can be an intimidating business. There's likely to be a multitude of airlines and travel agents hoping to separate you from your money, and it is always worth putting aside a few hours to research the current state of the market. Start early: some of the cheapest tickets have to be bought months in advance, and some popular flights sell out early. Talk to other recent travellers. Look at the ads in newspapers and magazines, consult reference books and watch for special offers. Then phone a variety of travel agencies for bargains. Airlines can supply information on routes and timetables; however, except at times of inter-airline war, they do not supply the cheapest tickets. Find out the fare, the route, the duration of the journey and any restrictions on the ticket. (See Restrictions in the Air Travel Glossary in this chapter.) Then sit back and decide which is best for you.

> ## Warning
>
> The information in this chapter is particularly vulnerable to change: prices for international travel are volatile, routes are introduced and cancelled, schedules change, special deals come and go, and rules and visa requirements are amended. Airlines and governments seem to take a perverse pleasure in making price structures and regulations as complicated as possible. You should check directly with the airline or a travel agent to make sure you understand how a fare (and ticket you may buy) works. In addition, the travel industry is highly competitive and there are many lurks and perks.
>
> The upshot of this is that you should get opinions, quotes and advice from as many airlines and travel agents as possible before you part with your hard-earned cash. The details given in this chapter should be regarded as pointers and are not a substitute for your own careful, up-to-date research.

Air Travel Glossary

Baggage Allowance This will be written on your ticket and usually includes one 20kg item to go in the hold, plus one item of hand luggage.

Bucket Shops These are unbonded travel agencies specialising in discounted airline tickets.

Bumped Just because you have a confirmed seat doesn't mean you're going to get on the plane (see Overbooking).

Cancellation Penalties If you have to cancel or change a discounted ticket, there are often heavy penalties involved; insurance can sometimes be taken out against these penalties. Some airlines impose penalties on regular tickets as well, particularly against 'no-show' passengers.

Check-In Airlines ask you to check in a certain time ahead of the flight departure (usually one to two hours on international flights). If you fail to check in on time and the flight is overbooked, the airline can cancel your booking and give your seat to somebody else.

Confirmation Having a ticket written out with the flight and date you want doesn't mean you have a seat until the agent has checked with the airline that your status is 'OK' or confirmed. Meanwhile you could just be 'on request'.

Courier Fares Businesses often need to send urgent documents or freight securely and quickly. Courier companies hire people to accompany the package through customs and, in return, offer a discount ticket which is sometimes a phenomenal bargain. In effect, what the companies do is ship their freight as your luggage on regular commercial flights. This is a legitimate operation, but there are two shortcomings – the short turnaround time of the ticket (usually not longer than a month) and the limitation on your luggage allowance. You may have to surrender all your allowance and take only carry-on luggage.

Full Fares Airlines traditionally offer 1st class (coded F), business class (coded J) and economy class (coded Y) tickets. These days there are so many promotional and discounted fares available that few passengers pay full economy fare.

ITX An ITX, or 'independent inclusive tour excursion', is often available on tickets to popular holiday destinations. Officially it's a package deal combined with hotel accommodation, but many agents will sell you one of these for the flight only and give you phoney hotel vouchers in the unlikely event that you're challenged at the airport.

Lost Tickets If you lose your airline ticket an airline will usually treat it like a travellers cheque and, after inquiries, issue you with another one. Legally, however, an airline is entitled to treat it like cash and if you lose it then it's gone forever. Take good care of your tickets.

MCO An MCO, or 'miscellaneous charge order', is a voucher that looks like an airline ticket but carries no destination or date. It can be exchanged through any International Association of Travel Agents (IATA) airline for a ticket on a specific flight. It's a useful alternative to an onward ticket in those countries that demand one, and is more flexible than an ordinary ticket if you're unsure of your route.

No-Shows No-shows are passengers who fail to show up for their flight. Full-fare passengers who fail to turn up are sometimes entitled to travel on a later flight. The rest are penalised (see Cancellation Penalties).

Air Travel Glossary

On Request This is an unconfirmed booking for a flight.

Onward Tickets An entry requirement for many countries is that you have a ticket out of the country. If you're unsure of your next move, the easiest solution is to buy the cheapest onward ticket to a neighbouring country or a ticket from a reliable airline which can later be refunded if you do not use it.

Open Jaw Tickets These are return tickets where you fly out to one place but return from another. If available, this can save you backtracking to your arrival point.

Overbooking Airlines hate to fly empty seats and since every flight has some passengers who fail to show up, airlines often book more passengers than they have seats. Usually excess passengers make up for the no-shows, but occasionally somebody gets 'bumped' onto the next available flight. Guess who it is most likely to be? The passengers who check in late.

Point-to-Point Tickets These are discount tickets that can be bought on some routes in return for passengers waiving their rights to a stopover.

Promotional Fares These are officially discounted fares, available from travel agencies or direct from the airline.

Reconfirmation If you don't reconfirm your flight at least 72 hours prior to departure, the airline may delete your name from the passenger list. Ring to find out if your airline requires reconfirmation.

Restrictions Discounted tickets often have various restrictions on them – such as needing to be paid for in advance and incurring a penalty to be altered. Others are restrictions on the minimum and maximum period you must be away, such as a minimum of 14 days or a maximum of one year.

Round-the-World Tickets RTW tickets give you a limited period (usually a year) in which to circumnavigate the globe. You can go anywhere the carrying airlines go, as long as you don't backtrack. The number of stopovers or total number of separate flights is decided before you set off and they usually cost a bit more than a basic return flight.

Stand-By This is a discounted ticket where you only fly if there is a seat free at the last moment. Stand-by fares are usually available only on domestic routes.

Transferred Tickets Airline tickets cannot be transferred from one person to another. Travellers sometimes try to sell the return half of their ticket, but officials can ask you to prove that you are the person named on the ticket. This is less likely to happen on domestic flights, but on an international flight tickets are compared with passports.

Travel Agencies Travel agencies vary widely and you should choose one that suits your needs. Some simply handle tours, while full-service agencies handle everything from tours and tickets to car rental and hotel bookings. If all you want is a ticket at the lowest possible price, then go to an agency specialising in discounted fares.

Travel Periods Ticket prices vary with the time of year. There is a low (off-peak) season and a high (peak) season, and often a low-shoulder season and a high-shoulder season as well. Usually the fare depends on your outward flight – if you depart in the high season and return in the low season, you pay the high-season fare.

You may discover that those cheap flights are 'fully booked, but we have another one that costs a bit more ...' Or the flight is on an airline notorious for its poor safety and leaves you in the world's least favourite airport in mid-journey for 14 hours. Or they claim only to have the last two seats available for India for the whole of July, which they will hold for you for a maximum of two hours. Don't panic – keep ringing around.

If you are travelling from the UK or the USA, you will probably find that the cheapest flights are being advertised by obscure bucket shops whose names haven't yet reached the telephone directory. Many such firms are honest and solvent, but there are a few rogues who will take your money and disappear, only to reopen elsewhere a month or two later under a new name. If you feel suspicious about a firm, don't give them full payment at once – leave a deposit of 20% or so and pay the balance when you get the ticket. If they insist on a full cash payment in advance, go somewhere else. And once you have the ticket, ring the airline to confirm that you are actually booked on the flight you paid for.

You may decide to pay more than the rock-bottom fare by opting for the safety of a better-known travel agency. Firms such as STA Travel, who have offices worldwide, Council Travel in the USA or Travel CUTS in Canada are not going to disappear overnight, leaving you clutching a receipt for a nonexistent ticket, but they do offer good prices to most destinations.

Once you have your ticket, write its number down, together with the flight number and other details, and keep the information somewhere separate. If the ticket is lost or stolen, this will help you get a replacement.

It's sensible to buy travel insurance as early as possible. If you buy it the week before you fly, you may find, for example, that you're not covered for delays to your flight caused by industrial action.

Travellers with Special Needs

If you have special needs of any sort – a broken leg, you're vegetarian, in a wheelchair, taking the baby, terrified of flying –

you should let the airline know as soon as possible so that they can make arrangements accordingly. You should remind them when you reconfirm your booking (at least 72 hours before departure) and again when you check in at the airport. It may also be worth ringing around the airlines before you make your booking to find out how they can handle your particular needs.

Airports and airlines can be surprisingly helpful, but they do need advance warning. Most international airports will provide escorts from check-in desk to plane where needed, and there should be ramps, lifts, accessible toilets and reachable phones. Aircraft toilets, on the other hand, are likely to present a problem; travellers should discuss this with the airline at an early stage and, if necessary, with their doctor.

Guide dogs will often have to travel in a specially pressurised baggage compartment with other animals, away from their owner, though smaller guide dogs may be admitted to the cabin. All dogs will be subject to quarantine laws (six months in isolation etc) when entering or returning to countries currently free of rabies such as Britain or Australia. Deaf travellers can ask for airport and in-flight announcements to be written down.

Flying with Children

Children under two travel for 10% of the standard fare (or free, on some airlines), as long as they don't occupy a seat. They don't get a baggage allowance either. Bassinets should be provided by the airline if requested in advance; these will take a child weighing up to about 10kg. Children between two and 12 can usually occupy a seat for half to two-thirds of the full fare, and do get a baggage allowance. Strollers can often be taken as hand luggage.

Round-the-World Tickets & Stopovers

India is a very popular stop on most RTW tickets; great value if you are on a big trip. A popular option is to fly into Delhi and then fly out of Kolkata (Calcutta), or vice versa. A typical RTW ticket costs A$1950 to

A$2400, UK£600 to UK£940 and US$1250 to US$2500, depending on the number of stops. See the Air Travel Glossary boxed text.

Another option is a stopover ticket which will enable you to visit two countries in one trip, for example Delhi, en route to Bangkok or Sydney. These usually don't cost much more than a straight return.

Cheap Tickets in India

Although you can get cheap tickets in Mumbai (Bombay) and Kolkata (Calcutta), it is in Delhi that the real wheeling and dealing goes on. There are a number of 'bucket shops' around Connaught Place, but inquire with other travellers about their current trustworthiness. See the Air Fares from Delhi boxed text for some sample one-way fares.

Air Fares from Delhi

The following one-way fares were quoted at time of research. They are meant as a guide only as final fare will depend on the carrier, season of travel and travel agent. Fares are given in both rupees and US dollars at exchange rates current at time of research, (tickets are normally paid for in rupees).

Auckland	Rs 27,500
	US$640
Bangkok	Rs 9500
	(specials as low as Rs 4800)
	US$220
	(specials as low as US$110)
Hong Kong	Rs 17,000 to Rs 22,000
	US$400 to US$510
Karachi	US$180
Kathmandu	US$142
Lahore	US$100
London	Rs 13,000 to Rs 16,000
	US$300 to US$370
Los Angeles	Rs 27,000 to Rs 35,000
	US$630 to US$810
New York	Rs 22,000 to Rs 30,000
	US$510 to US$700
Sydney	Rs 22,500
	US$520

Although Delhi is generally the best place for cheap tickets, if you're heading east from India to Bangladesh, Myanmar (Burma) or Thailand, you'll probably find much better prices in Kolkata, even though there are fewer agents.

Departure Tax

For flights to neighbouring SAARC countries (Pakistan, Sri Lanka, Bangladesh, Nepal) the departure tax is Rs 100. To other countries it's Rs 500.

This airport tax applies to everybody, even to babies who do not occupy a seat. The method of collecting the tax varies but generally you have to pay it before you check in, so look out for an airport tax counter as you enter the check-in area. The departure tax may have been worked into the price of your ticket, even if bought abroad, so check with the airline in advance or you'll end up with a wad of rupees to spend in the crummy airport shops.

The UK

Various excursion fares are available from London to India, but you can get better prices through London's many cheap-ticket specialists, affectionately known as 'bucket shops'. Check the travel page ads in the *Times, Business Traveller* and the weekly entertainment guides such as *Time Out*, or check give-away papers like *TNT*. Two reliable London shops are Trailfinders (☎ 020-7938 3939) 194 High Street Kensington, London W8 7RG, and (☎ 020-7938 3366) 42-50 Earls Court Rd, London W8; and STA Travel (☎ 020-7938 4711) 74 Old Brompton Rd, London SW7, or 117 Euston Rd, London NW1 (opposite Victoria Station). Also worth trying are Flightbookers (☎ 020-7757 2444, Web site www.flightbookers.co.uk) or Bridge the World (☎ 020-7911 0900) at 47 Chalk Farm Rd, Camden Town, London NW1.

From London to Delhi, fares range from around UK£159/308 one way/return in the low season, or UK£176/341 one way/return in the high season – cheaper short-term fares are also available. The cheapest fares are usually with Middle Eastern airlines like

Gulf Air or Emirates. Uzbekistan Airlines currently offers the cheapest return fares to Delhi at UK£320, with a stop at Tashkent. Call HY Travel (☎ 020-7935 4775), 69 Wigmore St, London, for fares. Thai International always seems to have competitive fares despite its high standards.

If you want to stop in India en route to Australia expect to pay around UK£800. You might find fares via Karachi (Pakistan) or Colombo (Sri Lanka) slightly cheaper than fares via India.

Most British travel agents are registered with the Association of British Travel Agents (ABTA). If you have paid for your flight to an ABTA-registered agent who then goes out of business, ABTA will guarantee a refund or an alternative. Unregistered bucket shops are riskier but are also sometimes cheaper.

Continental Europe

Fares from continental Europe are mostly far more expensive than from London, although Amsterdam is edging in, with good deals with Middle East Airlines from Amsterdam to Delhi. NBBS in Amsterdam is a popular travel agency.

Paris to Mumbai or Delhi costs approximately 3360FF, and to Chennai 3620FF.

Australia & New Zealand

STA Travel (Web site www.sta-travel-group.com) and Flight Centres International (Web site www.flightcentre.com.au) are major dealers in cheap air fares in both Australia and New Zealand. Check travel agencies' ads in the *Yellow Pages*, travel magazines, the weekly travel section of newspapers like *The Age* and *Sydney Morning Herald* and ring around.

The high season is 22 November to 31 January. Advance purchase tickets from the east coast of Australia to India range from A$1200 to A$1700 depending on the season and the destination. Fares are slightly cheaper from Darwin or Perth, and to Chennai and Kolkata. Fares from Australia to the UK via India range from A$1950 to A$2300.

There are no direct flights between India and New Zealand so most airlines offer stopovers in Asia. Air fares to Delhi from Auckland with Malaysian Airlines cost from NZ$1745 return (NZ$1945 between November and January). There are a few cheaper combinations with Air India and Garuda.

The USA & Canada

The cheapest return fares from the US west coast to India are around US$1348. Another way of getting there is to fly to Hong Kong and get a ticket from there. Low season tickets to Hong Kong cost from US$550 one way and around US$776 return from San Francisco or Los Angeles, higher in summer. Singapore Airlines also offers some very good deals.

From the east coast most air routes take you via Europe. Return tickets to Mumbai or Delhi will be around US$1400, or to Kolkata somewhere between US$1500 and US$1700. The cheapest one-way ticket to Delhi will be around US$880. An alternative way of getting to India from New York is to fly to London and buy a cheap fare from there.

High season for flights to India runs from June to August and from December to January. Low season runs from March to around mid-May and September to November.

Check the Sunday travel sections of papers like the *New York Times, San Francisco Chronicle/Examiner* or *Los Angeles Times* for cheap fares. Good budget travel agents include the student travel chains STA, and Council Travel (☎ 800-226 8624). The magazine *Travel Unlimited* (PO Box 1058, Allston, Mass 02134) publishes details of the cheapest air fares for destinations all over the world from the USA.

Fares from Canada are similar. From Vancouver the route is like that from the US west coast, with the option of going via Hong Kong. From Toronto it is easier to travel via London. *Travel Cuts* is Canada's national student travel agency and has offices in all major cities. The *Toronto Globe & Mail* and the *Vancouver Sun* carry travel agents' ads.

Africa

There are plenty of flights between East Africa and Mumbai due to the large Indian population in Kenya. Typical one-way fares from Mumbai to Nairobi are US$440 with Ethiopian Airlines, Kenya Airways, Air India or Pakistan International Airlines (PIA, via Karachi).

Asia

Bangladesh Biman Bangladesh Airlines and Indian Airlines fly between Kolkata and Dhaka (US$80) and between Kolkata and Chittagong (US$106) in Bangladesh. Many people use Biman from Kolkata through to Bangkok – partly because it's cheap and partly because it flies through Yangon (Rangoon) in Myanmar. Biman should put you up overnight in Dhaka on this route but be careful – it appears they will only do so if your ticket is specifically endorsed that you are entitled to a room. If not, tough luck – you can either camp out in the hot transit lounge or make your way into Dhaka, pay for transport and accommodation, and get hit for departure tax the next day.

Nepal Royal Nepal Airlines Corporation (RNAC) and Indian Airlines share routes between India and Kathmandu. Both airlines give a 25% discount to those under 30 years of age on flights between Kathmandu and India; no student card is needed. Delhi is the main departure point for flights between India and Kathmandu. The daily one-hour Delhi to Kathmandu flight costs US$142. Other cities in India with direct air connections with Kathmandu are Mumbai (US$257), Kolkata (US$100) and Varanasi (US$79). The flight from Varanasi is the last leg of the popular Delhi-Agra-Khajuraho-Varanasi-Kathmandu tourist flight. If you want to see the mountains as you fly into Kathmandu from Delhi or Varanasi, you must sit on the left side.

The Nepali airlines Necon Air recently started flying from Kathmandu to Patna, and at the time of research had plans to fly from Lucknow as well. Buddha Air was also, at the time of research, planning to start flights between India and Nepal. Necon Air also flies out of Kathmandu with four flights per week to Patna (US$75) and three flights to Kolkata via Biratnagar (Nepal).

Pakistan Pakistan International Airlines (PIA) operates flights from Delhi to Karachi for US$119 and to Lahore for about US$78. Flights are also available between Karachi and Mumbai on PIA and Indian Airlines.

Elsewhere in Asia Not many travellers fly between **Malaysia** and India because it is so much cheaper from Thailand, but there are flights between Penang or Kuala Lumpur and Madras. The one-way economy fare from Kuala Lumpur to Delhi is US$280.

There are no land crossing points between **Myanmar (Burma)** and India (or between Myanmar and any other country), so your only choice from India is to fly there. Myanmar Airways flies Kolkata-Yangon (Rangoon) (US$155); Biman Bangladesh flies Dhaka-Yangon.

The one-way economy fare from **Singapore** to Delhi is around US$400.

There are flights between Colombo in **Sri Lanka** and Mumbai, Chennai, Tiruchirappalli or Thiruvananthapuram (Trivandrum) in South India. Fares from Chennai to Colombo are Rs 3889.

For **Thailand**, Bangkok is a popular departure point from South-East Asia into Asia proper. Bangkok to Kathmandu with Thai International is US$190 one way, US$380 return for a ticket valid for three months. Bangkok to Kolkata via Yangon (Myanmar) can by done for US$255 by combing a Thai International ticket from Bangkok to Yangon with an Indian Airline ticket from Yangon to Kolkata (this ticket must be ordered three days in advance). Bangkok to Kolkata one way costs US$190 with Thai International.

LAND

Drivers of cars and riders of motorcycles will need the vehicle's registration papers, liability insurance and an international driver's permit in addition to their domestic licence. Beware: there are two kinds of international permits, one of which is needed mostly for former British colonies. You will also need a *carnet de passage en douane*, which is effectively a passport for the vehicle, and acts as a temporary waiver of import duty. The carnet may also need to have listed any more-expensive spares that you're planning to carry with you, such as a gearbox. This is necessary when travelling in many countries in Asia, and is designed to prevent car import rackets. Contact your local automobile association for details about documentation.

Liability insurance is not available in advance for many out-of-the-way countries, but has to be bought when crossing the border. The cost and quality of such local insurance varies wildly, and you will find in some countries that you are effectively travelling uninsured.

Anyone planning to take their own vehicle with them needs to check in advance what spares and petrol are likely to be available. Lead-free fuel is not available in India, and neither is every part for your car.

Cycling is a cheap, convenient, healthy, environmentally sound and, above all, fun way of travelling. Some intrepid souls revel in the challenge posed by cycling in the Himalaya, and some agencies can even provide backup support services for touring cyclist groups. See the Getting Around chapter for information. One note of caution: before you leave home, go over your bike with a fine-toothed comb and fill your repair kit with every imaginable spare. As with cars and motorcycles, you won't necessarily be able to buy that crucial gizmo for your machine when it breaks down somewhere in the back of beyond as the sun sets.

Bicycles can travel by air. You *can* take them to pieces and put them in a bike bag or box, but it's much easier simply to wheel your bike to the check-in desk, where it should be treated as a piece of baggage. You may have to remove the pedals and turn the handlebars sideways so that it takes up less

space in the aircraft's hold; check all this with the airline well in advance, preferably before you pay for your ticket.

For more details on using your own vehicle in India, see the Getting Around chapter.

Bangladesh

The situation with crossings between India and Bangladesh is vague. The main crossings are at Benapol/Haridispur (near Jessore, on the Kolkata route), Chilahati/Haldibari (in the far north, on the Shiliguri-Darjeeling route) and more recently along the entire eastern border with India (eg at Tamabil/Dawki, in the north-east corner of the Shillong route, and east of Brahmanbaria on the route to Agartala in the Tripura region). If officials tell you that you cannot cross elsewhere, be sceptical because we have letters to the contrary from travellers. In recent years travellers have crossed at Bhurungamari/Chengrabandha (in the north, well east of Chilahati, an alternate route to Shiliguri and Darjeeling), Hili/Balurghat (north-west of Bogra) and Godagari/Lalgola (west of Rajshahi on the Padma River, an alternate route to Kolkata). It may also be possible to pass at Satkhira (south-west of Khulna).

The problem is that these lesser crossings witness so few westerners (maybe only once or twice a year) that everyone assumes it's impossible. Getting the correct story from Indian and Bangladeshi officials is virtually impossible. The truth is probably that crossing at these lesser routes is simply more variable and never certain. If you do use one of the minor crossings, be sure you don't leave the border without a stamp in your passport, otherwise you'll run into problems when leaving the country.

No exit permit is required to leave Bangladesh. But if you enter Bangladesh by air and leave by land you do need a road permit, which can be obtained from the Passport & Immigration office, 2nd floor, 17/1 Segunbagicha Rd, Dhaka. It's open Thursday to Saturday 8 am to 1 pm. Two passport photos are required and the process takes about 24 hours; there is no fee. If you are driving from Bangladesh in your own vehicle, two permits are required: one from the Indian High Commission (☎ 504879), House 120, Road 2, Dhanmoni, Dhaka; and one from the Bangladesh Ministry of Foreign Affairs (☎ 883-260/261), Pioneer Rd, facing the Supreme Court in Segun Bagicha (in the city centre).

Dhaka to Kolkata The Dhaka to Kolkata route is the one used by the majority of land travellers between Bangladesh and India. Coming from Dhaka it's wise to book your seat on the bus at least a day in advance. The buses that operate overnight between Dhaka (departing 8 to 11 pm) and the border are direct; they reach Benapol (the Bangladeshi border town) at dawn. From Benapol to the border, it's about 10 minutes by cycle-rickshaw (Tk 6). There are no daytime buses between the border and Benapol. Crossing the border takes an hour or so with the usual filling in and stamping of forms. From the border at Haridispur (India) it's about 10km (Rs 17, 20 minutes by cycle-rickshaw, or Rs 90 by auto-rickshaw) to Bangaon. It's possible to change money at Bangaon where the rate is better than at the border.

Alternatively, you can take a Coaster (minibus) from Jessore to Benapol (Tk 14), from where you can proceed to the border and India.

Chilahati to Darjeeling The Bangladesh border point at Chilahati can be reached by train, although it's much quicker to take the bus. From Chilahati to Haldibari (the Indian border checkpoint), it's a 7km walk along a disused train line. The train trip from Haldibari to New Jalpaiguri takes two hours and costs Rs 15. From New Jalpaiguri to Darjeeling you can take the fast buses or the slower more picturesque toy train (if running). Note that changing money in Chilahati is virtually impossible. There are moneychangers at Haldibari.

Shiliguri to Bhurungamari This northern border crossing is rarely used by travellers. Getting to the Indian border town of Chengrabandha from Shiliguri is easy. There are buses every 45 minutes between 6 am and 1 pm. The 70km trip costs Rs 24 and takes 2½ hours. The Indian immigration office opens at 9 am. Outside you can change Indian rupees into taka. Bhurungamari is 1km from the border. It's a tiny village and if you're caught here for the night your only option may be to sleep on the floor of one of the bus offices. You can take buses direct to Rangpur (5½ hours), Bogra (eight hours) or Dhaka (15 hours).

Sylhet to Shillong It takes 2½ hours to get to Tamabil from Sylhet by bus from where it's a 15 minute hike to the border. It is then a farther 1.5km walk to Dauki in India, from where buses run to Shillong (3½ hours).

Europe

The classic way of getting to India has always been overland. Sadly, the events in the Middle East and Afghanistan have turned the cross-Asian flow into a trickle. Afghanistan is still off-limits but the trip through Turkey, Iran and into Pakistan is straightforward.

The Asia overland trip is certainly not the breeze it once was, but it is definitely possible. Many travellers combine travel to the subcontinent with the Middle East by flying from India or Pakistan to Amman in Jordan or one of the Gulf states. A number of the London-based overland companies operate their bus or truck trips across Asia on a regular basis. Check with Exodus (☎ 020-8673 0859), 9 Weir Rd, London SW12 0LT, UK; Encounter Overland (☎ 020-7370 6845), 267 Old Brompton Rd, London SW5 9LA, UK; or Top Deck Travel (☎ 020-7370 4555) for more information.

For more detail on the Asian overland route, see the Lonely Planet guides to *Pakistan, Iran* and *Turkey*.

Nepal

There are two border entry points in the Himalayan regions covered in this book: at Banbassa, in the Kumaon district of Uttarakhand (the UP hills), which is the closest village to the western Nepal border village of

Mahendranagar; and Paniktanki, in northern Bangla (West Bengal), opposite the eastern Nepal border town of Kakarbhitta.

To/From Uttarakhand It is also possible to cross the border at Nepalganj, Dhangadi and Mahendranagar in the far west of Nepal. The entry at Mahendranagar, just over the border from the Uttarakhand (UP) village of Banbassa, is the most interesting possibility. It's a beautiful ride, though the road can be flooded in summer so try to check in advance. From Delhi to Banbassa it's a long 12 hour bus journey. From Almora, in the Kumaon region of Uttarakhand, it's seven hours (Rs 85), and from Pithoragarh, in the eastern Kumaon district, and an access point for the Milam Glacier trek, it's eight hours (Rs 78). Banbassa is also connected by rail to Bareilly.

From Banbassa, you can catch a cycle-rickshaw (20 minutes) to the border and across to Mahendranagar. There are direct night buses from Mahendranagar to Kathmandu, but they take a gruelling 25 hours. The countryside is beautiful and fascinating, so it's much better to travel during the day and to break the journey at Nepalganj. If you can't get a direct bus for the nine-hour trip from Mahendranagar to Nepalganj, take a bus to Ataria (at the junction for Dhangadi) and from there to Nepalganj. There are plenty of buses from Nepalganj to Kathmandu (day and night, 16 hours) and to Pokhara (night, 15 hours).

To/From Bangla (West Bengal) From Shiliguri, the major transport hub en route to Darjeeling and Sikkim, it is only one hour to the Indian border town of Paniktanki. Buses run regularly on this route (Rs 10) or there are jeeps for Rs 30 per seat. A cycle-rickshaw across the border to Kakarbhitta costs Rs 10. Buses depart Kakarbhitta daily at 4 pm for Kathmandu (Nepali Rs 250, 17 hours). Visas are available at the border for US$25 cash.

Once in Nepal, buses travel west as far as Narayanghat on the Mahendra Hwy, skirting the foothills and passing a number of interesting places and sights on the Terai (Nepali plains); from Narayanghat the road climbs through the Siwalik Hills to Mugling and the Trisuli River valley, where you double back towards Kathmandu. If it isn't too hot, consider travelling by day, so you can see the sights and stop in Janakpur and/or the Royal Chitwan National Park.

Avalanches and floods can sometimes delay the bus. The road is in very poor condition in the vicinity of the Kosi Barrage and there's another very bad section on the Prithvi Highway (the Pokhara to Kathmandu road) between Mugling and Kathmandu. Many travellers consider it to be one of the roughest bus journeys on the entire subcontinent!

There are day buses from Kakarbhitta that go to many other places on the Terai, including Janakpur (Nepali Rs 153), and there are night buses to Pokhara (Nepali Rs 339).

From Delhi There are direct buses from Delhi to Kathmandu (36 hours), but these generally get bad reports from travellers. It's cheaper and more satisfactory to organise this trip yourself.

If you are heading straight to Nepal from Delhi or elsewhere in western India, then the Gorakhpur to Sunauli route is the most convenient. Gorakhpur is an important railway junction: the 783km (14½) hour trip to or from Delhi costs Rs 211/737 in 2nd/1st class.

From Bihar It is also possible to enter Nepal from the insalubrious town of Raxaul, near Muzaffarpur, in Patna (Bihar), opposite the equally insalubrious Nepali border town of Birganj. Buses for Raxaul go from the main bus terminal in Patna (Gate 6; Rs 70, seven hours).

There are other roads into Nepal from northern Bihar to the east of Birganj but they are rarely used by travellers, and a couple of them are closed. One is the crossing between Jogbani (near Purnia) and Biratnagar. Additionally, the narrow-gauge railway from Jaynagar (near Darbhanga) which crosses the border to Janakpur is also closed.

Pakistan

Due to the continuing unstable political situation between India and Pakistan, there's only one border crossing open. There have been signs that cross-border links will be strengthened (with the introduction of a direct bus link between Delhi and Lahore) and this may well have an effect on the ease of travel between these rival nations.

Lahore to Amritsar The crossing at Attari is open daily to all traffic and can be crossed by bus, rail or in your own vehicle. It may be worth checking the situation in the Punjab with the Home Ministry in Delhi or the Indian High Commission in Islamabad, Pakistan, before you travel, as regulations may change if political tensions are running high. In 1999 a nonstop Delhi-Lahore bus link was inaugurated by tourism officials from both sides of the fence. It remains to be seen whether or not this becomes a regular service, and whether foreigners will be allowed to use it, but there's a good chance that it will be up and running by the time this book is out.

From Lahore (Pakistan) to Amritsar (India) the daily *Amritsar Express* leaves Lahore City station at 11 am and reaches Amritsar about 3 pm after a few hours at the border passing through immigration and customs. Going the other way, the *Indo-Pak Express* leaves Amritsar at 9.30 am and arrives in Lahore about 2 pm. Sometimes, however, border delays can make the trip much longer.

From Amritsar you cannot buy a ticket until the morning of departure and there are no seat reservations – arrive early and push. Moneychangers on the platform offer good rates for Pakistan rupees. The 4607 *Indo-Pak Express* leaves Amritsar at 9.30 am on Monday and Thursday, reaching Lahore in Pakistan at 1.35 pm. It can be delayed for hours at the border.

The road crossing at Wagah, about 4km beyond Attari, is quicker. The border is open daily 9 am to 3.30 pm (winter) or 4 pm (summer), and most people walk across. There are hourly buses till about 3 pm from Amritsar to Attari (Rs 13, one hour), but not all continue on to Wagah. It's easy to get a rickshaw between Attari and Wagah. Taxis from Amritsar cost around Rs 400, or look for minibuses by the train station (Rs 60).

Minibus No 12 leaves from just outside Lahore City railway station all day for Pak Rs 9; normally you change at Jallo for the remaining 5km to Wagah. Occasional buses run between the border and Amritsar or you can take a rickshaw (Rs 10) for the 3km ride to Attari, where there are regular buses for the one hour ride to Amritsar.

Pakistani time is 30 minutes behind Indian Standard Time. If you're stuck on the Pakistan side you can stay at the *PTDC Motel*, where there are dorm beds and double rooms.

Travellers have reported that whichever direction you're travelling, the exchange rate between Indian and Pakistan rupees is more advantageous to you on the Pakistan side of the border, though be aware that it's illegal to take Indian rupees into or out of India. And don't put them in your socks – everyone does that!

On both sides of the border you must clear immigration and then customs as well as two further security checks and then carry your luggage across 100m of no-man's-land.

South-East Asia

In contrast to the difficulties of travelling overland in central Asia, the South-East Asian overland trip is still wide open and as popular as ever. From Australia the first step is to Indonesia – Timor, Bali or Jakarta. Although most people fly from an east-coast city or from Perth to Bali, there are also flights from Darwin and from Port Hedland in the north of Western Australia. The shortest route is the flight between Darwin and Kupang on the Indonesian island of Timor.

From Bali you head north through Java to Jakarta, where you either travel by ship or fly to Singapore or continue north through Sumatra and then cross to Penang in Malaysia. After travelling around Malaysia you can fly from Penang to Madras in India or, more popularly, travel north to Thailand and eventually fly out from Bangkok to India, perhaps with a stopover in Myanmar (Burma). Crossing by land from Myanmar to India (or indeed to any other country) is forbidden by the Myanmar government.

An interesting alternative route is to travel from Australia to Papua New Guinea and from there to Irian Jaya, then to Sulawesi in Indonesia. There are all sorts of travel variations possible in South-East Asia and the region is a delight to travel through. See the Lonely Planet guide to *South-East Asia.*

SEA

There is no longer a ferry service running between Rameswaram and Talaimannar in Sri Lanka. The service between Chennai and Penang (Malaysia) ended some years ago. The shipping services between Africa and India only carry freight (including vehicles), not passengers.

ORGANISED TOURS

There are numerous foreign 'eco-travel' and adventure travel companies that can provide unusual and interesting trips and treks, in addition to companies that provide more standard tours. There are too many to include them all; check newspapers and travel magazines for ads. Many change their programs each year so the tours mentioned here are a guide only.

Companies that organise tours to various parts of the India Himalaya include the following:

Australia & New Zealand

Adventure World (Explore's Australasia agent)
(☎ 02-9956 7766, fax 9956 7707)
3rd floor, 73 Walker Street, North Sydney, NSW 2059, Australia
(toll-free ☎ 0800-652 954, 09-524 5118, fax 520 6629, email discover@adventureworld.co.nz)
101 Great South Road, Remeura, Auckland, New Zealand

Exodus Expeditions (see also the UK)
(toll-free ☎ 1-800-800724 or 02-9925 5439, fax 9251 5432)
Suite 5, 1 York St, Sydney, NSW 2000, Australia

Ferris Wheels Classic Motorbike Safaris
(☎/fax 02-9904 7419) 61 Elizabeth St, Artarmon, NSW 2064, Australia. Supported Enfield motorbike safaris from Delhi to Leh (over the highest motorable road in the world) and from Shiliguri to Kalimpong, Gangtok, Darjeeling (for Christmas) and Kathmandu.
Web site www.ferriswheels.com.au

Peregrine Adventures
(☎ 03-9663 8611, fax 9663 8618)
258 Lonsdale St, Melbourne 3000, Australia. Also offices in Sydney, Brisbane, Adelaide, Perth and Hobart.

Venturetreks
(☎ 09-379 9855, fax 377 0320)
164 Parnell Rd, PO Box 37610, Parnell, Auckland, New Zealand

World Expeditions
(☎ 02-9264 3366, fax 9261 1974)
3rd Floor, 441 Kent St, Sydney, NSW 2000, Australia
(☎ 09-522 9161, fax 522 9162)
Remuera Rd, Newmarket, Aukland. New Zealand. Well-established and experienced.

Canada

Worldwide Quest International
(☎ toll free 1800-387 1483 or 416-221 3000, fax 221 5730)
36 Finch Ave West, Toronto, Ontario MSN 2G9. Tours to Sikkim and Bhutan and trekking in Zanskar.
Web site www.worldwidequest.com

France

Allibert Guides
(☎ 04 76 45 22 26, fax 04 76 45 50 75)
rue Longifan, 38 530 Chapareillan
(☎ 01 40 21 16 21, fax 01 40 21 16 20)
14 rue de l'Asile Popincourt, 75011 Paris

The UK

Encounter Overland
(☎ 020-7370 6845, fax 7244 9737)
267 Old Brompton Rd, London SW5 9JA

Exodus Expeditions
(☎ 020-8673 0859, fax 8673 0779)
9 Weir Rd, London SW12 OLT.
Web site www.exodustravels.co.uk.

Explore Worldwide
(☎ 01252-319448, fax 343170, email info@explore.co.uk)
1 Frederick St, Aldershot, Hants GU11 1LQ UK. Trekking in Ladakh, boat tour down the Ganges via Rishikesh and Nainital, jeep safari and Pin Valley trekking tour in Spiti and Sikkim/Bhutan cultural tour. Web site www.explore.co.uk

Himalayan Kingdoms
(☎ 0117-923 7163, fax 974 4993)
20 The Mall, Clifton, Bristol, BS8 4DR, UK. Trekking and mountaineering.

Imaginative Traveller (overseas reservation office)
(☎ 020-8742 3113, fax 8742 3046)
14 Barley Mow Passage, Chiswick, London
W4 4PH, UK.
Web site www.imaginative-traveller.com

KE Adventure Travel
(☎ 017687-73966 or 72267, fax 74693,
email keadventure@enterprise.net)
32 Lake Rd, Keswick, Cumbria CA12 5DQ).
Tours, treks and mountaineering, including
Leh-Manali mountain bike trips and ascents of
Stok Kangri in Ladakh.
Web site www.keadventure.com

OTT Expeditions
(☎ 0114-258 8508, fax 255 1603,
email andy@ottexpd.demon.co.uk)
South West Centre, Suite 5b Troutbeck Rd,
Sheffield S7 2QA. Mountaineering tours, including Stok, Kangri (6121m) in Ladakh.
Web site www.ottexpeditions.co.uk

Steppes East
(☎ 01285-810267, fax 810693,
email sales@steppeseast.co.uk)
Castle Eaton, Swindon, Wiltshire SN6 6JU.
Tailor-made itineraries to Ladakh, plus
trekking in Sikkim.
Web site www.steppeseast.co.uk

Travelbag Adventures
(☎ 01420-541007, fax 541022)
15 Turk St, Alton, Hants GU34 1AG.
Web site www.travelbag-adventures.co.uk

World Expeditions
(☎ 020-8870 2600, fax 8870 2615,
email worldex@dircon.uk)
4 Northfields Prospect, Putney Bridge Rd,
London SW1 1PE

The USA

Adventure Center
(☎ 800-227 8747 or 510-654 1879, fax 654 4200)
1311 63rd St, Suite 200, Emeryville, CA

94608. Can book passengers on a wide variety
of adventure travel companies. This is the
US agent for Explore Worldwide and Encounter Overland (see The UK entry earlier
in this section).
Web site www.adventure-centre.com

All Adventure Travel.
(☎ 303-440 7924) PO Box 4307, Boulder,
CO 80306

Asian Pacific Adventures
(☎ 800-825 1680 or 213-935 3156, fax 935 2691)
826 S. Sierra Bonita Ave, Los Angeles, CA
90036. Arunachal Pradesh tour and customised
tours to India.

Geographic Expeditions/InnerAsia Expeditions
(☎ 800-777 8183 or 415-922 0448 , fax 346
5535, email info@geoex.com)
2627 Lombard St, San Francisco, CA 94123,
USA. Trekking in Nubra, Sikkim and Manali-
Zanskar, tours in Ladakh and Arunachal
Pradesh.

Himalayan High Treks
(☎ 800-455 8735 or ☎/fax 415-861 2391)
241 Dolores St, San Francisco, CA 94103.
Treks around Zanskar, Ladakh's Markha
Valley and Sikkim.
Web site www.himalayanhightreks.com

Mountain Travel-Sobek
(☎ 800-227 2384 or 415-527 8100, fax 525 7710)
6420 Fairmount Ave, El Cerrito, CA 94530,
USA. Ladakh treks and tours.

Turtle Tours
(☎ 888-299 1439, fax 602-488 3406)
Box 1147, Carefree, AZ 85377.
Customised cultural tours to Ladakh.
Web site www.turtletours.com

Journeys
(☎ 0800-255 8735) 4011 Jackson, Ann Arbor,
MI 48103, USA.
Trekking and cultural tours in Ladakh.
Web site www.journeys-intl.com

Getting Around

AIR

While there are numerous air services between the Indian Himalaya and Delhi and Kolkata (Calcutta) there are only a couple of scheduled flights between centres in the hills region. Addresses and phone numbers of relevant airlines are included in the relevant town entries. See also the Gateway Cities chapter.

Compared to other modes of transport to the Himalayan regions, flights are still comparatively expensive, but are a speedy, efficient and comfortable means of covering the large distances. (Flying to Leh in winter is the *only* means of getting there.)

Airports & Airlines

Himachal Pradesh has two functioning airports: at Bhuntar, 10km south of Kullu, serving the Kullu and Parvati valleys; and at Jubbarhatti, 23km south of Shimla. Gaggal airport, 15km south of Dharamsala, had suspended flights at the time of research but may resume a service to Delhi.

In Uttarakhand, Jolly Grant is the closest airport to Dehra Dun (25km) and Haridwar (35km), as well as Mussoorie and Rishikesh. Other airports in the region are at Pantnagar, 71km south of Nainital, and at Pithoragarh, in eastern Kumaon, though at the time of research there were no scheduled flights to any of these airports.

The closest airport serving the hills region of Bangla (West Bengal) and Sikkim is at Bagdogra, 12km west of Shiliguri, 90km south of Darjeeling, and 114km south of Gangtok.

For Arunachal Pradesh the nearest airport to Itanagar is 216km away at Tezpur in Assam. There's also an airport at Dibrugarh in Assam. Many people transfer through Gauhati, which has connections to both Delhi and Kolkata (Calcutta), as well as essential services like changing money.

With the deregulation of the Indian skies, Indian Airlines no longer has a monopoly on domestic air services, and at least half a dozen new airlines, known as Air Taxi Operators (ATOs), have started services (though many folded soon after opening). Those that currently serve the Indian Himalaya are Jagson, Jetair, Archana and Sahara. Alliance Air is a fully owned subsidiary of Indian Airlines.

Booking Flights

Indian Airlines has computerised booking at all but the smallest offices, so getting flight information and reservations is relatively simple – it's just getting to the head of the queue that takes time. Nevertheless, all flights are still heavily booked and you need to plan as far in advance as possible. The private operators are all reasonably efficient, and most have computerised booking or authorised agencies in major tourist centres. Theoretically, you should be able to make reservations on all scheduled flights operating in India before leaving your home country, but in practice it can prove problematic. If your agent can book domestic tickets they may not be able to actually issue tickets and it may be necessary to reconfirm and pay for the flight on arrival in India, which should be done as soon as possible.

Tickets & Conditions

The following conditions apply to Indian Airlines; regulations, student discounts and restrictions applying to smaller operators should be checked when booking your ticket.

- The ticket must be paid for with foreign currency credit card, or rupees with encashment certificates. Change is given in rupees.
- Refunds on adult tickets attract a charge of Rs 100 and can be made at any office within an hour of departure. There are no refund charges on infant tickets. If you fail to show up 30 minutes before the flight, this is regarded as a 'no show' and you forfeit the full value of the ticket.

- Beware that check-in baggage limits for Jagson and Archana is a paltry 10kg – after this you pay a pricey excess of around US$2/kg.
- If you lose your ticket Indian Airlines will absolutely not refund lost tickets, but may issue replacements at their discretion.

Fares

All Indian Airlines tickets have a foreigner's US dollar rate that is higher than the local's Indian rupee rate. Private airlines usually charge the same as Indian Airlines on identical routes but don't offer discounts to passengers under 30 years.

Infants up to two years old travel at 10% of the adult fare, but only one infant per adult can travel at this fare. Children two to 12 years old travel at 50% of the adult fare. There is no student reduction for overseas visitors, but there is a youth fare for people 12 to 29 years old – 75% of the US dollar fare.

If you are planning to visit other areas of India before or after the Himalaya, Indian Airlines' 15/21 day 'Discover India' pass, which costs US$500/750, can be reasonable value. This allows unlimited travel on its domestic routes. There's a 25% discount if you're under 30. There is also a 'Wonder Fare' of US$300, which allows unlimited travel within any one of Indian Airlines's sectors. Neither is of much use if you are sticking to the Himalaya. For individual fares, see the relevant regional chapters.

Check-In

Check-in time is one hour in advance. With all flights to and from Srinagar, an extra hour is required to get through the heavy security checks. On some internal routes, as a security measure, you are required to identify your checked-in baggage on the tarmac immediately prior to boarding. Don't forget to do this or it won't be loaded onto the plane.

BUS

Due to the paucity of train services in the Himalayan region, unless you can afford to hire a private vehicle, you'll probably find that you'll spend a good deal of time aboard buses. Between Delhi and the more popular tourist regions such as the hill stations, there is often a choice between luxury two-by-two seat (2x2) deluxe coach services (often run by government tourist bureaus), and ordinary, rattle-you-silly services. See the Gateway Cities chapter for details. However, between the hill stations and up into the more remote regions, there's simply a choice of either being squashed inside buses that would be rejected by scrap-metal

---

Warning – Travelling on the Roof

If the weather's fine, for short trips, travelling on the roof can present a pleasant alternative to the confined conditions inside the bus. Not only is there generally more space up here, but the 360° panoramic views can be truly awe-inspiring. Bear in mind, however, that in matters of hours, you can ascend from sunny valley bottoms to thousands of metres above sea level, so make sure you have warm gear to don when it gets chilly.

You should also beware of low-hanging power lines, particularly when the bus halts and you stand up to clamber down from the roof. The section of road between Manali and Dharamsala is particularly notorious for low lines, and in 1995 a westerner was electrocuted when he stood up on a bus roof at a *chai* (tea) halt along this route. Fortunately his life was saved by timely first aid, but remember to be vigilant. Also beware of low branches – if your fellow passengers suddenly collectively dive for the floor, they are probably not praying to Mecca, but are sparing themselves from being brained by a fast approaching branch. Travelling on bus roofs is particularly dangerous along the Parvati Valley and in Lahaul and Kinnaur, due to overhanging rocks.

merchants in some countries, or successively freezing and sweltering on their roofs.

Ordinary buses generally have five seats across (3x2) though if there are only five people sitting in them consider yourself lucky! There are usually mounds of baggage in the aisles and chickens under seats. These buses tend to be frustratingly slow, are usually in an advanced state of decrepitude and stop frequently – often for seemingly no reason – and for long periods, and can take forever. They're certainly colourful and can be an interesting way to travel on short journeys; on longer trips you'll probably wish you'd stayed at home. In the Himalaya, even the longest trips are compensated for by the magnificent scenery – you'll spend half your time agonising over the centimetres which separate you from the abyss below and the rest gazing in awe at perennially snow-covered peaks.

Government-run bus companies operate in each state in the Indian Himalaya, and their services are usually supplemented by private buses – although they may only operate on certain routes and sometimes only during season. Unlike state bus companies, private operators are keen to maximise profits; therefore, maintenance is less and speed more – a dangerous combination. In addition, drivers who would have been pensioned off years before in some countries, may present an alarming spectacle straining to see through their bifocal lenses.

The thing foreigners find hardest to cope with on buses is the music. Hindi pop music is usually played at maximum volume and seems to screech without end. Requests to turn it down are usually greeted with amusement and complete disbelief. Video buses seem to have been phased out in the Himalaya, an act of compassion worthy of the Buddha himself. If you do have the misfortune to have to catch an overnight bus, you may find you have finally slipped off into a shallow slumber when you are awoken by the blaring of the bus horn and/or the cassette suddenly turned to an ear-splitting, sleep-shattering volume. If it's any consolation, if you're awake, there's a good chance that the driver is also! In general, night buses are a little more expensive than daytime buses and are not as safe.

During the pilgrimage season (April to November) in the Garhwal Himalaya, you may find you've joined a group of pilgrims en route to pay homage at the four holy shrines (Char Dham) of Yamunotri, Gangotri, Kedarnath and Badrinath. In this case, you'll be assailed by collective songs in praise of the presiding deities at the shrines, which is not necessarily unpleasant.

In the mountainous areas of Himachal Pradesh and Uttarakhand (the UP hills), buses usually stop at shrines and temples at particularly hairy sections of the road. The resident *pujari* (person who performs an offering) will pass a tray of *prasaad* (sacred food offerings) through the window, which will be passed from passenger to passenger, who will take a portion and smear their forehead with bright orange or red *tikka* powder, and leave a small donation.

Road Conditions

The roads in the Indian Himalaya, although remarkable feats of engineering, are, with a few exceptions (notably in the hills region of Bangla), enough to induce terror in even the hardiest traveller. Roads are frequently unsealed, always narrow and invariably windy, and perch precariously on the sides of valleys, often with precipitous drops that plunge hundreds of metres to valley floors.

During the monsoon season (mid-June to September, with some regional variations), roads can be washed away or rendered impassable by landslides. Flexibility is the key to travelling during the monsoon, as the best laid plans can be hopelessly sent awry, and you may find yourself stranded for days.

In Sikkim and parts of Himachal Pradesh, frequent roadblocks have given rise to the institution of 'transshipping'. This simply means that you'll be dumped on one side of a landslide which you will have to scramble over to the opposite side, laden with your gear, where a veritable convoy of vehicles will be waiting to ferry you to your destination. It's not unusual for a

PATRICK HORTON

CRAIG PERSHOUSE

CRAIG PERSHOUSE

PATRICK HORTON

Top left: Monks with prayer drums and cymbals, Leh. **Top right:** A woman carries her goods, Central Market, Srinagar. **Middle:** Ornate Buddhist statue in Tiske Gompa. **Bottom:** Costumed monks perform their hypnotic ritual dance with masks and skulls.

GARRY WEARE

KERRY LORIMER

GARRY WEARE

Gompas, chörtens, locals, and even visitors – all must learn to adapt to the elements of the rugged Himalayan landscape. These images are taken from the regions around Ladakh.

small settlement of chai stalls and *dhabas* (cheap restaurants) to spring up on either side of the roadblock to provide hot chai and sustenance to drenched and mud-caked passengers.

Labourers clearing blocked roads are a ubiquitous sight throughout the Himalaya. Men, women and children, usually from the poorer areas down on the plains, frequently from Bihar, engage in the backbreaking and seemingly never-ending task of keeping the major highways of the Himalaya open to traffic.

Getting a Seat

If there are two of you, work out a bus boarding plan where one can guard the gear while the other storms the bus in search of a seat. The other accepted method is to pass a newspaper or article of clothing through the open window and place it on an empty

seat, or ask a passenger to do it for you. Having made your 'reservation' you can then board the bus after things have simmered down. This method rarely fails.

Catching a bus involves comparatively little predeparture hassle. You can, however, often make advance reservations at bus stations for a small additional fee. You may have to ask several people before you locate the correct ticket counter, and then join the inevitable queue. A prepurchased ticket should result in a confirmed seat, and you can request a window or aisle seat. Make sure you don't get there too late; we arrived at one bus station in Kinnaur with a reserved ticket smugly in hand only to find that we couldn't physically get inside the packed bus, let alone make it to the tantalisingly empty seat. In the remote areas of Ladakh, Kinnaur, and Lahaul and Spiti, it is every man, woman, child, goat and chicken

Some Indian Rules of the Road (Seriously)

Drive on the Left Theoretically vehicles keep to the left in India – as in Japan, the UK or Australia. In practice, most vehicles keep to the middle of the road on the basis that there are fewer potholes. If in doubt remember that traffic coming from the left has priority. So has traffic from the right, and also traffic in the middle.

Overtaking In India it is not strictly necessary to ascertain that there is space to complete the overtaking manoeuvre before pulling out. Overtaking can be attempted on blind corners, on the way up steep hills or in the face of oncoming traffic. In fact on particularly dangerous bits of road this is mandatory. Every moving vehicle must at least try to overtake every other moving vehicle, especially if it has just overtaken you. Smaller vehicles unexpectedly encountered in mid-manoeuvre can be expected to swerve apologetically out of the way. If a larger vehicle is encountered it is to be hoped that the overtakee will pull over, career off the road or otherwise make room for the overtaker.

Use of Horn Although vehicles can be driven with bald tyres or nonexistent brakes, it is imperative that the horn be in superb working order. Our surveys during research revealed that the average driver uses the horn 10 to 20 times per kilometre, so a 100km trip can involve 2000 blasts of the horn. A blast of the horn can mean anything from 'I am travelling too fast to stop (and if you don't get out of the way we shall both die)' (long desperate blast) to 'Hey you there in the bazaar, aren't you a friend of the brother of the guy I once met in Chennai?' (Casual blast) to 'I haven't used my horn for several minutes' (bored blast). Signs prohibiting use of horns are not to be taken seriously.

Seat Belts In the absence of seat belts both drivers and passengers should wear garlands of marigolds, which must be kept fastened at all times.

for themselves! It is harder to get a seat if you catch a bus halfway through its journey. If there are dozens of people waiting for a through bus, try walking a few hundred metres up the road in the direction the bus is coming from. It will probably stop to let you on board before it stops again to let everyone else in.

Private luxury coach services can be booked through travel agencies in popular tourist destinations like hill stations. Scheduled services on popular routes are often advertised on boards outside the agency.

Baggage

Baggage is generally carried for free on the roof, but take a few precautions. Make sure it's tied on properly and that nobody dumps a tin trunk on top of your (relatively) fragile backpack. At times a tarpaulin will be tied across the baggage – make sure it covers your gear adequately. Some travellers even chain their pack to the roof rack – not a bad idea, although thieves have been known to simply slash packs with a knife and remove the contents. Carry your valuables on board with you. If you're travelling in the Indian Himalaya during the monsoon season, no matter how carefully you've covered your pack, there's a good chance that it will arrive sodden and drenched at your destination. Try to insist that it be placed inside the bus, even if this means you have to sit cross-legged on top of it! A drenched pack is no joke, and getting your gear dry during the monsoon can be virtually impossible – it will probably go mouldy first. If your pack must travel on the roof, cover it with a plastic bag or sheet.

Keep an eye on your bags at chai stops. There's not much you can do if potential thieves are riding on board the top of the bus. Having a large, heavy-duty bag into which your pack will fit can be a good idea for bus and air travel.

If someone carries your bag onto the roof, expect to pay a few rupees for the service.

Toilet Stops

On long-distance bus trips, chai stops can be far too frequent or, conversely, agonisingly infrequent. Long-distance trips can be a real hassle for women travellers – toilet facilities are generally inadequate to say the least. Forget about modesty and do what the local women do – wander a few yards off or find a convenient bush.

TRAIN

There are very few railway lines in the Himalayan regions, and those that do exist are generally narrow-gauge and of interest more for their novelty value than as a means of covering long distances. However, travelling *to* the hills by train from either Delhi or Kolkata (Calcutta) is a good alternative to the buses. For details of these services see the Gateway Cities chapter.

The first step in coming to grips with Indian Railways is to get a timetable: *Trains at a Glance* (Rs 20) is a handy, 100 page guide covering all the main routes and trains. It is usually available at major train stations and sometimes on news stands in the larger cities. If you can't find it, a regional timetable provides similar information, including the local train services, and a pink section with timetables for the major mail and express trains (the fast ones) throughout the country. Indian Railways publishes its timetable on an Internet site (www.indianrailway.com), where you can work out the best train for your route.

There is also the 300 page *Indian Bradshaw* (Rs 50) that covers every train service in the country. It's more detailed than most people need and can be frustratingly difficult to find things. It's probably only useful if you are planning to travel beyond the Himalayan regions to other parts of India. Thomas Cook's *Overseas Timetable* has good train timetables for India, although it's not available in India.

Timetables indicate the kilometre distance between major train stations and a table at the back shows the fares for distances from 1km to 5000km for the various train types. With this information it's easy to estimate the fare between any two train stations.

A factor to consider with Indian trains is that getting there may not always be half the fun but it is certainly 90% of the experience. Fortunately, travelling from either Delhi or Kolkata (Calcutta) to the Himalayan regions doesn't entail some of the long, gruelling and dusty trips that it does in other parts of the country, unless you're considering taking the *long* (1628km) trip from Delhi to New Jalpaiguri, the railhead for Shiliguri, gateway to the Bangla (West Bengal) hills and Sikkim. All services to the railheads in the foothills of the Himalaya, or just below them, on the plains, generally take less than 12 hours.

Classes

There are generally two classes – 1st and 2nd – but there are a number of subtle variations on this basic distinction. For a start there is 1st class and air-con (AC) 1st class. The air-con carriages only operate on the major trains and routes. The fare for AC 1st class is more than double normal 1st class. A slightly cheaper air-con alternative is the AC two tier sleeper, which costs about 25% more than 1st class. These carriages are a lot more common than AC 1st class on trains serving the Himalayan regions.

Between 1st and 2nd class there are two more air-con options: the AC three tier sleeper and AC chair car. The former has three levels of berths rather than two, while the latter, as the name suggests, consists of carriages with aircraft-type layback seats. Once again, these carriages are only found on the major routes, and the latter only on day trains. The cost of AC three tier is about 70% of the 1st class fare; AC chair is about 55% of the 1st class fare. Most budget travellers will opt for a 2nd class sleeper (also known simply as sleeper class), which gives you a berth in a three tier non-air-con carriage.

When making a reservation it's possible to request a particular berth. Top berths are a good bet from the security aspect, as you can haul your pack up there (and even secure it with a chain and padlock), making it less easy to be silently spirited away.

In 2nd class, unreserved travel can be a nightmare since the trains are often hopelessly crowded, and not only with people.

Indians seem unable to travel without the kitchen sink and everything that goes with it. Fans and lights have a habit of failing during prolonged stops so that air stops moving through the carriage, and toilets can get a bit rough towards the end of a long journey. Worst of all are the stops. Trains seem to stop often, interminably and for no apparent reason.

In 2nd-class reserved it's a great deal better since, in theory, only four people share each bench but there's inevitably the fifth, and sometimes even the sixth, person who gets the others to bunch up so they can get part of their bum on the seat. This normally doesn't happen at night or in 1st class, where there are either two or four people to a compartment, and the compartment doors are lockable.

On some routes there are special high speed Rajdhani and Shatabdi trains. These are more comfortable but much more expensive than normal express trains or the buses. For Rajdhani trains there are three classes only: AC three tier, AC two tier and AC first class. Shatabdi trains normally offer AC chairs for the shorter trips. The price of the ticket includes meals and mineral water.

Reservations

In Delhi and Kolkata (Calcutta) there are special tourist booking facilities at the main booking offices. These are for any foreign tourists and they make life a lot easier.

Reservations can be made up to six months in advance though you can normally get a reservation a few days in advance. There is a reservation fee of between Rs 15 and Rs 35, depending on the class of your ticket. Your reservation ticket will indicate which carriage and berth you have, and when the train arrives you will find a sheet of paper fixed to each carriage listing passenger names and berth number. Usually this information is also posted on notice boards on the platform. It is Indian railway efficiency at its best.

As at many bus stations, there are separate women's queues. Usually the same ticket window handles the male and female queues, taking one at a time. This means that women can go to the front of the queue, next to the first male at the window, and get almost immediate service.

If the train you want is fully booked, it's often possible to get an RAC (Reservation Against Cancellation) ticket. This entitles you to board the train and have seating accommodation. Once the train is under way, the TTE (Travelling Ticket Examiner) will find a berth for you, but it may take an hour or more. This is different from a waitlisted ticket, as the latter does not give you the right to board the train. The hassle with RAC tickets is that you will probably get split up if there are two or more of you.

If you've not had the time to get a reservation or been unable to get one, it's worth just getting on the train in any reserved carriage. Although there's the risk of a small fine for 'ticketless travel', most TTEs are sympathetic. If there are spare berths/seats they'll allot you one, and charge the normal fare plus reservation fee. If all the berths/seats are already reserved, you'll simply be banished to the crush and confusion in the unreserved carriages. This trick only works well for day travel. At night, sleepers are generally booked out well in advance, so if you can't get one (or a RAC ticket) then sitting up in 2nd class is your only choice.

If you plan your trip well ahead, you can avoid all the hassles by booking in advance from abroad. A good travel agent who specialises in India will book and obtain tickets in advance and have them ready for you on arrival, though you'll probably pay more. Another option is to allow a couple of days in either Delhi or Kolkata (Calcutta) to arrange a ticket.

Refunds

Booked tickets are refundable but cancellation fees apply. If you present the ticket more than one day in advance, a fee of Rs 10 to Rs 50 applies, depending on the class. Between 24 and four hours before departure, you lose between 25% and 50% of the ticket value (depending on the distance of the journey). Any later than that and you can keep the ticket as a souvenir.

When presenting your ticket for a refund, you are officially entitled to go straight to the head of the queue, the rationale being that the berth/seat you are surrendering may be just the one required by the next person in the queue.

If you lose your ticket you can still travel on that reservation by paying between 10% and 25% of the original fare.

Getting a Seat

If you want a sleeper and there are none left then it's time to try and break into the quotas. Ask the stationmaster, often a helpful man who speaks English, if there is a tourist quota, station quota or if there is a VIP quota. This last option is often a good bet because VIPs rarely turn up to use their quotas.

If all that fails, then you're going to be travelling unreserved and that can be no fun at all. To ease the pain, get yourself some expert help. For, say, Rs 10 baksheesh you can get a porter who will absolutely ensure that you get a seat if it's humanly possible. If it's a train starting from your station, the key to success is to be on the train before it arrives at the departure platform. Your porter will do just that, so when it rolls up you simply stroll on board and take the seat he has warmed for you.

Women can ask about the Ladies' Compartments that many trains have and are often a refuge from the crowds in other compartments.

Himalayan Trains

Due to the precipitous terrain, there are few railway lines in the Himalayan regions, and those that do exist are all narrow-gauge services, meaning long, slow hauls between destinations that can be much more speedily accessed on bus services.

Nevertheless, if time is not a problem, travelling along even part of these amazing routes can be a memorable experience, and you'll marvel at the ingenuity of the early engineers who planned and also laid these tracks.

When it's running, you can't beat the toy train trip from New Jalpaiguri or Shiliguri, on the Bangla (West Bengal) plains, up to the hill station of Darjeeling. Construction of the line started in 1879, and in 1881, was finally completed. The train navigates some extraordinary loops and steep grades, covering the 90-odd kilometre in about nine hours.

From Pathankot, in the north of the Punjab, a narrow-gauge line wends its way through the Kangra Valley to Joginderna-gar, a trip taking some nine hours, passing en route the ancient capital of the valley at Kangra and the township of Baijnath, with an ancient temple dedicated to Shiva as Lord of the Physicians. The terminus at Jogindernagar must be one of the most picturesque stations in India.

The third narrow-gauge line serves Shimla, the capital of Himachal Pradesh, starting at Kalka, in Punjab and Haryana, and covering the 96km in about five hours.

Road Safety

In India there are 70,000 road deaths per year, which is an astonishing total in relation to the number of vehicles on the road. In the USA, for instance, there are 43,000 road fatalities per year, but it also has more than 20 times the number of vehicles.

The reasons for the high death rate in India are numerous and many of them fairly obvious – starting with the congestion on the roads and the equal congestion in vehicles. When a bus runs off the road there are plenty of people stuffed inside to get injured, and it's unlikely too many of them will be able to escape in a hurry. One newspaper article stated that 'most accidents are caused by brake failure or the steering wheel getting free'!

Many of those killed are pedestrians involved in hit-and-run accidents. The propensity to disappear after the incident is not wholly surprising – lynch mobs can assemble remarkably quickly, even when the driver is not at fault.

Most accidents are caused by trucks – for on Indian roads might is right and trucks are the biggest, heaviest and mightiest. You either get out of their way or get run down. As with so many Indian vehicles, they're likely to be grossly overloaded and not in the best condition. Trucks are actually licensed and taxed to carry a load 25% more than the maximum recommended by the manufacturer. It's staggering to see the number of truck wrecks by the sides of the national highways, and these aren't old accidents, but ones that have happened in the last 24 hours or so – if they haven't been killed, quite often the driver and crew will be sitting around, wondering what to do next.

The karma theory of driving also helps to push up the statistics – it's not so much the vehicle that collides with you as the events of your previous life that caused the accident. Therefore, the driver takes less responsibility for road safety than might normally be expected.

If you are driving yourself, you need to be extremely vigilant at all times. At night there are unilluminated cars and ox carts, and in the daytime there are fearless bicycle riders and hordes of pedestrians. Day and night there are the crazy truck drivers to contend with. Indeed, at night, it's best to avoid driving at all along any major trunk route unless you're prepared to get off the road completely every time a truck is coming in the opposite direction! The other thing you have to contend with at night is the eccentric way in which headlights are used – a combination of full beam and totally off (dipped beams are virtually unheard of). A loud horn definitely helps since the normal driving technique is to put your hand firmly on the horn, close your eyes and plough through regardless. Vehicles always have the right of way over pedestrians and bigger vehicles always have the right of way over smaller ones.

For more information on these trips, see the Himachal Pradesh and Bangla Hills chapters.

CAR RENTAL

While it's possible to rent cars in major centres such as Delhi and Kolkata (Calcutta), if you're planning to head beyond the relatively easily accessible hill stations, it's probably not a good idea. Not only do road conditions vary from poor to impassable, roads can be treacherous, and you'll be liable for any damage. In addition, insurance may not cover damage sustained by the vehicle in the more remote regions of the Himalaya.

Nevertheless, if you are still considering hiring a vehicle, self-drive in Delhi isn't cheap at around Rs 1400 per 24 hours (150km minimum) plus Rs 7 per extra kilometre. Alternatively, a seven day unlimited mileage deal costs around Rs 9500. Fuel is extra and a deposit of Rs 1000 is payable (returnable if there's no damage whatsoever to the car – a scratch constitutes 'damage', so check the car thoroughly before you take it). You will need an international driver's licence.

All the above price examples assume you'll be driving an Ambassador. These sturdy old beasts have been known to traverse some pretty rugged country, but during the monsoon period in the higher reaches of Uttarakhand and beyond the hill stations in Himachal Pradesh, and in Ladakh and Zanskar, forget it – you'll need a 4WD vehicle such as a Gypsy jeep, and, unless you have an advance drivers' diploma in mud scrambling, your safest bet is to hire an experienced driver who knows the terrain. The other and cheapest rental option is a Maruti van, which seats three or four. They are only good for short trips and are rarely hired without a driver.

Long-distance car hire with driver is becoming an increasingly popular way of getting around parts of India. With costs shared among say, four people, it's not overly expensive and you have the flexibility to go where you want, when you want. It's easy to hire a car and driver, either from the local state tourist authority, at a taxi stand or taxi union office, or privately through your hotel. By western standards the cost is quite low, certainly cheaper than a rented car (without driver) in the west. Almost any local taxi will happily set off on a long-distance trip in India.

Charges vary from town to town but there is generally a minimum charge per day for a set number of kilometres after which there is an additional per kilometre charge. For example an Ambassador in Delhi costs Rs 1350 per day for up to 250km, and then an additional Rs 5 per kilometre. In Manali the charge is around Rs 900 per day for 150km and then Rs 6 per kilometre. In McLeod Ganj this changes to Rs 700 for 80km and then Rs 5.5 per kilometre. Overnight charges will be added to the hire fee for a multi-day trip. In Ladakh, for example the overnight fee is Rs 250. In Himachal Pradesh it is Rs 100.

MOTORCYCLE

The motorcycle section is based largely on information originally contributed by intrepid Britons Ken Twyford and Gerald Smewing, with updates from Jim and Lucy Amos.

Travelling around India by motorcycle has become increasingly popular in recent years, and the number of intrepid souls who have covered the long northward haul to Leh is increasing every year. Motorcycling offers the freedom to go when and where you like – making it the ideal way to get to grips with the vastness that is India.

What to Bring

An international driving licence is not mandatory, but is handy to have.

Helmets should definitely be brought with you. Although Indian helmets are cheap, it is often hard to find one that fits well, and the quality is suspect. Leathers, gloves, boots, waterproofs and other protective gear should also be brought from your home country. A few small bags will be a lot easier to carry than one large rucksack.

It is always a good idea, and vital in remote areas, to carry spare tubes and chains. A tent and sleeping bag are handy where accommodation is scarce, and essential in areas where you may be caught in bad weather (which can happen at any time of the year).

Regulations & Road Rules

In Delhi, helmets are required for all drivers (but not pillion passengers), but are rarely used. Although helmets are not compulsory in the Indian Himalayan regions, they are highly advisable.

Despite stated permit regulations, travel on a motorcycle in the restricted regions of Ladakh, Kinnaur, and Lahaul and Spiti *is* allowed, either alone or in a group of less than four. However, in remote regions, travelling with a passenger, or even better, with another biker, is always the preferable and more enjoyable option.

Organised Motorcycle Tours

Classic Bike Adventure (☎ 0832-273351, fax 276124, 277343), Casa Tres Amigos, Socol Vado No 425, Assagao, Bardez, Goa, is a German company that organises bike tours on well-maintained Enfields with full insurance. Tours last two to three weeks and cover Rajasthan, the Himalaya between Kullu/Manali and Gangotri, and the south from Goa.

Ferris Wheels (☎/fax +61 02-9904 7419, email safari@ferriswheels.com.au), Box 743, Crows Nest, NSW 2065, Australia, also organises tours through the Himalaya and Rajasthan on classic Enfields. You can find out more about the tours they run, plus useful information and links to other related sites on their Web site www.ferriswheels.com.au.

Rental

Motorcycles can be rented from companies in Delhi for a negotiable price, including insurance, for about Rs 10,000 per month for a 500cc or Rs 8000 for a 350cc, or from Rs 400 per day (with third party insurance). Rental companies in Delhi will want a substantial bond of about US$500 – some unused travellers cheques will probably do – or your flight ticket home. It is also possible to rent bikes by the day in popular travellers' centres such as Manali and McLeod Ganj. You used to be able to hire bikes in Leh but this seems to have stopped now.

Buying & Selling

Motorcycles can be bought and sold, or exchanged with those of other foreigners in Delhi and Kolkata (Calcutta). See the Delhi section of the Gateway Cities chapter for details of a couple of companies. As an example, in Delhi or Kolkata (Calcutta) you could probably pick up a three or four-year-old Enfield 500cc for around US$1000, depending on its condition and your bargaining power. Older bikes will be cheaper but will need more maintenance.

New bikes are generally purchased through a showroom. You'll have to have a local address and be a resident foreign national. However, unless the dealer is totally devoid of imagination and contacts, this presents few problems.

When you are buying a second-hand bike, all you need to do is give an address. It is best to engage the services of an 'auto-consultant' – who acts as go-between from buyer to seller. They will usually be able to show you a number of machines to suit your price bracket. These agents can be found by asking around in mechanics districts, or may sometimes advertise on their shop fronts.

For around Rs 1000 (which usually covers a bribe to officials) they will assist you in transferring the ownership papers through the bureaucracy. Without their help this could take weeks.

When the time comes to sell the bike, don't appear too anxious to get rid of it. Regardless of which bike it is, you'll be told it's the 'least popular in India'. Don't hang around in one town too long, as word gets around the autoconsultants and the offers will get smaller as the days go by. The overall appearance of the bike doesn't seem to affect the price greatly. Dents and scratches don't reduce the cost much, and added

Which Motorbike?

One of the Enfield Bullet series, usually 350cc or 500cc, is a popular choice for foreigners because the Bullets are easier to buy and sell, and spare parts are generally readily available. Attractions are the traditional design, thumping engine sound, and the price, which is not much more than the new 100cc Japanese bikes. They're wonderfully durable bikes, easy to maintain and economical to run, but mechanically they're a bit 'hit and miss', largely because of poorly engineered parts and inferior materials – valves and tappets are the main problem areas.

Another drawback is the lack of an effective front brake on the 350cc– the small drum brake is a joke, totally inadequate for what is quite a heavy machine. The Bullet is also available in a 500cc single-cylinder version. It has a functional front brake and has 12-volt electrics which are superior to the 350's six-volt. If you opt for a 350cc, consider paying the Rs 4000 extra to have the 500cc front wheel fitted.

Current prices for a new 350cc Enfield run from Rs 51,000 for a Standard, Rs 54,000 for a Deluxe and Rs 58,000 for a Machismo. The last two come fitted with the 500cc double front brake. The price for a new 500cc model is around Rs 60,000 (US$1500), including ownership papers. The price of a two or three-year-old 500cc will drop to around Rs 40,000.

If you are buying a new Enfield with the intention of shipping it back home, it's definitely worth opting for the 500cc as it has features – such as folding rear foot-rest and longer exhaust pipe – which most other countries would require. The emission control regulations in some places, such as California, are so strict that there is no way these bikes would be legal. You may be able to get around this by buying an older bike, as the regulations often only apply to new machines. Make sure you check all this out before you go lashing out on a new Enfield, only to find it unregisterable at home. Madaan Motors and Inder Motors both on Karol Bargh in Delhi (see the Gateway Cities chapter) will ship a bike anywhere in the world for around Rs 13,500, including the crate, packing and insurance.

Many countries lift heavy import duties and/or sales tax provided you have owned the bike in India for a minimum of three months. In Australia, if you have owned the bike for three months, you can import the bike under the personal import scheme, which requires few, if any, modifications.

extras don't increase it by much. If you get a reasonable offer, grab it.

Ownership Papers A needless hint perhaps, but do not part with your money until you have the ownership papers, receipt and affidavit signed by a magistrate authorising the owner (as recorded in the ownership papers) to sell the machine, not to mention the keys to the bike and the bike itself!

Each state has a different set of ownership transfer formalities. Get assistance from an autoconsultant or from one of the many 'attorneys' hanging around under tin roofs by the Motor Vehicles office. They will charge you a fee of up to Rs 300, which will consist largely of a bribe to expedite matters. Alternatively you could go to one of the many typing clerk services and request them to type out the necessary forms, handling the matter cheaply yourself – but with no guarantee of a quick result. Check that your name has been recorded in the ownership book and stamped and signed by the department head.

If you intend to sell your motorcycle in another state it is vital to get a 'No Objections Certificate'. This confirms your ownership and is issued by the Motor Vehicles department in the state of purchase, so get it immediately when transferring ownership papers to

Which Motorbike?

The Rajdoot 350 is an imported Yamaha 350cc. It's well engineered, fast and has good brakes. Disadvantages are that it's relatively uneconomical to run, and spares are hard to come by. These bikes are also showing their age badly as they haven't been made for some years now. A Rajdoot 175cc costs US$800 new.

The Yezdi 250 Classic is a cheap and basic bike. It's a rugged machine, and one that you often see in rural areas.

There's a good Web site (www.indiabikes.com) where you can get plenty of information on different Indian bikes and their specs, as well as touring routes and tour companies.

BRADLEY MAYHEW

your name. The standard form can be typed up for a few rupees, or more speedily and expensively through one of the many attorneys.

Insurance & Tax As in most countries, it is compulsory to have third-party insurance. The New India Assurance Company or the National Insurance Company are just two of a number of companies that can provide it. The cost for fully comprehensive insurance is Rs 720 for 12 months, and this also covers you in Nepal. Third-party insurance runs at about Rs 200.

Road tax is paid when the bike is bought new. This is valid for the life of the machine

and is transferred to the new owner when the bike changes hands.

On the Road

In the event of an accident, call the police straight away, and don't move anything until the police have seen exactly where and how everything ended up. One foreigner reported spending three days in jail on suspicion of being involved in an accident, when all he'd done was take a child to hospital from the scene of the accident.

Don't try to cover too much territory in one day. As such a high level of concentration is needed, long days are tiring and dangerous.

Riding High

The 4th of July, 1994. Independence Day. What more auspicious day could there be to set off from Manali to Leh on my newly-acquired Enfield Bullet, to ride across the highest passes in the world?

The map said 475km. Piece of cake, I thought, two days easily. That was my first mistake. Such a distance is a pretty hard two days' ride *anywhere* in India, but in the extreme altitude of the Himalaya it's nigh on impossible. But I set off with my grossly overloaded panniers and rucksack on the back (second mistake), giving very little traction to the front wheel. I wobbled across the 3978m Rohtang Pass, straight into an arctic crosswind that had me keeled over like a yacht just to keep going straight ahead. Mistake number three; should've had some warm clothes. A pair of woolly socks over your hands does nothing to improve reflex lever control.

Over the course of the five long days that it actually took me to accomplish my foolhardy independent crossing of the Himalaya, I got bogged in axle-deep mud, got stuck in a glacial creek and had to be rescued, shorted out the spark plug and had to borrow a spare, dropped the bike in loose gravel and again in mushy snow, unrolled my sleeping bag to find it was soaked right through, had a puncture and had to hitch 35km to the next tyre-wallah, and finally (mistake number 37) ran out of petrol 15km shy of Leh. To say I had been a little un-prepared would be stating the ever-so-bleedin' obvious.

But I loved it so much that five years later I've now done that same road 18 times. It is simply the most awesome scenery I have ever found anywhere in the world, and the best way to see it is on a motorbike. Every sweeping corner into a new valley brings a breathtaking change of colour, texture, formation and usually, climate.

On a bike, unlike a bus, you're free to just stop and look and soak it all in. And don't let anyone tell you it's too dangerous; you're much better off with your own rapid means of evasive action than you are sitting on a bus with 48 other people wondering if the guy up front prayed loudly enough to Kali this morning as that overloaded Tata truck screams down the hill towards you.

But whether you join an organised commercial group or do your own thing, *be prepared* for many unforseen delays and don't underestimate the road. It commands respect.

Mike Ferris

On the busy national highways expect to average 50km/h without stops; on smaller roads, where driving conditions are worse, 10km/h is not an unrealistic average. On the whole you can expect to cover between 100km and 150km in a day on good roads. In the mountains, reduce this by half to a third.

Night driving should be avoided at all costs.

Repairs & Maintenance Anyone who can handle a screwdriver and spanner in India can be called a mechanic, or *mistri*, so be very careful. If you have any mechanical knowledge it may be better to buy your own tools and learn how to do your own repairs. This will save a lot of arguments over prices. In remote areas, do-it-yourself is essential. If you are getting repairs done by someone else, don't leave the premises while the work is being done or you may find (without proof) that good parts have been ripped off your bike and replaced with dodgy old ones.

Original spare parts bought from an 'Authorised Dealer' can be rather expensive compared to the copies available from your spare-parts-*wallah* (man).

If you buy an older machine you would do well to check and tighten all nuts and bolts every few days. Indian roads and engine vibration tend to work things loose and constant checking could save you rupees and trouble. Check the engine and gearbox oil level regularly. With the quality of oil available, it is advisable to change it and clean the oil filter every couple of thousand kilometres.

Punctures Chances are you'll be requiring the services of a puncture-wallah *(punkucha-wallah* in Hindi) at least once a week. They are found everywhere, often in the most surprising places, but it's advisable to at least have tools to remove your own wheel and take it to the puncture-wallah.

If you buy a second-hand bike it's worth lashing out on new tyres. A new rear tyre for an Enfield costs around Rs 600.

Fuel Petrol costs Rs 24 per litre; diesel is much cheaper. Petrol is usually readily available in all larger towns and along the main roads so there is no need to carry spare fuel along these routes. In remote areas, however, petrol supplies are scarce, and what little there is may be allocated for 'essential vehicles' – so take enough to get from one major town to another. (Some maps, such as those produced by Nest & Wings, indicate which places have petrol supplies.)

Road Safety
In many Himalayan regions, the roads are permanently rocky, muddy, wet, snowy or dusty, so wear wet-weather gear, including a good jacket and boots – and have some protection against the sun. In case of a breakdown, you and your bike may be able to hitch a lift on a passing truck for a negotiable fee, but check how the driver ties up your bike in the back of the truck. Travelling with a passenger or another biker is advisable.

One final piece of advice: be very, very careful – roads are often windy, treacherous, narrow and rough, and most other drivers are certifiable maniacs.

BICYCLE
The cycling information from Ann Sorrel includes updates from various travellers.

Every day millions of Indians pedal along the country's roads; for stalwart cyclists, a touring trip to the Himalaya is not out of the question. Nevertheless, long-distance and mountain cycling is not for the faint of heart. You'll need physical endurance to cope with the roads and the climate, plus you'll face cultural challenges – 'the people factor' – being stared at, crowds forming around your bike, even getting stones thrown at you; cyclists are very much exposed.

Useful Information
Before you set out, read some books on bicycle touring such as the Sierra Club's *The Bike Touring Manual* by Rob van de Plas (Bicycle Books, 1993). Cycling magazines provide useful information including listings for bicycle tour operators and the addresses of spare-parts suppliers. They're also good places to look for a riding companion.

For a real feel of the adventure of bike touring in strange places read Dervla Murphy's classic *Full Tilt – From Ireland to India on a Bike*, or Lloyd Sumner's *The Long Ride*, and *Riding the Mountains Down* (subtitled 'A Journey by Bicycle to Kathmandu') by Bettina Selby (Unwin Publications, 1984).

The International Bicycle Fund (IBF, ☎/fax 206-767 0848, email ibike@ibike .org), 4887 Columbia Drive South, Seattle, Washington 98108-1919 USA, has two publications that may help you prepare for your biking adventure. These are *Selecting and Preparing a Bike for Travel in Remote Areas* and *Flying with Your Bike*. Each is US$2 plus postage and handling (in the USA it's US$1 for first item and US$0.50 for each additional item; in other countries US$2 for first item and US$1 for each additional item). The IBF is also happy to help prospective long-distance cyclists with information and advice.

Using Your Own Bicycle

If you are planning to tour the Himalaya by bicycle, forget a touring bicycle – you'll need a sturdy mountain bike. Their smaller, sturdier construction makes them more manoeuvrable, less prone to damage, and allows you to tackle rocky, muddy roads.

Crossing international borders with a bicycle is relatively uncomplicated. Unlike a car or motorcycle, papers need not be presented. Do not be surprised, however, if the bike is thoroughly inspected for contraband!

Bringing your own bicycle does have disadvantages. Your machine is likely to be a real curiosity and subject to much pushing, pulling and probing.

Spare Parts   If you bring a bicycle to India, prepare for the contingencies of part replacement or repair. Bring all the tools you'll need, spare tyres, tubes, patch kits, chassis, cables, freewheels and spokes. Ensure you have a working knowledge of your machine. Bring a compact bike manual with diagrams in case the worst happens and you need to fix a rear derailleur or some other strategic part. Indian mechanics can work wonders and illustrations help overcome the language barrier. Most of all, be ready to make do and improvise.

Roads don't have paved shoulders and are very dusty, so keep your chain lubricated.

Although India officially uses the metric system, tools and bike parts follow 'standard' or 'imperial' measurements. Don't expect to find tyres for 700c rims, although 27 x 1¼ tyres are produced in India by Dunlop and Sawney. Some mountain bike tyres are available but the quality is dubious. Indian bicycle pumps cater to a tube valve different from the Presta and Schraeder valves commonly used in the west. If you're travelling with Presta valves (most high-pressure 27 x 1¼ tubes) bring a Schraeder (car type) adaptor. In India you can buy a local pump adaptor, which means you'll have an adaptor on your adaptor. Bring your own pump, as well; most Indian pumps require two or three people to get air down the leaky cable.

In major cities, Japanese tyres and parts (derailleurs, freewheels, chains) are available, but pricey – although so is postage, and transit time can be considerable. If you receive bike parts from abroad, beware of exorbitant customs charges. Say you want the goods as 'in transit' to avoid these charges. They may list the parts in your passport!

There are a number of shops where you may locate parts. Try the cycle bazaar in the old city around Esplanade Rd, Delhi and Nundy & Company, Bentinck St, Kolkata (Calcutta). Alternatively, take your bicycle to a cycle market and ask around – someone will know which shop is likely to have things for your 'special' cycle.

If you are riding an Indian bike there is no real need to carry spare parts. Just take a roll of tube-patch rubber, a tube of Dunlop patch glue, two tyre irons and the wonderful 'universal' Indian bike spanner, which fits all the nuts. There are plenty of puncture-wallahs in all towns and villages who will patch tubes for a couple of rupees.

Luggage   Your cycle luggage should be as strong, durable and waterproof as possible. As you'll be frequently detaching luggage when taking your bike to your room, a set designed for easy removal from the racks is a must. (*Never* leave your cycle in the lobby or outside your hotel – take it to bed with you!) Bike luggage that can easily be reassembled into a backpack is also available.

Theft   If you're using an imported bike, try to avoid losing your pump (and the water bottle from your frame) – their novelty makes them particularly attractive to thieves. Don't leave anything on your bike that can easily be removed when it's unattended.

Don't be paranoid about theft – outside the major cities it would be well-nigh impossible for a thief to resell your bike as it would stand out too much. And not many folk understand quick-release levers on wheels. Your bike is probably safer in India than in western cities.

Buying & Selling an Indian Bicycle

Finding an Indian bike is no problem: every large town will have at least a couple of cycle shops. Shop around for prices and remember to bargain. Try to get a few extras – bell, stand, spare tube – thrown in. Centre-pull and side-pull brakes are also available but at extra cost and may actually make the bike more difficult to sell. There are many brands of Indian clunkers – Hero, Atlas, BSA, Raleigh, Bajaj, Avon – but they all follow the same basic, sturdy design. A few mountain-bike lookalikes have recently come on the market, but they have no gears. Raleigh is considered the finest quality, followed by BSA. Hero and Atlas both claim to be the biggest seller.

Reselling the bike is no problem. Ask the proprietor of your lodge if they know anyone who is interested in buying a bike. Negotiate a price and do the deal personally or through the hotel. Most people will be only too willing to help you. Count on losing a couple of hundred rupees or about 30%, depending on local prices. Retail bike stores are not usually interested in buying or selling second-hand bikes. A better bet would be a bike-hire shop, which may be interested in expanding its fleet.

On the Road

Try to avoid the major highways up north like the NH1 through Haryana, and the NH2 – the Grand Trunk Road between Delhi and Kolkata (Calcutta). They're plagued by speeding buses and trucks. A basic knowledge of Hindi will help you to translate the signs, although at least one marker in five will be in English.

Another option is to follow canal and river paths. It's also possible in some areas to bike along railway tracks on maintenance roads. Do make inquiries before venturing off-road.

I once travelled most of a day before discovering the reason I had not encountered any pedestrian traffic: a major railway bridge was down and no ferry in service to ford the raging waters!

Ann Sorrel

If you've never before cycled long distances, start with 20 to 40km a day. In the hills region, from 10 to 20km a day is respectable. You can increase this as you gain stamina and confidence. For an eight hour pedal a serious cyclist and interested tourist will average 125 to 150km a day on undulating plains, or 80 to 100km in mountainous areas.

Inexpensive lodges are widely available and there are plenty of tea stalls and restaurants (called 'hotels') so there's no need to bring a tent. On major highways stop at *dhabas* (small restaurants), the Indian version of a truck stop. The one with the most trucks parked in front generally has the best food (or serves alcohol). Dhabas have *charpois* (string beds) to serve as tables and seats or as beds for weary cyclists. You should keep your cycle next to you throughout the night. There will be no bathroom or toilet facilities but plenty of road noise. Dhabas are not recommended for single women.

Asking directions can be a real frustration. Always ask three or four different people just to be certain, using traffic police only as a last resort. Try to be patient; be careful about 'left' *(baya)* and 'right' *(daya)* and be prepared for instructions like 'go straight and turn here and there'.

Transporting your Bike

Sometimes you may want to quit pedalling. For sports bikes, air travel is easy. With luck, airline staff may not be familiar with procedures. Tell them the bike doesn't need to be dismantled and that you've never had to pay for it. Remove all accessories and let the tyres down a bit. You may have to remove the pedals and turn the handlebars sideways.

Bus travel with a bike varies from state to state. Generally it goes for free on the roof. If it's a sports bike stress that it's lightweight. Secure it well to the roof rack, check it's in a place where it won't get damaged, and take all your luggage inside.

Train travel is more complex – pedal up to the train station, buy a ticket and explain you want to book a cycle for the journey. You'll be directed to the luggage offices (or officer) where a triplicate form is prepared. Note down your bike's serial number and provide a good description of it. Again leave only the bike, not luggage or accessories. Your bike gets decorated with one copy of the form, usually pasted on the seat, you get another, and who knows what happens to the third. Produce your copy of the form to claim the bicycle from the luggage van at your destination. If you change trains en route, *personally* ensure the cycle changes too.

Mountain-Bike Tours

Mountain-bike touring is catching on in the Himalaya. Several agencies in Dharamsala offer mountain-bike tours for visitors, as do some of the posher resorts on the outskirts of the Corbett National Park. Gurudongma Travels (☎ 03592-55204) in Kalimpong, in the Bangla hills, has Indian-made 10 and 18 speed mountain bikes for touring, and can also provide support services for cycling groups, such as backup vehicles, meals, guides and accommodation in tents and guesthouses.

Some foreign travel agencies, such as Exodus Expeditions and KE Adventure Travel (refer to Organised Tours in the Getting There & Away chapter), organise mountain-bike tours along incredible routes such as between Leh and Manali. Himalayan Journeys in Manali will also organise mountain-bike treks to Lahaul and Spiti, and Leh. And you thought the bus along this road was rough!

Final Words

Just how unusual is a cycle tourist in India? I'd venture to guess that currently 2000 foreign cyclists tour for a month or more each year somewhere on the subcontinent. That number appears to be growing rapidly. Perhaps 5000 Indians tour as well – mostly young men and college students.

If you're a serious cyclist or amateur racer and want to contact counterparts while in India, there's the Cycle Federation of India – contact the Secretary, Yamun Velodrome, New Delhi.

HITCHING

Hitching is never entirely safe in any country in the world, and we don't recommend it. Moreover in India it's generally not a realistic option. There are not that many private cars streaking across India so you are likely to be on board trucks. You are then stuck with the old quandaries of: 'Do they understand what I am doing?'; 'Will the driver expect to be paid?'; 'Will they be unhappy if I don't offer to pay? Of if I do?'. But it is possible. In Ladakh & Zanskar, travelling by truck is a legitimate mode of transport, particularly along the Manali to Leh and Leh to Kargil routes.

Travellers who decide to hitch should understand that they are taking a small but potentially serious risk. You will be safer if you travel with a partner and let someone know where you are planning to go. It's a particularly bad idea for women to hitch. Remember India is a developing country with a patriarchal society far less sympathetic to rape victims than the west. A woman in a truck on a lonely road may be seen to be tempting fate.

There are of course other dangers; two Israelis were killed in 1998 when their truck plunged off the road between Leh to Manali.

LOCAL TRANSPORT

Although there are comprehensive local bus networks in most major towns, unless you have time to familiarise yourself with the routes you're better off sticking to taxis, auto-rickshaws, cycle-rickshaws and hiring bicycles. The buses are often so hopelessly overcrowded that you can only really use them if you get on at the starting point – and get off at the terminus!

Where the fare is not ticketed, fixed or metered, agree on the fare beforehand. If you fail to do that, you can expect enormous arguments and hassles when you get to your destination. And agree on the fare clearly – if there is more than one of you, make sure it covers all of you. If you have baggage, make sure there are no extra charges, or you may be asked for more at the end of the trip. If a driver refuses to use the meter, or insists on an extortionate rate, simply walk away – if he really wants the job the price will drop.

Taxi & Jeep

There are taxis in most of the larger towns in the Indian Himalaya, and drivers in many centres have joined cooperatives, or unions, so long-distance fares are standardised and should be posted at the taxi booth. In Ladakh and the Kullu Valley, *all* fares are fixed, and difficult to negotiate. Nevertheless, in the low season, it's worth bargaining – fares can be reduced up to 40%.

In many centres (but not the remote regions of eastern Himachal Pradesh), share taxis or jeeps ply the major routes between important towns and hill stations. You'll find share jeep, sometimes called 'trekker', stands in Haridwar, Rishikesh and Dehra Dun, in the lower reaches of Uttarakhand, in Shiliguri and some of the major towns in the Bangla (West Bengal) hills, such as Darjeeling and Kalimpong, and in most of the major towns in Sikkim. Jeeps generally depart when there are 11 passengers on board, and fares in the rear of the jeep are usually slightly cheaper than in the middle bench seat and in the front with the driver. Rates are up to double the cost of the equivalent bus fare, but jeeps are faster and relatively more comfortable.

Auto-Rickshaw

An auto-rickshaw (also known as scooter or auto) is a noisy three-wheel device powered by a two-stroke engine with a driver up front and seats for two (or more) passengers behind. It doesn't have doors and has a canvas top. They're generally about half the price of a taxi, usually metered and follow the same ground rules as taxis. If the meter is 'broken', establish a firm rate before you set out.

Because of their size, auto-rickshaws are faster than taxis for short trips and their drivers are decidedly nuttier – hair-raising near-misses are guaranteed and glancing-blows are common; thrillseekers will love it!

In busy towns you'll find that, when stopped at traffic lights, the height you are sitting at is the same as most bus and truck exhaust pipes – copping dirty great lungfulls of diesel fumes is part of the fun of auto-rickshaw travel. Also, their small wheel size and rock-hard suspension makes them supremely uncomfortable; even the slightest bump will have you instantly airborne. The speed humps and huge potholes found everywhere are the bane of the rickshaw traveller – pity the poor drivers.

Tempo

Somewhat like a large auto-rickshaw, these ungainly looking three-wheel devices operate, rather like minibuses or share-taxis, along fixed routes. They are particularly conspicuous in Dehra Dun, where they are known locally as Vikrams, and ply between Rishikesh and Haridwar. Unless you are spending large amounts of time in one city, it is generally impractical to try to find out what the routes are. You'll find it much easier and more convenient to go by auto-rickshaw.

Cycle-Rickshaw

This is effectively a three-wheeler bicycle with a seat for two passengers behind the rider. Although they no longer operate in most of the big cities except in the old part of Delhi and parts of Kolkata (Calcutta), you will find them in all the smaller cities and towns, where they're the basic means of transport.

Fares must always be agreed on in advance. Avoid situations where the driver says something like: 'As you like'. He's punting on the fact that you are not well acquainted with correct fares and will overpay. Invariably, no matter what you pay in situations like this, it will be deemed too little and an unpleasant situation often develops. Always settle on the price beforehand, though even this doesn't guarantee anything. There is a greater possibility of a post-travel fare disagreement when you travel by cycle-rickshaw than by taxi or auto-rickshaw.

It's quite feasible to hire a rickshaw-wallah by time, not just for a straight trip. Hiring one for a day or even several days can make good sense. Drivers can also double as guides.

Other Transport

In some places, *tongas* (horse-drawn buggies) and *victorias* (horse-drawn carriages) still operate. You'll see them patiently waiting for custom in Rishikesh at the bus station. Kolkata (Calcutta) has an extensive tram network and India's first underground railway. Once upon a time there used to be people-drawn rickshaws but today these only exist in parts of Kolkata (Calcutta).

Bicycle

India is a country of bicycles – it's an ideal way to get around the sights in a city or even for longer trips – see Bicycle earlier.

Bicycles for hire in hill stations and other touristed spots, such as Haridwar and Leh, are generally low-tech bum-bruising contraptions that can be hired from around Rs 5 per hour or Rs 15 per day; Rs 200 per day for stronger mountain bikes. In some places bicycle vendors may be unwilling to hire to you since you are a stranger, but you can generally offer an ID card as security, or by paying a deposit (around Rs 500).

If you get a puncture, you'll soon spot men sitting under trees with puncture repair outfits at the ready – it'll cost just a couple of rupees to fix it.

If you're travelling with small children and would like to use bikes a lot, consider getting a bicycle seat made. If you find a shop making cane furniture, they'll quickly make a child's bicycle seat from a sketch. Get it made to fit on a standard-size rear carrier and it can be securely attached with cord.

Horse & Pony

If you're not an avid trekker, one of the finest ways to enjoy the Himalaya is astride a sturdy mountain pony near Shimla! See the Activities section of the Facts for the Visitor chapter for more information on where you can hire some four-legged transport.

TREKKING

Two-legged transport is one of the most common means of getting around, and sometimes the only way of getting to remote areas. Details of treks are included as boxed text in the regional chapters. See the Facts for the Visitor chapter for information about equipment, health and issues affecting the trekker. For comprehensive coverage, pick up a copy of Lonely Planet's *Trekking in the Indian Himalaya* by Garry Weare.

ORGANISED TOURS

At almost any place of tourist interest in the Indian Himalaya (and in quite a few places where there's not much tourist interest), there will be tours operated either by the Government of India tourist office, the state tourist office or the local transport company – sometimes by all three. These tours are usually excellent value, particularly in towns where the tourist sights are spread out.

These tours are not strictly for western tourists; you will almost always find yourself far outnumbered by local tourists, and in many places just a little off the beaten track you will often be the only westerner on the bus. Despite this, the tours are usually conducted in English – which is possibly the only common language for the middle-class Indian tourists in any case. These tours are an excellent place to meet Indians.

The big drawback is that many tours try to cram far too much into too short a period of time. In Gangtok, for example, half and full-day tours that take in the renowned Rumtek Gompa leave you little time actually at the monastery to take in the magnificent wall paintings and religious artefacts. If a tour looks too hectic, you're better off doing it yourself at a more appropriate pace or taking the tour simply to find out to which places you want to devote more time.

Gateway Cities

Most international travellers bound for the hills will find themselves transiting through either Delhi (for Ladakh, Himachal Pradesh and Uttarakhand) or Kolkata (Calcutta; for Bangla (West Bengal), Sikkim and Arunachal Pradesh). Basic stopover and getting there & away information is given here; for more detail see Lonely Planet's *Delhi* and *India* guides.

Delhi

☎ 011 • pop 11 million

Delhi is the capital of India and its major international transport hub. During the summer (when most visitors pass through en route to the Himalaya) the city is uncomfortably hot, with temperatures regularly over 40°C. Most people only spend one or two days here, arranging money, flights or train tickets to the hills. That said, Delhi is without doubt an endlessly fascinating city and there are plenty of interesting things to see and do (and buy) if you take time to explore.

ORIENTATION

Delhi actually consists of two parts. Old Delhi is a warren of bazaars and backstreets that contains most of the city's Muslim and Mughal monuments. Here you will find the Red Fort, the Jama Masjid (Friday Mosque) and the famous shopping street of Chandni Chowk, as well as Old Delhi railway station, and a little farther north the main interstate bus station at Kashmiri Gate.

New Delhi is by contrast a planned and spacious city, created as a colonial capital by the British. Its hub is the huge circle known as Connaught Place, where you will find most airline offices, banks, travel agents, tourist offices and mid-range hotels. It is divided up like slices of a pie and these blocks are named alphabetically.

Janpath, running south of Connaught Place, is one of the most important streets and

Warning – Scams in Delhi

There are more scamsters in Delhi than most travellers are prepared for. Don't be paranoid, but keep your eye out for the following scams:

- Some taxi drivers try to persuade tourists that there are riots in Paharganj and offer to take you elsewhere, often Karol Bagh.

- Beware that touts hanging around the Government Tourist Office in Connaught Place will try to hustle you into nearby private tourist concerns while claiming that these are the official tourist offices.

- Steer clear also of the dozen or so 'tourist information centres' across the road from the New Delhi railway station. Touts from these offices will try to sell you overpriced bus and train tickets, as well as dubious tours of Kashmir.

has several tourist offices and many handicraft stalls. South of here are government buildings, museums, residential districts and Chanakyapuri, the diplomatic enclave.

In between Old and New Delhi is the area known as Paharganj. This has become the main budget travellers hangout and there are dozens of guesthouses, restaurants, fax and email offices etc. At the eastern end of Paharganj is New Delhi Railway station, where most foreigners buy their tickets.

INFORMATION
Tourist Offices

The Government of India tourist office (☎ 332 0005, fax 332 0342) is at 88 Janpath near Connaught Place. It is helpful at answering most questions, has some free literature (including a good map of Delhi) and

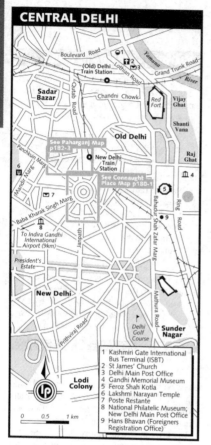

CENTRAL DELHI

1   Kashmiri Gate International Bus Terminal (ISBT)
2   St James' Church
3   Delhi Main Post Office
4   Gandhi Memorial Museum
5   Feroz Shah Kotla
6   Lakshmi Narayan Temple
7   Poste Restante
8   National Philatelic Museum; New Delhi Main Post Office
9   Hans Bhavan (Foreigners Registration Office)

offers good value ITDC bus tours of both Old and New Delhi – a good way to see the city in a short period of time. The morning tour of New Delhi (Rs 125, five hours, 8 am) includes the Qutab Minar, Humayun's tomb, India Gate, the Jantar Mantar and the Lakshmi Narayan temple. The afternoon Old Delhi tour (Rs 100, 2.45 pm) includes the Red Fort, Jama Masjid, Raj Ghat, Shanti Vana and Feroz Shah Kotla. If you take both tours on the same day it costs Rs 200.

The Himachal Pradesh Tourism Development Corporation (HPTDC) (☎ 332 4764) is on the first floor of the Chandralok Bldg, 36 Janpath. You can book seats on HPTDC buses to Shimla and Manali and can reserve any HPTDC accommodation here. They also sell basic maps of Himachal Pradesh.

The Uttar Pradesh tourist authority (☎ 332 2251), in the same building, acts as the office for KMVN and GMVN. You can get all kinds of free literature here. The office runs tours to Corbett Tiger Reserve and Pindari Glacier. See the Corbett Tiger Reserve entry in the Uttarakhand chapter for details.

Other Himalayan tourism offices include:

Bangla (West Bengal)
    (☎ 373 2695) A2 State Emporium Complex, Baba Kharak Singh Marg
Jammu & Kashmir
    (☎ 334 5373) 201-203, Kanishka Shopping Plaza, 19 Ashoka Rd
Sikkim
    (☎ 611 5346) New Sikkim House Bldg, 14 Panchsheel Marg, Chanakyapuri

Money

There's a 24 hour State Bank of India and a Thomas Cook counter in the international arrivals hall, before you go through customs and immigration.

Central Bank in the Ashok Hotel in Chanakyapuri is open 24 hours. Almost all foreign banks (see following) change money. With a Visa/Plus card you can get cash rupees from 24 hour ATMs at Citibank, Hong Kong & Shanghai Bank and Standard Chartered Bank. You can still get cash advances over the counter during normal working hours.

American Express (☎ 332 5221) has an office at Wenger House, A Block, Connaught Place. Sita World Travels (☎ 331 1133), 12 F-block Connaught Place is the place to pick up or arrange a money transfer with Western Union. Other banks include:

ANZ Grindlays
    (☎ 372 1242) 10 H-block Connaught Place

Bank of America
(☎ 371 5565) Hansalaya Bldg, 14
Barakhamba Rd. Access your account with a
Versateller card and cheque book.
Citibank
(☎ 371 2484) Jeevan Bharati Bldg, Outer
Circle, Connaught Circus
Hongkong & Shanghai Bank
(☎ 331 4355) ECE House, 28 Kasturba
Gandhi Marg
Standard Chartered
(☎ 336 0321) 17 Sansad Marg (Parliament St)
State Bank of India
Indira Gandhi International Airport (24 hours)
Thomas Cook
(☎ 336 8359) Hotel Imperial, Janpath.
Arrange money transfers here.

Post & Communications

There is a small post office in A-block,
Connaught Place but the main post office
can be found on the roundabout on Baba
Kharak Singh Marg, 500m south-west of
Connaught Place.

Poste restante mail can be collected
nearby from the Foreign Post Office on
Market Rd. The poste restante office is
around the back and up the stairs (Monday
to Friday, between 9 am and 5 pm). Beware
that poste restante not marked to 'New
Delhi' will end up at the inconveniently situated Old Delhi post office. American Express will hold mail for its card or travellers
cheque holders.

There are plenty of private STD/ISD call
offices for international phone calls or faxes,
especially around Paharganj, and most places
allow you to be called back free of charge.

There are several places in Paharganj to
send/receive emails. The cheapest and most
convenient place at time of research was
the Gold Regency Hotel (Rs 100, one hour).
It is open 24 hours and also serves decent
pastries.

Visa Extensions & Permits

The Foreigners' Regional Registration Office
(☎ 331 9781, fax 375 5183) at Room 104, 1st
floor, Hans Bhawan, Tilak Bridge, is the
place to come for visa extensions or permits
for Arunachal Pradesh. See the information in
the Facts for the Visitor chapter. The office is
open Monday to Friday, 9.30 am to 1 pm, and
2 to 4 pm.

Travel Agencies

Some ticket discounters around Connaught
Place are real fly-by-night operators, so take
care. Those recommended by readers include:

Aa Bee Travels
Hare Rama Guest House, Paharganj
Cox & Kings
(☎ 373 8811, fax 331 7373)
Indra Place, H-block, Connaught Circus
Cozy Travels
(☎ 331 2873), BMC House, 1 N-block
Connaught Place
Sita World Travels
(☎ 331 1122, fax 332 4652)
12 F-block Connaught Place
Y Tours & Travel
(☎ 336 1915, fax 374 6032)
YMCA, Jai Singh Rd

Adventure Tour Operators

Local Himalayan tour operators are listed
under town headings.

The following tour operators arrange
adventure sports in the Himalaya:

Amber Tours Pty Ltd
(☎ 331 2773, fax 331 2984)
Flat 2, Dwarka Sadan, 42 C-block Connaught
Place. Yoga and mystic tours, river rafting,
trekking, fishing for the mahseer, and private
jet or helicopter flights over the Himalaya.
Himalayan River Runners
(☎ 685 2602) 5 F-block Hauz Khas Enclave.
Rafting expeditions in the western Himalaya.
Mercury Travels Limited
(☎ 336 2008/2091, fax 373 2013/334 4068)
Jeevan Tara Building, Sansad Marg, New
Delhi. Mercury specialises in organised treks
in the western Himalaya.
Shikhar Travels
(☎ 331 2444, fax 332 3660)
209 Competent House, 14-block Middle Circle,
Connaught Place. Trekking and mountaineering tours, also runs expeditions for beginners.
World Expeditions
(☎ 698 3358, fax 698 3357)
1 G-block, MG Bhawan 7, Local Shopping
Centre, Madangir. Fully inclusive treks to all
areas of the Indian Himalaya.

CONNAUGHT PLACE (DELHI)

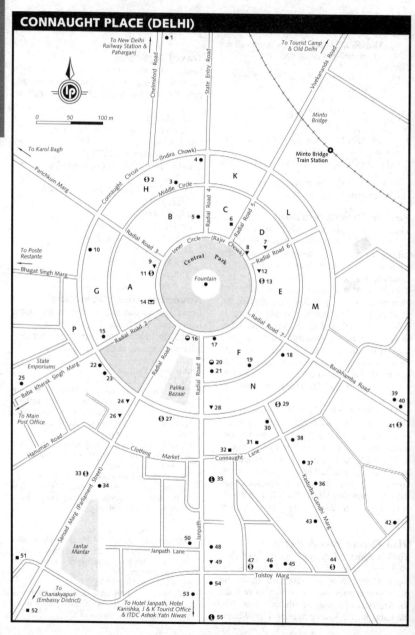

To New Delhi Railway Station & Paharganj

To Tourist Camp & Old Delhi

Vivekananda Road

Minto Bridge

Minto Bridge Train Station

To Karol Bagh

Panchkuin Marg

Connaught Circus

(Indira Chowk)

State Entry Road

Chelmsford Road

Middle Circle

Radial Road 4

Radial Road 5

Radial Road 3

Inner Circle — (Rajiv Chowk)

Central Park

Fountain

Radial Road 6

To Poste Restante

Bhagat Singh Marg

Radial Road 2

Radial Road 1

Radial Road 7

State Emporiums

Baba Kharak Singh Marg

Barakhamba Road

To Main Post Office

Hanuman Road

Radial Road 8

Palika Bazaar

Clothing Market

Connaught Lane

Sansad Marg (Parliament Street)

Kasturba Gandhi Marg

Jantar Mantar

Janpath

Janpath Lane

Tolstoy Marg

To Chanakyapuri (Embassy District)

To Hotel Janpath, Hotel Kanishka, J & K Tourist Office & ITDC Ashok Yatri Niwas

CONNAUGHT PLACE (DELHI)

PLACES TO STAY
6 Hotel Palace Heights
31 Sunny Guest House
32 Ringo Guest House; Don't Pass Me By Café; Don't Pass Me By Travels
51 YMCA Tourist Hotel; Y Tours & Travels
52 YWCA International Guest House; VINstring Holidays

PLACES TO EAT
8 Pizza Express
9 Wenger's
12 Kovil Pizza Hut
24 El Arab Restaurants; The Cellar
26 Kwality Restaurant; People Tree
28 Wimpy
49 Sona Rupa Restaurant; Royal Nepal Airlines Corporation (RNAC)

OTHER
1 Railway Booking Office
2 ANZ Grindlays Bank
3 Cox & Kings
4 Plaza Cinema
5 Bookworm
10 Gulf Air
11 American Express; Gulf Air; Singapore Airlines; Jet Airways
13 ANZ Grindlays Bank
14 Post Office
15 Malaysian Airlines; Royal Jordanian
16 Prepaid Auto-Rickshaw Kiosk
17 Sita World Travels
18 Aeroflot
20 EATS Airport Bus
21 Indian Airlines
22 Calculus Cyber Centre
23 Regal Cinema
27 Citibank; Air India
29 Hongkong & Shanghai Bank
30 Air France
33 Standard Chartered Bank; Allahabad Bank
34 British Airways; Swissair
35 Government of India Tourist Office
37 American Centre
38 Pakistan International Airways (PIA)
39 Emirates; Wheels Rent-a-Car
40 Kuwait Airways; Saudia
42 KLM; Uzbekistan Airways
43 British Council
44 Credit Lyonnaise
45 Jagson Airlines
47 Deutsche Bank; Cathay Pacific Airlines
48 Lufthansa Airlines
50 Map Sales Office
53 Thomas Cook
54 Central Cottage Industries Emporium
55 Chandralok Building (Haryana, Himachal Pradesh & Uttar Pradesh Tourist Offices; Delta Airlines Druk Air; Japan Airlines; Lufthansa Airlines)

Film & Photography

There are dozens of places to buy and process film in Connaught Circus. Mahatta & Co (☎ 332 9769), 59 M-Block, Connaught Place is India's sole Canon agent and the best place to come for repairs. The other main centre for camera repair is Chandni Chowk in Old Delhi.

Medical Services

The East West Medical Centre (☎ 462 3738, 469 9229), near Delhi Golf Course at 38 Golf Links Rd has been recommended by many travellers and expats. Charges are high by Indian standards, but worth it for the good treatment.

There is a convenient 24 hour pharmacy at Super Bazaar in Connaught Place. To call an ambulance dial ☎ 102, but don't hold your breath.

Motorcycle Shops

If you are in the market for a new or second hand Enfield motorcycle try Inder Motors

(☎ 572 8579, fax 578 1052), 1744/55 Hari Singh Nalwa St or Madaan Motors (☎ 573 5801, fax 723 5684), 1767/53 Naiwala St, both in Karol Bagh. Madaan Motors also stocks old Nortons and Matchless bikes. The Karol Bagh district consists of dozens of motorbike-related industries.

THINGS TO SEE

The major highlights are the huge Mughal buildings of the **Jama Masjid** (Friday Mosque) and **Red Fort** in Old Delhi and the colonial architecture of the Rajpath and parliament buildings in New Delhi. Visitors to the Jama Masjid should remove their shoes at the door and may have to borrow a robe if arms or legs are not adequately covered. The Red Fort has a sound and light show every evening. English shows are at 7.30 pm (Nov-Jan), 8.30 pm (Sept-Oct and Feb-Apr), and 9 pm (May-Aug). Tickets cost Rs 20.

Less-visited sights include the **Nizam-ud-din Tomb** in south Delhi and the National Museum. If you've been to Ladakh, Spiti or

MacLeod Ganj you might be interested in visiting **Tibet House** (☎ 461 1515), Lodi Rd in southern New Delhi. The museum is open Monday to Saturday from 10 am to 1 pm, and 2 to 5 pm. Admission is Rs 1. See Lonely Planet's *Delhi* guide for more details.

PLACES TO STAY
Paharganj
Most backpackers stay in an area known as Main Bazaar, Paharganj, which is a side road leading off from New Delhi train station.

It's best to ask around a few hotels when you get there but a few popular ones include the *Hotel Vivek* (☎ 351 2900, 1534-50 Main Bazaar), *Hotel Payal* (☎ 352 0867, 1182 Main Bazaar), *Anoop Hotel* (☎ 352 9366, 1566 Main Bazaar) and *Hare Krishna Guest House* (☎ 753 3017, 1572 Main Bazaar). Rooms cost anything from Rs 150 or Rs 300 with bath.

Hotel Namaskar (☎ 752 1234, 917 Chandiwalan) is a friendly place where singles/doubles cost Rs 150/200. It's also a reliable travel agency.

Major's Den (☎ 752 9599, 2314 Laksmi Narayan St), is a clean and well-run place with spacious rooms for Rs 150 and Rs 350.

Hotel Kelson (☎ 752 2646, Rajguru Rd) and *Roxy*, next door, both have small but clean rooms with hot water bath for Rs 250, or Rs 400 with air-con and Star TV, plus free tea and coffee.

Mid-range places include the *Hotel Gold Regency* (☎ 354 0101, fax 354 0202, 4350 Main Bazaar), with rooms for Rs 700 and Rs 900 and *Metropolis* (☎ 352 5492, fax 752 5600, 1634 Main Bazaar), with small air-con rooms from Rs 660 to Rs 1100.

Connaught Place
The other main accommodation centre is Connaught Place, a more civilised but pricier place to stay. A popular place is *Hotel Palace Heights* (☎ 332 1419, D-block, Connaught Place), with average singles/doubles for Rs 275/375, with air cooler and common bath or Rs 690 for air-con doubles. The shabbier *Ringo Guesthouse* (☎ 331 0605, 17 Scindia House, Connaught Lane) and *Sunny Guesthouse* (☎ 331 2909, 152 Scindia House, Connaught Lane) guesthouses cost 125/250 or Rs 350 to 400 with bath.

Mid-range places include the *YMCA Tourist Hotel* (☎ 336 1915, fax 374 6032, Jai Singh Rd) with singles/doubles for Rs 500/570 or Rs 950/1400 with air-con and bath, and the *YWCA International Guest House* (☎ 336 1517, fax 334 1763, 10 Sansad Marg), with rooms for Rs 550/850 (plus 10% service charge and 10% luxury tax on rooms over Rs 500). Both are popular and are worth booking in advance. The *ITDC Ashok Yatri Niwas* (☎ 332 4511) is just a 10 minute walk from Connaught Place on Ashoka Rd at the intersection with Janpath. It's a huge tower block. Rooms and service vary wildly and cost Rs 550/700/800 single/double/triple (plus 10% luxury tax).

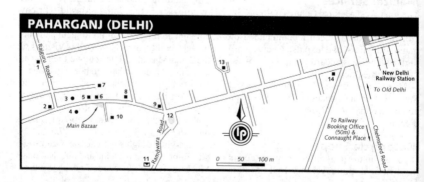

PAHARGANJ (DELHI)

PLACES TO EAT

Most hotels in Paharganj have good rooftop restaurants. Some of the best include the Anoop, Vivek and Hare Rama. The best place to eat in Paharganj is *Metropolis* restaurant. It's pricier than the rest, but the food is top notch. You can get great lassis and hot milk from a stand nearby.

Restaurants in Connaught Place tend to be mid-range. *Sona Rupa* on Janpath has good value Indian vegetarian food. Over near the Regal Cinema is the excellent *Kwality* and nearby *El Arab*, a Moroccan restaurant which has a daily buffet for Rs 150. Also a bit of fun is *Rodeo's (12 A-block, Connaught Place)* serving Mexican and Italian food. The staff dress as cowboys, and the menus flip out from cardboard guns. Open until late.

SHOPPING

Delhi is an excellent place to buy cheap books on India and Tibet as well as cheap western and Indian music. Most bookshops are in Connaught Place and there are ad hoc stalls all around the circle. Bookworm *(Radial Road, B-Block)* is one of the best. There are several good music shops in the underground Palika Plaza. Paharganj has a couple of second hand bookstalls and street stalls selling cheap copies of Time and Newsweek.

PAHARGANJ (DELHI)

1 Hotel Kelson
2 Metropolis Tourist Home; Metropolis Restaurant
3 E-Mail Centre
4 Book Exchange; Bicycle Hire
5 Hotel Vishal; Lords Café; Hare Krishna Guest House
6 Anoop Hotel
7 Major's Den
8 Hotel Vivek
9 Hotel Payal
10 Hare Rama Guest House; Aa Bee Travels
11 Paharganj Post Office
12 Vegetable Market
13 Hotel Namaskar; Smyle Inn
14 Hotel Gold Regency

The various State Emporiums are the best place for souvenirs. The Central Cottage Industries Emporium on Janpath has a fixed price array of goods from all over India. Most other state emporiums, including Himachal Pradesh are on Baba Kharak Singh Marg. Kashmiri and Tibetan souvenirs are found in the stalls along Janpath. Haggling is the key here. Paharganj has mostly clothes, oils and perfumes.

GETTING THERE & AWAY
Air

Delhi is the main international and domestic gateway to the Himalaya. For details of domestic flights see the Flights from Delhi boxed text. See also To/From the Airport later in this section.

Arrival Many international flights to Delhi arrive and depart in the small hours of the morning. Take special care if this is your first foray into India and you arrive exhausted and jet-lagged. It is possible to stay put in the airport until dawn, but most people get a prepaid taxi into town. You can also reserve a room in advance and informing the hotel of your arrival time, or by calling a hotel yourself from the airport. Alternatives are to ask the 24 hour Government of India tourist office or the hotel reservation counter in the airport arrivals hall to book a room for you. Be particularly aware of scams at this time of night.

If you have a direct connection to the Himalaya you will need to transfer to the domestic terminal (Terminal I), 7km away. Delhi Transport Corporation buses connect the international and domestic terminals (Rs 10) and there is also a free IAAI bus between the two terminals, although service can be patchy. The bus stop is just outside the international terminal to the left. EATS (see To/From the Airport) will also take you between terminals on their roundabout route.

Departure If you're leaving Delhi in the early hours of the morning, book a taxi the afternoon before. They'll be hard to find in

Flights from Delhi

destination	airline	frequency	foreigner's price US$
Bagdogra (for Shiliguri)	Jetair	daily	185
Bagdogra (via Gauhati)	Indian Airlines	2 weekly	185
Dibrugarh (via Gauhati)	Sahara	4 weekly	254
Gauhati	Indian Airlines	5 weekly	210
	Sahara	4 weekly	210
Jammu	Indian Airlines	daily	105
	Jetair	2 daily	108
Kolkata (Calcutta)	Indian Airlines	2 daily	180
	Jetair	2 daily	188
	Alliance	4 weekly	180
Kullu	Jagson	3 weekly	150
Leh	Indian Airlines	weekly	105
	Alliance Air	3 weekly	105
Shimla	Jagson	3 weekly	105
Srinagar	Indian Airlines	2 weekly	115
	Jetair	2 daily	121

the night. When leaving Delhi with Air India (domestic or international flights) all baggage must be X-rayed and sealed, so do this at the machine just inside the departure hall before you queue to check in. For international flights the departure tax (Rs 500) must be paid at the State Bank of India counter in the departures hall, also before check-in, though you should check that the tax hasn't already been figured into the cost of your ticket, as it is in most cases.

There are retiring rooms at both the domestic (☎ 329-5126) and international (☎ 545-2011) terminals, which you can use if you have a confirmed departure within 24 hours, but you'll need to ring in advance, as these are often full.

Airline Offices
Domestic Airlines The following airlines also have offices at the domestic terminal and this can be a good place to make a booking (you might even be able to get a same day connection):

Archana Airways
 (☎ 684 2001, airport ☎ 566 5519)
 41-A Friends' Colony East, Mathura Rd
Indian Airlines
 (☎ 331 0517, airport ☎ 141, 462 0566)
 Malhotra Bldg, F Block, Connaught Circus,
 Web site www.nic.in/indian-airlines
Jagson Airlines
 (☎ 372 1593, airport ☎ 566 5545)
 12-E Vandana Bldg, 11 Tolstoy Marg
Jet Airways
 (☎ 685 3700) Jetair House, 13 Community
 Centre, Yusuf Serai

International Airlines International airlines are:

Aeroflot
 (☎ 331 2843) BMC House, 1st Floor,
 1 N-block Connaught Place
Air France
 (☎ 331 2853) 7 Atma Ram Mansion,
 Connaught Circus
Air India
 (☎ 331 1225) Jeevan Bharati Bldg, 124
 Connaught Circus, Web site
 www.airindia.com

British Airways
(☎ 332 7428) DLF Bldg, Sansad Marg (Parliament St)
Cathay Pacific
(☎ 332 1286) 809/810 Ashoka Estate Bldg, Barakhamba Rd
Emirates
(☎ 332 4665) Kanchenjunga Bldg, 18 Barakhamba Rd
Gulf Air
(☎ 332 7814) 12 G-block, Connaught Circus
KLM – Royal Dutch Airlines
(☎ 372 1141) Prakesh Deep Bldg, 7 Tolstoy Marg
Kuwait Airways
(☎ 331 4221) DCM Bldg, 16 Barakhamba Rd
Lufthansa
(☎ 332 3310) 56 Janpath
Malaysian Airlines
(☎ 332 4308) 55 G-block, Connaught Place
Pakistan International Airlines (PIA)
(☎ 331 3161) Kailash Bldg, 26 Kasturba Gandhi Marg
Qantas
(☎ 332 9372) Mohan Dev Bldg, 13 Tolstoy Marg
Royal Nepal Airlines Corporation
(☎ 332 1164) 44 Janpath

Thai International Airways (THAI)
Park Royal Hotel, American Plaza, Nehru Place
Uzbekistan Airways
(☎ 335 8687) Prakash Deep Bldg, 7 Tolstoy Marg

Bus

Delhi's large Interstate Bus Terminal (ISBT) is at Kashmir Gate, north of the Old Delhi train station. Facilities here include 24 hour left-luggage (Rs 10 per day), a State Bank of India branch, post office and a couple of restaurants. There is a general inquiries office at the entrance to the building on the first floor. State transport offices operating here include:

Delhi Transport Corporation (DTC)
(☎ 335 4518), counter 34
Haryana Roadways
(☎ 296 1262), counter 35
Himachal Roadways Transport Corporation (HRTC)
(☎ 296 6725), counter 40
Jammu & Kashmir Roadways
(☎ 332 4422, ext 2243)

Bus Services from Delhi to the Western Hills Regions

company	destination	duration	ordinary/semideluxe/ superdeluxe (Rs)
HRTC	Shimla (ISBT)	10 hrs	150/222/265
	Dharamsala (ISBT)	12 hrs	200/249/357
	Manali (ISBT)	16 hrs	242/301/407
	Kullu (ISBT)	14 hrs	-/272/382
UP Roadways, DTC	Dehra Dun (ISBT)	7 hrs	85/105/150/250 (AC)
	Mussoorie (ISBT)	8 hrs	-/127/-
	Haridwar (ISBT)	8 hrs	68/84/115
	Rishikesh (ISBT)	6 hrs	78/96/-
HPTDC	Manali (ISBT)	15 hrs	450
	Leh (ISBT)	3 days	1000
	Shimla (ISBT)	9 hrs	290
	Nainital (AV)	9 hrs	137
	Ranikhet (AV)	12 hrs	165
	Almora (AV)	12 hrs	150
	Banbassa (AV)	12 hrs	125
	Ramnagar (AV)	7 hrs	90

ISBT = Buses from Delhi ISBT   AV = Anand Vihar Bus Station   AC = Air-conditioned

Punjab Roadways
(☎ 296 7842), counter 37
Uttar Pradesh Roadways
(☎ 296 8709), central block

The Anand Vihar bus station, 15km north, handles all public services to Kumaon. Delhi Transport Corporation (DTC) buses shuttle run the two stations from lanes no 45 and 46.

Private companies in Paharganj also offer deluxe buses to the hills. Approximate fares are Manali (Rs 250), Shimla (Rs 300), McLeod Ganj (400), Mussorie (300), Dehra Dun Rs (350), Haridwar/Rishikesh (Rs 175 to 250), Nainital (Rs 180 to Rs 250), Kathmandu (Rs 650, 32-36 hrs).

Potala Tours (☎ 294 6262, email potala@giasd01.vsnl.net.in), 1011 Antriksh Bhawan, 22 Kasturba Marg (not far from Connaught Place) runs a good overnight service to McLeod Ganj (Rs 350) at 6 pm. The only snag is that the bus departs from their office at Majnuka Tilla, a ten minute taxi ride north of the ISBT. See the box for details of services to the hills. HPTDC's services are particularly popular; bookings should be made at their office (see Tourist Offices earlier).

Train

Delhi is an excellent place to make rail reservations. The best place to go is the foreign tourist booking office upstairs in New Delhi train station. Don't believe the touts who say it has closed. Opening hours are Monday to Saturday 7.30 am to 5 pm and it can get very busy. You can pay in foreign currency (cash, travellers cheques or credit cards) at the desk to the left and in rupees (with an encashment certificate) on the right. Make sure you fill out a reservations slip.

Major Trains from Delhi

destination	train no & name	departs	arrives	fare (sleeper/1st) (Rs)
Dehra Dun	4041 *Mussoorie Exp*	10.05 pm OD	8.00 am	113/377
	2017 *Shatabdi Exp*	7.10 am ND	12.35 pm	465/910[2]
Gauhati	5622 *North East Exp*	7.00 am ND	6.45 pm	369/1895
(for Arunachal)	2424 *Rajdhani Exp*	5.00 pm ND	7.30 pm	1350/2760/4920[3]
Haridwar	2017 *Shatabdi Exp*	7.10 am ND	11.21 am	465/910[2]
	4041 *Mussoorie Exp*	10.05 pm OD	6.00 am	113/377
Howrah	2302/2306 *Rajdhani Exp*	5.00 pm ND	10.45 am	1345/2190/3825[3]
	2382/2304 *Poorva Exp*	4.25 pm ND	4.15 pm	302/1102
Jammu	4645 *Shalimar Exp*	4.10 pm ND	6.30 am	174/604
Kathgodam (for Nainital)	5013 *Ranikhet Exp*	11.00 pm OD	6.10 am	105/361
New Jalpaiguri	5622 *North East Exp*	7.00 am ND	9.40 am	317/1615
	2424 *Rajdhani Exp*	5.00 pm ND	2.00 pm	1470/2365/4130[3]
Pathankot	4033 *Jammu Mail*	9.10 pm OD	7.25 am	149/520
	1077 *Jhelum Exp*	9.20 pm ND	8.45 am	149/520
Ramnagar (for Corbett)	5013A *Corbett Park Link Exp*	11.00 pm OD	4.30 am	90/489
Shimla	4095 *Himalayan Queen*[1]	6.00 am ND	11.25 am	120/410

OD = Old Delhi, ND = New Delhi
[1] Change at Kalka for narrow gauge to Shimla (departing noon, 5½ hrs)
[2] Fares for *Shatabdi Express* trains are AC Chair/AC Executive Class
[3] Fares for *Rajdhani Express* trains are AC Three Tier/AC Two Tier/AC First Class

The main ticket office is on Chelmsford Rd between New Delhi train station and Connaught Place. It is well organised, but incredibly busy. Take a numbered ticket from the counter as you enter the building, and then wait at the allotted window. Even with 50 computerised terminals, it can take up to an hour to get served. The office is open 7.45 am to 9 pm Monday to Saturday, and until 1.50 pm on Sunday.

Remember that there are two main train stations in Delhi – Delhi train station in Old Delhi, and New Delhi train station at Paharganj. If you're departing from the Old Delhi train station you should allow 30 minutes to an hour to wind your way through the traffic snarls of Old Delhi. Between the Old Delhi and New Delhi train stations you can take the No 6 bus for just Rs 1, or catch an auto-rickshaw, which will cost about Rs 40.

Many travellers opt for the buses when travelling to Himachal Pradesh, but for Dalhousie or Dharamsala (for McLeod Ganj), it's possible to travel overnight by train to Pathankot, in the Punjab, from where it is only 3½ hours by bus to either of these hill stations. It's a longer trip than on the bus, but if you find you simply can't sleep on the buses, it can offer a good alternative.

Uttarakhand's train terminals are Dehra Dun and Haridwar. Rishikesh is only 24km north of Haridwar, and the hill station of Mussoorie lies only 34km north of Dehra Dun. There are numerous convenient bus services connecting these towns throughout the day. For the Kumaon district of Uttarakhand, the closest train stations are at Kathgodam, 35km south of Nainital, and Ramnagar, for Corbett Tiger Reserve.

See the Major Trains from Delhi boxed text on the opposite page.

Car Hire

There are several car hire companies in Delhi, though it's a better idea to rent a taxi (see following). An average of six people are killed in traffic accidents in Delhi every day. Car rental companies include:

Hertz
  (☎ 619 7188) Ansal Chambers, 8687 Bhikaji Cama Place
Wheels Rent-a-Car
  (☎ 331 8695,
  email wheels.racdel@elnet.ems.vsnl.net.in)
  18 Barakhamba Rd

Taxis

Taxis can be hired in Delhi for multi-day trips into the Himalaya. There are several taxi companies along Janpath. Ambassadors cost around Rs 1350 a day for 250km, with driver. After this you add on Rs 4.75/km. You will also have to pay a passenger tax for the taxi to cross state borders (around Rs 300 to Rs 400).

GETTING AROUND

Auto-rickshaws are the most popular way to get around Delhi, though you will have to haggle for a reasonable price. Fares are around Rs 15 from Paharganj to Connaught Place and Rs 40 from Paharganj to Old Delhi Train station. There are pre-paid (fixed price) auto-rickshaw stands in Connaught Place and the Interstate bus terminal bus stand. Fares from the latter are Rs 25 to Paharganj, Rs 32 to Connaught Circus and Rs 12 to Old Delhi railway station. Bus 753 goes from ISBT bus stand to Old Delhi railway station.

To/From the Airport

The international terminal (Terminal II) is 20km from the centre and EATS (Ex-Servicemen's Air Link Transport Service; ☎ 331-6530) has a regular bus service between both the international and domestic terminals and Connaught Place. The fare is Rs 30 plus Rs 5 per large piece of luggage, and they will drop you off or pick you up at most of the major hotels en route if you ask. There is also an EATS city-to-airport service which departs regularly from opposite Palika Bazaar on Radial Rd 8 (Janpath) in Connaught between 4 am and 11.30 pm.

A regular Delhi Transport Corporation bus service runs from the airport to the New Delhi train station and the Interstate bus terminal. The fare is Rs 30 plus Rs 5 per large piece of luggage, and they will drop you off at most of the major hotels en route and at the entrance to New Delhi train station for Paharganj. At New Delhi train station it uses the Ajmer Gate side. There is also a public bus service to the airport (No 780) from the Super Bazaar at Connaught Place, but it can get very crowded.

Just outside the international terminal is a prepaid taxi booth. Don't give the driver your chit (voucher) until you have arrived at your destination. A prepaid taxi from the domestic terminal to Connaught Place costs Rs 135; fares are Rs 170 to Paharganj, plus Rs 5 per bag. From Connaught Place or Paharganj to the airport most hotels will book a taxi for Rs 200; if you flag one down it should cost a little less. Auto-rickshaws will run out to the airport too, but you'll be covered in exhaust fumes.

Kolkata (Calcutta)

☎ 033 • pop 12 million

Densely populated and frequently polluted, Kolkata can be an ugly and desperate place. Yet it's also one of the country's more fascinating centres and has long been acknowledged as the cultural capital.

At the time of research, this capital of British India until the beginning of the 20th century, was changing its name to Kolkata. The city is of course closely associated with the work of Mother Teresa's Calcutta mission.

ORIENTATION

Kolkata sprawls north-south along the eastern bank of the Hooghly River. If you arrive from anywhere west of Kolkata by rail, you'll come into the immense Howrah Station and have to cross the Howrah Bridge into Kolkata proper.

For visitors, the more relevant parts of Kolkata are south of the bridge in the areas around BBD Bagh and Chowringhee. BBD Bagh, formerly Dalhousie Square, is the hub of the central business district (CBD). Here you will find the main post office, the international telephone office, the Bangla (West

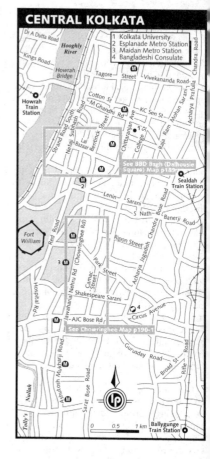

CENTRAL KOLKATA

1 Kolkata University
2 Esplanade Metro Station
3 Maidan Metro Station
4 Bangladeshi Consulate

See BBD Bagh (Dalhousie Square) Map p189

See Chowringhee Map p190-1

0   0.5   1 km

Bengal) tourist office, the American Express office and various train booking offices.

South of BBD Bagh is the open expanse of the Maidan along the river, and east from that is the area known as Chowringhee. Sudder St runs off Chowringhee Rd and is the core of the Kolkata travellers' scene. Most of the popular cheap hotels are along Sudder St so it is well known to any taxi or rickshaw-wallah. Most of the budget and midrange hotels are concentrated in this area, together with many of the banks, airline offices, restaurants, travel agencies and the Indian Museum. At the southern end of Chowringhee you'll find the Government of India tourist office and the British Council (and library) on Shakespeare Sarani and, nearby, the Victoria Memorial.

Getting around Kolkata is slightly confused by the recent renaming of city streets. Most taxi-wallahs still use the old names, however.

INFORMATION
Tourist Offices
The helpful Government of India tourist office (☎ 282 5813, fax 282 3521) is at 4 Shakespeare Sarani on Chowringhee.

The Bangla tourist office (☎ 248 8271) is at 3/2 BBD Bagh – the opposite side to the post office. It is open Monday to Friday, 10.30 am to 5.30 pm, but don't expect to find many brochures or much useful infor-

mation. Both the state and national tourist offices have counters at the airport (☎ 511 8299), and Bangla has an office at Howrah Station (☎ 660 2518) open daily, 7 am to 1 pm. Other state tourist offices include:

Arunachal Pradesh
   (☎ 228 6500) 4B Chowringhee Place
Assam
   (☎ 298 3313) 8 Russel St
Himachal Pradesh
   (☎ 271792) 2H, 2nd floor, Electronic Centre, 1-1A, BAC St
Sikkim
   (☎ 226 8983/6717) 5/2 Russel St
Uttar Pradesh
   (☎ 220 7855) 12A Netaji Subash Rd

Money
American Express (☎ 282 0623, fax 248 8896) is at 21 Old Court House St. The Thomas Cook office (☎ 247 4560, fax 247 5854) is in the Chitrakoot Building, 230 AJC Bose Rd.

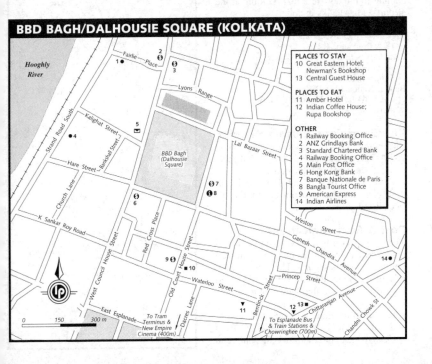

BBD BAGH/DALHOUSIE SQUARE (KOLKATA)

PLACES TO STAY
10 Great Eastern Hotel; Newman's Bookshop
13 Central Guest House

PLACES TO EAT
11 Amber Hotel
12 Indian Coffee House; Rupa Bookshop

OTHER
1   Railway Booking Office
2   ANZ Grindlays Bank
3   Standard Chartered Bank
4   Railway Booking Office
5   Main Post Office
6   Hong Kong Bank
7   Banque Nationale de Paris
8   Bangla Tourist Office
9   American Express
14 Indian Airlines

Hooghly River

Fairlie Place
Lyons Range
Kalighat Street
Strand Road South
Baneshai Street
Hare Street
Church Lane
K Sankar Roy Road
Red Cross Place
West Council House Street
East Esplanade
Lal Bazaar Street
BBD Bagh (Dalhousie Square)
Weston Street
Ganesh Chandra Avenue
Old Court House Street
Waterloo Street
Dacres Lane
Bentinck Street
Princep Street
Chittaranjan Avenue
Chandni Chowk St

To Tram Terminus & New Empire Cinema (400m)
To Esplanade Bus & Train Stations & Chowringhee (700m)

0   150   300 m

On Chowringhee Rd there are branches of Citibank, the State Bank of India, Standard Chartered and ANZ Grindlays (near Park St metro station). ANZ Grindlays has another branch on Shakespeare Sarani. All these banks have ATMs with 24 hour access, in which you can use credit, Giro and Cirrus cards. ANZ Grindlays and Standard Chartered also have branches with ATMs near the main post office, as does the Hong Kong Bank on the corner of Hare and West Council House Sts, and the Reserve Bank of India, which changes torn notes.

Near the Bangla tourist office, in the Stephen Building, is RN Dutt, a licensed private moneychanger who deals in just about any currency. On Sudder St there are a few licensed moneychangers. Travellers' Express Club, at 20 Mirza Ghalib St, is one of the few places you can change money on a Sunday.

The State Bank of India has a 24 hour counter in the new terminal building at the airport. Other banks include:

Algemeene Bank Nederlands
    18-A Brabourne Rd
Bank of America
    (☎ 242 2829)
    8 India Exchange Place
Banque Nationale de Paris
    4-A BBD Bagh East, next to the Bangla
    tourist office.

Visa Extensions & other Permits

The Foreigners' Registration Office is at 237 Acharya J C Bose Rd (☎ 247 0549) and is the place for visa extensions.

Permits for Sikkim and Arunachal Pradesh can be obtained from the tourist offices listed above.

Post & Communications

The main post office is on BBD Bagh and has an efficient poste restante (to claim mail you need your passport). The New Market post office is far more conveniently located if you're staying in the Sudder St area. The Park St post office is reliable for posting parcels than the main post office.

There are lots of Public Call Offices (PCOs) to make international calls and send

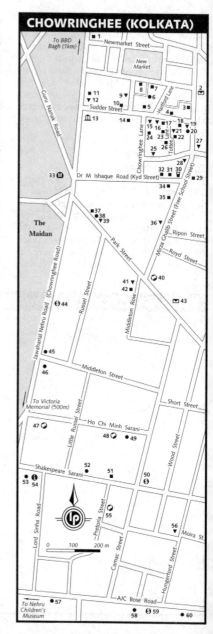

faxes. American citizens can make collect calls to the USA from the US Consulate.

Email & Internet Facilities Many of the old PCOs in and around Sudder St now have computer terminals connected to the Internet and more are springing up around the city, almost on a daily basis. The cost of using the Internet is generally Rs 3 per minute and Rs 5 to Rs 10 per A4 printout; some centres have block-time charges.

The British Council Library (☎ 282 5944), 5 Shakespeare Sarani, charges nonmembers Rs 100 for 30 minutes or Rs 50 for members (including 5 free pages of print-out). Another block-time place is the Cyber Empire Internet Cafe, in the New Empire Cinema near New Market; charges are Rs 25 for 15 min, Rs 2 per page for printout.

Travel Agencies

Travellers' Express Club at 20 Mirza Ghalib St (Free School St) offers competitive prices on airline tickets. Rail tickets can be purchased from several little outlets around Sudder St. The Bengal Travel Service, 4 Sudder St, charges Rs 40 commission on tickets, but they can usually get seats at short notice and saves a lot of time.

Film & Photography

Behind the YMCA at 24 Chowringhee Rd, Latif's is recommended for camera repairs. Camera Craft at 24 Park St, on the 1st floor, is also good. Slide film can be bought from the processing shop/PCO, Electro Photo Lab, next to Khalsa Restaurant off Sudder St.

Medical Services

Dr Paes at Vital Medical Services (☎ 282 5664, fax 282 5656), 6 Ho Chi Minh Sarani, is open 9.30 to 11 am. Wockhardt Medical Centre (☎ 475 4320/4096), 2/7 Sarat Bose (Lansdowne) Rd, is open 11.30 am to 2 pm. Alternatively, medical queries should be directed to any of the large hospitals.

CHOWRINGHEE (KOLKATA)

PLACES TO STAY	35 Classic Hotel	13 Indian Museum
1 Oberoi Grand Hotel	37 Park Hotel; Trinca's	20 English Wine Shop
3 Centrepoint Guest House;	Restaurant	30 Off cum On Rambo Bar
Hotel Diplomat; Hotel	42 YWCA	33 Park St Metro Station
Astoria; Travellers' Express	51 Astor Hotel	38 Cambridge Book &
Club		Stationary Company
4 Hotel Plaza; Astoria	**PLACES TO EAT**	40 French Consulate
5 Fairlawn Hotel	9 Khalsa Restaurant	43 Park St Post Office
7 Hotel Lindsay; Gujral Lodge;	12 Zaranj Restaurant	44 State Bank of India
Jharokha Restaurant	15 Blue Sky Cafe; Curd Corner	45 British Airways; RNAC;
8 CKT Inn	16 Zurich's	Air France; Citibank
10 Lytton Hotel; Sun Set Bar	19 Khwaja	46 Cathay Pacific; KLM
11 YMCA	21 JoJo's Restaurant	47 British High Commission
14 Salvation Army Guest	25 Abdul Khalique Hotel	48 US Consulate
House	27 Princess Restaurant & Bar	49 Vital Medical Services
17 Hotel Maria; Titrupati's	28 Hong Kong Restaurant	50 ANZ Grindlays Bank
18 Shilton Hotel	36 Mocambo's; Armenian	52 British Council & Library
22 Modern Lodge	College (Thackery's	53 Sahara Indian Airlines
23 Hotel Paragon;	Birthplace)	54 Government of India
Hotel Galaxy	39 Kwality Restaurant	Tourist Office
24 Hotel Palace; Cybercafe	41 Peter Cat	55 Japanese Consulate
26 Timestar Hotel	56 Hare Krishna Bakery;	57 Foreigners' Registration
29 Sonali Guest House	ISKCON	Office
31 Neelam Hotel		58 Gulf Air
32 Hotel Crystal; PCO	**OTHER**	59 Thomas Cook
(24 Hour Telephone)	2 New Market Post Office	60 Thai Airways
34 East End Hotel	6 Treasure Island Market	International

THINGS TO SEE

Amongst the squalor and confusion, Kolkata has places of sheer magic: flower sellers beside the ethereal Hooghly River, the majestic sweep of the Maidan and the grand beauty of the Victoria Memorial.

Conveniently situated on the corner of Sudder St and Chowringhee Rd, the **Indian Museum** (Rs 5) is a beautiful colonial building which displays India's finest collection of treasures; open daily except Monday 10 am to 5 pm.

ORGANISED TOURS

The Government of India tourist office (☎ 282 5813) at 4 Shakespeare Sarani has a full-day tour for Rs 100, departing daily (except Monday) at 8 am from their office. It covers Belur Math, Dakshineswar Temple, the Jain temple, Victoria Memorial, Indian Museum, Nehru Children's Museum and the zoo.

The Bangla tourist office has a similar tour for Rs 75 or a second tour that crams in even more for Rs 100.

There are private walking tours of Dalhousie Square (BBD Bagh) and North Kolkata (including Tagore's House and humble, off the tourist circuit areas). These fascinating and informative tours, conducted by architect and conservationist, Manish Chakraborti, leave from the Great Eastern Hotel, and cover the historic buildings, heritage sites and general history of the areas. Contact Footsteps (☎ 337 5757), AA171A Salt Lake, Kolkata 700 064.

PLACES TO STAY

Budget travellers' accommodation is centred on Sudder St. Kolkata also has a collection of Ys (singles/doubles around Rs 300/500) but they're often full. Places listed in this section start at budget, with midrange towards the end. Aim to arrive in Kolkata before noon or you may have great difficulty in finding a cheap bed.

Salvation Army Guest House (☎ 245 0599, 2 Sudder St) is popular with volunteers. Dorm beds are Rs 60 and private doubles are Rs 100 up to Rs 700.

Hotel Maria (☎ 245 0860), farther down Sudder St, is equally popular, with dorm beds for Rs 70. There are also singles/doubles for Rs 150/180, or Rs 200/250 with bath. It has a nice rooftop meeting area, its own PCO and a strict no drugs, no alcohol policy.

Centrepoint Guest House (☎ 244 8184, 20 Mirza Ghalib St) is a bustling, popular place. Top floor, clean dorm beds are Rs 70. Doubles are Rs 200 or Rs 450 with air-con, and there's a lounge with TV.

Yatri Nivas (☎ 660 1742), in the new building next door to Howrah Station, has dorm beds for Rs 85 and doubles with bath for Rs 300, or Rs 450 with air-con. You can only stay here with a train ticket for 200km or more, and then only for three nights. There are also *Retiring Rooms* at Howrah and Sealdah stations, Rs 130 for doubles with bath. For transit passengers, there are also rooms at *Kolkata Airport*. Check at the reservations desk at the terminal.

Central Guest House (☎ 274876, 18 Prafulla Sarkar St) is good value with clean rooms with bath for Rs 190/250.

There's a bunch of mid-range places within easy walking distance of BBD Bagh. *Hotel Crystal* (☎ 226 6400, fax 246 5019, 11 Dr M Ishaque Rd (Kyd Street)), is good-value and close to the action, with a PCO in the courtyard. Rooms with TV and phone cost Rs 300/425, or Rs 750 with air-con. *CKT Inn* (☎ 244 0047, 12A Lindsay St), is a small friendly place with rooms for Rs 700/1100, with air-con TVs and bath. *Hotel Astoria* (☎ 2454 9679, fax 244 8589, 6/2 Sudder St), is all air-con. Huge rooms with bath, TV and phone are Rs 770/895.

Fairlawn Hotel (☎ 245 1510, fax 244 1835, 13A Sudder St), is a piece of Kolkata where the Raj still lives, albeit in a decidedly eccentric manner. The hotel is crammed with memorabilia and pre-war furnishings. Singles/doubles cost US$40/50 plus tax. The tariff includes three meals (set menu), plus afternoon tea (20% discount Apr-Sept).

PLACES TO EAT

Finding good food at reasonable prices is no problem in the Sudder St area. Places to try include the *Blue Sky Cafe*, just off Sudder St, for good breakfasts and snacks, *Titrupati's,* a great little street stall outside Hotel Maria, and the popular *Zurich's* farther along Sudder St. *Khwaja*, is a little more expensive, but a good place to escape the furore of the street.

Khalsa Restaurant, in the street opposite the Salvation Army Guest House, has been popular with both locals and travellers for many years. *Indian Coffee House*, near Kolkata University, is an institution with young undergraduates.

Hare Krishna Bakery, on the corner of Hungerford and Moira Sts, is the place for good bread and takeaway snacks.

Jharokha is a rooftop restaurant on the 10th floor above Hotel Lindsay. It offers sweeping views over Kolkata and is a great place to take photos. The meals, at an average of Rs 50, are very generous.

With the exception of hotel restaurants, most of the mid-range and upmarket restaurants are on or around Park St. *Kwality Restaurant* (17 Park St) has a small menu with main dishes around Rs 65.

Amber Hotel (☎ 248 6520, 11 Waterloo St) is often voted by residents of Kolkata as the best place to eat in the city. Prices are very reasonable. Ring to reserve a table.

Astor Hotel has a pleasant garden that's good for a relaxing drink (beers are Rs 60) or a barbecue (daily between 6 and 11 pm). On Saturday evenings there's live music.

ENTERTAINMENT

Kolkata is famous for its culture. Pick up *Calcutta This Fortnight* from tourist offices.

In the Sudder St area, the *Sun Set Bar* at the Lytton Hotel is a good place for a drink. Similar is the open-air bar in the forecourt of the *Fairlawn Hotel*.

Paris Bar & Restaurant (SN Banerji Rd), is an interesting combination of Indian pub and nightclub. Open from noon to 11pm, they have singers, live bands and sell all the really mind-altering beers like Thunderbolt. Thursday is a 'dry' day in Kolkata and some licensed restaurants are closed.

SHOPPING

There are numerous interesting shops along Chowringhee Rd selling everything from carpets to handicrafts. The Central Cottage Industries Emporium at 7 Chowringhee Rd is good. New Market, formerly Hogg Market, is the best place for bargain shopping. The AC Market on Shakespeare Sarani specialises in imported food.

The main bookshop area is along College St, opposite the university. Elsewhere, in the same building as the Indian Coffee House, Rupa has a good range that includes its own publications. Newman's, in the same block as the Great Eastern Hotel, runs one of Kolkata's oldest bookshops.

Others worth trying include The Cambridge Book & Stationery Company at 20D Park St; and Booklands, at the eastern end of Sudder St. Seagull Bookstore & Publishers, just off Chowringhee, opposite Rabindra Sadan metro station, is a treasure trove; they serve tea and biscuits while you browse.

GETTING THERE & AWAY
Air

For details of flights from Kolkata (Calcutta) to the eastern Himalaya see the Flights from Kolkata boxed text on the following page.

Most international airline offices are around Chowringhee:

Aeroflot
   (☎ 282 9831/3765)
   58 Chowringhee Rd
Air France
   (☎ 226 6161) 41 Chowringhee Rd;
   enter from Middleton St
Air India
   (☎ 282 2356) 50 Chowringhee Rd
Bangladesh Biman
   (☎ 229 2844) 30C Chowringhee Rd
British Airways
   (☎ 226 3450/3454)
   41 Chowringhee Rd; enter from Middleton St
Cathay Pacific
   (☎ 240 3312/3211)
   1 Middleton St
Gulf Air
   (☎ 247 7783/5576)
   230A AJC Bose Rd

Flights from Kolkata to the Himalaya

destination	airline	frequency	foreigners' price (US$)
Bagdogra	Indian Airlines	4 weekly	80
	Jetair	3 weekly	80
Delhi	Indian Airlines	2 daily	180
	Jetair	2 daily	188
	Alliance	4 weekly	180
Dibrugarh (for Arunachal)	Indian Airlines	4 weekly	95
Gauhati	Indian Airlines	6 weekly	70
	Jetair	5 weekly	71
Tezpur (for Arunachal)	Alliance	2 weekly	80

Indian Airlines (domestic)
(☎ 262548, 264433)
39 Chittaranjan Ave. Open 24 hours seven days a week; also an office in the Great Eastern Hotel.
Jet Airways (domestic)
(☎ 229 2813/2660)
18 Park Street
Royal Nepal Airlines (RNAC)
(☎ 246 8534) 41 Chowringhee Rd, enter from Middleton St
Sahara India Airlines (domestic)
(☎ 282 9067) 2A Shakespeare Sarani
Thai International Airways (THAI)
(☎ 280 1630/1635)
229 AJC Bose Rd

Kolkata is a good place for competitive air fares to other parts of Asia, Europe and the east coast USA. You'll find the best deals is by word of mouth and frequent checks with agencies and airlines.

Bus

The only buses that travellers use with any regularity are those from Kolkata to Shiliguri and New Jalpaiguri (for Darjeeling). The 'Rocket Service' (2x2 push-back seats) costs Rs 160 and leaves Kolkata at 8 pm, arriving the next morning. It's much rougher than going by train and only a Rs 30 saving.

Buses generally depart from the Esplanade bus stand area at the northern end of the Maidan, but there are a number of private companies with their own stands.

Train

If you've just flown into Kolkata, check the rail reservation desk at the airport, as they have an air-travellers' quota for same-day or next-day travel on the main expresses.

Kolkata has two major train stations. Howrah, on the west bank of the Hooghly River, handles most trains, including services to Delhi and the western Himalaya. Trains to New Jalpaiguri for Darjeeling, Sikkim or the north-east, leave from Sealdah train station on the east side of the Hooghly River. For times and fares for the major trains, see the Major Trains from Kolkata boxed text.

The tourist train booking office is on the 1st floor at 6 Fairlie Place, near BBD Bagh. It's open Monday to Saturday, 9 am to 1 pm and 1.30 to 4 pm, and until 2pm on Sunday. Another booking office nearby, at 14 Strand Rd, sells advance tickets on routes into and out of Delhi, Chennai (Madras) and Mumbai (Bombay). Both these places attract long queues and the staff at Fairlie Place office demand to see exchange certificates if you pay in rupees.

For a small fee (about Rs 40), agents in and around Sudder St can get tickets for you, often at short notice.

GETTING AROUND

Beware of pickpockets on any of Kolkata's public transport.

Major Trains from Kolkata

destination	train no & name	departs	arrives	fare (sleeper/1st) (Rs)
Delhi	2305 *Rajdhani Exp*	1.45 pm H	10.00 am	1375/2290/3975[1]
	2303 *Poorva Exp*	9.15 am H	9.25 pm	302/1102
Dehra Dun/ Haridwar	3009 *Doon Exp*	8.15 pm H	7.25 am	311/1156
Gauhati	3045 *Saraighat Exp*	10.00 pm H	5.00 pm	245/849
	5657 *Kanchenjunga Exp*	6.25 am S	4.00 am	245/849
Kathgodam (for Nainital)	3019 *Kathgodam Exp*	9.45 pm H	4.20 am	
New Jalpaiguri	3143 *Darjeeling Mail*	7.15 pm S	8.15 am	174/604
(for Darjeeling and Sikkim)	5657 *Kanchenjunga Exp*	6.25 am S	6.25 pm	174/604
Pathankot (for Dharamsala)	3073 *Himgiri Exp*	11.00 pm	10.30 am	343/1331

H = Howrah, S = Sealdah
[1] Air-con only; fare includes meals and drinks, fares are for AC three tier, AC Two Tier, AC First Class

Kolkata's bus system is hopelessly crowded. Fares are from Rs 1.50. Take a No S7 or S27 bus between Howrah station and Sudder St; ask for the Indian Museum. There is a secondary private minibus service, which is quite a bit faster and slightly more expensive, with fares starting at Rs 1.75.

There's a public tram service, but the dilapidated trams are like sardine tins in rush hour. Fares start at Rs 1.20. Out of rush hour they are a relatively fast, cheap way to get to areas outside the city centre.

India's first underground train system is still being built in Kolkata, almost totally by hand. It's the current southern sector, from Chandni Chowk to Tollygunge station, and the north sector to the west of BBD Bagh, that are of most use to visitors; there's a station near Sudder St. Tickets are Rs 3 to Rs 7.

As with Delhi's taxis, you will have to negotiate hard to get a fair price before you get in the cab. Few meters work or are used. At Howrah station there's a pre-paid taxi rank outside (Rs 39 to Sudder St) although it can take 15 minutes or more to get to the front of the queue. If you want to avoid the queue, other sharks will offer to take you around Rs 120.

Kolkata is the last bastion of the human-powered rickshaw, apart from at resorts like Mussoorie where they're just for the tourists. Rickshaws only exist in small parts of central Kolkata and they are restricted to the small roads. Across the river in Howrah or in the suburbs, there are auto and cycle-rickshaws.

To/From the Airport

The airport is 17km north-east of the city centre. It's possible to exchange travellers' cheques at the international terminal. In the adjacent domestic terminal, there's an accommodation booking service and a train reservation desk.

A public minibus (No S10) runs from BBD Bagh to the airport (Rs 8). At the northern end of the Maidan, bus No L33 goes from the Esplanade bus stand to the airport (Rs 5). There's also an airport minibus from Babu Ghat. The metro also goes to Dum Dum, but stops 5km short of the airport. A bus from the metro is Rs 5 and a taxi Rs 40.

For a taxi from the airport, it's cheaper to go to the prepaid kiosk where you'll be assigned one (Rs 130 to Sudder St or the Oberoi Grand Hotel). In the opposite direction expect to pay 25% extra or more.

Jammu & Kashmir

The regions of Jammu & Kashmir – including Srinagar, the summer capital, and the city of Jammu, the winter capital – form part of the vast state of Jammu & Kashmir (J&K for short). The regions of Jammu and Kashmir (with the exception of Ladakh and Zanskar) have been subject to political unrest since the late 1980s. The following information is included for background information for interest only and travellers are strongly advised to contact their embassy in Delhi before thinking about travelling to these regions.

The state of J&K (population 9.67 million) is a region of wide cultural and geographical contrasts. The Kashmir Valley is a fertile, verdant region, once a vast inland lake, which is enclosed by the high snow-capped ridges of the Pir Panjal to the west and south, and the main Himalaya Range to the east. It is famous for its scenic beauty, fine crafts and high quality saffron. Its population is predominantly Sunni Muslim and the region has formed the heart of Sufi Islam in India since the 14th century.

South of the Kashmir Valley is the region of Jammu, the former capital of the Hindu Dogra kingdom. It includes the city of Jammu, situated on the north Indian plains, a short distance from the rolling Siwalik Hills. North of the Siwaliks, the rest of the Jammu region is drained by the Chenab River whose vast catchment area includes several narrow valleys that extend deep into the high Himalaya. The region of Jammu is predominantly Hindu, although small Muslim communities can also be found near Banihal and Kishtwar immediately south of the Kashmir Valley.

Security in Kashmir

Pakistan and India have fought two wars over Kashmir, in 1948 and 1965, and the region remains a flash point between the two countries. From 1989 militant activity increased substantially in Kashmir and it is

Warning

! Lonely Planet strongly advises against travelling to the regions of Jammu & Kashmir. While the Indian Government has not placed restrictions on visiting Jammu & Kashmir, it is still foolhardy to visit the regions until all the militant groups have confirmed that tourists are not targets. The situation is exacerbated by the naive advice offered by travel agencies and even the J&K Tourist Office in Delhi which even after July 1995 persisted with the notion that the situation in Kashmir is under control. It is therefore essential to contact your embassy in Delhi for up-to-date information. See the Government Travel Advice boxed text in the Facts for the Visitor chapter for advice. At the time of research the Australian, British, Canadian and US governments were all strongly advising their citizens not to travel to Kashmir.

As this book went to press, Indian and Pakistani military authorities had agreed on a plan that brought the bloody fighting at Kargil in mid-1999 to an end. Under the agreement, Muslim militants in the disputed Kashmiri region withdrew from the Indian-controlled sector. Almost immediately, most Indian guns fell silent, but the conflict is still far from resolution amid fears that the conflict could escalate into a full-blown war between the world's newest nuclear powers.

estimated that over 30,000 Kashmiris have died in the fighting, which continues to smoulder. For details on the conflict see the Kashmir Problem boxed text in the Facts about the Region chapter. The political violence, bombings and kidnappings have rightly discouraged most travellers from visiting the region.

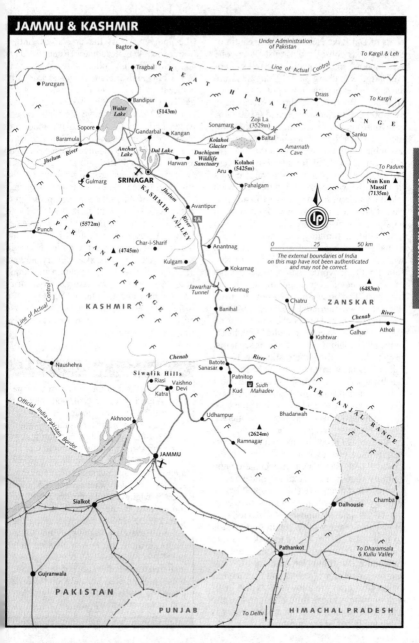

JAMMU & KASHMIR

Until 1989, a stay on the famous houseboats of Dal Lake close to the city centre of Srinagar was considered a must for anyone visiting northern India, while the treks out of Gulmarg, Sonamarg and Pahalgam were among some of the most popular in the Himalaya. Before the outbreak of violence, over 600,000 Indian tourists and 60,000 foreign tourists visited Kashmir during the summer months, a figure that quickly dropped to a combined total of less than 7000.

Flagging levels of foreign tourism were brought to a bloody halt by the tragic events of July 1995, when six foreign trekkers were taken hostage in the Aru area of Pahalgam, east of Srinagar. The men were kidnapped in an attempt to ensure the release of 15 militants held in Indian jails. One American managed to escape, but a Norwegian man was beheaded the following month and found with the words 'Al Faran', the name of a little-known guerilla group, carved into his chest. The other four men remain missing, presumed murdered in December 1995.

In the region of Jammu, the situation is no better. There have been sporadic bomb blasts in the city of Jammu since 1992, as separatist groups have shifted their attention to the Hindu majority in the south. The town of Kishtwar has also been subject to separatist activity, and the Indian Army has actively discouraged foreigners from visiting the area. Recent hotspots of political violence include Doda, Tangmarg, Kupwara and Punch.

A veneer of normalcy has returned to Srinagar since elections in 1996, though the city still feels like it's under occupation and military checkpoints remain in place everywhere. Most hotels are still occupied by the military and all bars and cinemas have been closed for fear of fundamentalist violence. Houseboat owners often retain bodyguards to look after the trickle of tourists who are cautiously returning to the area. Security procedures for flights into and out of Srinagar are extremely rigorous and no carry-on bags or batteries are allowed. It is also difficult to post packages from Srinagar. Despite the trickle of tourists in the area, trekking is completely out of the question.

Particularly tense dates include 27 October (the anniversary of the arrival of Indian troops in 1947), 26 January (Republic Day) and major Muslim holidays. A closely connected but quite different danger occasionally comes from Pakistan shelling along the Srinigar Hwy. In May 1999 Pakistani militants captured Tiger Hill above the highway between Drass and Kargil and the road was closed for two months. Though a few travellers are again making the trip from Srinagar to Leh, Lonely Planet still strongly advises against travel to and around Kashmir; see the Warning! boxed text earlier in this chapter.

In spite of this, there are no special permits necessary to visit J&K. In July 1990, certain areas of the Kashmir Valley were declared 'disturbed areas'. That is to say, the Indian military and reserve police forces in Kashmir were given extraordinary powers of arrest, similar to the situation in Punjab after 1984. However, there are no restrictions on movements in he state except those which were already in force, such as the ban on travel close to the India-Pakistan cease fire line, or to areas under curfew.

Sri Amarnath Yatra

At the full moon in the month of Sravana (July/August), thousands of Hindu pilgrims make the *yatra* (pilgrimage) to the Sri Amarnath Cave when a natural ice *lingam* (symbol of Shiva), reaches its greatest size. Although at this time the yatra is less a trek than a long queue, the spirit of this immense pilgrimage is amazing. In 1995, despite an escalation of tensions in J&K, over 60,000 pilgrims made the long trek to the cave, with the deployment of more than 20,000 security personnel along the Jammu-Pahalgam highway. The *Chari Mubarak* (holy mace) was installed in a bullet-proof vehicle under constant armed guard en route to the sacred cave. Despite these precautions, several bomb blasts along the route killed one security officer and injured several pilgrims.

JAMMU REGION
Jammu
☎ 0191 • pop 257,000

Jammu is J&K's second-largest city and its winter capital. It sits on the plains, so in summer it is a sweltering, uncomfortable contrast to the cool heights of Kashmir. From October onwards it becomes much more pleasant. Jammu is actually two towns. The old town sits on a hilltop overlooking the river, and several kilometres away across the river is the new town of Jammu Tawi.

Jammu to Srinagar

On the Jammu to Srinagar route are the hill resorts of Kud, Patnitop and Batote. The important Sudh Mahadev Shiva temple is 8km from Kud and Patnitop. Also on this route is Sanasar, a beautiful valley which is a centre for the Gujar shepherds each summer.

During the winter months, Srinagar was often completely cut off from the rest of India before the Jawarhar Tunnel was completed. The 2.5km-long tunnel is 200km from Jammu and 93km from Srinagar and has two separate passages.

From Banihal, 17km south of the tunnel, the Kashmiri region begins in earnest and people speak Kashmiri as well as Dogri. At the northern end of the tunnel is the green, lush Vale of Kashmir.

KASHMIR VALLEY

This is one of the most beautiful regions of India but over the last decade or so it has been racked by political violence.

The Mughal rulers of India were always happy to retreat from the heat of the plains to the cool green heights of Kashmir, and indeed Jehangir's last words, when he died en route to the 'happy valley', were a simple request for 'only Kashmir'. The Mughals developed their formal garden-style art to its greatest heights in Kashmir.

Among Kashmir's greatest attractions were undoubtedly the Dal Lake houseboats. During the Raj period Kashmir's ruler would not permit the British (who were as fond of Kashmir's cool climate as the Mughals) to own land here. So they adopted the solution

of building houseboats – each one a little bit of England, afloat on Dal Lake. A visit to Kashmir, it was often said, was not complete until you had stayed on a houseboat.

Srinagar
☎ 0194 • pop 725,000

Srinagar, the summer capital of Kashmir, stands on Dal Lake and the Jhelum River.

It is a city with a distinctly Central Asian flavour. Indeed the people look different from those in the rest of India; when you head south from Srinagar the trip is always referred to as 'returning to India'.

The old city is near the Hari Parbat Hill and the picturesque Jhelum River and includes a labyrinth of alleyways, mosques and houses, constituting the commercial heart of the city. The more modern part of the city is farther up the Jhelum River (above its famous seven bridges) that sweeps through Srinagar.

North-east of the city is **Dal Lake**. Much of Dal Lake is a maze of intricate waterways. It comprises a series of lakes including Nagin Lake some 8km from the city centre. Most of the more modern houseboats are on these lakes. The famous Mughal gardens including the Shalimar Bagh and Nishat Bagh are on the far (east) side of Dal Lake.

There are a number of interesting places in the Kashmir Valley near Srinagar including **Harwan**, **Sangam** (a centre for the production of cricket bats), and **Verinag**, where the Jhelum River has its source.

Pahalgam
• alt 2130m

Pahalgam is about 95km from Srinagar, at the junction of the East and West Lidder rivers, and was a popular base for trekking before the present troubles. The **Sri Amarnath yatra** still endures, however, and each year in July-August thousands of Hindu pilgrims approach the Amarnath Cave from this area.

Gulmarg
• alt 2730m

The large meadow of Gulmarg is 52km south-west of Srinagar at 2730m. The name means Meadow of Flowers and in spring it's just that. This was also a popular trekking base and before the terrorist activity it was India's premier skiing resort.

South of Srinagar

Interesting places in the south-west of the Kashmir Valley include Yusmarg, reputed to have the best **spring flowers** in Kashmir, which was, before the terrorist activity, a good base for treks farther afield. **Char-i-Sharif** is on the road to Yusmarg. Its famous *ziarat* (shrine) of Kashmir's patron saint Sheikh Nooruddin Noorani was burnt down in May 1995. Yusmarg (en route to Pakistan) is subject to separatist control. **Aharbal** was a popular resting place for the Mughal emperors when they made the long trip north from Delhi.

Srinagar to Kargil

Out of Srinagar is the **Dachigam Wildlife Sanctuary**, once a royal game park, and **Anchar Lake**, rarely visited but close to Srinagar, has a wide variety of water birds. The Jhelum River flows into **Wular Lake**, one of the largest freshwater lakes in India.

Sonamarg, at 2740m, is the last major town before Ladakh, and before the terrorist activity was an excellent base for trekking. Its name means Meadow of Gold, which could derive from the spring flowers or from the strategic trading position it once enjoyed.

Baltal, an army camp, is the last place in Kashmir, right at the foot of the Zoji La. The route from Baltal to Amarnath Cave is subject to landslides and is extremely dangerous for this reason, as well as the political problems. The **Zoji La** (3529m) is the watershed between Kashmir and Ladakh – on one side you have the green, lush scenery of Kashmir while on the other everything is barren and dry.

The road up the pass is breathtaking, even more so than the road up the much higher Taglang La (5328m) on the Leh-Manali road. The road clings to the edge of sheer drops.

Drass is the first main village after the pass. From Drass, it is then another 56km to Kargil.

For more information on the road from Kargil to Leh, refer to the Leh to Kargil section in the Ladakh & Zanskar chapter.

Ladakh & Zanskar

Ladakh – the land of high passes – is the Trans-Himalaya zone marking the boundary between the peaks of the western Himalaya and the vast Tibetan plateau. Since it was opened up to tourism in 1974 Ladakh has been known as 'the Moonland', 'Little Tibet', and even 'the last Shangri La'. Whatever the description, Ladakh is one of India's most remote regions.

The culture of Ladakh is predominantly Buddhist, with once close cultural and trading links with Tibet. This is particularly evident in the most populated region of Leh and the Indus Valley, with its many whitewashed *gompas* (monasteries) and forts.

Padum, the capital of the more remote Zanskar Valley, shares this Buddhist heritage. Likewise, ancient gompas and tiny whitewashed villages are found in the depths of this rugged, arid mountainscape.

Kargil and the Suru Valley is the third main region of Ladakh. While its geography is similar to the rest of Ladakh, its people are Shi'ah Muslim and share a cultural affinity with Baltistan (now in Pakistan).

Travel to Zanskar, Leh, and along the Manali road is allowed without permits, as long as you don't stray too close to sensitive border areas. Heavy fighting between Drass and Shergol in 1999 displaced thousands of refugees. Check with your embassy about the current situation, taking note that local authorities want to play down the crisis.

History

Ladakh was first populated by Khampa nomads, who grazed their yaks, goats and sheep on the high, windswept pastures. It was not until the coming of the Mons, Buddhist pilgrims from India on their way to Mt Kailash in Tibet, that settlements were established along the upper Indus.

The remnant Brokpa people live in a handful of villages in the Indus Valley downstream from Khalsi. The Brokpas (also known as Dards) are an ancient Indo-Iranian

Ladakh & Zanskar at a Glance

Population: 140,000 (year 2000 estimate)
Area: approx 96,701 sq km
Capitals: Leh & Kargil
Main Languages: Ladakhi, Purig, Tibetan & English
Best Time to Go: May to Oct
Trekking Areas: Padum to Darcha, Lamayuru & Leh; Spituk to Markha Valley & Hemis; Lamayuru to Chilung; Likir to Temisgam

Highlights

- **Leh** – Explore the labyrinthine alleyways of the old town and wander up to Leh Palace, Ladakh's 'mini Potala'.

- **Hemis** – Examine the beautiful frescoes at this important gompa.

- **Matho** – Witness the extraordinary austerities performed by the monks at this gompa's annual festival.

- **Tikse** – Visit this stunningly set gompa with its important library and exquisite artwork.

- **Nubra Valley** – Follow the old trading route that once connected Tibet with Turkistan, and traverse the world's highest motorable mountain pass.

- **Tso Moriri** – Visit the region of the nomadic Khampa people, and take in a diverse range of wildlife.

- **Alchi** – Stand in awe before some of the finest artwork in the Buddhist world.

- **Lamayuru** – Explore one of Ladakh's finest and most stunningly set gompas.

- **Suru Valley** – Visit one of Ladakh's most scenic and least visited valleys.

- **Zanskar** – Trek across the high mountain passes of this isolated region.

tribe with Mediterranean features and bacchanalian fertility festivals, and are the last of the Dard peoples to remain Buddhist.

In the 7th century, Mongol influences increased with Tibetan migrants. During the Lha-chen dynasty, founded in 842, forts and palaces such as that of Shey were constructed, and the power of Ladakh for the first time stretched beyond the Indus Valley. In the 11th century, the Buddhist scholar Ringchen Zangpo established 108 Buddhist gompas throughout western Tibet and Ladakh. In the late 14th century the famous Tibetan pilgrim Tsongkhapa (born 1357) visited Ladakh and popularised a new Buddhist teaching, headed by the first Dalai Lama. The Gelukpa order, as it was known, gained popularity in Ladakh, and gompas at Tikse, Likir and Spituk were founded during this period.

Polyandry & Primogeniture

In the tough farming environments of Ladakh, Zanskar and Spiti the land can only physically support a limited population. For this reason family fields are rarely divided. The eldest son traditionally inherits the land and house when he has children old enough to help in the fields. At that point the father either moves into a smaller home, or builds a new one.

Less common these days but still prevalent among the older generations, is the system of polyandry, where a woman marries two brothers. Both husbands are regarded as the fathers of any offspring. Equally, a man might have two sisters as wives if his first wife was unable to have children. The basis of the system was to have only one marriage per household in each generation. If another couple wished to marry, they had to set up their own house and had no claim on the family property. Men and women who didn't marry always have the option of joining a monastery or nunnery. Otherwise the only option was a life without a partner working on the family fields.

During the following centuries, Ladakh was vulnerable to a number of attacks from combined Balti-Kashmir armies. The upper fort above Leh known as the Peak of Victory was built to commemorate Ladakh's successful defence against these invaders.

However, Ladakh did not completely escape intruders. In the 16th century it fell subject to the rule of Ali Mir of Baltistan. The Ladakhi king, Jamyang Namgyal, was forced to marry one of the Mir's daughters.

Under Singe Namgyal (1570-1642), Ladakh's fortunes improved. During the early 17th century, the Ladakhi royal family assisted Drukpa monks to establish gompas at Hemis and Stakna. Soon Ladakhi forces were called on to face a combined Mongol-Tibetan army and help was sought from the Kashmir governor. This involved symbolic tribute to the Mughal empire and the mosque in Leh bazaar was the price Aurangzeb extracted. This time also marked the beginnings of the Sunni Muslim Arghon community of traders, who still live mainly in Leh. A community of Shi'ah Muslims from Baltistan also put down roots at Chuchot, just across the Indus from Choglamsar.

After the conflict with Tibetan forces, trade relations resumed and Leh was able to re-establish its influence over Zanskar and farther south to Lahaul and Spiti. Ladakh's fortunes changed again in the 1830s when the Dogra army from Jammu invaded Ladakh and exiled its king to Stok. The famous general Zorawar Singh, who was appointed by the first maharaja of Kashmir, Gulab Singh, led the Dogras.

Ladakh was integrated into the maharaja's vast state in 1846 and remained under the control of Jammu & Kashmir after Independence, until some autonomy was granted in 1995 following several years of political and social unrest.

Ladakh is still a sensitive area and its borders with both Pakistan and China are disputed. India's war with China in 1962 exacerbated the problem and was one of the main reasons why Ladakh was closed to outsiders until 1974. While China and India are approaching accord on the border dispute,

LADAKH & ZANSKAR

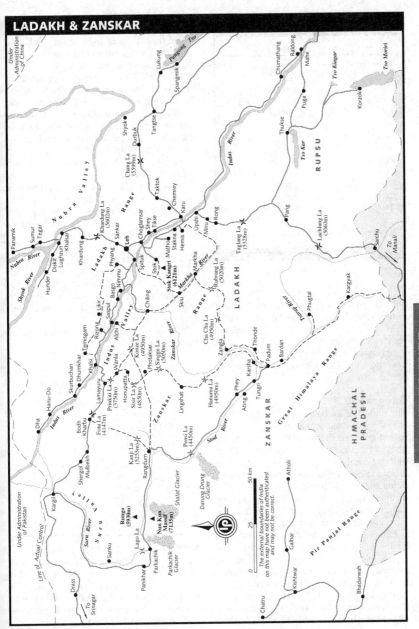

The external boundaries of India on this map have not been authenticated and may not be correct.

0   25   50 km

Festivals of Ladakh's Gompas

gompa	date
Chemrey	Nov
Diskit	Feb
Hemis	Jun/Jul
Karsha	Jul
Leh	Feb
Likir	Feb
Losar	Dec
Matho	Feb/Mar
Phyang	Jul/Aug
Spituk	Jan
Stok	Feb/Mar
Taktok	Jul/Aug
Tikse	Oct/Nov

New Year Festival is celebrated at all gompas.

heavy fighting continues between India and Pakistan on the Siachen Glacier, to the north of the Nubra Valley (see the Highest Battlefield on Earth boxed text in the Facts about the Region chapter) – a conflict that ensures a significant military presence in Ladakh. Travellers are forbidden to travel near the border area.

Geography

The region of Ladakh is part of the Trans-Himalaya, a vast and complex mountain region between the main Himalaya Range and the Tibetan plateau. The region receives only minimal rainfall each year, which is diverted along irrigation canals. Here barley fields and lines of poplar trees in the depths of the valleys contrast with the barren ridges and mountains that define the region's geographical character.

Ladakh is bordered to the south and west by the Great Himalaya Range, which includes many impressive ice-capped peaks, including Nun (7135m) and Kun (7087m), the highest peaks in the Kashmir Himalaya. North and parallel to the Himalaya is the Zanskar Range, which is the main range between the Himalaya and the Indus Valley.

The region is drained by the Zanskar River, which flows into the Indus River just below Leh, and the Suru River, which flows into the Indus downstream of Kargil.

The Stok Range, immediately south of Leh, is an impressive outlier north of the Zanskar Range, while north of Leh is the snowcapped Ladakh Range. North of the Ladakh Range the Nubra and Shyok rivers drain the huge peaks of the eastern Karakoram including Rimo 1 (7385m) and Teram Kangri 1 (7464m) that define the northern border of Ladakh.

In the east of Ladakh are several beautiful *tsos* (lakes), including Pangong Tso, forming the border with Tibet and Tso Moriri, set in a high altitude desert characteristic of the Tibetan plateau.

Tourist Offices

Jammu & Kashmir (J&K) tourist offices throughout India handle inquiries for travel to Ladakh and Zanskar, and can help with some up-to-date maps and information before you arrive.

Tourist offices in the major cities throughout India are:

Chennai
  (☎/fax 044-834335) 837 Anna Salai Rd
Delhi
  (☎ 011-332 5373, fax 371 6081)
  201-203 Kanishka Shopping Plaza,
  19 Ashoka Rd
Kolkata (Calcutta)
  (☎ 033-248 5791) 12 Chowringee Rd
Mumbai
  (☎ 022-218 9040, fax 218 6249)
  25 North Wing, World Trade Centre,
  Cuffe Pde

Leh

☎ 01982 • pop 15,000 • alt 3505m

Leh is set in a broad valley just to the north of the Indus Valley. Until 1947 it had close trading relations with Central Asia, with yak trains setting off from the Leh bazaar to complete the stages over the Karakoram Pass to Yarkand and Kashgar. Today Leh is

LADAKH & ZANSKAR

Average Temperatures for Leh & Kargil

month	Leh		Kargil	
	max	min	max	min
January	-3	-14	-4	-13
February	1	-12	-2	-12
March	6	-6	5	-5
April	12	-1	14	3
May	17	3	22	9
June	21	7	26	14
July	25	10	30	18
August	24	10	29	17
September	21	5	25	12
October	14	-1	19	5
November	8	-7	10	-1
December	2	-11	1	-8

All temperatures are given in degrees Celsius (see the conversion table on the inside back cover for the Fahrenheit equivalents).

an important strategic centre for India. The large military presence is a reminder that Ladakh is alongside India's troublesome borders with Pakistan and China.

Leh's character also changed when Ladakh was opened up to foreign tourists in 1974. Since then, well over 100 hotels have been established and many of the shops in the main bazaar and on Fort Rd sell Ladakhi and Kashmiri arts and crafts. At the height of the tourist season traffic jams occur on Fort Rd, perhaps the first in Ladakh.

Leh is dominated by the dilapidated nine storey Leh Palace. Until the 1830s this was home to the Ladakhi royal family, before they were exiled to Stok. Above the palace at the top of the Namgyal Hill is the Victory Fort, built to commemorate Ladakh's victory over the Balti-Kashmir armies in the 16th century.

The old town of Leh is at the base of Namgyal Hill, a labyrinth of alleys and houses stacked with wood and dung – fuel to withstand the long winter months. This area is the heart of Leh's Sunni Muslim Arghon community. To the south of the old town is the polo ground where weekly matches are contested between Leh and the outlying villages of the Indus Valley. The mosque at the head of the Leh bazaar was commissioned by the Mughal Emperor Aurangzeb. All around the old town are many dogs; the Buddhists forbid any culling so the only natural population control is the freezing winter.

In the first two weeks of September, Leh plays host to the Ladakh Festival (see the Festivals of Ladakh section in this chapter).

See the Life & Death in Ladakh boxed text on p.218 for details on the region's culture.

At Changspa, an outlying village of Leh surrounded by neatly farmed barley fields and poplar trees, are important Buddhist carvings dating back to the 8th and 9th centuries when Ladakh was converted to Buddhism. Close by is the quiet village of Sankar, the site of a gompa serving much of the Leh Valley. Leh's main Buddhist place of worship is the Soma Gompa, close to the mosque.

Orientation

Leh is small enough to find your way around easily. The road from the airport goes past

Buddhists, Muslims & Christians

Relations between the Buddhist and Muslim communities of Leh have improved vastly since the social conflicts of the early 1990s, but tensions remain. One unmistakable sign is the war of the loudspeakers between the Jama Masjid and the Buddhist Soma Gompa, the headquarters of the Ladakh Buddhist Association. Some days when the mosque broadcasts the *azan*, the Muslim call to prayer ('Allah-o-Akbar' – God is great) the nearby gompa sees fit to retaliate with a high-volume broadcast of Buddhist choral singing with flutes. As one Muslim leader put it, there's a cold war going on.

Traditionally relations between Buddhists and the Muslim Arghon community were very close, and intermarriages were common. Even today there aren't many people in Leh who don't have both Muslim and Buddhist relatives. This began to change when an uprising started in Kashmir in the 1980s. The Buddhists of Ladakh began agitating to separate from Muslim-majority Jammu & Kashmir and become a Union Territory. As the number of tourists slumped and the economy faltered because of the conflict in Kashmir, tensions grew. In 1989 the Ladakh Buddhist Association ordered and enforced a social boycott of Muslims. Suddenly neighbours didn't speak to each other, families were split and even violence erupted on occasion.

Eventually the government in Delhi banged enough heads together to work out a compromise; Ladakh's Buddhists could be a majority in their own Ladakh Autonomous Hill Development Council as long as the social boycott ended. The boycott was called off in 1993 and the new administration was set up in 1995.

Other causes of dispute linger. Buddhists resent that many intermarriages result in a Buddhist girl becoming Muslim, while Muslims feel unhappy that Buddhists, who own much of the land, get the bulk of income from tourists. The Muslims, traditionally traders, also feel encroached upon by the mainly Kashmiri businessmen who arrive every year for the tourist season.

Leh's tiny Christian community of 30 or so families, which began with the arrival of the German Moravian mission in 1885, seems to get along with both sides. Every Christian family has relatives belonging to another religion. The Moravian Mission School on Changspa Lane is regarded as the best in Leh and children of all faiths attend.

the new and old bus stands, then turns into the main street, Main Bazaar Rd, where there are plenty of shops and restaurants. South of the Leh Palace, around the area of Fort Rd, is the most popular area to eat, arrange travel in the region and spend money. To the north-west of the town and about 2km out of Leh is the village of Changspa, with its many guesthouses and long-term visitors. A similar distance to the north, the village of Sankar also has many family-run guesthouses.

Information

Tourist Offices The Tourist Reception Centre (☎ 52297) is rather pointlessly 3km from the town centre, on the road to the airport. For general inquiries, the small counter in the same building as the Foreign Exchange is far handier. Both tourist offices are open 10 am to 4 pm Monday to Saturday. There is a small tourist information counter at the airport, but this really just handles foreigners' registration forms.

Permits Permits are not required for Leh. However, you will be required to fill out a foreigners' registration form at the airport, and again at your hotel. For permits to the restricted regions of Ladakh (Nubra Valley, Pangong Tso, Tso Moriri and the Dha-Hanu Region), you can either pay Rs 100 for a travel agency to handle the bureaucratic formalities, or battle the red tape yourself at the District Magistrate's Office (☎ 52210), open normal business hours, just above the polo ground. For more details on permits, see the Ladakh Regions section later in the chapter.

Money Facilities are poor, to say the least, but Leh is the only place to change money between Manali and Kargil. The only bank that changes money is the State Bank of India, which has a Forex (Foreign Exchange) counter at the Tourist Information Centre on Fort Rd. In high season the queues are phenomenally long and you can expect to wait for four or more hours to be served by the sole, overworked teller.

The Forex is open Monday to Friday, 10.30 am to 4 pm (but you'll need to be there by 1 pm in high season to be served); and on Saturday 10.30 am to noon. You must fill out two copies of a currency form, detailing the numbers on your travellers cheques or currency notes. Don't rely on credit cards.

The Singge Palace and Khangri hotels also change money at slightly lower rates; the Jammu & Kashmir Bank on Old Leh Rd near the corner of Main Bazaar Rd may offer moneychanging facilities in the future. Some travellers prefer to change US dollars cash at a slightly better rate with the shopkeepers on Fort Rd.

Post The main post office – open Monday to Saturday 10 am to 1 pm and 2 to 5 pm – is hopelessly inconvenient, over 3km from the centre of Leh. The smaller post office on the corner of Fort and Main Bazaar roads is open 10 am to 4 pm, Monday to Saturday. The poste restante at the main post office is not particularly reliable, and too far out to go every day to check, so use your guesthouse or the tourist office on Fort Rd as a mailing address, but warn them first so that they hold onto the letters.

Telephone & Fax All around Leh are small telephone booths that have long-distance facilities. Calls within India cost Rs 40 per minute; to Europe, North America, Australia

and New Zealand, it's Rs 80 per minute. Faxes are far more expensive (Rs 3 per second, which can easily become Rs 500 for a single page), but machines are available. In high season the telephone lines are seriously overloaded in the evenings, but there's a much better chance of getting through during the day.

Email You can send emails from the Gypsy's World office in the White House building on Fort Rd for Rs 100 per message, but you can't access the Internet to check Web based emails. Messages can take a day or so to reach the outside world and another day for replies to reach Leh, so be prepared for a visit or two. Receiving emails is free (email matin.chunka@gems.vsnl.net.in).

Travel Agencies Many travel agencies operate in the summer. Almost all agencies work on a commission basis, selling tickets for other companies' buses and tours.

It is easy enough to organise your own tours to the restricted areas of Ladakh, by arranging a taxi or going by public bus. Travel agencies can organise tours, but they often do little more than arrange the taxis themselves and take a commission. As a general rule of thumb, if booking an organised tour, deal with an agency in an upmarket hotel; while you may pay more, the quality and reliability is more likely to be there. Of course, one of the best ideas is to talk to other travellers.

Travel agencies recommended by travellers include:

Druk Travels
    Hotel Ibex complex, Fort Rd
Explore Himalayas
    (☎ 52727) Main Bazaar Rd
Fantasy Trek & Tour
    White House Bldg, Fort Rd
Gypsy's World
    (☎ 52935) White House, Fort Rd
Paradise Trek & Tour
    (☎ 52818) Fort Rd
Rimo Expeditions
    (☎ 53348) near the police station, Ecology
    Centre Rd

LADAKH & ZANSKAR

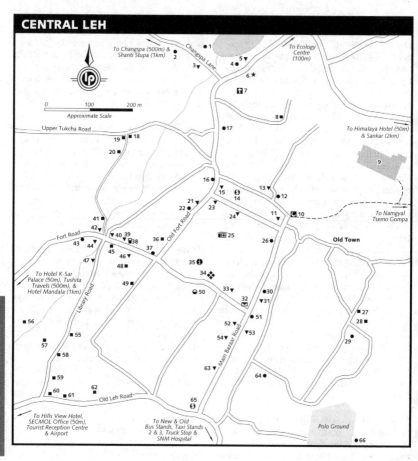

CENTRAL LEH

Equipment Hire Several travel agencies rent sleeping bags, tents and so on, but the gear can be of low quality and poorly maintained and a hefty deposit is demanded for each item. Check the gear carefully before you take it. Some places that rent gear, including mountaineering equipment, are the Traveller Shop (☎ 52248) in the White House building and Mero Expeditions across the road. Approximate rental prices per day are: two person tent, Rs 100; sleeping bag, Rs 70; and gas stove, Rs 30 – all

plus a deposit. A deposit on a tent can be as high as Rs 3000.

Rafting Agencies Several agencies in Leh run white-water rafting trips on the Indus, Zanskar and Shyok rivers, either as part of a trek or separately. The season only lasts from about early July to mid-September. A three hour, calm trip from Hemis to Choglamsar, or a more exciting one from Phey to Nimmu, costs Rs 750 per person. Better rafting from Nimmu to Alchi or to

CENTRAL LEH

PLACES TO STAY
8   Khan Manzil Guest House
18 Jigmet Guest House;
    Streamview Guest House
19 Ti-Sei Guest House
20 Dehlex Hotel
27 Tak Guest House
28 Old Ladakh Guest House
36 Hotel Ga-Ldan Continental
41 Indus Guest House;
    Bimla Hotel
45 Hotel Yak Tail Travels
48 Dreamland Hotel &
    Restaurant
49 Hotel Khangri
55 Hotel Bijoo; Leh District
    Library
56 Yasmin Guest House;
    Padma Guest House
57 Hotel Choskor
58 Pangong Hotel
59 Kang-La Hotel
60 Hotel Dragon
61 Nezer View Guest House
62 Singge Palace

PLACES TO EAT
3   Mentokling Restaurant
5   Mona Lisa Bar & Restaurant

11 Budshah Inn
13 Ladakhi Bakeries
15 Tibetan Restaurant Devi
21 Pumperknickel German
    Bakery
23 La Terrasse
24 Banana Leaf Curry House
31 Kokonor Tibetan
    Restaurant
33 Tibetan Friends Corner
    Restaurant
39 Gezmo
40 Poora Barba
42 Penguin Bakery
44 Tibetan Kitchen
46 Summer Harvest
47 Instyle German Bakery;
    Kailash Expeditions
52 La Montessori
53 Wok Tibetan Kitchen
54 Amdo
63 Mughal Darbar

OTHER
1   Moravian Mission School
2   Mahabodhi Meditation
    Centre
4   Rimo Expeditions
6   Police Station

7   Moravian Church
9   Leh Palace
10 Jama Masjid
12 Syed Ali Shah's Postcard
    Shop
14 State Bank of India
16 Dzomsa Laundry & Water
    Refills
17 Artou Bookshop
22 Parkash Booksellers
25 Soma Gompa
26 Pharmacy
29 Delite Cinema
30 Explore Himalayas
    Office
32 Post Office
34 Hotel Ibex Complex
35 Tourist Office; Foreign
    Exchange
37 HPTDC Bus Office
38 Namra Bar
43 White House
50 Taxi Stand 1;
    Taxi Union Office
51 Lost Horizon Books
64 Ladakh Art Palace
65 Jammu & Kashmir Bank
66 District Magistrate's
    Office

Khalsi will cost Rs 1200 for the day. Longer, customised rafting trips for the adventurous cost about US$65 per day, including all transport, gear, food and a guide. Rafting is not allowed downstream of Khalsi.

Two of the better travel agencies in Leh for rafting trips are Indus Himalaya, in the Hotel Ibex complex, and Rimo Expeditions (see Travel Agencies earlier).

Bookshops & Libraries Both Artou Bookshop and Lost Horizon Books on Main Bazaar Rd have good selections of books on Ladakh and Tibet, as well as novels. The Tibetan Handicraft Emporium, on Main Bazaar Rd, is also good for Tibetan literature.

The Ecology Centre (see later in this section) has a very good library with books on local issues and ecological matters, open Monday to Saturday 10 am to 4 pm. Next to the Hotel Bijoo, the small Leh District Library is a good place to read (mainly old) books about Ladakh. It is open Monday to Saturday 10.30 am to 4 pm. For more serious study of Buddhism and Tibet, try the Central Institute of Buddhist Studies (CIBS) library in Choglamsar.

Newspapers & Magazines English-language Indian newspapers and slightly dated foreign magazines can be obtained at Parkash Booksellers. The bilingual (English and Ladakhi) quarterly magazine *Ladags Melong* is an interesting source of information on Ladakhi culture, education, history and so on. It is sold at bookshops.

Film & Photography Several places along Fort and Main Bazaar roads sell print and slide film, but always check the expiry date. The Gemini Lab on Fort Rd, opposite the Hotel Yak Tail, does a passable job with developing print (not slide) film. You can also buy film and some wonderful prints of photos of old Ladakh from Syed Ali Shah's postcard shop.

Courses Buddhist study centres have been set up in Leh, and in nearby Choglamsar. The Mahabodhi Meditation Centre on Changspa Lane (look for the sign on the way to the Shanti Stupa) has summer meditation sessions at 5 pm Monday to Saturday. The Centre also holds study camps lasting from four days. The New Age scene has arrived in Leh, so if you're into discovering the past lives of your inner child look for posters in the bakeries or along the road to Changspa.

Laundry Dzomsa is an environmentally friendly laundry that washes clothes away from streams to avoid contaminating the precious water supply. They charge Rs 15 for pants and Rs 10 for shirts, and do an excellent job. Dzomsa also refills water bottles with filtered water for Rs 7, which is not only cheaper than buying bottled water, it also spares Leh yet more plastic rubbish. There are other laundries around town, including one opposite the State Bank of India.

Medical Services Leh is at an altitude of 3505m, so it is important to acclimatise to avoid Acute Mountain Sickness (AMS). If you suspect you are suffering from the symptoms of AMS, medical advice is available (☎ 52014 from 10 am to 4 pm, ☎ 52360 from 4 pm to 10 am). For more information on AMS, see the Health section in the Facts for the Visitor chapter. Leh has several clinics and pharmacies that can dispense advice and medicines for low-level complaints, but for anything serious, go to the public Sonam Norbu Memorial (SNM) Hospital (☎ 52014), nearly 3km south of Leh. The doctors there have a good reputation but the facilities aren't the best. You can also contact a doctor through one of the upmarket hotels. The pharmacy near the mosque on Main Bazaar Rd sells western toiletries such as tampons.

Leh Palace

Looking for all the world like a miniature version of the Potala in Lhasa, Tibet, Leh Palace was built in the 17th century, but is now dilapidated. The Archaeological Survey of India has moved in to do restoration work at their legendary easy pace, so it's no longer possible to catch the view from the roof. Admission costs Rs 10, which includes a look at the central prayer room. It's open 7 am to 9 pm; watch out for holes in the floor.

The palace is just an amble up any old laneway at the back of the mosque. Going by the road is much longer if you are on foot.

Namgyal Tsemo Gompa

The Tsemo (Red) Gompa contains a fine three-storey-high Maitreya Buddha (the Future Buddha) image and ancient manuscripts and frescoes. It's open 7 to 9 am, assuming the monk from Sankar gompa who unlocks the doors arrives. The red-walled *gönkhang* (chapel of protector deities) nearby has an unusual portrait in a court scene fresco just to the left of the door, thought to be the great Ladakhi king Tashi Namgyal. However, women aren't traditionally allowed to enter gönkhangs. The king built the gönkhang in the 16th century, as well as a now ruined fort farther up this steep crag (the views of Leh from it are superb). The steep path to the gompa starts from the road to the Leh Palace, or you can take a return taxi for Rs 150 (it's a killer climb if you've just arrived in Leh by plane, allow 20 minutes).

Sankar Gompa

It's an easy 25 minute stroll to the 150-year-old Sankar Gompa, north of the town centre. (A return taxi costs Rs 135.) This interesting little gompa, which belongs to the Gelukpa order, is only open 7 to 10 am and 5 to 7 pm. A donation of Rs 10 is requested. The gompa has electric lighting so an evening visit is worthwhile. Upstairs is an impressive representation of Avalokiteshvara (Tibetan: Chenresig), the Bodhisattva of Compassion, complete with 1000 arms and 1000 heads, a library, and great views from the roof. Sankar is home to Ladakh's most senior Gelukpa monk, the Kushok Bakula, who is also head of Spituk Gompa; the *rinpoche* (revered lama) has an apartment above the main building.

Shanti Stupa

Looming impressively, especially at night when it is illuminated, this stupa was built by a Japanese sect who intended to spread Buddhism by building temples throughout the world. With some eventual financial assistance from the Japanese government, it was opened by the Dalai Lama in 1983.

From the top, there are great views, especially at sunset. The stupa is at the end of Changspa Lane, about 3km from Fort Rd. If on foot, there is a very, very steep set of steps – not to be attempted if you have just arrived in Leh. By taxi (Rs 135 return) or with your own transport, a longish, winding (but less steep) road goes straight to the top.

Jama Masjid

Leh's charming Friday mosque is more impressive from the outside than the inside, although the dusty carpeted prayer hall has some distinctly Ladakhi features that make it unique, such as the carved roof beams and the curling edges of the *mihrab* (niche indicating the direction of Mecca). The ground floor of the building is occupied by shops, a literal sign of the Arghon community's roots in trade. The mosque was built in about 1666.

Try not to visit during prayer times, especially Friday's noon prayers. It is respectful to cover your head before entering.

Soma Gompa

The 'new monastery', also called the Chokhang Vihara, is about 40 years old, and is the biggest Buddhist monument in downtown Leh. In the main hall stands a 2m-high statue of Shakyamuni, flanked by a modern Buddha on the left and Padmasambhava on the right. Except for the richly decorated beams the wooden-floored hall is quite sparse, except for murals above the main statue. There is *puja* (prayers) at 9.30 am and 4.30 pm, otherwise the hall is usually closed. Look for the large ornate wooden gates below the Banana Leaf Curry House.

The Ecology Centre

Known locally as the Ecology Centre, this is the headquarters of the Ladakh Ecological Development Group (LEDeG). Founded in 1983, it initiates and promotes 'ecological and sustainable development which harmonises with and builds on the traditional culture'. This includes environmental and health education, strengthening the traditional system of organic farming, and publishing books in Ladakhi. LEDeG has had great success with its simple design for greenhouses, which you'll see all over Ladakh.

The video *Ancient Futures – Learning from Ladakh* is shown at the Ecology Centre, usually at 4.30 pm every second day except Sunday if the demand is there. It's worth seeing for an insight into Ladakh, and the problems associated with tourism. An earnest discussion group follows the video. The small library is very good, and the handicraft shop has a good, if a little pricey (but it is nonprofit), selection of locally made goods. For further information about LEDeG, contact the Ladakh Project/ISEC at offices in the US and UK (see Volunteer Work in the Facts for the Visitor chapter)

Students' Educational & Cultural Movement of Ladakh (SECMOL)

SECMOL (☎ 52421) was founded in the late 1980s to organise cultural shows, promote traditional art forms, and organise youth activities. People interested in conducting English conversation classes may join the summer camps at Phey village near Phyang Gompa (board and food cost about Rs 80 per day). The camps help local students prepare for the state exams, which are held in English or Urdu, not Ladakhi. It also produces a local magazine, *Ladags Melong*, and a Ladakhi phrasebook. The

SECMOL offices, usually open during the afternoon from Monday to Friday, are just off Old Leh Rd.

Sauna & Massage

To help unwind after a trek, Thagang Sauna and Massage in Changspa opposite the Eagle Guest House offers a sauna for Rs 100 and massage for Rs 300.

Places to Stay

There is an amazing number of hotels and wonderful budget guesthouses in Leh, almost all of which are only open during the tourist season. Prices are technically set by the local tourist authorities, but what you pay depends more on tourist demand – prices can soar in the high season, especially after the arrival of a full flight. In low season, even a day or two after the season ends, prices can drop dramatically, sometimes by up to 50%. Prices quoted here are for the high season, but, remember, the cost of a hotel will change from day to day. A lot of upmarket places will also charge an arbitrary 'service tax' of about 10%.

The electricity supply is spasmodic, so torches (flashlights) and candles may be needed. Before paying extra for hot water, inquire how regular it is; often it runs only for one or two hours a day. Leh's dog population tends to sleep all day and bark all night, so it is worth finding somewhere quieter on the outskirts. If you're staying for some time in Leh, it is a good idea to check into one place for the first night, then spend your first day, while acclimatising, finding a place that really suits.

Places to Stay – Budget

Budget accommodation can be found in three main areas: the old town, which is a little noisy and smelly, but has character; the 'newer', greener areas along, or not far from, Fort Rd; and in the peaceful village of Changspa. Most other accommodation is in the newer parts of Leh.

Old Town Under the Leh Palace, along a quiet road to the Sankar Gompa, are several

good places, and there are a couple of characterful places in the old town. The water supply here can be erratic.

Himalaya Hotel (☎ 52746) has a charming setting among brooks and willow trees. This small, rustic family-run place has doubles with bath for Rs 300.

Khan Manzil Guest House (☎ 52681) not far from Syed Ali Shah's postcard is a 200-year-old place built around a courtyard – the owner says he has avoided renovations to keep the character of the building. Single/double rooms with common bath are Rs 80/100.

Old Ladakh Guest House (☎ 52951) has doubles with common bath for Rs 180, and two charming doubles with bath for Rs 250 and Rs 300.

Tak Guest House nearby is a simple little place with shared bath. Dark rooms downstairs are Rs 100, and a big airy double upstairs is Rs 150.

Changspa Changspa, about a 15 minute walk from the town centre, is very popular with budget travellers. Many of the older places are basic, with toilets outside the main building, but are usually very friendly, and surrounded by colourful gardens. Following are recommended places among the dozens around or on the way to Changspa.

Eagle Guest House (☎ 53074) has singles/doubles for Rs 150/200.

Tsavo Guest House is a very basic, authentic Ladakhi home with doubles from Rs 100.

Stumpa Guest House is another family home with rustic triple rooms for Rs 200.

Asia Guest House (☎ 53403) is one of the nicer family-run places, with doubles for Rs 150 plus a terrace restaurant by a big garden.

Oriental Guest House (☎ 53153), run by a very friendly family, has doubles from around Rs 120 up to Rs 300 for a big double with a view.

Goba Guest House is a very peaceful farmhouse with simple but decent singles/doubles for Rs 80/150.

Karzoo Guest House (☎ 52324) has plain doubles with common bath for Rs 150, and a lovely garden.

Greenland Guest House (☎ 53156) is a pleasant family home with doubles for around Rs 150.

Rainbow Guest House (☎ 52211) is a friendly place with doubles for Rs 100 downstairs, Rs 120 upstairs. It is surrounded by fields and has a nice garden.

Other Areas Along the lane known as Library Rd (which the library isn't actually on) are several good places. There are also a couple on nearby Old Leh Rd.

Pangong Hotel is verging on the mid-range, but has airy, bright singles/doubles with hot water for Rs 200/300.

Kang-La Hotel is a cheery family-run place with creaky stairs and shared bath for Rs 150/200.

Hills View Hotel (☎ 52058) has rooms for Rs 100/150 with a slightly shabby common bath, Rs 250 for a double with private bath.

Nezer View Guest House has rooms from Rs 120 with common bath.

Up the lane beside the Penguin Bakery are several guesthouses.

Ti-Sei Guest House (☎ 52404) has a nice garden and a traditional Ladakhi kitchen, with rooms for Rs 80/150.

Dehlex Hotel (☎ 52755) is fairly rustic but it's central with a big garden; all rooms have common bath for Rs 80/150.

Jigmet Guest House (☎ 53563), on Upper Tukcha Rd, not far away, is tidy and has large rooms for Rs 80/150 with common bath and Rs 300 with private bath.

Streamview Guest House (☎ 52745) next door has very pleasant rooms with common bath for Rs 100/150.

Places to Stay – Mid-Range

A few of the places that used to be in the budget range are now are a little overpriced despite improvements. These include several strung out along the lane next to the Penguin Bakery.

Bimla Hotel (☎ 52754) is nicely decorated; prices range from Rs 100 for a single with shared bath up to Rs 500 for a big double with hot water and great views.

Indus Guest House (☎ 52502) close by has big clean doubles all with hot water for Rs 300 to Rs 400.

There are several options on or near Fort Rd. *Dreamland Hotel* (☎ 52089) is a very central but reasonably quiet older hotel, with rooms for Rs 350/400. *Yasmin Guest House* (☎ 52405) has good doubles with bath and hot water for Rs 300.

Padma Guest House (☎ 52630) is deservedly popular; rooms range from doubles with shared bath in the old house for Rs 180 to larger doubles in a new wing with private bath for Rs 700.

Hotel Choskor (☎ 52462) is a rambling old place with big doubles for around Rs 300.

At the time of writing the *Hotel Sun-n-Sand* (☎ 52468) and the *Hotel Ri-Rab* (☎ 53108), both in Changspa, were willing to drop their rates from Rs 1400 to Rs 400.

Milarepa Deluxe Guest House (☎ 53218), on the way to Sankar, has some beautiful double rooms for Rs 400 and Rs 500. Walk about 500m up the Sankar road from the Himalaya Hotel and then head left down a lane for another 150m.

Places to Stay – Top End

Prices for these places are high, and offer little value; a room may have some form of heating or air-conditioning, and hot water, but no other extras. If not many tour groups paying full price have booked in, the prices are highly negotiable. Many places offer an 'American Plan', which includes three meals for an additional Rs 500 to Rs 600 per day and are usually the advertised price. It may seem a reasonable deal, but there are plenty of good cheap places to eat in Leh, and why always eat at the same place?

The central *Hotel Khangri* (☎ 52311), the *K-Sar Palace* (☎ 52348), the *Singge Palace* (☎ 53344) and the quiet but isolated *Hotel Mandala* (☎ 52330) are all top-end places charging Rs 1720/2070 for a single/double with all meals.

Central, around Fort Rd are the *Hotel Yak Tail Travels* (☎ 52118), with rooms from Rs 800/950, and the *Hotel Ga-Ldan Continental* (☎ 52436), with singles/doubles from Rs 1250/1500.

Hotel Bijoo (☎ 52131), on Library Rd, has a nice garden and charges Rs 1500/1800 with all meals. *Hotel Dragon* (☎ 52139) is a superior place nearby charging Rs 1720/2070 with all meals.

Gypsy's Panorama Hotel (☎ 52660), at the foot of the Shanti Stupa hill, boasts of being the first with central heating.

Hotel Omasila (☎ 52119), Changspa, charges Rs 1720/2070.

Places to Stay – Winter

Almost every place to stay in Leh closes in winter, mainly because no one can get to the area. Prices at those places that remain open in the low season are still high because of a charge for room heating, which is certainly needed as the temperature in winter can plummet to about -35°C.

Some places that are reliably open in winter include the first and original *Old Ladakh Guest House*, which has remained open every day since 1974; the *Indus Guest House*; the *Hotel Khangri*; and the popular and centrally heated *Gypsy's Panorama Hotel*.

Dongmo
tea churner.

Gur-Gur & Chang

A trip to Ladakh would be incomplete without sampling *gur-gur* tea and *chang* beer. Similar to Tibet and other Tibetan-influenced areas like Spiti in Himachal Pradesh, gur-gur tea (also known as *soldja*) is made with yak butter (which is either rancid or fresh depending on the region of Ladakh). The butter is mixed with salt, soda, milk, a prepared green leaf tea and hot water. The churning of the liquid in a *dongmo* (wooden tube) makes a 'gur-gur' sound – hence the name of the tea. Gur-gur tea, which is often mixed with *tsampa* (barley flour) is usually kept hot in a copper kettle and placed on a stove.

You will be offered gur-gur during the two traditional culture shows put on for tourists in Leh. A monk may offer you a small cup from the gompa kitchen, or during a puja, a child novice will continually refill the monks' and visitors' cups. In a Ladakhi home, a family will sit around a low table known as a *chogtse* and drink dozens of cups in a few hours. If you are offered some Ladakhi tea, remember that you may offend if you don't finish your cup, and whenever you do finish it, the cup will be refilled immediately. Novices will probably appreciate gur-gur more if they expect soup and not a cup of tea.

Chang, made from excess barley during the harvests, is a dominant part of many Buddhist rituals and celebrations. Drunk by women and men, chang helps to loosen the body and mind during traditional dancing, is an integral part of the celebration of a birth, and is drunk in large quantities while negotiating a wedding, and at the marriage ceremony itself. Chang is enjoyed by most Ladakhis, including monks, but not by Muslims (who live mainly in western Ladakh and Leh) because of its alcohol content.

Chang has a sour taste that is a easier to get used to than gur-gur. You may be offered some rough home-brewed chang in a Ladakhi home, or you can buy some in shops and restaurants in non-Muslim regions of Ladakh. Chang is especially welcome during long, cold evenings, but be careful – its intoxicating effect will be made worse by the high altitude.

Places to Eat

There is no shortage of places to eat in Leh (although supplies are sometimes scarce), and it's a joy to sample various types of food from a multitude of good places. Almost all places serve a range of cuisines. If you want to eat at a popular place in the high season, you'll need to get there before 7 pm to get a table.

Indian Cuisine The *Mughal Darbar (Main Bazaar Rd)* is recommended. Although the servings are small, a great meal will only set you back about Rs 100 per person.

Poora Barba (Fort Rd), opposite the Hotel Yak Tail, is the place for no-frills, cheap Indian food, such as filling plates of vegetable curries and rice.

Ibex Bar & Restaurant in the Hotel Ibex complex does terrific meals for about Rs 150 per person.

Banana Leaf Curry House, on the first floor of the Soma Gompa gateway, is a decent mid-range place.

Budshah Inn, near the mosque and worth a visit; specialises in Kashmiri cuisine.

Tibetan Cuisine Leh has a sizable Tibetan refugee population, which naturally has influenced the cuisine and increased the number of Tibetan restaurants. Along Main Bazaar Rd, mostly on the 2nd or 3rd floors, are several good, cheap (and well-signed) places to try Tibetan specialities, including *Kokonor Tibetan Restaurant*, the *Wok Tibetan Kitchen* and the two *Amdo* cafes, which also serve reasonable western and Chinese food.

Tibetan Kitchen (Fort Rd) is the best restaurant in town and charges accordingly: around Rs 250 for dinner. The varieties of Tibetan cuisine are explained on the menus for the uninitiated. It will do a famous *gyarhcee* (Tibetan hotpot) for at least four people with a day's notice.

Dreamland Restaurant, central, in the hotel of the same name, is popular for its Tibetan specialities, among other types of food.

Tibetan Restaurant Devi, an unpretentious place near the State Bank of India, has maintained its reputation for cheap, nourishing food.

La Montessori (Main Bazaar Rd) serves up big portions of very tasty Chinese, Tibetan and some western favourites.

Tibetan Friends Corner Restaurant, near the taxi stand, is another established local favourite.

Western Cuisine The *Summer Harvest (Fort Rd)* near the Hotel Yak Tail is very popular, and deservedly so.

Gezmo (Fort Rd) is a popular place for breakfast and coffee and has a useful notice board.

La Terrasse, near the Soma Gompa, has a pleasant upstairs terrace with umbrellas, though it is better for breakfast or snacks than main meals.

Mona Lisa Bar & Restaurant is a relaxed open-air place near the Ecology Centre. It serves pizzas and Ladakhi bread with felafel for about Rs 60. See also under Bars, later in this section.

Bakeries Though the fresh cinnamon rolls, croissants smothered in chocolate and other tasty cakes are generally very good for around Rs 30, the bakeries in Leh generally aren't so good at meals.

Instyle German Bakery, on Library Rd, is a great place for a cup of coffee and a cake, sandwiches and breakfast, including piping hot porridge. Their attempts at dishes such as chow mein, however, are dire.

Penguin Bakery, on Fort Rd, is not a bad place for a snack.

Pumperknickel German Bakery, on Old Fort Rd, is very popular; specialities include lasagne and a big set-price breakfast (Rs 40).

Hot, fresh Indian and Tibetan-style bread can be bought in the early morning from the *Ladakhi Bakeries* in the street behind the mosque, near Syed Ali Shah's postcard shop. Get there early to watch them make the bread. It is great with locally made jam.

Entertainment

Bars If you're desperate for a bottle of Turbo Extra Strong Lager, there are a

LADAKH & ZANSKAR

couple of bars. *Chang* (Tibetan barley beer) is hard to find; ask at your hotel if they can acquire some.

Namra Bar, a bit dark and seedy but popular with local tour guides, is opposite the Hotel Yak Tail.

Mona Lisa Bar & Restaurant (see Places to Eat) is a relaxing place that serves cans of beer for Rs 60 and has Western popular music.

Shelden Green Restaurant (Changspa) serves beer rather more quickly than it serves the usual mix of western, Chinese and Indian meals, but the shady garden is pleasant.

Mentokling Restaurant near the Moravian Mission School is another open-air place selling beer.

There is a shop selling bottles of Indian beer and whiskey at the *Hotel Ibex complex*, slightly ominously just across from the taxi stand where the drivers hang out.

Cultural Performances The *Cultural & Traditional Society* (CATS) puts on a

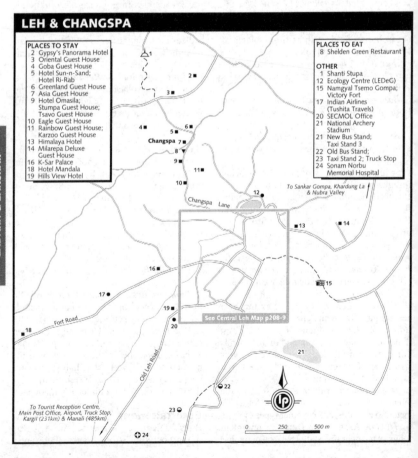

LEH & CHANGSPA

PLACES TO STAY
2 Gypsy's Panorama Hotel
3 Oriental Guest House
4 Goba Guest House
5 Hotel Sun-n-Sand;
   Hotel Ri-Rab
6 Greenland Guest House
7 Asia Guest House
9 Hotel Omasila;
   Stumpa Guest House;
   Tsavo Guest House
10 Eagle Guest House
11 Rainbow Guest House;
   Karzoo Guest House
13 Himalaya Hotel
14 Milarepa Deluxe
   Guest House
16 K-Sar Palace
18 Hotel Mandala
19 Hills View Hotel

PLACES TO EAT
8 Shelden Green Restaurant

OTHER
1 Shanti Stupa
12 Ecology Centre (LEDeG)
15 Namgyal Tsemo Gompa;
   Victory Fort
17 Indian Airlines
   (Tushita Travels)
20 SECMOL Office
21 National Archery
   Stadium
21 New Bus Stand;
   Taxi Stand 3
22 Old Bus Stand;
23 Taxi Stand 2; Truck Stop
24 Sonam Norbu
   Memorial Hospital

Changspa

Changspa Lane

To Sankar Gompa, Khardung La & Nubra Valley

See Central Leh Map p208-9

Fort Road

Old Leh Road

To Tourist Reception Centre,
Main Post Office, Airport, Truck Stop,
Kargil (231km) & Manali (485km)

0   250   500 m

cultural show each summer evening opposite the Hotel Yak Tail at 6 pm (which is not particularly pleasant if you have a room nearby); tickets cost Rs 50. In competition to this, the **Ladakh Artists' Society** of Leh also puts on a show of Ladakhi songs and dances every day at 5.30 pm outside the Leh Palace, costing Rs 70. It's an entertaining show, at a great location. Bring a torch (flashlight) for the walk back.

While they *are* set up for tourists, these shows are likely to be the closest you'll get to see some traditional songs and dances, and to try (if you dare) some Ladakhi *gurgur*. It's a good idea to avoid the front rows unless you want to become part of the spectacle at the end of the show.

Cinemas Fans of Hindi musicals with gory fight scenes can get their fix at the **Delite Cinema** in the old town.

Shopping

Prices in Leh are generally quite high; you may find exactly the same Tibetan-inspired items on sale at lower prices in Delhi, Dharamsala or Nepal. Thangkas, dorjes and tons of cheap jewellery make up the bulk of what's on offer, along with Kashmiri carpets from the many stores open during the tourist season. Only buy something because you like it, not because you have been told it is 'unique', 'antique', sellable for a huge profit back home or any other standard selling spiel.

Some reasonable places for local goods are the Ladakh Art Palace in the old town, the Ecology Centre, or around the shops in the old part of town behind Main Bazaar Rd. In the latter you can find much more authentic goods than the bulk of the souvenir junk sold on Fort Rd, including Ladakhi clothes, tables and kitchenware. If you are around Leh at the time of the Ladakh Festival (first two weeks of September), there are good exhibitions and stalls selling local handicrafts and clothes.

Getting There & Away

Air Lots of travellers have a nightmarish time flying out of Leh in the high season;

going by road via Manali to Delhi is a more secure option at this time of year. From June to September Indian Airlines (IA) has at least four return flights a week between Leh and Delhi (US$105/155 economy/1st class and via Chandigarh each Wednesday (US$70, economy). There are also direct flights once a week from Leh to Srinagar (US$55/80), and twice a week to Jammu (US$65, economy). They can be a useful, indirect, way of getting out of Leh if the Leh to Delhi flights are hopelessly overbooked. IA is currently the only airline flying to Leh, as compensation for the loss-making flights it must maintain during the winter.

From October to May IA generally still flies into Leh four times a week from Delhi, but this depends greatly on weather conditions. If/when flights from Leh are delayed, IA will pay for passengers' overnight accommodation in Leh.

IA warns passengers it cannot depart Leh with more than 70 to 80 passengers because of the altitude, climatic conditions and short runway. So, at peak periods, flights can be heavily overbooked. To avoid this, book well ahead but be prepared for disappointment. If you can't get a booking in economy class, it's worth trying for 1st class.

Another answer is to get to the airport early on the day you want to go, because even if you are waitlisted up to number 100, there is still a chance you will get on a flight, and a sudden improvement in conditions may result in a larger passenger load. Many people get caught out by booking their flight to Delhi and flight home for the same day, only to find that they get stranded in Leh; add some more days into your schedule to avoid this.

Bus There are only two overland routes to Leh: the road from Srinagar, and the road from Manali in Himachal Pradesh. A complication when trying to leave Leh for Srinagar or Manali is that you may not be able to buy tickets on the local buses (or private buses at the end of the season) until the evening before departure, because buses may not turn up from either of these places. Thus you can't be certain you will be leaving until the last moment. Try to book ahead, if possible, especially in the high season, at the new bus stand in Leh, from where the public buses leave.

Srinagar The Leh to Srinagar road is usually open from the beginning of June to October, but in practice the opening date can vary. In recent years the section of the road from Kargil to Srinagar was closed to foreign tourists for a time because of Pakistani shelling; check at the tourist office for more information. The trip takes two days, about 12 hours travel on each day, with an overnight halt at Kargil. There are two classes of public bus, but you may not get the class you want on the day you want. When the road is open, Jammu & Kashmir State Transport Corporation (J&KSTC) buses to Kargil/Srinagar cost Rs 145/220 in A class (more room and softer seats), Rs 110/175 in B class. They leave Leh at 5.30 am from the new bus stand every day, in season.

At the time of research, the deluxe/tourist private buses, which used to connect Srinagar and Leh, were cancelled due to lack of demand.

Manali The Leh to Manali road is open for a shorter period, usually from July to mid-September, sometimes up to mid-October; again, the opening and closing dates can be variable depending on climatic conditions. There is a good selection of private and public buses for this route, indicating its popularity. (For more information on the buses, and the trip, see Leh to Manali later in this chapter.)

Life & Death in Ladakh

For seven days following the birth of a child the father stops working and a birth feast, called *tsan ton*, is celebrated. The mother remains indoors for one month following her confinement. One year after birth the naming ritual known as *ming ton* is held. The child is taken before a lama who, upon receipt of payment or produce, bestows a name on the child, after which a feast concludes the ceremony.

The *bag ton*, or marriage ritual, proceeds following presentation of the man at the bride's family bearing a bowl of *chang* and negotiations regarding the offer proposed by the groom to the family of the bride. The ceremony is performed at the home of the groom, officiated by lamas, and the celebrations concluding the ceremony continue for several days.

The funeral ritual, known as *shid ton* can be a modest or elaborate affair according to the relative affluence or importance of the deceased. Cremation can take place up to 20 days following death, during which time prayers are recited and a piece of cloth suspended over the doorway signifies the period of mourning. After death the lama whispers directions into the deceased's ear from the *Bardo Thodol* or Book of the Dead to help them through the various stages of *bardo* (the intermediate stages between death and rebirth).

Following the cremation of a highly revered man, the ashes are collected and formed into an image of the deceased, which is interned in a *chörten*. High lamas are placed in coffins with the knees drawn up against the body and personal and religious effects placed around it. The traditional form of disposing of the body in Tibet, where wood for cremation was scarce, was the sky burial. The body, after being dissected and ground in a mortar with parched maize, was taken to a lofty site and left for wild animals and birds of prey to devour. Another ceremony is normally held 49 days after death at which time the soul is thought to have passed through bardo and been reincarnated.

Jeep & Taxi Long-distance jeeps and taxis are an expensive, but useful, alternative to the buses.

'Indian jeeps' take five passengers, and 'Japanese jeeps' and Ambassador taxis take four passengers, plus driver. Fares are listed at the taxi stands in Leh and Kargil. Extra charges are Rs 250 if staying overnight; waiting for the second and third hours (the first is free) is set at Rs 115 per hour.

The two day trip from Leh to Manali (including an overnight stop) will cost Rs 16,335. If hiring a jeep or taxi for a long trip, try to get a driver who speaks English and knows the area. This is not always possible because the next driver on the Taxi Union list gets the fare, regardless of his talents. Taxi drivers in Leh and Kargil are unionised; they must wear uniforms, and have to go through union checkpoints on all routes outside Leh.

While officially 'fixed', jeep and taxi fares for longer, more expensive, trips are negotiable outside of the high season.

Truck Trucks are a worthy, and acceptable, method of travelling to, or to places on the way to, Manali or Srinagar. Talk to the drivers at the old bus stand in Leh the day before you want to travel.

Getting Around
To/From the Airport The bus service from the airport to Leh costs Rs 5 but it doesn't run regularly, if at all. Rates for jeeps and taxis are set at Rs 80 to Leh, or Rs 125 to Changspa.

Bus All public buses leave from the new bus stand, where it's difficult to secure information on schedules. Both tourist offices have an updated, but often incomplete, timetable for public buses. To get to the new bus stand find the lane and follow people through the areas with the chörtens; don't follow the long road.

Jeep & Taxi A taxi from the old and new bus stands to Fort Rd for those tired from a long journey and/or with loads of gear will

cost about Rs 30. Prices from Leh for day trips to nearby gompas are:

Sankar, Spituk & Phyang: Rs 580
Shey, Tikse & Stok: Rs 685
most gompas around Leh: Rs 1950

Taxis in Leh congregate around three designated stands; they generally don't go around the streets looking for customers – you will have to approach them. Taxi drivers are unionised and accept only the union rate; fares are listed at the taxi stands. The biggest stand, taxi stand No 1 (☎ 52723), on Fort Rd, is open 7 am to 7 pm, but there are taxis hanging around Fort Rd in the very early morning, waiting for fares to the airport or the new bus stand. Taxi stand No 2 is at the old bus stand, where a few old taxis loiter; and No 3 is at the new bus stand, but you may find it hard to get a taxi from here.

Motorcycle Motorcycles are just about the perfect way of travelling around the area near Leh, but unfortunately local businesses don't seem to find it profitable to rent them out. Ask around and you may be able to hire a Vespa scooter for about Rs 500 per day, plus petrol. Ensure that you have comprehensive insurance coverage in the event of an accident in which either yourself or a local person is injured.

Bicycle Bicycle rental is just catching on. Mountain bikes – a great way to visit the more accessible villages (but you may have to walk up to the gompas, anyway) – can be hired from Wisdom Travels on Fort Rd near the Hotel Yak Tail for Rs 200 per day.

AROUND LEH
There are many beautiful gompas and villages that can be visited in day trips from Leh. Unless you have a taxi or your own transport, you will probably only be able to visit one or two in one day. Even though there is often no need to stay overnight, the villages are usually pretty and quiet, and sometimes a worthy alternative to Leh.

LADAKH & ZANSKAR

Places are listed in alphabetical order for ease of reference.

Chemrey Gompa

Chemrey village has a well-maintained and quiet gompa that sees few tourists because it is a little difficult to get to. Built to commemorate the death of King Singge Namgyal in 1645, the gompa belongs to the Drukpa order, and is where invading Dogras defeated a Tibetan army in the 1840s. The friendly monks can show you the impressive ancient library, and lovely Buddhist images on the wall of the prayer room. Nearby is a **cave gompa**.

To get to Chemrey, catch the bus to Taktok, get off at Chemrey village, and be prepared for a long (about an hour) and steep walk (it's steeper than that to Tikse Gompa). By car, you can take a road to the top, but it is very narrow and windy. From Leh, return taxis cost Rs 860, or you could try to arrange a side trip to Chemrey and Taktok if you're going on to Pangong Tso. There is nowhere to stay in Chemrey, but plenty of camping spots. However, before setting up your tent check with the villagers as to the correct places to camp.

Choglamsar

Choglamsar has become an important centre for the study of Tibetan culture and history, and Tibetan Buddhism. Around the Tibetan refugee camp, just off the main road from Leh, there is a Tibetan library, medical centre, handicraft shops, study centre, bookshops, plenty of restaurants, and the Central Institute of Buddhist Studies.

Any of the buses heading south from Leh will drop you off at Choglamsar, or a one-way taxi will cost Rs 130. There are a couple of crummy guesthouses along the very noisy main road, but none worth recommending, especially as Choglamsar is so close to Leh.

Hemis Gompa

Also known as Chang-Chub-Sam-Ling (or the Lone Place of the Compassionate Person), Hemis Gompa, which belongs to the Drukpa order was founded in the early 17th century. Now it is one of the most accessible (45km from Leh), famous and, therefore, most popular and touristy gompas around. Cradled in a lovely valley, surrounded by streams and fronted by long *mani stone* (stone carved with Tibetan Buddhist mantra) walls, it is certainly worth a visit. The gompa is also important for Ladakhi Buddhists, who are meant to visit it once in their lifetime.

The gompa has an excellent library and well-preserved frescoes, showing Kashmiri influence. The large dukhang on the right side of the building is quite austere. Upstairs there are several smaller shrines. This is the sort of place where you may be invited to see a puja. The largest *thangka* in Ladakh, over 12m long, is at Hemis, but is only exhibited every 12 years (the next unveiling is in 2004). To commemorate the birth of the renowned Indian sage, Padmasambhava, the famous annual Hemis festival is held on the 9th to 11th days of the 5th Tibetan month. (See the Festivals of Ladakh colour section in this chapter.) Hemis is worth staying over for a night to explore the **Gotsang Hermitage Gompa**, along a trail for an hour behind the gompa. There are also some **caves** nearby.

There are no guesthouses near Hemis Gompa, but the *East West Guesthouse* in the village, a long 20 minute walk away, has doubles for Rs 150. Several places near the gompa allow camping: you can set up your own tent next to it for Rs 35, or rent a preset two person tent for Rs 50. Book at the nice outdoor *restaurant*, next to the gompa entrance, which serves unexciting but welcome Chinese food, tea and beer.

A daily bus for Hemis leaves Leh at 9.30 am; returning from Hemis at 12.30 pm, which allows you an hour or so to look around. Return taxis from Leh cost Rs 860.

Matho Gompa

Built in the early 16th century, but virtually destroyed in subsequent wars, the gompa at Matho belongs to the Sakyapa order. The festival here is famous for the incredible activities of the monks and novices, who often go into trances, and inflict wounds on them-selves that miraculously either do not draw blood or, if they do, heal immediately.

There are some impressive thangkas in the very old library and a rather tacky mu-seum (which includes a stuffed yak). It is a busy place, with a school for 30 children, and the 20 or so monks can be seen making intricate silver and gold decorations for stupas. From the roof are staggering views of the 'moonscapes' of Ladakh.

Currently, the 5km road to Matho from the back of the Stakna Gompa (see Stakna Gompa entry later in this section) is not passable for vehicles, but the two gompas can be reached along this road on foot. If you are keen, and like walking, it is not difficult to combine a visit to Matho and Stakna on the same day. Take the bus to Hemis, get off at the sign to the Stakna Gompa, walk to Matho via Stakna, and re-turn the same way. Otherwise, catch the Leh to Matho bus that leaves at 9 am and 5 pm, and returns to Leh at 10 am and 6 pm. It's about a 20 minute steep walk from the vil-lage bus stop to the gompa.

A return taxi from Leh to both Stakna and Matho will cost Rs 785. A return taxi just to Matho costs Rs 725. There is nowhere to stay in Matho, but loads of pretty (but wet) places to camp.

Shey Gompa

Shey, 15km from Leh, was the former sum-mer palace of the kings of Ladakh. The gompa is partially used, and is still being re-stored. There is a small library and a collec-tion of thangkas, and some stupas and mani walls nearby. The magnificent 12m Shakya-muni Buddha statue, made of copper but gold plated, is the largest in the region. It was built by King Singge Namgyal's son. More crumbling **chörtens** are scattered around the nearby fields. About 1km towards Leh, where the road sweeps around a rocky spur, there is an ancient carving of the five Bud-dhas of meditation; the images are thought to date back to the 8th century.

Shey is easy to get to and can be easily combined with a visit to Tikse by any form of transport. Catch any bus from Leh going to Tikse or Hemis and disembark at Shey; by taxi, it will cost Rs 265 return.

The only place to stay is the pleasant and large *Shil Kar Hotel & Restaurant* near the road up to the gompa. Rooms with bath cost Rs 150.

Spituk Gompa

On a hilltop above the Indus River, 8km from Leh, Spituk Gompa was built in the 15th century under the Gelukpa order. It is next to the airport, and so has an ugly view at the front, but the back looks onto the pretty local village. The two prayer rooms have some nice Buddha statues, only unveiled once a year during the annual fes-tival, held usually in December. The red-walled *gönkhang* (protector chapel) at the top of the hill is particularly spooky. There is a strongly worded warning aimed at visiting Hindus that the fearsome guardian deities are not to be worshipped as the goddess Kali.

Spituk has nowhere to stay or eat, as it is so close to Leh. From Leh to Spituk is a long, hot walk past ugly army camps; a bike would be ideal. Alternatively, take one of the buses from Leh that go past Spituk every 15 minutes or so. Taxis from Leh cost Rs 225 return.

Stakna Gompa

The gompa at Stakna – which means 'tiger's nose' – is another set spectacularly on the Hemis side of the Indus River. Built by King Singge Namgyal's step-brother, as part of the Drukpa order, it is not difficult to get to, and can be combined with a trip to Matho on the same day (see the Matho Gompa entry).

A brightly restored courtyard leads to several new and old prayer rooms, one of which has a lovely silver chörten. From the roof are some of the best 'moonscape' views to be had of Ladakh.

To get there, take the Leh-Hemis bus, and get off at the roadside sign to the gompa. Cross the bridge, and walk for 30 minutes across the shadeless fields and up the steep

Treks in Ladakh

Treks out of Leh and the Indus Valley include the popular trek from Spituk, just below Leh, to the Markha Valley and Hemis Gompa, and the trek from Lamayuru Gompa to Chiling village on the Zanskar River. These treks can be completed from the end of June until mid-October when the first of the winter snows settle on the high passes. Proper acclimatisation is also necessary as many of the passes are around 5000m. Indeed, a few days in Leh (3505m) is recommended before commencing your trek.

There are many trekking agencies in Leh offering inclusive treks with a guide, pack horses, food and supplies for around US$50 per day. If you are making your own arrangements, pack horses can be hired from Spituk or Lamayuru for around Rs 200 per horse per day. It is recommended that all camping gear including sleeping bag and tent are brought with you even on *inclusive* treks, as the gear provided may not be adequate. Food supplies should also be carried with you from Leh as village lodges and tea houses are not available on all stages of the treks.

Spituk to Markha Valley & Hemis via the Kongmaru La

The trek from Spituk Gompa follows the Jingchen Valley to the Ganda La (4920m). At least one rest day should be included before crossing the pass. Thereon, it is a steady descent to the Markha Valley and the village of Skiu. It is a further stage to Markha village, before ascending to the yak grazing pastures at **Nimaling**. Above the camp is the impressive peak of Kangyaze (6400m). The Kongmaru La (5030m) is the highest pass on the trek and affords great views, south to the Zanskar Range and north to the Ladakh Range. After crossing the pass there is one further camp site at the village of Chogdo before reaching Hemis Gompa. From Hemis there is a daily bus (at 12.30 pm) back to Leh.

Stage 1	Spituk to Rumbak	(6-7 hrs)
Stage 2	Rumbak to Yurutse & camp	(4-5 hrs)
Stage 3	Yurutse to Skiu via the Ganda La	(6-7 hrs)
Stage 4	Skiu to Markha	(7-8 hrs)
Stage 5	Markha to Nimaling	(7-8 hrs)
Stage 6	Nimaling to Chogdo via Kongmaru La	(6 hrs)
Stage 7	Chogdo to Hemis	(4-5 hrs)

path. A return taxi from Leh costs Rs 630. There is no guesthouse in the village, but it should be possible to camp back near the Indus.

Stok Gompa

Over the bridge from Choglamsar, the Stok Gompa is where the last king of Ladakh died in 1974. Built in 1814, it is a popular place because it is so easy to get to. There are over 80 rooms, only a few of which are open to the public.

The **museum** has a unique display of rare ornaments from the royal family, thangkas, and traditional clothing and jewellery. There's also a rather grotesque stuffed snow leopard suspended from the ceiling. Entry is Rs 20, and it's open in summer from 8 am to 7 pm. Photography is not permitted. The gompa, which has some fine masks and frescoes, is behind the museum.

One of the only nearby places to stay is the elegant *Hotel Highland* (☎ 3783), just under the museum, with doubles for Rs 600. There are other smaller places to stay towards the main road.

An option for those with money to burn is the *Ladakh Sarai* (☎ 42013), costing

Treks in Ladakh

Lamayuru to Chiling via the Konze La & Dung Dung La

From Lamayuru the trek crosses the Prinkiti La (3750m) to the ancient gompa and village at Wanla. It is a further stage to the village of Hinju at the base of the Konze La where an additional day is recommended for acclimatisation before crossing the pass. From the Konze La (4950m) there are impressive views of the East Karakoram Range before a short descent to the village of **Sumdo Chinmu**. The following days' climb to the Dung Dung La (4820m) is rewarded with views of the Zanskar Range and a birds eye view of the swirling Zanskar River before a long and tiring descent to the village of **Chiling**. From Chiling you can either return to Leh or continue to the Markha Valley. The stage from Chiling to the village of Skiu in the Markha Valley can be completed in three hours. It's an interesting stage that includes crossing the Zanskar River by a pulley bridge that is maintained and operated by villagers (Rs 100).

Stage 1	Lamayuru to Wanlah via Prinkiti La	(3-4 hrs)
Stage 2	Wanla to Hinju	(4-5 hrs)
Stage 3	Hinju to Sumdo Chinmu via Konze La	(6 hrs)
Stage 4	Sumdo Chinmu to Dung Dung La base	(3 hrs)
Stage 5	Camp to Chiling via Dung Dung La	(6 hrs)

Likir to Temisgam

This trek can be completed in a day if you are fit! From Likir Gompa the trail crosses a small pass to the village of **Yantang**, a short distance from Rizong Gompa. The next stage leads to the village of **Hemis-Shukpachu**. It is a further short stage over two minor passes to the roadhead at **Temisgam**. The trek can be completed throughout the year. Horses can be hired from Likir while supplies and a tent must be brought from Leh.

Road building will eventually render this trek obsolete. Until then there is a daily bus service to Likir from Leh, while there is a bus from Temisgam back to Leh each day around noon making it possible to complete the third stage of the trek and be back in Leh that evening.

Stage 1	Likir to Yangtang	(4-5 hrs)
Stage 2	Yangtang to Hemis-Shukpachu	(3 hrs)
Stage 3	Hemis-Shukpachu to Temisgam	(3-4 hrs)

US$135/200 for a single/double, including sightseeing, activities (rafting, trekking), food and accommodation. It is a deluxe camp of Mongolian yurts with all modern conveniences; book with Mountain Travel India in New Delhi (☎ 011-752 5032).

Direct buses to Stok leave Leh at 8 am and 5 pm, or you could get there by mountain bike or motorcycle. A taxi will cost Rs 370 return from Leh.

Taktok Gompa

With at least five different spellings, Taktok is the only gompa in the upper Indus Valley belonging to the Nyingmapa order. Built around a cave above the village of Sakti, the actual date of construction varies depending on who you talk to, but there have been some recent additions. The frescoes have been damaged over the years, but there are some intricate rugs and paintings to see.

Taktok is a little difficult to get to, and not on the usual 'gompa trail'. Tourists are not common, so you may have to find a monk to open the prayer rooms for you. Two festivals are held each year, from the 9th to 11th days of the sixth month (July/August), and from the 26th to 29th days of the ninth month (around November) of the Tibetan calendar.

The **J&KTDC Tourist Bungalow** opposite the gompa has passable doubles for Rs 35, but no running water and only meagre food. However, there are excellent camping sites everywhere. One or two early-morning daily buses go past Taktok from Leh, but departure times change regularly, so check at the tourist offices in Leh. There is at least one late afternoon bus back from Taktok to Leh every day. A return taxi from Leh costs Rs 980.

Tikse Gompa

The Tikse Gompa, 17km from Leh, belongs to the Gelukpa order and is a good example of how donations have been put to good use through extensive restoration work. It is a bit garish and some may feel it has a slightly oppressive feudal atmosphere, but the setting is absolutely stupendous. Beside the car park you are able to see the small **Zan-La Temple**.

The Tikse Gompa has an important collection of Tibetan books in its library, some excellent artwork and a new Maitreya temple. It's a busy place, with almost incessant chanting and music, and there is a good chance to witness a puja. Go to the roof for great views of the valleys and villages. There is even a small (and welcome) cafe and shop. The gompa is open daily 7.30 am to 6 pm. Permission is required to use video or movie cameras.

The only place to stay in Tikse is the **Skalzang Chamba Hotel (☎ 47004)**, right at the start of the road leading to the gompa. It is a well-run and pleasant place with a small garden, and costs Rs 200 per room. There is also a restaurant. Serious students (male only) of Buddhism, but not ordinary backpackers, may possibly be able to stay at the gompa.

A bus from Leh to Tikse leaves about every hour or, alternatively, take the Hemis bus, which leaves Leh at 9.30 am. From the bus stop, it is a fair walk up to the gompa, as with most gompas. A return taxi from Leh will cost around Rs 400.

Ladakh Regions

This section deals with areas that have been opened up by the Indian authorities to allow travellers (with permits) to visit.

Permits

Permits are required (except for Ladakhi and Zanskari Indians) for all of the four restricted areas in Ladakh: the Nubra Valley, Pangong Tso, Tso Moriri and the Dha-Hanu region. Quite possibly the regulations for these new areas will be relaxed, or even abolished – although you are unlikely to ever get permission to go anywhere you want in the region, because it remains sensitive.

At the time of writing, permits were only valid for seven days, and although four people must *apply* for a permit together, checkpoints do not require that you actually need to *travel* together. Take your permits with you at all times – there are several checkpoints along most roads. If you need a group, leave messages around notice boards in Leh or let your travel agent organise things.

At the travel agency you must fill out the application form, which your travel agent will have. List every place you think you may go to, within the permitted regions. It costs another Rs 100 per person for the travel agent to organise the permit, which includes a special 'fee' for speedy service at the District Magistrate's Office. This usually takes a day.

Take a photocopy of the permit for yourself. These permits must be shown at checkposts, and hotels in the regions may also require details of your permit. You are allowed to travel to the regions by public or private transport, or by taxi, alone, or in a group of less than four as long as there are four names and passport details on the permit. Travel agencies usually have old photocopies of other passports to help 'fill up' the required numbers for your 'group'.

Don't even think about going without a permit, going to forbidden areas or overstaying your allotted seven days. If you get caught breaking the rules a visit to an Indian jail is not unlikely, and your travel agency will be severely penalised.

Climate

Average summer (Jun-Sept) and winter (Oct-May) temperatures for the four regions are:

region	summer max/min	winter max/min
Dha-Hanu	29/15°C	-3/-15°C
Nubra Valley	28/15°C	-3/-15°C
Pangong Tso	18/5°C	-12/-25°C
Tso Moriri	17/6°C	-10/-22°C

What to Bring

For the two lake regions, Pangong Tso and Tso Moriri, there are currently no guesthouses, or shops to buy supplies. You must take all your own food, and sleeping and cooking equipment – which can be hired in Leh. In the more populated Dha-Hanu and Nubra Valley areas, there are a few guesthouses for accommodation and food, and small shops for basic supplies. To liven up a boring plate of *dhal* and rice or *thukpa*, or to please locals if you are willing to share, it's a good idea to bring some canned meat and fresh vegetables from Leh.

Even in the height of summer, temperatures in some valleys in all regions can be extremely cold. The days can be hot, causing dry skin and sunburn, so a good hat, sunscreen and so on are important. Other items worth considering are torches (flashlights) and candles, as electricity, if there is any, is unreliable in all regions; and binoculars to admire the wildlife, which is guaranteed to disappear when you get too close.

Organised Tours

Tours, organised by reputable travel agencies in Leh, are the easiest, most comfortable, but, naturally, most expensive way to go. If you want to pay more for a guide and some comfort, make sure the tour is not just a local taxi-driver-cum-guide, because you can organise one of them yourself at the taxi-stand in Leh for far less. The quality of jeep, tent accommodation, food, destination and guide, and the demand affects the price of organised tours, but a rough idea of the sort of costs per day per person for an up-market trip are: a five day package to the Nubra Valley for US$50; and to Tso Moriri for four days US$60.

NUBRA VALLEY

The Nubra Valley – *nubra* means 'green' – used to be on the trading route that connected Tibet with Chinese Turkistan, and was the envy of Turkistan, which invaded it several times. Also known as the Ldomra (Valley of Flowers), Nubra has always been well cultivated and fertile, with the best climate in Ladakh, so fruits, such as apples and apricots, and grains, have always been plentiful. The Nubra people are 90% Buddhist.

The valley is a wonderful area to visit, dominated by an incredible broad, empty valley between the Nubra and Shyok rivers. Camels might be seen near Hunder. There are pretty, villages spread along alluvial fans at the edges of the valleys, small forests, wild lavender growing everywhere and some wildlife, but, inevitably, the area is becoming slowly more affected by the increasing number of travellers who make the effort to visit. Remember that your permit only allows you to travel as far as Hunder along the western valley, and to Panamik, in the northern valley. For details on travelling to the Nubra Valley, see Getting There & Away at the end of this section.

Special Events

Nubra Valley isn't as crowded with gompas as the area around Leh, so festivals tend to be less religious and more sport-oriented. As part of the **Ladakh Festival** in September each year, there are many activities in the Nubra Valley that should not be missed, including a camel safari between Diskit and Hunder. They are generally centred on the main villages of Diskit and Sumur (see the Festivals of Ladakh colour section in this chapter).

Leh to Khardung

The road to the Nubra Valley goes through the highest motorable pass in the world at

Khardung La (5602m). The pass is almost permanently covered in fog and snow, and is likely to be bitterly cold at the top regardless of the time of year. The pass is occupied by a grubby military camp and stacks of oil drums, so it isn't the most scenic place to visit. In the summer, you may see the world's highest traffic jam of trucks and buses too. The traffic over the pass goes in one direction one day and the opposite direction the next.

The road between Leh and Khalsar is reasonable, except between the miserable road-building camps of South Pullu and North Pullu, just before and after Khardung La, where the road is atrocious. Every winter the road is damaged, and the unhappy job of fixing it goes to teams of workers from Bihar and Nepal. Near the pass, there are many places to stop for views, if you can, such as the intriguing-sounding Siachen Toggler's Gate.

The road then continues to Khardung village, which, most disappointingly, has no tea stall, one very basic shop, and an unused Government resthouse. A small office may collect Rs 40 for 'wildlife' – perhaps to buy some.

Khalsar

The Nubra Valley really starts at the village of Khalsar, where there are several tea houses and a huge amount of discarded army equipment. The road then bisects – the road to the left goes to Hunder and beyond in the valley following the Shyok River; that to the right goes farther north, to Panamik and beyond, following the Nubra River.

Diskit

To Diskit, the road suddenly turns left, along an awesome, wide and dry riverbed for about 3km. Truck and bus drivers know where to turn off (there are no signs), so if you have your own transport, ask and follow the other vehicles. Diskit is about 10km farther up the hill.

The **Diskit Gompa**, with about 70 monks, is the oldest – over 350 years old – and the biggest of its kind in the Nubra Valley, and

shouldn't be missed. It is particularly famous for its murals, and the scenery from the roof is wonderful. According to legend, there is a statue in the gompa that has the head and arm of an invader from over five centuries ago. There are three prayer rooms, on different levels, as well as a library, some very old frescoes, and a few nice thangkas. From the village, it is a 40 minute walk. The gompa is slightly hidden, up the hill, and can be confusing to find, so, if in doubt, keep asking locals for directions.

Between Diskit and Hunder is an area of **sand dunes**, not unlike the Saharan regions (if you can ignore the snow-capped Himalaya in the background!). You may be lucky enough to see a few semi-wild and domesticated Bactrian (double-humped) camels. If you want to risk a ride, ask at your guesthouse or around the villages. Sometimes, camel safari races are held between the two villages.

Places to Stay & Eat About 50m from the gompa is *Olthang Guest House & Camping*. It has a nice garden, and costs Rs 300 per room, with a bath.

Sun Rise Hotel, on the main road near the Olthang, is OK for Rs 150 a room.

Sand Dune Guest House in the village centre has good rooms for Rs 100/150.

Your hotel will rustle up something basic like dhal and rice and there are little tea houses along the main street.

Hunder

Hunder is a pretty village, set among lots of trees, and mingling streams. It is nicer than Diskit, but Diskit is bigger with slightly better facilities. From Diskit, it is only about 7km to Hunder; some visitors enjoy the walk from one village to another, either along the main road or across the sand dunes. (But watch out for wild camels!)

The **gompa** at Hunder is about a 2km walk above the village, including a short, but steep, rocky climb. There is only a small Buddha statue, and some damaged frescoes, but the climb is worth it for the views and the rather eerie atmosphere. Don't wander too far up the road because of the heavy military presence there.

Places to Stay & Eat Hunder is a spread out village, like many others, full of cobbled streets, with no centre and street signs. There is no way to find out the name and location of a guesthouse – they are often just a few rooms at the back of someone's home; it is a matter of constantly asking directions.

One of the better places is the *Nerchung Pa Guesthouse*, owned by the local headmaster. It is friendly, set in a nice garden, costs Rs 150 per person including three meals, and is very hard to find.

Sumur

Sumur is the first major village along the Nubra River side of the valley. It is also a pretty place, and worth staying and exploring.

The **Samstem Ling Gompa** at Sumur, over 150 years old, is a large complex with seven temples. Inaugurated by the Dalai Lama in 1962, it is a busy, friendly place with about 45 children busy chanting, or cultivating apples and apricots. The prayer rooms open to the public house an impressive collection of thangkas and excellently restored frescoes.

By road, it is a fair distance from Sumur village to the gompa: about 3km towards the village of **Tegar**, from where a 3km road to the gompa starts. It's far quicker on foot (about 1km), as you can go up the hill from the village and avoid the road, but you will have to ask directions. It can be confusing, because the gompa near the start of the road to the Samstem Ling Gompa is actually the Tegar Gompa. The Samstem Ling Gompa is more colourful closer to Sumur.

Places to Stay & Eat Along the main road in Sumur is the dingy *Hotel Sumur* for rock-bottom price and comfort.

Tsering Angchok Hotel is another no-frills place but cheapish at Rs 100 per person – just follow the signs from the main road.

Stakray Guest House, farther up – ask for directions – owned by the local headmaster, has rooms for about Rs 200 a person

with three meals. You get good, friendly service and mountain views.

Hotel Yarab Tso is an upmarket place just opposite the road leading to the Samstem Ling Gompa, near Tegar village. For a rather overpriced Rs 600, you get a large, clean room and immaculate bath with hot water.

You may be able to stay at the Samstem Ling Gompa if you are a serious (male) Buddhist student. There are some shops near the main road in Sumur with limited supplies, and some tea stalls that serve basic food.

Panamik

Panamik is another small village, famous for centuries for its **hot springs**, and is the first or last stop along the ancient trade route between Ladakh and Central Asia. Panamik is as far north as foreigners are permitted to travel in India; farther north lies the high altitude battlefield of the Siachen Glacier.

While Panamik may be a long way to come for some hot springs, they are worth visiting if you're in the Nubra Valley. Unfortunately soldiers sometimes pollute the pool by using it to do their laundry. The water, which is meant to cure rheumatism, among other ailments, is pumped in by pipe from the Nubra River, about 2km from the village. It is usually easier for men to have a bathroom or shower; unfortunately, women will have to be a bit more modest and careful about their attire. There are also a couple of craft shops in the village, where you can buy some weaving and woodcarvings.

The 250-year-old **Ensa Gompa**, perched on a cliff on the far side of the river, is farther than it seems – a couple of hours at least. However, if you do want to get there, walk about 5km to Hargam, then cross the bridge for some more walking. Strictly speaking this means going beyond the permit zone, so the soldiers might insist you go back. Some travellers have tried to cross the river by swimming or wading and nearly came to a tragic end. Be sensible and take the bridge.

Places to Stay & Eat The only place to stay is the *Silk Route Guest House*, which

LADAKH & ZANSKAR

costs Rs 200 for a big double room; dhal, rice and tea will cost more. There are one or two small shops for supplies, but they offer little.

Getting There & Away

As with most of Ladakh, the road to the Nubra Valley (because of the very high Khardung La), and, therefore, the valley itself, is only open for three to four months of the year, from about June to September.

Bus Buses travel to both sides of the Nubra Valley from Leh every few days. The timetables are irregular, so check with local bus and tourist agencies. The buses are slow and crowded, as expected in this region, but are fun. Buses between Leh and Diskit travel on Friday (Rs 65, about six hours); they leave Leh at 6.30 am. A bus to Sumur and Panamik (about 10 hours to Panamik, Rs 79), leaves Leh at 6.30 am on Monday and Wednesday.

Truck Lifts on trucks, even military ones – in fact, anything travelling along the roads to, and around the Nubra Valley – are quite acceptable for tourists and locals alike, although women should travel in pairs. As usual, negotiate a fare (around the cost of the bus fare, ie Rs 65) the day before, and prepare yourself for a rough old ride.

Taxi Hiring jeeps or taxis may be the only alternative, and with a group it is often a good option. A one-way/return taxi to Diskit from Leh will cost Rs 3355/4425. A taxi from Leh to Panamik will cost Rs 3520, or Rs 4700 return. A return trip from Leh visiting Diskit, Hunder, Sumur and Panamik for three days will cost about Rs 8000 per taxi. If there are taxis around Diskit, they will offer full-day tours around the area on the southern side of the valley for Rs 950; or Rs 1250 including both sides. From Diskit to Panamik, it will be Rs 1155/1490; from Diskit to Sumur, Rs 770/970.

Getting Around

Buses from Diskit to Panamik and back go on Monday and Wednesday. The bus will drop you off in the main street of Diskit, a little way off the main road.

DHA-HANU

Dha-Hanu consists of a handful of villages along a road leading north-west from Khalsi, which is west of Leh, midway to Kargil. The steep bare walls of the Indus give the terraced fields more light and heat than other parts of Ladakh, which combined with the lower altitude ensures rich crops of vegetables and fruits (especially apricots).

It is a small region and doesn't get many visitors, which is not a bad reason to visit. The definite pluses are its accessibility by bus, along a reasonable road, the charming villages and the people, who have different traditions and appearances to the rest of the population of Ladakh. Currently, permits will allow you to go only as far as Dha village.

The area is probably most famous for its inhabitants, known as Dards or Brokpas, 'people of the land', an ancient Indo-Iranian tribe. Despite their proximity to Pakistan and other Islamic regions, they are traditionally not Muslims (though there are a few mosques in the area) but retain their own Buddhist traditions and beliefs. They belong to the whiter-skinned Indo-Aryan tribal group, who migrated to the area over 1000 years ago from the Gilgit area in far northern Pakistan. Two of their most unusual traits are their intense distaste for onions and cows, and anything bovine such as milk and beef.

The Brokpas often wear traditional clothes. Men wear coats similar to those worn in Leh, and some are made from goatskin. Women often wear caps (rather than the *gondas* found in Leh) adorned with jewellery, flowers and peacock feathers, have long, ornate chains, heavy earrings, and wear their hair long.

Places to Stay & Eat

There are a handful of basic guesthouses in the village of Dha.

Skyababa Guesthouse at the Leh end of the village has basic doubles for Rs 100, and the family is friendly.

Chunu Guesthouse in the heart of the village has very rustic doubles for Rs 60.

Lhariemo Shamo Guesthouse nearby is similar but charges Rs 100 for a double.

There are recognised *camping sites* at the villages of Dhumkhar, Skurbuchan, Hanu, Biama and Dha, and plenty of other legal, but unofficial, places along the way. The one or two shops at Dha and Skurbuchan offer little food; your guesthouse will provide something to eat, or bring your own.

Getting There & Away
Buses from Leh to Dha leave daily at 9 am (Rs 20, six hours); and from Leh to Dha via Skurbuchan daily at 10 am. A taxi to Dha from Leh will cost Rs 2486, and Rs 3393 return over two days.

TSO MORIRI & TSO KAR
Known as 'mountain lake', Tso Moriri is in the Rupshu Valley, only about 140km, but a rough and tumble six or so hours by jeep, from Leh. The lake is about 28km long and 8km at its widest, and at an elevation of over 4000m. Surrounded by barren hills, which are backed by snow-covered mountains, Tso Moriri is not in a really spectacular setting, but it's a good place to relax, visit the nearby **gompas** and walk around. On the way from Leh to Tso Moriri is another, brackish, lake the smaller Tso Kar, or 'white lake'. On a slight – and legal – detour off the track linking Tso Kar and Tso Moriri is the smaller lake of **Tso Kiagar**.

This is an area of nomadic people, known as Khampas, who can often be seen taking advantage of the summer and moving herds of goats, cows and yaks from one grazing spot to another. Khampas live in large, movable, family tents, or in solid winter-proof brick huts.

Another great aspect of this region is the amount of wildlife – the best (accessible) place in Ladakh for it. Commonly seen are wild asses, known as kiangs, foxes, and cuddly marmots busy waking up from their last hibernation, or preparing for the next. On the lakes, you may see black-necked geese in large flocks.

Tso Moriri
• alt 4400m
The small collection of huts on the shore of Tso Moriri is simply called Tso Moriri. Here you must register and show your permit. You can pitch your tent here, but there is nothing stopping you from camping anywhere else. Tso Moriri village does have a toilet.

Korzok
A 1km or so path at the back of the huts leads to the delightful village of Korzok, inhabited by friendly people. The **gompa** there is quite unusual because it is inhabited predominantly by about 30 women, who often spend their days making beautiful garments for themselves, but which are not for sale. The gompa was built in about 1850, replacing one destroyed during a Dogra invasion.

Thukse
On Tso Kar, the village of Thukse has a small **gompa** and a collection of solid brick huts set up for the dramatic winters. You will have to find the monk to let you in the gompa.

Places to Stay & Eat
In short, there is nowhere to stay in the region at all. You must bring your own tents and all equipment. There are pre-set two person tents at the astronomical price of Rs 800 at Tso Moriri village; these are set up for upmarket, organised tour groups.

There is no place to eat in the region, so, again, bring your own food and cooking equipment. This is a very fragile environment, so take out, and back to Leh, everything that you bring in – cans, bottles, papers, *everything*.

Getting There & Away
There are two ways that your 4WD jeep is physically able, and permitted, to enter or leave the region. The first route is over the Mahe bridge (near Raldong, along the Indus Valley road) through Puga, and then to one or both lakes. The other route is the road south from Upshi, over the Taglang La (5328m), then a detour off the road – look

LADAKH & ZANSKAR

out for the yellow sign. Once you get off any main road, there are no signs (or maps) at all.

There is no public transport that even remotely goes near the lakes. The area has no signposts, and quality maps of the area are nonexistent, so motorcycles are not recommended unless you have a guide (you could easily burn out the clutch in the sand drifts as well). There will be very few people around to give you directions – the marmots around here outnumber humans by about 50 to one!

Taxi A round trip from Leh to Tso Moriri over three days costs about Rs 9000 via Tso Kar and Taglang La; the shorter, more direct way is Rs 7500. From Leh, a two day round trip just to Tso Kar will be Rs 6500. Travel agencies in Leh can organise a three day 'jeep safari' from Rs 7500 to Rs 10,000 per vehicle, including meals and tent accommodation, depending which way you go.

Trekking With a guide, trekking is possible, and has been completed successfully by several travellers. On foot, you can enter the region from anywhere; the best starting point would be the Mahe bridge – it is easy to get a bus or truck there from Leh. But remember that suitable maps do not exist of the area.

CHUMATHANG

Not far from the Mahe bridge is the uninspiring village of Chumathang, set around a huge yard of rusting asphalt drums. Its claims to fame are its hot springs and rafting. You can organise yourself a private bathroom of hot sulphurous water, which is not worth the effort. There are a few tea stalls in the village, and one or two charmless guesthouses.

PANGONG TSO
• alt 4250m

The salty Pangong Tso – *pangong* means 'hollow' – is the highest lake in Ladakh at about 4300m, and is flanked by massive peaks over 6500m high. The lake is 150km long, but is only 4km at its widest, and

extends almost in a straight line, way into Tibet; in fact, only a quarter of the lake is in India. Unfortunately visitors are usually only allowed to spend an hour or two at the lake itself and some travellers have reported that the army make it clear they would prefer you didn't visit at all. Many visitors find the long trip and quick turnaround a waste of time and money. Permits allow travel from Leh to Pangong Tso via Karu, Chang La (5599m), Durbuk, Tangtse, Lukung and only as far as **Spangmik**, the first village on the north-western side of the lake.

The area around **Tangtse**, on the way to the lake, is of historical significance, as it was an important stop on the old trade routes. There is a small **gompa** and, nearby, some **inscriptions**, possibly 1000 years old, on some hard to find rocks.

Places to Stay & Eat
There are no guesthouses in the villages except a *Government resthouse* in Tangtse, which is not strictly for tourists, so you will have to bring your own tents and all your own supplies. Foreigners are no longer permitted to camp by the lake. Official camping sites are at Durbuk, Tangtse and Lukung; otherwise, just take your pick of any unofficial spot in the countryside. Lukung is about the best area for camping. There are several little villages along the lake, and on the way to it, but they offer little, if anything, in the way of supplies.

Getting There & Away
From Leh, the road is reasonable to the military town of Karu, goes over the Chang La (5599m), and then becomes terrible down to Tangtse, another military site. It then alternates between bad and barely adequate until Lukung, and then Spangmik, which is as far as your permit will allow; a 4WD vehicle is necessary for this section.

By Indian or Japanese jeep from Leh the one-way/return fare to Tangtse is Rs 2915/3630. A more leisurely two day trip, which is about all you may need, will cost Rs 5250 per vehicle from Leh. You may be able to fit in a side trip to the gompas at

Tikse and Chemrey along the way to Tangtse.

There are occasional buses from Leh to Tangtse, but taking one will severely limit your ability to explore the area, as there is no local public transport there.

Leh to Manali

Since opening to foreigners in 1989 the Leh-Manali road has become a popular way into and out of Leh. The only other road to Leh goes through Kashmir and along a stretch between Drass and Kargil, made more hazardous than usual by Pakistani artillery, and there is often difficulty in getting flights into and out of Leh. There is nothing much to see along the road in the way of villages or gompas; it is the raw high altitude scenery that will certainly impress and is reason enough for travelling this way.

The road to Manali is the world's second-highest motorable road (the highest runs from Leh to the Nubra Valley), reaching 5328m at Taglang La. As only about half of the 485km between Leh and Manali is paved, it can be a rough journey. For much of the way the only inhabitants of the high plateaux are Khampa nomads, soldiers and teams of tar-covered workers from Bihar and Nepal struggling to keep this strategic road open. Whatever form of transport, it will take at least two days, with an overnight stop at a tent camp, probably in Sarchu.

Sudden changes in weather are common, even in the mid-summer month of August, causing delays of several days. It is worth having some cold and wet weather gear with you in the bus because the weather, especially around the highest passes, can be very cold and/or wet. The road is usually open between early June and mid-October.

LEH TO UPSHI

Leaving Leh, from the main road you will get your last glimpse (or your first, of course, if coming from Manali) of the magnificent gompas at Tikse, Shey and Stok.

For an hour or so before Upshi, along a paved, but dusty, road, there are plenty of ugly military sites, such as at Karu, where there is the turn-off to the Pangong Tso area and the gompas at Taktok and Chemrey.

UPSHI

The first checkpoint of Upshi is the turn-off south to Manali. Although permits are not needed for this trip, foreigners have to register at the police hut. If travelling on a bus with plenty of other foreigners, there is lots of time

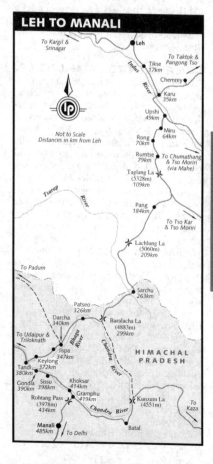

for tea, a greasy 'omlate', or to stock up on supplies of chocolate and other goodies.

UPSHI TO TAGLANG LA

At Miru, there is a crumbling little hillside **gompa**, surrounded by chörtens. There is nowhere to stay or eat, but plenty of camping sites. Lato has a huge **chörten** on the side of the road, but there is no village to speak of. From here the road starts to climb for about three hours to Taglang La (5328m), where there's a little shrine, and possibly the world's highest 'Gents Urinal' and 'Ladies Urinal'. The bus will stop for a rest and a look around, but if coming from Manali and you haven't acclimatised to the altitude, take it easy.

TAGLANG LA TO LACHLUNG LA

Not long after Taglang La, the road surprisingly flattens out along the Morey Plain, and becomes paved. This area is only occasionally inhabited by Khampa nomads. If going on to Tso Moriri or Tso Kar, you will have to look out for the sign. (See the Ladakh Regions section earlier.) The road to Pang is good, through a windswept valley, then becomes hopelessly potholed. About 5km before Pang the road descends through a dramatic **series of gorges** before reaching the tea house settlement.

Pang, at the bottom of these gorges, has several restaurants in tents set up by the river where most buses stop for lunch. A plate of rice, dhal and vegetables costs about Rs 30, and you may be able to stock up on mineral water and biscuits. Most tents have a mattress where you can unroll your sleeping bag for around Rs 50 per night. There are some rather grim toilets nearby.

At 5060m, Lachlung La is the second-highest pass on the Leh-Manali road. Nearby is an incredible 20km of switchback roads, including the spine-tingling 21 Gata Loops, or hairpin bends, on one side of a mountain.

SARCHU

• alt 4100m

Sarchu is just inside Himachal Pradesh, and is where most buses stop overnight. It is just a collection of tents, dotted over a length of 15km or so, which all pack up for eight months of the year (ie October to May). Just opposite the striped Himachal Pradesh Tourist Development Corporation (HPTDC) tent camps, you must register, again, with the police. Your bus driver may collect passports and do it himself, but it still involves a lot of waiting.

HPTDC buses stop at HPTDC's own **tent camps**. They are the best of the lot: clean two person tents with camp beds and mountains of blankets are Rs 115 per person. A **tent kitchen** does passable dhal and rice for dinner, and omelettes for breakfast, all costing about Rs 40.

Public and other private bus drivers seem to have some sort of 'arrangement' with other tent site owners, so you may have little choice but to stay in a tent camp not even remotely as good as the HPTDC site, but for around the same price. Travellers on buses that arrive late at the camps have the least choice. Although the driver may try to dissuade you, you can sleep on the bus for free, where it will be warmer. There are plenty of places to put your own tent.

Just over the bridge from the HPTDC camp are several **tent restaurants** that serve dhal and rice, tea, omelettes, curried noodles, and, for those long cold evenings, a shot of whiskey or chang (take it easy though; alcohol is more powerful at high-altitude).

BARALACHA LA

It's only a short climb to this 4883m pass, which means Crossroads Pass because it is a double pass linking both the upper Chandra and Bhaga valleys with the Lingti Valley and vast Lingti plains around Sarchu. About an hour farther on is the **police checkpoint** at Patseo. Here the road begins to hug the Bhaga River to Tandi, where it meets the Chandra River.

DARCHA

Darcha is the other major tent site on this road. Faster buses from Leh, or slower ones from Manali, may stay here, depending on the time and the state of the road around Baralacha La, but Sarchu is more commonly used as a stopover. Like Sarchu, Darcha is just a temporary place, with some crummy tents for hire, and a few tent restaurants in the area. Shortly after Darcha, you pass through Jispa, where there is yet another large army camp.

Darcha is the start of a popular trekking option to get into Padum, and in winter it is the only way. From here, you can also trek into places such as Hemis (about 11 days). If you have your own transport, try to get to the little lake of **Deepak Tal**, about 16km from Darcha. It is a great spot for camping and exploration.

KEYLONG TO MANALI

Keylong is the first town of any size on the journey from Leh to Manali, and the administrative centre of Lahaul & Spiti. From Keylong, it isn't far to the T-junction at Tandi. From here there is a road that goes sharply to the north-west along the Chenab River to the little-visited parts of Himachal Pradesh towards Udaipur and the famous temple site of **Triloknath**. See the Around Keylong section of the Himachal Pradesh chapter for details.

The road to Manali heads south-east, and climbs steadily past Gondla, Sissu and Khoksar. There are *PWD resthouses*, which you may be able to use, in all three places, but nothing much else. There is a nice **waterfall** near Sissu, set under spectacular peaks. Farther on, at Gramphu, the road continues to climb along Lahaul & Spiti – get off at Gramphu or at Keylong if you want to continue to Kaza – or heads south to Manali.

Rohtang Pass (3978m) – not high, but treacherous all the same – starts the descent to Manali.

See the Himachal Pradesh chapter for more details on Keylong and Manali.

GETTING THERE & AWAY
Bus

As the road goes up to 5328m at its highest point, most people suffer the effects of alti-

tude (headaches, nausea) from the rapid ascent, as well as the high altitude, unless they have spent time acclimatising in Leh.

If you plan to fly one way, then fly into Leh and take the bus out because the effects of the altitude on the Leh-Manali journey will not be so great as in the other direction. Many people coming from Manali spend an uncomfortable night at Sarchu, where the altitude is around 4100m.

All buses leave Leh at about 6 am to get an early start for the long haul to the overnight stop. Make sure you know your bus number because at this early hour, in darkness, it can be quite confusing finding your bus among several others.

There are three types of buses that travel between Leh and Manali, all of which generally run daily during the season, more often if there is demand. Most bus services will not start until about early June and then cease in about mid-October, possibly later, if there is demand and the weather holds. Late in the season, the availability of buses from Leh depends on the demand for passengers travelling in the other direction, ie from Manali to Leh. From Manali, it is easy to get a connection on a deluxe bus almost straight away to Delhi for about Rs 400 or to many other places; less for the public bus.

HPTDC Bus The most comfortable bus is operated by the HPTDC. Bookings and departures are from the HPTDC office on Fort Rd in Leh, or the HPTDC Marketing Office (☎ 01902-52360) on The Mall, Manali. Tickets cost Rs 700 (Rs 600 from Leh to Keylong), or Rs 1000 including a tent, dinner and breakfast in Sarchu. This extra Rs 300 is not worth it, as you can stay in the same tent and order the same meals yourself in Sarchu for about half this. Try to book your bus ticket as far in advance as you can, especially if you intend travelling at the end of the season.

Private Bus Many privately owned (mostly by travel agencies in Manali) buses offer an alternative. All private buses cost around the same: about Rs 800, plus accommodation

LADAKH & ZANSKAR

and food in Sarchu or Darcha – but the price can, and does, change according to the demand. In Leh, you must buy your tickets from any of the travel agencies, which means you probably won't know what bus you have a ticket for until you get on. In Manali, bookings can, and should, be made directly with the bus agencies themselves, or any of the travel agencies in Manali will sell you a ticket. Some of the bus companies in Manali servicing the Leh to Manali route on a regular basis are:

Enn Bee Tours & Travels
   (☎ 01902-52650) The Mall (opposite the bus station)
Ibex Tours
   (☎ 01902-52480) Hotel Ibex, The Mall
Swagtam Tours
   (☎ 01902-52390) Mission Rd .

Public Bus The third alternative is the less comfortable, and generally slower, but certainly cheaper, public bus. They leave, according to demand, every one or two days from Leh and Manali at about 4 am. Superdeluxe (a bit of a misnomer) costs Rs 525; A class (more comfortable) is Rs 500; and B class is Rs 345. Subtract about Rs 70 from the fare if you plan to get off at Keylong.

Truck
Trucks can often be quicker than buses, and should be cheaper. They may not stop at Sarchu, but instead drive through the night, which is not a great idea; or they may stop overnight anywhere alongside the road – also not much fun. Trucks are more comfortable if there are only a couple of people in the cabin; women probably won't want to travel alone. Plenty of trucks travel this route, in season. It is just a matter of organising a lift the day before where the trucks stop in Leh or Manali. Around Rs 300 is a reasonable price. The truck stop in Leh is on the road to the airport.

Taxi
An option – which is not outrageous if in a group – is a taxi between Leh and Manali

for Rs 16,335. Discounts of up to 40% are possible outside the high season. This can be arranged at the Taxi Union on Fort Rd in Leh, or on The Mall, Manali. It will cost more for each day you take, but it allows you to stop, take photos, visit villages, and, theoretically, have some control over your maniacal driver.

Motorcycle
Motorcycles are a popular means of travelling between Leh and Manali, and places beyond. This, of course, gives you the option of taking several days to admire the spectacular scenery.

It is worth remembering that there are no villages between Leh and Keylong, so you will have to take all your spare parts, particularly spare chains and tubes – and enough spare parts to get out of Leh, too, because it doesn't have much to offer either. Some tent sites may sell limited (and sometimes even diluted) petrol at twice the Leh or Manali price; there are petrol stations at Tandi and Keylong, but nowhere else. At all times, it is advisable to wear cold and wet weather gear, including boots, because the road is always muddy, wet and dusty in places.

Leh to Kargil

This section refers to places on, or near, the main road from Leh to Kargil. The places below are listed in order of distance from Leh. See the Leh to Kargil map for distances.

There are a number of buses that ply the 231km to Kargil. Trucks are also a good way of getting a lift and for hitching between villages. Taxis may seem outrageous, but with a group sharing the cost, you can visit several gompas on the way to, say, Alchi or Lamayuru. For instance, a taxi from Leh to Alchi, stopping at Phyang, Basgo, Likir and Rizong, will cost about Rs 1200.

PHYANG
Not far past Spituk (refer to the Around Leh section for further details on Spituk), a long,

roughish track off the main road leads to the pretty village of Phyang. Mani walls lead to the little-visited **gompa** that was built around the 15th century by King Tashi Namgyal, and now houses about 50 monks who belong to the Drigungpa branch of the Kagyupa order.

The gompa is in need of restoration, but it's a good place to scramble around and explore, if you can find a monk to show you around. There's a bronze Buddha statue reputedly almost one thousand years old, and some huge thangkas, one of which is unrolled once a year during the annual Phyang Festival held around July/August.

Direct buses from Leh leave daily at 7.30 am, 2 and 5 pm (Rs 9.5). Hitching is not really possible as very few vehicles make the detour to Phyang. Taxis from Leh cost Rs 495 return. From Phyang, there is a trekking route that almost parallels the main road, passing through some lovely villages such as Likir and Temisgam, before returning to the main road near Khalsi. Part of this trek is described in the Treks in Ladakh boxed text earlier in this chapter.

NIMMU

Nimmu is a pleasant place to stop for tea. The only notable thing about Nimmu is that about 8km east, towards Leh, is the junction of the differently coloured Indus and Zanskar rivers. If you can, get out and admire this really spectacular sight. To Nimmu, take any bus going from Leh beyond Nimmu; a one-way/return taxi from Leh costs Rs 577/715.

BASGO

It's only 6km farther on to Basgo, which was the former capital of lower Ladakh, before the Ladakh kingdom was united at Leh. The 400-year-old **gompa** is up some winding, steep tracks. It is often deserted, so ask around for one of the handful of monks in the village to open up. The prayer room in the **Ser Zung Temple** has great frescoes; another temple has an enormous gold and copper statue of the Maitreya Buddha (the Future Buddha), and some elaborate roof and wall frescoes. The views from the roof are wonderful.

Lagungpa Guest House, next to the gompa, offers basic, but reasonable, doubles

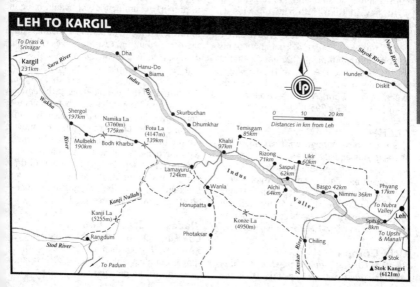

LEH TO KARGIL

for Rs 100. Daily buses from Leh go direct to Basgo at 1 and 4 pm (these times are changeable, so check at the tourist office in Leh for an update); or catch one of the daily buses to Alchi or beyond. A one-way/return taxi to Basgo from Leh will cost Rs 660/825.

LIKIR

Five kilometres from the main road, just before Saspul, is another magnificent **gompa**, overlooking the village of Likir. Known as the Klu-kkhyil (Water Spirits) Gompa, it was founded in the 14th century, and was the first gompa in Ladakh known to have been built under the direction of Tibetan monks. The present gompa was rebuilt in the 18th century, re-dedicated to the Gelukpa order, and is now inhabited by almost 150 monks.

There is a small museum upstairs, with an impressive collection of thangkas up to 500 years old, as well as some interesting Buddha figures. Unfortunately the wall paintings have suffered much water damage. There is no entrance fee, but there's a donation box for voluntary contributions. Among other things, the monks ask that visitors do not engage in '... smooching or hugging'.

To stay in Likir, return to the village, about 30 minutes walk across the fields. The pleasant *Norboo Guest House* has a large, authentic Ladakhi kitchen. Rooms here, including all meals, are good value at Rs 150 per person. A bus to Likir village, which continues to the gompa, leaves Leh every day at 3 pm. A one-way/return taxi from Leh costs Rs 795/890.

ALCHI

Alchi is a busy village with several good places to stay and eat. It is a pretty place, especially at the end of summer when villagers are harvesting. There's also a lovely walk down to the Indus River. It's worth staying to break up the long haul between Leh and Kargil or Srinagar, or as a base for exploring places such as Likir, Basgo and Rizong.

Alchi Gompa

The *chos-kor* (religious enclave) at Alchi is one of the great art treasures of the Buddhist world, one of the very few remaining examples of Indian Buddhist art from the 11th century. This collection of five small temples has a miraculously preserved series of statues and frescoes in a style quite different from the rest of Ladakh's gompas. The finest of the temples is the **sumtsek** (three-storey temple), with ornate wooden carvings at the entrance and three remarkable statues of Buddha inside. Take a torch (flashlight) to examine the miniature paintings on the robes of the Buddhas, but don't use a camera as the flash will damage the art.

In the niche on the left is a statue of Avalokiteshvara, with scenes of court life painted on its clothing. The statue of Manjushri on the right has images of pilgrimages and palaces, while Maitreya, the central statue in the niche at the rear has figures in Tantric positions. The three statues protrude into the upper storey, reached by a rickety ladder. Around the walls are numerous mandalas.

The nearby **dukhang** (main prayer room) is the oldest building in Alchi and has six beautiful mandalas and a stunning statue of the Vairocana Buddha. The courtyard is partially open to the sky but you'll need a torch to properly examine the Vairocana statue in the niche at the back of the inner hall. Behind the guilded statue and on either side there are some interesting friezes of fierce deities, royalty and ancient armies.

The small temple next to the dukhang contains an image of **Ringchen Zangpo**, who founded the gompa in the 11th century on his return from India, which accounts for the Indian and, particularly, Kashmiri, influences. The **Lhakhang Soma** or 'new' temple to the left of the sumtsek is painted with incidents from the life of Buddha.

One of the more enjoyable aspects of this gompa is that it is the only one in the Ladakhi region on flat ground, so no knee-breaking climbing is involved.

Places to Stay & Eat

Choskor, a family-run place in the village, a short walk from the temples, offers good, simple doubles/triples for Rs 120/150, and basic meals in a nice garden.

Zimskhang Guest House, closer to the temples, has doubles without/with bath for Rs 100/200.

Pota La Guest House has airy rooms with bath for Rs 150. It also has a restaurant and camping site. *Samdup Ling Guest House*, nearby, is a similar price and standard.

Lotsava, is simple but good value. Rooms are Rs 60/100 with shared bath.

Alchi Resort near the car park has two-room huts with bath and hot water set around a courtyard for a negotiable Rs 500.

Getting There & Away

There is one direct bus to Alchi every day, leaving Leh at 3 pm (Rs 30). Otherwise, take any other daily bus to places beyond Alchi, and get off at the bridge about 2km past Saspul (tee it up with the bus conductor or driver). It is a fairly easy 3km walk from there (taking short cuts) to Alchi. A one-way/return taxi from Leh costs Rs 935/1155.

SASPUL

Saspul is a village on the main road, over the river from the turn-off to Alchi. Apparently there is a small **cave temple** nearby, but nobody seems to know much about it. While Saspul is nice enough, Alchi has far more to offer.

Chakzoth Guest House, on the main road in Saspul, has small rooms for Rs 50.

Hotel Duke (☎ 194106-27021) is a decent, new mid-range place, painted with Ladakhi murals. Comfortable doubles are Rs 500; and dinner is Rs 120.

RIZONG

About 6km along a rough road leading off the main road is the start of the area with the **nunnery** of Julichen and the **gompa** of Rizong. The gompa, belonging to the Gelukpa order, entails a very steep climb. Founded only 100 years ago, it is less notable artistically than some others, but is known for its frescoes. The lamas and *chomos* (nuns) follow a strict lifestyle.

There is no village at Rizong, so there is nowhere to stay or eat, but you may be able to stay at the gompa (men only) or the nunnery (women only) if you ask, and bring your own supplies. Alternatively, near the turn-off to Rizong, about 200m towards Alchi on the main road, is the pricey *Uley Tokpo Camping Ground* with mildly luxurious tents for Rs 800 for two, Rs 1650 with meals. The camp is set among apricot trees.

There is no direct bus to Rizong from Leh, so it is a matter of getting a bus bound for somewhere beyond Lamayuru. If coming from Alchi, it is not difficult to hitch a ride on a truck or bus for 20 minutes between the turn-offs for Alchi and Rizong. As an alternative, a taxi one way from Leh to the bottom of the walk up to the gompa will set you back Rs 1330.

KHALSI

There has been some sort of bridge over the Indus River, and a turn-off to the Dha-Hanu region, at Khalsi for many centuries. Now it is a major military area, where your passport will be checked regardless of where you are going, and your permit checked if you're going to the Dha-Hanu region.

LAMAYURU

After exploring villages around the area, it comes as a surprise to find that Lamayuru is a scruffy little place. But it is completely overshadowed by one of the most famous and spectacularly set gompas in Ladakh.

It is the location perched above the drained lake on an eroded crag overlooked by massive mountains, that makes it special. Belonging of the Kagyupa order, and the oldest known gompa in Ladakh (dating back beyond the 10th century) it has been destroyed and restored several times over the centuries. Once criminals were granted asylum here (not any more, you'll be glad to know!), which explains one previous name for the gompa: Tharpa Ling or Place of Freedom. Try to get there early to witness a mesmerising puja. There are renowned collections of carpets, thangkas and frescoes.

Take a wander through the wonderful stone passages and courtyards of the lower part of the complex and try to locate the **Singge Gang lhakhang**, an Alchi-era temple with guardian deities in an adjacent chamber. It isn't easy to find; look out for the white and red walls.

About three hours walk from Lamayuru is the small **Wanla Gompa**, set on the popular trekking route to Padum in Zanskar.

Places to Stay & Eat

The options aren't so fantastic. The better places to stay are in the village, not on the main road.

Hotel Shangri-La, near the main road, has nice views and rooms for Rs 100.

Hotel Dragon is a slightly better option (no dirt floors); just follow the ubiquitous signs. It offers large rooms, with shared bath, for Rs 150 per room.

Both hotels offer some food, but it's usually little more than dhal, rice or noodles. It's also possible to stay at the gompa's very basic lodgings for Rs 50.

Getting There & Away

There are no buses from Leh or Kargil directly to Lamayuru, so take the Leh to Kargil/Srinagar bus and get off at the truck stop at the top of the village. A better option is a ride on one of the many trucks that stop there. Trucks leave Lamayuru in the early morning; ask around at the truck stop for expected departure/arrival times. A one-way taxi in one long day from Leh costs Rs 1952. You can easily walk from the main road to the gompa and the village.

MULBEKH

From Lamayuru the road traverses Fotu La (4147m), the highest pass on the route, then Namika La (3760m) before suddenly turning into a lovely green valley. Mulbekh is the last vestige of Buddhism, as you shortly head into the Muslim-dominated regions near Kargil and beyond.

Mulbekh's main claim to fame is the impressive 8m-high **Maitreya statue**, an image of a future Buddha, cut into the rock face, dating back to about 700 CE (common era). Unfortunately, all buses stop for food and a rest at the village of **Wakha**, only 2km from Mulbekh, so this gives you no opportunity

to inspect the statue on the way, but you can see it from the bus window.

There are also two gompas: **Serdung** and **Gandentse**, which offer great views of the valley. As in other smaller villages, it is wise to inquire if the gompa is open before making the ascent. If it's not, somebody from the village may have keys and accompany you.

Paradise Hotel & Restaurant, right opposite the Chamba statue, costs Rs 80 per room. The *Namchung Hotel* is similar.

J&KTDC Tourist Bungalow has rooms for Rs 40 per person.

From Leh, take the Kargil/Srinagar bus. Mulbekh makes a decent day trip from Kargil. A couple of buses leave Kargil for Mulbekh every day. A return taxi from Kargil plus an hour or so in Mulbekh will cost Rs 800.

SHERGOL

About 7km farther on towards Kargil, along a fertile valley, is the small village of Shergol. Meaning Lord of the Morning Star, Shergol is set on the opening of the Wakha River, and has a tiny **cave gompa** perched halfway up the steep, eastern slope of the mountain. It is almost deserted, and is really for those who can't get enough of gompas and stiff walks up mountains. The view, of course, is magnificent. Below the gompa is a **nunnery**, home to a dozen or so chomos.

Kargil & the Suru Valley

The valleys of Suru, Drass, Wakha and Bodh Kharbu lie midway between the alpine valleys of Kashmir, and the fertile reaches of the Indus Valley and Ladakh. The region is politically part of India, ethnically part of Baltistan, and geographically an integral part of Ladakh. It is the only region of India with a Shi'ah Muslim majority (see the Shi'ahs of Ladakh boxed text).

Geographically, there is little doubt that one has crossed the Himalayan watershed.

The Shi'ahs of Ladakh

Kargil and the Suru Valley is the only region of India where the majority are Shi'ah Muslims. Isolated from both their Sunni Muslim neighbours in Kashmir and the Buddhists of the Indus Valley, the Shi'ahs look far afield, to Iran and the city of Lucknow in Uttar Pradesh, the centre of Shi'ah India. Books and other religious materials come from Lucknow, while the area's religious leaders study in Iran (the great Shi'ah centres in Iraq are off limits for now). Religious students from Iran regularly visit Kargil and hold public lectures.

Shi'ah Islam broke away from the majority Sunni school over the issue of the successor to Mohammed, or Imam. Shi'ahs hold that the Imamate rightfully belonged to Mohammed's cousin Ali and his descendants, including his martyred son Hussain. The major Shi'ah festival in Kargil is during the Islamic month of Muharram, commemorating the battle of Karbala in modern-day Iraq when Hussain was killed. Shi'ahism also differs from Sunni Islam with its hierarchy of clerics; currently the highest authority is the Supreme Leader of Iran, Ayatollah Khamenei, although a dispute over self-flagellation has led to a split that has reached even Kargil.

During the Muharram processions it is customary for men to whip themselves in mourning for Hussain. Ayatollah Khamenei says the custom should be stopped and that it would be better to give blood to a blood bank, but Ayatollah Shirazi, a senior Iranian cleric, argues the custom should continue. You can sometimes tell which side of the debate a Kargil shopkeeper stands on by portraits stuck on the wall; some are of the rather jolly looking white-bearded Ayatollah Shirazi, others show the bespectacled Ayatollah Khamenei.

The spiritual leaders of Kargil's Shi'ahs are known as Aghas, descended from the missionaries who started converting the population, apparently peacefully, in the 15th century. Many of those missionaries were Syeds, direct descendants of the Prophet Mohammed. The Syeds are recognisable by their black turbans. Shi'ah clerics who are not Syeds wear white turbans.

The Shi'ahs of Ladakh have lagged behind their Buddhist neighbours economically; perhaps because Islam doesn't have the same exotic appeal to foreign tourists as Buddhism, the Shi'ahs have received only a tiny share of the tourist dollar. Nevertheless, relations between the two communities are quite good; the Shi'ahs have never taken part in the Islamic extremism that has wreaked Kashmir.

A new generation of mullahs in Kargil has gradually lifted many of the old prohibitions, in particular on music, polo, female education and learning English. One of the old mullahs ordered that people wishing to learn another language should learn Arabic, to prepare them for paradise, where only Arabic is spoken. Increased literacy has changed the relationship between mullahs and lay Shi'ahs; people are now encouraged to study their faith themselves and to ask their mullahs questions on law, theology and ethics, while in turn the mullahs are expected to be knowledgeable in all aspects of the faith.

Nevertheless, the Suru Valley is still a conservative area without the familiarity that people in Leh have with foreigners; taking photos of women is not appreciated and non-Muslim visitors to the Jama Masjid (Friday Mosque) aren't really welcome.

The steep barren hills now stretch to the snow line. As the snows melt, the waters flow freely down into the heavily irrigated valleys. Here Tibetan-style settlements thrive. Whitewashed mud and stone houses contrast with deep-green barley fields. Mosques are the only sign that one has not yet entered Buddhist Ladakh.

The earliest settlers of these isolated tributaries of the Indus were the Dards. According to the noted historian AH Franke, the Dards were already acquainted with the Buddhist teachings prevalent in north-west India, and had absorbed them into their culture some time before 500 CE. Later, as the Tibetan forces invaded Ladakh, much of the Dardic culture was abandoned, although isolated pockets of their heritage remain significantly intact, notably at Drass.

The full cultural shift came far later, in the 15th century, shortly after the Kashmiris were converted to Islam. Most Dardic groups were also converted, including the people of Drass. What remain today are Dardic groups, distinct from the Baltis in both language and religion – the Dards are Sunni Muslims, and the Baltis are Shi'ah. To complete this cultural patchwork, there are some isolated Dardic communities, in the Dha-Hanu region below Khalsi, which are still Buddhist.

In the Suru, Wakha and Bodh Kharbu valleys, the cultural similarities with Baltistan are more apparent. Trade links were also strong between Gilgit and Kargil, so the region's attention focused along the Indus Valley. Isolated Buddhist communities still remain at Mulbekh in the Wakha Valley, and in the tiny kingdom of Heniskot in the upper Bodh Kharbu Valley.

The regions of Dardistan and Baltistan maintained a degree of independence from both the Mughal armies that held Kashmir, and the Mongol-Tibetan armies intent on taking Ladakh. In the 1830s, however, the Suru Valley was invaded by the army of Jammu's Dogra leader Zorawar Singh, who was intent on invading Ladakh. As a result of the Dogra forays, Ladakh and Baltistan came under the influence of Jammu, and in 1846 became an integral part of the maharaja's state of Jammu & Kashmir. A century later the region was divided, and the cease fire line between Pakistan and India was drawn across the state of Jammu & Kashmir just north of Kargil, though in the 1971 war the frontier moved back about 12km from the town. As a consequence, the regions down the valley from Kargil are strictly no-go areas for foreigners.

Kargil can be a little hotter than Leh. In summer (May to October), the average maximum/minimum temperature is 28/16°C and in winter (November to April), it is -2/-12°C.

KARGIL
☎ 01985 • pop 5500

The importance and influence of Kargil has changed dramatically over the past century. It was, until 1947, an important trading centre linking Ladakh with Gilgit and the lower Indus Valley. There were also important trading links between the villages of the Suru and Zanskar valleys, and not much more than 20 years ago it was not uncommon to see yak trains making their way from Padum into the Kargil bazaar.

Continuing political problems in Kashmir and the proximity of the town to the Pakistani army have seriously affected the number of visitors to Kargil, and the existing hotels survive from the handful of visitors making their way from Leh to Padum and the Zanskar Valley. The town has been shelled by the Pakistani army several times in recent years; when artillery duels flare up, the town is declared off limits. At the time of writing fighting was continuing, in the most serious escalation of violence in 20 years, in an attempt to dislodge the rebels and most locals had been evacuated to neighbouring areas. Dras and large areas of Kargil were evacuated during the emergency and the Srinigar-Leh Hwy was closed. Check developments carefully before heading to Kargil.

The people of Kargil are mostly Shi'ah Muslims: Arabic script is everywhere; women are rarely seen, and if so, are usually veiled; and mosques dominate the town.

Orientation & Information

Kargil, next to the roaring Suru River, is the second-largest town in Ladakh but is really little more than one long main road called Main Bazaar Rd, with lots of lanes jutting off. Along Main Bazaar Rd are plenty of

FESTIVALS OF LADAKH

Festivals are an integral part of Ladakhi religion and agriculture, usually coinciding with the commemoration of religious events and the end of the harvest. These festivals often used to take place in winter, but many have now moved to the summer to coincide with another important part of the year: the tourist season. Major festivals are held each year at Spituk, Matho, Hemis, and most other gompas in the region. The annual dates for these gompa festivals, which are determined according to the Tibetan lunar calendar, are listed in this chapter.

Now that tourism is flourishing in the region, the annual Ladakh Festival has been extended and is now held in the first two weeks of September in a blatant attempt to prolong the tourist season. Nevertheless, the festival should not be missed. Regular large, colourful displays of dancing, sports, ceremonies and exhibitions are held throughout Ladakh, but mainly in Leh, which has the highest population and receives the most visitors.

The first day of the festival starts with a spectacular march through the main streets of Leh. People from all over Ladakh, monks in yellow and orange robes, polo and archery troupes and Tibetan refugees from Choglamsar, walk proudly in traditional costume, wearing the tall, bright *perak* hats and the curled *papu* shoes. The march culminates in a day-long cultural display at the polo ground in Leh. (If you want the best view of the opening ceremonies, ignore the march and go early to the polo ground to get a good seat.)

Other activities during the two weeks include mask dances, which are serious and hypnotic when performed by monks, or cheeky and frivolous when performed by small children. There are also archery and polo competitions, concerts and other cultural programs throughout

Inset: Tibetan Gelugpa monks. Photo: Bradley Mayhew
Left: Boy monks with splendid Berak hats and incense.
Right: Bright and cheeky – a mask dance performed by a child.

PATRICK HORTON

CHRISTOPHER WOOD

RICHARD I'ANSON

Ladakh. From year to year, handicraft, food, wildlife and *thangka* exhibitions are held in Leh. The tourist offices in Leh hand out free programs that list the locations and dates of the various activities.

Apart from Leh, other smaller, associated festivals are held in Changspa, Tangtse (near Pangong Tso), Shey, Basgo, Korzok (on the shore of Tso Moriri) and Biama (in the Dha-Hanu region). In the Nubra Valley, Diskit and Sumur hold the biggest festival outside Leh with camel races, 'warfare demonstrations' (not quite as violent as they sound), ibex and peacock dances, traditional marriage ceremonies, some sword dancing from Baltistan, flower displays and archery competitions.

CHRISTOPHER WOOD

Top: Young women in colourful traditional dress for a festival at Alchi.
Bottom: Unveiling of a huge thangka at Hemis – the most important gompa in Ladakh & Zanskar.

places with long-distance and international telephone facilities, as well as the post office and the State Bank of India, which changes money 10 am to 2 pm weekdays and 10 am to noon on Saturday. It's a lot faster changing money here than at the Forex in Leh.

If you have some time to kill, walk up Hospital Rd for some decent views of the area, or there are some nice fields and villages across the Qatilgah bridge, at the end of Balti Bazaar Rd. It's a longer walk uphill to the outlying village of Goma Kargil.

The Tourist Reception Centre, not to be confused with any similarly named government office, is next to the taxi stand, just off Main Bazaar Rd. Open 10 am to 4 pm, Monday to Friday, it has no great information on local areas, or on Zanskar. It does, however, rent out trekking gear: tents are Rs 40 per day, sleeping bags are Rs 16 per day, plus a deposit (around Rs 1500 for a tent).

The best place to arrange trekking and travel is through the Siachen and Greenland hotels.

Places to Stay

Kargil used to be full of grotty places to stay overnight for those travelling between Srinagar and Leh, or onwards to Zanskar. A few places on Main Bazaar Rd linger on, but they are really awful – it is not hard to get somewhere without the bugs, mould and noise.

J&KTDC Tourist Bungalow (☎ 2348) has clean rooms, good views and costs only Rs 40 per person, although it is a steep walk up from Main Bazaar Rd.

Hotel International is a dilapidated place with passable singles/doubles with bath and cold shower for Rs 100/150.

Hotel Tourist Marjina (☎ 33085) has rather dark rooms with shared bath for Rs 100 set on a courtyard; you enter through a streetside restaurant.

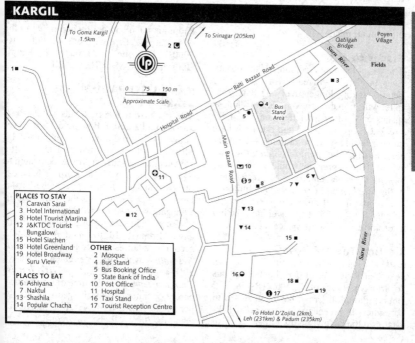

KARGIL

PLACES TO STAY
1 Caravan Sarai
3 Hotel International
8 Hotel Tourist Marjina
12 J&KTDC Tourist Bungalow
15 Hotel Siachen
18 Hotel Greenland
19 Hotel Broadway Suru View

PLACES TO EAT
6 Ashiyana
7 Naktul
13 Shashila
14 Popular Chacha

OTHER
2 Mosque
4 Bus Stand
5 Bus Booking Office
9 State Bank of India
10 Post Office
11 Hospital
16 Taxi Stand
17 Tourist Reception Centre

To Goma Kargil 1.5km
To Srinagar (205km)
Qatilgah Bridge
Poyen Village
Suru River
Fields
Balti Bazaar Road
Bus Stand Area
Hospital Road
Main Bazaar Road
Suru River
0 75 150 m
Approximate Scale
To Hotel D'Zojila (2km), Leh (231km) & Padum (235km)

LADAKH & ZANSKAR

Hotel Greenland (☎ 2324), farther south near the taxi stand, has quiet rooms with a veranda, some with nice baths (some with hot water) for Rs 150/200. The manager is an experienced trekker and useful for arranging a trip to Zanskar.

Hotel Broadway Suru View (☎ 2304) is a new place near the Greenland with rather incompetent staff, but it has decent double rooms with bath for a bargain Rs 200.

Hotel Siachen (☎ 2221) has excellent singles/doubles for Rs 350/500; it has a very nice garden, hot water and is good value. They can change money, and there's a travel agency.

Caravan Sarai (☎ 2278) in upper Kargil is a nice place, catering for the upmarket trekking crowd. It has rooms with hot water and views for Rs 1000/1400, including breakfast.

Hotel D'Zojila (☎ 2360), about 2km out of Kargil, is overpriced but they will negotiate if there are lots of empty rooms; singles/doubles are Rs 600/800 including bath and hot water, or up to Rs 2070 for a double with all meals.

Places to Eat

There is not much to recommend the restaurants in Kargil – it really isn't set up for people staying longer than one day. Your hotel will probably do some bland Chinese dishes and some omelettes and bread for breakfast. On and near Main Bazaar Rd are some bearable small restaurants – the *Naktul*, *Shashila* and *Popular Chacha* – all of which claim to prepare 'Chine's' food. Also worth a try is the *Ashiyana*. The restaurants at the *Siachen* and *Greenland* are quite adequate and they'll discreetly serve a bottle of beer for Rs 125 in the evening (alcohol is prohibited in Kargil, hence the price).

Getting There & Away

Bus The daily early-morning bus to Leh leaves at 5 am (Rs 145, 12 hours); the bus to Srinagar leaves at 4.30 am (Rs 145, 12 hours), though the road has been closed to foreigners in recent years because of Pakistani shelling. Towards Leh, there are also two daily buses to Mulbekh and one to Shergol; towards Srinagar, there are regular daily buses to nearby Drass.

There are at least two buses a day to nearby Panikhar and Parkachik. To Padum, in Zanskar, there is a 4.30 am bus on alternate days for Rs 150/220 for the B/A class bus (check at the bus stand for up-to-date information); the trip takes about 15 hours.

The Kargil bus stand is divided into two adjoining lots, just off Main Bazaar Rd. The office where you can book a bus ticket a day ahead for long trips, which is recommended, is in a burnt-out old building in the northern bus stand. There may be some more reliable and comfortable private buses between Kargil, Leh and Srinagar if and when the demand picks up. Buses often have their destinations in Arabic script. If you have a ticket, go by the bus number (written in English).

Taxi In one day, a taxi from Leh can get you to Kargil for Rs 3355, or from Kargil to Srinagar for Rs 3100. A taxi from Kargil to Padum is not a bad option compared to the bus, but the trip will cost a hefty Rs 7000/12,000 one way/return. The Kargil taxi stand is on Main Bazaar Rd.

KARGIL TO PADUM
Sanku

The road from Kargil heads south-west, away from Padum, following the Suru river valley. It is predominantly inhabited by Muslims, who converted to Islam in the 15th century; a **Muslim shrine**, dedicated to Syed Mir Hashim, is in Karpo-Khar near Sanku. Sanku can also be reached from Drass, west of Kargil on the main road to Srinagar, on a two to three day trek.

There is a bus from Kargil to Sanku every day at 3 pm (Rs 18, four hours). At Sanku, accommodation is limited to a *Government Resthouse*, which may be rented (about Rs 50 per person), and a *J&KTDC Tourist Bungalow*, which at the time of writing was barely operational but charged only Rs 40 per person. Taxis from Kargil to Sanku demand Rs 700/1050 one way/return.

Panikhar & Parkachik

Farther down the Suru Valley, Panikhar and Parkachik are the places to get off and admire, or even get closer to, the twin mountains of Nun (7135m) and Kun (7087m). It is a lovely area in summer, often full of flowers. In Panikhar, the best option is a room at the comfortable *J&KTDC Tourist Bungalow* for Rs 40 per person. It is a four hour walk to and from the Lago La, from where you can catch a breathtaking view of the Nun-Kun massif. Walk about 3km up the road in the direction of Padum, cross the suspension bridge over the Suru River, walk down the valley for about 1km and then head up the foot trail to the pass. The last part of the walk is quite hard, but the view is more than worth it.

From the top you can either walk down the other side to Parkachik and head back along the road, but it's quicker to return the way you came. There is another *J&KTDC Tourist Bungalow* at Parkachik charging Rs 40 per person. A few kilometres farther up the road from Parkachik a great tongue of ice from the **Parkachik Glacier** descends to the Suru River.

Between Panikhar and Kargil, buses cost Rs 35 (five to six hours), and leave twice a day in the morning; or there's a Kargil-Padum bus that leaves on alternate days. Taxis from Kargil to Panikhar cost Rs 1200/1800 one way/return.

Rangdum

About halfway in time, but not distance, between Kargil and Padum, is Rangdum, where trucks (but not buses) may stop for the night. You can visit the 18th century **Rangdum Gompa,** which serves as a base for about 35 monks and many novices. The *J&KTDC Tourist Complex* has basic facilities for Rs 40 per person. Several village *tea houses* offer very basic fare. From Rangdum, there is another good trek through the Kanji La (5255m) that links up with the Leh-Kargil road at Lamayuru.

The road from Rangdum heads in a more southerly direction and crosses the Pensi La (4450m). As the road descends from the pass you can see the vast **Darung Drung Glacier,** the source of the Stod River. On the way to Padum is Ating, from where you can visit the **Zongkul Gompa.** As you approach Padum, the valley becomes more populous with small villages such as Tungri, Phey and Sani.

Zanskar

The isolated region of Zanskar (Land of White Copper) is composed of a number of small mountain-locked valleys to the south of Ladakh. The valleys are bounded to the north by the Zanskar Range, and to the south by the main Himalaya. To the east and west, high ridges linking the Himalaya and Zanskar mountains ensure that there is no easy link between Zanskar and the outside world.

Zanskar essentially comprises the Stod Valley in the west, and the Lunak Valley in the east, which converge at Padum, the administrative centre of the region. The fertile region of Padum and its outlying villages and gompas form the nucleus of Zanskar. It is a small Himalayan kingdom by any standards. The valley is no more than 20km wide at its broadest, while 50km north of Padum the Zanskar River enters the impressive gorges of the Zanskar Range as it flows down to the Indus Valley.

Zanskar's location on the lee side of the main Himalaya Range ensures that it attracts considerably more snow than any other region of Ladakh. Snow can fall for over seven months of each year. Passes are often snowbound for more than half the year, and the winter temperatures of -20°C make it one of the coldest inhabited places in the world. In the depths of winter, all the rivers freeze over. Even the fast-flowing Zanskar River freezes on the surface, and the Zanskaris walk on the ice to reach the Indus Valley near Nimmu – an otherwise inaccessible route.

Until a generation ago it took villagers a week or more to reach the roadhead. However, in 1981 a jeep road linking Kargil and Padum was completed, creating direct

LADAKH & ZANSKAR

access to Kashmir or the Indus Valley for three or four months a year. The Pensi La, linking the Suru Valley with Zanskar, is generally clear of snow by early July. The road lifeline has taken its toll on the traditional culture of Zanskar. Anyone searching for some long-lost Shangri La should look elsewhere. However, the yak and pony trains still make their way over the more remote passes to Lahaul, Kullu, Kashmir and the Indus Valley.

Zanskar's uninterrupted Buddhist heritage has been principally due to its isolation. It can be traced back to a time when the Buddhist monks first made their way over the high passes from Kashmir. The gompa at Sani, founded in the 10th century, is an example of the earliest Buddhist influence. Indeed, legend has it that the sage Naropa meditated at the Sani chörten during his journeys through Ladakh. The original sites of such gompas as Phugtal, Karsha and Lingshat may also be attributed to this period. In many respects, the development of the Buddhist orders in Zanskar were the same as in other regions of Ladakh. The Dalai Lama's order – the Gelukpa – was established in the 15th century, and the well-preserved gompas at Karsha, Lingshat and Mune date from this period. The order supported by the King – the Drukpa – established its presence at Bardan and Zangla and 'colonised' the gompa at Sani in the 17th century.

Today, the Gelukpa gompas have established ties with Likir Gompa in the Indus Valley, while Bardan, Sani and Zangla have administrative and financial links with the gompa at Stakna, close to Leh.

The influence of Islam did not affect Zanskar until the 19th century. The presence of Muslim families in Padum dates from the 1840s, when the Dogras opened up the passes to Muslim traders from the Kishtwar area. The Dogra forces made their way over the passes from Kishtwar, and established their presence both here and in Ladakh. The fort at Pipiting below Padum was built as a fitting testimony to the Dogra times, when the powers of royal families

in both Zangla and Padum were reduced to the same nominal status as the royal families in Ladakh.

In 1995 foreigners were discouraged from visiting Zanskar, due to resentment that the bulk of earnings from tourism was going to trekking agencies based outside the region. However, in January 1996 Zanskar leaders issued a statement saying there would be no impediment to foreign tourists who may 'come and go as freely as before'. There is also some resentment that this overwhelmingly Buddhist area is administratively lumped in with Kargil rather than with Leh, a situation that will probably remain at least until a road is built linking Zanskar with the Indus Valley.

PADUM
☎ 01983 • alt 1000m

Padum is the administrative headquarters of the Zanskar region but was once an ancient capital. It is not a particularly attractive place, with incongruous government buildings that were constructed when the road from Kargil was completed in 1981. This has resulted in the town gaining a character similar to roadheads everywhere. Vehicles are repaired, diesel cans are discarded and much that is not used is disposed of here. The main camp site and the small hotel area is close by the newly constructed mosque (the only one in the Zanskar region), which serves the small Sunni Muslim community. The only telephone office is at the Hotel Ibex. There is a tourist office at the J&KTDC Tourist Bungalow (see following). Horses can be hired for around Rs 200 per day.

Padum is also the starting point for a number of difficult long-distance treks. See the Zanskar Treks boxed text.

Places to Stay & Eat
There's a limited choice of a few basic guesthouses and one more comfortable option.

Hotel Shapodok-la, in the centre of town, has cheap dorm beds. *Hotel Haftal View*, by the bus stand, is a bit grubby. Rooms are Rs 100/150. *Hotel Chorala* nearby is somewhat better, also with doubles for Rs 150.

AROUND PADUM

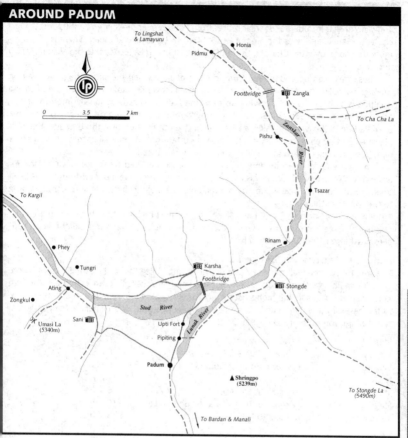

To Lingshat & Lamayuru

Honia

Pidmu

Footbridge · Zangla

To Cha Cha La

Pishu

Zanskar River

Tsazar

To Kargil

Rinam

Phey

Tungri

Karsha

Footbridge

Stongde

Ating

Zongkul

Stod River

Lung River

Sani

Umasi La (5340m)

Upti Fort

Pipiting

Padum

▲ Shringpo (5239m)

To Stongde La (5490m)

To Bardan & Manali

J&KTDC Tourist Bungalow has fairly big rooms with bath (cold water only) for Rs 50 per person.

Hotel Snowland is one of the better choices, with a nice garden and rooms for Rs 100/150. It is set in the fields about 100m behind the Hotel Chorala.

Hotel Ibex (☎ 45012) is the best in town, with decent doubles set around a sheltered courtyard for Rs 300 (no singles).

There isn't much to eating in Padum. The east worst place is the restaurant at the *Hotel Ibex*. The *Lhasa Tibetan* restaurant across the road from the Ibex is OK, as is the *Hotel Chorala* and the Tibetan *restaurant* at the bus stand under the Campa Cola sign.

Getting There & Away

Bus The road connecting Padum and Kargil is only open July to early October. It's completely impassable the rest of the year, effectively isolating the Zanskari people. In season, a bus runs between Padum and Kargil every alternate day (check with local

Zanskar Treks

Treks in Zanskar include the popular routes from Padum over the Shingo La (5090m) to Darcha and Manali, and over the Singge La (5050m) to Lamayuru and Leh. There is also a remote trek north over the Cha Cha La (4950m) and Rubrang La (5020m) to the Markha Valley and Leh.

These treks can be undertaken from the end of June when the snows begin to melt on the high passes to the middle of October before the first winter snow falls. There are of course exceptions as heavy storms blowing up from the Indian plains occasionally interrupt itineraries in August and September. River crossings are also a problem particularly on the trek from Padum to the Markha Valley and it is advisable not to undertake this trek until the middle of August when waters subside. It is also important to note that all of these treks involve high pass crossings of around 5000m so proper acclimatisation is essential.

If making your own arrangements pack horses can be hired from Padum or Karsha for around Rs 200 a day although this can increase during the harvest period from late August to early September. A local guide is also a valuable asset, particularly on the trek from Padum to the Markha Valley.

Camping gear including a tent and sleeping bag must be brought with you as there are a number of stages on these treks where there are no villages to stay for the night. Food supplies must also be brought from Leh.

Padum to Darcha via Shingo La

This trek follows the well-defined route up the Tsarap Valley for the first three stages before diverting to Phugtal Gompa, one of the oldest gompas in Zanskar. The trek continues through a number of villages to the highest settlement at Kargyak. From here it is one farther stage to the base of the Shingo La (5090m) before traversing the Great Himalaya Range. A final stage brings you to the roadhead at Darcha.

Stage 1	Padum to Mune	(6 hrs)
Stage 2	Mune to Purne	(8 hrs)
Stage 3	Purne to Phugtal Gompa & Testa	(6 hrs)
Stage 4	Testa to Kargyak	(7 hrs)
Stage 5	Kargyak to Lakong	(6-7 hrs)
Stage 6	Lakong to Rumjak via the Shingo La	(6-7 hrs)
Stage 7	Rumjak to Darcha	(6-7 hrs)

Padum to Lamayuru via Singge La

This trek may commence from either Padum or Karsha Gompa, the largest in the Zanskar region. The trek follows the true left bank of the Zanskar River for two stages before diverting towards the Hanuma La (4950m) and Lingshat Gompa. It is one farther stage to the base of

bus stations for up-to-date information), departing at about 4.30 am. The cost of the bus between Kargil and Padum is Rs 150/220 for B/A class (it depends which bus shows up), and the trip takes about 15 hours.

The trip between Kargil and Padum is spectacular, even impressing those jaded travellers who thought that they had seen it all along the Leh to Kargil road. But as usual in this part of the world, the road is also narrow, winding and slow. The trip usually takes about 15 hours, but can take a lot longer. You can and should book your ticket the day before in Padum or Kargil. You can the Singge La (5050m) before crossing the Zanskar Range. From the pass there are dramatic views of the Zanskar gorges while to the south are the snowcapped peaks of the Great Himalaya Range. The Singge La is not a particularly demanding pass crossing and the gradual descent to the village of Photaksar can be completed in one stage.

From Photaksar the trail crosses the Sisir La (4850m) to the village of Honupatta. It is a further stage to the ancient gompa at Wanla before finally crossing the Prinkiti La (3750m) to Lamayuru Gompa and onward transport by bus or truck to Leh.

Stage 1	Padum to Karsha	(2 hrs)
Stage 2	Karsha to Pishu	(4-5 hrs)
Stage 3	Pishu to Hanumil	(4-5 hrs)
Stage 4	Hanumil to Snertse	(5 hrs)
Stage 5	Snertse to Lingshat via Hanuma La	(5-6 hrs)
Stage 6	Lingshat to Singge La base	(5-6 hrs)
Stage 7	Base camp to Photaksar via Singge La	(5-6 hrs)
Stage 8	Photaksar to Honupatta via Sisir La	(6 hrs)
Stage 9	Honupatta to Wanla	(5 hrs)
Stage 10	Wanla to Lamayuru via Prinkiti La	(3-4 hrs)

Padum to Leh via Cha Cha La, Rubrang La & the Markha Valley

This challenging trek is followed by only a handful of trekkers each season. From Padum the trail heads north to the village of Zangla before diverting from the Zanskar Valley to the Cha Cha La (4950m). From the pass there are uninterrupted views south towards the Great Himalaya Range. Heading north the trail enters a series of dramatic gorges that support rare wildlife including brown bears, bharal and snow leopards. It takes a minimum of two stages to reach the Rubrang La (5020m) and the crest of the Zanskar Range before a steady descent to the villages of the Markha Valley. From Markha village it takes a further three stages to cross the Kongmaru La (5030m) to Hemis Gompa and the Indus Valley.

Stage 1	Padum to Zangla	(7 hrs)
Stage 2	Zangla to Cha Cha La base	(3 hrs)
Stage 3	Base camp to Gorge camp via Cha Cha La	(6 hrs)
Stage 4	Gorge camp to Tilat Sumdo	(6 hrs)
Stage 5	Tilat Sumdo to Rubrang La base	(5-6 hrs)
Stage 6	Base camp to Markha via Rubrang La	(6 hrs)
Stage 7	Markha to Nimaling	(7-8 hrs)
Stage 8	Nimaling to Chogdo via Kongmaru La	(6 hrs)
Stage 9	Chogdo to Hemis	(4-5 hrs)

get off anywhere you want on the road between Kargil and Padum, but you may have to then wait a day or so for another bus, or rely on hitching a lift on an infrequent truck.

Taxi By taxi, it costs Rs 7000/12,000 one way/return from Kargil to Padum. This is a

great way to really admire the amazing scenery. This trip can be done in one long day with about 12 hours driving, or you can stop at Rangdum, Parkachik or Panikhar.

Truck Trucks occasionally go along this route, but not nearly as often as the

Kargil-Leh road, because so few people live in and around Zanskar. Nevertheless, hitching rides on a truck, if you can find one, is normal practice, and most drivers will take you for a negotiable fee, maybe about the same as the bus fare.

Getting Around
Jeep & Taxi The Padum Taxi Union office across from the Hotel Haftal View charges exorbitant rates: Rs 650 return to Sani Gompa, Rs 800 return to Karsha Gompa, and Rs 5500/7000 one way/return to Rangdum. Not surprisingly, few visitors get around by taxi.

AROUND PADUM
Padum itself has little to offer, but serves as a good base for exploring nearby gompas, all of which need some trekking to get to as motor transport is very expensive.

Bardan Gompa
The remote gompa at Bardan is about 12km south of Padum, on the trekking route to Darcha. It belongs to the Drukpa order, and was built in the 17th century.

Karsha Gompa
This is one of the largest and most important gompas in Zanskar, dating back to about the 11th century, and belonging to the Gelukpa order. A large white complex housing over 100 monks, the Karsha Gompa holds pujas, often different from those in Ladakh, which should be witnessed, if possible. There is a Rs 20 fee to see the dukhang. There is also a 500-year-old **nunnery** nearby, on the other side of the ravine. It takes about three hours to walk to Karsha from Padum, but the return journey is made

much harder by the strong headwinds in the afternoon.

Hotel Mayur in Karsha village below the nunnery has basic doubles for Rs 150, all with shared bath. Another place to stay was being built at the time of research.

Sani Gompa
About two hours walk from Padum, Sani is believed to be the oldest Ka-ni-ka (named after the former king of Kashmir) gompa in Zanskar. Unlike most in Ladakh and Zanskar, it is built like a castle on flat ground, and involves no steep climbs, making it more accessible than the average gompa. There is a red wooden phallus just above the door, suggesting this gompa is associated with the fertility of surrounding farms.

There is an impressive prayer room full of Buddhist statues and plenty of frescoes and thangkas to delight. There is also a famous **stone carving** of the Maitreya Buddha on a large rock near the gompa.

Stongde Gompa
On the way to Zangla is the Stongde Gompa, nearly 20km from Padum. With about 50 Gelukpa monks, Stongde is now the second-largest gompa in Zanskar, after Karsha. The village of Tsazar, between Stongde and Zangla, also has an impressive gompa.

Zangla Gompa
The path continues past Tsazar to the village and gompa at Zangla, which belongs to the Drukpa order. It is also where the king of Zanskar has his castle. Zangla is 35km from Padum, and can be included in one of a few popular three or four day treks around the area. There is a small **nunnery** nearby that is also worth exploring.

Himachal Pradesh

Himachal Pradesh – the land of the eternal snow peaks – is a large amalgam of peoples, religions and former hill states, separated by offshoots of the Greater Himalaya. The Kullu Valley with its developed and tourist-oriented economy can be considered the backbone of the state. Off to the east is the Parvati Valley, popular with long-stay visitors. In the Chamba and Kangra regions can be found typical British hill stations and small but beautiful temple complexes.

The residence of the Dalai Lama is in Upper Dharamsala, known as McLeod Ganj, which has become a centre for Buddhism, as well as the headquarters of the Tibetan Government in Exile. Shimla, the famous colonial hot-weather capital of the Raj, remains Himachal's seat of government. Some locals even claim a Greek addition to the gene pool. Certainly, Alexander the Great (known locally as Iskander or Sikander) and his troops reached the Beas River in the 4th century BCE, though a mutiny among his troops soon pushed him reluctantly homeward.

The northern and eastern areas of Lahaul, Spiti and Kinnaur (labelled officially as 'tribal districts') are vast, barren and remote regions where travel can be rough. The region is dotted with Tibetan Buddhist *gompas* (monasteries), often in settings as spectacular as those found in Tibet and Ladakh. Gompas can be visited, as long as you are appropriately dressed and show proper respect.

Himachal also has many interesting Hindu temples. The best examples in stone are found at Baijnath (Kangra Valley), Bajaura (Kullu Valley), Mandi and Chamba. Popular pilgrimage sites include Jawalamukhi, in the Kangra Valley, where tongues of fire are thought to emanate from holes in the ground. The Bhimakali Temple at Sarahan, in the Sutlej Valley, is the best example of a distinct Himachali style.

'Himachal' is pronounced with the stress on the second syllable.

Himachal Pradesh at a Glance

Population: 6.13 million (year 2000 estimate)
Capital: Shimla
Main Languages: Hindi, English, Pahari, Bhoti, Kinnauri (Homskad)
Best Time to Go: central and west (Apr to Jun and Sept to Nov); east, north and northeast (Jun to Oct)
Trekking Areas: Dharamsala, Kangra Valley, Brahmaur, Chamba Valley, Manali and Kullu (Jun, mid-Sept to mid-Oct); Spiti and Pin valleys (mid-Jun to Sept)

Highlights

- **Shimla** – Ride the toy train to experience the decrepit grandeur of the Raj in this pleasant hill station.

- **McLeod Ganj** – Visit the home of the Dalai Lama and headquarters of the Tibetan Government in Exile, *the* place to head if you are interested in Tibetan Buddhism or chocolate cake.

- **Kullu Valley** – Enjoy the scenically pretty valley and adventure playground of Himachal Pradesh. If the crowds get too much head for the laid-back Parvati Valley.

- **Chamba** – Explore this beautiful town with ancient Hindu temples hidden in winding backstreets.

- **Temples** – Take in the ambience of ancient temples. Of the thousands in the region, our favourites are the Basheshar Mahadev at Bajaura (Kullu Valley) and the Baidyanath Temple at Baijnath (Kangra Valley).

- **Spiti** – Seek out the ancient Tibetan Buddhist monasteries of Dhankar, Ki and Tabo in this remote and desolate area.

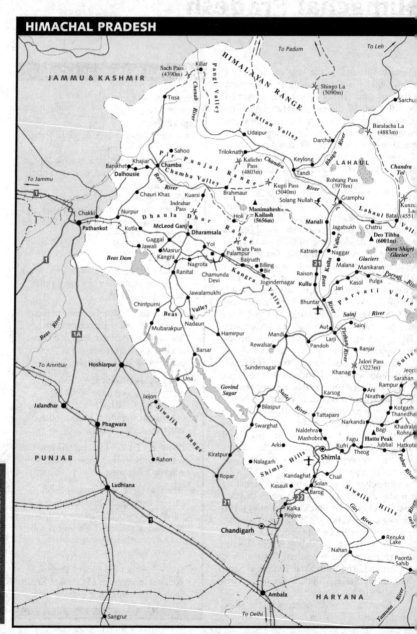

HIMACHAL PRADESH

JAMMU & KASHMIR

Spiti River

Shilla (7026m)

Kibber
Ki
Kaza

Spiti Valley

CHINA
TIBET

SPITI
Mikkim

Dhankar   Tabo   Sumdo

Nako

Manerang (6593m)

Leo Purgyal (6791m)

Shipki La (5669m)

Pin River   Pin Valley

KINNAUR   Puh

Kalpa   Rekong Peo   Morang

Valley
Wangtu
Nichar   Tapri

Sutlej   River

Kinnaur Kailash (6050m)

Sangla   Valley

Sangla   Chitkul

Seema

UTTAR
PRADESH

0   30   60 km

The external boundaries of India
on this map have not been authenticated
and may not be correct.

Mussoorie

Dehra Dun

Rajaji Wildlife
Sanctuary

History

As with most other Himalayan states, Himachal has a racial mix of Mongol and Aryan and often you find interior villagers with two names – Hindu and Buddhist – in an attempt to straddle this dual inheritance. The aboriginal hill people are associated with the Indus Valley civilisation, perhaps as a result of Alexander the Great's visit. Indeed, the Shimla state museum has Greek coins from Chamba.

Astride ancient trade routes to Tibet (over the Shipki La) and Central Asia (via the Baralacha La and Leh), as well as commanding the Sach Pass that led to Kashmir, the regions that today comprise Himachal produced a proliferation of wealthy feudal rulers. Rajas (kings), ranas (queens) and *thakurs* (titled rulers from Lahaul) ran their rival *rahuns* and *thakurais*, the regions over which they presided, making Himachal a patchwork quilt of tiny states. Only Kangra and Kullu (and later Chamba) had the power to break out of the petty feuding system.

Chamba's distinguished history began in Brahmaur under the Varman dynasty in 680 CE (common era). It extended its boundaries to include the town of Chamba in 920. Several Himachal states were ruled by kings from Bengal, who had fled from Muslim armies that had spread south and east in the centuries following Mahmud of Ghazni's raid on Kangra in 1009. The best known of these Bangali states is Mandi, founded as late as 1527. Bushahr, originally centred on the Baspa Valley of Kinnaur and later relocated to Rampur on the Sutlej River, was another important state, which controlled the trade routes to Tibet. With the exception of the bigger states, most of the later hill states were founded by Rajput adventurers from the plains in the early medieval period.

The first westerners to the region were Jesuit missionaries in search of the legendary kingdom of Prester John; they made few inroads, however, as both Hinduism and Buddhism were sufficiently entrenched to retain their adherents. Maharaja Ranjit Singh took Kangra Fort as his pay-off for

HIMACHAL PRADESH

Festivals of Himachal Pradesh

Festivals, fairs and ceremonies play an integral part in the life of the people of Himachal Pradesh. They usually celebrate religious events, domestic occasions such as a birth, death or marriage, or the start or finish of the season or harvest. In the remote regions of Lahaul and Spiti, festivals celebrate both Hindu and Buddhist religious events, agricultural events, to commemorate a birthday *(pingri)*, death or marriage *(paklen)* and often just to fill in the long winter months when this region is isolated from the rest of the world. Dancing, singing and drinking are a vital part of each festival. In most cases, dates of festivals in Lahaul and Spiti are determined according to the Tibetan calendar.

January/February
Phagul Also known as *Suskar*, this Kinnauri festival lasts about two weeks in January (February in Sangla) and is held to appease local forest gods. Gods are invited into the home and offered fine foods so they don't bother the village for the rest of the year.
Sazo Held each January in Kinnaur, villagers bathe in natural springs, or if brave, in the freezing Sutlej River. This is eagerly followed by a large feast.
Dachang Called the Festival of Arrows, this is held over six days in many villages of Lahaul & Spiti. Men shoot arrows into the air to ensure that good prevails over evil.
Phagli Held in Lahaul's Pattan Valley, Phagli is the New Year celebration. Flowers are gathered and offered as greetings, especially to the elder members of the family.

February/March
Losar Tibetan New Year is celebrated all over Spiti. It's a great time to be in McLeod Ganj, where the Dalai Lama gives week-long teachings.
Shivaratri Shivaratri is celebrated throughout India in late February/early March, and is dedicated to Shiva, who danced the *tandava* (the Dance of Destruction) on this day. In Himachal Pradesh, Mandi, at the gateway of the Kullu Valley, hosts the most interesting Shivaratri. The celebrations continue for weeks and deities from all over Mandi district are carried into the town. Large numbers of people have *darshan* (viewing of a deity) at the 16th century Bhutnath Temple in the centre of the town. The Baidyanath Temple at Baijnath, enshrines a sacred lingam, is also the centre of a good deal of devotional activity during Shivaratri.

March/April
Sui Mata Festival This four day festival is held at Chamba town. Sui Mata, the daughter of an ancient raja, gave her life to save the inhabitants of her father's kingdom. She is particularly revered by Chamba women, who carry her image from the old palace up to her small shrine, accompanied by singing and dancing.
Opera Festival Convened by the Tibetan Institute of Performing Arts (TIPA), at McLeod Ganj in April, this festival includes traditional *lhamo* opera plus contemporary and historical plays.

April/May
TIPA Anniversary Festival From 27 May, a three day festival at McLeod Ganj celebrates the anniversary of the foundation of TIPA, with performances by artists from the school.
Hang-Gliding Rally This rally at Billing, in the Kangra Valley, attracts both national and international hang-gliders.

Festivals of Himachal Pradesh

May/June
Summer Festival Shimla's summer festival has a broad appeal with golf and other sporting tournaments, a flower show and cultural performances including folk dancing.

Dhungri Festival This festival is celebrated at Manali's Dhungri Temple, and includes sacrifices to the goddess Hadimba.

July/August
Chaam Festival Lamas wearing masks perform dances during this festival, held at Ki Gompa in Spiti in late June/early July.

Dalai Lama's Birthday His Holiness the Dalai Lama celebrates his birthday on 6 July, and this is a special time to visit McLeod Ganj, his home, as Tibetans pray for the long life of their leader.

Dakhrain Held on 16 July, this festival celebrates the start of the rainy season in southern Kinnaur. Plenty of food, particularly dairy products, is enjoyed by everyone.

Ladarcha This is a famous trade fair held near Kaza (Spiti) in July.

Chishu This festival held in Lahaul & Spiti celebrates the birth of the greatly revered Buddhist sage, Padmasambhava, in July.

Minjar Festival This festival is celebrated in late July/early August in Chamba town.

Manimahesh Yatra Pilgrims from all over north India converge on the small village of Brahmaur, in the Chamba Valley, to commence the pilgrimage to the sacred lake of Manimahesh, below the peak of Manimahesh Kailash (5656m), 28km from Brahmaur.

August/September
Ukiang Also known as the *Phulech* or *Flaich* Festival, this is celebrated in many villages throughout Kinnaur between August and November beginning in the village of Rupi and culminating at the village of Nesang. All able villagers gather flowers and congregate in neighbouring pastures. A male goat is often sacrificed.

Pauri This three day festival at Triloknath, near Udaipur (Lahaul & Spiti), attracts thousands of Hindu and Buddhist pilgrims every August.

September/October
Dussehra Dussehra is celebrated India-wide as the victory of Rama over Ravana, the demon king of Lanka. In Kullu, Rama is worshipped in his form as Raghunath, whose image is borne through the streets on a wheeled *rath* (chariot) which is pulled by pilgrims. Following the procession, villagers perform dances in traditional dress. Dussehra is celebrated at Sarahan with sacrifices.

Namgan This celebrates the new harvest in Lahaul & Spiti. Local people dress up in traditional clothing and participate in horse races.

November/December
Chaam Festival Late October/early November sees chaam dances at Tabo Gompa in Spiti.

Lavi Fair This trade fair is held at Rampur, 140km north-east of Shimla on the banks of the Sutlej River. Inhabitants of the remote regions of Lahaul & Spiti, and Kinnaur congregate at the town to trade locally made produce and horses.

Chaam Festival This chaam festival is held at Dhankar Gompa (Spiti) in November.

helping Chamba Raja Sansar Chand expel marauding Gurkhas who had allied themselves with alienated local princes. Before the Sikh maharaja annexed it, the fort at Kangra had attracted several other prominent rulers since the days of Mahmud of Ghazni, including the mad Afghan Tughlaq and Tamerlane. Tughlaq's successor raided the nearby temple of Jawalamukhi to obtain Hindu texts he wished to translate. The emperor Akbar was fascinated by the eternal gas flame of Jawalamukhi, as was the Sikh maharaja, who raised a gold canopy over it.

The British discovered Himachal after their wars with the Sikhs and the Gurkhas in the early 19th century. Himachal was found to be ideal apple-growing country. An American missionary, the Reverend NS Stokes, developed the Kotgarh orchards (near Narkanda – his family still runs them) and the apple industry quickly spread to Kullu. Little bits of England were created at Shimla, Dalhousie and Dharamsala during the late 19th century. The narrow-gauge railway to Shimla was built in 1903 and another line was added through the Kangra Valley. In the interior, however, feudal conditions remained; men were forced to work without pay and women were regarded as chattels.

The new state of Himachal Pradesh comprising only six districts was formed in 1948. By 1966, the Pahari-speaking parts under Punjab administration, including Kangra, Kullu, Lahaul and Spiti, were added. Full statehood was achieved in 1971.

Geography

Himachal Pradesh is dominated by mountains, and associated rivers and valleys. The highest peaks, Shilla (7026m), Manerang (6593m) and Shipki (5669m), are all in the east. Some of those you are more likely to see are Leo Pargial (6791m), near Nako, in Kinnaur; Deo Tibba (6001m), not far from Manali; and Kinnaur Kailash (6050m), which dominates the views from Rekong Peo and Kalpa in Kinnaur.

The passes, such as the Rohtang Pass (3978m), Baralacha La (4883m) and Kun-

zum La (4551m), are pivotal points between culturally distinct regions. (*La* is a Tibetan word meaning pass.) In winter, Lahaul and Spiti are completely isolated when these and other passes are blocked by snow.

Himachal Pradesh can be easily segregated according to its various valleys. Lahaul consists of the Chandra and Bhaga valleys. It is drained by the Chandra River, which turns into the Chenab, before flowing west into Kashmir. Farther east, the Spiti River is joined by the Pin and Lingti rivers before joining the Sutlej River in Kinnaur. The Sutlej flows all the way to the Punjab. The Kullu Valley is drained by the Beas River (pronounced 'bee-ahs') and stretches from Mandi to Manali. It is joined by the Parvati Valley from the east.

In the west, the beautiful Kangra Valley stretches from Mandi to Shahpur, near Pathankot. To the north of the Kangra Valley, on the other side of the Dhaula Dhar Range, is the Chamba Valley, which is separated from the remote Pattan Valley (upper Chenab River valley) by the Pir Panjal Range. The Ravi River flows through Chamba and on to Lahore in northern Pakistan.

Tourist Offices

The Himachal Pradesh Tourist Development Corporation (HPTDC) provides some useful services. Every major town has a HPTDC tourist office, which offers local information and maps, runs local tours and sometimes handles bookings for local airlines.

HPTDC manages about 50 hotels in Himachal Pradesh. These are usually luxurious log huts, modest guesthouses or expensive hotels and are often the only hotels in remote destinations. Some HPTDC hotels offer low-season discounts but most don't. All offer a 25% discount to single travellers staying in a double room. All HPTDC tourist offices and most HPTDC hotels can make bookings for another HPTDC hotel.

In season, HPTDC organises 'deluxe' buses for tourists between Shimla, Kullu, and Manali, and links these places with Delhi and Chandigarh. HPTDC buses are more expensive than public buses but are a better option because they are quicker and far more comfortable. HPTDC also organises daily sightseeing tours out of Dharamsala, Shimla and Manali, which can be a useful way of visiting local areas.

HPTDC has a Web site with some useful information (www.hptdc.com) and there's a department of tourism magazine (www.himachaltourism.com). HPTDC offices elsewhere in India can also provide worthwhile information:

Kolkata (Calcutta)
 (☎ 033-271792) 2H, 2nd floor, Electronic Centre, 1/1A, BAC St, 700072
Chandigarh
 (☎ 0172-708569) Inter State Bus Terminal, Sector 17
Delhi
 (☎ 011-332 4764) Chandralok Bldg, 36 Janpath
Chennai (Madras)
 (☎ 044-827 2966) 28 Commander-in-Chief Rd
Mumbai (Bombay)
 (☎ 022-218 1123) 36 World Trade Centre, Cuffe Parade

Permits

Inner line permits are currently required for some areas of Spiti and Kinnaur. Regulations, and their implementation, have noticeably relaxed in the past year or so, and may relax further or even be abolished entirely. You'd be advised to check the current regulations with the relevant authorities or other travellers.

Foreigners can travel between Leh and Manali and between Leh, Manali and Kaza (the capital of the Spiti sub-division) without a permit. From Tabo to Rekong Peo, you need a permit, but no permit is required from both Rekong Peo to Shimla and Kaza to Tabo.

Permits can be obtained from the District and Sub-Divisional Magistrates' offices in most regional centres but are most easily processed in Kaza or Rekong Peo. See the Inner Line Permits boxed text in the Kinnaur section later in this chapter for more information.

Shimla

☎ 0177 • pop 105,000 • alt 2206m
Best Time to Go: mid-Sep to late Nov
High Season: mid-Apr to mid-Jul, mid-Sep to late Oct, mid-Dec to mid-Jan

Shimla was once part of the Nepalese kingdom, and called Shyamala, another name for the goddess Kali, but Shimla never gained any fame until it was first 'discovered' by the British in 1819. Three years later, the first 'British' house was erected, and in 1864 Shimla became the summer capital of India. Every summer until 1939 the government of India would pack its bags and migrate 1200 miles from the sweltering heat of Kolkata (Calcutta) – and later Delhi – to the cool heights of Shimla. After the construction of the Kalka to Shimla railway line in 1903, the exodus began in earnest and Shimla blossomed until the 'Britishers' packed up and finally went home. Following Independence, Shimla was initially the capital of the Punjab, then became the capital of Himachal Pradesh in 1966.

Today, Shimla is a pleasant, sprawling town, set among cool pine-clad hills, with plenty of crumbling colonial charm. Some travellers find the place too 'touristy' but nostalgic history buffs will love it. It has good facilities, although accommodation, particularly in the high season, is expensive and hard to find. For reasons of cost and weather, it is important to time your visit well (see the Himachal Pradesh at a Glance boxed text at the start of this chapter for information.) Remember to bring warm clothes after October; snow can be common in winter.

Orientation

There are only two roads in the central part of Shimla. Cart Rd circles the southern, lower side of Shimla, where the Inter State Bus Terminal (ISBT), taxi stands and train station are located. The higher (and pedestrianised) Mall runs east-west, reaching its highest point at Scandal Point (or Scandal Corner) – immortalised by Rudyard

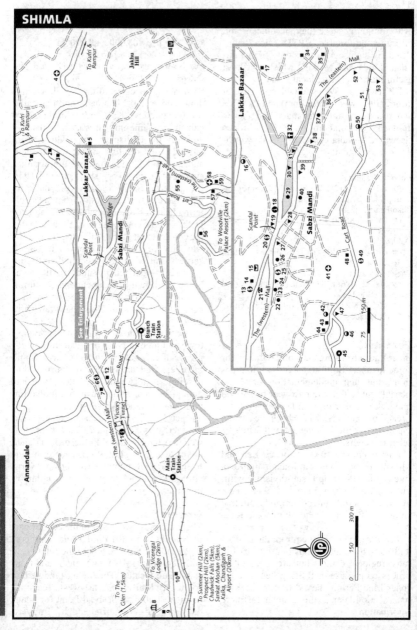

SHIMLA

SHIMLA

PLACES TO STAY			
1	Hotel Auckland	27	Alfa Restaurant
2	Hotel Chanakya; Hotel White	28	Baljee's; Fascination
3	Hotel Diplomat	30	Ashiana;
5	Hotel Uphar		Goofa;
7	Hotel Dalziel; Hotel Classic;		Quick Bite
	Hotel Prakash	31	Park Cafe
9	Spars Lodge	36	Sher-e-Punjab
10	The Cecil	38	Chung Fa
12	Hotel Gulmarg; Hotel	39	Himani's
	Fontaine Bleau	47	Local Dhabas
14	YWCA	52	Krishna Bakers
17	Hotel Dreamland	53	Embassy Restaurant
33	YMCA		
34	Hotel Mehman		OTHER
35	Deogar Hotel	4	Indira Gandhi Snowdon
43	Vikrant Hotel		Hospital
44	Hotel Ranjan	6	State Bank of India
48	Hotel Basant; Hotel Kohinoor	8	Himachal State Museum
56	HPTDC Hotel Holiday Home	11	HPTDC Tourist Information
57	Oberoi Clarke's Hotel		Centre (branch)
59	Hotel Shingar; Hotel Sangeet	13	UCO Bank
		15	Main Post Office
PLACES TO EAT		16	Rivoli Bus Stand;
19	Rendezvous		Skating Rink
24	Indian Coffee House; Devicos	18	HPTDC Tourist Office
	Restaurant		(main)
		20	ANZ Grindlays Bank

21	Central Telegraph Office
22	District Magistrate's Office
23	Himachal Emporium
25	Punjab National Bank;
	Span Tour & Travels
26	Kumar Studio Lab
29	Gaiety Theatre; Trishool's
	Bakery
32	Christ Church
37	Maria Brothers
40	Minerva Bookshop;
	Asia Book House
41	Deen Dayal Upadhayay
	(Ripon) Hospital
42	Kalka-Shimla Taxi Union
	Stand
45	Branch Train Station
46	Inter State Bus Terminal
	(ISBT)
49	Bank of Baroda
50	Vishal Himachal Taxi
	Operators' Union Stand
51	Passenger Lift
54	Jakhu Temple
55	Tibetan Refugee Handloom
	Shop
58	Kamal Nehru Hospital

Kipling, and the de facto centre of town. The Mall area known as The Ridge runs from Scandal Point up to Christ Church. A network of lively and colourful bazaars connects Cart Rd to the Mall and there is also a passenger lift connecting Cart Rd to The (eastern) Mall.

Information

Tourist Offices There is a confusing set of tourist offices in Shimla. Disregard the Directorate of Tourism, next to the YMCA, and the tourist booth at the train station; the latter offers very basic information and is hardly ever open. The HPTDC Tourist Information Centre branch office on Cart Road is run by an informative local guidebook author, but has a really inconvenient location. There is yet another small office next to the ISBT.

The best office to use however is the HPTDC tourist office (☎ 252561) at Scandal Point on the Mall. It provides basic local information and maps, takes bookings for HPTDC buses and local tours and acts as an agent for Archana and Jagson Airways. It's open 8 am to 8 pm daily in the high season; from 9 am to 6 pm in the low season.

Money There are several places to change money, but ask about encashment fees and rates first. Most banks are open Monday to Friday from about 10 am to 3.30 pm; and 10 am to noon on Saturday. The State Bank of India, along The (western) Mall, charges Rs 20 per transaction, plus Rs 3 for every travellers cheque cashed. The UCO Bank, above the Central Telegraph Office, charges no commission, so is a good option. ANZ Grindlays Bank, at Scandal Point, charges an outrageous Rs 195 fee to change travellers cheques but does allow advances on Visa Card and MasterCard for a reasonable Rs 75 per transaction. It closes at 2.30 pm.

HIMACHAL PRADESH

Colonial Shimla

From 1822, when the first 'British' home (Kennedy House at The Glen) was built in Shimla, it took only 40 years before the town became the official summer capital of the British Raj. By the end of the 19th century, Shimla boasted opulent colonial mansions (such as the Viceregal Lodge and Wildflower Hall), grand hotels (including the famous Cecil Hotel at The Glen) and huge churches. For many overheated and disgruntled expats the town was a tonic for ill health and, according to an expat Brit 'the first place in India that had been worth all the trouble of reaching'. At the height of Shimla's popularity over 10,000 locals a year were employed to haul luggage up from the plains. Shimla became a 'centre of empire', a place of 'philandering and frivolity', home to 'the cad, the card, the fortune-hunter and the flirt'. To this day the town still carries faint echoes of Curzon, Kitchener and Kipling, all of whom spent many years living and working in Shimla.

Until the end of WWII, and Independence shortly afterwards, the British continued to enjoy their cricket at Chail, golf at Naldehra and gymkhanas, polo and horse racing at Annandale. In Shimla itself, there was an endless round of bridge, ballroom dancing, cocktail parties, balls at Viceregal Hall and promenades down the Mall, where exclusive British boutiques such as the Army and Navy store sold the latest fashions from London next to imported jars of Crosse & Blackwell jams.

After a hard day of bridge what could be better than a visit to the Gaiety Theatre, (modelled after the Garrick Theatre in London) for a Shakespearian comedy or the latest offering from Agatha Christie or Noel Coward? Rickshaw pullers would wait patiently outside the theatre dressed in their customised uniforms (the Mall was closed to all other Indians except the highest aristocracy). Occasionally the local gentry got their own back; Scandal Point was given its name after a young memsahib (married European lady) eloped with the dashing maharaja of Patiala, returning after several days to face scandalised Shimla society.

Kipling used Shimla as a backdrop to parts of *Kim*, his classic novel of Great Game espionage, and also *Plain Tales from the Hills*, a collection of short stories mostly written in Shimla. Both are worth picking up for their insights into Shimla's faded colonial past.

The two chaotic Punjab National Bank branches, either side of the Indian Coffee House, change money, with no fee, but are wary of any cheques other than Thomas Cook or Amex. They may ask for a photocopy of the front page of your passport. The Bank of Baroda, down on Cart Rd, gives cash advances on a Visa card.

It's worth changing extra money in Shimla as there are no exchange facilities at Kinnaur, Lahaul or Spiti.

Post & Communications The main post office, not far from Scandal Point, is open 10 am to 6 pm, Monday to Saturday; 10 am to 4 pm on Sunday and public holidays.

Poste restante is held at counter 13 in a building next door (to the right as you exit).

The Central Telegraph Office (CTO) (fax 202598), west of Scandal Point, is open 24 hours and is the cheapest place to make telephone calls and to send and receive faxes. Faxes cost the standard government charge of Rs 116 per page to the US, Rs 100 to the UK and Rs 10 to receive.

Bookshops Maria Brothers, 78 The (eastern) Mall, has a fascinating, jumbled collection of antique local books, some very rare and pricey. It's a great place to browse around. Minerva Bookshop, opposite the Gaiety Theatre, near Scandal Point, has a good selection of cheap and popular English-language novels and books on the history and culture of Himachal Pradesh. It also has a good range of maps, so buy any you may need here rather than other places, which won't have the same selection. A few shops away, the Asia Book House is good for popular novels and magazines.

Medical Services The Indira Gandhi (or Snowdon) Medical College and Hospital (☎ 252646) is not far from Lakkar Bazaar. Deen Dayal Upadhayay (or Ripon) Hospital (☎ 252802) is near the centre of Shimla, close to Cart Rd. The Kamal Nehru Hospital is for women only. An ambulance service (☎ 3463 or 3464) is also available.

Film & Photography Shimla is well set up, so if you're heading farther north, especially to Lahaul, Spiti or Kinnaur, it may be a good idea to stock up on film. Along the (western) Mall, the Kumar Studio Lab is one of several reliable places to develop print, but not slide film.

Himachal State Museum

About 2.5km west of Scandal Point, the State Museum has a good collection of statues, coins, photos and other items from around Himachal Pradesh and is worth a visit. The ground floor is devoted to Buddhist and Hindu stonework and a selection of the region's famous Pahari and Kangra style of miniatures (for more on these see the Arts section of the Facts about the Region chapter). Upstairs holds an eclectic mix of more paintings, guns, swords, 2000-year-old Greek coins from Chamba, Devi masks, statues from Sarahan and a room devoted to the life of Mahatma Gandhi.

Entry to the museum is free, and it's open daily 10 am to 5 pm; closed on Monday and public holidays. Photography is prohibited.

Viceregal Lodge & Botanical Gardens

The Viceregal Lodge, also known as Rashtrapati Niwas, was formerly the residence of the British viceroy Lord Dufferin, and is

Monkey Business

Upper Shimla is a haven for cute-looking families of monkeys grooming each other on hotel rooftops, but be aware that they do bite, scratch and steal things. Before Independence the local British police were even forced to open a secret 'Monkey Incident' file to keep tabs on simian crime. Still today, when you check into the YMCA you'll be warned to keep your windows closed to stop monkey thieves bursting in SAS style. In early 1996 a monkey grabbed a bag containing money belonging to a Shimla trader and scattered the cash from a rooftop over the streets, which was quickly snatched by the delighted crowd!

where many decisions affecting the destiny of the subcontinent were made. Incredibly, every brick of the six storey building was transported by mule (the train hadn't been built at that stage). The lodge was eventually finished in 1888.

There are magnificently kept lawns, botanical gardens, and a small cafe. The lodge now houses the Indian Institute of Advanced Study – look for this sign, rather than any other, as you approach. As you enter the institute complex, walk around the front building – the lodge is at the back.

The lodge is a pleasant 2km walk farther west from the museum – about 4.5km from Scandal Point. It's open daily 9 am to 8.30 pm in summer, and closes a little earlier during the rest of the year. It costs Rs 6 for a guided tour of the lodge (closed 1 to 2 pm), or Rs 3 to look around the gardens only.

Himalayan Aviary

Right next to the entrance of the institute complex is the Himalayan Bird Park or Aviary. As expected, it has a collection of species found around Himachal Pradesh, such as the Himalayan monal (the state bird of Himachal Pradesh), various types of pheasants, and the national bird of India, the Indian peafowl. The aviary is open daily,

HIMACHAL PRADESH

except Monday, 10 am to 5 pm. Entrance is Rs 5, but a still camera costs an extra Rs 25, and a video camera, Rs 100.

Christ Church

The second-oldest church in northern India (the oldest is in Ambala), Christ Church was built between 1846 and 1857. The clocks were added three years later, but none of them now work. One of Shimla's major landmarks, the church is also renowned for its stained glass windows. You can discreetly have a look inside the church, or attend English-language services every Sunday morning during the tourist season. The neo-Tudor building next door is the local library.

Jakhu Temple

Dedicated to the monkey god, Hanuman, Jakhu Temple is at an altitude of 2455m near the highest point of the Shimla ridge, east of the town centre. It offers a fine view over the surrounding valleys, out to the snowcapped peaks, and over Shimla itself. Appropriately, there are many monkeys around the temple. It's a steep 45 minute walk from Scandal Point. Take the footpath that heads east past the Hotel Dreamland. Sunrise is a good time to be there if you can face the early start.

Bazaars

There are two main bazaar, or *mandi*, areas in Shimla. Just below the western end of the (eastern) Mall, the bustling **Sabzi Mandi** (Vegetable Market), also known as Lower Bazaar, is a maze of steep, twisting lanes full of stalls selling food and just about everything imaginable. The kinetic chaos of the streets is a refreshing contrast to the genteel, British-influenced Mall.

Beyond The Ridge, the small, busy **Lakkar Bazaar** is the place to buy souvenirs, although most shops seem to sell fairly tacky wooden stuff.

Walks

In addition to a promenade along the Mall and the walk to the Jakhu Temple, there are a great number of interesting walks around Shimla. For information on places farther afield, refer to the Around Shimla section.

The Glen, about 4km west of Scandal Point, is one of the former playgrounds of rich British colonialists. The turn-off is on the way to the State Museum, and goes through **Annandale**, another lovely area. This was the site of a famous racecourse, and cricket and polo are still played here.

Summer Hill is 5km away, on the Shimla-Kalka railway line, and has pleasant, shady walks. It's also famous because Mahatma Gandhi once stayed at the Raj Kumari Amrit Kaur mansion here.

Chadwick Falls are 67m high, but are only really worth visiting during or just after the monsoons – from July to October. The falls are 7km from Shimla and can be reached via Summer Hill.

Prospect Hill is about 5km west of Shimla, and a 15 minute climb from the village of Boileauganj. The hill is a popular picnic spot with fine views over the surrounding country. The **Kamna Devi Temple** is nearby.

Sankat Mochan, 7km from Shimla, on the road to Chandigarh, has a Hanuman temple, and fine views of Shimla. It can also be reached by taxi.

Tara Devi Temple is 10km from Shimla. Tara Devi is a Hindu version of the Tibetan goddess Drölma. It is situated on top of a hill, and another temple, dedicated to Shiva, is nearby. It's about 3km up a path from the Tara Devi station on the Shimla-Kalka railway, or you can take a taxi there.

Organised Tours

For a look around the areas near Shimla, an organised tour is not a bad idea. HPTDC (book at the office on the Mall) organises the following daily sightseeing tours in season. Buses leave from Rivoli bus stand at 10 am:

destination	fare (Rs)
Chail via Kufri	150
Fagu, Theog and Narkanda for great views	165
Kufri, Fagu, Mashobra and Naldehra	130
Naldehra, Tattapani hot springs	150

HIMACHAL PRADESH

Taxi unions offer similar itineraries by private car. See Taxi in the Getting There & Away section for details.

Special Events
The Shimla Summer Festival is held every year at the end of May or beginning of June and features displays of folk dance, crafts and concerts of local music. Accommodation can be tight at this time.

Places to Stay
Accommodation in Shimla is expensive, particularly during the high seasons, when even the crummiest room costs around Rs 200. But in the low season, or when business is quiet, prices will drop by up to 50%. Prices quoted below are for the high season.

Places to Stay – Budget
YMCA (☎ 252375, fax 211016) is probably the best budget choice, especially in season, when it can be booked out (reservations are accepted by phone and men and women can stay). In the low season, however, it doesn't drop its prices and you can often negotiate a better deal at a private hotel. Check in can feel like arriving at boarding school but the facilities are comfortable and spotlessly clean.

There are singles/doubles for Rs 145/210; both prices include seven day YMCA membership, breakfast, and shared bathrooms with hot water from 7 pm to 9 am. Doubles with bathroom cost Rs 390, again with membership and breakfast. Telephone calls, faxes and laundry are a bit pricey, though the restaurant *thalis* (plate meals) are good value. The YMCA is not far behind Christ Church, up a lane near a cinema.

YWCA (☎ 203081), above the main post office, isn't quite as good value but it's a convenient, friendly old place for men and women, with great views. Small rooms with bathroom cost Rs 200 in the high season (Rs 150 in the low season), while larger 'suites' cost Rs 200 (Rs 250 in the low season). There is a Rs 20 temporary membership charge. Water supply can be erratic so keep a bucket of water filled just in case.

Meals are an extra Rs 25, and a bucket of hot water is available for Rs 5.

Near the bus station are several relatively cheap but noisy places.

Hotel Ranjan (☎ 252818) is clean, with large rooms for Rs 180, Rs 200 with bath.

Vikrant Hotel (☎ 253602), nearby, has singles for about Rs 150 and doubles for Rs 303 or Rs 413 with bath.

Hotel Basant (☎ 258341, Cart Rd), farther east, is quite basic and not great value in the low season. Singles with common bath cost Rs 110; doubles with bath cost Rs 165 to Rs 220. Hot water comes by the bucket, at Rs 5.

Hotel Kohinoor (☎ 202008), next door, is more expensive but much nicer. Rooms with bath and running hot water cost about Rs 325 (Rs 225 in the low season).

Hotel Dreamland (☎ 206897) is a popular place in the Lakkar Bazaar area, a steep climb past The Ridge. Rooms range from Rs 250/400 for a single/double to Rs 600 for a deluxe double.

Hotel Uphar (☎ 257670), nearby, is clean, friendly and used to backpackers. Doubles with bathroom and hot shower cost Rs 275, or around Rs 400 with a view and small balcony. There is a 50% low-season discount.

Hotel Fontaine Bleau (☎ 23549) is a quaint, family-run place just downhill from the State Bank of India, at the western end of the Mall. It has a friendly landlady who speaks English well, and rooms from Rs 175 to Rs 400 with common bath.

Hotel Gulmarg (☎ 253168), next door, is a huge and rambling place with charmless, windowless and bathroomless economy singles/doubles starting at Rs 250/350, or Rs 350/520 with bathroom.

If you're getting an early or late train, the *retiring rooms* at the Shimla train station are standard Indian Railways issue. Comfortable but noisy rooms cost Rs 150, with a 50% discount in the low season.

Places to Stay – Mid-Range
The majority in this range will usually include TV (often cable) and a bathroom with hot

water. They are particularly good value in the low season, when a nice double room with cable TV and hot water will cost you about Rs 200.

Just off the (western) Mall, a steep walk uphill from the train station, there are three reasonable places.

Hotel Prakash (☎ 213321) has somewhat overpriced, but OK, rooms for Rs 400 and Rs 600.

Hotel Classic (☎ 253078), friendly and comfortable, has nasty singles but decent doubles with good views ranging from Rs 400 to Rs 500.

Hotel Dalziel is probably best value here, with rooms from a negotiable Rs 300 and up to Rs 500.

North of The Ridge, and around the Lakkar Bazaar area, are several good places, though they are a long hike from the bus or train stations.

Hotel Chanakya (☎ 254465) is clean and comfortable, with rooms ranging from Rs 250 to Rs 480.

Hotel Diplomat (☎ 257754), just a few doors away, is better, with doubles from Rs 500, or Rs 620 with a view (50% discount in the low season).

Hotel White (☎ 255276), near the Chanakya, has comfortable doubles for Rs 425 and Rs 500 with good views. The more expensive the room, the better the views.

A couple of minutes walk east of Christ Church is a sprinkling of newish places with a quiet, convenient location.

Deogar Hotel (☎ 208527) is a good choice, with flexibly priced doubles from smallish 1st-floor rooms for Rs 300 to the excellent rooftop suite at Rs 800. There are fantastic views over Shimla from the rooftop balcony.

Hotel Mehman (☎ 213692), nearby, is new and still sports spotlessly clean carpets and bathrooms. Comfortable rooms vary from Rs 550 to Rs 800, dependent largely on the views, with a 50% discount in the low season.

There are two good places across from the Oberoi Clarke's Hotel, at the bottom end of the (eastern) Mall.

Hotel Shingar (☎ 252881) has rooms for Rs 700, or Rs 900 with a view. It's well run and good value.

Hotel Sangeet (☎ 202506) is another good place. Standard rooms are clean, bright and best value at Rs 600.

HPTDC Hotel Holiday Home (☎ 212890), on Cart Rd, is friendly and well set up with a bar and coffee shop, but it's inconveniently located, and doesn't give low-season discounts. Rates are Rs 500 for economy rooms to Rs 2300 for a luxury room.

Spars Lodge (☎ 257908) affords a quiet stay on the colonial edges of Shimla, 2km west of Shimla centre, near the State Museum. Rooms are homely and nicely decorated with clean, bright bathrooms and great food. Singles/doubles cost Rs 600/900.

Places to Stay – Top End

Woodville Palace Resort (☎ 223919), 2km south past the Oberoi Clarke's on the (eastern) Mall, is the place to come for luxury and old colonial charm. This ivy-covered building was constructed in 1938 by Raja Rana Sir Bhagat Chandra, the ruler of the former princely state of Jubbal. It's a small place, set among very pleasant gardens. Double rooms are Rs 2000, and suites start at Rs 3000 – bookings are recommended.

Oberoi Clarke's Hotel (☎ 251010), down the far end of the (eastern) Mall, past the lift, is one of Shimla's earliest hotels. The luxurious rooms start at US$108/120 (plus 10% tax), including the compulsory three meal 'American Plan'.

The Cecil (☎ 204848), on the (western) Mall, offers sheer opulence. Used by Rudyard Kipling as a summer retreat, the building was made into a hotel in 1906. In 1924 Mr Oberoi, the eventual owner of the Oberoi hotel chain, worked here as a restaurant cashier, returning years later to buy the hotel after mortgaging all his assets. Rooms start at Rs 4700/6200 for a single/double in the low season, so bring a credit card.

Places to Eat

Indian Cuisine Shimla has a lot of places serving Indian (primarily southern) food.

Baljee's, on the (eastern) Mall, is one of the more popular restaurants. It has a delicious range of Indian and western food, and the service is good. Prices can be a little high at around Rs 100 for a meat dish (but the seats are very comfortable). Upstairs, the associated restaurant, *Fascination*, is similarly priced and just as popular.

Alfa Restaurant, also near Scandal Point, is about the same standard, price and popularity as Baljee's.

Himani's (49 The (eastern) Mall) does tasty southern Indian snacks and meals, and has a bar.

Rendezvous, at Scandal Point, has Indian and Thai food at moderate prices but service is slow.

Good cheap Indian food is available from many restaurants and *dhabas* (small restaurants) around the Sabzi Mandi and bus station. One of the better places is the *Sher-e-Punjab* on the (eastern) Mall. The special *channa* (chickpeas) is recommended at Rs 25.

Indian Coffee House, on the (western) Mall, is where traditionally dressed waiters serve pretty good coffee (but no tea) and southern Indian snacks.

Western & Chinese Cuisine One of the newer, better places, and worth the stroll, is the *Embassy Restaurant*, on the (eastern) Mall, not far from the top of the lift. It's self-serve and no-nonsense, and has great individual pizzas and hamburgers, as well as Indian and Chinese food.

Devicos Restaurant, on the (western) Mall, near Scandal Point, is a clean, trendy place that does good, but a little overpriced, fast food.

Park Cafe, on the (eastern) Mall, up some stairs, serves western treats like pizza (Rs 35 to Rs 50) and burgers and is popular with backpackers. It's good for milk shakes, breakfasts, and laid-back late-evening music listening.

HPTDC has a building on The Ridge with three places to eat. The *Ashiana* is about the best (and most expensive) place around the area for decor and service. The

Goofa, downstairs, is nowhere near as classy or good, but serves a reasonable (and early) breakfast. In the same complex, the *Quick Bite* has cheap pizzas, and Indian food – or, for a combination of both, try its 'keema pizza'.

Oberoi Clarke's Hotel is a good place for a splurge in luxurious surroundings; the set menu costs Rs 250 plus 8% tax.

Chung Fa, down some steps just off the Mall, is the best place for cheap Chinese food. It is run by an expat Chinese couple and there's a good range of noodles, dumplings and main dishes, all for less than Rs 40 a dish.

Just about every place serves hot, western breakfasts, but many don't open until about 9 am – Shimla is not a place for early starters.

Bakeries Next to the Gaiety Theatre, *Trishool's* is recommended.

Baljee's has a bakery counter at the front, and is a great place for morning or afternoon teas.

Krishna Bakers, on the (eastern) Mall, does good burgers, cakes and pastries.

Entertainment

Probably the most popular, and best, entertainment is to stroll along the Mall and The Ridge (vehicle-free!) and watch everyone else watch everyone else. This is especially pleasant in the evenings when the views and lights are wonderful. An *ice-skating rink* is open in winter – follow the signs from Scandal Point.

The lovely old *Gaiety Theatre* often has some shows or recitals, which are worth checking out, particularly during the Shimla Summer Festival.

There's a bar at *Himani's* and another (dingy and unwelcoming) at the *Rendezvous* on Scandal Point. The expensive hotels usually serve alcohol.

Shopping

The Himachal Emporium on the (western) Mall has a reasonable collection of local handicrafts. The Tibetan Refugee Handloom

Shop, at the other end of the Mall, is the showroom for a local development project and sells carpets, clothes and other Tibetan crafts.

Getting There & Away

Air Jagson Airlines flies small 17-seat Otters to/from Delhi (US$105) daily. Flights continue on to Kullu (US$67). Archana Airways flies daily to/from Delhi only (US$105). Bookings are possible at the HPTDC tourist office at Scandal Point or reliable agencies such as Span Tour & Travels (☎ 206850), 4 The (western) Mall. Shimla's airport is actually at Jubbarhatti, 23km south of town.

Bus The large and chaotic Inter State Bus Terminal (ISBT) on Cart Rd is set up on the reasonable assumption that most foreigners take the train or a tourist bus. However, there is a very handy private computer booking booth (counter 9) at the terminal, where the staff speak English, and you can book a ticket on any public bus up to a month ahead (worth doing in the high season). There is a second booking office just next to the HPTDC office at Scandal Point.

Buses to destinations east of Shimla depart from the Rivoli bus stand, on the northern side of the main ridge, below the HPTDC office.

Public Bus For local places, such as Tattapani, Kasauli, places on the way to Kalka, and places on the way to Narkanda such as Kufri and Theog, catch one of the regular local buses along Cart Rd.

Farther afield, to Manali (11 hours), there are two ordinary (Rs 106) and two semideluxe buses (Rs 139 daytime, Rs 174 overnight); all buses stop in Kullu (Rs 119 to Rs 149). One overnight semideluxe bus goes to Dharamsala (Rs 159, 10 hours). There are 10 buses a day to Bilaspur (Rs 49) and Mandi (Rs 83), or jump on any Manali-bound bus.

There is one overnight and one early-morning deluxe bus to Delhi (Rs 264, 10 hours), plus ordinary buses every hour (Rs 118). Ordinary buses to Chandigarh leave every half hour. Two buses depart every morning to Dehra Dun via Nahan (Rs 67), Paonta Sahib (Rs 90) and Haridwar (Rs 113, nine hours).

Rivoli bus stand has seven buses between 4 am and 11.30 am to Rekong Peo (Rs 120, 10 hours) via Rampur (Rs 60) and Narkanda (Rs 32, three hours). There is one bus at 7.30 am to Sangla and a couple of buses around 9.30 am to Sarahan (Rs 87). There are also hourly buses to Naldehra.

Private Bus Travel agencies along the Mall offer private overnight 'deluxe' (2x2) buses to Manali (Rs 225) and Delhi (Rs 275). These are neither regular nor reliable, and run only in the high season, after the bus from Manali or Delhi arrives with passengers. Prices change according to demand and the season.

HPTDC Bus HPTDC offers daily daytime buses in the high season to Manali (Rs 275, 10 hours) and overnight buses to Delhi (Rs 290, 10 hours) via Chandigarh. HPTDC buses are best booked at the tourist office at Scandal Point but actually depart from the office at Victory Tunnel.

Train There are two train stations in Shimla. All trains arrive at and depart from the main station on the western edge of town; some (but not all) trains also depart from the central branch station. The railway reservation office (☎ 252915) at the main station can arrange bookings for the Shimla-Kalka-Delhi line, and (in theory) for other trips in northern India. It's open Monday to Saturday 10 am to 1.30 pm and 2 to 5 pm; 10 am to 2 pm on Sunday.

The train journey to Shimla involves a change from broad gauge to narrow gauge at Kalka, a little north of Chandigarh. The narrow-gauge trip to Shimla takes about five hours. It's great fun as the little train winds its way around the mountains, although in summer it can get uncomfortably hot and crowded. There are three classes: 2nd class (Rs 14) uses old coaches with

Shimla's Toy Train

A 95.5km narrow-gauge track (69cm wide) was constructed in 1903 under the auspices of Lord Curzon, then Viceroy of India, to link Shimla (2206m), the flourishing resort and summer capital of India, with Kalka (656m), only 25km north of Chandigarh.

The tiny trains travel at speeds of between 15 and 25 km/h, so the trip can take up to five hours, and sometimes longer. The 102 tunnels total over 8km. The second-longest tunnel, at Koti, takes about three minutes to pass through; the longest tunnel, near Barog, is 1143m long, and it takes five minutes before you emerge at the other end. Some carriages have no lights, so it's completely dark in the tunnels. There are 845 bridges, which, like the tunnels, are all numbered. The line cost about 20 million rupees (in 1903!).

At least four toy trains travel each way between Shimla and Kalka every day. Barog, about 37km from Kalka, has always been regarded as the suitable halfway stop for food and drink, though the cucumber sandwiches have long been replaced by 'cutlets' and ketchup.

wooden seats, and can be crowded; chair car (Rs 114) is modern and comfortable; but 1st class (Rs 169) is definitely the way to travel, if you can afford it. It's worth inquiring about the Rail Car service (Rs 216), which runs occasionally in the summer season. The special compartment has glass sides so you get great views. Normally, there are four daily trains each way between Shimla and Kalka, and usually three more in the high season.

To travel from Delhi to Shimla by train in one trip, the best and most reliable way is to catch the *Himalayan Queen* from New Delhi station at 6 am, arriving in Kalka at 11.40 am. Then cross to another platform from where the noon toy train leaves, arriving in Shimla at 5.20 pm. Reservations can be made all the way to Shimla and it costs Rs 400 in AC chair car class (where seats are like an aeroplane's). Some travellers have found their ticket or reservation valid only to Kalka so check when you buy it.

In the opposite direction, the only way to do the Shimla-Delhi trip in one day is to catch the 10.55 am train from Shimla, which connects with the *Himalayan Queen* at Kalka and arrives into New Delhi station at 10.30 pm. The best overnight connection is the *Shivalik Express*, which leaves Shimla at 5.30 pm to connect with the *Kalka-Howrah Mail*, arriving in Delhi at 6.25 am. Fares are Rs 130 for 2nd sleeper, Rs 589 for 2nd AC sleeper.

If you don't want to bother with the toy train, a one-way taxi from Shimla to Kalka costs Rs 700. The Kalka-Shimla Taxi Union in Shimla also arranges shared taxis to Kalka for Rs 115 a seat.

Taxi There are two agencies with fixed-price taxis, which are almost impossible to bargain down, even in the low season. They are the Kalka-Shimla Taxi Union (☎ 258225) on Cart Rd, near the bus station, and the Vishal Himachal Taxi Operators' Union (☎ 205164), at the bottom of the lift on Cart Rd. Both are about the same price. Taxis are either Gypsy jeeps; 'multivans' that take three passengers plus driver; or the Ambassador taxi that can take four passengers, plus driver and costs about 10% more than the prices below.

Examples of one-way taxi fares from Shimla to other destinations in the Indian Himalaya are:

destination	fare (Rs)
Chandigarh	800 - 1000
Dehra Dun	2000 - 2250
Delhi	2500 - 3000
Dharamsala	2200
Kalka	700
Kullu	1800 - 2000
Manali	2200
Rampur	1200
Rekong Peo/Kalpa	2500

HIMACHAL PRADESH

Both taxi companies also offer one-day sightseeing tours, stopping at various places en route:

destination	fare (Rs)
Chail/Kufri	710
Naldehra via Mashobra	410
Narkanda via Fagu and Theog	760
Tattapani via Mashobra and Naldehra	710

For taxi fares to destinations around Shimla see the Getting There & Away sections of the Around Shimla entries.

Getting Around

To/From the Airport A fixed-price taxi costs Rs 400 from the airport to Shimla, but if you are staying anywhere along or near the Mall, you may have to walk the last bit because it is closed to traffic. HPTDC runs an unreliable bus service to/from the airport, otherwise local buses headed to Nalagarh go past the airport.

Passenger Lift At the eastern end of Cart Rd, next to the Vishal Himachal taxi stand, is a lift that goes up to the eastern end of the Mall (Rs 3). It certainly does save a steep climb. (There should be more in Shimla!)

Porters At the bus or train stations you will be besieged by porters to carry your luggage for Rs 4 to Rs 20, depending on weight and distance – not a bad idea, especially when you arrive. From the train station, for instance, it's a long, steep climb to the Mall, and, particularly, to somewhere like the Hotel Dreamland. Porters naturally double as hotel touts so stand your ground if you have a particular hotel in mind. Keep up with your porter; after all he has all your possessions on his back!

Around Shimla

There are a number of points of interest around Shimla that can be visited on day

trips from the hill station, including short walks around Kasauli, horse rides around the village of Kufri, golf at Naldehra and relaxing at the hot springs at Tattapani. For information on HPTDC and taxi tours to these places see the Shimla section.

SHIMLA TO KALKA

The road from Shimla to Kalka is lined with cafes and restaurants offering gorgeous views. Buses ply the road regularly, but visitors usually take the famous Shimla-Kalka train. You can get off and on the train at most stations along the way.

Solan
☎ 01792 • alt 1342m

Solan is known as the home of the Mohan Meakan brewery, built in 1835, and is the capital of the Solan district. It pretends to be another hill station but doesn't have the scenery, facilities or charm of nearby Shimla.

Most of the hotels in Solan are in the mid-price range.

Flora Holiday Resort (☎ 23492), near the bus stand, has rooms from Rs 200 to Rs 550, with hot water, views and a restaurant.

Hotel Utsav (☎ 20074), on the Mall, has singles/doubles from Rs 200/250.

Mayur Hotel (☎ 23670), near the Mall, has rooms from Rs 150/255.

Kumar Hotel (☎ 23847) is better value at Rs 100 a room.

HPTDC Tourist Bungalow (☎ 23733) has typically comfortable rooms for Rs 200 to Rs 400. There are dormitories (in theory at least) for Rs 50 a bed.

Solan is a major stop on the Shimla-Kalka railway line and there are regular buses to Shimla and Chandigarh. A one-way/return taxi between Solan and Shimla costs about Rs 400/550.

Barog

Barog is not a bad place for a day trip by train from Shimla. There are nice walks nearby, including to the 3647m Churdhar mountain.

HPTDC Hotel Pinewood (☎ 01792-38825) has rooms, some with great views, ranging from Rs 900 to Rs 1100, all with hot water and TV.

There are several mid-range places such as the **Kohinoor** with rooms from about Rs 250. The railway *retiring rooms* cost from Rs 50 to Rs 100.

Kasauli

☎ 01793 • alt 1927m

About 12km from the main road between Shimla and Kalka, Kasauli is a charming place. It's a good detour between Shimla and Kalka, a popular side trip from Shimla, or an alternative to staying in Shimla.

There are numerous lovely walks around Kasauli, including to **Sanawar**, another picturesque hill town, and the location of a famous colonial college. Only about 4km away, **Monkey Point** has no monkeys (unlike Shimla) but it's a nice walk there, with great views. These days, the area is owned by the Indian Airforce, so you'll have to get their permission (at the gates) as you walk to Monkey Point.

Places to Stay   Most places to stay are in the mid-price range.

Alasia Hotel (☎ 72008) has rooms from Rs 600.

Maurice Hotel (☎ 72074) has good value singles/doubles from Rs 250/350.

Anchal Guest House (☎ 72052) is OK at Rs 350 a room.

HPTDC Hotel Ros Common (☎ 72005), in a nice location, has rooms with TV from Rs 750 to Rs 1000, and has a nice location.

Getting There & Away   Regular local buses connect Shimla with Kasauli. By train, get off at the Dharampur station, and catch a local bus, or hitch a ride 12km to Kasauli. A one-way/return taxi from Shimla to Kasauli costs about Rs 700/1000.

WILDFLOWER HALL

Wildflower Hall, at **Charabra**, 13km from Shimla, was built as the residence of the then British commander-in-chief Lord Kitchener, specifically it seems, to irritate his rival Viceroy Lord Curzon whose official residence was the Viceregal Lodge in Shimla.

Before it was severely damaged by fire in 1993, HPTDC ran the place as the *Wildflower Hall Hotel*. The hotel is currently being renovated and is due to open in 2000 as a top-end heritage hotel.

CHAIL

☎ 01792

Chail was created by the maharaja of Patiala as his summer capital after he was expelled from Shimla. The town is built on three hills – one is topped by the Chail Palace, one by the village itself, and the other by the Snowview mansion.

Three kilometres from the village is the world's highest **cricket ground** (2444m), built in 1893. There is also a **wildlife sanctuary**, 3km from Chail, with a limited number of deer and birds. This is also great hiking country.

Places to Stay & Eat

Built in 1891, the palace is an example of pure colonial luxury. It's now the *HPTDC Palace Hotel (☎ 48141, fax 48142)*, with a range of suites, cottages, log huts, and rooms set among 28 hectares of lawns. Modest luxury starts at Rs 800 for a log hut, or Rs 1000 for a regular room, and moves up to Rs 4700 for the four bed 'Maharaja suite'. There is also a top-class restaurant, cafe and bar.

The *HPTDC Hotel Himneel (☎ 48337)* has more modest accommodation at Rs 600 a double.

The *Hotel Deodar (☎ 48318)* has rooms from Rs 300.

The *Pine View Tourist Lodge* has rooms from Rs 100 to Rs 250.

Getting There & Away

Chail can be reached from the Shimla-Kalka road via Kandaghat, or more commonly via the turn-off at Kufri. A return taxi from Shimla, via Kufri, costs Rs 700. There are occasional local buses (more in the high season) to Chail from Shimla and Chandigarh.

NORTH OF SHIMLA
Mashobra
☎ 0117

About 11km from Shimla, the small village of Mashobra has some pleasant walks, including to Sipi, where there is a fair every May and a wooden **temple** dedicated to Shiva.

About 3km from Mashobra, along a lovely trail, is the resort of **Craignano**, named after an Italian confectioner who settled here in the 19th century. You can book a room at the *Municipal Rest House* (☎ 224850) in Craignano through HPTDC in Shimla. The only other place to stay in or around Mashobra is the *Gables Resorts* (☎ 480171), which offers rural luxury from Rs 1600 upwards. The village has one or two *dhabas*.

Naldehra
☎ 0117 • alt 2050m

Fifteen kilometres farther north, Naldehra is a pleasant little village – so pleasant in fact that Lord Curzon named his youngest daughter after it. It is mostly famous for its **golf course**, one of the oldest, highest and most spectacular in India (and certainly the only one partly designed by a viceroy of India – Curzon again). There is even a temple, the **Mahunag Mandir**, in the middle of the course.

If you feel like a spot of golf, the green fees are Rs 400 (Rs 100 for Indians) for 18 holes (twice around the course), plus Rs 100 to hire golf clubs and balls, and Rs 50 for a caddy. You'll also need a wad of rupees to replace lost golf balls (it's very hilly).

The *Hotel Golf Glade* (☎ 487739) has six luxurious log cabins from Rs 1000 to Rs 1500, and better-value rooms from Rs 800 to Rs 1000.

Paradise Restaurant, on the main road, is the only decent place worth eating at outside the hotel.

Tattapani
☎ 0117 • alt 655m

Tattapani is famous only for its hot sulphurous springs. They are not as well developed or as nice as the ones in Vashisht, near Manali, or Manikaran, along the Parvati Valley, but the setting is great and the village is small and relaxed. The hot water is piped from a section of the Sutlej River to the two guesthouses on the bank.

Places to Stay & Eat The *HPTDC Tourist Inn* (☎ 485949) has three run-down rooms from Rs 200 to Rs 350. Plush new baths (for guests only) at the back of the hotel should be open soon but nonguests can use the old baths for Rs 10.

There are also some very basic *dorm rooms* for an unbeatable Rs 30 back at the entrance to town but you'd need your own bedding. They aren't easy to find; head up a lane about 100m to the left from the bridge before the village, turn sharp left again and look for a large wooden house.

Spring View Guest House (☎ 485958), down on the riverside, is a friendly and relaxed place, with rooms for Rs 100, or Rs 150 with a balcony overlooking the river. There's also a decent restaurant here and a free hot pool for guests.

Anupam Guest House, up in the village, only has two rooms but they are probably the best value in town. Prices are negotiable.

Hotel Springdale is a cheap place in the village of Sunni, which is about 5km south of Tattapani.

There are several reasonable places to eat by the bridge to Tattapani and both the riverside guesthouses have restaurants.

Getting There & Away Get off the bus just after the bridge over the Sutlej, about 10 minutes past Sunni. The guesthouses and springs are about 400m farther up, by the river. The village itself is up the road to the left before the guesthouses. A local bus leaves Shimla every hour from the Rivoli bus stand for Sunni, and normally continues to Tattapani. The last bus back to Shimla passes through Tattapani around 6.30 pm. A return taxi from Shimla to Tattapani costs Rs 710, including some waiting time while you soak your weary limbs.

EAST OF SHIMLA

Kufri

☎ 0117 • alt 2510m

Kufri is a nondescript little village, but the nearby countryside offers some good hiking, including to nearby Mahasu peak. Horses can be hired for trips around the valleys and hills.

The **Himalayan Nature Park** has a collection of animals and birds unique to Himachal Pradesh, but you won't see much unless you have your own vehicle or you're on a tour. There is a Rs 10 entrance fee, plus Rs 30 extra for a camera, and it's open 10 am to 5 pm every day. Nearby, the **Indira Tourist Park** has great views, the *HPTDC Cafe Lalit*, horse riding and a chance to have your photo taken standing next to a yak.

Kufri is promoted for its skiing (from December to February) but the snow isn't reliable and the location isn't particularly good. In winter, tobogganing is a popular and cheaper alternative.

Places to Stay & Eat The *Hotel Snow Shelter*, on the main road in the village, has cosy rooms, great views and hot water at a reasonable Rs 400.

Kufri Holiday Resorts (☎ 480341) is a very upmarket place where rooms cost from Rs 1150.

Atri Food Center and *Deluxe Food Corner*, on the main road, both serve reasonable food.

Getting There & Away Kufri is a stop for any of the regular buses that travel between Shimla, Narkanda and Rampur. A one-way taxi from Shimla to Kufri costs about Rs 400.

Fagu

Fagu is another unexciting village, but it serves as a good base for exploring the pleasant nearby countryside.

HPTDC Hotel Peach Blossom (☎ 0117-39522) is the only place to stay and is recommended if you want some solitude and views in a colonial setting. The six rooms are enormous, and have old fireplaces.

Doubles currently cost from Rs 275 to Rs 350 but you can expect prices to rise in the wake of recent renovations; check with HPTDC. Bookings are advisable.

Hatkoti Area

Along the Pabar River, the villages of **Hatkoti**, **Rohru** and **Seema** are rarely visited because the roads in the area are undeveloped, and most travellers follow the main road towards Narkanda instead. It is a very pretty area of apple orchards and hillside villages, and there is good *mahseer* fishing. There is a famous **temple** at Hatkoti dedicated to Durga and Shiva, who fought each other here. Nearby, the ancient village of **Jubbal**, once a princely state, is also pretty. Rohru has a famous festival at the **Devta Shikru Temple** in April.

HPTDC Hotel Pabbar (☎ 017815-8269) in Hatkoti has nice doubles for Rs 500 and dorm beds for Rs 50. Rohru has several basic hotels, the best of which are the *Anupam* and *New Prem*.

Irregular local buses link the area with Shimla (115km) and Narkanda.

Narkanda

☎ 01782 • alt 2708m

Halfway between Shimla and Rampur, Narkanda is basically a truck stop town, but it is a popular place for hiking (3300m Hattu peak and its hilltop temple, 8km to the east, makes for a good day hike) and for skiing, in season.

Skiing The ski season here lasts from January to mid-April. The road to Shimla usually remains open in winter, which makes Narkanda accessible and popular. But Narkanda is not as well set up for skiing as the other major site in the region, Solang Nullah, north of Manali.

The HPTDC office in Shimla or the Hotel Hatu in Narkanda can provide details of current skiing courses. Seven-day packages cost Rs 3500 including board, lodging, equipment and tuition. Better-organised 15-day basic and intermediate packages with Manali's Mountaineering Institute & Allied

Sports cost US$262. Unless you are in a group you'll have to join one of the fixed date packages for both of these. There are good opportunities for cross-country skiing around Narkanda if you have the equipment and experience.

Places to Stay & Eat The *Hotel Mahamaya* (☎ 8448) has lovely, large rooms with hot water, balcony and views for the up-market price of Rs 400 to Rs 800. It should offer discounts in the low season.

Hotel Snow View has cheaper rooms but an unoriginal name. Dorm beds (in the lobby!) cost Rs 38, or a ramshackle private room with bathroom costs Rs 220; amazing views and friendly staff make the place tolerable. Look for the sign from the village centre.

HPTDC Hotel Hatu (☎ 8430) is a secluded place 250m up a track east of the main road (look for the sign). Nicely furnished doubles cost Rs 750 and Rs 900 in the high season, Rs 525 and Rs 630 at other times.

There are several basic but friendly *dhabas* in the centre of town. For knives and forks try the restaurant at the *Hotel Hatu*.

Getting There & Away Local buses travel in either direction along the main road at least every 30 minutes. Shimla and Rampur are both about three hours and Rs 30 away. A return taxi from Shimla will cost about Rs 750.

SUTLEJ VALLEY
Nirath
About 20km west of Rampur, the small, revered Hindu **Surya Mandir**, or Sun Temple, at Nirath, sits invitingly across the other side of the wide Sutlej. A small footbridge leads to the temple, which is worth a look if you have your own transport.

Rampur
☎ 01782 • alt 1005m
Rampur was once a stop on the ancient trade route between India and Tibet, and is a former centre of the mighty Bushahr empire, which spread deep into Kinnaur.

Rampur is not a particularly exciting place to stay overnight, but there are one or two things to see if you do stop.

The **Lavi Fair** is held in Rampur every year in the second week of November, traditionally the time when shepherds descend to the warmer valley floor. With its origins in the trade between Pahari herders and Tibetan herders, the trade fair is still a fascinating occasion, as hill people from nearby regions trek into town to sell their summer produce and stock up on supplies for the encroaching winter.

The major attraction in town is the **Padam Palace**, built in 1925, on the side of the main road. You can't go inside, but there are lovely gardens, flanked by a Hindu temple, which you can wander around.

The older part of town, by the river and below the palace, is the most interesting place to explore. It's a maze of tiny lanes, full of shops and temples, such as the Hindu **Raghunath Temple** and the Buddhist **Sri Sat Nahan Temple**, built in 1926.

Places to Stay & Eat The *Narindera Hotel* (☎ 33155), 150m north-east of the bus station, has a variety of decent double rooms overlooking the river, with hot-water bathroom, from Rs 150 to Rs 250. Air-con rooms are Rs 500. There's a good restaurant.

Hotel Bhagwati (☎ 33117), down in the old town (look for the huge sign on its roof), remains deservedly popular. There are singles for Rs 75 and doubles for Rs 125 or Rs 175. All have bathrooms with a geyser.

There are several cheaper dosshouses in town but none amount to much.

Hotel Highway Home, on the main road as you come from Shimla, costs Rs 60 for a basic room with common bathroom. The restaurant is pretty good.

HPTDC Cafe Sutlej is worth the 1km walk from the palace towards Shimla for views and good food. The old town has plenty of *dhabas*, and several pretty good *bakeries*.

Getting There & Away Rampur is a major transport hub, so is well connected by (normally full) buses. There are buses every 30 minutes between 5.30 am and 4 pm to Narkanda (Rs 33, two hours), and then on to Shimla (Rs 60, six hours). To Rekong Peo there are buses at 5, 5.30 and 8.30 am; the 5.30 am departure goes on to Kalpa. Buses to Sarahan depart every two hours or so until 6.30 pm but beware that the last bus of the day is often packed. There is one gruelling bus a day to Kullu at 6.30 am. A one-way taxi from Shimla to Rampur will cost Rs 1200.

Sarahan
☎ 01782 • alt 1920m

Former summer capital of the Bushahr empire, Sarahan is a wonderful little village set high above the valley floor in a beautiful region of deodar forests. It is definitely worth a visit – there are spectacular views of Srikhand Mahadev (5227m) to the north and hiking opportunities to nearby villages such as **Ranwin**, and **Bashal peak**. Also visible in the valley below is the 28km-long tunnel of the new Jakhri hydroelectric project, one of the longest in the world.

Bhimakali Temple This Hindu temple, which has some Buddhist influences, dominates the village and is one of the finest examples of local Himachali architecture. There are some entry rules: you must wear a cap (which can be borrowed from inside the temple), no leather goods (belts, wallets etc) are allowed (they can be left with the guards), photography is only allowed outside the two main temples, and shoes must be removed.

As you pass through to the inner courtyard look out for the stunning silver doors dating from the 1920s, and the elaborately carved wooden roofs of the two main towers – the sun and moon symbols show Tibetan influence.

The two main towers each have five storeys, and are made of earthquake-proof layers of timber and stone. The right-hand tower is actually the older of the two (up to 800 years old) but is now considered structurally unsafe. Stairs ascend the left-hand

temple to the 2nd floor where the main statue of Bhimakali (a local version of Durga) is housed, surrounded by images of Parvati, Buddha and Annapurna, among others, all under a beautiful filigree silver canopy. Stairs descend to the 1st floor where there is a statue of Parvati, wife of Shiva.

In the far right of the courtyard is a small display of lamps and weapons. Next door is the **Lankra Vir Temple**, where human sacrifices were performed until the 19th century to appease Bhimakali, and the well into which the dead bodies were subsequently thrown. Sacrifices are still carried out a couple of days before the annual Dussehra festival in Sept/Oct, though the blood is now limited to that of a few goats and chickens. There are also processions of the temple gods during this time and huge crowds, making it a good time to visit Sarahan.

There are a couple of other temples in the complex, which are dedicated to Narsingh and Raghunath.

Places to Stay & Eat Inside the temple complex, the excellent *temple guesthouse* is the best budget bet, with a handful of clean, quiet rooms with bathroom for Rs 150, Rs 200 or Rs 300.

Snow View Hotel (☎ 74260), at the top of town near the bus stop, is a friendly place. The toilets are pretty grim but the ramshackle rooms are passable at Rs 200. The hotel's *Ajay Restaurant* is pretty good.

HPTDC Hotel Shrikhand (☎ 74234), set at the edge of a bluff, dominates the view as you come up the hill. Large, quiet, comfortable rooms, with TV and hot water, are good value. One room in the old cottage block costs Rs 300 but most rooms in the new block cost Rs 550, Rs 600 or Rs 900. There are dorms for Rs 50 when not booked out by extended Indian families. The restaurant here is excellent, and there are also a few *dhabas* in the village.

Getting There & Away There are a few direct buses from Shimla (Rs 87), Narkanda (Rs 57) and Rampur but generally it's easier to get a through bus to the junction at

Jeori and wait for a local bus (every hour or two) for the steep 17km climb to Sarahan. A taxi from Rampur to Sarahan is pricey at around Rs 500 but will save a lot of time; from Jeori to Sarahan costs about Rs 200.

To get from Sarahan to Shimla in one day (about seven hours), take the 6.30 or 7.30 am daily bus. To get to Rekong Peo or Kalpa in one day, take the early Shimla or Rampur bus, get off at Jeori, and wait for one of the hopelessly crowded buses heading north-east.

Kangra Valley

The beautiful Kangra Valley starts near Mandi, runs north, then bends west and extends to Shahpur near Pathankot. To the north, the valley is flanked by the Dhaula Dhar (White Ridge) Range, to the side of which clings Dharamsala and McLeod Ganj. There are a number of places of interest along the valley, including several important temples and McLeod Ganj, home of the Dalai Lama and the headquarters of the Tibetan Government in Exile.

The main Pathankot to Mandi road runs through the valley, and there is a narrow-gauge railway line from Pathankot as far as Jogindernagar. The famous Kangra school of painting developed in this valley, which is also famous for its tea.

DHARAMSALA
☎ 01892 • alt 1250m

While Dharamsala is synonymous with the Tibetan Government in Exile, the actual headquarters is about 4km above Dharamsala at Gangchen Kyishong, and most travellers hang out at McLeod Ganj, strung along a high ridge 10km above Dharamsala. Dharamsala itself is of little interest, although Kotwali Bazaar, at the foot of the roads leading up to McLeod Ganj, is an interesting and colourful market, and you can visit the Kangra Art Museum, which has examples of the miniature paintings for which the Kangra Valley was once renowned.

Information
Tourist Office The HPTDC tourist office (☎ 24212) is in Kotwali Bazaar. It can book HPTDC accommodation and runs local tours, in summer only, to Kangra, Jawalamukhi and Chamunda Devi Temple (Rs 150) or to Palampur and Baijnath (Rs 150). It also runs luxury buses to Manali (Rs 250, 10 hours) in summer only. The office is officially open Monday to Saturday 9 am to 8 pm.

Money The main branch of the State Bank of India is near the tourist office in Kotwali Bazaar. The main brands of travellers cheques in US dollars and pounds sterling are accepted. Farther down the main road the Punjab National Bank also accepts major travellers cheques. The Bank of Baroda, nearby, doesn't accept travellers cheques, but can give cash advances on Visa cards within 24 hours.

Foreigners' Registration Office Fifteen-day extensions of visas are granted at this office (☎ 22244) in exceptional circumstances (ie for medical problems). The office is in the southern part of town and is open Monday to Friday and every second Saturday 10 am to 5 pm.

Kangra Art Museum
This museum is a few minutes' walk down from the tourist office and is worth a half hour of your time. In addition to the famed miniature paintings, the museum has elaborately embroidered costumes of Kangra adivasis (tribal people), woodcarvings and tribal jewellery. There are some great oddities among the dross, like the sword disguised as a walking stick, the gargantuan elephant saddle and a beautiful multi-faced *paan* (betel nut leaves for chewing) box. The museum is open Tuesday to Sunday 10 am to 5 pm. Entry is free.

Places to Stay & Eat
Sood Guest House on Cantt Rd, Kotwali Bazaar, has doubles with bath for Rs 250 (Rs 100 in the low season) and hot water is available in buckets for Rs 5.

Top: Echoes of the British Raj – Christ Church and the State Library in Shimla. **Middle left:** Bright Buddhist chörten in Kinnaur. **Middle right:** Tibetan monk praying at Dharamsala. **Bottom:** Expansive views of the Parvati Valley.

Despite this harsh landscape of Himachal Pradesh, life flourishes in the Indian Himalaya. A baby monkey **(middle right)** and a vulture **(middle left)** are telling reminders of the continual cycle of death and rebirth.

B Mehra Hotel, a few doors up on the opposite side of the road, is slightly less salubrious. Scruffy doubles (with brilliant views!) are Rs 100 with bathroom and geyser. Singles with common bathroom are Rs 75.

Hotel Rainbow Bridge, just west of Kotwali Bazaar, is clean and quiet, with rooms from Rs 150 to Rs 400.

Shimla Guest House, down some steps off the main thoroughfare, is another decent choice. Rooms are spacious and clean for Rs 250 with bathroom and geyser and there's a pretty nice sitting area. The staff, however, are clueless.

HPTDC Hotel Dhauladhar (☎ 24926) has standard rooms for Rs 500/700, and better-value deluxe rooms for Rs 550/850 in the low/high season. There's a restaurant and bar here, with excellent sunset views.

Cloud's End Villa (☎ 24904) is the residence of the Raja of Lambagraon-Kangra and although inconveniently located halfway between Dharamsala and Gangchen Kyishong, it's a great place for a splurge. The five rooms range from Rs 770 to Rs 1250 and have all the classic colonial trappings.

Rising Moon Restaurant, on Cantt Rd, opposite the Sood Guest House, has continental breakfasts, and Tibetan cuisine. It's run by a very friendly Tibetan man.

Potala Restaurant, up a narrow flight of stairs opposite, has good veg and nonveg Tibetan and Chinese cuisine.

Shopping

The shoemaker Chhotu Ram, in the store with the sign 'Specialist in Dingo Shoes', on Cantt Rd, close to the Rising Moon Restaurant, makes fine men's leather shoes to order from Rs 450.

Getting There & Away

Buses for the 30 minute trip up to McLeod Ganj (Rs 9) depart every half hour throughout the day. The easiest place to catch one is at the top end of Kotwali Bazaar. Cramped passenger jeeps also run a shuttle service up to McLeod Ganj for the same price per seat. A Maruti van taxi should cost

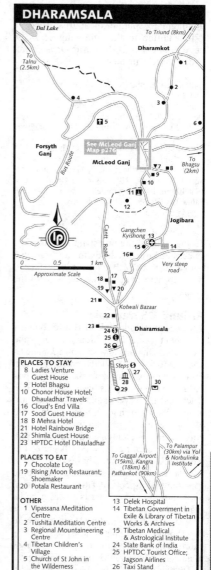

DHARAMSALA

PLACES TO STAY
8 Ladies Venture Guest House
9 Hotel Bhagsu
10 Chonor House Hotel; Dhauladhar Travels
16 Cloud's End Villa
17 Sood Guest House
18 B Mehra Hotel
21 Hotel Rainbow Bridge
22 Shimla Guest House
23 HPTDC Hotel Dhauladhar

PLACES TO EAT
7 Chocolate Log
19 Rising Moon Restaurant; Shoemaker
20 Potala Restaurant

OTHER
1 Vipassana Meditation Centre
2 Tushita Meditation Centre
3 Regional Mountaineering Centre
4 Tibetan Children's Village
5 Church of St John in the Wilderness
6 Tibetan Institute of Performing Arts (TIPA)
11 Tsuglagkhang (Dalai Lama's Temple)
12 Dalai Lama's Residence
13 Delek Hospital
14 Tibetan Government in Exile & Library of Tibetan Works & Archives
15 Tibetan Medical & Astrological Institute
24 State Bank of India
25 HPTDC Tourist Office; Jagson Airlines
26 Taxi Stand
27 Punjab National Bank; Bank of Baroda
28 Kangra Art Museum
29 Bus Stand
30 Post Office

HIMACHAL PRADESH

Rs 80 one way; there's a stand on the main thoroughfare, south of the tourist office.

In addition to the following services, there is one service to Haridwar at 3 pm. Other services include:

Dalhousie/Chamba (Rs 80/113, 6/8 hours, 8.30 am)
Dehra Dun (Rs 225, 14 hrs, 9 pm)
Delhi (Rs 107, 13 hours, 5, 7.20 am, 1, 5, 8 pm, Rs 204 deluxe, 6, 8 pm, Rs 145 semideluxe, 9.30 pm)
Kullu/Manali (Rs 110/136, 10/12½ hours, 5, 11 am, 5.30, 8.30 pm)
Mandi (Rs 72, six hours, 4, 5, 11 am, 6 pm)
Shimla (Rs 160, 10½ hours, 6.40, 8.30 am, 9.30 pm, Rs 170 semideluxe, noon, 7.45 pm)
Pathankot (Rs 39, 3½ hours, hourly 5.45 am to 5 pm)

To the right of the bus stand building is a steep staircase that leads to the vegetable market at Kotwali Bazaar – it's quicker to walk up here than to take the road to the bazaar.

Around Dharamsala

The beautiful **Norbulinka Institute** complex lies about 14km from McLeod Ganj, and 4km from Dharamsala, set amid Japanese-style gardens with shady paths, wooden bridges across small streams and tiny waterfalls. Norbulinka has been established to teach and preserve traditional Tibetan art, such as woodcarving, *thangka* (rectangular cloth) painting, goldsmithing and fine embroidery. Presently, new arrivals from Tibet are learning these skills here, but Norbulinka will eventually become a Centre for Higher Studies, where laypeople can study all aspects of Tibetan Buddhism, and study traditional crafts under Tibetan masters.

Nearby is the **Dolmaling Nunnery**, where the Women's Higher Studies Institute is shortly to be opened, offering nuns' courses at advanced levels in Buddhist philosophy.

There is a *guesthouse* at Norbulinka with doubles for Rs 550, and suites for Rs 850.

To get here, catch a Yol-bound bus and ask to be let off at Sidhpur, near the Sacred Heart School. At this crossroad is a signpost to Norbulinka, from where it is about a 20 minute walk. A taxi from McLeod Ganj will cost Rs 150.

MCLEOD GANJ
☎ 01892 • alt 1982m
High Season: mid-Apr to mid-Jun, mid-Sep to mid-Nov, Tibetan Holidays

Before Upper Dharamsala, or McLeod Ganj (named after the Lieutenant Governor of Punjab David McLeod) was established in the mid-1850s as a British garrison, it was the home of the seminomadic Gaddi tribe, who lead their flocks of sheep and goats up to the high alpine pastures of the Dhaula Dhar every summer. There is still a sizable number of Gaddi families in the villages around McLeod Ganj. The British developed the settlement as an important administrative centre for the Kangra region, and it became a popular hill resort.

On 4 April 1905, disaster struck in the form of a major earthquake. Many buildings were destroyed, numerous lives were lost, and the British decided to move their administrative headquarters farther down the mountainside to Lower Dharamsala, 10km by road below McLeod Ganj.

McLeod Ganj is best known as the headquarters of the Tibetan Government in Exile, and is the home of the 14th Dalai Lama, Tenzin Gyatso. His Holiness the Dalai Lama was recognised as the 14th incarnation of Chenresig, the Tibetan guardian deity of universal compassion, in 1937 at the age of two. Dalai means 'the Embodiment of the Ocean of Wisdom', and is a title that has been conferred on the rulers of Tibet since the 16th century.

In 1950, one year after the Chinese communists led by Mao Zedong wrested control in China from Chiang Kai-Shek, the Chinese marched on Lhasa, soon declaring the 'liberation' of Tibet.

In 1959, the Dalai Lama fled Tibet and was granted political asylum in India. In 1960, Nehru offered the exiled leader and the 80,000 devotees who followed him into exile the virtually abandoned settlement of

McLeod Ganj. It is from here that the Tibetans continue their struggle to regain their homeland. In 1989, the Dalai Lama was awarded the Nobel Peace Prize, presented to him primarily for his endeavours to find a peaceful solution for the liberation of Tibet.

Today McLeod Ganj is one of the most popular Himalayan destinations for foreign tourists. Accommodation can be especially tight during Losar (Tibetan New Year – February/March), the Dalai Lama's birthday (6 July) and other Tibetan festivals. March 10 is the anniversary of the uprising in Lhasa in 1959 and is an important date in McLeod Ganj.

Orientation

The heart of McLeod Ganj is the bus stand. From here roads radiate to various points around the township, including the main road back down to Dharamsala, which passes the church of St John in the Wilderness and the cantonment area of Forsyth Ganj. Other roads lead east and north-east to the villages of Bhagsu and Dharamkot. To the south, Temple Rd proceeds to the Tsuglagkhang Temple, about 800m to the south, from where it's possible to take a short cut down to the administrative area of Gangchen Kyishong (Tibetan for Happy Valley of Snow), where you'll find the Library of Tibetan Works & Archives, a walk of some 20 minutes. The other road through the bazaar, Jogibara Rd, also wends its way down to Gangchen Kyishong via the village of Jogibara.

Information

Tourist Office There's a new HPTDC office in McLeod Ganj, opposite Bookworm, open daily 10 am to 1.30 pm and 2 to 5 pm. It doesn't actually do anything yet and doesn't even have a phone, but this should change soon.

Tibetan Offices & Institutions As the headquarters of the Tibetan Government in Exile are in McLeod Ganj there are numerous offices and organisations concerned with Tibetan affairs and the welfare of the refugee community. These include the Tibetan Welfare Office, Refugee Reception Centre, Tibetan Youth Congress, Tibetan Children's Village (TCV), and the Tibetan Women's Association. Interested visitors are welcome at many of these.

All offices and institutions are open Monday to Friday 9 am to 5 pm (closed for lunch 1 to 2 pm in summer, and noon to 1 pm in winter), other than on Tibetan holidays and three Indian national holidays (26 January, 15 August and 2 October).

Money The State Bank of India is near the post office. It's open Monday to Friday 10.30 am to 1.30 pm and Saturday 10.30 to 11.30 am. It changes American Express, Thomas Cook and Visa travellers cheques in US dollars and pounds sterling only.

Post The post office is on Jogibara Rd, just past the State Bank of India. To post parcels you need to complete a customs form (in triplicate!), which you can get at the Office of Tibetan Handicrafts, opposite the State Bank of India (Rs 3). This form is not required for bookpost. There are several places that offer a parcel packing service, including a couple on Jogibara Rd. Letters sent c/o poste restante, GPO McLeod Ganj are held for one month.

Telephone & Fax The telecom office (fax 21528) is up a flight of stairs behind the bus stand. You can make international calls and send faxes at government rates. In theory you can also receive faxes here but be aware that they turn the machine off at night (when most overseas faxes will arrive) and at weekends. The office is open Monday to Saturday 10 am to 6 pm. Most hotels charge around Rs 3 per minute to receive incoming international calls.

Email & Internet Access McLeod Ganj has the best Internet facilities in the Himalaya. The Tibetan Youth Congress Computer Section (email tyc@del2.vsnl.net.in) will send a one page email for Rs 40, including 20 minutes typing time. Receiving

HIMACHAL PRADESH

emails costs Rs 5 per page. You can use the computer (offline) for Rs 50 per hour.

At the Green Cyber Cafe (email green@chi.vsnl.net.in) you can receive/send emails for Rs 10/25 per page. Internet use (for accessing Web-based email accounts) costs Rs 140 per hour or Rs 35 for 15 minutes, though this will likely drop soon. The Himalaya Cafe and Himachal Travels also offer a similarly good service.

Travel Agencies There are numerous travel agencies in McLeod Ganj. One reliable outfit is Potala Tours & Travels (☎ 21378, fax 21427), opposite the Hotel Tibet. Potala can book air, train and bus tickets (see under Getting There & Away), as well as arrange tours. Other reliable travel agencies include:

Himachal Travels
   (☎ 21428, fax 21528, email katoch@vsnl.com) Jogibara Rd. This agency is good for train and local and deluxe bus tickets. It reconfirms international air tickets for Rs 100, or the cost of the telephone call plus Rs 50. You can book local bus tickets for a Rs 30 service charge. Internet connection costs about Rs 100 per hour.
Dhauladhar Travels
   (☎ 21158, fax 21246)
   Temple Rd. Arranges domestic and international air bookings.
Tibet Tours & Travels
   (☎ 21966, fax 21528)
   Temple Rd. Good for specialist and Buddhist tours as well as most other services.

Trekking Outfits Eagle Height Trekkers & Travellers can organise porters and guides, as well as arrange treks in the Kullu, Chamba, Lahaul or Spiti valleys and Ladakh, from US$40 per day including porter, guide, cook, meals, tents and sleeping bag. Transport is extra. They are in the process of moving offices so you will have to check on their present location.

Yeti Trekking (☎ 21887, fax 21578) also arranges tailor-made treks to most areas, with accommodation en route in huts and houses. It can be found in a fine old building, which is reached through a gate off the

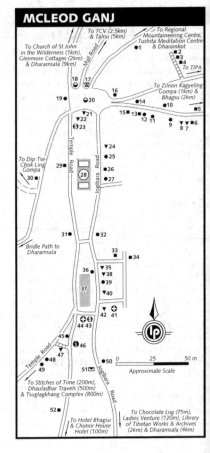

Dharamkot road. Sample prices include Rs 4800 for a seven day trek to Brahmaur and Rs 2800 for a four day trek to Indrahar Pass and back. Prices are per person, per day, based on a group of two or three people, and include food, porters and a guide.

Regional Mountaineering Centre This centre (☎ 21787) is about 15 minutes' walk north of McLeod on Dharamkot Rd. The centre mainly runs week-long mountaineering, rock-climbing (Rs 2100) and trekking

MCLEOD GANJ

courses (Rs 2960) for groups, but individuals can tag along if there's a course already running. You can get advice here on treks and mountaineering in the Chamba and Kangra valleys, and there's a useful list of registered local guides and porters. It's a good idea to advise the centre if you are planning a trek in the region.

Basic equipment is for hire, but only if it's not being used by a group. You can also purchase Survey of India trekking maps (Rs 15) and the paperback *Treks and Passes of Dhauladhar and Pir Panjal* (Rs 150) by SR Saini, the centre's director.

Bookshops There's an excellent selection of new books at Bookworm, up the road to the right of the State Bank of India. The Tibetan Bookshop & Information Centre on Jogibara Rd also has a comprehensive selection of books as well as government publications on the Tibetan struggle for independence and Tibetan Buddhism. The nearby Charitrust Bookshop has probably the town's best collection of books on Tibetan travel, history and Buddhism. Youtse Bookshop, on Temple Rd, is also worth a look.

Nowrojee & Son (est 1860) is a great old-style general store that also sells daily English-language newspapers.

Tibetan Publications *Chö-Yang* is a glossy journal published occasionally by the Department of Religion & Culture. There are seven volumes, which include scholarly essays on Buddhism and Tibetan culture. Other journals published in McLeod include the *Tibetan Bulletin* and *Rangzen* (Freedom), published by the Tibetan Youth Congress. *Contact* is a free local magazine that has a useful 'what's on' listing, plus information on local courses and volunteer work.

Laundry Several laundries on Bhagsu Rd, such as Sky Laundry and Quick Pick Laundry, offer a same day service if you get your clothes to them before 10 am. T-shirts cost around Rs 8, trousers Rs 10 to Rs 15. The government-run Premier Laundry is twice as expensive but more reliable.

HIMACHAL PRADESH

Medical Services Delek Hospital (☎ 22053) in Gangchen Kyishong often has volunteer western doctors on staff, as well as an ECG and x-ray machine and a dental department. For Tibetan medicine try Dr Yeshi Dhonden's clinic or the Dr Lobsang Dolma Khangsar Clinic, both near the State Bank of India.

Tsuglagkhang Complex

This complex, five minutes' walk south of McLeod Ganj, comprises the official residence of the Dalai Lama, as well as the Namgyal Gompa, bookshop and cafe and the Tsuglagkhang itself.

The **Tsuglagkhang**, or Central Chapel, is the exiled government's equivalent of the Jokhang Temple in Lhasa and as such is the most important Buddhist monument in McLeod Ganj. Although a relatively modest structure, it enshrines three magnificent images, including an enormous 3m-high gilt statue of Sakyamuni Buddha. To the left of this (and facing Tibet) are statues of Avalokiteshvara (Tibetan: Chenresig), the Tibetan deity of compassion, of whom the Dalai Lama is considered to be an incarnation, and Padmasambhava (Tibetan: Guru Rinpoche), the Indian scholar who introduced Buddhism and Tantric teachings to Tibet in the 8th century. Inside the Avalokiteshvara statue are several relics rescued from the Jokhang Temple during the Cultural Revolution.

Also housed in the temple is a collection of sacred texts known as the *Kangyur* which are based on the teachings of the Buddha, as well as the *Tangyur*, which are translations of commentaries based on the Buddha's teachings. The mural to the side depicts the trio of ancient Tibetan kings who oversaw the introduction of Buddhism into Tibet.

Next to the Tsuglagkhang is the **Kalachakra Temple**, built in 1992, which houses a stunning mural of the Kalachakra (Wheel of Time) mandala. Sand mandalas (constructed with coloured sand on the ground) are created here annually on the 5th day of the 3rd Tibetan month. There is also a display

Public Audiences with His Holiness the Dalai Lama

When the Dalai Lama is not touring around the world to raise awareness of the fate of Tibet at the hands of the Chinese, he resides in Dharamsala, and according to his schedule, gives 10 to 12 public audiences each year. To find out when the next audience is, check at the Branch Security Office on Bhagsu Rd in McLeod Ganj, or the Office of the Dalai Lama (☎ 21879, fax 21813) near the Tsuglagkhang. You need to register your name two to three days in advance when the scheduled audience is confirmed, and your passport details are required.

On the day of the audience, it's best to get to the temple about one hour in advance to get through the security checks. Cameras, bags and rucksacks are strictly prohibited, and you should wear respectable dress and carry your passport. As you join the hundreds of other devotees, you file past the Dalai Lama, who will shake your hand, and probably grin broadly and, if you're lucky, utter a few words. His monk attendant will give you a red *jyendue* (sacred thread).

highlighting the case of the Panchen Lama, whose reincarnation the Tibetan and Chinese governments are in dispute over. Photography is allowed in the Tsuglagkhang, but not the Kalachakra Temple.

The remaining buildings form the **Namgyal Gompa**, which offers ritual assistance to the Dalai Lama during the highly complex Kalachakra ceremony. Unusually, the monastery performs prayers and rituals for every school of Tibetan Buddhism. It is possible to watch monks debate here most afternoons, sealing points of logic with a great flourish and a clap of the hands.

Most Tibetan pilgrims make a *kora*, or circuit, of the Tsuglagkhang complex. Take the road to the left, past the entrance to the temple, and after a few minutes, where the road veers around to the left (towards Gangchen Kyishong), a small path leads off to the right, eventually looping all the way around the Dalai Lama's residence back to the entrance to the temple. The path is flanked by colourful mani stones and prayer flags, and at one section there is a series of small prayer wheels. The kora should be made in a clockwise direction only.

Dip Tse-Chok Ling Gompa

This beautiful little gompa lies at the bottom of a steep track, which leads off the lane past the Om Guest House. The main *dukhang* (prayer hall) houses an image of Sakyamuni, as well as two enormous drums covered in goat skin and painted around the rim, which were made by monks at the gompa. Also here are some superb butter sculptures. The butter is mixed with wax and sculpted into various forms. They are made during Losar (Tibetan New Year), and destroyed during Losar the following year. Sand mandalas are also made here.

Tibetan Institute of Performing Arts (TIPA)

This institute promotes the study and performance of the Tibetan performing arts to ensure the preservation of Tibet's traditional cultural heritage (a heritage largely destroyed in Tibet itself). The most important

of the arts taught and practised at the institute is traditional *lhamo* opera. Lhamo incorporates dance, mime and singing, with performers, most of whom wear masks and richly coloured costumes, accompanied by drums and cymbals. Lhamo draws on both Tibetan historical events and adaptations of plays from India. A small museum has recently opened at the site.

In April each year TIPA convenes an opera festival, which also includes folk dancing and contemporary and historical plays. There is also a three day festival from 27 May, the anniversary of the foundation of TIPA. Details of these and other performances at TIPA are posted around McLeod Ganj.

Library of Tibetan Works & Archives

The library at Gangchen Kyishong, halfway between Dharamsala and McLeod, is the repository of Tibet's rich literary heritage, containing about 40% of Tibet's original manuscripts, as well as an excellent general reference library open to all. Membership costs Rs 15 per month and entitles you to borrow two books at a time. Opening hours are Monday to Friday, 9 am to 1 pm and 2 to 5.30 pm in summer; lunch break an hour earlier in winter.

There's also a **Tibetan Cultural Museum** on the 1st floor, with some excellent exhibits including fine statues, rare Tibetan stamps and banknotes and a medal from the Younghusband mission to Lhasa. Opening times are the same as the library and entry costs Rs 5.

Also worth a visit near the library complex is the **Nechung Monastery**, home to the Tibetan state oracle. Inside the main chapel there is a fine *torma* (barley meal and butter) sculpture of Dorje Drakden, the protector deity who has been advising the Tibetan government on matters of state for centuries through the medium of the Nechung oracle. The current oracle is a monk in his 30s who revealed himself when the previous oracle died in 1984. It's possible to look around the monastery, which also has a good restaurant near the library.

HIMACHAL PRADESH

Tibetan Medical & Astrological Institute (Mentsikhang)

This institute is at Gangchen Kyishong, about five minutes' walk below the main entrance to the library area. There's a museum, library, research unit, and a college, at which Tibetan medicine and astrology is taught. There are two forms of astrological consultation. *Kartsi* considers aspects of astronomy and cosmic influences on human beings according to the configurations of the stars, moon and planets. *Nagtsi* is a system of astrology based on the elements of fire, water, earth, iron and wood. Calculations are made according to the year in which you are born. It's possible to have a life horoscope prepared for US$30.

The museum (opened on request) has a well-displayed exhibition of materials used

---

Traditional Tibetan Medicine

The origins of Tibetan medicine date back some 2500 years. It is based on a holistic approach, which considers both the psychological and physiological bases of disease, known as Sowa Rigpa. The Buddha in his manifestation as Sangsrgyas Smangbla is attributed with the original medicinal teachings, which found their way into Sanskrit texts in the 4th century CE (common era) and were later translated into Tibetan where they were received at the Tibetan royal court in the 8th century. They were known as the Four Secret Oral Tantras on the Eight Branches of the Essence of Nectar. Later Tibetan scholars contributed to this body of medicinal knowledge, which details eight branches of medicine – the body, including anatomy and embryology; paediatrics; gynaecology; disorders related to the impact of harmful influences; disorders caused by wounds; toxicology; geriatrics; and fertility.

Suffering, according to Buddhist philosophy, is a result of delusion and ignorance, which in turn give rise to attachment in the form of greed and desire. The physiological bases of disease are attributed to the fact that we are all composed of five cosmo-physical elements: earth, water, fire, air and ether. An imbalance between these energies results in disease, and can be attributed to factors such as an unbalanced diet, emotional disturbance and other external influences.

However, the real essence of traditional Tibetan medicine lies in diagnosis, and three diagnostic techniques are employed: visual diagnosis, particularly of the tongue and urine; sphygmology, which determines the nature of the disorder through an examination of the pulse; and interrogation.

Even if you're not sick, it's worth visiting Dr Yeshi Dhonden's clinic on Jogibara Rd in McLeod Ganj. The doctor determines the nature of an ailment by taking the patient's pulse, and appropriate pills are prescribed. There are six different types of pills: for migraines; for nervous disorders; for digestion; for blood purification; for food poisoning; and as a general tonic. The herbs from which the pills are made are collected mostly from those regions bordering Tibet, including Ladakh, Lahaul & Spiti, Bhutan and Nepal. They are first dried and then ground into powder, which is then mixed with hot water. A pill-making machine forms them into round balls, and they are left to dry in the sun, and then polished. The most precious of these pills are individually wrapped in silk, and tied with a coloured thread secured with a wax seal.

Dr Yeshi's clinic is open Monday to Friday, 8 am to noon, and 1 to 4 pm. Medicines can be sent overseas (US$25 including postage and packing), which is enough for one month's supply. (Check the customs laws of the country of destination.) Consultations are free, and one month's supply of pills costs from Rs 90 to Rs 300.

in Tibetan medicines, including herbs, cowrie shells, precious and semiprecious stones, fossils and metals. Exhibits are well labelled in both Tibetan and English, giving their scientific name and medicinal uses.

St John in the Wilderness

Dharamsala was originally a British hill resort, and one of the most poignant memories of that era is the pretty church of St John in the Wilderness (1852) and the tomb of Lord Elgin, the eighth viceroy of India, who died here in 1863. The church is only a short distance below McLeod on the main road towards Dharamsala. Services are held every Sunday at 11.30 am.

Walks

There are many fine walks and even finer views around McLeod Ganj. The sheer rock wall of the Dhaula Dhar Range rises behind the township. Interesting walks include the 2km stroll east to **Bhagsu** and the 3km walk north-east to the little village of **Dharamkot**, where there are fine views. From Dharamkot, you can continue east down to Bhagsu and walk back to McLeod along the main Bhagsu road.

An 8km trek from McLeod Ganj will bring you to **Triund** (2827m) at the foot of the Dhaula Dhar. It's a steep but straightforward ascent, with the path veering off to the right across scree just beyond Dharamkot. The views of the Dhaula Dhar from here are stunning. It's another 5km to the snow line at **Ilaqa**. There's a *Forest Resthouse* here for overnight accommodation (Rs 200); to book it ask at the HPTDC office. From Ilaqa, it's possible to continue over the Indrahar Pass to the Chamba Valley. See the Trekking from Dharamsala boxed text later in this chapter.

A shorter 5km walk can take you past the TCV Handicraft School and polluted **Dal Lake**, up to the hamlet of **Talnu** (also known as Naddi). There are more good views of the Dhaula Dhar wall from here and you can hire horses here (ask around for Mr Omni) for trips up to Triund (Rs 300/500 half/full day). Trails also lead to **Kareri Lake**,

around 26km away. There are six buses a day between Talnu and McLeod Ganj.

Buddhist Philosophy Courses

About 20 minutes' walk above McLeod is the Tushita Meditation Centre. One path heads off to the right near a small white *chörten* (stupa) just beyond the Regional Mountaineering Centre, another leads from Dharamkot village. The centre has facilities for retreats, as well as offering a monthly 11 day introductory course in Buddhist philosophy led by western and Tibetan teachers. Tushita (the name of a Buddhist paradise) was founded by the venerated lama Yeshe Rinpoche, whose reincarnation (a Spanish boy from Barcelona) was recognised in the late 1980s.

There is a small library at Tushita, which is open to students and nonstudents, and there are books on Buddhism for sale. Sex, cigarettes and alcohol are forbidden. Tuition, food and accommodation costs around Rs 240 per day. The office (☎ 21866) is open Monday to Saturday 9.30 to 11.30 am and 1 to 4.30 pm.

Behind Tushita is the Dhamma Sikhara Vipassana Meditation Centre (☎ 21309), which offers 10-day courses in Indian Hinayana Buddhism.

Down at the Tibetan library (☎ 22467) in Gangchen Kyishong, classes in specific aspects of Buddhist philosophy are led by Tibetan lamas and translated into English. Subjects are divided into two-week chunks, as outlined in the prospectus available from reception. They take place Monday to Friday, 9 to 11 am, and cost Rs 100 per month, plus Rs 50 registration. If you're not sure you want to commit yourself to what are quite advanced studies, it's possible to attend the first class free.

Tibetan Language Courses

Pema Youdon is a friendly Tibetan woman who teaches Tibetan language from her home opposite the post office. It costs Rs 40 per hour, and there is a discount for two-hour sessions. The Kalsang Guest House offers private language tuition for Rs 80 per

HIMACHAL PRADESH

hour. It's also possible to study Tibetan at the Library of Tibetan Works & Archives. Classes are held Monday to Friday 10 to 11 am and are divided into terms of three months. Beginner and advanced courses both cost Rs 200 per month, plus Rs 50 registration.

Volunteer Work
If you're interested in teaching English or computer skills to newly arrived refugees, check notice boards at the Library of Tibetan Works & Archives as well as *Contact* magazine (see Tibetan Publications, earlier in this section).

Places to Stay – Budget
There's a wide range of places to stay in McLeod Ganj. Most budget rooms are dismally dark and only the pricier rooms have a view.

Kalsang Guest House (☎ 21709), on TIPA Rd, is very popular with travellers. There's a range of rooms, including tiny singles/doubles with common bathroom for Rs 45/85. Doubles with hot showers (but no external windows) cost Rs 135 to Rs 180, or there are bright rooms with great views upstairs for Rs 275. Top-floor rooms can be noisy. You can get a hot shower in the common bathroom for Rs 10, but 30 minutes' advance notice is required. It's possible to store bags here if you are going on a trek.

Loselling Guest House, just above the Kalsang, is monastery-run. Rooms are small and viewless but clean and pretty good value. Rooms with a double bed and hot shower cost Rs 180; small singles with common bath are good value at Rs 60. A hot shower in the common bathroom costs Rs 10.

Paljor Gakyil Guest House (☎ 21443), just above the Loselling, has doubles for Rs 70, and doubles with bathroom from Rs 110 to Rs 132 (with cold water) or Rs 155 to Rs 220 (with hot water). Top-floor rooms with a view cost Rs 275.

Green Hotel (☎ 21000), on Bhagsu Rd, is a long-time favourite with travellers. Small spartan rooms are Rs 55 to Rs 80, and with bath, Rs 150 (cold water) or Rs 250

(hot water). Deluxe rooms are overpriced at Rs 350. Some rooms have great valley views, and there's a good restaurant here.

Tashi Khansar Guest House, opposite the Green, has basic single rooms with common bath (hot water) for Rs 70, and singles/doubles with bathroom for Rs 120/135, some with excellent views.

Kailash Hotel (☎ 21044) is very centrally located, opposite the chörten. There are doubles/triples for Rs 70/80, all with common bathroom (with 24 hour hot water). Rooms at the back have great views, but are pretty rustic.

Om Guest House (☎ 24313), on a path leading down from the bus stand behind the Kailash, is another popular place. Ground floor doubles are Rs 100, but the upper floor rooms with bath are much nicer at Rs 225 or Rs 250 and have great valley views. Hot water in buckets is Rs 8. There's a good restaurant but this means that the rooms can be noisy in the evening.

Shangrila Guest House, on the other side of the chörten, is monastery-run, with doubles with common bath for Rs 55, and hot water available in buckets for Rs 10.

Snow Lion Guesthouse, next door, is friendly, with clean, well-maintained rooms with bath and hot water for Rs 150, and Rs 200 with private balcony and good views.

Drepung Loseling Guest House (☎ 23187, Jogibara Rd), down an alley, is popular with long-term volunteers. It has doubles with bath and cold shower for Rs 150, or with a hot shower for Rs 190 and Rs 250, including breakfast. The more expensive rooms have their own balcony and great valley views.

Tibetan Ashoka Guest House (☎ 21763), next door, has a range of rooms, with dingy doubles from Rs 55 to Rs 90, Rs 162 with bathroom on the ground floor, and some of those on the top floor have their own balconies for Rs 275 and Rs 330. Hot water is Rs 10 a bucket.

Ladies Venture (☎ 21559), on Jogibara Rd, is a very quiet and friendly place, down past the Chocolate Log (see under Places to Eat). Rooms with bath but no view are

Rs 150/225, or Rs 200 sharing a bathroom with one other room. Comfortable rooms with a view cost Rs 300 and Rs 400. Six-bed dorms are available for Rs 50 a bed but these are often full.

Dip Tse-Chok Ling Gompa Guesthouse is a peaceful place, about 300m down a path that leads off the lane beyond the Om Guest House. Rooms are Rs 80, and have fine views over the valley.

It's also possible to stay at the *Zilnon Kagyeling Nyingmapa Gompa Guesthouse*, about 1km from McLeod on Bhagsu Rd. Rooms are Rs 60, and a hot shower is Rs 10. There is a rooftop cafe here.

Several other gompas offer accommodation to volunteers and local students only, as does the Library of Tibetan Works & Archives. There are also several hotels around Gangchen Kyishong.

Places to Stay – Mid-Range & Top End

Hotel Tibet (☎ 21587, fax 21327), on Bhagsu Rd a few steps from the bus stand, has standard/semideluxe/deluxe doubles for Rs 450/500/800. All rooms have carpet, cable TV and bath. There's a very good restaurant and bar here.

Hotel India House (☎ 21144) is bright, comfortable and a good option, though it lacks the Tibetan touch. Rooms cost Rs 800, Rs 1100 and Rs 1400 and most have a balcony with excellent views.

There are a couple of other large Indian-run hotels on the road past Bookworm.

Hotel Natraj (☎ 21574) has doubles on the ground floor for Rs 400, and semideluxe rooms for Rs 600; neither with views. Deluxe rooms with good views are Rs 800.

Hotel Him Queen (☎ 21184) and *Surya Resorts (☎ 21418)* have rooms from Rs 750 to Rs 1200 and you should be able to negotiate a good discount in the low season.

HPTDC Hotel Bhagsu (☎ 21091) is at the end of this road. It has a range of doubles from Rs 600 to Rs 1500, half this in the low season.

Chonor House Hotel (☎ 21006, fax 21468), nearby, is a very stylish place owned by the Norbulinka Institute. Doubles range from Rs 1300 to Rs 1700 (with a Rs 200 discount for single occupancy) and are beautifully decorated with traditional Tibetan artefacts. There's also a good Tibetan restaurant and bakery here. Bookings are recommended.

Glenmore Cottages (☎ 21010) is about 2km above McLeod, along a track that branches off the main Dharamsala road. It has comfortable accommodation in five peacefully located cottages. Rates range from Rs 990 to Rs 2250, and all rooms have heaters and geysers.

Places to Eat

Green Hotel has a very popular restaurant, with a range of excellent home-made cakes (the carrot cake is recommended), as well as vegetarian dishes like spinach quiche. It's also a good place for breakfast.

Himalaya Cafe, nearby, also has good food and a wonderful rooftop balcony with views over the plains, though the service is terrible. You can get filter coffee here and refill your bottle with boiled and filtered water for Rs 5.

Nick's Italian Kitchen, next door, has good cakes, quiches and Italian food.

Hotel Tibet has one of the best restaurants in town and features Tibetan, Chinese and Indian cuisine. There's a convivial bar here.

McLlo Restaurant, right above the bus stand, has an extensive menu, good food and a bar, though it's a little overpriced.

Friend's Corner, nearby, serves excellent Chinese food and prices are reasonable for the large portions.

Bhakto Restaurant, beneath the Kailash Hotel, has traditional and cheap mutton *momos* (Tibetan dumplings) and noodle soup. It's popular with local Tibetans, and is usually only open around lunchtime.

Malabar Cafe on Jogibara Rd, on the opposite side of the chörten, is a pleasant little place serving good Indian, Chinese and continental cuisine.

Cafe Shambhala, nearby, is also popular.

Gakyi Restaurant, on Jogibara Rd, serves the best special muesli in town (Rs 35) and there's a good range of healthy vegetarian food such as tofu and brown rice. In the morning you can get freshly baked brown bread for Rs 20.

Snowland Restaurant, nearby, is recommended for cheap and tasty Tibetan food.

Ashoka Restaurant on Jogibara Rd has the best Indian food in town. The chicken *korma* (braised curry) is excellent, and there's also good tandoori chicken (Rs 70 for a half portion), chicken Mughlai (Rs 100), and a very good *malai kofta* (cheese and vegetable balls in a rich cream-based sauce). There are also continental dishes such as pizza (Rs 40) and spaghetti. **Aroma Restaurant**, nearby, offers cheap Israeli cuisine.

Om Guest House has a popular restaurant. The vegie burger here is served with salad, a banana and chips; there's also a good sound system, plus spectacular sunset views.

Dreamland Restaurant, down a staircase to the right, just beyond Bookworm, has good salads. The chef is from Delhi, and also dishes up very good, and very reasonably priced, veg and nonveg Tibetan and Chinese cuisine.

Hotel Bhagsu has a pricier restaurant, but the food is very good and there are cold beers. However, it's a dark, gloomy and cavernous place. On sunny days, tables are set up in the gardens, and you can eat out here, a much more pleasant proposition.

McLeod Ganj is a great place for those with a longing for coffee and cake.

Chocolate Log *(Jogibara Rd)*, a few minutes' walk down past the post office, is an old favourite, serving western dishes such as pizza and various types of cakes (chocolate, black forest, banana).

Take Out is a place beneath the Hotel Tibet where you can buy freshly baked bread, cakes and doughnuts.

Snow Lion Guest House also serves great cakes, as well as good Tibetan food.

Shopping

McLeod Ganj is a good place to stock up on souvenirs and the upper parts of Temple and Jogibara Streets Rds are lined with handicraft and jewellery shops.

Tibetan textiles such as bags, *chubas* (the dress worn by Tibetan women), hats and trousers can be found at the Office of Tibetan Handicrafts, just north of the State Bank of India. Here you can have a chuba made to order with your own fabric (Rs 80), or with fabric supplied by the centre (Rs 350 to Rs 450).

Just opposite is the Tibetan Handicrafts Cooperative. The coop employs about 145 people, many of them newly arrived refugees, in the weaving of Tibetan carpets. Fine New Zealand wool carpets, with 90 knots per sq inch cost Rs 4972 per sq m, while those of 48 knots per sq inch are Rs 2603 per sq m, depending on the design. The society can pack and post purchases home, and visitors are welcome to watch the carpet makers at work on traditional looms.

Stiches of Time, farther downhill on Temple Rd, is run by the Tibetan Women's Association, and also makes chubas and other clothes to order.

Tara Herbal Gift Shop, near the bus stand, has traditional Tibetan herbal incense and books on Tibetan medicine. At the Green Shop, Bhagsu Rd, you can buy hand-painted T-shirts and recycled handmade paper.

Entertainment

There are several *video halls* in the town centre on Jogibara Rd. They show new releases and documentaries on Tibet all day and evening, with the program posted out the front. Tickets are Rs 5 to Rs 10. *TIPA* (see earlier in this section for details) has occasional performances of Tibetan opera and drama.

Getting There & Away

Air Gaggal airport, 15km south of Dharamsala, currently has no flights but services might soon resume to Delhi, Kullu and/or Shimla, so check at travel agencies.

Bus The Himachal Roadways Transport Corporation (HRTC) booking office is at the bus stand. Services can take you to Dehra Dun, leaving at 7.30 pm (Rs 225, 12 hours), Delhi in deluxe 2x2, leaving at 6pm

(Rs 300, 12 hours), Manali, leaving at 5am (Rs 100, 11 hours) and then again at 6 pm (Rs 125, 11 hours) and Pathankot, leaving at 9, 10 and 11 am, and 4 pm (Rs 47, 4 hours). If you need services to other destinations, you'll have to make your way down to Dharamsala.

Potala Tours & Travels, opposite the Hotel Tibet, has a deluxe service to Delhi, which leaves at 6 pm (Rs 350, 12 hours). Numerous other agencies offer deluxe buses. When booking a bus to Delhi take care to check that it will take you to Connaught Place and/or Paharganj, not just the Inter State Bus Station at Kashmir Gate. Quoted prices at Himachal Travels were: Manali (Rs 250) and Leh (Rs 1050). The Leh bus departs McLeod at 9 pm, arrives at Manali at 6 am and then departs Manali at 7 am, arriving at Leh the following evening (with an overnight stop en route).

Himachal Travels can also book ordinary buses departing from Dharamsala, for a charge of around Rs 25 per ticket.

Train Many travel agencies will book train tickets for services out of Pathankot, down on the plains in the Punjab (for details see the Pathankot section). It's worth booking as early as possible, preferably a week in advance. Generally a Rs 75 booking fee is levied. There's a railway booking office at the bus stand in Dharamsala, but it has only a tiny quota of tickets. It's only open 10 to 11 am, and is closed on Sunday.

The closest train station to McLeod is either Kangra or Nagrota, both around 20km south of Dharamsala. Both are on the small narrow-gauge line that runs along the Kangra Valley connecting Pathankot with the small settlement of Jogindernagar, 58km north-west of Mandi. It's a slow, five hour

Trekking from Dharamsala

The trek over the Indrahar Pass is one of many that can be undertaken over the Dhaula Dhar Range. It can be completed from mid-May to the end of June although you must be prepared for trekking through snow when approaching and crossing the Indrahar Pass. The monsoon rains continue from early July till mid-September, and from then until mid-October is an ideal time to trek.

Arrangements can be made at one of the trekking agencies in McLeod Ganj. If you have not trekked before a local guide is imperative, while porters can be hired for around Rs 200 per day. Sleeping bags and tents together with food supplies and kerosene must be carried with you.

McLeod Ganj to Chamba via the Indrahar Pass

The trek over the Indrahar Pass starts from the bus stand at McLeod Ganj and follows the well-defined trail past the village of Dharamkot and on to the meadow at Triund. It is a further stage to the base of the pass and an overnight at a rock cave before completing the long, and in places arduous, ascent over scree and boulders to the Indrahar Pass (4350m). From the pass there are rewarding views south towards the Indian plains, while the Pir Panjal Range provides an impressive backdrop to the north. The trek continues with a short steep descent to the camp at Chatru Parao before continuing to the village of Kuarsi. It is a further stage to Machetar to catch the bus for the four to five hour drive to Chamba.

Stage 1	McLeod Ganj to Triund	(3-4 hrs)
Stage 2	Triund to Lahesh Cave	(4-5 hrs)
Stage 3	Lahesh Cave to Chatru Parao via Indrahar Pass	(6-7 hrs)
Stage 4	Chatru Parao to Kuars	(5-6 hrs)
Stage 5	Kuarsi to Machetar	(6 hrs)

haul between Nagrota and Pathankot – the bus is much faster – but if you have the time, it's worthwhile taking the four hour trip east from Nagrota to Jogindernagar, which wends through the Kangra Valley affording fine views of the Dhaula Dhar Range to the north. To Jogindernagar, there are six trains a day, passing through Palampur (one hour) and Baijnath (two hours).

Taxi McLeod's taxi stand (☎ 21034) is next to the bus stand. A taxi to Pathankot is around Rs 800. To hire a taxi for the day, covering less than 80km, costs Rs 700. Local operators have also devised the following fixed-rate taxi tours to points of interest around McLeod Ganj and in the Kangra Valley:

Bhagsu Temple, Tsuglagkhang, Dal Lake, St John's Church and Talnu (Rs 180, three hours)
Norbulinka, Chinmaya Ashram at Tapovan, Chamunda Devi Temple, Kangra and Jawalamukhi Temple (Rs 900, eight hours)
Norbulinka, Tapovan, Chamunda Devi Temple, Palampur and Baijnath (Rs 950, eight hours)

Getting Around

Unfortunately, McLeod Ganj now has several auto-rickshaws – to Bhagsu the charge is Rs 35. Taxis cost Rs 50 to Gangchen Kyishong, Rs 80 to Dharamsala's Kotwali Bazaar and Rs 90 to Dharamsala bus station. There are also buses for the 40 minute trip down to Dharamsala (Rs 9), departing every 30 minutes between 4.15 am and 8.30 pm. Cramped passenger jeeps also run when full for the same price.

You can currently hire motorcycles from the New Karyana Shop (☎ 21510) on Temple Rd, though the arrangements are a bit ad hoc. Bikes cost Rs 350 a day, which includes a helmet but no insurance or petrol.

AROUND MCLEOD GANJ
Dusallan & Bhagsu

Many travellers planning to stay long term rent rooms from villagers in the settlements around McLeod Ganj. Between McLeod and Bhagsu, below the Bhagsu road (take the path beside the Green Hotel) is the tiny village of **Dusallan**. There are several places that rent rooms but you'll have to ask around. Rates are around Rs 40 per day, including a bucket of hot water, and some have magnificent views down over the terraced fields.

Two kilometres east of McLeod is the village of **Bhagsu**, or Bhagsunath, which has springs and a small Shiva temple, built by the raja of Kangra in the 16th century. There's also a waterfall here.

Places to Stay & Eat The *Hotel Triund* (☎ 21122) is on the left as you enter Bhagsu. It has brand new deluxe carpeted rooms with hot water for Rs 700, as well as superdeluxe rooms for Rs 800, and VIP suites for Rs 995.

Hotel Meghavan is another large hotel catering largely to Indian tourists, with rooms for Rs 600 to Rs 800.

Pink White Guest House, nearby, has good upper floor rooms with balcony and views for around Rs 150 to Rs 250, though you may have to negotiate the price.

If you walk up the path leading uphill from the main bus stop you come to three guesthouses aimed squarely at western backpackers.

Samgyal Guest House is first, with rooms with common bathroom for Rs 100 and Rs 150 (front-facing), as well as nicer rooms at the back with bath for Rs 250.

Seven Seas Lodge has clean and spacious marble-clad rooms for Rs 150 (ground floor) and Rs 200 (1st floor)

Omni Guest House has basic but pleasant rooms for Rs 80. There's a decent restaurant here and a free common hot shower.

New Blue Heaven, 10 minutes' walk up towards Dharamkot, has good-value rooms with hot-water bathroom for Rs 150, or Rs 200 with balcony. You can also get here by dropping down from the Dharamkot road.

Trimurti Restaurant in Bhagsu has good and very cheap vegetarian food and there's a notice board detailing local yoga and massage courses. There's a bakery a couple of doors down.

HPTDC Cafe Jaldhara is nearby and offers south Indian dishes.

Shiva Cafe is a good spot for a *chai* (tea), above the waterfall in Bhagsu.

EAST OF DHARAMSALA
Chamunda Devi Temple
☎ 01892

This popular temple, 15km east of Dharamsala on the bank of the Baner River, is dedicated to Chamunda, a particularly wrathful form of Durga. The idol in the main temple is considered so sacred that it is completely concealed beneath a red cloth.

The gateway to the complex is surmounted by brightly painted images of Rama, Krishna and Chamunda, and the road to the temple is flanked by stalls selling *prasaad* (food offerings for the gods) alongside electronic goods and tacky souvenirs. Mendicant *sadhus* (ascetic or holy person) recline in the shade after paying homage at the temple to attain *shiv shakti* – the power of Shiva. More colourful statue groups along with two squatting stone ganja-smokers can be seen around a pool in which young children splash and swim.

HPTDC Yatri Niwas (☎ 36065) has doubles for Rs 400 and Rs 550 and dorm beds for Rs 50. The nearby *Chaumunda* and *Vatika* hotels both have rooms from Rs 300 to Rs 600.

Buses between Dharamsala and Palampur can drop you at the Chamunda Devi Temple.

Palampur
☎ 01894 • alt 1260m

A pleasant little town surrounded by tea plantations, Palampur is 30km south-east of Dharamsala. A four day trek takes you from Palampur to Holi via the Waru Pass. There are no trekking agencies in Palampur so make arrangements in McLeod Ganj. A shorter walk can take you to the **Bundla chasm**, just outside town, from which a waterfall drops into the Bundla stream.

Places to Stay & Eat The *HPTDC Hotel T-Bud* (☎ 31298), 1km north of Main Bazaar, has doubles with bathroom from

Rs 550 to Rs 800 (Rs 330 to Rs 450 in the low season).

Hotel Highland Regency (☎ 31222), next to the new bus station, has pleasant rooms and clean bathrooms for Rs 275, Rs 400 or Rs 550. It also has a good restaurant.

Hotel Sawhney (☎ 30888), on Main Bazaar, has basic doubles for Rs 165, or Rs 250 with TV.

Pine's Hotel (☎ 32633), down near the old bus station, is better, with a wide range of good-value rooms from Rs 100 to Rs 125 for a single, and Rs 175 to Rs 250 for a double. It also has a good-value restaurant.

Joy Restaurant, 100m from the Hotel Sawhney, has cheap fare, including a very good egg chicken *dosa* (paper-thin pancakes made from lentil and rice flour) for Rs 30.

Sapan Restaurant, in Main Bazaar opposite the main post office, has Indian and Chinese cuisine.

Getting There & Away The new bus stand is 1km south of Main Bazaar; a taxi will charge Rs 15. Buses to Dharamsala take two hours and cost Rs 20. To Mandi, it's four hours and Rs 45, and to Pathankot, four hours and Rs 60 (last bus at 1.30 pm). A taxi from Dharamsala costs Rs 425/625 one way/return.

Maranda, 2km west of Palampur, is on the narrow-gauge line between Pathankot and Jogindernagar. There are six trains daily between Maranda and either Kangra to the west (for Dharamsala), or the end of the line at Jogindernagar, to the east.

Tashijong Gompa

This friendly gompa, 5km north-west of Baijnath, is the focus of a small Drukpa Kagyud community of 150 monks and 400 refugees from Kham province in eastern Tibet. The monastery complex consists of an assembly hall, a Lineage Temple (to the left) and the Kungar Rawa Hall (to the right). Hermits spend up to eight years in hillside cave retreats behind the monastery.

Local artisans run some carpet-making, thangka-painting and also woodcarving workshop, whose products are sold only in the cooperative workshop. A *chaam* (dance performed by lamas wearing masks) is held here on the 10th day of the second month of the Tibetan lunar calendar (mid-March).

It's possible to stay at the *Monastery Guesthouse*, where double rooms cost from Rs 100 to Rs 150. There is a second, cheaper *guesthouse* above the village clinic.

Two kilometres south of Tashijong, at Taragarh, is the extraordinary *Palace Hotel* (☎ *018946-3034)*, the summer palace of Dr Karan Singh, the son of the last maharaja of Jammu & Kashmir. The hotel is set in beautiful gardens complete with tennis court, aviary, and swimming pool. Portraits of the royal family are displayed throughout the hotel, which has the usual assortment of tiger skins and colonial furnishings. Doubles range from Rs 950; the suites, which are beautifully furnished with old bureaus and dressers, cost up to Rs 2300.

Tashijong village is a 2km walk north from the main Palampur-Baijnath road. Get off the bus at the bend in the road by the bridge.

Baijnath

The small town of Baijnath, 46km to the south-east of Dharamsala, is an important pilgrimage place due to its ancient stone **Baidyanath Temple**, dedicated to Shiva as Lord of the Physicians. It is said to date from 804 CE, although according to tradition it was built by the Pandavas, the heroes of the *Mahabharata*, when they were in exile following the slaying of their kin, the Kauravas. Large numbers of pilgrims make their way here for the Shivaratri Festival in late February/early March.

The temple features intricate carvings on the exterior walls, including those of Surya, the sun god, at the rear of the temple, and the marriage of Shiva and Parvati. The ceiling of the *mandapa*, or forechamber, is supported by four stone columns that were carved, along with their capitals, from single blocks. On either side of the inner sanctum are carvings of the Ganges and Ya-muna rivers personified as goddesses, to the left and right respectively. Beneath the windowsills are two crouching Garudas supporting the sill with their raised arms, while on the opposite side, the sill is supported by two stone lions.

Baijnath itself is an unremarkable town, although the Dhaula Dhar provides a fine backdrop. If you should find yourself stuck here, the *Hotel Shanker View* (☎ *01894-63831)*, 300m out of town on the road to Mandi, has singles/doubles from Rs 125/150 to Rs 200/250. Deluxe rooms are overpriced at Rs 350.

The narrow-gauge railway line passes through Baijnath to Pathankot (six hours), and Jogindernagar (1½ hours). The station is at Paprola, 1km west of the main bus stand. A taxi from Dharamsala costs Rs 650/850 one way/return.

Bir & Billing

Nine kilometres from Baijnath, along a track 4km to the north off the main road to Jogindernagar, is the settlement of Bir (2080m). Just below the village, a road to the west leads to a tiny Tibetan settlement with a fine gompa, which belongs to the Nyingmapa order of Tibetan Buddhism. It's a beautiful, peaceful location, and the monks, who are unused to visitors, are very friendly. There are several chai stalls here, but little else.

Fourteen kilometres north of Bir is Billing, known for the international hang-gliding competition that is held here annually. For information about hang-gliding, contact the tourist office in Shimla.

There is one bus daily from Jogindernagar to Bir, leaving at 9 am (45 minutes), and returning at 1 pm.

Jogindernagar

There's little reason to visit Jogindernagar, halfway between Dharamsala and Mandi, except to pick up the narrow-gauge train, which weaves through the Kangra Valley, terminating at Pathankot.

HPTDC Hotel Uhl (☎ *01898-22002)* has comfortable rooms for Rs 350 and Rs 550. *Tourist Hotel* at the bus and taxi stand has small but comfortable rooms for Rs 60 or Rs 100 with bath. However, the nicest place to stay is the *retiring rooms* at what could well be the quaintest train station in India (with the friendliest stationmaster). Rooms are around Rs 50.

There are two daily train services from Jogindernagar to Pathankot at 7.50 am and 12.20 pm, passing Baijnath (1½ hours), Palampur (3½ hours), Nagrota (for Dharamsala, four hours), Kangra (five hours) and Pathankot (nine hours).

SOUTH & WEST OF DHARAMSALA
Kangra
☎ 01892 • alt 615m

There is little to see in this ancient town, 18km south of Dharamsala, but at one time it was a place of considerable importance as the seat of the Chand dynasty, which ruled over the princely state of Kangra. The famous **Bajreshwari Devi Temple** was of such legendary wealth that every invader worth their salt took time to sack it. Mahmud of Ghazni carted off a fabulous fortune in gold, silver and jewels in 1009. In 1360 it was plundered once again by the Afghan ruler Tughlaq but it was able to recover and, in Jehangir's reign, was paved in plates of pure silver. The temple is in the bazaar, at the end of a labyrinthine series of alleyways flanked with stalls selling prasaad.

The British took possession of the ancient fort of Kangra, 2.5km south of modern Kangra, according to the terms of the Jawalamukhi Treaty in 1846, and established a garrison here. The disastrous earthquake that shook the valley in 1905 destroyed the fort and the temple, though the latter has since been rebuilt.

Nagar Kot, site of the ruined fort, is an evocative and beautiful place, perched high on a windswept ridge overlooking the confluence of the Manjhi and Baner rivers. It can be reached from Kangra by autorickshaw (Rs 35).

Places to Stay There's a *PWD guesthouse* at Purana (Old) Kangra, near the fort.

There are also several places to stay in Kangra itself, including the *Hotel Maurya*

(☎ 65875), on Dharamsala Rd, between the bus station and town centre, which has singles for Rs 150, and doubles for Rs 250 and Rs 350, all with bathroom and the doubles with hot water.

Jai Hotel (☎ 65568), on Dharamsala Rd, has rooms for Rs 100 and Rs 150.

Getting There & Away Kangra's bus stand is 1.5km north of the bazaar along Dharamsala Rd. There are buses to Dharamsala every 15 minutes (Rs 9, 45 minutes) and to Palampur every 20 minutes. Kangra has two train stations: Kangra station, 3km south of town and Kangra Mandir station, 3km east and 500m from the nearest road. A taxi from McLeod Ganj to Kangra will cost Rs 300/450 one way/return.

Masrur
South-west of Dharamsala, via Gaggal, is the small settlement of Masrur, which has 15 richly carved rock-cut temples in the Indo-Aryan style, hewn from the sandstone cliffs in the 10th century. They are partly ruined but still show their relationship to the better known and much larger temples at Ellora in Maharashtra. This is a beautiful, peaceful place, fronted by a small artificial lake and a pleasant lawn compound. The sculptures are badly eroded, but three crude statues of Sita, Rama and Lakshmi can still be made out in the dimly lit sanctum of the central temple. Several more badly damaged sculptures can be seen leaning against the low wall by the lake in front of the temples.

There are buses to Masrur from Kangra, but from Dharamsala you'll probably have to change at Gaggal. A taxi from McLeod Ganj will charge around Rs 550/700 one way/return to get to Masrur, and the road affords some magnificent views, particularly on the section between Gaggal and Masrur.

Jawalamukhi
Jawalamukhi (Mouth of Fire), the goddess of light, is 34km south of Kangra. Pilgrims descend into a tiny square chamber where a priest, while intoning a blessing on their behalf, ignites natural gas emanating from a

copper pipe, from which a blue flame, worshipped as the manifestation of the goddess, briefly flares. The temple is one of the most sacred sites in the Kangra Valley, and is topped by a golden dome and spire, the legacies of Ranjit Singh and the emperor Akbar.

HPTDC Hotel Jawalaji (☎ 01970-22280) has doubles from Rs 425 to Rs 850, all with bath. Dorm beds are Rs 50. There's a 30% low-season discount.

Buses to Dharamsala (Rs 30) leave throughout the day from the stand below the road leading up to the temple.

Nurpur

Only 24km from Pathankot, on the Dharamsala road, this town was named by Jehangir in honour of his wife Nurjahan. Nurpur Fort is now in ruins, but still has some finely carved reliefs. A ruined temple dedicated to Krishna, also finely carved, stands within the fort, which looms over the main road.

PWD Rest House (☎ 01970-2009), has large, very clean doubles for Rs 100.

PATHANKOT
☎ 0186 • pop 147,000

The town of Pathankot, in the extreme north-east of the Punjab, is important to travellers mainly as a railhead for trains to/from Delhi and as a bus centre for departures up to Dalhousie and Dharamsala. It is a chaotic and uninspiring city, and you probably won't want to stay here for a moment longer than necessary.

The dusty bus stand and the main train station are only about 400m apart. Chowkibank train station is 3km from Pathankot main station.

Places to Stay & Eat

There are a number of fairly unsavoury lodgings to the right as you exit the main Pathankot train station.

Green Hotel has clean but noisy rooms for Rs 250.

Hotel Darshan, nearby, has grim rooms with cold-water bathroom for Rs 100.

Hotel Tourist, farther down the road, is much better with a good variety of rooms set around a pleasant courtyard. Singles cost Rs 80, or Rs 130 with air-cooler and geyser. Air-cooled doubles range from Rs 175 to Rs 250, or Rs 350 with air-con.

Hotel Parag (☎ 29867) is another good choice. It is a 300m walk to the right as you leave the bus station, or a five to 10 minute walk left out of the main train station.

Trains from Pathankot Main Station

destination	train name	departure time	duration (hrs)
New Delhi	4034 *Jammu Mail*	6.40 pm	12
Old Delhi	4646 *Shalimar Exp*	11.25 pm	12
New Delhi	1078 *Jhelum Exp*	0.25 am	10½
Moradabad*	3152 *Jammu-Sealdah Exp*	9.30 pm	13½
Jodhpur	4805 *Jammu-Jodhpur Exp*	11 am	19

* for Corbett National Park and Nainital

Trains from Chowkibank

destination	train name	departure time	duration (hrs)
Old Delhi	2404 *Jammu-Delhi Exp*	8.40 pm	12
New Delhi	9368 *Malwa Exp*	10.40 am	8
New Delhi	2472 *Swaraj Exp*	1.30 pm	8

Comfortable air-cooled rooms with private hot-water bathroom cost Rs 250.

All the hotels have decent restaurants, though the *Vatika Restaurant* at the Hotel Parag is the best.

Getting There & Away
There are buses to Dalhousie (Rs 39, 3½ hours) and Chamba (Rs 57, five hours) every 90 minutes or so from 6.40 am to 5 pm. There are also numerous buses to Dharamsala (Rs 39, 3½ hours), from where regular buses run up to McLeod Ganj. A few morning buses continue to McLeod Ganj (Rs 47).

Overnight trains to Delhi are a popular option as they save time and a night's accommodation. Fares vary according to train but are roughly Rs 150 for 2nd sleeper, Rs 420 for AC three tier sleeper and Rs 734 for AC two tier sleeper. There are also several trains a day to Jammu (three hours).

There is a 24 hour taxi stand at Pathankot main station; to McLeod Ganj the fare is Rs 800 and to Dalhousie, Rs 820.

Getting Around
A cycle-rickshaw from Chowkibank to Pathankot main train and bus stations will cost Rs 25.

Chamba Valley

Separated from the Kangra Valley to the south by the high Dhaula Dhar Range and the remote Pattan Valley to the north by the Pir Panjal Range, is the beautiful Chamba Valley, through which flows the Ravi River. For over 1000 years this region formed the princely state of Chamba, the most ancient state in northern India. Few travellers find their way here, and of those who do, few continue down the valley beyond the hill station of Dalhousie. The valley is renowned for its fine *Shikhara* temples, with excellent examples in the beautiful town of Chamba, 56km from Dalhousie, and at the ancient capital of Brahmaur, a farther 65km down the valley

to the south-east. Brahmaur is also the starting point for some fine treks, including those to sacred Manimahesh Lake, and across the high Kugti Pass (5040m) to the Chandra Valley and Lahaul.

DALHOUSIE
☎ 01899 • alt 2036m
High Season: mid-Apr to mid-Jul, mid-Sep to mid-Nov, mid-Dec to early Jan

Sprawling over five hills at around 2000m, Dalhousie was, in the British era, a sort of 'second string' hill station, mainly used by people who lived in Lahore and could not aspire to life in Shimla. It was acquired from the raja of Chamba by the British and was named after Lord Dalhousie, then viceroy of India, by David McLeod (after whom McLeod Ganj was named). Dalhousie is famous for its public schools.

Dalhousie is popular with Punjabi tourists and getting accommodation during the early summer and peak Indian holiday periods can be extremely difficult. In October and November when the crowds have faded away, the climate is great and views of the snowcapped Pir Panjal are excellent. At this time, with its dense forest, old British houses and nice walks, Dalhousie can be a good place to spend a few days.

Orientation
Dalhousie is quite spread out. Most of the shops are clustered around Gandhi Chowk, about a 15 minute walk up from the bus stand. Gandhi Chowk is connected to Subhash Chowk (also with a high concentration of hotels and restaurants) by the Mall. This is actually two roads, the highest of which is a pedestrian-only road locally known as Garam Sarak (Hot Road) as it receives more sunshine than the other road, known as Thandi Sarak (Cold Road). A road also connects the bus stand with Subhash Chowk, which is a steep, five minute uphill walk.

Be careful if you are walking along Garam Sarak at night. It's badly lit, and some sections are in pitch darkness. Bring a torch (flashlight).

HIMACHAL PRADESH

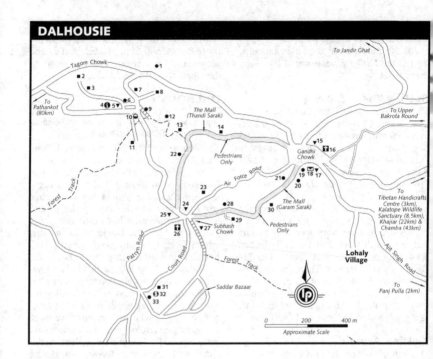

DALHOUSIE

To Jandir Ghat

Tagore Chowk

To Pathankot (80km)

The Mall (Thandi Sarak)

To Upper Bakrota Round

Gandhi Chowk

Pedestrians Only

Air Force Road

The Mall (Garam Sarak)

Pedestrians Only

Subhash Chowk

Forest Track

To Tibetan Handicrafts Centre (3km), Kalatope Wildlife Sanctuary (8.5km), Khajiar (22km) & Chamba (43km)

Lohaly Village

Ajit Singh Road

To Panj Pulla (2km)

Parryn Road

Court Road

Forest Track

Saddar Bazaar

0   200   400 m
Approximate Scale

There are many registered porters around the bus stand. In the low season, they charge Rs 20 between the bus stand and Gandhi Chowk, and Rs 10 to Subhash Chowk. Expect to pay double in the high season.

Information

Tourist Office The Dalhousie tourist office (☎ 42136) is on the top floor of the telegraph office, just below the bus stand. It's open Monday to Saturday 10 am to 5 pm, and during the tourist season on Sunday until 1 pm. During the season it runs full-day tours to points of interest around Dalhousie including Khajiar and Chamba, for Rs 100.

Money The Punjab National Bank is about five minutes walk from Subhash Chowk, next to the Aroma-n-Claire Hotel. It's the only bank that exchanges travellers cheques. It is open Monday to Friday, 10 am to 2 pm,

and 10 am to noon on Saturday (no foreign exchange transactions on Wednesday).

Travel Agencies Span Tours & Travels (☎ 40281, fax 40341) can book luxury coaches during the season to Delhi, Manali and Dharamsala, and can also make train and air reservations. Nearby Trek-n-Travels (☎ 40277) can arrange porters/guides for Rs 125/200 per day. It has trekking gear for rent.

Newsagencies You can get English-language newspapers at the bus stand, and at Dayal News Agency on Gandhi Chowk.

Emergency Police: ☎ 42126; Civil Hospital: ☎ 42125.

Things to See & Do

About midway along Garam Sarak, between Gandhi and Subhash chowks, you'll pass

DALHOUSIE

PLACES TO STAY		17	Lovely Restaurant	12	Cinema
2	Youth Hostel	24	Restaurant Preet Palace	16	St John's Church
3	Hotel Manimahesh	25	Moti Mahal Restaurant	18	Post Office
7	Hotel Mount View	27	Amritsari Dhaba;	19	Tibetan Handicrafts
8	Hotel Grand View		Sher-e-Punjab Dhaba;		Centre Showroom;
11	Hotel Satpushp		Alishan Dhaba		Bengali Sweet Shop
13	HPTDC Hotel Geetanjali			20	Dayal News Agency
14	Hotel Shangrila	**OTHER**		21	Tara Devi Shrine
23	Hotel Goher	1	English Cemetery	22	Himachal Handloom
29	Hotel Crags	4	HPTDC Tourist Office;		Industry Emporium
30	Monal Guesthouse; Jasmine		Telegraph Office	26	St Francis Catholic
	Guesthouse; Arti Guesthouse	6	Dalhousie Club		Church
31	Aroma-n-Claire Hotel	9	Tibetan Market;	28	Tibetan Rock
			Span Tours & Travels;		Paintings
PLACES TO EAT			Trek-n-Travels	32	Punjab National
5	Glory Restaurant	10	Bus Stand;		Bank
15	Kwality Restaurant		Taxi Stand	33	DC Khanna & Sons

brightly painted low-relief pictures of Tibetan deities, including Sakyamuni Buddha, Padmasambhava (Tibetan: Guru Rinpoche) and Avalokiteshvara (Tibetan: Chenresig), as well as Tibetan script bearing the sacred mantra Om Mani Padmi Hum (Hail to the Jewel in the Lotus). Close to Gandhi Chowk is a rock painting of Tara Devi, and a little shrine has been constructed here. There's a small **Tibetan market** just above the bus stand.

Kalatope Wildlife Sanctuary is 8.5km from Gandhi Chowk. The sanctuary is home to a variety of species including black bears and barking deer, as well as an abundant variety of birdlife. There's a checkpoint at **Lakkar Mandi**, on the perimeter of the sanctuary, which has fine mountain views. It's possible to get a taxi here (Rs 150 return), and walk 3km into the sanctuary. To take a vehicle into the sanctuary, you require a permit from the District Forest Officer (DFO) in Chamba. There's a *Forest Resthouse* here, but to reserve a room, you'll need to contact the Chamba DFO (☎ 01899-42639).

From April until November, Lakkar Mandi is home to an itinerant group of villagers who originally hail from Mandi, in the Kangra Valley. Their main source of income is derived from preparing charcoal, which they sell to the hotels in Dalhousie.

Walks

One leisurely stroll can take you down Court Rd, and back via Patryn Rd. En route you'll pass **DC Khanna & Sons**, a great old-fashioned store where you can grab a bottle of flavoured milk and sun yourself outside.

A more rigorous walk is the **Upper Bakrota Round**, around 5km from Gandhi Chowk. For information on this and other hikes to such places as **Mt Dainkund** (2745m), the highest hill around Dalhousie, ask at the travel agencies or tourist office.

Places to Stay – Budget

Dalhousie has over 50 hotels, although a fair number of them have a run-down, left-by-the-Raj feel. Prices given below are for high season but remember that most give a 50% discount whenever business is quiet.

The *youth hostel (☎ 42189)*, rather run-down but friendly, is a five minute walk from the bus stand. Rates remain constant all year. For Rs 20 (Rs 40 for nonmembers) you can get a bit of foam on the dorm floor, or there are a couple of doubles with bath for Rs 80 (Rs 100 for nonmembers). The hostel is closed 10 am to 5 pm.

Hotel Satpushp (☎ 42346), near the bus stand, has cheap rooms from Rs 100 to Rs 200, all with bath and hot water. This is good value in season for Dalhousie.

HIMACHAL PRADESH

Hotel Goher (☎ 42253), just off Subhash Chowk, has dingy singles with cold-water bath for Rs 200, but nice bright doubles with hot water from Rs 400 to Rs 500. Rooms are good value in the low season when there's a 50% discount.

Hotel Crags (☎ 42124) is a five minute walk along Garam Sarak, just below the road. It has front-facing doubles for Rs 200 and huge doubles for Rs 400 to Rs 600, with a 50% discount most of the time. All rooms have bathrooms and hot water. It's a somewhat dilapidated place, but it's in a quiet location and has a nice sitting area with fine views out over the valley.

Farther around Garam Sarak, near Ghandi Chowk, is a cluster of guesthouses, including the *Arti*, *Jasmine* and *Monal*; the last of these is probably the best of the bunch. Outside of the summer you can get a comfortable room with good views for around Rs 150 to Rs 250.

Places to Stay – Mid-Range
Aroma-n-Claire Hotel (☎ 42199), on Court Rd, is an atmospheric hotel about five minutes' walk to the south of Subhash Chowk. Construction on this large rambling hotel commenced in 1925, with materials especially shipped from Belgium. Rates range from Rs 600 to Rs 1200. It's slightly ramshackle, but has wonderful eclectic decorations and rooms of all shapes and sizes. There's a small borrowing library for guests.

HPTDC Hotel Geetanjali (☎ 42155) is just off Thandi Sarak, on the hill above the bus stand. It's a lovely, if slightly rundown, old building. Rooms are enormous, and all have bathrooms with hot water. The dining hall here has magnificent views. Doubles range from Rs 500 to Rs 650. The new *HPTDC Hotel Manimahesh*, near the youth hostel, should open by the time this book goes to press.

Hotel Shangrila (☎ 42314), nearby on Thandi Sarak, has a range of doubles from Rs 800 to Rs 1000 and singles for Rs 500. All rooms have views of the Pir Panjal, and the more expensive ones have a separate sitting area. The staff are helpful.

Hotel Grand View (☎ 42623), just above the bus stand, has doubles for Rs 1000 and double suites for Rs 1300. This is a beautifully maintained place, and better value than other hotels in the same price category.

Hotel Mount View (☎ 42120), nearby, and with less character, has doubles for Rs 1000, Rs 1200 and Rs 1400. Both hotels offer a 30% low-season discount.

Places to Eat
Restaurant Preet Palace, on Subhash Chowk, features reasonably priced Mughlai, Kashmiri and Chinese cuisine.

Moti Mahal Restaurant, nearby, serves south Indian food and also has a bar.

Better value are the dhabas just off Subhash Chowk. Best of the lot is probably the *Amritsari Dhaba*, though the *Sher-e-Punjab* and *Alishan* are also worth checking out. Dalhousie's dhabas are a cut above the usual Indian dhaba.

Lovely Restaurant, on Gandhi Chowk, is open all year, and there's a sunny terrace with outdoor seating. The menu features south Indian and Chinese cuisine.

Kwality Restaurant, also on Gandhi Chowk, has an extensive menu, and this place is very popular. In the high season, you might have to wait for a table.

Bengali Sweet Shop, on Gandhi Chowk near the Tibetan Handicrafts Showroom, has a range of sticky favourites such as *ras malai* and *gulaab jamun*.

In the Tibetan market, above the bus stand, there's a tiny *Tibetan restaurant* serving fried momos for Rs 10, and very cheap chow mein.

Glory Restaurant serves all-you-can-eat Gujarati thalis for Rs 60.

Shopping
Dalhousie is a good place to pick up a woollen shawl. The Himachal Handloom Industry Emporium on Thandi Sarak has a good selection.

At the Tibetan Handicrafts Centre (☎ 42119), 3km from Gandhi Chowk along the Khajiar road, you can have Tibetan carpets made to order. There are over 180 traditional designs to choose from. You can buy carpets, bags and purses from the Tibetan Handicraft Centre Showroom, on Garam Sarak. The shops nearby sell a range of goods, including Kashmiri shawls.

Getting There & Away
The booking office at the bus stand is open daily 9 am to 5 pm (closed 2 to 3 pm). There are buses every couple of hours to Pathankot (Rs 39, four hours). For Dharamsala (six hours) there is one bus at 8.30 am but the service seems unreliable. Another option is to take the Pathankot bus and change at the junction of Chakki. There are two daily services to Shimla (Rs 120, 12 hours) and one to Manali.

Buses to Chamba leave at 9.30 am, and 3.30 and 4.40 pm (Rs 30, three hours) and most go via Khajiar (Rs 10, 1½ hours). Private tourist buses usually depart at 9.15 and 10.10 am for Khajiar, wait an hour or so, and then continue to Chamba. You can pay for only one leg of the trip if, for example, you are just going to Khajiar.

Rates quoted at the taxi stand (☎ 40220) include Pathankot (Rs 820 one way), Chamba (Rs 550 one way or Rs 820 return via Khajiar), Khajiar (Rs 410 return), Brahmaur (Rs 1300 one way), Kalatope (Rs 360 return) and Dharamsala (Rs 1350 one way).

Getting Around
From the bus stand to Gandhi Chowk, taxis charge Rs 30, and to Subhash Chowk, Rs 36.

KHAJIAR
☎ 01899 • alt 1960m
This grassy *marg*, or meadow, is 22km from Dalhousie towards Chamba, and you can get here by bus or on foot in a day's walk. Over 1km long and nearly 1km wide, it is ringed by pine trees with a pond in the middle. The 12th century **Khajjinag Temple** has fine woodcarving on the cornices, and some crude carvings of the five Pandavas, the heroes of the *Mahabharata*, installed in the temple by the raja of Chamba in the 16th century.

It's possible to do a circuit of the marg by horseback (Rs 40).

Places to Stay & Eat
HPTDC Hotel Devdar (☎ 36333) has cottages right on the edge of the marg for Rs 450, and doubles for Rs 550. There's also a dorm with beds for Rs 50.

HPTDC Khajiar Cottage is a more basic place with dorm beds for Rs 50 on the north side of the marg.

Parul Guest House (☎ 36344), behind the temple, has a couple of pleasant rooms overlooking the marg for Rs 400; other rooms aren't half as nice.

Puri Guesthouse, nearby, has comfortable rooms without a view for Rs 300.

Gautam Guest House (☎ 36355), a couple of minutes' walk east of the marg, is the best budget choice. Clean and bright rooms with bathroom and hot water cost Rs 250 (Rs 150 in the low season) and there's a nice sitting area.

PWD Guest House on the east side of the marg has very pleasant rooms with bath for Rs 200. Bookings should be made through the Executive Engineer in Dalhousie (☎ 01899-42145).

There are also several *restaurants* on the marg.

Getting There & Away
Buses from Dalhousie to Khajiar (Rs 15, 1½ hours) leave at 9.30, 10.10, and 11.10 am, and 4.30 pm but timings are a little unreliable. From Khajiar, they return at 8.30 am and 4 pm. To Chamba, they depart at noon and 4.30 pm (Rs 15, 1½ hours). Tourist buses to Chamba stop at Khajiar for an hour – if you want more time then catch the 9.30 am bus from Dalhousie (if it's running) and proceed on to Chamba that afternoon. A taxi from Khajiar to Chamba is around Rs 450.

CHAMBA
☎ 01899 • alt 926m
It's a beautiful, if somewhat hair-raising 56km trip from Dalhousie to Chamba. The views down over the terraced fields are spectacular, with tiny villages clinging to the sheer slopes of the valley. Chamba lies in a valley at an altitude of 926m – quite a

bit lower than Dalhousie, so it's warmer in the summer. Perched on a ledge flanking the Ravi River, it has often been compared to a medieval Italian village and is famed for its ancient temples.

For 1000 years prior to Independence, Chamba was the headquarters of a district of the same name, and was ruled by a single dynasty of maharajas. The town was founded by one Raja Sahil Varman, who shifted the capital here from Brahmaur and named it after his daughter Champavati.

Chamba has a grassy promenade known as the Chowgan, which is the focus for the **Minjar Festival**, held each year in late July/early August (see the boxed text), and the **Sui Mata Festival**, held in March/April.

Information

The tourist office (☎ 22671) is in the Hotel Iravati on Court Rd, and there's a divisional tourism development office in the white building adjacent to the Iravati, but neither is of much use.

A better source of information is Mani Mahesh Travels (☎ 22507), close to the Lakshmi Narayan temple complex. You can arrange porters/guides here for Rs 150/250 per day, and the friendly staff can also tailor treks for most budgets in the valleys around Chamba. You can hire tents (Rs 100 per day), mats (Rs 40) and cooking equipment (Rs 50). The owner's son can provide a commentary on Chamba's beautiful temples (Rs 200) and his daughter acts as a guide for female trekkers when required.

The State Bank of India is open Monday to Friday, 10 am to 2 pm, and on Saturday, 10 am to noon. It will change Visa, American Express and Citicorp travellers cheques, as will the Punjab National Bank on Hospital Rd.

You can send and receive faxes at the telegraph office (fax 25333), hidden in the backstreets not far from the Rishi Hotel. The office is open Monday to Saturday 8 am to 7.30 pm, and 8 am to 3 pm Sunday. There are many private telephone booths in town.

You can get English-language newspapers at Pandit Badri Prasad, Museum Rd,

Minjar Festival

The origins of Chamba's Minjar Festival, held in late July/early August, are said to date back to 935 when the founder of Chamba, Raja Sahil Varman, returned to the town after defeating the raja of Kangra. It more probably evolved from a harvest festival to celebrate the annual maize crop. *Minjars*, silk tassels worn by men and women, represent sheaves of maize, and are distributed during the festival. The festival culminates with a colourful procession and at this time there are busy crowds of Gaddi, Churachi, Bhatti and Gujjar people. An image of Raghuvira is carried aloft at the head of the procession and images of other gods and goddesses are borne in palanquins. The procession proceeds to the banks of the Ravi River, where the minjars are thrown into the water.

Chowgan Bazaar. There's no English sign so look for the green doors.

Emergency Police: ☎ 22736; Ambulance: ☎ 22392.

Lakshmi Narayan Temple Complex

The six temples in this complex, all featuring exquisite sculpture, are representative of the Shikhara style, although they also share characteristics distinctive to the Chamba Valley. Three of the temples are dedicated to Vishnu, and three to Shiva. The largest (and oldest) temple in the group is that of **Lakshmi Narayan** (Vishnu), which is directly opposite the entrance to the complex. According to tradition it was built during the reign of the founder of Chamba, Raja Sahil Varman, in the 10th century. It was extensively renovated in the 16th century by Raja Partap Singh Varna. The image of Lakshmi Narayan enshrined in the temple dates from the temple's foundation. Some of the fine sculptures around the temple include those of Vishnu and Lakshmi, Narsingh (Vishnu in his lion

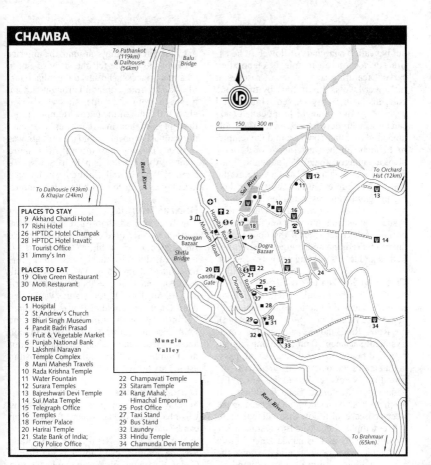

CHAMBA

To Pathankot (119km) & Dalhousie (56km)

Balu Bridge

0   150   300 m

Ravi River

To Dalhousie (43km) & Khajiar (24km)

Sal River

To Orchard Hut (12km)

To Dalhousie (43km) & Khajiar (24km)

Hospital Road

Museum Road

Chowgan Bazaar

Shitla Bridge

Dogra Bazaar

Court Road

Chowgan

Gandhi Gate

Mungla Valley

Ravi River

To Brahmaur (65km)

PLACES TO STAY
9   Akhand Chandi Hotel
17 Rishi Hotel
26 HPTDC Hotel Champak
28 HPTDC Hotel Iravati;
    Tourist Office
31 Jimmy's Inn

PLACES TO EAT
19 Olive Green Restaurant
30 Moti Restaurant

OTHER
1   Hospital
2   St Andrew's Church
3   Bhuri Singh Museum
4   Pandit Badri Prasad
5   Fruit & Vegetable Market
6   Punjab National Bank
7   Lakshmi Narayan
    Temple Complex
8   Mani Mahesh Travels
10 Rada Krishna Temple
11 Water Fountain
12 Surara Temples
13 Bajreshwari Devi Temple
14 Sui Mata Temple
15 Telegraph Office
16 Temples
18 Former Palace
20 Harirai Temple
21 State Bank of India;
    City Police Office

22 Champavati Temple
23 Sitaram Temple
24 Rang Mahal;
    Himachal Emporium
25 Post Office
27 Taxi Stand
29 Bus Stand
32 Laundry
33 Hindu Temple
34 Chamunda Devi Temple

form), and Krishna with the *gopis* (milk-maids). A small niche at the back harbours a beautiful sculpture of a goddess churning the ocean with Sheshnag, the snake of Vishnu, to bring the poison up from the bottom.

The fourth temple from the right, the **Gauri Shankar Temple**, is dedicated to Shiva. Its stone carving of the Ganges and Yamuna rivers personified as goddesses on either side of the door frame is renowned.

The complex is open 6 am to 12.30 pm and 2.30 to 8.30 pm.

Bajreshwari Temple

A five minute walk through the old town north-east of the Lakshmi Naryan temple complex leads you to the diminutive **Surara temples**. There's also a beautiful old **water fountain** nearby, more examples of which can be found in the Bhuri Singh Museum.

A further five minute walk leads up to the ancient **Bajreshwari Devi Temple**. The temple conforms to the Shikhara style, and is topped by a wooden *amalaka* (fluted medallion-shaped flourish). The sanctum

HIMACHAL PRADESH

enshrines an image of Bajreshwari (a form of Durga), although it is difficult to make out beneath its garlands of flowers. The entire surface of the temple is elaborately carved, featuring two friezes of rosettes at the lower levels. It is fronted by two stone columns with richly carved capitals and bases. A form of ancient script called *takri* can be seen crudely incised on the right column, and on other spots around the temple. In the niche on the western side of the temple is a damaged image of Undavi, the goddess of food, with a bowl and a ladle. At the rear of the temple, Durga can be seen slaying the giant Mahisasur and his buffalo vehicle. The giant is dwarfed by Durga, who is standing astride him with her foot on the buffalo. On either side of the door jambs, the rivers Yamuna and Ganges are personified as goddesses holding pitchers of water.

Chamunda Devi Temple

A terrace before this hilltop temple gives an excellent view of Chamba with its slate-roof houses (some of them up to 300 years old), the River Ravi and the surrounding countryside. It's a steep 30 minute climb along a path that begins above the bus stand, passing a small rock outcrop smeared with saffron that is revered as an image of the goddess of the forest, Banasti. When you reach the road, you can either proceed up the steep staircase, or follow the road to the left.

The temple is dedicated to Durga in her wrathful aspect as Chamunda Devi. Before the temple is her vehicle, a lion. Almost the entire wooden ceiling of the mandapa (forechamber) is richly carved, featuring animal and floral motifs, and depictions of various deities. From it are suspended brass bells, offered to the goddess by devotees.

Just before ascending the steps to the temple is a small pillar bearing the footprints of the goddess. Behind the temple is a very old, small Shikhara-style temple dedicated to Shiva.

Sui Mata Temple

About 10 minutes' walk from the Chamunda Devi Temple is a small modern temple dedicated to Sui Mata. You can also get here easily from the Bajreshwari Devi Temple.

Colourful paintings around the interior walls of the temple tell the story of Sui, a Chamba princess who saved the inhabitants of Chamba from a dreadful drought. After a message from the gods, she was buried alive at the site of the current temple. From the place of her incarceration, a stream miraculously appeared, and the drought was broken. During the month of Chaitra (March/April), a fair is held in Sui Mata's honour. Women and children can be seen here laying wildflowers before the temple.

Harirai Temple

This fine stone Shikhara-style temple, at the north-west side of the Chowgan, near the fire station, dates from the 11th century. It is dedicated to Vishnu, and enshrines a fine triple-headed image of Vaikuntha Vishnu reputedly made from eight different materials. In April 1971, the statue was stolen from the inner sanctum. It was discovered by Interpol on a ship destined for the USA seconds before the boat was to sail, and was returned to Chamba. At the rear of the temple is a fine sculpture of Vishnu astride six horses.

Other Temples

Several other temples lie hidden in Chamba's maze of backstreets; finding them can be half the fun.

Not far from the Rishi Hotel is the **Rada Krishna Temple**, also known as the Bhansi Gopal. Follow the alley south to the **Sitaram Temple**, devoted to Rama.

Behind the City Police Office is the **Champavati Temple**, dedicated to the daughter of Raja Sahil Varman. The dimly lit mandapa features four solid wooden carved pillars with floral and bird motifs.

Rang Mahal

The Rang Mahal, or Colourful Palace, was once home to the royal court, but now houses the **Himachal Emporium**. Here you can purchase *rumals* – small cloths featuring very fine embroidery in silk, a

HIMACHAL PRADESH

traditional craft executed by the women of Chamba for almost 1000 years. The stitching is very fine, and the reverse side of the cloth features a mirror image of the design – there is no evidence of knots or loose threads. Popular images portrayed on the cloths include Krishna and Radha, and those of Gaddi shepherds. A finely stitched rumal can take up to a month to complete, and costs from Rs 300 upwards.

You can also purchase repoussé brass plates and Chamba shawls here, and above the showroom is a workshop where you can see the shawls being made. An elaborately decorated shawl can take up to 45 days to make on a traditional wooden loom.

The emporium is open Monday to Friday 10 am to 1 pm, and 2 to 5 pm.

Bhuri Singh Museum

This museum has an interesting collection representing the art and culture of this region – particularly the miniature paintings of the Basohli and Kangra schools. There are also some murals that were recovered from the Rang Mahal after it was damaged by fire. The 1st floor has displays on local costume, woodcarving and jewellery. Look out for the treaties inscribed on copper tablets and the 19th century snakes and ladders board.

The museum is open Tuesday to Friday, Sunday and every second Saturday 10 am to 5 pm. Entry is free.

Gandhi Gate

This bright orange gateway at the southwest side of the Chowgan was built in 1900 to welcome Viceroy Lord Curzon to the city. This was the main entrance into the city before the new road was built.

Places to Stay

HPTDC Hotel Iravati (☎ 222671, fax 22565), on Court Rd only a few minutes' walk from the bus stand, has doubles with bathroom for Rs 450, Rs 600, Rs 700 and Rs 800 (30% discount in the low season). There's 24 hour room service and rooms are spotless.

HPTDC Hotel Champak (☎ 22774), behind the post office, is cheaper. Large doubles are good value at Rs 200 with common bath, or Rs 250 with hot-water bathroom. Dorm beds cost Rs 50.

Jimmy's Inn (☎ 24748) is a friendly family-run place opposite the bus stand. Small but clean rooms with cold-water bathroom cost Rs 150. Larger and nicer doubles with TV cost Rs 250. Hot water is available in buckets for Rs 5.

Rishi Hotel (☎ 24343), on Temple Rd right opposite the Lakshmi Narayan temple complex, is popular with travellers. Doubles for Rs 150 and Rs 250 have geysers, TV and unbeatable views over the temples. There are cheaper rooms at the back for Rs 100, but they are a little gloomy and share a cold-water bathroom. The dining hall here looks like a bargain but the food really isn't up to much.

Akhand Chandi Hotel (☎ 22371), in the shadow of the Rada Krishna Temple, has a beautiful shady garden surrounded by a lovely wooden veranda and is a great place to stay. All rooms are clean and carpeted, with bathroom and hot water, for Rs 200. At the time of research the hotel was changing hands and might even close, but it's worth checking out.

Orchard Hut (☎ 22607) is in a lovely tranquil spot in the Saal Valley, 12km from Chamba. The owners can point out local herbs and birds and advise on local treks (ask about their hut in nearby Rulpulli). You can even learn Indian cookery here for Rs 100 per day. Pitch your own tent or use one of theirs for Rs 100, or there are basic rooms for rent at Rs 200. With all meals, it's Rs 350. There's a communal bathroom with buckets of hot water. Check at Mani Mahesh Travels first (see under Information earlier in this section), as getting there isn't easy – you'll have to take a bus to Chaminu and then cross the river over a rickety bridge.

Places to Eat

Olive Green Restaurant, is upstairs in Dogra Bazaar on Temple Rd. It's a quiet and clean place, with good, reasonably

HIMACHAL PRADESH

priced veg and nonveg dishes and is the best option in town. You can also sample the local dish Chamba *madhra* (kidney beans with curd and ghee).

Moti Restaurant near the bus stand serves good standard Indian dishes. There's also a decent restaurant at the *Hotel Iravati* (nonguests welcome) but it doesn't serve dinner until 7.30 pm.

Chamba is known for its *chukh* – a chilli sauce consisting of red and green peppers, lemon juice, mustard oil and salt. You'll find it in most of the provision stores in Dogra Bazaar for around Rs 25 a jar.

Getting There & Away
Bus It's a somewhat nerve-shattering trip up-valley to Brahmaur. If there are no buses to Dalhousie you could take the Pathankot bus and change to a local bus at Banikhet. Services from Chamba include the following:

Brahmaur (Rs 32, 3½ hours, six daily 6.30 am to 4.30 pm)
Dalhousie (Rs 30, three hours, 6, 7.30, 11 am, 2, 6 pm)
Dharamsala (Rs 113, 10 hours, 11.30 am, 9.30 pm)
Khajiar (Rs 15, 1½ hours, 7.30 am, 2 pm)
Pathankot (Rs 57, five to six hours, nine daily)

Taxi To Khajiar, a taxi will cost Rs 400; to Brahmaur, it's about Rs 550.

BRAHMAUR
☎ 01090 • alt 2195m
Sixty-four kilometres south-east of Chamba is the ancient slate-roofed village of Brahmaur. It's a spectacular trip along a fairly precarious road up the Ravi River valley.

Before Raja Sahil Varman founded the new capital at Chamba in 920 CE, Brahmaur was the ancient capital of the princely state of Chamba for over 400 years, and the well-preserved temples are a testament to its wealth.

Brahmaur is a centre for the seminomadic Gaddi people, pastoralists who move their flocks up to alpine pastures during the summer, and descend to Kangra, Mandi and

Bilaspur in the winter. For more on the Gaddi see the Himalayan Peoples section in the Facts about the Region chapter.

Some fine treks commence from Brahmaur, though at the time of research treks north into the Pir Panjal were off limits due to the Indian army's efforts to flush out Kashmiri separatists from the western end of the range. Check at the Mountaineering & Allied Sports Sub-Centre (☎ 25036) in town. In any case it's well worth advising them if you are planning a trek in the region. They have some reference maps and can arrange guides and porters for Rs 200 to Rs 250 per day.

Chaurasi
In the heart of the village is a magnificent group of well-preserved ancient temples. The site is called the Chaurasi (84 in Hindi), as there are 84 temples here, although some are tiny shrines, less than 1m high.

The 84 temples relate to the legend that the only son of a pious woman of Brahmaur died of shock when his pet partridge was killed by a farmer. The boy's mother was overwhelmed with grief and threw herself on her son's funeral pyre. The villagers were so moved by this act of love that they accorded the woman the status of a deity and built a temple in her honour, at which she was worshipped as Brahmani Devi.

En route to Mt Kailash in Tibet, Shiva passed through Brahmaur with 84 holy saints. Unimpressed by her celestial guest, Brahmani Devi appeared before Shiva and asked him and his entourage to vacate the village immediately. Asserting his divine prerogative, Shiva refused to budge, and Brahmani Devi retreated to her temple. However, the next morning the 84 saints had vanished, and in their place stood 84 stone linga, today encompassed within the temple complex of the Chaurasi.

The oldest temple in the group, dedicated to Lakhna Devi, the mother of the gods, was built in the 7th century during the reign of Raja Meru Varman. It's made of wood and features fine carvings, such as the beautiful rosettes on the ceiling of the mandapa and the intricate carving on the capitals of the pillars. The entrance to the mandapa is also elaborately carved. In the inner sanctum is enshrined a brass image of the goddess, who is depicted standing.

Dominating the group is the large Shikhara-style **Manimahesh Temple**, dedicated to Shiva. The temple's lingam is protected by a massive brass cobra coiled around it. Opposite is a smaller Shikhara-style temple dedicated to Vishnu in his lion form as **Narsingh**. It enshrines a fine 1.5m-high statue of the god in its inner sanctum. To its left is the **Dharmeshvar Temple**, sacred to Shiva. It was originally built in the 14th century, but has been renovated over subsequent years.

Brahmani Mata Temple

From Brahmaur it's possible to walk to the small temple of Brahmani Mata. Follow the road up past the Chaurasi, which leads in about five minutes to a small village. Beyond here a path leads in 20 minutes to the larger settlement of Makotta, from where it takes about two hours to reach the temple. There are no houses between Makotta and the temple, so carry water with you. There's a small chai stall at the temple, and a pool in the freezing waters where devout pilgrims bathe.

Manimahesh Lake

The important *yatra*, or pilgrimage, to sacred Manimahesh Lake, at the base of Manimahesh Kailash (5656m), starts in Brahmaur in August. Tourist camps are normally set up at this time but facilities are generally stretched to breaking point.

Brahmaur is inundated with pilgrims, who travel hundreds of kilometres to undertake the 28km pilgrimage. Prior to the pilgrimage, a seven day fair is held at Brahmaur, followed by wrestling competitions and folk dances by pilgrims from distant villages. Fifteen days after the start of the festival, the pilgrims are led by priests to Manimahesh. Pilgrims normally go by road to Hardsar and then trek 7km (three hours) to Dancho. The next day they continue three hours up to the lake, and return the same

day. Parents blessed with a baby boy take the child on the pilgrimage, during which time the boy's hair is ceremonially cut.

At the lake there is an ancient and very beautiful temple dedicated to Lakshmi Devi in her form as slayer of the buffalo demon (Mahishasuramardini). The image of the goddess enshrined in the inner sanctum dates from the 7th century.

Places to Stay

Chamunda Guest House (☎ 25056) is about five minutes' walk up from the bus stand. Pleasant rooms are Rs 100/200. *Krishna Lodge*, at the bus stand, has very basic rooms that open onto a balcony with superb views. Doubles are around Rs 70. *Jamuna Lodge*, nearby, has doubles with common bath and good views for Rs 100, and hot water free in buckets. There are also doubles with bath for Rs 125, but they don't have a valley view.

Getting There & Away

There are a number of buses to Chamba between 6.30 am and 5.30 pm (Rs 32, 3½ hours). Occasional landslides around Garah can block the road for a few days after heavy rain.

Kullu & Parvati Valleys

High Season: mid-Apr to mid-Jun, mid-Sep to early Nov, Christmas and New Year

The Kullu Valley, and to a lesser extent the Parvati Valley, has been a popular place to hang out and take in some mountain scenery ever since the hippie invasions of the 1960s. Recent tourist spillover from the political violence in Kashmir has, however, had a profound effect on the valley and Manali, in particular, has developed rapidly, threatening the valley's peaceful and unhurried atmosphere.

Originally known as Kulanthapitha (End of the Habitable World), and later as Kuluta, the first recorded inhabitants of the Kullu Valley date back to the first century CE.

HIMACHAL PRADESH

KULLU & PARVATI VALLEYS

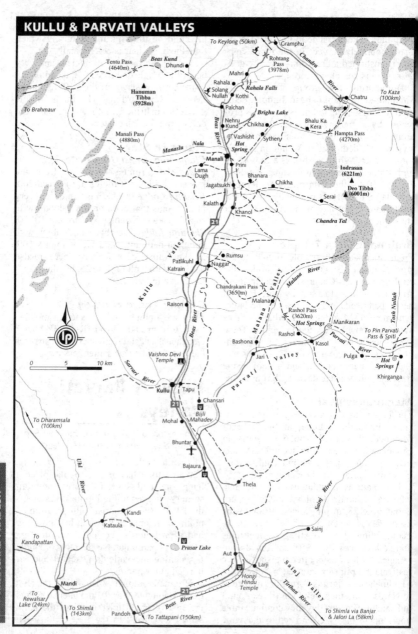

Alexander the Great, Buddha and the Tantric sage Padmasambhava all passed through the valley at some point. The first capital was at Jagatsukh, then moved to Naggar, before the British moved it to Kullu town. The Kullu Valley, about 80km long and often less than 2km wide, rises northward from Mandi at 760m to the Rohtang Pass at 3978m, the gateway to Lahaul and Spiti. With its alpine scenery, ancient history and rich handicraft tradition the valley enjoys striking similarities with Pakistan's Swat Valley.

The entire Kullu and Parvati valleys, from Mandi to Manali, are serviced by the airport at Bhuntar, 10km south of Kullu town. For flight information, see Getting There & Away in the Kullu section.

MANDI
☎ 01905 • alt 760m

Formerly a Bangali princely state and an important staging post on the salt route to Tibet, Mandi is the gateway to the Kullu Valley, and the junction of roads from Kullu, Kangra, Shimla and the plains. Mandi, which means market, is quite a good place to break the journey between Shimla and the Kullu Valley – a far better option to stay than, say, Bilaspur. There are some cheap hotels, you can dig out some of the 81 Hindu temples in the area, and take a day trip to the Tibetan Buddhist settlements at holy Rewalsar Lake. At less than 800m above sea level, Mandi is considerably hotter than other regional areas.

Orientation & Information
The centre of Mandi is the town square, dominated by a clock tower and a huge plaza of shops called the Indira Market. Most of the hotels and places to eat are around or very near the square. Over the Suketi River, to the east, is the newer area, where the bus station is located. Mandi is easy to walk around; from the bus station to the town square takes only about 15 minutes on foot.

The only place to change money is the Evening Plaza Hotel in the main square,

Warning – Bhang

The Kullu Valley area and especially villages along the Parvati Valley are famous for marijuana, sometimes known as *bhang*. It is esteemed by connoisseurs, and grows wild in the valleys. But don't be fooled by the fact that you see it growing everywhere, or that everyone else is smoking the stuff – like anywhere, it's still very much illegal and the police can and will bust you and you'll find yourself in trouble you could do without.

which changes cash and American Express travellers cheques only, for a 1% commission. You can get a cash advance off a Visa card at the Bank of Baroda, five minutes' walk from the main square. There's a 1% commission, plus a Rs 100 communication charge to verify the transaction. Get there before 1 pm.

The post office is cleverly hidden around the back of the court house, north of the main square, and is open Monday to Saturday, 7.30 am to 5.30 pm.

Tarna Hill
For a cool respite from the town, take an auto-rickshaw (about Rs 30 return) up the very steep four or five kilometres to Tarna Hill – it's too far and steep to walk, unless you enjoy that sort of thing. At the top of the hill, the Rani Amrit Kaur Park (opened by the Dalai Lama in 1957) has superb views of the area, and there's a nice cafe for lunch or a snack. In the park, the 17th century Hindu Syamakali Temple, also called the Tarna Devi Temple, is worth a look.

Temple Walks
Mandi's Shivaratri Festival, held in February/March, is one of the most interesting festivals in Himachal Pradesh. Much of the activity takes place at the multicoloured 16th century Bhutnath Temple in Moti Bazaar, just off the square to the west of the town square. See the Festivals of Himachal

HIMACHAL PRADESH

Warning – Missing Persons

Between 1996 and 1998 over a dozen foreign tourists have disappeared from the Kullu Valley. Persons have been reported missing from the villages of Naggar, Malana, Manali, Manikaran and Kasol. During your travels you may well see posters for Ian Mogford, a student from Bristol who disappeared in 1996, and Ardeven Taherzadeh, a Canadian who disappeared in 1997. Though some relatives have found the local police less than cooperative, a concerted Israeli investigation into a missing airforce pilot eventually discovered he had been murdered in his sleeping bag. It is not known what has happened to the other disappeared but the region is a centre for *charas* (marijuana) production and the local drug mafia are suspected of being involved. It's possible that some disappeared while trekking alone through remote regions or have even lost themselves (both physically and spiritually) in some kind of spiritual search.

If going to the area we recommend you avoid trekking alone, be cautious of locals offering tea and other substances, register fully at guesthouses and hotels, and be a little wary of befriending *sadhus* – not all of whom are holy men. A Foreign Missing Persons Bureau has been set up in Delhi and can be contacted through the British High Commission (☎ 011-687 2161).

Pradesh boxed text at the start of this chapter for details.

It's not hard to stumble across many other new and old, restored and decaying, Hindu temples around Mandi. From the Bhutnath Temple head north into the cloth bazaar and continue down to the Beas and its collection of riverside temples and *ghats* (steps leading down to the water). Just across Victoria Bridge is the **Triloknath Temple**, dedicated to Shiva. Back at the ghats you can continue along the riverbank until you hit another bridge, this one crossing the Sukheti. Just over the bridge is the **Panjvaktra Temple**, which depicts the five aspects of Shiva. From here you can recross the bridge and head up through the bazaar back to the main square.

Other temples you can dig out, if so inclined, include the Ardhanarisvara and Magru Mahadev temples. Ask for directions.

Places to Stay

Raj Mahal (☎ 22401), the rambling former palace of the raja of Mandi, oozes colonial timewarp, but it has budget prices, and is the best place to stay. It's at the back of a decrepit building, just behind the grandstand at Indira Market, next to the district library. Set around large gardens, comfortable singles/doubles with common bath cost Rs 98/127, while rooms for Rs 198/275 are well furnished, with a hot-water bathroom, and worth the extra money. There are also suites for Rs 350 and Rs 400. Look out for the hotel's private temple and the excellent old photos in the huge dining hall.

HPTDC Hotel Mandav (☎ 35503, fax 35551) is up a lane just behind the bus station. Comfortable, quiet economy doubles in the old block come with hot-water bath and a balcony with great views for Rs 250. The more modern rooms are comfortable but not as good value at Rs 500, or Rs 800 with air-con. There are no dorms.

Around the town square, there are places of all types and prices.

Standard Hotel (☎ 22948) is a popular place that charges Rs 55 for a small single and Rs 100, Rs 145 and Rs 160 for a double with bath. Rooms vary considerably so have a look at more than one. There's a restaurant and bar that serves beer for Rs 55 with one pappadam.

Hotel Shiva (☎ 24211) has rooms from Rs 125 to Rs 275 but is noisy.

Evening Plaza (☎ 25123) and *Mayfair* are two mid-range places with rooms for around Rs 300 to Rs 400, or air-con rooms for around Rs 600, but neither are up to much.

Along the road across the bridge from the bus station, there are a number of cheap,

HIMACHAL PRADESH

noisy, places for about Rs 40/60. The better ones are the *Hotel Anand* (☎ *22515*), which is cramped but reasonably clean; the *Hotel Koyal* (☎ *22248*); and the *Sangam Hotel* (☎ *22009*), which offers some views.

Vyas Guest House is a five minute walk from the bus station (just follow the signs), not far from the Panjvaktra Temple. Clean and cool rooms range from Rs 100 to Rs 200 and there's a friendly atmosphere.

Hotel Comfort is another relaxing place, five minutes' walk from the main square, above the Bank of Baroda. The three ground-floor rooms are Rs 200 and there's a nice sitting area.

Places to Eat

Copacabana Bar & Restaurant at the Raj Mahal is a popular open-air place where good food is served.

Hotel Mandav is worth the walk up for a good selection, breakfasts, and the bar (cold beer is Rs 60 a bottle). Dinner isn't served until 7 pm.

HPTDC Cafe Shiraz, just behind the main square, serves very average snacks in a dingy atmosphere.

Treet Restaurant, on the ground floor of the Indira Gandhi Plaza, is probably the best place in town, serving Chinese and south Indian food in dark but clean surroundings. Prices are reasonable.

Most of the hotels around the Indira Market serve pretty good food, including the *Hotel Standard* for good, cheap food. Plenty of *dhabas* and stalls selling just about everything are scattered around the market.

Getting There & Away

As the junction for the Kangra and Kullu valleys, Mandi is well served by local public buses. The bus station – where you can make advance bookings – is across the river in the eastern part of town.

There are buses every hour or so until 1 pm to Shimla (Rs 80, six hours) via Bilaspur, until 12.30 pm for Dharamsala (Rs 72, six hours) and all day up the Kullu Valley road to Bhuntar (for the airport and Manikaran), Kullu and Manali.

Taxis congregate outside the bus station, and at a stand on the eastern side of the town square. A one-way trip by taxi from Mandi to Kullu costs Rs 600.

AROUND MANDI
Rewalsar Lake
☎ 01905

Rewalsar Lake is high up in the hills, 24km south-west of Mandi and set beside the village of Rewalsar. It's a peaceful area, with some pretty scenery, and is worth a day trip, or an overnight stay.

The small lake (Tibetan: Pema-tso, or Lotus Lake) is revered by Buddhists because it is from here Padmasambhava (Tibetan: Guru Rinpoche) departed for Tibet. Most of Rewalsar's chapels have the guru as their central statue (look out for the curly moustache, staff and thunderbolt), flanked by Avalokiteshvara (Tibetan: Chenresig), Tara or Sakyamuni Buddha. Three Buddhist sects are represented at the lake; the Nyingmapa (closely connected with Padmasambhava), Drigung Kagyud and Drukpa Kagyud. Every year, shortly after the Tibetan New Year (February or March), many Buddhists make a pilgrimage here, especially from Dharamsala.

Hindus also revere the lake because it was here the sage Rishi Lomas did his penance as a dedication to Shiva, who, in return, gave Lomas the seven lakes in the vicinity, including Rewalsar.

Please note that as this is a Buddhist holy site you should walk around the shrines and the lake in a clockwise direction.

Things to See & Do As you enter the lake area, the **Drigung Kagyud Gompa**, immediately on the right, is full of monks who will show you around. The friendly **Tso-Pema Ogyen Heru-kai Nyingmapa Gompa & Institute**, farther around the lake, may be a bit of a mouthful, but it's worth a visit. Built in the 19th century, it has a huge butter lamp in the corner, a photo of the former head lama of the Nyingmapa sect and colourful murals. You can buy *katag* (ceremonial scarves) and prayer flags at the shop.

Around the lake, there are also **Hindu temples** to Rishi Lomas, Shiva and Krishna.

The Sikhs have the huge **Guru Govind Singh Gurdwara** on the east side of the lake. It was built in 1930 by Raja Joginder Sen and dedicated to Govind Singh, who stayed at Rewalsar Lake for a month. The *gurdwara* is especially active during the Baisakhi festival in April.

There is a cave associated with Padmasambhava and also several meditation chambers high in the hillside above the lake, just below the relay tower. You could make a day hike up to the cave or catch the daily bus there at 10 am. Auto-rickshaws start the bidding at Rs 200.

Places to Stay & Eat The *HPTDC Tourist Inn (☎ 80252)* has dorm beds in the old building for Rs 50, and nice doubles with common bath for Rs 200, or Rs 250 with hot-water bathroom (a better deal). Triples/quads are Rs 300/400. Most rooms have a balcony (although most do not actually overlook the lake).

All three monasteries have guesthouses: just choose your sect. The Drikung Gompa offers cosy little rooms in its *Peace Memorial Inn* for Rs 50 or Rs 130 with bathroom.

Tibet Hotel at the Ogyen Heru-kai Gompa has good value, bare-bones rooms on the lakeside for Rs 25/50 single/double and deluxe rooms for Rs 150 with hot-water bath.

The Zigar Gompa *guesthouse* has rooms with bathroom for Rs 40/80.

Tibetan Food Corner at the Zigar Gompa is very good value, with good Tibetan and western food and cross-cultural experiments like Tibetan bread with honey.

Sonam Tibetan Corner Hotel is a restaurant and serves up pretty good Tibetan food.

Tourist Inn has a decent restaurant in pleasant surroundings. There are several Indian *dhabas* along the main road.

Getting There & Away Rewalsar isn't actually on the way to anywhere, so you will have to travel to and from Mandi, whether you stay overnight in Rewalsar or not. Buses from Mandi go to Rewalsar village, every 30 or 40 minutes, so it is an easy day trip along a pretty, but fairly rough, road (Rs 12, one hour). A return taxi from Mandi costs about Rs 300.

Prasar Lake

Prasar is another lovely little lake in a great area for camping and hiking. It's more difficult and expensive to get to than Rewalsar, so will only appeal to the hardened few. The small lake is located at 2730m – about 2000m higher than Mandi. Alongside the lake there is a small, pretty, deserted **temple** dedicated to the sage Prasar Rishi.

There are no buses to the lake, so there are two alternatives. One is an irregular local bus from Mandi to the nearest accessible village, Kataula, and then a tough, steep 14km walk to the lake, or a 16km trek to the lake from the Kandi-Bajaura road. The other option is a return taxi from Mandi or Kullu (both cost a hefty Rs 1000 because the road is so rough).

There's one *Forest Inspection Hut*, which can be booked with the District Forestry Officer (DFO) in Mandi (☎ 22160), and the setting is perfect for camping. Of course you would need to carry in your gear, including drinking water and food.

MANDI TO KULLU

Pandoh

About 2km north of Pandoh, the impressive **Pandoh Dam** diverts water from the Beas River along two 12km tunnels to Baggi. The water then joins the Sutlej River near Bilaspur, eventually feeding into the huge artificial Govind Sagar. Pandoh Dam would be a nice place to visit and look around except for the gun-toting guards everywhere.

On the main road, 8km past Pandoh towards Kullu, is the revered **Hongi Hindu Temple**, set among dramatic cliffs. Your bus or taxi driver will probably stop here to give a small prayer or buy some prasaad to ensure a safe passage.

Sainj Valley

The Kullu Valley road passes the dismal little village of **Aut**, about 20km past Pandoh.

Aut functions as a turn-off to the Sainj Valley, and marks the true start of the Kullu Valley. Only a few kilometres along the road through the Sainj Valley is the pretty village of **Larji**, from where there is a turn-off to the village of Sainj. Larji, set at the spectacular junction of the Sainj and Tirthan rivers, is a centre for trout fishing, but you will need a licence from the HPTDC office in Kullu or the Fisheries office in Patlikhul. The road along the Sainj Valley continues as far as Banjar.

Bajaura

Back on the main road, 15km south of Kullu, is the village of Bajaura. It's the home of the **Basheshar Mahadev Temple**, the largest and most attractive stone temple in the Kullu Valley. Built in the 8th century from finely carved stone blocks, the temple has a central Shiva lingam, as well as images of Surya (the sun god), Vishnu, Ganesh, and a fearsome Durga standing on a *makara* (mythical crocodile) and a *kuccha* (tortoise) and slaying a buffalo demon. Outside, there is a sign with explanations in English.

The Basheshar Mahadev Temple is at the end of a 200m trail leading from the main road currently with a sign overhead reading 'Indo Italian Fruit Dev'.

Bhuntar

☎ 01902 • alt 1100m

Bhuntar's claim to fame is its airport, which serves all of the Kullu Valley, and its position as the turn-off to the Parvati Valley on the other side of the Beas. Otherwise, Bhuntar is only 10km from Kullu and not a particularly interesting place but if you have an early or late departure or arrival, staying here may be handy. You may *have* to stay here during Dussehra if Kullu's hotels are full.

Most hotels are in the main town, about 500m north of the airport and bus station. Jagson Airlines (☎ 65222) has an office next to the airport and there are several travel agencies around the village.

Places to Stay & Eat Best of a bad bunch near the airport/bus station is the *Hotel*

Airport-End, with clean but noisy rooms for a negotiable Rs 150 to Rs 450.

About 500m north of the airport, towards Kullu, are some mid-range places with TV, hot water, and modern rooms.

Hotel Sunbeam (☎ 65790) has rooms for Rs 300, Rs 350 and Rs 450. *Hotel Amit* (☎ 65123), next door, has doubles for Rs 400.

Hotel Trans Shiva (☎ 65623), farther north near the junction to the Parvati Valley, has rooms for Rs 250, Rs 300, Rs 400 and Rs 600. These three hotels offer a 50% discount in the low season.

Noble Guest House (☎ 65077), 400m east of the Trans Shiva, on the east bank of the Beas, is a good choice. Small but clean rooms with hot-water shower cost Rs 300 (Rs 150 when things are slow).

Hotel Silver Face (☎ 65797), nearby, is the best hotel in town, with rooms for Rs 500 to Rs 1200.

Around the bus station, several *dhabas* serve basic Indian and Chinese food, and some stalls have fantastic, fresh fruit juices. The *Malabar Restaurant* opposite the airport entrance is probably the best of the lot.

Lazeez Restaurant at the Sunbeam and the restaurant at the Amit have both good food and ambience. Nonveg dishes are around Rs 70, veg dishes around Rs 30. Service at the Trans Shiva is so bad it's almost funny.

Getting There & Away As the regional airport and the junction for the Parvati Valley, Bhuntar is well served by buses, leaving from outside the airport entrance. Most buses go to Kullu, where you may have to change for destinations farther north. All buses between Manali and anywhere south of Kullu stop at, or very near, Bhuntar.

Bhuntar has the valley's most frequent buses to Manikaran (and all places in between) from 7.30 am to 6.30 pm. You may have to change here if coming from Manali or Kullu.

Sample taxi fares include Kullu (Rs 80), Manikaran (Rs 475) and Manali (Rs 600). Taxis hover around the bus station.

For details of flights from Bhuntar see the Kullu Getting There & Away section.

Shopping in the Kullu Valley

The road along the Kullu Valley, particularly from Bhuntar airport to Kullu town, is lined with shops selling Kullu shawls and other locally produced handicrafts. Once an important part of household and village life, the manufacture and sale of Kullu shawls and other goods is now a thriving local industry. It's worth having a look at some of these shops to see the weaving in action, or to visit a farm of pashmina goats or angora rabbits – although there will be some real pressure to buy.

Pattoos are thick woollen shawls worn by local women, and fastened with a *gachi* (rope). Kullu caps, known as *topis*, are always colourful, and worth buying if trekking in cold climates. Other items include a *gudma*, often used as a sort of blanket, or a *pullan*, which is a type of slipper worn in the home.

The shops between Bhuntar and Kullu cater more for the tourist crowds, and despite an obvious overabundance of places, they don't offer particularly competitive prices. The best places to buy Kullu gear are the market stalls and cooperatives along the Mall in Manali, and Akhara Bazaar in Kullu town.

KULLU

☎ 01902 • alt 1220m

Kullu is the district headquarters of the valley but it is not the main tourist centre – that honour goes to Manali. Kullu is reasonably set up with hotels and other facilities, and is not a bad place, especially around Dhalpur, but many visitors do not bother to stay long in Kullu because there are nicer places around the valleys. Kullu is a particularly interesting place to witness the Dussehra festival; see The Valley of the Gods – Dussehra in Kullu boxed text.

Orientation

Kullu is small enough to walk around. The *maidan* (field) area at Dhalpur, where Kullu's festivals are held, is the nicest part of town. The 'centre' of town is probably the area around the taxi stand. From there a busy footpath heads down towards the bus station area (don't take the road if walking; it's longer) called Sarvari, full of shops and cheap guesthouses. The road from the bus station then heads towards Manali through Akhara Bazaar, which is a good place to buy Kullu shawls and other handicrafts.

Information

The HPTDC tourist office (☎ 24605) is by the maidan at Dhalpur. It's open daily 9 am to 7 pm in summer, and 10 am to 5 pm in winter but is only really useful for booking HPTDC buses, leaving outside the office.

The only place that changes money is the State Bank of Patiala, at the northern end of Akhara Bazaar. It's open Monday to Friday, 10.45 am to 2 pm. This branch accepts most travellers cheques (except Citicorp) but doesn't change cash.

The main post office, up from the taxi stand, is open Monday to Saturday, 10 am to 5 pm. You can send (and receive) faxes at government rates from the telegraph office (fax 22720) in Akhara Bazaar.

Temples

In the north of the town, the **Raghunath Temple** (built in 1660) is dedicated to the principal god in the valley. Although it's the most important temple in the area, it's not terribly interesting and is only open before 9 am and after 5 pm.

In the village of Bhekhli (3km from Kullu), is the **Jagannathi Devi Temple**. It's a stiff 1½ hour climb, but from the temple there are great views over Kullu. Take the path off the main road to Akhara Bazaar after crossing the bridge. Alternatively, take a one-way/return taxi for Rs 200/250, or an auto-rickshaw for far less. There are supposed to be two buses a day to Bhekhli at 8.30 am and 12.30 pm but don't count on it.

Places to Stay

Like Manali, and most places along the Kullu Valley, prices for hotels and guest-

HIMACHAL PRADESH

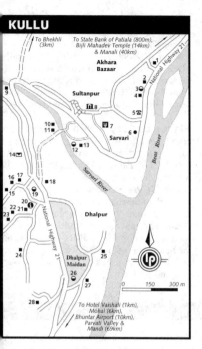

KULLU

To Bhekhli (3km)
To State Bank of Patiala (800m), Bijli Mahadev Temple (14km) & Manali (40km)
National Highway 21
Akhara Bazaar
Sultanpur
Beas River
Sarvari
Sarvari River
National Highway 21
Dhalpur
Dhalpur Maidan
0   150   300 m
To Hotel Vaishali (1km), Mohal (6km), Bhuntar Airport (10km), Parvati Valley & Mandi (69km)

houses in Kullu town vary according to the season, and, more commonly, the current tourist demand. Below are prices for the high season – but they vary considerably from one week to another.

Places to Stay – Budget

Dhalpur The *Hotel Bijleshwar View* (☎ 22677), right behind the tourist office, remains popular and pretty good value. The cheaper rooms cost Rs 300 and the larger, newer ones, with a balcony, are Rs 400 to Rs 500. All rooms have hot water and there's *at least* a 50% discount in the low season.

Around the maidan are several other good places. *Hotel Rohtang* (☎ 22303) is good value at Rs 200 a room, and Rs 450 for a room with four beds, but some rooms are dark. *Hotel Daulat* (☎ 22358) has slightly overpriced rooms with a balcony for Rs 200 to Rs 350.

Bhaga Sidh Guest House, up a lane at the back of the tourist office, has cheap singles/doubles in a family home for Rs 80/100. *Hotel Vimal*, nearby, has much the same for Rs 150.

New Vikrant (☎ 22756), farther up the road, has an excellent range of rooms from Rs 150 to Rs 375 and some nice communal sitting areas.

Across the other (eastern) side of the maidan are a couple of cheap places.

Fancy Guest House (☎ 22681) isn't bad at Rs 100, Rs 125 and Rs 250 for rooms with bath and constant hot water.

Sa-Ba Tourist Home is a clean friendly place that is probably better value, with genuine single rooms for Rs 75, and doubles for Rs 150.

HIMACHAL PRADESH

Hotel Rock-n-River (☎ 24214) has a somewhat inconvenient but pleasant location on the banks of the Sarvari River. Clean and bright rooms with a nice view are very good value at Rs 300 and Rs 400, with a 50% low-season discount.

Bus Station Area The *Aaditya Guest House* (☎ 24263), right by the river, is on the path that connects the central taxi stand area with the main bus station. Bright doubles cost Rs 100 or Rs 220 with hot-water bath.

Madhu Chandrika Guest House, behind it, is slightly more expensive.

The Nest (☎ 22685), near the bus station, has enormous doubles for Rs 250 and smaller ground floor rooms for Rs 150. Both have bathrooms but can be noisy.

Akhara Bazaar *Hotel Naman* (☎ 22667) has musty singles for Rs 100 and Rs 150, and doubles for Rs 150 to Rs 300. The cheaper rooms can be gloomy and the more expensive rooms noisy but it's not a bad place. There's a decent restaurant.

Central Hotel (☎ 22482) is a friendly place, and the oldest in Kullu. It has an almost infinite range of threadbare rooms from Rs 30 to Rs 200, most of them with at least some kind of attached bathroom.

Places to Stay – Mid-Range

Hotel Shobla (☎ 22800), in the centre of town by the river, has luxury rooms for Rs 550, Rs 770 and Rs 935, plus about Rs 360 for three meals.

HPTDC Hotel Sarvari (☎ 22471) is a little south of the maidan, and a short walk off the main road. It's a well-run place with clean and bright doubles in the old block for Rs 400 and dorm beds at Rs 45. Rooms in the new wing cost Rs 700 with a sitting area or Rs 900 with a balcony. The low-season discount is 30%.

The Valley of the Gods – Dussehra in Kullu

Nowhere highlights the complexity of popular Himachali religion better than the Kullu Valley. During the Dussehra festival in September/October, some 360 local village *devtas* (gods) are carried down from their village temples to pay homage to Raghunathji and attend the annual assembly of the gods. By the time the festival is in full swing Dhalpur Maidan is crammed with hundreds of tents, each housing a village god installed on his *rath* (chariot).

The opening day of the festival sees a procession of the main deity, accompanied by the sound of curved horns and drums, from Raghunath Temple to the maidan, where he is ceremonially installed. The sixth day sees the assembly of the gods. On the seventh day there are political speeches and staged folk dances until the afternoon, when there is a procession to the riverbank. Buffaloes are sacrificed and then human chains pull the huge rath back to the Raghunath Temple. That evening the village devtas are carried back to their villages, camping out for the night en route.

Dussehra has become an important trade fair. Hundreds of stalls are set up to supply highlanders with food, religious paraphernalia and consumer goods from the plains. The maidan is packed with funfairs and *sadhus*, palm-readers and sweet-sellers and there is also a cattle market.

Dussehra is a fascinating but wearying time to visit Kullu. Hotels double in price and you really need to get bunkered in a few days in advance, or at least make a reservation. If hotels are full it's easy enough to stay in Bhuntar, 10km away. Public transport out of Kullu is a nightmare on the final day – the roofs, and even the back ladders and grills of buses, are packed with revellers hanging on for dear life!

HIMACHAL PRADESH

Hotel Aroma Classic (☎ 23075) is another well-run place with rooms for Rs 400, Rs 550 and Rs 675, plus common balconies and a good restaurant.

Hotel Sidhartha (☎ 24243) is the best hotel in Akhara Bazaar, with clean but smallish rooms for Rs 400, Rs 500 and Rs 650 and a 50% low-season discount.

A few places south of Kullu, on the way to the airport, are in the top-end range but inconvenient unless you have your own transport. One of the best is the *Hotel Vaishali* (☎ 24225), with doubles from Rs 650 to Rs 850. It also handles Archana Airways bookings, and is more convenient and easier to find than the Archana Airways office near Bhuntar.

Places to Eat
HPTDC Monal Cafe, by the tourist office, serves good meals and snacks.

Hotstuff, just opposite, is a great place for pizzas, soup and just about everything else. Plenty of other cheap places around the bus stand, or the central taxi stand, serve basic Tibetan and Indian food.

Hotel Rohtang has nice views of Dhalpur maidan, with a good selection and prices; it's very good for breakfast

Hotel Aroma Classic looks expensive, but isn't – the setting, service and selection make it a good option.

Hotel Shobla has the best views, all the service you would expect, and good food at prices that aren't outrageous (pizzas Rs 40, omelettes Rs 20).

Getting There & Away
Air Jagson Airlines goes to/from Delhi (US$150) every day, with a stop in Shimla (US$67). Archana Airways flies direct daily between Delhi and Bhuntar (US$150). Flights are in small aircraft, mainly 15 to 20 seaters.

Archana Airways (☎ 65630) has its office at Mohal, 6km south of Kullu; alternatively book at the Hotel Vaishali, about 1km south of Kullu (☎ 24225). Jagson Airlines has an office at the airport in Bhuntar. Tickets are best booked through agencies in Kullu.

Bus Kullu has a large, busy bus station, with timetables displayed in English, and an advance booking system (inquiries ☎ 23466). The bus stand at the Dhalpur maidan is only good if you're going to Bhuntar, and, maybe, the Parvati Valley, but these buses may be full by the time they get to Dhalpur from the main Kullu bus station. It's better to go to the large station and get a seat or ticket as soon as you can.

There are several daily public buses to Mandi, or take any bus going to Shimla or Delhi; to Shimla, there are four buses each day. To Manikaran, a bus leaves every 30 minutes or so, or take a bus to Bhuntar and change there. There is a bus every 15 or 20 minutes between Kullu and Manali (Rs 25, two hours). To Naggar, buses leave every few hours from a bus stop in Akhara Bazaar, about 1km north of the main bus station. Alternatively take a Manali-bound bus to Patlikuhl and change there.

There are three public buses every day (one overnight) to Dharamsala. To Bajaura, Aut and the Sainj Valley (as far as Banjar), buses leave every hour or so. Regular daily express public buses go to Delhi (Rs 180, 14 hours) via Chandigarh. Direct daily buses to Chandigarh also leave several times a day.

HPTDC buses from Manali stop at the tourist office in Kullu and bookings can be made in advance here. Buses run daily in season to Dharamsala (Rs 250), Shimla (Rs 250), Delhi (Rs 450; overnight) and Chandigarh (Rs 275).

Travel agencies in Kullu sell tickets for deluxe private buses 'from Kullu', but these are really just part of the trips from Manali organised by bus companies in Manali. In season, daily overnight buses to Delhi cost Rs 350; to Dharamsala, Rs 250; to Leh, with a connection in Manali, Rs 800; and to Shimla, Rs 250.

Taxi Taxis from Kullu to Manali cost Rs 500 via the normal, quicker National Highway 21 (on the western side of the river), or Rs 650 if you take the slower, but more scenic, route via Naggar. For a few extra rupees, you

HIMACHAL PRADESH

should be able to stop at Naggar for a quick look around. With a group, a taxi is not a bad option, because it gives you more time to visit a few places along the way. Further examples of fixed one-way taxi fares include Manikaran (Rs 500), Katrain (Rs 200), Mandi (Rs 600), Delhi (Rs 4400), Dharamsala (Rs 1900) and Shimla (Rs 1900). To Bhuntar airport, the set price is Rs 100.

Kullu's Taxi Operators' Union (☎ 22332), just north of the Dhalpur maidan, offers the following return tours from Kullu:

Bhekhli Temple, Vaishno Devi Temple, Raghunath Temple, shawl factory, Bajaura (Rs 500, five hours)
Kasol, Manikaran (Rs 600, six hours)
Larji fishing trip (Rs 550, five hours)
Larji, Banjar, 3223m Jalori Pass (Rs 1500, eight hours)
Vaishno Devi Temple, Naggar Castle, Roerich Castle (Rs 500, five hours)

Getting Around
An auto-rickshaw is handy to get around, particularly if you have heavy gear, or want to visit the nearby temples. From Dhalpur to the bus station should cost about Rs 15, or to the airport at Bhuntar, Rs 60.

AROUND KULLU
Bijli Mahadev Temple
South of Kullu, across the river and high on a bluff, is the Bijli Mahadev Temple, surmounted by a 20m-high rod said to attract blessings in the form of lightning. At least once a year the image of Shiva in the temple is supposed to be shattered by lightning, then miraculously repaired by the temple *pujari* (priest).

The road to the temple is rough, which explains the high cost of transport there. A return taxi from Kullu will cost Rs 600 for the full day, including waiting time. Alternatively, take one of the few daily buses to Chansari (check by asking for the Bijli Mahadev Mandir). These normally leave from Tapu, on the east side of the Ramshila bridge, 1km north of Akhara Bazaar. From Chansari it's a steep 3km walk to the temple. Buses return to Kullu, at *around* 4 pm.

Vaishno Devi Temple
About 4km along the Kullu to Manali road is the modern Vaishno Devi Temple – a small cave with an image of the goddess Vaishno. You'll have to crawl in; it's not really worth the effort. There are several **temples** nearby dedicated to Rama, Shiva and Krishna.

PARVATI VALLEY
The pine-scented and craggy Parvati Valley is a beautiful and worthwhile side trip from Kullu. The three main settlements are popular with long-term, dope-soaked visitors but there are also some nice walks, beautiful alpine scenery and plenty of cheap places to stay. There are no places to change money in the valley; the nearest bank is in Kullu town.

Jari
• alt 1520m
Jari is halfway along the Parvati Valley, about 19km from Bhuntar. It has been developed to cater for the hippie crowd who have spilled over from Manikaran, or who prefer Jari's peace and cheap rooms. Treks start from here to Malana (see Treks around the Parvati Valley, later in this section), and Naggar (see the Trekking from Manali & the Kullu Valley boxed text in the Manali section).

There are several cheap, friendly, basic places to stay. The *Village Guest House* is a 10 minute uphill walk from the village centre but worth the hike. It's a peaceful, relaxed and well-run place, with decent rooms for Rs 50 or Rs 75. A hot shower costs Rs 10, or a bucket of hot water is Rs 5.

Back down in the village, the old wooden *Dharma Family Guest House* has OK rooms for Rs 50, as does the *Om Shiva Guest House*. *Roman Guest House* is Rs 70 or Rs 100. The best bet on the main road is *Golden Rays Hotel*, with clean, spacious doubles for Rs 60 or Rs 80 with bath. The toilets are the cleanest in the Parvati Valley.

Deepak Restaurant on the main road is the best place for food. *Rooftop Cafe* on top of the Om Shiva Guest House has great views.

Parvati Valley buses stop in the centre of town if required. A one-way taxi from Kullu to Jari is around Rs 350.

Kasol
• alt 1580m

Kasol is another tiny village along the Parvati Valley road that has slowly become a hang-out. It's very pretty, in a lovely setting among pines and streams with some trout. The village is actually divided into 'Old Kasol', on the Bhuntar side of the bridge, and 'New Kasol', on the Manikaran side. The village is a pleasant hour's walk downhill from Manikaran.

Rainbow Cafe & Guest House, in New Kasol, attracts many foreigners. It has a few charmless rooms for Rs 100, or Rs 150 with bathroom, and serves basic food and eastern 'herbs' all day.

Om Shanti Cafe, nearby (and similarly dope-soaked), is slightly cheaper.

HPTDC Tourist Hut, pleasantly sited, east of the Rainbow Cafe, has rooms for Rs 300 in the high season (Rs 150 in the low season), but you'll need to book in summer. Decent places to eat include the *Mountain Cafe* and *Nest Cafe*.

Old Kasol is generally a far nicer place to stay and there are plenty of guesthouses and cafes, some with nice gardens, which offer basic rooms for around Rs 50.

Yerpa's Guest House is by far the best of the bunch with clean rooms with common hot-water bathroom for Rs 100 and deluxe rooms with hot shower for Rs 250. There's a nice restaurant and a Tibetan-style sitting area (the owners are from Spiti).

Kasol Inn has less charm but is cheaper, with rooms for Rs 100 and Rs 150.

Village Moon Guest House, up in the village at the lower end of town, has basic rooms for Rs 50 but a nice location.

There are plenty of places to eat in old Kasol, including the *Namaste Garden Cafe*, *Shiva Mama's*, *Bhoj Cafe*, *Moondance Restaurant* and *Garden View Restaurant*, the last two of which also offer bare-bones rooms.

Manikaran
☎ 01902 • alt 1737m

Famous for its hot springs, which apparently cure anything from rheumatism to bronchitis and are hot enough to boil rice, Manikaran is another place where many foreigners have forgotten to leave. Manikaran means Jewel from the Ear in Sanskrit. According to the local legend, a giant Naga serpent took earrings from the goddess Parvati while she was bathing and then snorted them through its nose to create spaces where the hot springs spewed forth.

The town is split into two, over both sides of the roaring Parvati River. Almost all the guesthouses, places to eat and temples are on the northern side, where no vehicles are allowed. The first bridge you see as you approach from Bhuntar is a footbridge that leads to the hot springs under the enormous Sikh gurdwara, and then continues into the village. The second bridge is at the end of the Parvati Valley road, where there is a taxi and bus stand.

Temples The town is revered by both Hindus and Sikhs and is chock-a-block with sadhus, pilgrims and religious souvenir shops. The Hindu Shri Ramchander, or **Rama Temple**, dominates the centre of the town. It's a quiet place where you can discreetly have a look around, while the Indian sadhus and western freaks huddle around outside the temple trying to get some sunshine. Other temples include the stone Raghunath Temple, the nearby wooden Naini Devi Temple and the Shiva Temple by the gurdwara.

As you enter Manikaran, you cannot escape the extraordinary sight of the **Shri Guru Nanak Dev Ji** Sikh gurdwara.

Baths It's a good idea to have a hot bath while you're in Manikaran, if only to warm up. There are three alternatives: the crowded but free hot baths (separate for men and women) under the Sikh gurdwara; the Hotel Parvati (Rs 25/40 for one/two people, 20 minutes, plus Rs 5 per towel); or the free baths in most local guesthouses.

Places to Stay Like the rest of the region, prices vary according to demand.

HPTDC Hotel Parvati (☎ 73735) has clean doubles at Rs 400 (Rs 200 in the low season), which is not particularly good value around here.

Sharma Sadan (☎ *73703*) has a fine location right next to the wooden Naini Devi Temple on the main square and has nice rooms from Rs 100 (low season) to Rs 250 (June, July). There are nice hot baths here.

Of the cheaper places, the ***Sharma Guest House*** has lethargic staff but decent doubles for Rs 50 to Rs 120. It is close to the first footbridge – follow the signs around the village. ***Padha Family Guest House*** is nearby and of a similar standard. There is a wide range of rooms around a courtyard cafe, many with a balcony overlooking the river where you can sun yourself in the afternoon. Room rates vary from Rs 50 to Rs 300.

Paradise Guest House, nearby, has damp doubles for Rs 50 and Rs 100.

Shivalik Hotel, on the darker, southern side of the river, has clean but damp rooms for Rs 100, Rs 200 and Rs 300.

Dev Bhoomi Guest House, nearby, isn't up to much.

PWD Guesthouse, next door, is a bargain. The friendly *chowkidar* (caretaker) rents out two pleasant and spacious rooms with hot-water bathroom for Rs 100 or Rs 200 and you normally don't need a booking.

Places to Eat Manikaran is now set up for short and long-term staying foreigners.

Hot Spring Restaurant serves absolutely delicious pizzas.

O-Rest does similar food, and is popular.

Holy Palace has reasonable Italian and Israeli food for around Rs 40 a dish.

Shiva Restaurant, near the gurdwara, is also good but a little pricier than the rest. Around the village, several *dhabas* serve cheap Indian food and sweets.

Getting There & Away Buses between Kullu and Manikaran leave every 30 minutes or so, or, alternatively, take a regular bus going to Bhuntar, and catch another on to Manikaran (Rs 17, two hours). Buses link Manikaran with Manali six times a day (Rs 35, four hours). Another option is a day trip from Manali on a tourist bus for Rs

175, which stops at Kasol for a quick look on the way.

A return taxi from Manali to Manikaran will cost Rs 1100. A fixed-price taxi from the stand at the bus station in Manikaran will cost Rs 475 to Bhuntar (one way), and Rs 575 to Kullu (one way). A six hour sightseeing return taxi trip from Kullu along the Parvati Valley road costs Rs 600.

Treks around the Parvati Valley

From Manikaran, a well-defined trail leads 16km to the village of **Pulga** (five hours walk), where there are a couple of basic guesthouses and restaurants. The next stage (again four to five hours) continues on up the Parvati Valley to the hot springs at **Khirganga**, where Shiva sat and meditated for 2000 years. Here there are a number of basic teahouses to spend the night before returning directly to Manikaran in one long stage. Porters and guides can be hired in Manikaran – ask at any guesthouse or restaurant.

On the other side of the river from Jari, is the interesting Malana Valley. **Malana** (2652m) can be reached in a full-day trek from Jari. There are about 500 people in Malana and they speak a peculiar dialect with strong Tibetan elements. See the Legends of the Malana Valley boxed text for other cultural information. Malana is an isolated village with its own system of government and a caste structure so rigid that it's forbidden for visitors to touch either the people or any of their possessions. It's very important to respect this custom; wait at the edge of the village for an invitation to enter. See the Trekking from Manali & the Kullu Valley boxed text in the Manali section for information on hiking routes around Malana.

KULLU TO MANALI

There are a number of interesting things to see along both sides of the 42km valley between Kullu and Manali. There are two Kullu-Manali roads: the main highway, Highway 21, runs along the west bank of the Beas, while the rougher, but more scenic, road goes along the east bank, through Naggar.

Legends of the Malana Valley

Local legends have it that when Jamlu, the main deity of Malana, first came here, he bore a casket containing all the other Kullu gods. At the top of the pass he opened the casket and the breeze carried the gods to their present homes all over the valley.

At the time of the Dussehra Festival in Kullu, Jamlu plays a special part. He is a very powerful god with some demonic qualities. He does not have a temple image so, unlike other Kullu gods, has no temple *rath* (chariot) to be carried in. Nor does he openly show his allegiance to Raghunathji, the paramount Kullu god, as do the other Kullu deities. At the time of the festival, Jamlu goes down to Kullu but stays on the east side of the river from where he watches the proceedings.

Every few years a major festival is held in honour of Jamlu in the month of Bhadon. In the temple at Malana, there is a silver elephant with a gold figure on its back which is said to have been a gift from Emperor Akbar.

Raison

At a particularly wide and low part of the Kullu Valley 13km from Kullu is Raison.

HPTDC Adventure Resort (☎ 01902-40516) is right on the river. A hut with two bedrooms costs Rs 600 (Rs 300 in the low season), and a pretty camping spot is Rs 50.

Saga Guest House is a cheap place above the river, in the village.

Katrain

Katrain is on one of the widest points in the Kullu Valley.

HPTDC Hotel Apple Blossom (☎ 01902-40836) has doubles from Rs 250 to Rs 300, and a five bed dorm for Rs 50 per bed. The hotel has great views, but is looking a bit old and tired these days.

Nangdraj Guest House is cheap and family run, and the only other place in the village worth staying at.

A one-way taxi from Kullu to Katrain costs Rs 200.

Patlikuhl

Patlikuhl is the largest village between Kullu and Manali, and almost exactly halfway between the two towns.

Avtar Guest House (☎ 01902-84871) has basic facilities and rooms for Rs 75. Being so close to the lovely village of Naggar, just across the river, there seems little or no need to stay at Patlikuhl. There is a Fisheries Office at the northern edge of town where you can buy trout and get a fishing licence.

Naggar
☎ 01902 • alt 1768m

Naggar is a lovely little village, set on a hill and surrounded by forests. There are good facilities and quite a few interesting things to see and do. The village is also the trail head for treks over the Chandrakhani Pass (3650m) to Malana and the Parvati Valley (see the Trekking from Manali & the Kullu Valley boxed text in the Manali section later in this chapter). Naggar can be visited in a day trip from Manali or Kullu, but if you have time it's worth stopping over for a night or two.

Several of the hotels can help with trekking arrangements. The Ragini and Snow View hotels can arrange a porter and guide for Rs 500 or an all-inclusive trek for US$20 to US$25 per person, per day. The Poonam Lodge also runs a small trekking agency and rents out basic equipment.

Naggar Castle Naggar was capital of the Kullu Valley for nearly 1500 years. The castle, built about 500 years ago as the raja's headquarters, was converted to a hotel in 1978. The quaint old castle is built around a courtyard with verandas right around the outside, providing stupendous views out over the valley. Inside the courtyard is the small **Jagtipath Temple** containing a slab of stone that is said to have been carried there by wild bees, and a small **museum**. Renovations were carried out on the castle in 1998.

HIMACHAL PRADESH

Temples There are a number of interesting temples around the village. The grey sandstone Shiva **Gauri Shankar Temple** is at the foot of the small bazaar below the castle and dates from the 11th or 12th century. Almost opposite the front of the castle is the curious little **Chatar Bhuj Temple** dedicated to Vishnu. Near the Snow View Guest House is the pagoda-like **Tripura Sundari Devi Temple**, with some ornate woodcarvings. High up on the ridge above Naggar, near the village of Thawa, is the **Murlidhar Krishna Temple**.

Roerich Gallery One kilometre past the castle is the Roerich Gallery, a fine old house displaying the artwork of both the eccentric Professor Nicholas Roerich, who died in Naggar in 1947, and his son, Svetoslav Roerich, who died in Bangalore in

---

The Mystical Spy

Nicholas Roerich, born in 1874 in St Petersburg, must rank as one of the most enigmatic characters of the 20th century. As an artist, philosopher, and writer, Roerich expressed his deep spiritual convictions of humanity's harmonious link with nature. Among his many religious influences, Roerich drew inspiration from Pantheism, Hinduism, Buddhism, Theosophy, Yoga, as well as the theory of relativity. His artistic nature spurred his most valiant effort to preserve the great monuments of the world from careless wartime shelling, to the end that the Roerich Pact was signed in 1935 at the White House by US Secretary of Agriculture Henry Wallace (who later became vice president under the Roosevelt administration).

After successful exhibitions in America, Roerich embarked on his dream trip to India, where he settled, first in Darjeeling and later the Kullu Valley, in 1924. Inspired by the Himalaya, Roerich painted several series that represented his belief in the mystical Shambhala, the Tibetan Buddhist mythical 'Northern Paradise'. Roerich became convinced that the natural wonders of the Himalaya were manifestations of Shambhala, and therein lay a secret valley.

Roerich's greatest expedition took him twice over the Tibetan plateau, into Chinese Turkestan, Siberia, Mongolia and through the Gobi desert. His route made him target to espionage suspicions from the Chinese and British governments. Handing his diary over to the Soviet Consul in Ürümqi did nothing to diminish such rumours and his gift to the Soviet Commissar of Education, a painting of a giant head looming over the earth looking ominously to the east and entitled 'The Time Has Come', confirmed the distrust of many. In America, an editorial in the *New York Times* accused a power-hungry Roerich of forcing Wallace to sign the Roerich Pact via mystical charisma.

Spy or mystic, Roerich's talent as an artist has stood the test of time. His works can be viewed at The Nicholas Roerich Museum in New York or The Roerich Gallery in Naggar. His books published in English include *Adamant*, *Heart of Asia* and *Shambhala*.

1993; see the Mystical Spy boxed text. Its location is delightful and the views over the valley are great. It's open daily 9 am to 1 pm, and 2 to 5 pm and entry is Rs 10. Leave your shoes at the front door.

Just uphill from the gallery is the **Urusvati Himalayan Folk & Art Museum**. There's a collection of rumals and *aipans*, geometric folk designs painted on the floors and walls of family homes on auspicious occasions. Upstairs is a modern art gallery which sells postcards and copies of Roerich's paintings. Entry is included in the Roerich Gallery ticket.

Places to Stay The reputedly haunted *HPTDC Castle Hotel (☎ 47816)* has a good range of accommodation. The more basic rooms cost Rs 200 and Rs 300 with common bath and Rs 400 to Rs 1000 with bathroom. There are low-season discounts of around 30%. The more expensive rooms have a fireplace and a balcony with great views. Dorm beds for Rs 50 are often booked out. This is *the* place to stay. Try to book in advance, though, as it's very popular.

Poonam Mountain Lodge & Restaurant is right behind the castle. Good singles/doubles with hot water cost Rs 150/200 and the helpful owner is a mine of local information.

Hotel Ragini (☎ 47793) is a new midrange place with nice wooden decor and excellent rooms for Rs 300, Rs 350 (with balcony) and Rs 500.

Sheetal Guest House (☎ 47719), next door, has tired-looking rooms from Rs 250 to Rs 650.

Farther towards the Roerich Gallery are two cheap guesthouses.

Snow View Guest House (☎ 47325) has dark but OK doubles from Rs 100 to Rs 200 and small singles for Rs 50 and Rs 70.

Alliance Guest House (☎ 47363) is a simple but clean and comfortable place run by an expat Frenchman. Rooms with common hot-water bath range from Rs 80 to Rs 150, with a couple of rooms with bath for around Rs 300. Like anywhere in the Kullu Valley, these prices can drop significantly if business is quiet.

Places to Eat The *Castle Hotel* provides the best views, and certainly has the best atmosphere in the village. The food is pretty good, too.

Kailash Rooftop Restaurant at the Hotel Ragini and the *Cinderella Restaurant* at the Sheetal Guest House are also worth a try.

Poonam Restaurant has vegetarian food and a great location in the shadow of the Vishnu Hotel.

La Purezza Italian Restaurant, in the village on the main road, at the start of the road up to the castle, is surprisingly authentic with pasta dishes for around Rs 70.

Getting There & Away Naggar Castle and the guesthouses are at the top of a steep 2km road, off the eastern Kullu-Manali road. To get to the castle, get off the bus at the village on the main road, and walk up, or take one of the auto-rickshaws milling around. Buses go directly between the village of Naggar (on the main road) and Manali six times a day (Rs 10, one hour).

Another way is to get the bus to Patlikuhl (there are more buses along the western side of the river) from either Manali or Kullu. Then take a taxi (Rs 30) from Patlikuhl to Naggar Castle – or even walk, but it's steep, and about 7km.

A one-way/return taxi from Manali to Naggar Castle will cost Rs 300/400; a return taxi from Kullu is Rs 500. A Kullu-Manali taxi (Rs 500) will probably charge an extra Rs 150 for a quick stopover in Naggar. From Bhuntar airport, a taxi to Naggar Castle is Rs 450.

Jagatsukh

Between Naggar and Manali, Jagatsukh was another ancient capital of Kullu until it was supplanted by Naggar. There are some very old temples in the village, notably the **Shiva Temple**. Shooru village nearby has the old and historically interesting **Devi Sharvali Temple**.

Rishi Guest House is ordinary, but still costs about Rs 140 a room. Because Jagatsukh is so close to Manali, it's an easy half-day trip, or even a lovely walk along the road.

HIMACHAL PRADESH

From Jagatsukh, a steep four or five day trekking route leads towards Deo Tibba mountain (6001m) and Chandra Tal (lake) at 4800m.

Manali

☎ 01902 • alt 2050m
High Season: mid-Apr to end Jun, mid-Sep to early Nov, Christmas and New Year

At the northern end of the Kullu Valley and the Beas River sits the ancient site, but modern town, of Manali. It doesn't have the colonial history or charm of Shimla, nor the culture and spectacular settings common in Lahaul, Spiti and Kinnaur. But it is a pleasant, if overdeveloped, town with lovely forests and orchards nearby for hiking and good facilities for visitors.

In the 1970s and 1980s, Manali was very much a 'scene'. In the summer, the town would attract numerous western hippies and travellers drawn by the high quality marijuana that grows in the area. A lot of these people have moved to the nearby villages of Dhungri and Vashisht, or to Manikaran and Pulga, along the Parvati Valley. Now, the character of Manali has changed considerably; with literally hundreds of hotels and guesthouses, it's one of the most popular places in the country for honeymooning Indian couples.

Legend has it that Manu, Hinduism's Noah, stepped off a boat in Manali to re-create human life after floods had devastated the world. Manali is derived from Manu-Alaya, meaning Home of Manu.

Orientation

Manali is based around one street – the Mall – which is not nearly as charming as its namesake in Shimla. The Mall splits at Nehru Park, which has a statue of the great man, and heads left (north-west) uphill towards Old Manali, and right (east) across the Beas River to the Naggar Highway, and the nearby village of Vashisht.

Manali town can be divided into an area known as Model Town, a charmless 'suburb'

of new concrete hotels, one block west, halfway along the Mall; and the area unofficially known as the 'Tibetan area', dominated by a Tibetan market, a gompa and more guesthouses. The area north of Manali is made up of mid-range hotels and the outlying villages of Dhungri and Old Manali, both of which have become backpacker centres.

Information

Tourist Offices For tourist information go to the HPTDC Tourist Reception Centre (☎ 52175), which is the small, white hut, under the Hotel Kunzam. Open 10 am to 5 pm in summer (fewer hours in winter), the Tourist Reception Centre should not be confused with the far larger HPTDC Tourism Marketing Office (☎ 52360) next door, which sells bus tickets for HPTDC buses, arranges fishing permits and makes reservations for HPTDC skiing courses and hotels.

Money The State Bank of India, just past the end of the Mall, on the way to Old Manali, will only change Thomas Cook and American Express travellers cheques. The UCO Bank, opposite the HPTDC tourist offices, charges Rs 60 per transaction, and follows the same State Bank of India restriction regarding travellers cheques.

A moneychanger at the Solang Hotel, on School Rd, keeps more convenient hours and will change all major brands of travellers cheques as well as cash. There's a Rs 50 commission for every US$100. There's another moneychanger next to the Mayur Restaurant on Mission Rd.

If you are headed north of Manali then change some extra money here as there are no exchange facilities in Lahaul, Spiti and Kinnaur and nothing along the road to Ladakh until Leh.

Post & Communications The post office is conveniently located in Model Town, and is open Monday to Saturday, 9 am to 5 pm. The poste restante here is more reliable and convenient than those in Leh or Kullu town; mail marked for GPO Manali will

HIMACHAL PRADESH

arrive here even though this is officially a 'sub-post office'.

The Central Telegraph Office (fax 52404), a block north, is very helpful and you can make international calls and send/receive faxes here at government rates. It's open daily, 10 am to 6 pm. There are plenty of private STD/ISO telephone and fax booths in Model Town or along the Mall, and one or two in Old Manali.

Travel Agencies Of the many travel agencies in Manali, the following places, run by locals, are reliable, have been long established, and organise their own tours:

Antrek Tours
(☎ 52292, fax 52786)
Manu Market. For trekking, porters, guides, trekking equipment hire and skiing.
Druk Expeditions
(☎ 53135)
Model Town (a little west of the Gozy Restaurant). For trekking and mountaineering.
Himalayan Adventures
(☎ 52750, fax 52182)
The Mall (opposite the UCO Bank). For trekking, rafting, jeep safaris, jeep hire (US$45 per day) and trekking equipment hire. Fully inclusive local treks cost US$20 per person per day for a minimum of five people, rising to US$35 per person for just two people.
Himalayan Journeys
(☎ 52365, fax 53065,
email himjourn@del3.vsnl.net.in)
The Mall (near the State Bank of India).
North Face Adventure Tours
(☎ 52441, fax 52694)
The Mall (near the Mount View Restaurant). For paragliding and skiing.

Bookshops & Newsagencies The only bookshop in Manali is Bookworm (16, NAC Markets), at the back of the bus station. A good range of English and foreign-language novels can be bought or swapped here. Daily English-language newspapers are available in the afternoon from the Verma newsagency, under the Hotel Renuka, on the Mall.

Books & Maps Nest & Wings (India) puts out a fairly complete (but out of scale) *Tourist Guide Map to Manali* (Rs 20). *Tourist Paradise: Himachal* (International Publishers) has some historical information, and plenty of advertisements for Rs 50. Although both can be bought in Manali, they are more readily available in the bookshops along the Mall in Shimla.

Film & Photography Several places along the Mall sell slide and print film, although it is a little expensive, and could be out of date. Both on the Mall, Parkash Studio, next to the UCO Bank, and Tibet Colour Lab, next to the Hotel Ibex, are good places to develop your prints (but not slides).

Medical Services Some travellers have reported that the Mission Hospital (☎ 52379) down School Rd, just off the Mall, provides good facilities and care. You can try Tibetan medicine at the Mentsikhang clinic in the Tibetan area.

Dhungri Temple

The Dhungri, or Hadimba Temple, is a nice four storey wooden building in the middle of a lovely forested parkland, known as the Dhungri Van Vihar. Erected in 1553, the temple is dedicated to the goddess Hadimba. According to a local legend, Bhima, one of the Pandava brothers, killed the evil Hadimb and married his sister Hadimba. The temple has intricate woodcarvings of dancers and characters from various Hindu stories, and horns of bulls and other animals decorate the walls. Every May, there is a major festival at the temple, when sacrifices are carried out in honour of Hadimba.

On foot, follow the sign to the temple from the road out towards the HPTDC Log Huts. Alternatively, walk past the Hotel Hilltop through the apple orchards towards the Hotel Shrinagar Regency or the monstrous Hadimba Palace. It's an easy 20 minute walk; if you need directions, ask a local. A new road now goes all the way to the entrance of the park, near the temple, so a taxi or auto-rickshaw (Rs 20) is another option.

HIMACHAL PRADESH

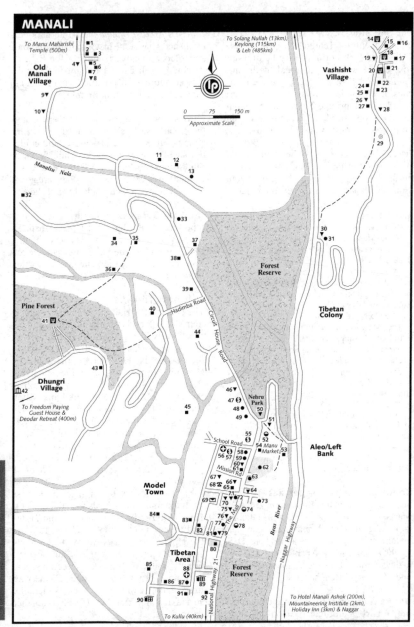

MANALI

PLACES TO STAY
1 Krishna Guest House
2 Diplomat Guest House
3 Dragon Guest House
5 Tourist Nest
6 Veer Paying Guest House
7 Kishoor Guest House
11 Hotel Riverbank; Hotel Him
    View; Tibetan Kitchen
12 Rising Moon; Hema Guest
    House;
    Mamta Paying Guest House;
    Jungle Bungalow
15 Bodh Guest House
16 New Dharma
17 Amrit Guest House
21 Kalptaru Guest House
22 Anand Hotel
23 Sonam Guest House
24 Janta Guest House
25 Surabhi Hotel
27 Hotel Bhrigu;
    Hotel Valley View
32 HPTDC Log Huts
34 Hotel New Highland
35 Hotel Kalpana
36 Hotel Chetna
37 Pinewood Hotel
38 Sunshine Guest House
39 John Banon's Hotel
40 HPTDC Hotel Rohtang
    Manalsu
43 Hotel Shrinagar Regency
44 Hotel Tourist
45 Hotel Hilltop
53 HPTDC Hotel Beas
54 HPTDC Hotel Kunzam;
    HPTDC Tourist Offices
61 Hotel Renuka; Verma
    Newsagency

65 Sukhiran Guest House
80 Hotel Ibex; Ibex Travels;
    Tibetan Market;
    Tibet ColourLab
82 Premier Hotel; Mona Lisa
83 Hotel Shishar; Lhasa Hotel
84 Mount View Hotel
85 Potala Hotel
86 Hotel Sunflower
91 Hotel Snow Drop
92 Samrat Hotel

PLACES TO EAT
4 Mount View Cafe
8 Little Tibet Cafe;
    Shiva Garden Cafe
9 Ish Cafe
10 Moon Dance Garden
19 Super Bake; Zodiac Cafe;
    Ranu Rooftop Cafe
26 Freedom Cafe
28 Rose Garden Inn
30 Phuntsok Coffee House
46 Johnson's Cafe
50 Sa-Ba Restaurant
51 HPTDC Juniper
    Restaurant
60 Sher-e-Punjab Restaurant
64 Mona Lisa Restaurant
66 Mayur Restaurant;
    Moneychanger
67 Swamiji's Madras Cafe;
    Sangam Restaurant
70 Moc Restaurant
71 Mahadev Food Corner
75 Mount View Restaurant;
    Chopsticks
76 Kamal Dhaba;
    Himalaya Dhaba
79 Gozy Restaurant

OTHER
13 HPTDC Club House
14 Hindu Temple
18 Hindu Temple
20 Hindu Temple
29 HPTDC Hot Baths Complex
31 The Enfield Club
33 Nirvana Travels
41 Dhungri Temple
42 Museum of Traditional
    Himachal Culture; Utopia
    Complex
47 State Bank of India;
    Archana Airways
48 Himalayan Journeys
49 Jagson Airlines
52 Taxi Stand
55 UCO Bank; Parkash Studio
56 Mission Hospital
57 Solang Hotel Moneychanger
58 Himalayan Adventures
59 Charitrust Tibetan Handicraft
    Emporium
62 Pace Antrek Tours
63 Himcoop
68 Central Telegraph Office
69 Main Post Office
72 Harrison Travel; Kullu-
    Kashmir Handicraft Coop
73 Bookworm
74 Bus Station
77 North Face Adventure Tours
78 Him-Aanchal Taxi Stand
81 Druk Expeditions
87 Inder Motors
88 Mentsikhang Clinic
89 Himalayan Nyingmapa
    Gompa
90 Gadhan Thekchokling
    Gompa

Museum of Traditional Himachal Culture

This small, privately funded museum near the Dhungri Temple is worth a quick visit. The curator has spent years collecting folk art and handicrafts from Manali's surrounding villages in a valiant attempt to protect the distinct and interesting traditions of the Kullu Valley.

Items on display include traditional woolspun clothes such as the *chola* cloak, *suthan* trousers and *gachi* (rope) waistband,

as well as carved wooden chests, columns and pots for distilling spirits. There are also several scale models of regional folk and palace architecture.

The museum should keep the same opening hours as the nearby Utopia Complex (see Entertainment, later in this section). Entry costs Rs 5.

Gadhan Thekchokling Gompa

Built by Tibetan refugees in the late 1960s, this gompa has some new but excellent

HIMACHAL PRADESH

Outdoor Sports in Manali

The environs of Manali afford a myriad of adventure and leisure activity opportunities, from rafting on the Beas to paragliding on the slopes of nearby Solang Nullah.

Fishing The hotel reservation counter at the HPTDC Marketing Office issues one-day fishing permits for Rs 100. You can also get permits at the Fisheries Office in Patlikhul. The best angling in the Kullu Valley is said to be at Larji, Katrain and Kasol.

Hiking There are several good day hikes from Manali. The 12km hike up the western side of the Beas River to the Solang Valley is a nice alternative to the bus. Lama Dugh meadow is a 6km hike up the Manaslu *nulla* (small river valley), west of Manali town and makes a nice day or overnight trip. Multi-day hikes in the Manali region include the three day trek to Beas Kund (3690m), the source of the Beas River, and the two or three day hike from Gullaba to Brighu Lake (4270m), returning via Vashisht. For a rundown of other treks in the region see the Treks from Manali and the Kullu Valley boxed text in the Manali section.

Mountain Biking Himalayan Journeys will rent you a bike and helmet and drop you up at the Rohtang Pass for Rs 800, though you need to find a minimum of four people. It can also arrange multi-day biking trips.

Paragliding In summer, several travel agencies organise paragliding on the slopes of Solang Nullah, north of Manali. Himalayan Journeys and North Face Adventure Tours both offer two-minute tandem 'joy rides' for Rs 400, or 10 to 15-minute 'high rides' for Rs 1500. Both run a one day beginners' course for Rs 700 per person and a week-long course for Rs 3000 to Rs 4000. Prices include accommodation (if applicable), food, equipment and a guide, but not transport.

Rafting Some basic rafting is available along the Beas River, depending on the weather and the state of the unpredictable Beas. The rafting season generally lasts from May to mid-June, and, depending on the monsoon, from mid-September to mid-October. Trips generally start

quality frescoes and a fine central statue of Sakyamuni Buddha, flanked by Tara, Padmasambhava, Maitreya (Tibetan: Jampa; the Future Buddha) and a 1000 armed Avalokiteshvara, among others. The main entrance has a superb painting of the Wheel of Life, with a particularly vivid depiction of hell. On the outside wall there is a list of Tibetan martyrs killed between 1987 and 1989, during the Chinese occupation. There is also a small Tibetan carpet workshop attached to the gompa.

The gompa, open from 6 am to 7 pm, dominates the 'Tibetan area' around the bottom of the Mall. Photos are permitted for Rs 2.

Nearby is the Himalayan Nyingmapa Gompa, which is worth a quick look.

Old Manali

The original settlement of Manali is about 2.5km north-west of 'new' Manali. It's a lovely (but rapidly developing) area of old guesthouses and orchards and it's worth a stroll around, even if you're not staying there. Past most guesthouses, the small **Manu Maharishi Temple** is where Manu meditated after he arrived in the area. To get to Old Manali, follow the road to the left at the top of the Mall and follow the signs – it's across the bridge, and up the left-hand road.

Outdoor Sports in Manali

at Pirdi and continue 16km down to Jhiri. Prices depend on the number of passengers and your bargaining power but are around Rs 800, including transport, equipment, lunch and a guide. North Face Adventure Tours charges Rs 650 with no transport or lunch. Longer trips go from Raison to Jiri (25km) for Rs 1200. For more adventurous rafting trips you will have to try the Indus or Zanskar rivers to the north, or maybe the Sutlej River, near Shimla.

Skiing Skiing for beginners is possible at Solang Nullah from January to March; the later the better, because January is very cold. Refer to Solang Nullah in the Around Manali section for details of courses. Skiing in summer, between April and June, is possible at Rohtang Pass, north of Manali. North Face offers skiing day trips to Mahri, near the pass, for Rs 900.

Ski gear can be rented from the Mountaineering Institute (following), North Face Adventure Tours and at Solang Nullah. All you'll need for a day's skiing will cost around Rs 300.

Heli-skiing is a relatively new sport. For about US$850 a day, you can be dropped onto any deep snowfields around the region. Himalayan Journeys can organise this if you have the money and experience.

Mountaineering Institute & Allied Sports The institute (☎ 52342) is about 3km south of The Mall, down a side road opposite the Ram Regency Honeymoon Hotel. It offers all sorts of tours and courses, which are outlined in a prospectus available from the institute for Rs 5. Established in 1961, the institute is an impressive complex with a library, museum and offices, and plenty of helpful experts if you want to try something adventurous around the region. Class sizes are large (about 20 to 30 students) but the cost is reasonable, even if foreigners have to pay about six times more than a Himachali (the institute is subsidised by the local government).

It offers fixed-date, single-sex, 25-day basic (US$293) and 27-day advanced (US$329) mountaineering courses, and two weeks of kayaking on the Beas River in October/November for US$189. Prices include food, gear, training and (dormitory) accommodation, but not transport. Refer to the Solang Nullah section for more details on its skiing courses.

Organised Tours

Tours are organised by the HPTDC Tourism Marketing Office and by local private bus companies (see Getting There & Away). They may be touristy, but are often the best way to visit local places, especially if you can't share the cost of a taxi. Each bus agency offers three identical day trips:

Naggar Castle and Roerich Gallery, via Jagatsukh temples (Rs 125)
Parvati Valley, stopping at Vaishno Devi Temple and Manikaran (Rs 175)
Rohtang Pass (3978m), via Nehru Kund (lake), Kothi, Rahala Falls and Mahri viewpoints (Rs 150)

Places to Stay

In Manali, prices are generally quite high, and vary considerably according to the season. Prices listed in hotel receptions are the authorised *maximum* price and most places will quickly offer a 'low-season discount' of up to 50%, even during the high season if things are quiet. Prices below are for the high season, but, remember, prices will vary, almost from day to day. It's also worth bearing in mind that different parts of Manali come into season at different times. For example, in September and October you can get excellent discounts in Old Manali's backpacker joints, just when the Indian honeymooner

HIMACHAL PRADESH

hotels in Model Town are at full occupancy. Conversely, from June to August the Model Town hotels offer good discounts, just as Old Manali hikes up its prices.

Places to Stay – Budget

Budget accommodation can be easily found in the nearby villages of Old Manali, Vashisht (see the Around Manali section) and Dhungri, but there aren't many cheap places in Manali itself.

Manali The *Sukhiran Guest House* (☎ 52178), at the back of the Mall, is basic but friendly and remains one of the best-value places in Manali. Doubles cost Rs 138 with common bathroom, and there are some dorm beds (eight in a room) available for Rs 25. A bucket of hot water costs Rs 5.

Hotel Renuka (☎ 52309) has a great central location but it can be noisy and rooms are nothing special for Rs 300/400, with hot water and balcony.

Mount View Hotel (☎ 52465), in Model Town, is friendly and has decent doubles with TV for around Rs 400, plus good low-season discounts and recommended food.

Samrat Hotel (☎ 52356), a little farther down past the Hotel Ibex, is pretty good value in the low season, with doubles from Rs 250.

In the Tibetan area are several basic, but comfortable, family-run and friendly guesthouses, which offer a convenient location and good discounts in the low season.

Hotel Snow Drop offers clean, airy rooms from Rs 100 to Rs 150, depending on the season.

Potala Hotel (☎ 53658) has clean and comfortable rooms for Rs 300 or Rs 425.

Hotel Sunflower (☎ 52419), nearby, is cheaper, with doubles for Rs 250 and Rs 350.

Old Manali Many travellers opt for the peace and low prices of Old Manali, a collection of old guesthouses and backpacker cafes, sometimes set among orchards. New places are opening all the time so it's worth asking around. Old Manali is a 3km uphill walk from the Mall, which can be a real drag if you have a lot of gear. Auto-rick-

shaws cost Rs 35 uphill, but as little as Rs 10 back down.

Over the bridge, and to the right, there are a few places that are a little more expensive than in Old Manali proper but have a nice location next to the river and are closer to town. Some of the popular cheapos are the *Rising Moon*, *Mamta Paying Guest House* and *Jungle Bungalow*, all of which have doubles for about Rs 100.

Slightly more upmarket (and less intimate) places include the *Hotel Riverbank* at about Rs 300 a double; *Hotel Him View*, with good-value rooms from Rs 150 to Rs 400; and the *Hema Guest House* from Rs 150 to Rs 250 a double.

Over the bridge and up the hill to the left is the village itself.

Tourist Nest (☎ 56520) is a new place with clean bright doubles with hot-water bathroom for Rs 200 to Rs 250. Ground floor rooms open onto a small garden, while upper rooms have a small balcony; both are excellent value.

Dragon Guest House, opposite, is clean and modern with rooms for Rs 200 and Rs 250. It is surrounded by an apple orchard.

Nearby, the old wooden *Veer Paying Guest House*, and the concrete *Kishoor Guest House* both have a nice garden setting and sociable sitting area and charge around Rs 125 for clean rooms with bath.

Diplomat Guest House has good views, and costs up to Rs 100 a room.

Krishna Guest House, a little farther on, is run by a nice family. Rooms cost a reasonable Rs 75/120.

Dhungri A newer, grungy alternative to Old Manali and Vashisht, Dhungri village is an easy 2km walk west of the Mall. Several old village family homes have been converted to guesthouses with cheap rooms, shared bathrooms and more often than not, a surplus of techno music and dope. There are several cheap restaurants in the village. Most joints close down outside of the summer.

Freedom Paying Guest House costs Rs 100 a double.

Deodar Retreat has very basic rooms for Rs 40/60. New places are being built so it's best to just ask around. (Refer to the Dhungri Temple section for more details on how to get there.)

Places to Stay – Mid-Range

A lot of the mid-range places are new concrete hotels all lined up in the charmless, uninspiring 'suburb' called Model Town, one block west of the Mall. Each hotel offers almost identical facilities – usually including TV and hot water – for an almost identical price of around Rs 450 for a double, in season. But this is a good area for low-season bargains, especially in summer; many places offer rooms at half the normal price. Of the dozens to choose from, some of the better hotels (close to the post office) are: the **Mona Lisa** (☎ 52447), the **Hotel Shishar** (☎ 52745), the **Lhasa Hotel** (☎ 52134) and the **Premier Hotel** (☎ 52473).

Most of the other places in this range are on the main road between Manali and Old Manali, catering mainly for the Indian family and honeymoon market. There are dozens of places, all of which offer TV, hot water and, often, some seclusion in lovely gardens.

John Banon's Hotel (☎ 52335) is an old Raj-era building with clean, large rooms for Rs 1000-plus (not to be confused with the super swish, very expensive Banon Resorts, nearby).

Sunshine Guest House (☎ 52320) is another old-style place with a nice lawn and good rooms from Rs 350 to Rs 600.

Pinewood Hotel (☎ 52118) is another good choice run by the Banon family, with doubles for Rs 650.

A secluded bunch of hotels can be found five minutes' walk west of the main road.

Hotel Chetna (☎ 52245), painted red, has lovely views of the pine forest and rooms from Rs 250 to Rs 500.

Hotel Kalpana (☎ 52413) has nice and secluded doubles from Rs 300 to Rs 550.

Hotel New Highland (☎ 52399), a little farther up, has rooms from Rs 650.

The HPTDC runs several places – bookings can be arranged at the HPTDC Tourism Marketing Office on the Mall.

HPTDC Hotel Beas (☎ 52832), on the eastern side of the Mall, has great views of the river, and rooms from Rs 250 to Rs 550.

HPTDC Hotel Rohtang Manalsu (☎ 52332), on the road to the Dhungri Temple, is a nice place, with good views across the valley. Doubles cost from about Rs 450 to Rs 650.

Places to Stay – Top End

Many of these places provide little extra in the way of service and facilities than the better places in the mid-range.

Holiday Inn (☎ 52262, fax 52562) has all the luxury you would expect, but is several kilometres from town. Rooms, including meals, cost from Rs 2300.

Hotel Manali Ashok (☎ 52331), halfway between the Holiday Inn and town, is a huge place with luxurious rooms with views from Rs 1700 to Rs 2400.

Hotel Shrinagar Regency (☎ 52292) is a huge place dominating the western part of town. It has doubles from Rs 1650.

HPTDC Log Huts (☎ 52407) offers something a little unusual, just off the road to Old Manali. A luxury hut with two bedrooms costs from Rs 3000 to Rs 4000.

Hotel Ibex (☎ 52480), back in town on the Mall, has rooms from Rs 600 to Rs 1000 and a handy location.

HPTDC Hotel Kunzam (☎ 53197), also on the Mall, has good rooms for Rs 900 and Rs 1150, 30% less in the low season.

Places to Eat

Manali For western food, such as hamburgers, pizzas and milk shakes, the **Sa-Ba** in Nehru Park, at the top of the Mall, is good, and in a nice location.

HPTDC Juniper Restaurant, right near the bridge, offers a vast selection, in a good setting, but with higher prices.

Just about every restaurant, regardless of what sort of food it may serve during the day, opens from about 8 am to serve good, hot western breakfasts.

Sher-e-Punjab, on the Mall, has a sterile setting, but its Indian food (as well as pizza and pasta) is recommended, and is popular with Indian visitors.

Gozy Restaurant has good service and a great selection of authentic Punjabi and Gujarati food at a reasonable price. It's on the Mall.

Down a little alley called Mission Rd, just off the Mall, is a group of cheap little places, all serving great vegetarian food.

Mayur Restaurant is very popular, and has cosy decor.

Swamiji's Madras Cafe has large thalis for Rs 35.

Sangam and *Neel Kamal*, in the hotel of the same name, are also worth a try.

Mahadev Food Corner, a block south, has dirt cheap Indian food and a nice sitting area next to a Hindu temple and *dharamsala* (pilgrims' lodging) complex.

Mount View Restaurant and next door, *Chopsticks*, are cosy, highly recommended places where you can order genuine Chinese food – and not just chop suey – as well as momos or Japanese sukiyaki.

Moc Restaurant, near the Sukhiran Guest House, shares the same menu and kitchen as the Chopsticks but its prices are significantly lower!

Mona Lisa, opposite the bus station, is another congenial place, popular for its Indian and western food at reasonable prices.

Along the Mall are several *dhabas*, serving cheap, authentic Indian food – great places for a cup of chai and a couple of samosas. The *Kamal* and *Himalaya* are the best two around. In the Manu Market, there are also a couple of even cheaper dhabas.

Johnson's Cafe is farther uphill and a bit more upmarket. The pleasant open-air garden cafe serves good pasta and pizza (Rs 100), excellent desserts (crème caramel!) and cold beer. Fresh trout costs Rs 200.

Phuntsok Coffee House is a Tibetan-run place at the junction of the Naggar Highway and the road to Vashisht, and is the best place in the Manali area. It's worth coming from Vashisht, Manali (or just about anywhere in India) for, among other delights,

its apple, banana or walnut cakes or pies with custard. Everything mentioned here is highly recommended!

Old Manali The best places are over the bridge, and up the road towards the village. There are several pleasant outdoor places, which are worth a visit and are great for taking an extended coffee break and swapping travellers' tales. All cater exclusively to westerners, so you'll be lucky to find any real Indian cuisine.

Moon Dance Garden, just over the bridge, is a typical laid-back, outdoor place with one of the many local 'German Bakeries'. *Ish Cafe*, farther up, is deservedly popular.

Little Tibet Cafe, nearby, serves wholesome, cheap Tibetan food. *Shiva Garden Cafe*, also nearby, has good Italian food, and serves Israeli cuisine.

Mount View Cafe, a bit farther up, is worth a visit for its wonderfully secluded location.

Tibet Kitchen, back by the bridge, is by far your best bet, with an excellent range of hearty Tibetan noodles and also western delicacies.

Entertainment

The **HPTDC Club House**, near the bridge on the way to Old Manali, offers some activities. For a Rs 5 one day temporary membership, you have access to the nice, but pricey, bar and restaurant, and a library where you can read (but not borrow) English-language books. Table tennis and snooker can be played if you pay a few extra rupees.

Utopia Complex (☎ 53846) is a new leisure centre near the Dhungri Temple, which plans to offer a full size snooker table (Rs 100 per hour), steam bath, gymnasium (Rs 25 per session) and carom (billiard-like game played with discs) boards, as well as a restaurant and small museum.

Shopping

There are plenty of places to buy clothes and souvenirs in Manali, particularly along the Mall. These places often claim to have 'fixed prices' but this is not strictly true. Some of the better places are the Charitrust Tibetan Handicraft Emporium on the Mall, or any of the cooperatives run by local women, such as the Kullu-Kashmir Handicraft Coop, opposite the bus station. For a top quality pashmina shawl (pashmina is shorn from the underbelly of the Ladakh snow goat) expect to pay upwards of Rs 10,000. Traditional pillbox-style hats (Afghan, Kullu and Kinnauri) are quite cheap.

Roadside stalls spring up in the evenings, especially around the Gozy Restaurant and the bus station. The Tibetan Market, spread around the back of the Hotel Ibex, has a good range of thangkas and silver and turquoise jewellery, but you'll find higher quality at the Tibetan and Nepalese shops near the post office. Manali has a better selection of woollen clothes than Leh, and better prices too.

For an indulgence, try some of the locally made pickles, jams and juices, made from apples and apricots and other fruits and nuts. Himcoop on the Mall is a good place to look. Natural oils for massages and shampoos are also available.

Getting There & Away

Air Manali's nearest airport is at Bhuntar, 52km south of Manali and 10km south of Kullu town. Refer to Getting There & Away in the Kullu town section for details on flights. There are no flights between Manali/Kullu (Bhuntar) and Leh. You can make bookings at the Jagson Airlines office (☎ 52843) in the north of Manali town (Visa cards accepted), and at most travel agencies. The official office for Archana Airways is Ambassador Travels (☎ 52110), next to the State Bank of India.

Bus The bus station is normally well organised. There are two booths – open 9 am to noon, and 2 to 5 pm – which provide computerised booking services. You can book a ticket up to a month in advance, which is very useful in the high season.

The companies that do long-distance trips from Manali (and local sightseeing tours) are listed below. Tickets can be bought from the respective bus companies or from any other travel agency in Manali.

Enn Bee Tours & Travels
  (☎ 52650) The Mall (opposite the bus station)
Harrison Travel
  (☎ 53319) The Mall
Ibex Travels
  (☎ 52480) Hotel Ibex, The Mall
Swagtam Tours
  (☎ 52390) Mission Rd

Leh Several daily deluxe and public buses connect Manali with Leh from about early July to mid-September, though the road is normally open several weeks before and after this. Private buses run up to a month later than the public buses according to the weather and the demand. This is a long, but truly spectacular, ride over two days, with a stopover at a tent site (normally Sarchu). Manali is not very high (2050m), so if you're not used to higher altitudes, take care along the way, especially at Baralacha La (4883m), Taglang La (5328m) and Sarchu (4100m). HPTDC runs a daily bus (which originates in Delhi) for Rs 1000, including overnight camp at Sarchu, dinner and breakfast, or Rs 700 without extras. Private agencies such as Enn Bee, Ibex and Swagtam cost around Rs 800 but normally don't include food or accommodation. Public buses cost from Rs 345 to Rs 525 and normally stop for the night at Keylong. Take some food, water and warm clothes and try not to sit at the back of the bus.

For details about the route, see Leh to Manali in the Ladakh & Zanskar chapter.

Kullu & Parvati Valleys Public buses shuttle between Manali and Kullu town every 15 minutes (Rs 25, two hours). Most buses travel via the quicker, western bank of the Beas. To Naggar (Rs 10, one hour), there are six daily buses from Manali, leaving every hour or so from 9.30 am.

Along the Parvati Valley, six public buses leave Manali from 6.30 am to 1.30 pm

Warning

! Beware of low-hanging power lines on the trip between Manali and Dharamsala if you're riding on the roof of the bus.

every day to Manikaran (Rs 35, 3½ hours). Alternatively get a bus to Bhuntar and change, as buses run from here to Manikaran until around 6pm.

Other Places   To Delhi (16 hours), every day in summer there is one public 'deluxe' bus (Rs 345), one semideluxe (Rs 298), at least one overnight HPTDC bus (Rs 450), and usually several overnight private buses (about Rs 400). Private companies and HPTDC also run daily buses, in season, to Shimla (Rs 250 to Rs 275, 10 hours), Dharamsala (Rs 250 to Rs 275, 10 hours), and Chandigarh (Rs 300, 10 hours). With demand, there may be private buses to Jammu and Dalhousie (Rs 400). You may find prices a little less in the low season.

Public bus services include:

destination	fare (Rs)	departs
Chandigarh	105	6 daily
Delhi	298*	5 daily
Dharamsala	131	3 daily (10 hrs)
Keylong	57	5 morning (6 hrs)
Mandi	45	5 daily (5 hrs)
Shimla	140*	4 daily

*semideluxe

For Spiti, catch the 4 am departure to Tabo (Rs 130, 14 hours) or the 6 am bus to Kaza (Rs 100, 12 hours).

Taxi   Long-distance taxis are available from the two Him-Aanchal Taxi Operators Union stands (☎ 52450 24 hours) on the Mall. A one-way/return taxi from Manali to Kullu is Rs 500/700, or Rs 850 returning via Naggar. A one-way/return to Naggar only is

Rs 300/400, to Solang Nullah is Rs 225/300 and to Manikaran is Rs 1000/1100. Other one-way fares include Kaza (Rs 5000), Dharamsala (Rs 2500), Keylong (Rs 2400) and Leh (Rs 11,000 for three days, two nights).

Getting Around

To/From the Airport   For buses between Bhuntar airport and Manali, take a regular Bhuntar-Kullu and a regular Kullu-Manali bus, or there may be a less regular one that goes directly between the airport and Manali. A taxi between Manali and Bhuntar costs around Rs 600.

Taxi   Taxis offer sightseeing trips to Vashisht, Old Manali and a couple of local temples for Rs 300, but this trip can be done just as easily on foot, or more cheaply in an auto-rickshaw. Taxi prices are fixed; the minimum charge is Rs 35; waiting costs Rs 40 per hour.

Auto-Rickshaw   Known locally as three-wheelers, these can take you, and your heavy luggage, to Dhungri, Old Manali and Vashisht, but not much farther, for a negotiable Rs 30 to Rs 40.

Motorcycle   There are several places to hire bikes in Old Manali and Vashisht, however only in summer. Nirvana Travels (☎ 53222), in north Manali, hires Enfields for Rs 275 per 24 hours, which includes third party insurance. For bike repairs or a tune-up before heading up to Leh, which is a good idea, try Inder Motors in Manali's Tibetan area or The Enfield Club by the turn-off to Vashisht.

AROUND MANALI
Vashisht

Vashisht is a lovely little village, high up on the hillside, about 4km from the Mall by road. Its hot springs are a great way to relax after a trek or the long trip from Leh, and a good place to go if your hotel has no hot water. There are several decaying temples in the village dedicated to the sage Vashisht Muni and the god Rama.

The footpath and road to Vashisht go straight past the **HPTDC Vashisht Hot Baths Complex**, which is open daily 8 am to 8 pm. It is a large area, full of little Turkish-style sauna rooms, where you can bathe in the hot sulphurous water. A 30 minute soak in the regular baths costs Rs 40 for one person, Rs 50 for two, or splash out in the deluxe baths for Rs 100 for two people. There's a cafe here. The common public baths (separate areas for men and women) in Vashisht village are free, but don't look very hygienic. These baths are open from 5 am to 9 pm every day.

Places to Stay Vashisht remains a very popular place for long-term budget travellers, who are attracted by its cheap facilities, great setting, and the availability of some locally grown 'horticultural products'. Most convenient places to stay are along the road leading up to the village, or crowded around the village centre and the temple.

New Dharma, a bit of a walk behind the temple, and the *Bodh, Amrit* and *Kalptaru* guesthouses all offer very similar, no-frills, older-style accommodation in the heart of the village, usually with a shared bathroom, from about Rs 60 and up to Rs 100 for a room.

Anand Hotel is newer and more clinical, but good value, with spacious rooms with bath for Rs 100. There are plans to open an Internet cafe here soon.

Just down the road from the village centre, the cheaper, Tibetan-style *Sonam* and *Janta* guesthouses have basic rooms from Rs 60.

Surabhi Hotel is more expensive, but still good value, with nice rooms, great views and a *real* bath with hot water for Rs 250 or Rs 350 – about half that in the low season.

Hotel Bhrigu (☎ 01902-8240), and the excellent *Hotel Valley View*, next door, offer good rooms and great views from Rs 300 to Rs 500 a room.

Places to Eat The cafe at the *HPTDC Hot Baths Complex* serves hot and cold drinks, and a selection of pretty good Chinese and Indian food.

Rose Garden Inn, across the road, has great views and pricey, but delicious, Italian and other 'continental' food.

Super Bake, in the village next to the temple, serves wonderful baked goodies, and one or two places around here provide cheap, authentic food.

Ranu Rooftop Cafe or the *Zodiac Cafe* are both good places to hang out.

Freedom Cafe, just down the road a bit, has a great outdoor setting, and serves pretty good western breakfasts and Israeli food, although it's a little more expensive than it used to be.

Hotel Valley View offers something a bit more upmarket, with daily specials and good views.

Getting There & Away Vashisht is connected by a good road, so a three-wheeler can take you there for around Rs 40 – which is a good idea, especially if you have loads of gear. On foot, it's quicker to take the unmarked trail, which starts about 200m past the turn-off to Vashisht, and goes all the way to the Hotel Valley View, via the HPTDC Hot Baths.

Solang Nullah

Some of Himachal Pradesh's best ski slopes are at Solang Nullah, about 13km northwest of Manali. There are 2.5km of runs, with black, red and blue routes mainly for beginners, and one 300m ski lift. February and March are the best months to ski; January is bitterly cold, and Christmas time can be busy with Indian tourists. But don't disregard Solang if it isn't snowing; the area is very pretty in spring and summer. If you want some seclusion, Solang Nullah is worth a stay for a few days. This is outstanding hiking country and a perfect place to day-trip out to when there's no snow.

There are several options for skiing courses. (Refer to the Travel Agencies section under Manali for details of agencies there involved in skiing.) Prices quoted here are only a guide – final prices will depend

HIMACHAL PRADESH

Treks from Manali & the Kullu Valley

There are many trekking possibilities out of the Kullu Valley. These include a number of five-day introductory treks such as the trek from Prini village over the Hampta Pass (4270m) to the Chandra Valley and Lahaul; the trek from Jagatsukh to the base of Deo Tibba and the trek from Naggar over the Chandrakhani Pass (3650m) to Malana and the Parvati Valley. There is also a more challenging trek from Manikaran in the Parvati Valley over the Pin Parvati Pass (4810m) to the Pin Valley and Spiti. See also LP's *Trekking in the Indian Himalaya*.

These treks can be completed in the brief pre-monsoon period in June before the Kullu Valley is subject to the first of the monsoon rains. The heaviest monsoon rains fall from early August through to mid-September. A settled period from mid-September until mid-October follows before the onset of the winter snows.

Experienced trekking agencies in Manali can organise trekking arrangements from US$50 per person per day. If making your own arrangements porters can be hired from around Rs 120 to Rs 150 per day, while pack horses with attendants cost upwards of Rs 150 per horse per day depending on the trek and the number of horses being hired. Tents and trekking equipment are not usually hired out by the agencies unless you are undertaking an inclusive trek. All food supplies should be purchased in Manali or Kullu as most treks go beyond the villages on at least some stages of the trek.

Manali to Chandra Valley via the Hampta Pass

This trek, one of the most popular in Himachal Pradesh, commences from Prini village climbing steadily to the village of Sythen. The trail then enters the meadows and conifer forests of the Hampta Valley. There is no shortage of idyllic camp sites leading to the base of the Hampta Pass (4270m). The climb to the pass is not unduly demanding. From the pass the peaks of Deo Tibba (6001m) and Indrasan (6221m) can be appreciated in the vicinity of the pass, while the summit of Hanuman Tibba (5928m) can also be seen on the far side of the Kullu Valley. The descent to the Chandra Valley and the settlement at Chatru takes another stage.

From Chatru, you can take a bus to Manali or continuing up the Chandra Valley to Chandra Tal and the Baralacha La – an interesting option if travelling on to Leh and the Indus Valley.

Stage 1	Prini village to Sythen and camp	(3-4 hrs)
Stage 2	Camp to Chikha	(3-4 hrs)
Stage 3	Chikha to Bhalu ka kera	(3 hrs)
Stage 4	Bhalu ka kera to Shiliguri via Hampta Pass	(7 hrs)
Stage 5	Shiliguri to Chatru	(3 hrs)

Chandra Tal & Baralacha La Option

Stage 6	Chatru to Chota Dara	(5-6 hrs)
Stage 7	Chota Dara to Batal	(5-6 hrs)
Stage 8	Batal to Chandra Tal	(6-7 hrs)
Stage 9	Chandra Tal to Tokpo Yongma	(6 hrs)
Stage 10	Tokpo Yongma to Tokpo Gongma	(6-7 hrs)
Stage 11	Tokpo Gongma to Baralacha La	(4 hrs)

Jagatsukh to the Base of Deo Tibba

This delightful trek commences from the village of Jagatsukh (8km south of Manali), winding through a series of villages to the grazing pastures at Khanol. From here there is a steady climb (steep in places) to the Gujjar shepherd camp at Chikha. The trail then heads through silver birch trees and flowered meadows to a magnificent camp set beneath huge hanging glaciers flowing from Deo Tibba (6001m). From the Gaddi shepherd camp at Serai a day trek

Treks from Manali & the Kullu Valley

can be made to the terminal glacial moraine at the base of Deo Tibba. The final stage back to Jagatsukh can be completed with time to catch the bus back to Manali the same day.

Stage 1	Jagatsukh to Khanol	(2-3 hrs)
Stage 2	Khanol to Chikha	(4- 5 hrs)
Stage 3	Chikha to Serai	(4-5 hrs)
Stage 4	Serai to Deo Tibba base and return	(7 hrs)
Stage 5	Serai to Jagatsukh	(7 hrs)

Naggar to the Parvati Valley via the Chandrakhani Pass and Malana

The village of Malana is an isolated community that has its own language, customs and law, governed by a system of village elders. The village beliefs are determined by the god Jumla, said to be pre-Aryan and independent of the Hindu gods that reside in the Kullu Valley. It is believed that the existence of the village is recorded in the Mughal annals. Until quite recently the villagers resisted outsiders from even passing through the area.

To reach Malana we trek from Naggar village and complete a long, steady climb through mixed forest and open meadows to the Chandrakhani Pass (3650m). From the pass there are bird's-eye views across to the upper Kullu Valley and to many of the peaks at the head of the Bara Shingri Glacier. The descent to Malana is steep even for the sure footed. After visiting the village there is a further stage to the Parvati Valley to the road head at Jari and the bus back to the Kullu Valley and Manali.

Stage 1	Naggar to camp above Rumsu village	(2-3 hrs)
Stage 2	Camp to base of Chandrakhani Pass	(5-6 hrs)
Stage 3	Camp to Malana village via Chandrakhani Pass	(6 hrs)
Stage 4	Malana to Jari	(4-5 hrs)

Manikaran to Spiti Valley via the Pin Parvati Pass

From Manikaran, a well-defined trail leads to the village of Pulga – the highest village in the Parvati Valley. It's a further stage to the hot springs at Khirganga where, after a day's bathing and meditation, there is the option to return direct to Manikaran. Beyond Khirganga the trail enters mixed conifer and deciduous forest before reaching a series of open meadows where Gaddi shepherds graze their flocks throughout the summer months. These stages include crossing the famous Pandu bridge, a natural rock bridge over the Parvati River, before reaching the rich alpine pastures alongside Mantakal lake. Beyond the glacially fed lake the trek becomes harder, ascending extensive moraine and boulder fields to the base of the Pin Parvati Pass (4810m). The pass is located at the head of a small snowfield and affords fine views of the Greater Himalaya Range while to the north the Zanskar Range can be appreciated beyond the Spiti Valley. Once over the pass it is two stages to the village of Sangam and the daily bus service to Kaza, the headquarters of Spiti region.

Stage 1	Manikaran to Pulga	(4-5 hrs)
Stage 2	Pulga to Khirganga	(4-5 hrs)
Stage 3	Khirganga to Bhojtunda	(5 hrs)
Stage 4	Bhojtunda to Thakur Khan	(4-5 hrs)
Stage 5	Thakur Khan to Mantakal Lake	(6-hrs)
Stage 6	Mantakal Lake to base of Pin Parvati Pass	(7 hrs)
Stage 7	Camp to Pin Valley camp via Pin Parvati Pass	(5 hrs)
Stage 8	Camp to Mud village	(8-9 hrs)
Stage 9	Mud village to Sangam	(4-5 hours)

HIMACHAL PRADESH

on the size of the group, type of accommodation and level of service:

HPTDC organises seven-day skiing packages. These include accommodation in Manali (which is not the least bit convenient if the road between Manali and Solang is snowed under), food, lessons and some sightseeing for Rs 3500 per person, from Manali. Some travellers have written complaining about poor tuition and service.

Antrek Tours in Manali, through the Raju Paying Guest House in Solang Nullah, offers seven to 10-day packages, including accommodation, all meals, porters and instruction, for around Rs 700 per day; Rs 200 extra per day for ski-gear hire. The Friendship Hotel in Solang offers similar week-long packages.

North Face Adventure Tours charges Rs 4660 for one week, Rs 3560 for three nights, four days, Rs 2860 two nights, two days; all inclusive, with accommodation in Solang.

Himalayan Journeys offers a week long course from Rs 6000 per person in a group of four to Rs 7500 for individual tuition. A two week course is Rs 11,000. Prices include accommodation, guide and equipment.

Himalayan Adventures runs a basic seven day course (minimum five persons) for Rs 3000.

The Mountaineering Institute & Allied Sports runs basic, intermediate and advanced all inclusive 15-day courses for US$262, which includes rental of gear, food and dormitory accommodation near the slopes – but not transport.

Places to Stay & Eat   All places are in the tiny, picturesque village, only a few hundred metres below the ski slopes. Prices listed are for the high season, but they will probably halve in the low season.

Friendship Guest House is a small place with large rooms for Rs 300, and Rs 150 for smaller rooms with a common bathroom.

Raju Paying Guest House has large doubles with nice wood panelling for Rs 200, or Rs 300 for a room with up to four beds.

North Face offers a more basic, but still comfortable, alternative but caters mainly for prearranged skiing packages.

Each hotel serves large plates of simple, hot vegetarian food, accompanied by loads of tea. There are several other good restaurants around the village catering to the tourist crowd, but these are usually closed in the low season.

Getting There & Away   Buses leave Manali at 8 am, and 1 and 4 pm every day to Solang Nullah (Rs 7). A nicer way is to take the bus to Palchan, the turn-off to Solang Nullah from the main road, and then walk for about an hour to Solang through gorgeous countryside. Taxis cost Rs 225/300 one-way/return from Manali. Roads may be blocked by snow in January and February.

Rohtang Pass
The Rohtang Pass crosses the massive Pir Panjal Range and links the Kullu and Lahaul valleys. Though not without its dangers (Rohtang means Pile of Corpses in Tibetan), the wide pass has for centuries served as an essential link on the trade routes to Leh, Yarkand and Kashgar. At 3978m it's now a popular place for excitable Bangali (Bengali) tourists to touch their first snow. There are several tea stalls where you can take in the stunning views of Sonapani Glacier to the north. The pass is 51km from Manali, and you can get there on any bus to Keylong.

Lahaul & Spiti

Best Time to Go: Lahaul (mid-Jun to late Oct); Spiti (Aug to Oct)
Region Isolated by Snows: Lahaul (mid-Nov to mid-Jun); Spiti (mid-Oct to mid-Jul)

Lahaul and Spiti, the largest district in Himachal Pradesh, is a vast area of high mountains and narrow valleys bound by Ladakh to the north, Tibet to the east, Kinnaur to the southeast and the Kullu Valley to the south. The Lahaul and Spiti valleys are quite distinct. Lahaul is often regarded simply as a midway point en route to Leh but it also has some little-visited gompas, Hindu temples and is the starting/finishing point for some great treks. The desolate but very beautiful Spiti Valley has only recently been opened to foreign tourists attracted to its friendly people, isolated Ladakhi-style scenery and superb Tibetan Buddhist gompas.

Lahaul consists of two regions – upper Lahaul, which includes the Chandra and Bhaga valleys, and lower Lahaul, which comprises the region of the Chenab Valley below the confluence of the Chandra and Bhaga rivers. Lahaul is wedged between the main Himalaya Range to the north, and the peaks of the Pir Panjal Range to the south.

The Spiti Valley is squeezed between the Himalaya and the Zanskar ranges. It is climatically very similar to Ladakh and consists mainly of high-altitude desert, though there are surprisingly rich pastures 600m above the valley floor. Spiti translates as Middle Land and has traditionally been divided into Sham (around Tabo), Pin, Bhar (around Kaza) and Tud (around Losar).

Both Lahaul and Spiti are cut off by heavy snow from the Kullu Valley for up to eight months of the year. The road over the Rohtang Pass linking the Kullu Valley and Lahaul was completed in the 1960s, and it is only relatively recently that a motorable road was constructed from Lahaul to Spiti over the 4551m Kunzum La. To combat Lahaul's winter isolation, a tunnel under the Pir Panjal is supposedly being constructed to provide year-round access to the Kullu Valley.

Both Lahaul and Spiti are cut off by heavy snow from the Kullu Valley for up to eight months of the year.

History

In many ways Lahaul and Spiti's historical backgrounds run parallel with that of Ladakh. Accounts recall how sages crossed the Rohtang Pass and the Baralacha La en route to Ladakh. In the 10th century, upper Lahaul was united with Spiti and Zanskar as part of the vast Guge kingdom of western Tibet. It then came under Ladakhi influence, which at this time stretched to the upper limits of the Kullu Valley.

Although political allegiances changed over the centuries, it was Ladakh's defeat by the Mongol-Tibetan armies in the 18th century that led to Lahaul being split into two regions. Upper Lahaul came under the influence of the Kullu raja, while lower Lahaul, across to the district of Pangi, came under the influence of the courts of Chamba. Trade agreements evolved between Kullu and Ladakh, and Lahaul was considered neutral territory. Records say trade was conducted during the summer months in a series of camps on the vast Lingti Plains, just beyond the Baralacha La at the junction of trails to Ladakh, Zanskar, Spiti and Lahaul.

Spiti has always been more isolated than Lahaul. It did not command any major trading crossroads and paid tribute to Ladakh until the Dogra army under Zorawar Singh installed a governor for a brief period between 1834 and 1839.

After the annexation of Kullu in 1841, the Sikhs extended their power north across Lahaul and for a time the entire region came under the influence of Ranjit Singh. Spiti remained part of Ladakh until 1846.

In 1847, Kullu and Lahaul came under the British administration as a division of the Kangra state, while Spiti became part of the newly formed maharaja's state of Jammu & Kashmir. However, in 1849 it was exchanged for other territories and came under the Kangra administration.

Under British administration, the region's trails were upgraded, and bridges were constructed along the main trading highways that linked Kullu, Lahaul and Spiti. Records recount how huge logs were hauled over the Rohtang Pass by upwards of 200 porters, while the system of *begar*, or forced labour, was the only means contractors had for improving the roads.

While the Nonos, or rulers, of Spiti tended to confine their trading activities to the Tibetan borderlands, the Thakurs of Lahaul secured many valuable trade agreements with Kullu and the towns to the south.

With the Chinese occupation of Tibet in 1949, the region's cultural links were cut. The exile of the Dalai Lama has, ironically, seen a resurgence in the cultural and religious life of Spiti. At the same time, improved communications set into motion after the 1962 Sino-Indian War have seen a

KINNAUR & SPITI

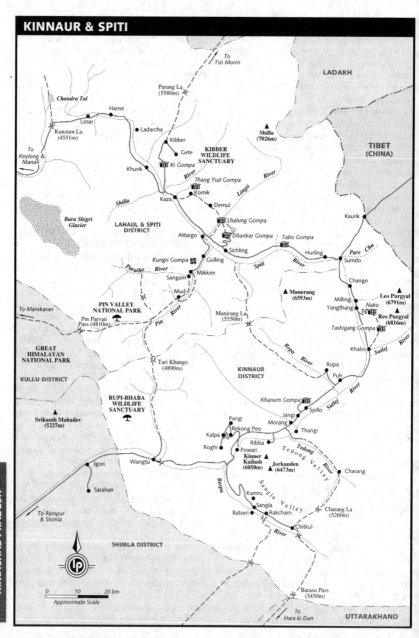

HIMACHAL PRADESH

rapid integration with the rest of India and the growth of a cash economy.

People & Culture

In Spiti and parts of Lahaul, most people are Tibetan Buddhists, and gompas and their lamas dominate village life. The main valleys are split between the Drukpa Kagyud (Lahaul), Gelukpa (Spiti) and Nyingmapa (Pin Valley) orders. In Lahaul, about half population is Hindu. In some Lahauli temples and homes, it is not unusual to see idols from both religions side by side.

The people of Lahaul and Spiti congregate into communal groups *(kotchis)*, which are then divided into smaller groups *(puttees)*. Farms, which are usually inherited by the eldest son, rely on natural springs or complicated irrigation systems, to grow crops. Barley *(no)*, wheat *(do)*, potatoes *(alu)* and peas are the main crops and goats, sheep, yaks and *dzo* (a cross between a cow and a yak) are reared. Lahaul and Spiti are the only areas in India where hops are grown, mainly for the manufacture of beer. *Kuth*, a famous medicinal herb, is exported to Europe.

Food and drink in the region is similar to Tibet and Ladakh – noodles called *thukpa*; fried or steamed dumplings called *momos*; *tsampa*, which is cooked or raw barley flour; *churpe*, dried cheese; barley beer called *chang*; yak butter tea; and a bread made from buckwheat called *kalhu*. A ubiquitous sight in most homes is the *dongpo* (butter tea churner).

During ceremonies and festivals, men and women sometimes decorate themselves with silver, amber and coral jewellery called *murki* and *kyanti*; women sometimes wear similar items called *kirkistsi*. The men in the region often wear a long thick coat called a *cholu*, fastened at the waist by a *gachi* (rope) – but this sort of traditional dress is slowly being replaced by modern clothes. You may see the men play a high-volume Tibetan dice game called *cholo*.

The main indigenous language of the area is Bhoti, which is very similar to Tibetan. There are several distinct, but mutually comprehensible, dialects in the region, such as Machat (spoken around Udaipur) and Gaheri (found near Keylong). If you have travelled to Ladakh, you'll be glad to know that the very handy word *jule* (pronounced Joo-Lay), which means hello, goodbye, please and thank you, is also used in Lahaul and Spiti.

Permits

Inner line permits are not necessary for travel from Lahaul to Spiti and you are now permitted to go as far down valley as Tabo. A permit is only necessary if you're travelling between Tabo and Rekong Peo, the capital of Kinnaur. For more information see the boxed text in the Kinnaur section.

When to Go

The area is very pleasant in summer (June to September) when it is warm during the day and the nights are cool. Both Lahaul and Spiti are effectively isolated from the annual monsoon so there is little rain. In winter, there is plenty of snow, which cuts off Lahaul, north Spiti and upper Kinnaur for six or seven months a year, and temperatures can drop to -30°C.

The Rohtang Pass to Lahaul is normally closed between mid-November and mid-June and the Kunzum La to Spiti is usually closed from mid-October to mid-July. A daily bus usually manages to run up the Sutlej Valley to Kaza year-round, except during periods of heavy snowfall in January and February. Beware of the burning power of the sun in this region – you can get burnt very easily even on cold days.

MANALI TO KEYLONG

At the northern base of the Rohtang Pass, **Gramphu** is the junction for the roads to Leh and Spiti. There are a couple of dhabas where you can wait for the bus to Keylong or Kaza. Five kilometres farther, **Khoksar** is regarded as the coldest inhabited place in Himachal Pradesh. There's a police checkpoint here and you'll need to get out and sign the register. Single women travellers have reported harassment here so be on your toes, especially at night or if you smell alcohol on anyone's breath.

The road continues on to Gondla, site of the seven storey **castle** of the thakur of Gondla and the starting point for a visit to the wooden **Guru Ghantal Gompa** at the village of Tupchiling, a steep 4km away. Founded about 800 years ago, but repaired extensively about 30 years ago, the gompa is linked to the one at Stakna, near Leh in Ladakh, and belongs to the Drukpa order. You can also hike to Tupchiling from **Tandi**, where the Bhaga and Chandra rivers join to form the Chenab.

KEYLONG
☎ 019002 • alt 3350m

Located in the small but fertile Bhaga Valley, Keylong, the capital of Lahaul and Spiti, is a reasonable place to break up the journey from Leh to Manali (although you're almost at Manali anyway) and is a good base for day hikes to several nearby Tibetan monasteries.

The bus station is on the main Manali-Leh road, from where it's a short walk down a series of steps to the town itself. There's a telegraph office in the north of town but nowhere to change money.

Drilbu Adventures (☎ 22207), next to the Gyespa Hotel, is a new travel agency that can help arrange porters and transport to Leh. Darcha, around 20km north-east, is the trail head for the week long trek to Padum (see the Treks In Zanskar boxed text in the Zanskar section of the Ladakh & Zanskar chapter).

Places to Stay & Eat
There are a couple of very basic dosshouses on the main road but the decent hotels are in the lower town.

Lamayuru Hotel is a good budget bet; spacious, but damp rooms with hot-water bathroom are Rs 125.

Gyespa Hotel, opposite, has dreary singles/doubles for Rs 100/150 and is an emergency option only.

Hotel Dubchen Keylong, nearby, is better, with doubles for Rs 175 downstairs or Rs 250 for brighter rooms upstairs, with a sunny balcony. All rooms have hot-water bathroom.

Hotel Snowland (☎ *22219)*, two minutes' uphill from the Lamayuru, has comfortable rooms with nice bath from Rs 300 to Rs 450.

HPTDC Tourist Bungalow (☎ *22247)* has a few overpriced doubles at Rs 350, and some dorm beds (six in a room) for Rs 50.

Hotel Dekyid (☎ *22217)* is a secluded place past the Tourist Bungalow. It is a favourite of adventure tour groups, with clean rooms for around Rs 300.

Tashi Deleg is another mid-range place with carpeted rooms with bath for Rs 200, Rs 300 and Rs 350.

The restaurants at the *Gyespa* and pricier *Tashi Deleg* are the best. There are numerous dhabas on the main road and a couple of dirt-cheap chow mien places in town itself.

Getting There & Away
Six daily buses travel between Keylong and Manali (Rs 57, six hours); book your ticket in advance at the ticket office. To Kaza there are sometimes direct buses; otherwise change at Gramphu.

From 15 July to 15 September the daily long-distance deluxe HPTDC buses between Leh and Manali stop in Keylong but it's very hard to get a confirmed seat. You may have to book the ticket from Manali to Leh and pay the full whack. The public bus costs about half the HPTDC price of Rs 600 and leaves Keylong at 4 am. Plenty of trucks ply the busy road and are a good alternative. (Refer to the Leh to Manali section in the Ladakh & Zanskar chapter for more details on travel to and from Keylong.)

AROUND KEYLONG
Shashur Gompa
High on the hillside above Keylong is the yellow Shashur Gompa (Shashur means Among the Blue Pines). Dedicated to the Zanskari missionary Deva Gyatso, the 16th century monastery is of the Drukpa Kagyud order. There are two main halls, currently undergoing reconstruction. The lower hall features a central Sakyamuni Buddha, in front of which is an image of Deva Gyatso. The left wall has murals of the Tibetan

saints Marpa, Milarepa (with his hand cupped behind his ear), Naropa and Tila – the founders of the Drukpa order.

An annual chaam festival, held every June or July (depending on the Tibetan calendar), is renowned for the mask dances performed by the lamas and the unfurling of a 5m-long thangka.

To get to the gompa follow the steep 3km (45 minute) horse trail that leads off the main road, 200m north of the bus station.

Khardong Gompa

The 900-year-old gompa at Khardong, formerly a capital of Lahaul, lies directly across the Bhaga Valley from Keylong. This Drukpa Kagyud monastery is the largest in the area with about 30 lamas and *chomos* (nuns). There are excellent frescoes on the 1st floor, a huge prayer wheel, and a famous library of ancient Kangyur and Tangyur scriptures, though you'll have to track down a nun to open the doors for you.

To get to the monastery head through the bazaar, follow the stepped path down to the hospital, continue to the bridge over the raging Bhaga River and then hike up the steep hillside to Khardong village.

Tayal Gompa

Four kilometres north of Keylong on the road to Leh, above the village of Satingri, is a gompa called Tayal, which means Chosen Place in Tibetan. The 300-year-old gompa has a library, a fine collection of thangkas and a 4m-high statue of Padmasambhava.

You could hitch the 4km or jump on a bus. The path up to the monastery leads off the main road just after a large tributary *nullah* (stream). It's possible to walk back to Keylong on the eastern side of the valley, via Khardong Gompa, but you'd have to ask directions to find the bridge over the Bhaga River.

Pattan Valley

The upper section of the Chenab Valley, from Tandi to Udaipur, is sometimes known as the Pattan Valley. It is a little-visited area, regularly bypassed by tourists travelling between Manali and Keylong, but not by the thousands of pilgrims who flock to the Triloknath Temple every August for the three day Pauri Festival.

The main town in the valley, **Udaipur**, has its own finely carved wooden temple, built in the 15th century and dedicated to the goddess Markula Devi. About 16km before Udaipur is the ancient **Triloknath Temple**, on a bluff near the village of Tunde. Once a Hindu temple, then rededicated to Buddhism with a white marble six-armed image of Avalokiteshvara, it is now sacred to followers of both religions, resulting in a curious mix of Buddhist prayer flags and the Hindu trident, lingam and Nandi bull. You can walk around the prayer wheels to see the original Hindu architecture. There are some strong Kashmiri influences in the temple's design.

Udaipur has a PWD and Forestry *Resthouse* and some basic *guesthouses*.

Buses ply the treacherous road from Keylong to Triloknath (Rs 23, three hours) and Udaipur at 10 and 11 am and 4 pm. From the main road it's a 4km uphill walk or hitch to the Triloknath Temple. A shorter path leads behind the Triloknath Temple, past a local school, back down to the main road, where you can catch the last bus back to Keylong between 4 and 5 pm. There are also direct daily buses to/from Manali.

MANALI TO KAZA

From the Gramphu junction, the bone-shaking 'road' heads up the boulder-strewn and heavily glaciated Chandra Valley. **Chatru**, 17km on, is the trail head for treks over the Hamta Pass to Manali and there are a couple of guesthouses in the village above the road. Batal, 24km farther, is the starting point for treks to nearby **Bara Shigri** (Big Glacier), up to 10km long and 1km wide, and one of the longest glaciers in the Himalaya. There are a couple of *dhabas* offering food.

From here the road switches back up to the stunning **Kunzum La** (4551m), where everyone piles out of the bus to do a kora of the flag-strewn Geypan Temple. From the pass, a 9km trail branches off to lovely

Chandra Tal (Moon Lake), at about 4250m, and continues to Baralacha La, on the road to Leh. There's a basic shelter on the pass and you could possibly spend the night here if you have a very good down sleeping bag and are properly acclimatised.

The first main village on the Spiti side is the pleasant hamlet of Losar (4079m), about 60km from Kaza. There are a couple of places to stay for Rs 50 to Rs 100, including the *Sam Song Hotel* and the *Kunzum* and *Sarchu* dhabas. A new gompa is being built nearby.

KAZA
☎ 01906 • alt 3640m

Kaza is the major transport hub and administrative centre of Spiti subdistrict. It's an easy-going place to spend a few days – to rest from the arduous bus trips, to visit some stunning monasteries or to wait for your inner line permit if you're headed on to Kinnaur.

Orientation & Information
Kaza's 'old town', around the new bus stand, is a maze of little shops, hotels and white-washed houses. The 'new town', across the creek, is a collection of tin-roofed government buildings, including the Sub-Divisional Magistrate's office (look for the Indian flag).

KD Studio, in the old town, develops three passport photos for Rs 60 and there are a couple of places nearby to make photocopies. The State Bank of India doesn't change money, though some shopkeepers might exchange small denomination US dollar notes.

There's a small Sakyapa gompa on the main road in new Kaza but there are more interesting gompas not too far away.

Places to Stay & Eat
In the old town, there are a couple of very average places by the bus stand. The charmless *Zambala Hotel* offers acceptable rooms for Rs 150, while *Rupa Sweets*, opposite, has a few cheap rooms if you can raise them from their torpor.

Mahabauda Guest House, at the top end of the old town by the main road, is a much better choice. This family-run place has cosy rooms with common bath for Rs 100 or Rs 150, excellent Tibetan cuisine and an in-house Tibetan doctor.

Snow Lion Hotel & Restaurant, next door, is also friendly and good value with clean rooms for Rs 100 or Rs 130. The food is also good here.

Milarepa Guesthouse, just across the creek, is quite basic, with good-value but scruffy singles/doubles for Rs 100/150.

Sakya's Abode (☎ 22254), next door, is a favourite of tour groups and set in a lovely garden. Good rooms cost Rs 200, Rs 300 and Rs 500 and there are dark and gloomy singles for Rs 100 and dorm beds for Rs 50. A bucket of hot water costs Rs 5.

Khangsar Hotel & Restaurant is about 500m from Milarepa's, on the main road to the north, and is a bit far out to be convenient. Musty rooms cost Rs 150 and Rs 200.

HPTDC Tourist Lodge, also in the new town, has five rooms with hot-water bathroom for Rs 300.

Sakya's Abode has a great dining hall, with good Spitian food, basic Indian meals and breakfast.

Layul Cafe is the best-value place in the old town and you can get a huge bowl of excellent *kiyu* (square noodles, potato, tomato and onion stew) here for Rs 25. Other places for food include the Tibetan-style *Ladakhi Hotel* and *Himalaya Hotel*.

Getting There & Away
The new bus stand is on the southern edge of town. Get to the bus early to make sure you get a seat. A bus to Rekong Peo (Rs 105, 12 hours) leaves Kaza at 7 am. There are one or two daily buses to/from Manali (12 hours, Rs 100) at 7 am and one to Kullu (Rs 120) at 4 am. One bus goes daily to Chango (Rs 50) at 2 pm. There are also irregular buses between Kaza and Keylong (eight hours); otherwise take a Manali-bound bus to Gramphu (Rs 68) and change there. For Tabo (Rs 30, two hours) take any east-bound bus.

HIMACHAL PRADESH

There's no official taxi stand or office, though minibuses often hang around the old town centre. Fares are high because of the lack of competition and petrol costs. A taxi to Manali costs a pricey Rs 4000.

AROUND KAZA
Ki Gompa & Kibber

Ki (pronounced 'key'), the oldest and largest gompa in Spiti, has a spectacular location (4116m) atop a conical bluff, 14km from Kaza. It was built by Ringchen Zangpo and belongs to the Gelukpa order. The gompa was invaded three times in the 19th century by Ladakhis, Dogras and Sikhs, then damaged by fire, and later partially destroyed by an earthquake in 1975. The Dalai Lama is due to perform a Kalachakra ceremony here in August 2000 to inaugurate a new assembly hall.

Although being restored (donations are expected), the gompa is still famous for its priceless collection of ancient thangkas, and for housing the reliquary chörten of Lotsawa Rinpoche, the reincarnation of Ringchen Zangpo. No photos are allowed inside the gompa. Ki has a chaam festival in June/July.

About 11km from Ki village is the small village of **Kibber**, also known as Khyipur. Kibber was once part of the overland salt trade, and is today a dramatic, if desolate, place, with a small monastery and several other shrines. At 4205m, it claims, somewhat dubiously, to be the highest village in the world (Gete, at 4270m, a village about 7km east of Ki, has a better claim to this honour). The **Ladarcha Festival**, held near Kibber each July, attracts Buddhists from all over the region.

Places to Stay & Eat It is usually possible to stay at Ki Gompa for a donation, otherwise the friendly *Samdup Tashi Khangsar Hotel & Restaurant* in the village below has nice rooms for Rs 50.

Kibber has three small guesthouses. The family-run *Sargaung Guest House* and *Hotel Rainbow* rent out no-frills rooms for Rs 50 and offer basic food. The *Resang Hotel & Restaurant* at the entrance to the village has carpeted rooms with bathroom for Rs 150. The new *Parang La Guest House* was under construction at the time of research.

Getting There & Away In summer, a bus leaves Kaza every day at 2 pm to Ki and Kibber (Rs 12). This will allow you time to see Ki Gompa while the bus goes to, and comes back from, Kibber, but you won't be able to see both Ki and Kibber in one day. A return taxi from Kaza to both Ki Gompa and Kibber village costs Rs 450 to Rs 500; to only Ki and back, Rs 300; or one way to Ki, Rs 250.

Some travellers have attempted to walk to both Ki and Kibber from Kaza in one day, but it is a very long walk (about 22km from Kaza to Kibber). Perhaps a better option is to get the bus to Kibber, walk down to Ki and stay the night there.

Thang Yud Gompa

About 13km east of Kaza, and 7km from Gete, the 14th century Thang Yud Gompa (also known as Hikim Gompa) belongs to the Sakyapa order. There is a dirt road to nearby Komik village but no public transport to this secluded gompa. It involves a steep three hour trek from Kaza, with a height gain of 800m, and you'll need reliable directions from local people.

DHANKAR GOMPA
• alt 3890m

Built nearly 1000 years ago, Dhankar Gompa has one of the most spectacular settings in the Buddhist world, huddled amid eerily eroded cliffs high above the Spiti River. Once the site of the capital of Spiti, and then a jail, the gompa has some outstanding thangkas (usually locked away) and some interesting sculptures and frescoes. A new monastery is being constructed 1km from the site and this is the place to look for a guide to open up the site. Dhankar has a chaam festival in November.

The gompa is also popular for the medicinal herbs grown here, which cure lung and heart complaints. Some lamas come from as far as Dharamsala to collect these herbs. There is a small **lake** about 3km behind Dhankar village.

It's possible to trek 15km from Dhankar to **Lhalung Gompa** – over 1000 years old and famous for its woodcarvings. From here, you can head down the Lingti Valley to the main road, or continue along the ridge on foot all the way to Kaza, overnighting in Lhalung, Demul and possibly Komik villages. You will need a guide, a tent and all your food for this trip as there is no formal accommodation en route.

Getting There & Away
From Kaza to Dhankar, take any buses headed down the valley and get off just before the village of Sichling, from where there is a steep 8km walk (including an altitude increase of about 600m), or, if you are lucky, there might be a daily bus between Sichling and Dhankar. A one-way/ return taxi from Kaza to Dhankar Gompa costs Rs 600/700.

PIN VALLEY
The Pin Valley starts just north of Dhankar and continues all the way to the Pin Parvati Pass. The valley has been declared a national park and is famous for its wildlife – tourist agencies refer to it as the 'Land of Ibex and Snow Leopard', though you are unlikely to see anything bigger than a marmot. The beautiful valley is much greener than the Spiti Valley and holds Spiti's only concentration of Nyingmapa Buddhism. The most important gompa in the valley is the 600-year-old **Kungri Gompa**, 2km off the main road near Gulling. A new concrete monastery is being built next to the ancient (and often locked) chapels.

This is trekking and camping country; the most popular treks lead over the Pin Parvati Pass to Manikaran and over the Pin Baba Pass to Wangtu in Kinnaur.

Accommodation is limited to the *Hotel Himalaya* at Gulling (Rs 120 a room) and the *Ibex* and *Narzang* guesthouses at Sangam (Rs 35 to Rs 50). Cherwang Dorje Zangpo, the owner of the Ibex guesthouse,

is a good person to talk to when arranging porters and guides for treks in the valley. From Sangam you can make day hikes up the Pin Valley 13km to Mud or up the lesser-visited Paraiho Valley. A guide is strongly recommended.

Public transport goes only to Mikkim, though a road is currently being built as far as Mud. A daily bus leaves at 9 am from Kaza (Rs 22), or wait for it at Attargo, at the junction with the main road. A one-way taxi from Kaza to Mikkim costs Rs 700.

TABO GOMPA
• alt 3050m

Tabo Gompa is one of the most important monastic sites in the Tibetan Buddhist world, and is planned as the place where the current Dalai Lama will retire. It was built in 996 CE by the Great Translator, Ringchen Zangpo, and its 1000 year anniversary was held in June 1996. Along with Alchi in Ladakh and Thöling in western Tibet, Tabo has some of the best-preserved examples of Indo-Tibetan art remaining in the world.

Tabo holds a chaam festival in October/November and has a prayer ceremony every morning at 6.30 pm. Be quiet and respectful if you wish to attend the ceremony and don't take photos.

Things to See
There are nine temples in the complex (collectively known as the *choskhor*), all at ground level and dating from the 10th to the 16th century. The most common combination of icons found in the gompa is the popular triad of Sakyamuni Buddha, flanked by Maitreya (left), the Future Buddha, and Manjushri (right), the Bhodhisattva of wisdom.

The main assembly hall of the **tsuglagkhang** is surrounded by 33 raised Bhodhisattva statues, which together form a 3D mandala. The main statue is a four sided Sarvarvid Vairocana, one of the five Dhyani Buddhas. You can walk around the *khorlam* (inner kora) path to a second set of Buddhas, above two lions, and a series of

Buddha wall paintings. The main image at the altar is that of Ringchen Zangpo.

To the left of the tsuglagkhang is the **Lhakang Chenmo**, featuring a central Sakyamuni Buddha and eight Medicine Buddhas. Farther left is the **Serkhang** (Golden Chapel), with statues of (going clockwise) the Medicine Buddha (blue), Amithaba (red), Vajrapani, Maitreya, Sakyamuni, Vairocana and Tara. The statue of Tara is particularly beautiful, showing the same fluid lines and coloured *dhoti* as seen in Alchi Gompa in Ladakh.

Around the back of the main complex is the **Kyil Khor** (Mystic Mandala Temple), with some beautiful but faded mandalas. The last two chapels to the north are the **Dromton Lhakhang**, notable for its Kashmiri-influence doorframe and the **Maitreya Chapel**, with a 6m statue of Maitreya (Tibetan: Jampa).

On the other side of the road, opposite Tabo village, are some **caves**, known locally as Pho Gompa, with some faded ancient murals, including images of the mythological snow lion, *maksura* (half elephant, half crocodile) and *naga* (serpent). Bring a torch (flashlight).

The **library** in the monastery guesthouse is open to all and is an excellent place to spend a few hours or days learning more about Tibetan Buddhism. There is also a **thangka painting school** nearby, founded by the Dalai Lama.

Places to Stay & Eat

The *gompa guesthouse* has good rooms for Rs 150 or Rs 250 with bath; dormitory beds are Rs 50. The family-run *Himalayan Ajanta Hotel*, next to the State Bank of India, has very peaceful, carpeted rooms for Rs 100 and Rs 150, with hot water by the bucket.

The best places to eat are the *Tenzin Restaurant* and *Millennium Monastery Restaurant* at the back of the gompa guesthouse.

Getting There & Away

From Kaza to Tabo (Rs 30, two hours), take the 7 am bus, which goes on to Rekong Peo.

Through-buses back to Kaza pass by Tabo sometime in the afternoon. There is also a daily bus to Kullu departing around 5.30 am. A taxi from Kaza costs Rs 1000.

Kinnaur

☎ 01786
Best Time to Go: Apr to Nov

Kinnaur is a remote mountainous district between Shimla and the Tibetan border. The region was derestricted in 1991 and travel to and around Kinnaur is now possible with easy-to-obtain permits; see the Inner Line Permits boxed text later in this section.

The early history of Kinnaur is sparsely recorded. Perhaps the most remarkable fact is that the region was (unlike nearby Lahaul, Spiti and Ladakh) *not* invaded by the forces of western Tibet (Guge). Connections with Tibet have always been strong though, and the old road up the valley – the Hindustan-Tibet Highway – has been traversed for centuries by pilgrims, saints, traders, and even the odd turn-of-the-century British official headed up to the Tibetan trade mission at Gartok. Until recently, Kinnauri apricots, *chilgoza* (pine nuts – an important local crop), cloth and iron goods were traded for Tibetan pashmina wool.

In the 19th century the region, as with the Shimla hill states, paid tribute to the Gurkha rulers and thereafter the British. A tribute was exacted by the superintendent of the Shimla hill states that included terms of military support, if required, and the provision of a system of begar (forced labour) to work on the construction of roads in the area. Following local protests, the system of begar was abolished in 1920-21. In 1960, Kinnaur became a district of Himachal Pradesh, with the capital at Kalpa. The capital was transferred to nearby Rekong Peo a few years ago.

Kinnaur is bound to the north by the formidable Zanskar Range, which forms the border with Tibet. To the south, the main Himalaya Range forms the backdrop of the

HIMACHAL PRADESH

region including the impressive Kinnaur Kailash Range, with the peaks Kinnaur Kailash (6050m), Jorkanden (6473m) and Phawarang (6349m). South of Kinnaur Kailash is the popular Sangla Valley, which has been described as one of the most scenic in the entire Himalaya.

Kinnaur is drained by the Sutlej River, which flows from close to Mt Kailash in Tibet and enters India through the 5669m Shipki La before joining the headwaters of the Spiti River. Thereon the region is characterised by deep gorges as the waters surge through the main Himalaya Range and flow south to Rampur. The roads in upper Kinnaur rank as some of the most spectacular in the Himalaya, passing through the Himalaya into the Trans-Himalaya region of upper Kinnaur and Spiti, without crossing a pass.

People & Culture

Because of regular references to them in ancient Hindu texts as 'celestial musicians', Kinnauris have always regarded themselves as a distinct people of the Aryan group. Nearer the Tibetan border, Tibetan and Mongol features are also obvious. Most Kinnauris follow a mixture of Hinduism, which they gained from the area's ancient links with the rest of India, and Tibetan Buddhism. Especially near the borders of Tibet, villages often have both Hindu and Buddhist temples, and lamas continue to hold a strong influence over village life. Kinnaur also has a rich spread of local gods, such as Purgyal in Nako and Naryan in the Sangla Valley, which live side by side with the more widely recognised Hindu and Buddhist deities.

Probably the most distinctive part of the Kinnauris' dress is the grey woollen cap worn by men and women. It is curled up at one side, edged with red or green felt strips, and is called a *thepang*. On men, the thepang is often accompanied by a woollen shirt called a *chamu-kurti* and a coat. Women wear dresses called a *sari dhori* covered by the all-purpose *choli* or *bergi* (shawl), fastened by a *digra*. Kinnauri shawls are famous for their quality and design.

Kinnauri houses are mostly made from either wood or wooden beams interspersed with stone, normally with a *togang*, or balcony, which always faces the sun, and topped with a slate roof. Kinnauris are mostly involved in subsistence agriculture and breed sheep, goats *(chigu)* and yaks. The climate and altitude is perfect for apples, apricots and walnuts *(akrot)*. Barley and wheat are the dominant crops, and peas and potatoes are often grown. Tradition forbids Kinnauris to consume chicken but they enjoy alcohol *(ghanti)*, such as *angoori* grape wine and *arak* made from fermented barley.

Kinnauri (often called Homskad) is the major indigenous language and it has about 12 different dialects. One of these is called Sangnaur, and is only spoken in the village of the same name, near Puh.

When to Go

The road up the Sutlej Valley remains open year-round, though the region is bitterly cold in winter and receives several metres of snow. The ideal time to visit the popular Sangla Valley is either in the springtime (from April to the end of May) or in the autumn (September and October) as unlike the rest of Kinnaur, it receives mild monsoon rains.

Permits

From the Shimla region, you can travel as far as Rekong Peo, Kalpa and the Sangla Valley without a permit. For travel to northern Kinnaur, past Jangi, and beyond to Tabo in Spiti, you currently need an inner line permit. These can be easily obtained from the office of the Sub-Divisional Magistrate in Rekong Peo (see the boxed text).

REKONG PEO

☎ 01786 • alt 2290m

Up a side road from the main highway through Kinnaur are the two main towns of Kalpa, the former capital, and Rekong Peo, the current capital of Kinnaur. Both places have the most stupendous settings in probably all of Himachal Pradesh – anywhere up the road will give you incredible views of the mighty Kinnaur Kailash mountain, among several others, at around 6000m. Rekong Peo has better facilities and transport connections, and it is where you will have to apply for an inner line permit, but Kalpa, 7km away and 600m higher up, is by far the nicer place to stay. Rekong Peo has a cultural festival in October, with local dance and music.

Orientation & Information

Rekong Peo is very small; everything is within a yak's spit of the bus stop in the centre of the village. The banks here do *not* change foreign currency. To get an inner line permit head for the office at the bottom of town. There are several places to make photocopies of permits and passports, and stock up on some necessities (mineral water is hard to find outside Peo). The Himachal Emporium, 100m past the Fairyland Hotel, sells Kinnauri caps, shawls etc.

Things to See

A lovely, brightly coloured gompa, the **Kinnaur Kalachakra Celestial Palace**, or Mahabodhi Gompa, is a 20 minute steep walk above the village, just behind the radio station. Inaugurated by the Dalai Lama in 1992, the gompa itself is not the major attraction – there is a huge outdoor Buddha statue, in an area overrun by apple orchards, and facing the mighty Kinnaur Kailash

Inner Line Permits

The Indo-Tibetan (Chinese) border is a touchy zone (the two countries were at war in 1962) and permits are currently needed for any travel within 40km of the Tibetan border. Regulations have relaxed considerably in the last few years and these permits are now a mere formality; there is even talk of scrapping them entirely. For now you'll need an inner line permit for travel between Kinnaur and Spiti. You may also need a permit for certain treks – check this before setting off. Indian nationals need no permit. You don't need a special permit to drive a car or motorcycle in the area – your biggest headache will be finding fuel between Rekong Peo and Kaza.

In theory, permits can be obtained from District Magistrates in Shimla, Rekong Peo, Keylong, Kullu and Chamba, or the Sub-Divisional Magistrate's office in Kaza, Rampur, and Nichar. In reality, Rekong Peo and Kaza are by far the easiest places to get a permit.

Officially you need a group of four people to apply but this rule has been relaxed in Kaza and Rekong Peo, as it is often difficult to get a group together. You need three passport-sized photos, a photocopy of the front pages of your passport (with your personal details and photo), an application form from the Magistrate's office and some patience – the whole process could take up to a day, assuming the official you need isn't 'out of station'.

In Shimla and Keylong you may also need a 'letter of introduction' from a travel agency. Most agencies will provide this for a small fee, or even arrange the whole permit for a little more.

Despite what may be written on the permit, you can stay in any village and camp anywhere along the main road between Kaza and Rekong Peo; you can travel on any form of public or private transport; and you can travel alone or in a group of any size. The form also states you 'shall not resort to photography' – there is no restriction, but be careful around any sensitive or military areas; and you cannot carry any 'maps' – you are allowed to do this, but most maps aren't very good anyway.

Checkpoints between Rekong Peo and Kaza are at Jangi, Chango and Sumdo. Never venture too close to the Tibetan border or too far from the main roads.

mountain. The setting alone is probably worth the trip to Kinnaur.

Places to Stay & Eat

There are a couple of reasonable places in Rekong Peo.

Fairyland Guest House (☎ 22477), 200m from the bus stop, is convenient. For Rs 200 you get a decent room with hot water. Rs 50 extra gives you fantastic views of Kinner Kailash without having to get out of bed.

Cheaper and infinitely crummier places include the noisy *Hotel Snow View* in the centre of town, with doubles for Rs 200; the *Hotel Rangin*, along the path to the bus station; and the *Shambhala Hotel*, 10 minutes' walk uphill from the bus station.

Shivling View Hotel & Restaurant (☎ 22421) has a quiet but inconvenient location five minutes walk west of town on the road to Kalpa. Pleasant doubles with hot water cost Rs 220. There's a good restaurant.

Manish Bhojnayla restaurant, right in the centre of town, is a small Tibetan-run restaurant that serves excellent *thugpa*, momos and sweet tea. Otherwise, the best bet for food is the *Snow View* or the *Fairyland*. The latter has a good selection of Indian food and good views.

Getting There & Away

Most arriving buses let passengers off in the centre of town but actually depart from the new bus station, a five minute walk uphill from the centre (take the short-cut pathway as it's much quicker). Most buses are through buses and so departure times and seat bookings are a little unpredictable.

There are occasional buses uphill to Kalpa (via Pangi), but it's a lot quicker to get a taxi (Rs 100), or even hitch.

There are daily buses to Kaza (Rs 105, 12 hours) at 7.30 am and to Sangla/Chitkul (Rs 25/35, 2½/four hours) at 9.30 am and 12.30, 1.30 and 4 pm. At least six buses a day, starting from 4.30 am, go to Shimla (Rs 120, 10 hours) and there are several private buses to Rampur. Unfortunately, some of these buses do not originate in Rekong Peo, so are often hopelessly full by the time they arrive.

For villages around Rekong Peo there are buses at 9.30 am to Morang; 6 am, 1.30 and 5.15 pm to Puh; 7.30 am, noon and 1.30 pm to Yangthang; and 4.30 pm to Thangi.

KALPA

☎ 01786 • alt 2960m

Known as Chini when it was the main town in Kinnaur, Kalpa is the legendary winter home of Shiva; during the winter, the god is said to retire to his home here and indulge his passion for hashish. In the month of Magha (January/February), the gods of Kinnaur supposedly meet here for an annual conference with Shiva. Kalpa was also a favourite resting place for several high-level British colonialists, including Lord Dalhousie.

Kalpa is a tiny collection of narrow lanes, 7km and 600 vertical metres from Rekong Peo. What it lacks in facilities, Kalpa makes up for with atmosphere, charm, a couple of old wooden temples and a large chörten.

Walks

There are some nice walks to be had around Kalpa. Try heading two hours up to **Pangi** village, where there is an interesting temple to the local god Shesering. Alternatively, head south-west of town through apple orchards, along the old Hindustan-Tibet Highway to **Roghi**, for views of the dramatic Sutlej gorge. There are also good views from pastures a couple of hours' hike above Kalpa.

The walk between Kalpa and Rekong Peo is much shorter (45 minutes) if you follow the short cuts rather than the winding road. Masochists only should try the walk uphill.

Places to Stay & Eat

HPTDC Hotel Kinner Kailash has quite good rooms for Rs 500, Rs 600 and Rs 800. More rooms and a restaurant are being built. It's a stiff five minute walk above the village centre – look out for the green roof.

Sivalik Hotel, nearby, offers acceptable rooms for Rs 200 or Rs 300. A new hotel is being built in the village centre.

Auktong Guest House (☎ 26019), set in a pleasant apple orchard five minutes' walk north-east of Kalpa village, is very friendly and the best budget place to stay. To get there from Kalpa bus stop, walk up to the HPTDC hotel, take a right and follow the road east. Pleasant rooms cost Rs 175, with common bathroom, nice views and free buckets of hot water. Cheap food is available.

Just downhill from the Auktong is the government *Circuit Rest House*. This is by far the most comfortable place but you need permission from the District Commisioner in Rekong Peo; just being a tourist isn't enough.

Timberline Trekking Camps, on the outskirts of the village, offers luxury tents (with hot water) in a pleasant location for Rs 650. The whole place packs up and goes back to Delhi from October to May.

Getting There & Away
Long-distance buses to Rekong Peo rarely continue to Kalpa, so you'll probably have to get to Rekong Peo first and then change. Taxis cost Rs 100/150 one-way/return to or from Rekong Peo.

There are somewhat unreliable buses between Kalpa and Rekong Peo (Rs 5, one hour) at 6.30, 9, 10 and 10.30 am. Most continue on to other destinations so if you are headed to Shimla or the Sangla Valley check first to see if there is a direct bus from Kalpa, otherwise head down to Rekong Peo.

SANGLA VALLEY
The Sangla, or Baspa, Valley has been called 'the most beautiful valley in the Himalaya'. This is pushing it a bit, but the valley is graced with fine traditional wooden architecture, friendly people and spectacular mountains, which wall the valley off from Garhwal to the south and Tibet to the east. The road into the valley must be one of the most hair-raising in the Himalaya.

The Sangla Valley is mildly affected by the monsoon and can be wet and miserable in the summer. Kinnauri festivals are celebrated with abandon here, including Phagul in February, Dakhrain in July and Phulech in September (see the Festivals boxed text at the beginning of the chapter for more details).

Sangla
☎ 01786 • alt 2680m

Sangla village is the largest in the valley. From here, you can hike 2km to Kamru, with a five storey wooden **fort** and a few small temples. Kamru is a former capital of the Bushahr empire, which once ruled Kinnaur.

Places to stay include the *Baspa Guesthouse (☎ 42206)*, with rooms for Rs 165, or Rs 220 with bathroom; the *Highland*, with basic rooms for Rs 150; and the *Kailash View*, just above the village, with good carpeted top floor rooms with hot water for Rs 300 and dormitory beds for Rs 75.

Monal Restaurant, in the centre of town, is a good place for Indian and Chinese food and breakfast. There are several buses a day to Chitkul, Rampur and Rekong Peo. A taxi down to Karcham costs Rs 25 per person.

The valley road continues to Batseri, and Rakcham (Rock Bridge), a good trekking base, with the pleasant *Rupin River View Hotel*. Rooms here are around Rs 200. You can make strenuous day hikes from here up to meadows at Shaone Thach.

Chitkul
• alt 3450m

The 44km valley road finishes at the pretty village of Chitkul, 1½ hours by bus from Sangla, where there are three 500-year-old **temples**, dedicated to the goddess Matha Devi, as well as a small gompa. Treks lead from Chitkul over the Barasu Pass to Garhwal but there's a border checkpoint about 3km up valley and you'll need an inner line permit to get farther than this.

There are a couple of small wooden guesthouses in the village but none are signposted so you'll have to ask around. The friendly *Anwar House* offers rustic but pleasant doubles/triples for Rs 100/150 and will cook up basic food. There's a basic *PWD Rest House* by the main road where you can get a room for Rs 150 if it's not already booked.

Buses leave for Rekong Peo at 6.30 am and 2 pm. Change at Karcham for destinations down valley.

REKONG PEO TO SUMDO

Between Rekong Peo and Tabo in Spiti, there is private accommodation at Nako only. If you make arrangements in Shimla, Kaza or Rekong Peo, you may be able to stay at the resthouses owned by the PWD at Puh, Jangi, Yangthang and Morang. There are plenty of suitable camping sites along the way.

About 20km north-east of Powari is **Ribba**. This pleasant little place is famous for its 1000-year-old gompa and angoori (grape wine). **Morang** also has a gompa, with renowned sculptures and carvings. Nearby **Jangi** village is the last place you can visit without an inner line permit. The village of **Spillo** is the usual lunch stop for buses en route to Kaza, but few travellers make it to ancient **Khanum Gompa**, on the hillside high above Spillo. Farther up the valley, at **Khabo**, the road leaves the Sutlej to follow the smaller Spiti River.

From Yangthang, it's 7km up the hillside to **Nako**, high above the valley at 3662m. Dominated by Leo Purgyal mountain, the peaceful village has a beautiful setting around a lovely small lake. The village is famous because of the legend that Padmasambhava created it by throwing a rock there. His footprints on a rock above the village are still worshipped. The 11th century **gompa**, of the Drukpa order, has four temples. The main tsuglagkhang has statues of the five Dhyani Buddhas. The small chapel in the corner is said to house Purgyal, the local pre-Buddhist god. There is also an interesting painting of Gesar, a Tibetan hero, sitting on a *kyang* (Tibetan ass). There is another chapel on the other side of the lake, which is surrounded by mani stones and houses a giant *dongyur* (prayer wheel).

You can stay overnight at the *yellow guesthouse* by the bus stop (Rs 100 to Rs 150) or the more basic *green guesthouse* in the village itself. Buses head up to Nako from Yangthang at 1.30 and 6 pm and head down at 6 am. It's an easy downhill walk. Buses pass through Yangthang at around 9 am for Rekong Peo and noon for Kaza.

If you have a sleeping bag, consider the hike over the Labche La, visible behind Nako, to **Tashigang Gompa**. You'd be wise to take a guide – this is no place to get lost.

A couple of kilometres from Yangthang the road crosses the Milling stream, a notorious spot for summer landslides. You may have to walk over the slide and catch another bus on the far side. Another 11km takes you to **Chango**, where there is a checkpoint and a gompa. The final checkpoint is at **Sumdo**, where a side road branches off 19km to the border town of Kaurik and the (closed) road to Tibet.

Uttarakhand

Traditionally the hills of Uttar Pradesh (UP) stretching between Himachal and the eastern border of Nepal are known as Uttarakhand – the 'northern parts'. Historically this is a spiritually evocative place for Hindus. Over the long centuries of Muslim domination of the Ganges plain these mountains were a bastion of Hinduism, and today Hindus aspire to make a pilgrimage at least once each lifetime to attain *moksha* (release) at the feet of the gods. Today Uttarakhand refers to eight hill districts of northern Uttar Pradesh that make up the culturally distinct provinces of Garhwal and Kumaon.

The region has several popular hill stations, including Nainital and Mussoorie, and many trekking routes – most of them little known and even less used. The pilgrimage sites of the Char Dham are in Garhwal. They are the four sacred *yatra* (pilgrimage destination) shrines marked by the sources of the Yamuna and Ganges and the temples of Kedarnath and Badrinath. More accessible pilgrimage centres include Rishikesh and Haridwar – where, according to Hindu tradition, the Ganges leaves the Himalaya.

History

Stone Age implements found in Garhwal date back to 8000 BCE (before common era). Waves of Aryan invaders and settlers in the millennia between 1500 BCE and 1500 CE (common era) pushed the aboriginal population and the Mongol highlanders to the periphery of society.

An Ashokan edict near Kalsi, west of Mussoorie, indicates the presence of Buddhism in the hills. The fact that the Chinese pilgrim Xuan Zhang spent time in the area in the 7th century, probably at Uttarkashi, is further evidence of this. The Hindu philosopher and reformer Shankaracharya is credited with restoring Brahmanic Hinduism in the 9th century CE.

Uttarakhand at a Glance

Population: 6.64 million (year 2000 estimate)
Best Time to Go: mid-May to mid-Jul; mid-Sept to mid-Nov
Main Languages: Hindi, English
Trekking Areas: Garhwal, Nanda Devi & Kumaon (May/Jun & Sept/Oct)

Highlights

- **Garhwal** – Join the pilgrims on a *yatra* (pilgrimage) to the sacred Himalayan shrines of Yamunotri, Gangotri, Kedarnath & Badrinath.

- **Mussoorie** – Enjoy a pre-dinner cocktail at a Raj-era hotel.

- **Haridwar** – Explore some of the hundreds of temples at this thriving sacred city.

- **Rishikesh** – Find a guru, and peace of mind, at an ashram.

- **Valley of Flowers** – Trek to this high-altitude meadow and take in some of the Himalaya's finest scenery.

- **Nainital** – Go rowing on an emerald-green lake at one of India's favourite hill stations.

- **Jageshwar** – Examine some exquisite temple architecture at this tiny village.

- **Kausani** – Take in the panoramic mountain vistas from Gandhi's favourite hill station.

- **Corbett Tiger Reserve** – Follow the trail of a tiger at this important national park.

Between the 8th and 14th centuries the Katyuri dynasty, which ruled from central Kumaon, held sway in Uttarakhand, leaving a legacy of beautiful temples in Joshimath, Baijnath (Garur) and Jageshwar. The Katyuri dynasty was succeeded by Kumaon's Chand rajas whose first capital was at Champawat but was later moved to Almora.

The Panwar dynasty, claiming descent from the famous Raja Bhoj of Dhar (in Madhya Pradesh), united Garhwal's 52 warring fiefdoms to make their capital in the 14th century at Chandpur. It was moved to Devalgarh in 1512 and then to Srinagar in 1517 (the latter a bad choice in view of the periodic flooding by the Ganges).

The Gurkhas invaded Uttarakhand from Nepal in 1803 and were not evicted until 1815 when British arms proved stronger. True to form the British came to stay, and only Tehri Garhwal survived as a native state with a new capital in sweltering Tehri.

In independent India the failure of the Uttar Pradesh administration in Lucknow to develop the region has led to demands for a separate hill state. The campaign also grew with pressure for lower caste job quotas in government and education in the early 1990s. The hill regions are poor but most of the people are upper caste, especially Brahmans and Rajputs, and bitterly opposed the discrimination against them in favour of the masses living on the plains. The Bharatiya Janata Party (BJP), which draws support from upper caste Hindus, backed the push for a new state, while the Congress-I government of PV Narasimha Rao rejected it, arguing that it was unhealthy for the country to create new states on caste lines.

Once the BJP came to power in 1998, however, the positions reversed – the BJP put the issue of statehood into bureaucratic limbo while Narasimha Rao, who had retired, came out to support it. At the time of research the issue was bogged down in debate.

The Udham Singh Nagar district, on the edge of the Kumaon foothills, was settled by Punjabi farmers after Partition – it is sometimes called 'Little Punjab'. These farmers, many of them Sikhs, have become relatively wealthy and are rejecting the new state because of a proposed ceiling on farm sizes. The Sikh Akali Dal party has vowed to remove support for the BJP if Udham Singh Nagar is included in the new state.

The BJP has sent the issue to a committee for discussion and appraisal (a typical Indian government way of sweeping potentially disruptive issues under the carpet). The question of which state Haridwar should join is also contentious.

In terms of population and geography Uttarakhand is comparable to Himachal Pradesh, and regional leaders hope to emulate that state in developing tourism. If and when the new state is created, it will probably be known as Uttaranchal, which means northern land, rather than Uttarakhand – the BJP believes the name Uttarakhand has sacred connotations that make it ineligible. One site proposed as the new capital is Gairsain, on the border of Garhwal and Kumoan, but at least for the first few years the new administration would divide its time between Dehra Dun in Garhwal and Nainital in Kumaon.

Geography

Uttarakhand encompasses an area comparable in size to the entire adjacent state of Himachal Pradesh. It has some of the most spectacular peaks in the Indian Himalaya – more than 100 are over 6000m, including, from west to east, Bandarpanch (6316m), Gangotri (6672m), Kedarnath (6940m), the peaks of Chaukhamba, with the highest at 7138m and those of Badrinath, with the highest at 6853m, Nilkantha (6957m), Dunagiri (7066m), Nanda Devi (7817m) and Trisul (7120m). Lying before these Greater Himalayan peaks are the mid and lesser Himalaya, culminating in the newest ranges of foothills, the Siwalik Hills. The Siwaliks, which extend east from Himachal Pradesh across southern Uttarakhand, are rising at a rate of about 3cm a year – among the fastest in the world.

The holy Yamuna and Ganges rivers have their sources in Garhwal. The affluents of the Ganges form a network across Garhwal, and the sites of their major confluences, of which there are five, form the Panch Prayag (*panch* means five, *prayag* is a sacred confluence). A pilgrimage to the Panch Prayag is deemed as spiritually meritorious, second only in importance to that to the confluence

UTTARAKHAND

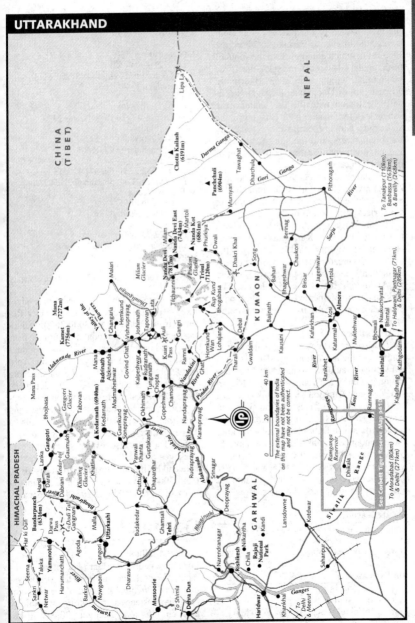

of the Yamuna and Ganges at Allahabad. The most sacred of the prayags is at Deoprayag, 68km east of Rishikesh. There the Bhagirathi, which emerges from the snout of the Gangotri Glacier at Gaumukh, meets the Alaknanda, which rises near Badrinath. Downstream of Deoprayag the river is officially bestowed with the title Ganga (the Ganges). Before reaching the Bhagirathi, the Alaknanda, flowing south-west, is joined by four other rivers, and the site of their confluences are revered as the remaining four of the Panch Prayag.

The Alaknanda meets the Dhauliganga at Vishnuprayag, 10km north of Joshimath. It is joined by the Nandakini at Nandaprayag, which rises to the south of the sacred Homkund (*kund* means lake). Farther south-west it meets the Pindar at Karanprayag. The Pindar emerges from the Pindari Glacier, to the north-east. Threading its way west, the next major confluence is at Rudraprayag, where the Alaknanda meets the Mandakini. The Alaknanda, supplemented by its union with the other rivers, finally meets the Bhagirathi.

Information

UP Tourism has offices in most major tourist centres (see the list, following). The Garhwal and Kumaon regions also have tourist organisations: Garhwal Mandal Vikas Nigam (GMVN), and Kumaon Mandal Vikas Nigam (KMVN), whose offices can be found in many larger towns in Uttarakhand. GMVN headquarters is in Dehra Dun, and a trekking and mountaineering division is in Rishikesh. GMVN has a Web site at www.gmvn.com.

There is a network of GMVN and KMVN tourist bungalows throughout Uttarakhand, with rates that vary according to season:

GMVN Seasons

High:	16 Apr to 30 Jun, 16 Sept to 31 Oct
Mid:	1 Jul to 15 Sept
Low:	1 Nov to 15 Apr

KMVN Seasons

High:	1 Apr to 15 Jul
Mid:	15 Sept to 15 Nov
Low:	16 Jul to 14 Sept, 16 Nov to 30 Mar

UP tourist offices throughout India include the following:

Ahmedabad
(☎ 0121-400 0752)
303 Ashwamedh House, 5 Smriti Kunj, Navrangpura
Chandigarh
(☎ 0172-707649)
SCO 1046-47, 1st floor, Sector 22B
Chennai (Madras)
(☎ 044-220 7855)
28 Commander-in-Chief Rd
Delhi
(☎ 011-332 2251, fax 371 1296)
Chandralok Bldg, 36 Janpath, New Delhi
Kolkata (Calcutta)
(☎ 033-220 7855)
12A Netaji Subhash Rd
Lucknow
(☎ 0522-232659)
Chitrahar Bldg, 3 Naval Kishor Rd
Mumbai (Bombay)
(☎ 022-218 5458)
World Trade Centre, Cuffe Parade, Colaba

UP Tourism in Delhi runs two/three-night fixed-departure tours to Corbett Tiger Reserve from Delhi for Rs 3000/3500, including transport, accommodation, entrance fees, guide and one elephant ride. It also operates package tours during the yatra season (April to October/November) to the Char Dham temples of Garhwal. Packages departing from Delhi feature luxury bus and accommodation: an eight day tour to Badrinath and Kedarnath costs Rs 4850, and there's also a 12 day tour to the four temples (Rs 7100).

UP Tourism also offers seven day taxi packages during the yatra season to Kedarnath and Badrinath: departing from Rishikesh (Rs 6300 per person for twin accommodation), or from Delhi (Rs 10,000 per person).

Garhwal

• pop 3.1 million

For many people the Garhwal region epitomises the essential spirit of the Himalaya; this is the *Dhev-bumi* (Land of the Gods) of Hinduism, steeped in history, mythology and religious lore. It covers 30,029 sq km

Festivals of Uttarakhand

January
Uttarkashi Fair On the day of Makar Sankranti (14 January), images of various Hindu deities are carried into Uttarkashi on palanquins by pilgrims from outlying centres. Pilgrims flock to rivers and temple tanks to bathe, and give alms to the poor.

Uttarayani Festival This trade fair held at Bhageshwar in Kumaon has its roots in the now defunct wool trade with Tibet.

February/March
International Yoga Festival Every year from 2 to 7 February the big guns of yoga from India and around the world gather in Rishikesh. See under Rishikesh later in this chapter for details.

Tapkeshwar Mahadev Mela This large fair is held in honour of Shiva at the Tapkeshwar Mahadev Temple near Dehra Dun. It generally corresponds with the nationwide celebration of Shivaratri.

April
Bissu This five day festival is held in the Yamuna Valley in late spring. Village idols are paraded in processions, as villagers prepare for the harvesting season.

July/August
Jayanti Festival This festival celebrates the birth of Shiva. At this time, pilgrims throng to the Vishwanatha Temple at Uttarkashi to pay homage to the god.

August/September
Nanda Devi Mela This three day fair is held at the Nanda Devi Temple in Almora.

October
Autumn Festival This festival, celebrated in Nainital in the first week of October, features dancing and music programs, and yachting on the Nainital lake.

November
Gauchar Fair This trade fair, one of the biggest fairs in Garhwal, is held from 14 to 21 November at the village of Gauchar, 12km west of Karanprayag on a wide terrace overlooking the Alaknanda River.

Kumaon Festival This annual cultural festival, from 4 to 6 November, rotates around the main centres of Kumaon. It features Kumaoni food, and dance and music programs. For more information check at a KMVN tourist office. The festival will be held at the following places in forthcoming years:

2000 Bhageshwar; 2001 Almora; 2002 Nainital

and is the source of the sacred Ganges and Yamuna rivers. It is scored by dramatic gorges studded with glacial lakes and cascading waterfalls, traversed by valleys that, during the monsoon, are carpeted with wild-flowers. The highlands are dotted with green *bugyals,* high-altitude meadows. Garhwal is also the site of the Char Dham, the busy holy pilgrimage sites of Yamunotri, Gangotri, Kedarnath and Badrinath.

Garhwal is a stronghold of the Shaivites (worshippers of Shiva). Shiva fled to the Garhwal Himalaya hotly pursued by the heroes of the *Mahabharata,* the five Pandava brothers, who sought atonement from the god after they slew their kinsfolk, the Kauravas. The Panch Kedar is the most important yatra for Shaivites, representing the five parts of Shiva that emerged after he attained the form of a bull and dived into the earth to escape the Pandavas at Kedarnath. The temple at Kedarnath is the most sacred, but after they have had *darshan* (presentation to the deity) here, devout pilgrims sometimes proceed to the other four temples, at Tunganath, Rudranath, Madmaheshwar and Kalpeshwar.

Many villages have their own deities; worship of the goddess Nanda Devi predominates in many of the regions within sight of the magnificent holy mountain, revered as a manifestation of the goddess. The Devi's marriage as Parvati to Shiva is commemorated annually in the Nandashthami Festival. In the remote Har ki Dun Valley, Duryodhana, the eldest Kaurava brother, is revered. The snow-melt lake of Hemkund, near the Valley of Flowers National Park, is held sacred by Sikhs, as it was on the shores of this lake that the Sikh guru Govind Singh is believed to have meditated.

Five of the hill districts of northern Uttar Pradesh are in Garhwal: Dehra Dun,

The Castes of Garhwal

As the Dhev-bumi, or Hinduism's Land of the Gods, it isn't surprising that 92% of the population is Hindu, with Muslim, Sikh, Buddhist and Christian communities of roughly equal sizes making up the remainder.

Brahmans, the priestly caste, make up an unusually high proportion of Garhwal's population – around 25%. Many of Garhwal's Brahmans are descended from refugees who fled Muslim rule in medieval north India, though the origins of some goes back farther than that. When the Hindu philosopher Shankaracharya re-established the temples at Kedarnath and Badrinath in the 9th century CE, he wanted to find priests who were 'pure' and untainted by Buddhism. He appointed priests from the Namboodiri Brahman caste of distant Kerala, believing these Brahmans had not been corrupted as Buddhism had not made deep inroads in the southern state. Other Brahman settlers came from as far afield as Karnataka, Maharashtra, Andhra Pradesh and Rajasthan.

The biggest caste in Garhwal is the Rajputs, a warrior caste who also migrated to the secure mountainous terrain of Garhwal during the centuries of Muslim rule. They make up about 40% of the population. The Rajputs have remained true to their martial roots, and many men serve in the Indian army. The esteemed regiment of the Garhwal Rifles is based in Lansdowne.

The Kols or Doms make up the lower castes, about 25% of the population. Members of these castes are the original inhabitants of Garhwal and generally have darker complexions than the dominant upper castes. Kol villages have preserved snake *(nag)* worship, and it is claimed they still have rituals centred on appeasing demons and goblins.

The tribal peoples of Garhwal are mostly of Indo-Tibetan origin and live in the high valleys of the Himalaya. They are often called Bhotias (Bhotia is an old Hindi name for Tibet). They used to follow a nomadic and seminomadic lifestyle but are now settled farmers. The Jadhs of the Uttarkashi area and the Marchas in the valleys above Chamoli are the biggest communities of Bhotias. With their ancient links to Tibet, the tribal religion they practise combines elements of Buddhism and Hinduism, similar to Nepal.

Chamoli, Uttarkashi, Pauri Garhwal and Tehri Garhwal. The remaining three districts lie in neighbouring Kumaon to the east. Garhwal is bordered by Himachal Pradesh to the east, and the watershed of the Greater Himalaya forms the border with Tibet to the north.

DEHRA DUN

☎ 0135 • pop 424,500 • alt 701m

Also spelt Dehra Doon (*dun* or *doon* means valley), this old centre of the Raj is situated in the broad Doon Valley between the Siwaliks, named after Shiva, and the front range of the Himalaya. To the east and west are the Ganges and Yamuna rivers respectively. The hill station Mussoorie, 34km away, can be seen on the high ranges above the valley. The town has lost some of its charm due to traffic congestion. Nevertheless Dehra Dun is blessed with a moderate climate year-round, several points of interest nearby, and a colourful bazaar.

The Indian Military Academy and the Survey of India (which sells large-scale maps of many Indian cities) are both based here. There are also several prestigious boarding schools including the Doon School, India's most exclusive private school, where Rajiv Gandhi was educated. Quite a few of the larger houses around the town are home to retired army officers. On the way to Mussoorie there are several Tibetan Buddhist gompas and colleges.

Orientation

The clock tower is the hub of the town and most of the budget hotels are near it or close to the train station and the Mussoorie and Delhi bus stands.

The mid-range and top-end hotels are in the area known as Astley Hall, about 1km north of the clock tower, and farther north on Rajpur Rd, the route to Mussoorie. (Astley Hall comprises an entire city block on the east side of Rajpur Rd, but the hall itself is mysteriously elusive.) The main market is Paltan Bazaar; high quality *basmati* (long-grain) rice for which the Doon Valley is famous is sold here.

The Delhi bus stand is about 1km from both the train station and the clock tower, on Gandhi Rd. The Mussoorie bus stand and taxi stand is adjacent to the train station, about 2km south of the clock tower. The main post office is just a few steps north of the clock tower. Just to the south of Astley Hall, extending east back to Lytton Rd, is Gandhi Park, a pleasant and shady place to relax.

Information

GMVN (☎ 654371) has an office at the Hotel Drona, near the Delhi bus stand at 45 Gandhi Rd. It's open Monday to Saturday 10 am to 5 pm (closed for lunch 1 to 2 pm).

The State Bank of India is close to the clock tower, at 11A Rajpur Rd, in the Windlass Shopping Complex, beneath the Hotel Ambassador. Most travellers cheques are accepted, but *not* Visa. The Central Bank, Astley Hall area, on Rajpur Rd, is one of the few banks that will exchange Visa travellers cheques.

BJ Travels (☎ 657888), about 200m north of the main post office at 15B Rajpur Rd, has a computerised reservation system and can provide instant confirmation on domestic and international flights. To arrange treks, contact Garhwal Tours & Trekking (☎ 627769), 151 Araghar Rd, or Trek Himalaya Tours (☎ 653005).

Forest Research Institute

Established by the British, the FRI, 5km north-west of the heart of town, is now reputedly one of the finest institutes of forest sciences in the world and houses a **museum**. Like many Indian museums established by the British, this one nowadays seems like a museum of a museum, with a faint odour of decay and rather rudimentary maintenance. It's set in large botanical gardens, with the Himalaya providing a spectacular backdrop. There's also a bookshop and library.

The institute is open from Monday to Friday 10 am to 5 pm and entry is free. To get there take a Vikram (six-seater tempo) from the clock tower to the institute gates, route No 8 (Rs 6).

Tapkeshwar Mahadev Temple

This pretty cave temple, to Shiva, is 6km north-west of the city centre, 2km beyond the FRI, at the village of Ghari. The temple gets its name from the perpetually dripping water that falls on a sacred lingam: *tapke* is the sound made by the water, and Ishwar is a collective name for the Hindu gods.

A large *mela* (fair) is held here on Shivaratri day (Feb/Mar). It's a colourful event, with carnival rides for children and food stalls catering to the thousands of pilgrims. A return auto-rickshaw from town costs about Rs 120.

Other Things to See

The Wadia Institute of Himalayan Geology has a museum with rock samples, semi-precious stones and fossils. The museum is on General Mahadev Singh Rd, and is open Monday to Friday 10 am to 5 pm. About 8km west of Dehra Dun is the Robber's Cave, a popular picnic spot 1.5km beyond Anarwala village. Local buses run to Anarwala.

The Survey of India has its headquarters off Rajpur Rd, 4km from the clock tower, in the Hathibarkala Estate. There's a rather motley collection, with illogical restrictions on buying maps of Uttar Pradesh because it borders Tibet, but not Sikkim or parts of the North-East Region, which also border Tibet. Some of the maps have barely been altered since the British left. The Survey of India is open Monday to Friday 10 am to 5 pm (closed 1 to 2 pm, though often until later – this is the Indian civil service, after all).

Other places to visit include the Lakshman Sidh Temple and the village of Sahastradhara (14km east of Dehra Dun) with cold sulphur springs and a *Tourist Rest House* (Rs 200 for a double; book through the GMVN in Dehra Dun – see under Information, earlier).

Organised Tours

GMVN (see Information earlier) runs day tours during May and June and in September and October around Dehra Dun (Rs 80), including the Forest Research Institute and Tapkeshwar Mahadev Temple, departing from the Hotel Drona at 10.30 am and returning at 5 pm. Day trips to Mussoorie and to Haridwar (Rs 120) both leave at 10 am and return at 7 pm, and there are also tours to Dakpathar at the western extreme of the Doon Valley (Rs 120), leaving at 10 am and returning at 6 pm. These tours are a good way of seeing the area, although some of the attractions en route such as river barrages and the horribly touristy Kempty Falls near Mussoorie are of limited interest. For trekking agencies, see Information earlier.

Places to Stay – Budget

GMVN Hotel Drona (see under Places to Stay – Mid Range & Top End) has dorm beds (men only) for Rs 60.

Hotel Nishima (☎ 626640) is a simple budget place with rooms for Rs 150/200, set off the street but close to the railway and bus stations. It's not in the most attractive part of town but it is noticeably cleaner than some of the other cheapies.

Hotel Meedo (☎ 627088) is a large place with singles for Rs 150, and doubles for Rs 250 to Rs 350, all with baths. Those at the back are quieter. There's a rather sleazy bar next door, but the Meedo itself is clean and friendly. (Don't confuse this place with the top-end Hotel Meedo's Grand.) Unusually for Dehra Dun, this hotel has 24 hour checkout.

Hotel Dai-Chi (☎ 658107), on Mahant Laxman Dass Rd, is also in a quiet part of town (unless it's sports day at St Joseph's Academy across the road). Large clean rooms with bath plus hot water cost Rs 250/350, and there's a vegetarian restaurant.

Places to Stay – Mid-Range & Top End

Dehra Dun has an excellent selection of mid-range hotels, most strung out along Rajpur Rd.

Hotel Ambassador (☎ 655831, fax 655830, 11A Rajpur Rd) on the top floors of the Windlass Shopping Centre, has air-cooled singles/doubles with colour TV from Rs 250/350. There's 24 hour room service and the staff are friendly.

Hotel Gaurab (☎ 654215), on Gandhi Rd, is a spanking new hotel, well soundproofed from the busy traffic outside. Pleasant rooms cost from Rs 270/370, to Rs 870 for a two-room suite. The Tripti restaurant here is also good.

Motel Himshri (☎ 653880, fax 650177, 17 Rajpur Rd) has ordinary rooms from Rs 275/350; larger deluxe rooms with air-con cost Rs 425/525.

The President (☎ 657082, fax 658883), Astley Hall, is charming and tastefully decorated – almost a boutique hotel. Air-cooled rooms cost Rs 800/900. There is a very good restaurant called The Pavilion, and a bar and coffee shop.

Hotel Meedo's Grand (☎ 747171, 28 Rajpur Rd), 3km from the train station, has rooms for Rs 400/500. Despite the ugly exterior the rooms are comfortable with wall-to-wall carpet and piped music. There's a restaurant and bar; credit cards are accepted.

GMVN Hotel Drona (☎ 654371, 45 Gandhi Rd) is next to the Delhi bus station. Reasonably large rooms with bath and hot water cost Rs 375/500, Rs 525/700 with air-con, but like so many government-run places it could be better. There's a restaurant and bar and a 10% mid/low-season discount.

Osho Resort (☎ 749544, fax 748535, 111 Rajpur Rd) describes itself as a 'retreat with a waterfall'. It's certainly the most unusual place to stay in town, with an open-air cafe facing the road and a jumble of buildings and cottages at the rear. It's part of the organisation of the late Osho, the guru once known as the Bhagwan Rajneesh. Rooms range from Rs 390/490 up to Rs 1090/1290; there are also wooden huts. Videos of the late guru are available and there's a meditation centre and a vegetarian restaurant.

Places to Eat

Kumar, on Rajpur Rd near Motel Himshri, serves up some of the best vegetarian food in town. Recommended are the *gajar ka halva* (made from carrot, spices and milk) and the *makki ki roti, sarson ka saag* (corn roti with mustard-leaf spinach) with lassi (Rs 50). Another *Kumar* 100m south serves

nonveg and Chinese food. Both are open 11 am to 4 pm and 7 to 11 pm.

Motimahal, one of the best in a string of eateries on the opposite side of Rajpur Rd, serves good veg and nonveg dishes. *A-One Grill*, nearby, is a hole-in-the-wall eatery serving take-away tandoori chicken and kababs from 8 pm until late.

Udipi Restaurant, on Lytton Rd, is a good south Indian place with air-con; *masala dosas* cost Rs 80.

Vegetarian by the Hotel President dishes up inexpensive (Rs 30 and under) but tasty meals. The bare dining hall doesn't have the most convivial of atmospheres. Above the Vegetarian is *Daddy's*, which offers Mughlai, south Indian and Chinese food, with decor frozen some time in the 1960s.

Standard Confectioners near the Vegetarian restaurant is one of several good bakeries in Dehra Dun; there are several good *sweet shops* near the clock tower.

Getting There & Away

Bus The Mussoorie bus stand, by the train station on Haridwar Rd, is for destinations in the hills. There are frequent departures to Mussoorie (Rs 17, 1½ hours). Other buses go to Nainital (Rs 125, 11 hours), Uttarkashi (Rs 90, seven hours) and Tehri (Rs 50, four hours).

The Delhi bus stand, beside the Hotel Drona, serves destinations on the plains. The seven hour trip to Delhi costs Rs 150/240/300 ordinary/semideluxe/deluxe. Deluxe buses leave hourly between 5.15 am and 10.30 pm; ordinary buses leave every 15 to 30 minutes.

Other destinations include:

destination	fare (Rs)	duration (hrs)	departs
Dharamsala	230	15	12.30 pm
Kullu/Manali	215	14	3.15 pm
Manali	250	16	3.15 pm
Lucknow	182	16	1.30, 6 pm
Rishikesh	15	1½	frequent
Shimla[1]	108	7	several am
Shimla[2]	130	9	7.25, 9.15 am

[1] via Paonta Sahib, Solan & Kumar
[2] via Saharanpur, Ambala & Chandigarh

Train Services to Dehra Dun, the terminus of the Northern Railway, include the speedy *Shatabdi Express*, leaving New Delhi at 7.10 am daily and reaching Haridwar at 11.20 am and Dehra Dun at 12.35 am. A chair car seat costs Rs 485 to Dehra Dun.

The *Mussoorie Express* leaves Dehra Dun at 9.15 pm, Haridwar at 11 pm and arrives at Old Delhi train station at 7 am. The journey costs Rs 118/643 in 2nd/1st class from Haridwar, slightly more from Dehra Dun. There are also services to Lucknow, Varanasi and Mumbai (Bombay).

The *Doon Express* operates between Lucknow and Dehra Dun. The 545km journey costs Rs 180/625 in 2nd/1st class. There are also services from Dehra Dun to Kolkata (Calcutta), Varanasi and Mumbai.

Taxi There's a share taxi stand in front of the Mussoorie bus stand on Haridwar Rd. Taxis leave for Mussoorie when full (five passengers required), and depart every hour or so between 6 am and 6 pm (Rs 60, 1¼ hours). You'll have more luck if you hang around the taxi stand when trains disgorge their passengers from Delhi. A second share taxi stand is by the Hotel Prince, on Haridwar Rd. Taxis and jeeps depart when full for Rishikesh (Rs 20), Haridwar (Rs 20), and Paonta Sahib, just over the border in eastern Himachal Pradesh (Rs 18). The jeep stops 1km before the border, from where you can catch a rickshaw.

A taxi to Mussoorie will cost Rs 300; to other destinations during the high season expect to pay: Rishikesh (Rs 300), Haridwar (Rs 400) and Uttarkashi (Rs 1200).

Getting Around

Six-seater tempos (Vikrams) belch diesel fumes all over the city, but are a cheap way to get around. They run on fixed routes for about half the price of an auto-rickshaw ride. Route No 1 runs from the clock tower along Rajpur Rd.

Cars can be hired through GMVN at its Rajpur Rd and Hotel Drona offices. You may be able to negotiate better rates through Ventures Rent a Car (☎ 22724), at 87 Rajpur Rd.

MUSSOORIE
☎ 0135 • pop 35,000 • alt 1921m
High Season – May to early July
Mid-Season – Apr, Oct
Low Season – mid-Nov to late Mar, late July to Sept

Mussoorie was founded by an Irishman, Captain Young, who stumbled upon the 15km ridge on which the town was later sited in 1827 while out enjoying a spot of hunting. He immediately recognised the potential of the site, with its salubrious climate and magnificent Himalayan vistas, as a hill station, and in less than 10 years a thriving town had emerged. Maharajas, British officers and their entourages were borne up to Mussoorie on ponies or carried up on *jhampanies* (chairs) with essential extras such as crystal chandeliers, billiard tables and grand pianos being hauled up on bullock carts. As the settlement developed, Mussoorie, the closest hill station to Delhi, became a favourite summer retreat of the British. The town they built was not so much British as a kind of homesick memory of Britain, and still today some of the outlying districts of the town such as Landour retain this atmosphere.

Today the once-glorious Victorian edifices are mostly dilapidated, jostled on all sides by ugly modern concrete constructions catering to the thousands of holiday makers who converge on the hill station in summer. With more hotels than any other hill station (350 and rising), the town suffers an acute water shortage in the summer. Outside the peak summer months of May and June, Mussoorie is a far more pleasant proposition, with good walks along the mountain ridges and fine views of the Himalayan massifs of western Garhwal from Gun Hill, rising 609m above the town.

Orientation

Despite initial impressions, the layout of Mussoorie is straightforward: the Mall extends 2km across the face of a long mountain ridge, oddly oriented to the south rather than towards the stunning Himalayan panorama. It connects the library end (Gandhi Chowk), at the west end of the Mall, with Kulri Bazaar to the east. East of Kulri Bazaar is the

Masonic Lodge bus stand (also known as the Picture Palace bus stand).

Buses or taxis will drop you at either the Library bus stand at Gandhi Chowk or the Masonic Lodge bus stands. If you arrive at the Library bus stand, walk west about 100m and you'll pass beneath a brightly coloured archway, announcing your arrival at the library area, which is riddled with hotels in all price categories (see under Places to Stay). Hotels are strung out along the Mall, with some a short distance off the Mall up steep roads and paths.

A 600m walk west of the Masonic Lodge bus stand brings you into the thick of Kulri Bazaar, even more crammed with places to stay. Looping north above the Kulri Bazaar end of the Mall is Camel's Back Rd, which was built as a promenade and passes a rock formation that looks vaguely like a recumbent camel. It also has a fair share of hotels. The main post office, State Bank of India and Bank of Baroda are all in the Kulri Bazaar area; there's nowhere to change money at the library end of the Mall.

Information
Tourist Offices There's a UP tourist office (☎ 632863) towards the Kulri Bazaar end of the Mall, near the ropeway station, and a GMVN office (☎ 632984) at the Hotel Garhwal Terrace, about 500m farther west along the Mall.

Money The State Bank of India at Kulri Bazaar will exchange American Express travellers cheques in US dollars only, and Thomas Cook and MasterCard cheques in US dollars and pounds sterling only. At the Bank of Baroda you can get cash advances on a Visa card. The only place it may be possible to change Visa travellers cheques is at the Trek Himalaya Tours office (see Organised Tours & Treks, later in this section), although the rate won't be very good.

Travel Agencies Try Ambica Travels (☎ 632238) at the Hotel Hill Queen, Upper Mall Rd, the Mall (west) can book deluxe non-air-con/air-con buses to Delhi

(Rs 150/270). They also book air and train tickets. Hire cars can be arranged through Kulwant Travels (☎ 632717) and Harry Tours & Travels (☎ 631747), both at the same Masonic Lodge bus stand.

Bookshops There's a good selection of books and maps at Cambridge Booksellers and Chander Book Depot, both at Kulri Bazaar.

Medical Services Try St Mary's Hospital (☎ 632845). James Chemist is a well-stocked dispensary near the Picture Palace; so too is A Kumar & Co, beneath the library at the west end of the Mall.

Emergency Police: ☎ 632013; Fire ☎ 632100; Ambulance ☎ 632829.

Things to See & Do
A 400m ropeway runs up to 2530m-high **Gun Hill** (Rs 25 return, 9 am to 7 pm daily and until 10 pm, 15 May to 15 July), so named because in British times there was a gun fired here every day at noon precisely. For early-morning views of the Himalaya including Bandarpunch (6316m), Kedarnath (6940m) and Nanda Devi (7817m) you have to walk up. At the top, photo agencies will (if you like) dress you up in sequined Garhwali dress and take your photo for Rs 30. At the Doon Studio, at the library end of the Mall, you can do the same and have your photo taken against a painted Himalayan backdrop (Rs 30 to Rs 60 for three postcard-sized prints; pictures ready in three to four days).

The walks around Mussoorie offer great views. **Camel's Back Road** was built as a promenade and passes a rock formation that looks like a camel – hence the name. You can rent ponies or cycle rickshaws (Rs 60). Another good walk takes you down to **Happy Valley** and the **Tibetan Refugee Centre** where there's a temple and a small shop selling hand-knitted sweaters. You can sample the local *chang* (beer) here in one of the small wooden eateries nearby, and the Tibetan students are usually keen to talk in

English. An enjoyable longer walk (5km) takes you through Landour Bazaar to **Childers Lodge** (Lal Tibba), the highest point in Mussoorie, and Sisters' Bazaar. There is a half-forgotten old British **cemetery** on Camel's Back Rd and also one at Landour Bazaar with tombstones erected in the Raj days.

About 15km north-west of Mussoorie are the **Kempty Falls**, a series of five falls that terminate in a pool in which hordes of day-trippers converge wearing rented swimming gear (towels can also be hired here). The falls are a poorly maintained tourist trap but if you're in need of a refreshing dip, GMVN runs tours here during the summer.

There's a small **Tibetan market** extending along the path leading from the Hotel Padmini Niwas towards Kulri Bazaar, but the merchandise is nearly all cheap plastic toys and the sort of drab woollen cardigans popular with Indian dowagers.

Other suggestions to while away your time include having your senses assailed by an Indian good-cop-meets-bad-guys-and-avenges-family blockbuster at the venerable **Picture Palace** (Rs 15/35 in the stalls/gallery); playing snooker in the fine old **billiard hall** at Hotel Clarks, Kulri Bazaar (Rs 60); or roller skating (Rs 40) on the wooden floor of **The Rink**.

If you're still at a loose end, you could sit in the reading room of the **Tilak Memorial Library**, to the east of Kulri Bazaar, and peruse the English-language dailies and read the tiger-hunting exploits of Jim Corbett (temporary membership Rs 25, security deposit of Rs 100 required to borrow books; open 9 am to noon and 4 to 8 pm).

If all else fails, there are people who can help you decide what to do in the future. Mr Jai Krishnan Singh, an **astrologer** with a small office next to the Hotel Ratan in the library area, promises to make 'a sincere attempt to probe your future'. For what it's worth, he picked that I was a writer within five minutes. Consultations cost around Rs 300 and take an hour or two. Mr GA Baig makes similar claims, and can be found in the shop called Jewellers – Astrologer, 5 The

Mall. Mr Baig only does readings in the morning, otherwise 'the sun is in the wrong place' for astrological purposes. He charges around Rs 200 for 30 minutes.

Language Courses

The Landour Language School (☎ 631487, fax 631917) in the attractively forested Landour area has introductory courses in Hindi, with most classes held in an old Methodist church (group/private Rs 45/70 an hour). The school is open 9 February to 11 December. Contact the principal, Mr Chitranjan Datt, Landour Language School, Landour, Mussoorie, 248179. Many students stay at the nearby Hotel Dev Dar Woods.

Organised Tours & Treks

There's a small GMVN booth (☎ 631281) at the Library bus stand at Gandhi Chowk, that runs tours to the over-touristed Kempty Falls (Rs 50, three hours) and day tours (Oct and Nov only, Rs 200), which include the picnic site of Dhanolti, set amid deodar forests and with excellent views of the Himalaya; and the Surkhanda Devi Temple, perched at 3050m and also affording magnificent views of a 300km-long stretch of the Himalaya.

A respected trek operator is Trek Himalaya Tours (☎ 630491, fax 631302), on Upper Mall just under the Ropeway. Neelu Badoni here can arrange treks in the Garhwal area, and jeep safaris to Kinnaur, Spiti and Ladakh, and can sort out the paperwork and necessary permits for these areas. Harry Tours & Travels (see Travel Agencies earlier) can also organise treks.

Places to Stay

With so many hotels competing for your custom, prices vary enormously according to the season. Rates given here are for the low season (November to March) unless otherwise stated but you may be able to negotiate a further reduction at this time. Note that some hotels are closed in January and February. Prices rise by up to 300% in the summer and finding anywhere to stay during the Hindu festivals of Dussehra

(Sept/Oct) or Diwali (Oct/Nov) can be very difficult. Porters from either bus stand to any hotel expect Rs 20. There are troupes of monkeys that raid luggage, so keep windows and balcony doors closed when you're gone!

Places to Stay – Budget
Kulri Bazaar & the Mall (East End)
GMVN Hotel Garhwal Terrace (see Mid-Range & Top End) has dorm beds for Rs 80.

Hotel Broadway (☎ *632243*) is a friendly, well-kept place with some nice views, and is deservedly popular. Doubles cost from Rs 125; there are a few singles for Rs 75. The rates include *bed tea* (early morning tea brought to your room), and the atmosphere is enhanced with a lovely tiled sunroom and friendly service by Mr Malik and his family. Food is available on request.

Hotel Valley View (☎ *632324*), on the Mall, is a well-managed place with great views and clean rooms for Rs 200/450. There is a nonveg dining hall. Fresh towels are provided.

Hotel Clarks (☎ *632393*) has plenty of Raj-era character and boasts a billiard room with a full-size table that wouldn't look out of place in a British club. Some of the rooms themselves are a little shabby; they range from Rs 200 to Rs 600. Still, the place has lots of character and it's right in the heart of things.

Hotel Vikram (☎ *632551*), close to the Tilak Memorial Library and Kulri Bazaar, has doubles for around Rs 300. It's a quiet place with decent rooms and great views over the Doon Valley.

Hotel Sunny Cot (☎ *632789*) is a friendly family-run hotel with clean doubles for Rs 200. However, it's a little tricky to find. Take the path leading up to the Hotel Rockwood and turn left at the Hotel Avenel; it's at the top of the hill.

Library Area & the Mall (West End)
Hotel Laxmi Palace (☎ *632774*) has clean, pleasant rooms and reliable hot water. The path down to the hotel is next to the arch on Gandhi Chowk. Doubles cost Rs 300.

Hotel India (☎ *632359*), just above the Mall, is run by a friendly Sikh family. It has doubles with bath for Rs 250 to Rs 500. The water is solar heated. This place seems particularly prone to monkeys trained to raid luggage, so keep windows and balcony doors closed. The rooms facing north have breathtaking views of the Nagtibba Range.

Prince Hotel (☎ *632674*), nearby, is an interesting old building with great views, but the rooms, while large, seem rather neglected (upstairs rooms are better). A double with bath and (unreliable) hot water costs Rs 250. This is another lovely old building in dire need of timely maintenance before the whole glorious edifice collapses. The views from the terrace are great, and from here you can ponder how on earth the gentlefolk of yore managed to get the grand piano up the mountainside and into the drawing room.

Hotel Shalimar, on Happy Valley Rd, is a well-kept old British place about 600m from Gandhi Chowk. It's in a quiet area surrounded by trees, although some of the views look over at piles of rubbish at the back of ugly concrete hotels closer to Gandhi Chowk. Doubles cost Rs 250.

Places to Stay – Mid-Range & Top End
Kulri Bazaar & the Mall (East End)
Hakman's Grand Hotel (☎ *632959*) is a place for Raj-era nostalgia buffs; there is even a cash register in the lobby calibrated in annas. The cavernous ballroom is a delight with pressed-tin ceiling and old prints on the walls. But the rooms have to be seen to be believed: cushioned vinyl bedheads, multicoloured polka dots on the walls, enormous 1920s armchairs and claw-feet baths. The rooms cost from Rs 320 to Rs 560.

Hotel Shipra (☎ *632662*), near the Masonic Lodge bus stand, has well-appointed rooms from Rs 1250 to Rs 1450, and a restaurant and bar. You'll be spirited up in a grubby but high-tech glass lift that gives you the odd sensation of levitating over the Doon Valley.

Hotel Horizon (☎ *631588*) is a very good small hotel opposite the Hotel Shipra with

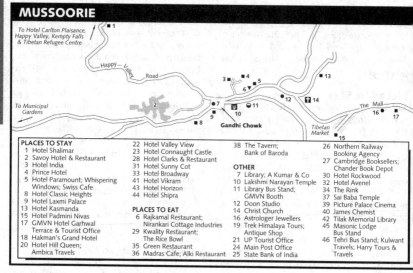

MUSSOORIE

To Hotel Carlton Plaisance,
Happy Valley, Kempty Falls
& Tibetan Refugee Centre

Happy — Valley Road

To Municipal Gardens

Gandhi Chowk

The Mall

Tibetan Market

PLACES TO STAY
1 Hotel Shalimar
2 Savoy Hotel & Restaurant
3 Hotel India
4 Prince Hotel
5 Hotel Paramount; Whispering Windows; Swiss Cafe
8 Hotel Classic Heights
9 Hotel Laxmi Palace
13 Hotel Kasmanda
15 Hotel Padmini Nivas
17 GMVN Hotel Garhwal Terrace & Tourist Office
18 Hakman's Grand Hotel
20 Hotel Hill Queen; Ambica Travels
22 Hotel Valley View
23 Hotel Connaught Castle
28 Hotel Clarks & Restaurant
31 Hotel Sunny Cot
33 Hotel Broadway
41 Hotel Vikram
43 Hotel Horizon
44 Hotel Shipra

PLACES TO EAT
6 Rajkamal Restaurant; Nirankari Cottage Industries; The Rice Bowl
29 Kwality Restaurant; Green Restaurant
35 Green Restaurant
36 Madras Cafe; Alki Restaurant

38 The Tavern; Bank of Baroda

OTHER
7 Library; A Kumar & Co
10 Lakshmi Narayan Temple
11 Library Bus Stand; GMVN Booth
12 Doon Studio
14 Christ Church
16 Astrologer Jewellers
19 Trek Himalaya Tours; Antique Shop
21 UP Tourist Office
24 Main Post Office
25 State Bank of India
26 Northern Railway Booking Agency
27 Cambridge Booksellers; Chander Book Depot
30 Hotel Rockwood
32 Hotel Avenel
34 The Rink
37 Sai Baba Temple
39 Picture Palace Cinema
40 James Chemist
42 Tilak Memorial Library
45 Masonic Lodge Bus Stand
46 Tehri Bus Stand; Kulwant Travels; Harry Tours & Travels

thick pile carpets, satellite TV and views across the valley. The decor includes odd concrete pressings moulded and painted to look like pine wood. Doubles cost Rs 840 or high season Rs 1400.

Hotel Connaught Castle (☎ *632210*) is up a long driveway leading off the Upper Mall Rd. It's a stylish modern place with marble corridors and luxurious rooms from Rs 1650. There's a generous noon checkout.

GMVN Hotel Garhwal Terrace (☎ *632682*) is a slightly shabby GMVN place with pink frilly decor. Rooms, all with satellite TV, cost Rs 500. There are two restaurants.

Library Area & the Mall (West End)
Hotel Paramount (☎ *632352*), on the Mall, is run by a friendly Sikh man. Rooms, although a little small, are reasonably airy with plenty of natural light and cost Rs 200 to Rs 500. There's no restaurant here, but room service is available.

Hotel Kasmanda (☎ *632424, fax 630007*), uphill from Christ Church, was formerly a palace of the maharaja of Kas-

manda. It has been beautifully maintained. There are 1.2 hectares of gardens and the rooms are decorated with pictures of tiger hunts and old lithographs. Rooms cost Rs 700/1100. There is room service and a small dining hall.

Hotel Carlton Plaisance (☎ *632800*), Happy Valley Rd, is a lovely old lodge with a nice garden about 2km from Gandhi Chowk, stuffed with old furniture, prints and the skins of unfortunate wild animals. Somehow it feels almost more British than Britain, a place where the ghosts of colonials would feel at home. Everest conqueror Sir Edmund Hillary has left a letter of recommendation. Doubles are Rs 700, suites Rs 1000.

Hotel Classic Heights (☎ *632514*), a short distance south of the library, has a range of doubles from Rs 480 or Rs 795 in the high season. The travel counter can arrange trekking, fishing and horse riding. The more expensive doubles have stadium-sized beds on two-stepped platforms, royal red carpet and Doon Valley views.

Hotel Padmini Nivas (☎/fax *632793*), about 600m east of the library, once be-

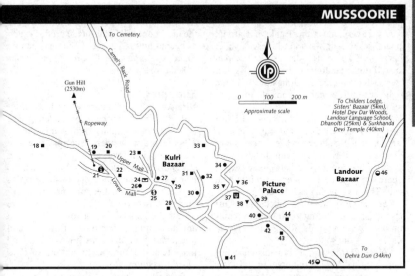

longed to the maharaja of Rajpipla. Doubles start from Rs 500; an apartment costs Rs 1500. The old world atmosphere is enhanced by a rose garden and wicker chairs on the patio. With advance notice, staff can arrange a yoga instructor, and there's a small library, comfortable drawing room and laundry facilities. There's also a Gujarati vegetarian restaurant.

Savoy Hotel (☎ 632010, fax 632001) is a vast decaying British pile covered with ivy and replete with faded touches of the Raj. It's so big it even has its own post office. On a foggy day it has a wonderfully Gothic atmosphere. Fittingly, it's said to have a resident ghost, one Lady Gore Ormsby, whose death allegedly provided inspiration for Agatha Christie's *The Mysterious Affair at Styles*. There are also tennis and squash courts, a beer garden, an enormous billiard room and of course a ballroom. It's overpriced, with doubles (with three meals) starting at Rs 1995, rising to Rs 2795 for a suite.

Sisters' Bazaar *Hotel Dev Dar Woods* (☎ 632644) is in a beautiful lofty wooded

location by Sisters' Bazaar. Popular with foreigners at the nearby language school, it's an interesting and pleasant place to stay. Rooms cost Rs 300 including breakfast; three meals are included for the same price if you stay more than 15 days.

Places to Eat

Most of the better hotels have their own restaurants, and there are a lot of very good (and good value) restaurants in the Kulri Bazaar area. Due to a steep hike in licensing fees, many restaurants no longer have bars. In the low season, restaurants generally close around 10 pm.

Kulri Bazaar & the Mall (East End)
Madras Cafe specialises in south Indian food, with 24 different types of dosa (Rs 10 to Rs 30), plus *idlis* (steamed rice cakes) with *dhal*, and *vadas* (deep fried doughnuts).

Alki Restaurant is a few doors down, with south Indian and Chinese dishes. Here a sweet *kulfi faluda* (kulfi ice cream with faluda: long chickpea-flour noodles) costs Rs 20.

Green Restaurant has good veg food; try the cheese *korma* (Rs 35).

The Tavern, near the Bank of Baroda, specialises in Mughlai and Chinese cuisine; the *reshmi kabab* (tender chicken kabab cooked in the tandoor) is excellent (Rs 90). There's live and recorded music here in the high season. It remains open late throughout the year.

Kwality Restaurant in the heart of Kulri Bazaar has reasonable food but a spartan canteen atmosphere. Nonveg dishes are around Rs 50, with most veg dishes under Rs 40. Next door is a fruit juice stand, where fresh juice is squeezed while you wait. The mango shakes are very good.

The Rice Bowl features Tibetan and Chinese cuisine, including good steamed mutton *momos* (dumplings, Rs 18) and special *thukpa* (noodle soup, Rs 22).

Clarks Restaurant, a short distance farther along the Mall at the hotel of the same name, serves good cappuccino, though the period ambience is somewhat spoiled by the masonite tables.

Library Area & the Mall (West End)
Whispering Windows is a popular spot to watch the holiday makers promenade along the Mall. During the high season there's dancing to recorded music on the tiled floor.

Rajkamal Restaurant, next door, has good cheap veg and nonveg food, and a dignified, ancient waiter resplendent in brass-buttoned livery.

Swiss Cafe next to the Hotel Paramount has Chinese and Indian food, as well as a selection of muffins and Danish pastries during the season.

Savoy Hotel meals are not cheap, with nonveg dishes around Rs 130, but you may be rewarded with a glimpse of the ghost of Lady Gore Ormsby. If you're feeling really magnanimous, shout your dining companions to a bottle of Moët et Chandon (Rs 2000). Beers are Rs 95. The writer Ruskin Bond, who is one of the very few British people still living in Mussoorie, usually spends an hour or two at the bar every night. Advance reservations are essential.

Sisters' Bazaar Superb cheddar cheese (Rs 150 to Rs 175 per kg; not made during the monsoon) and home-made produce such as peanut butter, jams and chutneys can be found at *A Prakash & Co*, a long-established grocery store.

Shopping
Nirankari Cottage Industries, at the library end of the Mall, has carved wooden boxes, brass statues of Hindu deities and Buddhas, Tibetan prayer wheels, ceramic Chinese vases and hand-carved wooden walking sticks made from oak. Queen Mary, then the Princess of Wales, took one of these walking sticks away with her as a souvenir of her visit to Mussoorie. There is an antique store next to the Trek Himalaya Tours office with an interesting collection of furniture and mementos from old British homes, a good place to search for ancient editions of *Boys Own Adventure* books.

Pure pashmina wool shawls can be purchased at Jewellers – Astrologer, 5 The Mall (near the GMVN Hotel Garhwal Terrace), but they're not cheap, with prices starting at Rs 7000, up to Rs 60,000 for antique Jamawar shawls, produced on wooden looms, and employing a method now lost.

Getting There & Away
Bus There are numerous buses from Dehra Dun's 'Mussoorie bus stand' (next to the train station) to Mussoorie between 6.30 am and 8.30 pm (Rs 18, 1½ hours). These go either to the Library bus stand (Gandhi Chowk) or Kulri Bazaar (Masonic Lodge bus stand). When travelling to Mussoorie from the west or north (ie Jammu) by train, it is best to get off at Saharanpur and catch a bus from there to Dehra Dun or Mussoorie, if there's no convenient train connection.

Buses to Dehra Dun leave regularly from the Library and Masonic Lodge stands (Rs 18). For Delhi, there's a deluxe overnight service from the Library bus stand (Rs 160), and an ordinary express overnight service (Rs 130) from the Masonic Lodge stand.

Buses to Hanumanchatti (for Yamunotri) originate in Dehra Dun and collect passengers in Mussoorie at the Library bus stand (Rs 90, 10 am, seven hours).

The Tehri bus stand is for buses to Tehri (Rs 40, five hours) and connections to Uttarkashi and Gangotri. The trip may be rough, but takes in some marvellous mountain scenery.

Train With at least 24 hours notice, train tickets can be arranged through the Northern Railway booking agency (☎ 632846), at the Kulri Bazaar end of the Mall. There is only a small allocation of tickets. The office is open Monday to Saturday 10 am to 4 pm, and Sunday 8 am to 2 pm.

Taxi Taxi fares from the Library and Masonic Lodge bus stands include: Rishikesh (Rs 600, 2½ hours), Haridwar (Rs 700, three hours), Sisters' Bazaar (Rs 120 one way, Rs 180 return with a half-hour wait, 30 minutes each way), Delhi (Rs 1800, seven hours) and Uttarkashi (for Gangotri, Rs 1500, 5½ hours).

Getting Around

The Mall is closed to traffic for most of the year, so to traverse the 2km between Kulri Bazaar and the library area, you can either walk, rent a pony (officially Rs 20 per km), or take a cycle-rickshaw. Expect to pay about Rs 20 to Rs 25 from the Ropeway to Gandhi Chowk.

HARIDWAR

☎ 0133 • pop 218,500 • alt 320m

Haridwar's propitious location, at the point where the Ganges emerges from the Himalaya to begin its slow progress across the plains, makes it a particularly holy place. It serves as a gateway to the holy pilgrimage sites of Badrinath, Kedarnath, Gangotri and Yamunotri farther north; Haridwar (or Hardwar) means 'gateway *(dwar)* of the gods (Hari)'. With such a distinguished spiritual pedigree, it is not surprising that it is a favourite place of pilgrimage for tens of thousands of Hindus, many of whom can be found at any one time bathing off the Harki Pairi *ghat* (landing, or series of steps),

Kumbh Mela

Aeons ago the gods and demons, who were constantly at odds, fought a great battle for a *kumbh* (pitcher). Whoever drunk the contents of this pitcher would be ensured immortality. They had combined forces to raise the pitcher from the bottom of the ocean, but once it was safely in their hands, Jayant, the son of Indra, grabbed it on behalf of the gods and ran. After a struggle lasting 12 days the gods eventually defeated the demons and drank the nectar – it's a favourite scene in illustrations of Hindu mythology. During the fight for possession of the pitcher four drops of *amrita* (nectar) spilt on the earth, at Allahabad, Haridwar, Nasik and Ujjain. The mela is held every three years, rotating among the four cities. Thus each has its own mela every 12 years (for a god's day is a human's year).

Holiest of these four sacred sites is Prayag in Allahabad where the Kumbh Mela returns in 2001.

revered as the precise spot where the Ganges leaves the mountains and enters the plains. The Ganges is actually diverted just to the north of the town by a barrage, with the city extending along the west bank of the Upper Ganges Canal.

Every 12 years the Kumbh Mela attracts millions of pilgrims who bathe here. Kumbh Mela takes place every three years, consecutively at Allahabad, Nasik, Ujjain and Haridwar. It is next due to take place in Haridwar in 2010.

There are many ashrams here but you may find Rishikesh (24km to the north) more pleasant, especially if you wish to study Hinduism. It is difficult to imagine how anyone could attain tranquillity and peace of mind in Haridwar's chaotic milieu. If you've just arrived from Delhi and want to immerse yourself in the colour and pageantry of a thriving Hindu *dham* (holy place) – or simply want to see some extraordinary examples of modern

UTTARAKHAND

temple architecture – Haridwar is not a bad place to spend a few days. The area around Jasharam Rd is a conservative district with some rather fine buildings from the 1930s, in an Indo-Art Deco style (Art Deco painted in a distinctly Indian riot-of-colour scheme). Haridwar is also a good point of access for the little-visited Rajaji National Park, just to the east of the city.

Orientation

Buses pull into the UP Roadways bus stand at the south-west end of town, on Railway Rd, the long road that runs parallel to the Upper Ganges Canal, connecting this end of town with Har ki Pairi (the main ghat), about 2.5km north-east. The train station is opposite the UP Roadways bus stand. The canal is traversed by the Laltarao Bridge, which you'll cross if you're coming from Rishikesh. The road over the bridge meets Railway Rd; the north-eastern section of Railway Rd (ie from Laltarao Bridge to Har ki Pairi) is known locally as Upper Rd. There are places to stay and eat scattered along the length of Railway Rd, with a lot of budget options in the area known as Shiv Murti, just to the north-east of the bus stand. Behind Har ki Pairi, running parallel to the canal, is the busy market area known as Bara Bazaar.

Information

Tourist Offices The GMVN tourist office (☎ 424240) is on Upper Rd, directly opposite the Laltarao Bridge. It's open Monday to Saturday 10 am to 5 pm. You can book Char Dham packages here, but the best source of local information is Sanjeev Mehta at Mohan's Fast Food, Railway Rd (see Places to Eat). Sanjeev is a keen photographer, and spends most of his free time stalking through the jungle endeavouring to capture its inhabitants on film. UP Tourism's regional office (☎ 427370; 10 am to 5 pm daily) is based at the Rahi Motel, farther west down Railway Rd, past the UP Roadways bus stand.

Money The Bank of Baroda, next door to the Hotel Mansarovar International, ex-changes American Express and Thomas Cook travellers cheques in US dollars and pounds sterling only. The State Bank of India on Sadhu Bela Marg also has foreign exchange facilities.

Post & Communications The main post office is on Upper Rd (Railway Rd) about 200m north-west of Laltarao Bridge.

Trekking Outfits & Tour Operators Ashvani Travels (☎ 424581), at 3 Upper Rd, can organise trekking (including equipment), white-water rafting (Sept to Mar) and ski packages to Auli (Jan/Feb). They can also provide guides and porters to take visitors around the salient spots of Haridwar.

Emergency Police: ☎ 426200; Fire ☎ 426000; Hospital: ☎ 426060.

Things to See

Haridwar is a very old town, mentioned by the Chinese scholar/traveller Xuan Zhang in the 8th century CE, but its many temples were constructed comparatively recently, and are of little historical interest, although they do have many idols and illustrated scenes from the Hindu epics.

The main ghat, **Har ki Pairi** (Footstep of God), is supposed to be at the precise spot where the Ganges leaves the mountains and enters the plains. Consequently the river's power to wash away sins at this spot is superlative and endorsed by a footprint Vishnu left in a stone here. The ghat is on the west bank of a canal through which the Ganges is diverted just to the north. Each evening at sunset priests perform the Ganga Aarti, or river worship, ceremony here, when lights are set on the water to drift downstream while priests engage in elaborate rituals. The glare from the sun's rays reflecting off the water and marble-paved bridges is phenomenal – bring sunglasses.

In addition to the main ghat, a series of smaller ghats extends along the canal bank, with large orange-and-white life-guard towers at intervals to ensure that bathing pilgrims don't get swept away.

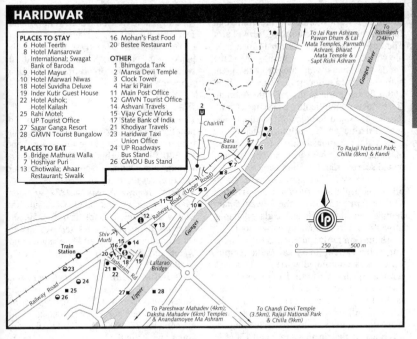

HARIDWAR

PLACES TO STAY
6 Hotel Teerth
8 Hotel Mansarovar International; Swagat Bank of Baroda
9 Hotel Mayur
10 Hotel Marwari Niwas
18 Hotel Suvidha Deluxe
19 Inder Kutir Guest House
22 Hotel Ashok; Hotel Kailash
25 Rahi Motel; UP Tourist Office
27 Sagar Ganga Resort
28 GMVN Tourist Bungalow

PLACES TO EAT
5 Bridge Mathura Walla
7 Hoshiyar Puri
13 Chotiwala; Ahaar Restaurant; Siwalik

16 Mohan's Fast Food
20 Bestee Restaurant

OTHER
1 Bhimgoda Tank
2 Mansa Devi Temple
3 Clock Tower
4 Har ki Pairi
11 Main Post Office
12 GMVN Tourist Office
14 Ashvani Travels
15 Vijay Cycle Works
17 State Bank of India
21 Khodiyar Travels
23 Haridwar Taxi Union Office
24 UP Roadways Bus Stand
26 GMOU Bus Stand

To Jai Ram Ashram, Pawan Dham & Lal Mata Temples, Parmath Ashram, Bharat Mata Temple & Sapt Rishi Ashram

To Rishikesh (24km)

To Rajaji National Park; Chilla (8km) & Kandi

To Pareshwar Mahadev (4km); Daksha Mahadev (6km) Temples & Anandamoyee Ma Ashram

To Chandi Devi Temple (3.5km), Rajaji National Park & Chilla (9km)

On the north side of the canal, between Har ki Pairi and the Upper Rd, is the colourful **Bara Bazaar**. Along with the usual religious paraphernalia (*prasaad* – food offered to the gods – images of the deities, religious pamphlets, etc) are scores of tiny stalls crammed along both sides of the bazaar selling an assortment of goods including tiffins, shawls, ayurvedic medicines, brassware, glass bangles, wooden whistles, bamboo canes and cane baskets.

It is worth taking the chairlift (Rs 20 return) to the **Mansa Devi Temple** on the hill above the city. The lift is not exactly state of the art, but it's well maintained. It operates 8 am to noon, and 2 to 5 pm. If you're feeling energetic, you can walk up (1.5km) and enjoy the view down over the city and the ghats at your leisure. Vendors sell colourfully packaged prasaad of coconuts, marigolds and other offerings to take up to

the goddess. Mansa is one of the forms of Shakti Durga. Photography is forbidden in the temple.

About 4km to the south of Haridwar is the **Pareshwar Mahadev Temple**. The temple, which was inaugurated by the late former president of India, Giani Zail Singh, houses a sacred lingam (symbol of Shiva) reputedly made of mercury. The **Daksha Mahadev Temple** (also known as Shri Dakheswar) is 2km farther along this route, on the riverbank at Khankhal. Daksha, the father of Sati (Shiva's first wife), performed a sacrifice here but neglected to invite Shiva. Sati was so angry at this unforgivable indiscretion that she managed to spontaneously self-immolate! Opposite this temple is the **Anandamoyee Ma Ashram**, which, since the death of this Bangali guru who counted among her devotees Indira Gandhi, has become an enormous mausoleum.

Other temples and buildings of note in the environs of Haridwar include the **Bhimgoda Tank**, about 1km to the north of Har ki Pairi. The tank is said to have been formed by a blow from Bhim's knee – Bhim is one of the Pandava brothers, who fought in the great battle described in the *Mahabharata*. About 150m farther north is the **Jai Ram Ashram**. Here the usual multicoloured deities characteristic of Hindu temples are strangely absent. Pristine white sculptures depict the gods and the demons battling for the waters of humanity. Also here are electronically animated scenes from the Hindu epics.

About 500m farther along this road, a turn-off to the right at a (usually) dry riverbed leads a farther 500m to the **Pawan Dham Temple**, famed for its fantastic glass and mirrorwork, and its elaborately garbed idols.

About 1km farther along this road, on the left, is the extraordinary **Lal Mata Temple**, which was completed in 1994. This is a replica of the Vaishno Devi Temple in Jammu & Kashmir, and it is completely faithful to the original – right down to the artificial hill on which the replica is sited. Adjacent is a perpetually frozen ice lingam, a replica of that in the Amarnath Cave in Jammu & Kashmir.

Farther along this road, which eventually rejoins the main Rishikesh road, is the **Parmath Ashram**, which has fine images of the goddess Durga. The road proceeds past the **Bharat Mata Temple**, looking like an apartment block with a central dome. It's eight storeys high and there's a lift to the top for lazy pilgrims. On the top floor is an image of Shankar (Shiva). Just before this route rejoins the main Rishikesh road is the **Sapt Rishi Ashram**, about 5km from Haridwar, named after the *sapt* (seven) *rishis* (Hindu saints) who prayed here for the good of humanity. According to tradition, the Ganges split here in order not to disturb the meditating rishis. Tempos (Vikrams) ply this route.

Chandi Devi Temple, erected on Nhil Hill by a Kashmiri raja, Suchet Singh, in 1929, and a number of other temples in the hills are reached by an approximately 4km walk to the south-east. Municipal approval has been granted for the construction of a ropeway cable car from Haridwar to Chandi Devi Temple.

You may see large **river turtles** on the banks of the Nildhara River, near Haridwar, which is over 2km broad during the rainy monsoon.

Places to Stay

Hotel Mayur (☎ 427586), on Upper Rd, near the chairlift, has very basic singles/doubles for Rs 170/220 in the low season, and Rs 300/500 in the high season (May/Jun). Rooms have bath, air-cooler and geyser, and those at the front are larger.

Hotel Marwari Niwas (☎ 427759), Subzi Mandi, is down the laneway beside the Mayur. Air-cooled doubles are Rs 250, and rooms with air-con are Rs 450. Rooms are set around a well, and all have running hot water and satellite TV. Room service is available.

The *Hotel Mansarovar International* (☎ 426501), on Upper Rd, towards Bara Bazaar, has comfortable but drab rooms with air-coolers for Rs 550/750, and with air-con, Rs 750/900. A 15% to 20% discount applies in the low season, and there's a good restaurant (the Swagat). Credit cards are accepted.

Hotel Teerth (☎ 425311), Bara Bazaar, is set right on the river, with great views over Har ki Pairi. Air-cooled doubles are Rs 500, air-con doubles are Rs 800. All rooms have balconies facing the river, the staff are friendly and helpful and there's a restaurant.

There's a cluster of budget and mid-range hotels in the area called Shiv Murti, just east of the bus stands and train station.

Hotel Kailash (☎ 427789), Jasharam Rd, has air-cooled doubles for Rs 300 and air-con doubles for Rs 650. Some of them have balconies, and there's a restaurant.

Hotel Ashok (☎ 427328), a few doors down, has basic singles with bath (cold water only) for Rs 75. Doubles with common bath are Rs 165, or with bath (running hot water), Rs 250. Air-cooled deluxe doubles are Rs 500. Rooms are spotless, and there's a travel desk and dining hall.

Hotel Suvidha Deluxe (☎ 427423), Sharwan Nath Nagar, is in a quiet location, about five minutes walk away. Pleasant doubles, all with colour TV, are Rs 600 with air-cooler, Rs 1100 with air-con, and there's a restaurant.

Rahi Motel (☎ 426430) is handy to the bus stands, but in a quiet location. It's also the home of UP Tourism's regional tourist office. Air-cooled singles/doubles are Rs 400/450; with air-con, they're Rs 650/850. Rates include breakfast, and there is also a six-bed dorm (Rs 70). All rooms have colour TV, and there's a restaurant.

Inder Kutir Guest House (☎ 426336), Sharwan Nath Nagar, is a friendly, family-run place close to the Upper Ganges Canal. Air-cooled doubles cost Rs 150 and Rs 250, and there's a dining hall.

GMVN Tourist Bungalow (☎ 426379), Belwala, is in a peaceful location right on the river, outside the main part of town. Singles/doubles are Rs 350/450. Dorm beds are Rs 100. There's no restaurant, but meals can be brought to your room.

Sagar Ganga Resort (☎ 422115) is a lovely Indo-Art Deco style lodge that once belonged to the king of Nepal, situated right on the river. Doubles cost Rs 750, and an enormous deluxe double costs Rs 1250.

Places to Eat

As a holy pilgrimage place, alcohol and meat are strictly prohibited; in fact, imbibing the one or consuming the other is a prosecutable offence. There is, however, a good selection of vegetarian restaurants.

Bestee Restaurant, Shiv Murti, has good shakes (in season, try the delicious *cheiku* shake – cheiku is a small brown fruit similar in appearance to a potato, but sweet). There are also snacks such as vegie rolls and cutlets.

Hoshiyar Puri has been serving *thalis* for over 50 years, and they're still good value. The special thali features cheese korma, muttar paneer, dhal and *kheer* (rice pudding).

Bridge Mathura Walla, Bara Bazaar, has a range of sticky temptations including *ras malai* – a milk and sugar based sweet

served in a banana leaf plate, floating in sugar syrup and sprinkled with pistachio nuts; *rabri*, a similar milky confection; and wedges of cashew-studded halva.

Mohan's Fast Food (*Chitra Cinema Compound, Railway Rd*), close to Shiv Murti, is deservedly popular. There are the usual offerings such as pizza and vegie burgers, with a few special Gujarati dishes thrown in for good measure, such as *batata vada* – four pakoras, green mint chutney and chilli (Rs 20), and *pao bhaji* – two buns with minced vegetables served in a thali with salad (Rs 20). There's also an astonishing range of ice creams and sundaes, and the friendly owner, Sanjeev Mehta, has a wealth of knowledge on sights around Haridwar, and on the Rajaji National Park.

Opposite the GMVN tourist office are three good upmarket dining places. *Ahaar Restaurant*, the pick of the bunch, specialises in Punjabi, south Indian and Chinese cuisine. It's downstairs next door to the Ahaar ice-cream parlour. The long-running *Chotiwala*, a few doors down, has good dosas. *Siwalik*, on the corner, is a multicuisine restaurant that specialises in Gujarati dishes.

Getting There & Away

Bus The UP Roadways bus stand (☎ 427037) is at the south-west end of Railway Rd. Services to other destinations in India include the following:

Agra (Rs 114, 12 hours, early-morning, late afternoon and evening departures)
Almora (Rs 128, 10 hours, 5, 7 am, 4, 5 pm)
Dehra Dun (Rs 20, 1½ to two hours, every 30 minutes)
Delhi (ordinary service, Rs 68, eight hours, every 30 minutes)
Nainital (Rs 132, Rs 158 express, eight hours, 6, 7, 8 am, 6.30, 9.30 pm)
Ranikhet (Rs 112, Rs 143 express, nine hours, 6 am, 4.30 pm)
Rishikesh (Rs 10.50, one hour, every 30 minutes)
Shimla (Rs 135, 14 hours, 6, 10, 10.40 am, 5, 7, 9.30 pm)
Tehri/Uttarkashi (Rs 56/87, five/10 hours, 5.30, 6.30, 8.30 9.30 am)

For Mussoorie, you'll need to change at Dehra Dun. For the Char Dham (Yamunotri, Gangotri, Badrinath and Kedarnath), you'll need to get to Rishikesh. As many of the buses to these pilgrimage sites leave in the wee hours, you'd better to stay overnight in Rishikesh.

To get to Chilla (for Rajaji National Park), see the Rajaji National Park section, later in this chapter.

Train See the Dehra Dun section for details of trains between Haridwar and Delhi. Other direct trains which connect to Haridwar are as follows (prices given are for air-con chair class):

destination	fare (Rs)	distance (km)	duration (hrs)
Kolkata	650	1472	35
Lucknow	325	493	11
Mumbai	700	1649	40
Varanasi	580	894	20

Taxi The Haridwar Taxi Union (☎ 427338), open 24 hours, is directly opposite the bus stand. Posted rates are as follows:

destination	fare (Rs)
Almora	2000
Chilla, for Rajaji National Park	305
Dehra Dun	405
Delhi	1305
Gangotri	2000
Hanumanchatti, for Yamunotri	2000
Mussoorie	705
Nainital	1800
Ranikhet	2000
Rishikesh	305
Shimla	3000
Tehri	905
Uttarkashi	1200

A nine day tour to the Char Dham is Rs 8000 (transport only). You may get more competitive rates from the travel agencies on Jasharam Rd in the Shiv Murti area such as Shakti Wahini Travels (☎ 427002) or Khodiyar Travels (☎ 423560).

Getting Around

You can get from the train station or UP Roadways bus stand to Har ki Pairi by cycle-rickshaw for Rs 10 or Vikram for Rs 5. Low-tech rattle-you-senseless bicycles can be hired from Vijay Cycle Works, Railway Rd, but for Rs 1.50 per hour, or Rs 10 per day, who's complaining?

RAJAJI NATIONAL PARK

This beautiful park, covering 820 sq km in the forested foothills east of Haridwar, is best known for its wild elephants, numbering around 150 in all. Unfortunately their future is in question since human competition for land has severed their traditional migration route, which once stretched from here to the area that is now part of Corbett Tiger Reserve, 170km to the east. Plans for a 'migration corridor' would involve moving several villages and have become bogged down in the usual bureaucracy. Nevertheless, increasing ecological awareness has brought about some advances, with large ducts having been constructed under the Chilla-Rishikesh road to enable the migrating animals to pass beneath. On a less happy note, there have been newspaper reports of well-connected Indians building lodges on the edge of the park and using it as a hunting reserve.

As well as elephants, the park contains some rarely seen tigers and leopards, chital (spotted deer), which can be seen in herds of up to 250 at one time, sambar (India's largest species of deer), wild boar, sloth bears, barking deer, porcupines, jungle fowl, hornbills and pythons.

Chilla has become the adoptive home of Raja, a baby elephant, who became an orphan when his mother, and several other elephants, were struck and killed by a train on the Rishikesh Rd.

Information

Open mid-November to mid-June, the entry fee is Rs 100 for up to three days, and Rs 50 for each additional day. Entry into the park is not permitted between sunset and sunrise. Photography fees are Rs 50 for a still camera, Rs 500 for a video camera.

The (rather unattractive) village of **Chilla**, 13km east of Haridwar, is the only area that currently has an infrastructure in place for visitors. From Chilla it is possible to take elephant rides (Rs 50 per person, up to four people; Rs 200 for solitary would-be mahouts, or elephant masters) into the park. The elephants are often said to be 'sick' however. Official hire rates for jeeps (available from Chilla) are Rs 20 per km. The Forest Ranger's office is close to the tourist bungalow at Chilla; pay entry fees and book elephant rides here.

About 1km beyond the entry gate is a *machaan* (hide), previously used by hunters, but now a vantage point from where visitors can unobtrusively view the park's inhabitants.

It may be possible to visit tribal villages in the park, where Gujars, who still live in their traditional clay huts and tend buffaloes, greet visitors with bowls of fresh, warm buffalo milk. Check at the Forest Ranger's bungalow in Chilla, or contact Sanjeev at Mohan's Fast Food, Railway Rd, Haridwar.

Places to Stay
The *GMVN Tourist Rest House* at Chilla has standard doubles for Rs 265, or Rs 400 for air-cooled. There are dorm beds for Rs 65; you may also be able to camp in the grounds.

Nine *Forest Rest Houses* are dotted around the park. Double rates at Beribara, Ranipur, Kansrao, Kunnao, Phandowala, Satyanarain and Asarodi are all Rs 150; at Motichur and Chilla, rates are Rs 300. At these places, other than at Chilla, you'll need to bring your own food. For bookings contact the Chief Forest Officer, Tilak Rd, Dehra Dun, or write to the Director, Rajaji National Park Office, 5/1 Ansari Marg, Dehra Dun (☎ 0135-621669).

Getting There & Away
Buses to Chilla leave from the Garhwal Motor Owners' Union (GMOU), Haridwar, close to the Rahi Motel, en route to Kandi. They depart at 7 and 9 am, and return at noon and 4 pm (Rs 9). If there are enough passengers, share taxis leave from the taxi stand opposite the UP Roadways bus stand (Rs 10). The official rate for a reserve taxi to Chilla from Haridwar is Rs 200/300 one way/return (although ensure that the driver knows how much time you plan to spend at the park). You could also cycle to Chilla; bikes are available for hire in Haridwar (see under Haridwar's Getting Around section).

To walk to Chilla from Haridwar, cross the Laltarao Bridge and walk to the roundabout, then turn left onto the Rishikesh road. Just before the cable bridge over the Ganges Canal, turn right. After 100m you'll reach a dam; cross the dam and turn left, where a short walk will bring you to a small artificial lake. Here you'll see migratory birds (winter only), including Siberian cranes, ducks and other waterfowl; in the evening wild animals, including elephants, come here to drink (although you should beware of wild elephants at dusk). The road flanking the lake leads to Chilla, 5km distant.

AROUND CHILLA
Situated 14km north-east of Chilla, 2km off the Chilla-Rishikesh road, is the small village of **Bindevasani**. Local buses ply between the village and both Chilla and Haridwar, with the section between Chilla and the turn-off to Bindevasani at a high elevation, affording good views out over the national park. There's a small **temple** sacred to Durga, a steep 15 to 20 minute walk above the village. The temple itself is not of great interest, but it commands an excellent position, overlooking the *sangam* (confluence) of the Bindedhara and Nildhara rivers.

About 14km north of Bindevasani is **Nilkantha**, with its Mahadev Temple, dedicated to Shiva. From Nilkantha, it is possible to continue to **Lakshman Jhula** (see the Rishikesh section), the suspension bridge that traverses the Ganges to the north-east of Rishikesh. The trail follows the original pilgrimage path, which affords magnificent forest scenery – beware of wild elephants, especially at dusk.

There are *dharamsalas* (pilgrims' rest houses) at Nilkantha. You'll need to be prepared to camp out and will require provisions at Bindevasani.

RISHIKESH
☎ 01364 • pop 82,000 • alt 335m

In spite of its claim to being the 'Yoga Capital of the World', Rishikesh is a quieter and more easy-going place than Haridwar. Though the town centre is a typically busy Indian town, the area upriver is much more peaceful and is surrounded by forested hills on three sides. The holy Ganges (almost clear here) flows through the town and, as in Haridwar, there are many ashrams along its sandy banks. This is an excellent place to stay and study yoga, meditation and other aspects of Hinduism.

Rishikesh has long been a holy place of pilgrimage, with sages and ascetics making their way here to pay homage to the great Mother Ganga en route to the pilgrimage sites farther north in the Himalaya. According to tradition, Rama and his brother Lakshmana stopped here after slaying the demon king of Lanka, Ravana. The town grew around the Bharat Mandir (*mandir* means temple), erected on the site where Vishnu appeared to two rishis – a father and son – who had impressed the god with their intense veneration.

In the 1960s Rishikesh gained instant fame as the place where the Beatles came to be with their guru, the Maharishi Mahesh Yogi (later immortalised as Sexy Sadie), which led Ringo Starr to say that the ashram experience was 'just like Butlins', the working class British holiday camps. Rishikesh is also the starting point for trips to Himalayan pilgrimage centres like Badrinath, Kedarnath and Gangotri.

Orientation
The main administrative and commercial sector is to the south of the (usually dry) Chandrabhaga River; the main and Yatra bus stands are here, as well as the main post office, banks and hotels. If you arrive by jeep you will probably be dropped on Haridwar Rd in this commercial area. The northern extension of Haridwar Rd is called Lakshman Jhula Rd. It goes past the GMVN tourist office to Shivanand Jhula; most of the temples and ashrams are to be found on either side of the river here. Lakshman Jhula (*jhula* means bridge) is 2km north. Here there are more ashrams and temples.

Information
Tourist Offices The UP tourist office (☎ 430209) is on Railway Station Rd. It's open Monday to Saturday 10 am to 5 pm (lunch 1.30 to 2 pm). The helpful GMVN tourist office (☎ 430372) is in the area known as Muni ki Reti (open Monday to Saturday 10 am to 5 pm; closed 2 to 3 pm). It's on Lakshman Jhula Rd, near Kailash Gate.

Money The State Bank of India is next to the Inderlok Hotel on Railway Station Rd. It exchanges most major travellers cheques, but *not* Visa or MasterCard. If you're carrying either of these, go to the Bank of Baroda, near the Yatra bus stand, which has a maddening policy of changing only US$100 per person per day. The only other place to change Visa travellers cheques is at the Hotel Ganga Kinare.

Travel Agencies Ajay Travels (☎ 432897), beneath the Hotel Neelkanth on Ghat Rd in the commercial district, can arrange taxis

---

Swami Alert

While many of Rishikesh's ashrams have charitable dispensaries and hospitals, the sheer opulence of some suggests an obsession with matters more material than spiritual, and the behaviour of some gurus falls well short of saintliness. In 1995, one of these 'holy' men, Swami Rameshwarand Giriji Maharaj, fell from grace when he murdered the husband of a female devotee with whom he had enjoyed a less than spiritual alliance. He allegedly told the woman that she could attain spiritual salvation only through sexual relations with a person closer to God – like him.

Swami Shivananda & the Divine Life Society

Swami Shivananda was born in 1887 in the south Indian village of Pattamadai, and named Kuppuswamy. As a young man, Kuppuswamy studied medicine, excelling in his final exams. After working as a doctor for several years, he went to Rishikesh in 1924, where he met Sri Swami Visvananda Saraswati. This encounter changed his life. He was initiated into the Sannyasa order, threw away the trappings of wealth, undertook various privations including long fasts and immersing himself for hours in the icy waters of the Ganges, and pledged to save humanity.

Among the thousands of pilgrims who came to the holy town of Rishikesh were many suffering from disease, and there was no shortage of patients the doctor-turned-swami could practise his healing craft upon, including people with cholera and smallpox. In 1927 he founded a charitable dispensary at Lakshman Jhula.

Swami Shivananda visited all of the most important pilgrimage places in India, and in 1936 returned to Rishikesh and founded the Divine Life Society, whose prime aims were the spreading of spiritual knowledge and service to humanity. The society continues to propagate the ideals of Swami Shivananda, with more than 500 branches worldwide. Swami Shivananda passed into what his followers call his *maha samadhi*, or final union with God, in 1963.

---

and bus travel to the Char Dham and elsewhere. Similar services are offered by Blue Hills Travels (☎ 431865), in the Swarg Ashram area. In theory it's possible to send email from the Blue Hills office, but in practice the connections are very erratic.

Meditation & Yoga Courses

There are lots of ashrams offering courses in meditation, yoga and Hindu philosophy. However, many foreigners report difficulties in finding one that satisfies them – some have extremely rigid rules, some only accept people for long-term study, and some see foreigners as the source of a quick buck. It is worth talking to other travellers first and going to a few lectures at different ashrams to find your guru, if you're looking for one. It is also possible to arrange for a yoga instructor to come to your hotel; it may not be as 'authentic' as an ashram but at least you know what you're getting.

Many westerners attend the Hatha yoga and *pranayama* (breath control) meditation classes at **Sri Ved Niketan Ashram** in Swarg Ashram, founded by Shri Vishwaguruji Maharaj Yogasamrat. Lectures on various aspects of Hindu philosophy are also given here (in English). Courses cost Rs 300 for a

week, and classes are held at 6.30 am and 6 pm. It is also possible to stay here (see the Places to Stay section).

Shivanand Ashram (☎ 430040) was founded by Swami Shivananda and is under the auspices of the Divine Life Society. The ashram is on the west side of Lakshman Jhula Rd, directly opposite the Shivanand Jhula. There are lectures, discussions and meditation and yoga classes daily, with courses from three days to two months (all free). It is possible to stay at the ashram (for a limited period, by donation) but one month's notice is required: write to the Divine Life Society, PO Shivanandanagar, 249192, District Tehri, Garhwal, Uttar Pradesh.

Close by, reached along a path leading up from Lakshman Jhula Rd, and set in lovely gardens high above the Ganges, is the **Yoga Niketan Ashram** (☎ 430227). Classes on meditation and the pranayama form of Hatha yoga are held throughout the year, although you must stay for a minimum of 15 days. It's possible to stay if you're attending classes (Rs 125 per day), and meals are available. Additional courses cost extra.

Above Yoga Niketan is the **Omkarananda Ashram** (☎ 430883), which runs courses (by donation) in a separate building called the Omkarananda Ganga Sadan, back down on Lakshman Jhula Rd, near the Shivananda Arch. If there are enough students (minimum 20 required), beginner courses are run in Hatha yoga. Regular yoga courses are held daily (except Sunday) 5.30 to 7 pm. Instruction in various forms of Indian classical dance is also given.

The reputable **Yoga Study Centre** (☎ 431196) at Koyalgati, south of the city centre, runs three-week courses in the Iyengar form of Hatha yoga during February, April and September for beginners, intermediate and advanced students. Payment is by donation and accommodation can be arranged.

In the Lakshman Jhula area, on the right when approaching the bridge from the west side of the river, is the **Vanmali Gita Yogashram** (☎ 431316). The ashram was founded by Sri Swami Jayendra Saraswati Maharaj Jagadguru Sankaracharya; two-hour classes in yoga and meditation are held at 4 and at 6.30 pm respectively.

International Yoga Festival

This festival, arranged by UP Tourism, is held annually 2 to 7 February. Yoga and meditation masters from around India converge on Rishikesh at this time to impart their wisdom. Seven-day packages including meals, hotel accommodation, transportation from your hotel to venues, lectures and air-con deluxe coaches between Delhi and Rishikesh are US$500 per person. Bookings should be made at least two months in advance to the Director, UP Tourism, Chitrahar Building, 3 Naval Kishor Rd, Lucknow (☎ 0552-228349, fax 221776).

Things to See & Do

The **Triveni Ghat** is an interesting place to be at dawn, when people make offerings of milk to the river and feed the surprisingly large fish. After sunset, priests set floating lamps *(diya)* on the water in the Ganga Aarti (river worship) ceremony.

Nearby is the **Bharat Mandir**, the oldest temple in Rishikesh. The temple is sacred to Bharat Ji Maharaj, an incarnation of Vishnu. The black image of the idol, formed from a single stone, is believed to have been installed by the Hindu reformer, Shankaracharya, in the 9th century. There are some large and unusual carvings around the exterior walls, including images of Narsingh and other incarnations of Vishnu. The temple is open 5 to 11 am and 1 to 9 pm.

Swarg Ashram, on the east side of the river over the Shivanand (or Ram) Jhula, is the spiritual heartland of Rishikesh, full of multicoloured ashrams, dharamsalas and marble bathing ghats, set against a beautiful backdrop of wooded hills. Bleary-eyed *sadhus* (ascetics) hang out here smoking Shiva's gift and favourite poison, *charas* (hashish). Barring the odd scooter this area is blissfully free of traffic.

About 2km north the suspension bridge **Lakshman Jhula** was built in 1929 to replace a rope bridge. This is where Rama's brother Lakshmana is said to have crossed the river on a jute rope, and the old **Lakshman Temple** is on the west bank. Across the river are some turreted oddities, including the 13 storey **Kailashanand Mission Ashram**, also known as Swarga Niwas – Heavenly Abode. A fair swag of the Hindu pantheon is represented by colourful statues on almost every floor, and there's a good view from the top. It's a pleasant 2km walk along this bank to the Shivanand Jhula. In October this area positively swarms with fireflies.

Pilgrims take Ganga water to offer at **Nilkantha Mahadev**, 11km from Rishikesh and a four hour walk from Lakshman Jhula on the east bank. There are fine views on the way up to the temple at 1700m but take something to drink and start early, it can get very hot. It's now possible to go by bus.

There are also great views from **Kunjapuri**, in the hills north of Rishikesh. It's a 3km walk from Hindola Khal (45 minutes by bus from Rishikesh), which all buses to Tehri pass through.

Organised Tours & Treks

At the GMVN tourist office (☎ 430372) you can book Char Dham packages, and there's

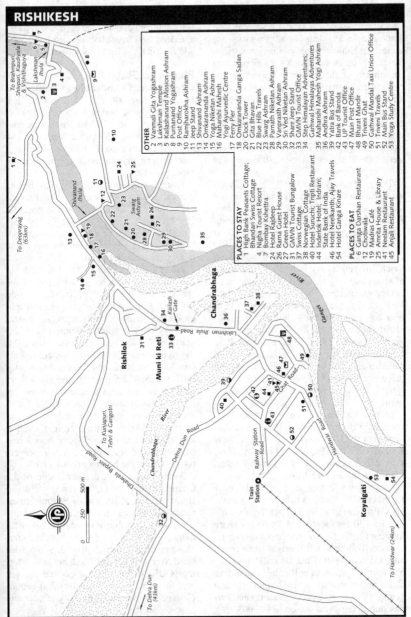

RISHIKESH

OTHER
2 Vanmali Gita Yogashram
3 Lakshman Temple
5 Kailashanand Mission Ashram
8 Purnanand Yogashram
9 Post Office
10 Ramjharokha Ashram
11 Jeep Stand
13 Shivanand Ashram
14 Omkarananda Ashram
15 Yoga Niketan Ashram
16 Maharishi Mahesh
   Yogi Ayurvedic Centre
17 Ferry Pier
18 Omkarananda Ganga Sadan
20 Clock Tower
21 Gita Bhavan
22 Blue Hills Travels
23 Swarg Ashram
28 Parnath Niketan Ashram
29 Vanprasth Ashram
30 Sri Ved Niketan Ashram
32 Share Jeep Stand
33 GMVN Tourist Office
34 Step Himalayan Adventures;
   Garhwal Himalayas Adventures
35 Maharishi Mahesh Yogi Ashram
36 Andhra Ashram
39 Yatra Bus Stand
42 Bank of Baroda
43 UP Tourist Office
47 Main Post Office
48 Triveni Ghat
49 Bharat Mandir
50 Garhwal Mandal Taxi Union Office
52 Main Bus Stand
53 Yoga Study Centre

PLACES TO STAY
1 High Bank Peasants Cottage;
  Bhandari Swiss Cottage
4 Bhandari Swiss Cottage
7 Bigtha Tourist Resort
  Bombay Kshetra
24 Hotel Rajdeep
26 Rama Guest House
27 Green Hotel
31 GMVN Tourist Bungalow
37 Swiss Cottage
38 Norwegian Cottage
40 Hotel Suruchi; Tripti Restaurant
44 Inderlok Hotel; Indrani;
   State Bank of India
46 Hotel Neelkanth; Ajay Travels
54 Hotel Ganga Kinare

PLACES TO EAT
6 Ganga Darshan Restaurant
12 Chotiwala
19 Madras Café
25 Little Italy
   Ganga Travels & Library
44 Neelam Restaurant
45 Anjali Restaurant

also a Trekking & Mountaineering division (☎ 430799, fax 430372) where you can hire tents, rucksacks, sleeping bags and mountaineering equipment, as well as book treks. Rates for treks start at Rs 1325 per day (minimum of three people required), including transport by deluxe coach or taxi, all meals, porters, guides and accommodation in tourist resthouses or tents. Treks include a nine day Har ki Dun trek, a 10 day trek to the lake of Rup Kund, an eight day trek to the Valley of Flowers, and a 14 day trek to the Khatling Glacier (all during the summer months only).

Triveni Travels (☎ 433979, fax 432989) on Haridwar Rd can arrange rafting on the Ganges at Brahmapuri, 10km from Rishikesh, or through the more exhilarating rapids at Shivpuri, 18km from Rishikesh. It costs Rs 300 from Brahmapuri or Rs 400 from Shivpuri, and includes transport, lunch, life jackets and helmets. A minimum of five people is required. They also have caving expeditions through the 200m-long Vishitha *gufa* (cave), 16km from Rishikesh near Shivpuri (Rs 500), and half-day elephant safaris in the Rajaji National Park for four people (Rs 750 each), as well as trekking and Char Dham packages. Triveni can also pick you up from Delhi airport and drive you straight to Rishikesh for Rs 1350 (phone or fax in advance with your flight number).

Step Himalayan Adventures (☎ 432581, fax 431558) and Garhwal Himalayas Adventures (☎ 433478, fax 431654), both near Kailash Gate near the GMVN tourist office, also offer rafting at comparable rates, wildlife tours and trekking.

From their camp at Kaudiyala near Rishikesh, UP Tourism offers rafting packages. Prices start at Rs 350 per day for rafting, Rs 150 for meals, and Rs 65 for share lodging (or Rs 100 for single occupancy).

From Rishikesh, UP Tourism offers coach and taxi tours to the Char Dham. A four day bus tour to Badrinath is Rs 1695, including share accommodation. To Yamunotri and Gangotri, a seven day tour departs each Friday during the yatra season (Rs 3200).

A 10 day taxi package to the Char Dham is Rs 8300 per person. The six day taxi package departing from Rishikesh to Kedarnath and Badrinath is Rs 5100 per person.

Places to Stay
City Centre, Chandrabhaga & Rishilok
Inderlok Hotel (☎ 430555), on Ghat Rd, has standard singles/doubles for Rs 500/600, or with air-con, Rs 770/880. Rooms are cool and comfortable, all with colour TV. The hotel has a travel desk and a resident yoga teacher who gives classes in the pleasant rooftop garden.

Hotel Suruchi (☎ 432269), right beside the Yatra bus stand, is built around a spacious atrium. Standard rooms cost Rs 250/350; air-cooled rooms are Rs 350/450. Attached baths have cold water only, but bucket hot water is free. The restaurant here is very reasonably priced.

Hotel Ganga Kinare (☎/fax 431658, 16 Virbhadra Rd) is a bit of a hike from the centre, about 2km south of Railway Station Rd. However, it's in a lovely peaceful spot on the west bank of the Ganges, and rooms are very well appointed, some (more expensive!) having beautiful river views. All rooms are centrally air-conditioned. Rooms cost Rs 1350/1650, and there are suites for Rs 1800/2800. Free meditation classes are held on the terrace, and guests can use the hotel's rowing boats. There's also a reference library on yoga, a travel desk that can arrange trekking, rafting, skiing, cycling and wildlife and cultural tours, and a reasonably priced restaurant. Evening prayers take place on the hotel's private ghat.

Swiss Cottage, on the north side of the Chandrabhaga River, is run by Swami Brahmananda, a disciple of Swami Shivananda. Rooms are set around a shady courtyard, and the jumble of rooms and colourful murals aren't easy to forget. Singles, doubles and triples are all Rs 50, some with bath. No meals are provided, but self-catering is OK. If this place is booked up, ask here for directions to the nearby *Norwegian Cottage*. It's equally as friendly, if not quite as atmospheric.

GMVN Tourist Bungalow (☎ *430373, Rishilok*) is a good place to stay and is set around lovely grounds. It is, in fact, the place that breaks the general rule that government-run places are not much good. There are ordinary doubles with common bath for Rs 150, or with bath, Rs 350 and Rs 450. The restaurant is good and you can store luggage in the cloak room for Rs 4 per bag per day.

Swarg Ashram Area *Green Hotel* (☎ *431242*), down a quiet lane, has clean, if spartan, rooms at Rs 75/125. Larger doubles with air-coolers are Rs 250, hot water is free by the bucket and there's a good restaurant.

Rama Guest House, behind the Green Hotel, has clean doubles with common bath for Rs 60 (there's one *tiny* single for Rs 40). The guesthouse is run by a very friendly man who hails from Chennai.

Hotel Rajdeep (☎ *432826, fax 433109*) is a good mid-range place in the lanes east of the bridge, but easy to find if you follow the signs. Standard doubles cost Rs 225, air-cooled doubles Rs 325 and air-con deluxe rooms Rs 775. They can arrange trekking and rafting, there are yoga classes held here, and there's a nice rooftop area.

Vanprasth Ashram is right on the Ganges, at the south end of Swarg Ashram, about a 10 minute walk from the Shivanand Jhula. There are lovely flower gardens and a resident yoga teacher, but you don't have to attend classes if you don't want to. Doubles (facing the Ganges) and triples are Rs 100 with bath (cold water only), and there's a room that can accommodate up to six people (Rs 300). There's a canteen, but you can use the ashram's kitchen facilities (free). Foreigners can stay only from 1 November to 31 March.

Sri Ved Niketan Ashram, next door, is an unmissable orange-and-turquoise edifice. There are daily yoga and meditation classes (see Yoga & Meditation, earlier), but no pressure to attend. Large but very spartan singles/doubles with hard beds are Rs 30/70 with bath (cold water only; bucket hot water free). The upstairs rooms at the front have good fantastic views over the Ganges.

Lakshman Jhula Area The following places are farthest from the bus and train stations (at least 4km), but it's a colourful and interesting area.

Bombay Kshettra is on the east side of the river. It's an atmospheric, colourful old building with rooms ranging from Rs 60 to Rs 80, depending on the size, all with common bath, and set around a pleasant courtyard.

Nigha Tourist Resort (☎ *434801*) is a passable modern place with some rooms overlooking the Ganges, which would be better if plastic waste wasn't marring the gardens. Doubles cost Rs 150, which includes a private bath.

High Bank Peasants Cottage (☎ *431167*) is set in beautiful flower gardens high above the Ganges. Take the road to the left, about 1km after the Shivanand Jhula; the cottage is about 500m up a track. Rooms are Rs 250/300 with bath (hot water free in buckets), and the balcony has wicker chairs where you can sit and contemplate the Ganges. Discounts are offered for stays of over a week. Each morning Lisa, the family dog, brings the newspaper up from the front gate. Good homely Indian meals (not too spicy!) using vegies from the garden are available, and you can arrange treks and river rafting here.

Bhandari Swiss Cottage (☎ *431534*), just above High Bank, is also very pleasant. The rooms are large and cost Rs 150 for singles and doubles, or Rs 250 for slightly larger rooms. Meals are available, and there are great views from the balcony. It's just the place to recover from the rigours of travel.

Farther up the track from High Bank several villagers rent out *rooms* for long-term visitors. Expect to be charged around Rs 150 per day.

Places to Eat

Rishikesh is a holy pilgrimage town, and is therefore strictly vegetarian.

Indrani at the Inderlok Hotel has a good range of Chinese cuisine (Cantonese and Manchurian), as well as specials such as *rajmah* – seasoned kidney beans (Rs 30) and gajar ka halva in season (Rs 20).

Anjali Restaurant, farther down Railway Station Rd towards Triveni Ghat, has very cheap dishes (most under Rs 10) in its mirrored dining hall-cum-*dhaba*.

Neelam Restaurant, run by the helpful Mr Singh, is a low-key place in a small lane just off Haridwar Rd. It's popular with westerners tempted here by dishes such as macaroni (Rs 30), spaghetti and good rice pud, as well as the standard Indian fare.

The *Madras Café*, on the west side of Shivanand Jhula, has a good range of dosas, and if you don't like it hot, you can ask the cook to exercise restraint with the spices. It's also worth trying the lassis and cold coffee here.

Amrita House & Library, Swarg Ashram, is tricky to find but worth the search. Go up the lane past the Chotiwala restaurants, turn left down the lane to the jeep stand, and then follow the signs and turn right into a laneway (locals seem accustomed to giving directions). It's a terrific little eatery with books for perusing while you tuck into your banana, raisin and curd pancakes. The owner also does excellent spaghetti and pizzas, made with homemade buffalo cheese.

Chotiwala, Swarg Ashram, is a long-time favourite for rooftop dining. The filling special thali is Rs 30, and there's a good range of Kwality ice cream.

Tripti Restaurant at the Hotel Suruchi has excellent fare, including *dhal makhani* (black lentils and red kidney beans with cream and butter) and the sublime Suruchi sundae with hot chocolate sauce and nuts (Rs 15).

Ganga Darshan Restaurant (Lakshman Jhula), opposite the Bombay Kshettra, is set right on the river, and has cheap, filling thalis for Rs 20, as well as south Indian food (dosas, idlis, etc).

Things to Buy

Rishikesh is a good place to pick up a *rudraksh mala*, the strings of beads used in *pujas* (offerings) made from the nuts of the rudraksh tree. Prices start from around Rs 100, with beads of the smaller nuts commanding higher prices. Flanking the waterfront on the east side of the river, in the Swarg Ashram area, are dozens of stalls selling devotional accoutrements such as prasaad, scriptural booklets and cassettes, as well as shawls and ayurvedic medicines. There's also a good range of ayurvedic medicines made from herbs from the Himalaya at the Maharishi Mahesh Yogi Ayurvedic Centre, on Lakshman Jhula Rd, opposite the pathway up to Yoga Niketan Ashram.

Getting There & Away

Bus From the main bus stand (☎ 430066) there are buses to Haridwar every 30 minutes from 4.30 am to 10.30 pm (Rs 10.50, one hour), and numerous buses to Dehra Dun between 6.30 am and 8 pm (Rs 13.50, 1½ hours). Between 4.30 am and 10.30 pm there are hourly buses to Delhi. The trip takes around six hours and costs Rs 78/225/300 ordinary/semideluxe/superdeluxe.

There's one bus at 8.15 am to Ramnagar (Rs 65, six hours) that continues to Nainital (Rs 88, 8½ hours). To Shimla, go first to Dehra Dun, from where there are several services between 5.30 and 11.30 am (Rs 82, seven hours).

From the Yatra bus stand (☎ 432013) buses leave regularly during the pilgrimage season (April to mid-November). Prices are 30% higher after 1 September. There are four buses to Hanumanchatti, the road head for Yamunotri, 5 to 8 am (Rs 96, 10 hours).

Badrinath (Rs 118, 3.30 to 5.30 am, 14 hrs)
Kedarnath (Rs 92, 3.45, 4.15 and 5 am, and 12.30 and 1 pm, 12 hrs)
Uttarkashi (Rs 60, 3.45, 5.30, 8, 10 and 11.30 am, and 12.30 pm, 7 hrs)
Gangotri (Rs 112, 6, 6.30, 7 and 7.30 am, 12 hrs)

Train Bookings can be made at the train station (☎ 131) 10 am to 4 pm (closed 1.30 to 2 pm). The station has a small allocation of seats for Haridwar. There are trains to Haridwar at 6.40 and 9.15 am, 2.10, 3.15 and 6.40 pm (Rs 4). The 6.40 am service arrives at Delhi at 5.20 pm. The 6.40 pm train connects with the *Mussoorie Express* for Delhi and with overnight trains to Lucknow and Agra. The 2.10 pm train connects with the *Jammu Tawi* express destined for Pathankot and Jammu.

Taxi & Jeep Official (low season) reserve taxi rates are: Delhi, Rs 1100; Dehra Dun, Rs 300; Mussoorie, Rs 550; Uttarkashi (for Gangotri), Rs 850; Tehri, Rs 600; Haridwar, Rs 250; and Ranikhet, Rs 1800. Expect to pay 20% to 50% more during summer. The main office for the Garhwal Mandal Taxi Union (☎ 430413) is on Haridwar Rd, just over Ghat Rd. Official rates for the Char Dham are Rs 7500, or for Badrinath and Kedarnath only, Rs 4200.

You can flag down share jeeps for Dehra Dun (Rs 20) anywhere along the Dehra Dun Rd. You may be able to get a share taxi to Haridwar (Rs 20) from the main bus stand. An alternative (and grubbier) proposition is to pick up a shared Vikram (Rs 10) anywhere along the Haridwar Rd.

Share jeeps to Uttarkashi and Joshimath leave from the corner of Dehra Dun Rd and Dhalwala Bypass Rd. There's no timetable as such – jeeps leave when full (or to be more accurate, when overloaded) between 7 am and 2 pm. Seats cost Rs 110 to Uttarkashi (five hours), or Rs 200 to Joshimath (eight hours).

Getting Around

Vikrams run from Ghat Rd junction up to Shivanand Jhula (Rs 3) and Lakshman Jhula (Rs 5). Shivanand Jhula is a pedestrian-only bridge, so you'll have to lump your backpack across if you're planning to stay on the east side of the Ganges (ie in the Swarg Ashram area). On the east bank of the river, a seat in a jeep between Lakshman Jhula and Shivanand Jhula costs Rs 3.

For Rs 5 you can cross the river to Swarg Ashram from 8 am to 7 pm by boat (particularly auspicious).

YAMUNOTRI
• alt 3165m
The Yamunotri Temple is one of the four holy dham, or Garhwal pilgrimage sites. It is near the source of the Yamuna River, the second-most holy river in India after the Ganges. It emerges from a frozen lake of ice and glaciers on the Kalinda Parvat at an altitude of 4421m. Hanumanchatti, a small village 12km from Yamunotri, is currently as close as you can get to the pilgrimage site by vehicle, though a road is being pushed through to Jankichatti, 7km up the trail. The 12km trek winds through fields and into a gorge, with fine views of the mountains.

Trail to Yamunotri

The 12km (five to six hour) trek up to the small settlement from the road head at Hanumanchatti offers a good taste of high Himalayan scenery. There are *dharamsalas* and several basic budget *hotels* for Rs 50 to Rs 100 per person around the main square at Hanumanchatti, or the *GMVN Tourist Bungalow* down a flight of steps near the river has expensive dorms beds for Rs 100, and doubles without/with bath for Rs 250/450.

From Hanumanchatti the trail passes through Phoolchatti, 1km from Hanumanchatti with several basic *chai* (tea) stalls, to the pleasantly sited hamlet of Jankichatti 6km farther on. There are several guesthouses here, as well as a *GMVN Tourist Bungalow* with dorm beds for Rs 100 and doubles with common bath for Rs 250. By taking a 1km detour across the river you reach the old village of **Kharsali**, where the *pandas* (priests) of Yamunotri live. The old houses here have traditional Garhwali slate roofs and carved wooden doorways, and there is a Shiva temple here.

The last leg of the trek is certainly the most rigorous, with the often slippery trail zigzagging up the side of a gorge. In some parts the trail has been hewn from the rock, in others it consists of concrete platforms jutting out. It may be nerve-racking but the views back down the valley are magnificent.

Yamunotri Village & Temple

The village itself is a shabby collection of chai stalls that use the river as a rubbish dump, but the setting partly makes up for it, with huge waterfalls behind Yamunotri falling like a curtained backdrop into the valley.

The temple itself is a modern edifice built over a hot spring regarded as the source of the river. Heavy rain and avalanches require it to be rebuilt every few years. The small silver image of the goddess Yamuna is virtually indistinguishable beneath garlands of flowers. According to tradition, the temple is built on the site of the hermitage of a holy man, Asit, a devout sage who received the blessings of both goddesses Yamuna and Ganga by regularly bathing in their waters. However, as he succumbed to old age and infirmity, he was unable to make the arduous pilgrimage to Gangotri, and the Ganga, in her benevolence, sprung from a rock at Yamunotri. The old sage was thus able to ritually bathe in both rivers daily, and did so until his death, when the Ganges mysteriously disappeared.

The priests of Yamunotri like to sit in a marble-floored pavilion near the temple, where volcanic heat warms the floor. Steaming hot springs here are used to cook potatoes and rice, which are either taken home as prasaad or holy food, or eaten at the temple. There is a small and rather grubby warm water tank at the foot of the pavilion, the Yamuna Bai Kund, which is used for holy baths.

Yamunotri is the least developed of the Char Dham, and apart from the temple there are only a handful of dharamsalas, ashrams and chai stalls. The *Ramananda Ashram* welcomes foreigners (donation only), and the *GMVN Tourist Bungalow* has dorm beds for Rs 100 and doubles with common bath for Rs 250.

Getting There & Away

GMVN operates seven day luxury coach tours to Yamunotri and Gangotri during the pilgrimage season from Rishikesh, costing Rs 3200 per person. There are four daily bus services from Rishikesh's Yatra bus stand to Hanumanchatti, costing Rs 96 and leaving between 5 and 8 am. Buses from Uttarkashi to Hanumanchatti cost Rs 42 and take about five to six hours. To charter a taxi to or from Rishikesh costs Rs 2000.

TEHRI
• **pop 33,000** • **alt 770m**

Buses from either Mussoorie or Rishikesh en route to Uttarkashi (and on to Gangotri) will usually detour off the town of Tehri for a chai halt. You may need to overnight here if you're travelling from Uttarkashi to Kedarnath or Joshimath. The town was founded in 1815 by Maharaja Sudarshan Singh to replace his former capital at Srinagar, which was ceded to the British. It remained the capital until 1924 when Maharaja Narendra Shah moved the capital and modestly named it after himself – Narendranagar.

There is little infrastructure for tourists in the town as it is planned to be flooded by the Tehri Dam in 2004 – why bother when the town will be under hundreds of metres of water in the near future? Nevertheless there are a few interesting relics of the days of the maharajas, including the **Raj Mahal** (palace), a 1km walk above the old town overlooking the confluence of the Bhagirathi and Bhilanganga rivers, and an old temple in a beautiful position on a shelf above the Bhagirathi, with stone steps leading down to the water's edge.

New Tehri will be built high above the old town, on the far side of the river, and already dam works have disfigured the landscape. The project has been highly criticised by environmentalists, not least because the dam is in a highly seismically active zone.

Places to Stay

The *New Krishna Hotel* has basic rooms for Rs 75/100 for singles/doubles. Directly above it is the *Hotel River View*, with slightly better rooms for Rs 90/120 or with bath, Rs 100/150.

Getting There & Away

Buses from Tehri's busy bus stand leave for Uttarkashi (Rs 30, three hours), continuing to Gangotri (Rs 80, seven hours). The interesting but arduous journey to Mussoorie takes around three hours (Rs 30). There are also numerous services south to Rishikesh and Haridwar and services east to Srinagar and Rudraprayag, with connections north to Joshimath.

UTTARKASHI
☎ 01374 • pop 20,000 • alt 1150m

Uttarkashi, 155km from Rishikesh, is the administrative headquarters of the district. Several trekking companies operate from here and the town is the base for the Nehru Institute of Mountaineering, where Bachhendri Pal, the first Indian woman to climb Mt Everest, was trained. The town is pleasantly sited on the flat valley floor of the Bhagirathi River, drawing pilgrims to its Vishwanatha Temple, sacred to Shiva. The town has mythological links with Varanasi, also known as Kashi – Uttarkashi is northern Kashi (uttar means north).

It is possible that you'll wind up here looking for a bed before proceeding farther north to Gangotri. You can stock up on supplies here if you're planning a trek, although the town has more to offer. On the day of annual Makar Sankranti (14 January), the town hosts a colourful fair, when deities are borne aloft into the town on palanquins from outlying villages.

Orientation & Information
UP Tourism (☎ 2290) only offers information and can be found in an office upstairs on Bhatwari Rd (the Gangotri road), where most of the hotels are situated, about 500m uphill from the main bus stand. There is nowhere in town to change money. The post office is down a laneway off Hanuman Chowk. The District Forest Officer (☎ 2444) is in a densely forested region called Kot Bangla, 2.5km south-east of the main market (rooms are available in the *Forest Rest House* here – about Rs 60 per night).

Things to See & Do
The **Vishwanatha Temple** is sacred to Shiva, and during the Jayanti Festival (Jul/Aug) villagers from the region throng to Uttarkashi to celebrate the god's birthday. In the courtyard is the **Shakti Temple**, dedicated to the goddess of energy, with a massive 8m brass trident, symbol of Shiva, projecting from it.

Remarkably these temples and the **Kuteti Devi Temple**, 2km to the south of Uttarkashi on the opposite side of the river, all escaped damage during the devastating 1991 earthquake. The Kuteti Devi Temple houses a simple statue of the mother goddess, and can be reached via a path that leads up from the vehicular bridge over the river. There are good views back over Uttarkashi from here.

About 11km before Uttarkashi, if coming from the south, is the Bhotia village of **Dunda**, where it's possible to buy woollen shawls, sweaters and blankets made by villagers. South of Uttarkashi (29km) is **Chaurangi Khal**, from where a 3km trek through dense forest leads to **Nachiketa Tal** (*tal* means lake). There is small temple on the lake shore.

It is possible to take a pleasant two day excursion to **Dodi Tal**. See the Trekking in Garhwal boxed text in this chapter.

Organised Tours & Treks
As the headquarters of the Nehru Institute of Mountaineering, it is not surprising that Uttarkashi has several reputable trekking-cum-mountaineering agencies.

A good first point of contact is Mount Support (☎ 2419, fax 2459), about 10 minutes walk north of the bus stand on Bhatwari Rd. The managers here can tailor treks to visitors' requirements, and offer packages including all meals, guides, porters, cook, tent and sleeping mat from Rs 1500 per day. High-altitude porters are Rs 350 per day; a cook is Rs 300 per day, and a mountain guide (a graduate from the Institute) is Rs 500. An ordinary porter costs Rs 100 per day. You can also hire gear here although you need to leave a substantial deposit. Two-person tents (Rs 100 per day) require a Rs 5000 deposit. Other equipment for hire includes sleeping bags (Rs 25); four-person tents (Rs 125); kitchen tents (Rs 60); and cooking gear (pots, pans, kerosene stove, etc – Rs 100). It's best to write in advance and give your proposed itinerary and requirements, but the managers can help you out if you turn up with no advance notice. Write to Mount Support, PO Box 2, Uttarkashi 249 193, Garhwal, Uttar Pradesh.

Places to Stay

Strangely, virtually none of the hotels in Uttarkashi take advantage of the excellent river and mountain views. Nearly all of them are instead crowded along the noisy Bhatwari Rd.

GMVN Tourist Bungalow (☎ 2222) is neither particularly friendly nor well-managed but at least it's on a quiet road that branches to the right off Bhatwari Rd, about 2km north of the bus stand. Dorm beds cost Rs 60, and doubles without/with bath are Rs 350/550.

The purple-tiled *Hotel Mandakini (☎ 3377)* on Bhatwari Rd, has decent doubles with bath and geyser for Rs 250.

Hotel Bhandari Annexe (☎ 2384), nearby, has singles/doubles with bath for Rs 150/230, and triples for Rs 280. A bucket of hot water costs Rs 5, and the rooms are basic but clean.

Hotel Relax (☎ 2893), on Bhatwari Rd, has pleasant enough doubles/triples with bath for Rs 250/350.

There are some cheap places at the bus stand for around Rs 100 per night, but the noise from the road barely abates all night.

Ekant Tourist Complex (☎ 2684), about 9km north of town at Netala, has very nice doubles for Rs 300; the hotel is in a peaceful location overlooking the Bhagirathi River with a few simple ashrams nearby.

Places to Eat

One of the best cheap eats is fresh Bhagirathi River trout, smothered in red chilli sauce, and dished up from trolleys at the bus stand. Expect to pay about Rs 25 per 250g. Other fare to tempt you on the trolleys is chunks of fresh liver, and goats' legs, complete with trotters. On Bhatwari Rd the *Preeti Restaurant* and the *Bhandari Restaurant* are reasonable little eateries serving Chinese and south Indian food.

Getting There & Away

Numerous buses depart for Gangotri between 6 am and 2 pm (Rs 42, five hours). To get to Kedarnath or Badrinath requires an overnight stop in Srinagar (Rs 65, seven hours); buses leave at 5 am and 2 pm. To Rishikesh there

are numerous buses between 5.30 am and 2 pm (Rs 65, eight hours). Buses leave for Hanumanchatti (for Yamunotri) at 6.30 and 7.30 am (Rs 42, six hours).

Share jeeps to Rishikesh leave when full from the bus stand in the morning (Rs 125, six hours).

The taxi union office at the bus stand charges Rs 800/1400 one way/return to Gangotri, Rs 1200 to Rishikesh, Rs 1400 to Hanumanchatti, and Rs 1100 to Srinagar.

UTTARKASHI TO GANGOTRI

The long and frequently nerve-racking journey from Uttarkashi to Gangotri affords spectacular forest and mountain scenery, although logging and the resulting erosion is scarring the landscape.

About 52km from Uttarkashi is the pleasant village of **Gangnani**, where there are hot springs and a nice bathing pool, a temple and a couple of simple and cheap hotels. It's a nice place to rest for a day or two.

On the final approach to Gangotri, the road climbs steeply from the valley floor to an elevation hundreds of metres above the river, with glimpses of the snow-clad peak of Sudarshan (6151m). About 20km before Gangotri is the small village of **Darali**, where bus passengers are assailed by villagers selling apples. Fourteen kilometres before Gangotri, the road crosses high above the Jadganga River on a 100m-long bridge just before the village of **Lanka**. At 3000m above sea level, and 123m above the gorge floor, this is reputedly one of the highest bridges in the world.

GANGOTRI
• alt 3042m

With the growing influx of pilgrims Gangotri is starting to lose the ambience of a small Himalayan village, but it hasn't been completely spoiled just yet. As Gangotri is snowbound for at least half the year, during the winter months the inhabitants retreat farther down the mountainside and the village is deserted. On the day of Akshaya-Tritiya (late April/early May), elaborate pujas announce the opening of this temple and the one at

The Divine Descent of the Ganges

The event leading to the Ganges falling at Gangotri has its origins in a struggle between King Sagar, who slew the demons troubling the earth, and Indra, ruler of the abode of the gods. Having dispatched the demons, King Sagar embarked on an *aswamedh yagya*, an elaborate religious ritual to proclaim his supremacy. Fearing his own power would be threatened, Indra set out to thwart the upstart king. Indra stole the king's horse and tethered it to the ashram of the sage Kapil, who was himself engaged in a deep trance. The 60,000 sons of the prolific king, and their half brother, Asamanjas, traced the horse to the ashram, but their noisy arrival disturbed the meditating sage. When Kapil opened his eyes, all those his gaze fell upon turned to ashes. Asamanjas was the only survivor. The sage advised the king's grandson, Anshuman, that the 60,000 brothers could only enter heaven if the Ganges was brought down to earth and the ashes of the incinerated brothers were cleansed in its divine waters.

The task of enticing the goddess Ganga to earth proved too much for Anshuman, but his grandson Bhagirath resolved not to move from the spot until the deed had been accomplished. He entered a state of deep meditation, and after several years was partly rewarded when the Ganges fell earthward but got tangled in Lord Shiva's matted hair. More intensive meditation on the greatness of Shiva was needed before the god released the waters of the Ganges. (According to another tradition, Shiva allowed the Ganges to fall through his hair, thus sparing the world from the destruction that would have been wrought if it had borne the river's full, undiluted, weight.) The water fell in seven distinct streams, including the Bhagirathi at Gangotri, and the 60,000 brothers finally gained entrance to heaven.

Yamunotri. On the day of Diwali in November the closing ceremonies are performed, and the idol of the goddess Ganga is removed to Haridwar, Prayagraj and Varanasi.

Orientation & Information

The town straddles both sides of the river, technically the Bhagirathi, but venerated as the Ganges. The bus stand and several guesthouses are on the north side of the river; a number of ashrams and more guesthouses, the GMVN Tourist Rest House and a tiny postal agent, beneath the Bhagirathisadan Ashram, are on the south side of the river. The two sides are connected by bridges, one near the temple, and one that crosses the river about 200m to the west. There is an ayurvedic clinic at the Kailash Ashram (on the right bank of the river near the Yoga Niketan Ashram) but you can't stay here.

Gangotri Temple

The Gangotri Temple is a relatively modest structure. The facade is painted silver and topped by four gilded spires on each corner and a large central spire, each surmounted by a golden flourish. The silver image of the goddess Ganga in the inner sanctum is surprisingly small. Before it lies an assortment of conch shells, *chattris* (silver umbrellas), bells and tridents. The idol is surrounded by a silver frame featuring floral and bird motifs. The temple was built in the 18th century by the Gurkha general Amar Singh Thapa, on the spot where the Pandava brothers of *Mahabharata* fame came to atone for killing their cousins the Kauravas. The 10 temple *pandas* or priests are chosen each year from the village of Mukhwa.

A few steps from the temple is a stone known as **Bhagirath Shila**, upon which King Bhagirath sat while endeavouring to cause the Ganges to fall to earth through the powers of intense meditation. According to tradition, it originally fell at Gangotri – in centuries past the Gangotri Glacier ended at Gangotri, though it is now 17km farther up the valley.

Trekking in Garhwal

There are many superb trekking opportunities in the Garhwal region. The region attracts many thousands of pilgrims; however, only a handful of trekkers discover the region's delights.

The treks in the Garhwal Himalaya include those to the Har ki Dun Valley, Dodi Tal, the Khatling Glacier and to Gaumukh and the source of the Ganges. (For treks in the region of Nanda Devi , see the Trekking around Nanda Devi boxed text later in this chapter.) The best time to trek is either in the pre-monsoon period (mid-May to end June, or from mid-Sept to mid-Oct) during the post-monsoon season. In July and August the region is subject to heavy rainfall.

UP Tourism's regional subsidiary, Garhwal Mandal Vikas Nigam (GMVN) in Rishikesh can organise inclusive treks, while there are a number of agencies here and in Uttarkashi, Joshimath and Mussoorie that can make similar arrangements. Budget for around US$50 per day. If making your own arrangements, porters are normally available at the road head for around Rs 200 per day while guide rates vary from Rs 300 per day upwards. The GMVN at Rishikesh have stocks of sleeping bags and tents for hire, although supplies may be limited. As with most treks in the Indian Himalaya experienced trekkers are advised to bring their own equipment.

Food supplies can be bought at Mussoorie or Uttarkashi. On these treks are many teahouses or PWD resthouses. However, on some stages – ie if going beyond Har ki Dun to Ruinsara Lake, or beyond Dodi Tal to Hanumanchatti, or beyond Gangi to the Khatling Glacier or beyond Gaumukh to Tabovan – it is essential to bring your own supplies.

Har ki Dun Valley & Ruinsara Lake

From Mussoorie it is a six hour drive to the road head at Sankri. From here the trek follows a tributary of the Tons River to the beautiful meadow of Har ki Dun. The initial stages of the trek lead through well-established settlements to the highest village of Seema. It is a further stage to Har ki Dun where a day or two could be spent exploring the side valleys north of the Swargarohini Range. It is also possible to extend the trek by returning to Seema and trekking to Ruinsara Lake with fine views of Swargarohini 1 (6525m).

Stage 1	Sankri to Taluka	(3 hrs)
Stage 2	Taluka to Seema	(5-6 hrs)
Stage 3	Seema to Har ki Dun	(4-5 hrs)
Stage 4	Har ki Dun to Dev Thach	(3 hrs)
Stage 5	Dev Thach to Ruinsara Lake & return	(7 hrs)
Stage 6	Dev Thach to Sankri	(6 hrs)

Uttarkashi to Hanumanchatti via Dodi Tal

From Uttarkashi it is a short bus ride to the road head at Sangamchatti from where you trek up the well-defined trail to the village of Agoda. It takes a further stage to reach Dodi Tal, an idyllic lake set in a forest of oak, pine, deodar and rhododendron. From Dodi Tal there is a short

The path to the temple is flanked by stalls selling prasaad. Sadhus sit in tiny cells before aromatic fires of burning deodar branches. Close to the temple, steps descend to the main bathing ghat, and pilgrims brave the freezing waters. Just downstream the dramatic waterfall of **Gaurikund** thunders away, near Dev Ghat where Kedar Ganga joins Bhagirathi.

Places to Stay & Eat

Most of the guesthouses and ashrams don't have electricity – generators generally run

Trekking in Garhwal

steep ascent to the Darwa Pass (4150m) before trekking along the ridges for views of Bandarpanch (6316m). An intermediary camp is necessary before descending to the Hanuman Ganga and Hanumanchatti (for the trek to Yamunotri), with buses to Uttarkashi or Mussoorie.

Stage 1	Sangam Chatti to Agoda	(2-3 hrs)
Stage 2	Agoda to Dodi Tal	(6 hrs)
Stage 3	Dodi Tal to Seema camp via Darwa Pass	(6-7 hrs)
Stage 4	Seema to Hanumanchatti	(4 hrs)

Gangotri to Gaumukh & Tabovan

Gangotri can be reached from Rishikesh by bus via Tehri and Uttarkashi (10-12 hrs). The trek to the source of the holy Ganges starts from the bustling pilgrim village of Gangotri and follows a bridle trail along the true right of the Bhagirathi River. There are a number of pilgrim rest stops with adequate shelter and food before reaching Gaumukh (3890m) the 'Cows Mouth' and the true source of the Ganges. Beyond Gaumukh the going gets harder with a demanding stage across moraine to the meadow at Tabovan. From the camp there are inspiring views of Shivling (6543m) while Bhagirathi 1 (6856m) rises dramatically on the far side of the Gangotri Glacier.

Stage 1	Gangotri to Bhujbasa	(6-7 hrs)
Stage 2	Bhujbasa to Gaumukh	(2 hrs)
Stage 3	Gaumukh to Tabovan & return	(5-6 hrs)
Stage 4	Gaumukh to Gangotri	(6 hrs)

Ghuttu to the Khatling Glacier

It is an eight hour bus ride from Rishikesh to the road head at Ghuttu. From Ghuttu (1520m) the trail follows the true right of the Bhilanganga to its source at the Khatling Glacier. To reach the glacier the trail leads through the established villages including Reeh (2130m) and Gangi (2590m) before ascending through mixed forest to the grazing meadows beneath the impressive peaks of Kirti Stambh (6270m), Bharte Khunta (6578m), Thalay Sagar (6361m) and Jogin (6465m). From the Khatling Cave (3650m) it takes a full day to scramble across rock and scree to reach the ice tunnel that marks the start of the Khatling Glacier (3710m).

Stage 1	Ghuttu to Reeh	(3-4 hrs)
Stage 2	Reeh to Gangi	(3-4 hrs)
Stage 3	Gangi to Kharsali meadow	(6 hrs)
Stage 4	Kharsali to Khatling Cave	(4-5 hrs)
Stage 5	Khatling Cave to Khatling Glacier & return	(6 hrs)
Stage 6	Khatling Cave to Gangi	(6-7 hrs)
Stage 7	Gangi to Ghuttu	(5-6 hrs)

for only a few hours in the evening. The nicer places are on the south side of the river away from the bus stand. The rates vary a lot depending on demand; the following prices are about average. As Gangotri is a holy site, meat is forbidden.

Just over the main bridge the *Ganga Niketan Guest House* overlooks the river and there is a reasonably good cafe here with tables set on a terrace right on the riverbank (not that Gangotri is a place for fine dining by any means). Simple

Greening Gangotri

The Himalayan Environment Trust has initiated a project to protect the Gangotri Basin of Uttarakhand, identified as the most polluted area in the Himalaya.

Each year 250,000 pilgrims visit the sacred shrine, in addition to over 70 mountaineering expeditions and some 25,000 trekkers. A staggering 50 tonnes of rubbish and refuse lies on the trails in the vicinity of the sacred village, and between it and the source of the Ganges above it, much of which finds its way into the river system. Trees and bushes flanking the main trail up to the source of the Ganges have been stripped for fuel for camp fires, and the environs of the basin have been denuded of forest cover.

The objectives of the Gangotri Conservation Project are to remove rubbish from the area with the assistance of the Indian army, mountaineering organisations and adventure tour operators, and to commence intensive afforestation of the area. In addition, the building of rubbish dumps, the supply of more ecologically sound forms of fuel to the region, the training of officers to enforce environmental regulations and the establishment of sustainable eco-development programs in local villages, along with other measures, will be introduced.

single/doubles cost Rs 40/75, and the friendly manager can arrange guides and porters to Gaumukh and Tabovan. Hot water in buckets costs Rs 10.

A path up behind the Ganga Niketan to the right leads to the *Yoga Niketan Ashram*, affiliated to the ashram of the same name in Rishikesh. Several of the rooms are in charming little wooden cabins made of deodar timber. It costs Rs 200 per day to stay here, which includes simple meals and Hatha yoga classes. *Sadaks* (students of yoga and meditation) are accommodated in individual rooms, and buckets of hot water

are free. Classes are held here from May to July; when there are no classes it costs Rs 100 per day to stay here. If you want to stay here and attend classes (although there's no pressure to attend), phone Yoga Niketan Ashram in Rishikesh (see the Rishikesh section for details).

Shri Krishna Ashram, on the south bank of the river, to the left after you cross the main bridge, is a simple old stone place with a balcony. Payment is by donation – say around Rs 50 for one person, Rs 75 for two.

Bhagirathisadan Ashram, nearby, has rooms for one to five people, all with bath and a balcony that catches the morning sun. The canteen below provides buckets of hot water for Rs 5. Again, payment is by donation.

GMVN Tourist Rest House is OK but not great. There are dorm beds for Rs 100, and doubles without/with bath for Rs 250/550. It's also on the south bank of the river, near the Yoga Niketan Ashram.

Getting There & Away

Buses depart regularly for Uttarkashi (Rs 42, five hours). The early-morning buses at 5, 6 and 7 am connect with services through to Rishikesh and Haridwar, while the 8 am bus connects with a service to Srinagar. Later buses terminate in Uttarkashi.

SRINAGAR
☎ 01388 • pop 22,000 • alt 610m

Srinagar is a midway point between Kedarnath/Badrinath and Gangotri, and many buses stop here overnight. It's a busy transit town on the east bank of the Alaknanda River, 60km south-east of Tehri and 118km short of Kedarnath. Srinagar was the capital of Garhwal from the 16th century, when it was founded by Raja Ajai Pal, until 1815, when it was ceded to the British by Maharaja Sudarshan Shingh as part payment for the former's help in expelling the Gurkha armies.

Once the cultural capital of Garhwal, successive floods and the Gurkha invasion have largely erased the city's former grandeur, and it is now not a particularly

CRAIG PERSHOUSE

Extreme conditions – sand dunes and rocky mountains near Hundar, Nubra Valley, Jammu & Kashmir.

GARRY WEARE

PATRICK HORTON

GARRY WEARE

GARRY WEARE

Whether it's your first or your tenth, each visit to the Indian Himalaya will provide a unique dose of wonder and surprises.

interesting place to linger. Set in a broad valley upstream from where the Ganges winds through the foothills to Rishikesh, the basin around Srinagar seems to be something of a heat trap; it's considerably warmer here than Rishikesh in summer.

UP Tourism (☎ 52210) is in the same building at the GMVN Tourist Rest House on Upper Bazaar Rd. The post office is about 200m east (ie towards Rudraprayag) of the bus stand.

Things to See
If you do have a few hours to fill in, the ancient Shiva temple of **Kamleshwar Mahadev** has an interesting history, having miraculously survived floods in 1893 and 1970. On the day of Vaikunth Chaturdashi (November), childless couples hold an all-night vigil here and keep ghee-fed lamps burning until dawn. In the older parts of town down from Upper Bazaar Rd you can still see a few old carved wooden Garhwali doorways.

Places to Stay & Eat
Hotel Alpine (☎ 52262) is right next to the noisy bus stand so you're unlikely to miss your bus. Reasonably good rooms with shared bath cost Rs 100/200.

Hotel Rajhans (☎ 52192) nearby has doubles/triples with bath for Rs 200/225. All the rooms are smallish but are carpeted and air-cooled. There's a fairly good vegetarian restaurant on the ground floor.

Motel Sudarshan Castle (☎ 53351), on Upper Bazaar Rd, is next to the Netaji Subhash Chandra Bose statue (the tubby guy with glasses), opposite the post office. It's a clean and friendly place with dorm beds for Rs 70, doubles/triples with air-cooler and bath for Rs 350/450.

Hotel Samrat, around the corner from the Motel Sudarshan Castle, has doubles with bath and air-cooler for Rs 350, and a triple room for Rs 500.

GMVN Tourist Rest House (☎ 52199) at the bus stand has dorm beds for Rs 70, doubles with bath for Rs 300 and air-con doubles for Rs 800, and there's a restaurant.

Some decent dhabas around the bus stand include the *Basera, Deep Kamal* and *Sanik* restaurants, all vegetarian.

Getting There & Away
Buses to Gaurikund (for Kedarnath) may require a change at Rudraprayag, 34km to the north-east. There's a railway booking agency (☎ 52199) at the GMVN Tourist Rest House, but as usual the allocation of tickets is tiny – tickets need to be booked at least 72 hours in advance.

SRINAGAR TO KEDARNATH
The road divides at **Rudraprayag**, 34km north-east of Srinagar; the route north goes to Gaurikund, the Kedarnath trail head, and the route east continues to Karanprayag, Joshimath and Badrinath. Rudraprayag is revered as the site where the Mandakini River meets the Alaknanda, one of the five holy confluences of the Panch Prayag. The legendary hunter Jim Corbett shot a killer tiger here in 1926, responsible for the deaths of 300 villagers. It's a crowded little town of few charms that has grown rapidly in recent years.

The route to Gaurikund is often blocked or slowed by landslides – the effects of deforestation are cruelly apparent on this road, with great barren scars evident where rock and earth have crashed down from high on the valley walls to the river below.

The route to Kedarnath passes through **Guptakashi** (*gupta* means hidden), where, according to the *Mahabharata*, Shiva dwelt temporarily incognito in an endeavour to elude the pursuing Pandavas (see the Shiva the Bull boxed text in the Kedarnath section). There are two important temples here, the Chadra Sekhara Mahadev and the Ardha Narishwar. The first is dedicated to Vishwanatha, a form of Shiva, and the presiding deity of Varanasi. The pond in front of the temple is believed to be fed by two springs with water from Gangotri and Yamunotri. The *pandas* of Kedarnath Temple live in the nearby villages.

From Guptakashi it is possible to undertake a 30km trek to **Madmaheshwar**, one of the Panch Kedar temples, marking the place where Shiva's middle emerged after he plunged into the earth in the form of a bull at Kedarnath to escape the Pandavas (see Panch Kedar, later in this chapter, for more information).

Just over 1km from Guptakashi is the tiny settlement of **Nala**, which is notable as one of the very few places left in Uttarakhand where a Buddhist shrine may be found, a vestige of the 1000 years of Buddhist dominance of the region before Shankaracharya heralded the revival of Hinduism in the 9th century. The road proceeds through **Rampur** and **Soneprayag**. From Soneprayag it is possible to walk (or drive, depending on the state of the road) 3km to the village of **Trijuginarayan**. A temple dedicated to Narayan (Vishnu) marks the site where, according to Hindu tradition, the wedding of Shiva and Parvati took place. Before the temple is a sacred fire, believed to have burned continually from the time of the divine union.

Gaurikund
☎ 01364 • alt 2000m

Gaurikund is the last village accessible by motor vehicle before Kedarnath. During the pilgrimage season busloads of pilgrims are unloaded at the bus stand and assailed by pony keepers and *dholi* (litter) bearers all vying for their custom.

This cramped little town has been completely overwhelmed by modern multistorey dharamsalas of a particularly unattractive nature, although the temple and hot springs at the heart of the old village retain some charm. The path towards Kedarnath leading up from the bus stand is flanked by stalls in which the relatively well looked after ponies breathe their steamy sweet breath over the throngs of pilgrims, some on horseback, others carried by dholi bearers, and the majority striding with determination to the object of their devotion, 14km away and 1600m closer to the heavens.

At Gaurikund, Parvati engaged in a protracted (several hundred years) meditation to impress Shiva with her devotion, finally being rewarded for her labours when Shiva took her as his consort. She is worshipped in the form of Gauri, along with Shiva as Mahadev, in an ancient temple almost hidden in a maze of lanes downhill from the Kedarnath path. The Tapt Kund hot springs are a bit farther along, and though it's tempting to take a warming dip the pool isn't especially clean.

There are places to store luggage at the bus stand near the start of the Kedarnath path and at the GMVN Rest House; both are called 'clock rooms' for some oddly consistent reason and both charge Rs 5 per piece per day.

Places to Stay & Eat There are dozens of places to stay in Gaurikund, from hotels to simple village lodgings for Rs 30 to Rs 50 per night. Prices vary greatly according to demand. Some of the more comfortable places include the following.

Deepak Lodge (☎ 69913) is above the Kedarnath path, with views across the jumbled rooftops to the forested far side of the valley. Clean double rooms with bath cost Rs 150 and Rs 200.

New Sunil Lodge is near Deepak Lodge, and also has views and doubles with bath for Rs 200. There is also a restaurant.

Hotel Shivlok (☎ 86921), on the square next to the hot springs, has double rooms are comfortable but a little overpriced at Rs 300.

GMVN Tourist Rest House is not especially good value and doesn't seem to get many visitors given the cut-throat competition among hotels in town; dorm beds are Rs 60, deluxe doubles with bath cost Rs 400. There's a little-used restaurant here.

There are numerous dhabas of similar standard flanking both sides of the path; down at the hot springs the friendly *Hotel Pawanhansh* has south Indian food like masala dosas for Rs 18.

Getting There & Away The dhaba-wallahs near the bus stand will help with information regarding bus schedules – an imprecise art due to the state of the road. There is a direct daily service to Badrinath at 5 am (Rs 93, 13 hours), which passes through Joshimath (Rs 90, 10 hours). If you don't wake up in time, there are later buses to Rudraprayag at 7, 8 and 10 am, noon and 2 pm (Rs 35, four hours), from where there are frequent services to Rishikesh and Joshimath.

Trail to Kedarnath

There's no need for a guide on the straightforward but steep ascent to the temple – just follow the throngs of pilgrims along the wide bridle path. The most pleasant way to tackle the ascent is on the broad back of a mountain pony. You'll need to engage in some heavy bargaining to get a fair rate for the pony and its owner, who'll accompany you on foot or on his own steed.

Make sure you know what you're paying for before you set out, or you might find you're forking out for the pony-wallah's meals and the pony's lunch of sugar and water, as well as hiring a horse blanket. In May and June expect to pay either Rs 400 one way or Rs 800 return; at other times you shouldn't pay more than Rs 300 up, Rs 150 down, or Rs 400 return.

The pony-wallahs cover the 14km in about five hours up and about three hours down. Lesser mortals on foot will take about seven hours up and four or five hours down. If you require the services of a porter, he'll charge upwards of Rs 200 each way (double that in May and June).

There is a great sense of camaraderie between the toiling pilgrims on the hike, who greet each other with a hearty 'Jai Kedar!' as they meet on the trail. The path affords beautiful views down the Mandakini River, with waterfalls plummeting down the sides of the valley and colourful alpine flowers bordering the trail. On a less happy note much of the forest along the path has been destroyed for firewood and to construct the numerous chai stalls along the way.

Rambara is the halfway point, 7km from Gaurikund, perched at the tree line. It is a messy little place, and there's no real point in staying at the *GMVN Tourist Rest House* here, which has dorm beds for Rs 100 and pleasant doubles with bath for Rs 400.

Above Rambara the landscape becomes more barren and the path steepens, until 5km past the town after a series of switchbacks and a particularly steep ascent, the extraordinary vision of the south flank of Kedarnath (6940m) looms into view, and the temple is visible 1km farther on.

KEDARNATH TEMPLE
☎ 01772 • alt 3581m

The object of devotion that lures pilgrims to these chilly heights is housed in a relatively plain grey stone temple, at the end of a path lined by drab grey ashrams and dharamsalas. Though the village is not especially interesting the views of the mountains are fantastic, especially on a clear moonlit night. In the temple's dim inner sanctum pilgrims pay homage to a large black rock protruding from the ground, which is worshipped as the hump on the back of the bull whose form Shiva assumed.

This holy object is one of the 12 *jyothirlinga*, lingams believed to derive currents of power *(shakti)* from within themselves as opposed to lingams ritually invested with *mantra-shakti* by priests.

The legend of the jyothirlingam (the lingam of light) stems from a long dispute for primacy between Brahma and Vishnu. During this dispute the earth split apart to reveal an incandescent column of light. To find the source of this column, Vishnu became a boar and burrowed underground, while Brahma took to the skies in the form of an eagle. After 1000 years of fruitless searching, Shiva emerged from the lingam of light and both Brahma and Vishnu acknowledged that he was the greatest of gods.

On the walls of the *mandapa*, or outer chamber, are relief sculptures of the five Pandavas and their wife, Draupadi, and in the centre of the chamber is a small recumbent Nandi bull, the vehicle of Shiva, reputedly made from eight different materials. Between the mandapa and the inner sanctum is a small vestibule with a sculpture of Ganesh engaged passionately with his consort.

In the dark inner sanctum, priests anoint the sacred lingam with holy water from

Shiva the Bull

According to the Hindu scriptures, Shiva, while seeking to elude the pursuing Pandavas who sought forgiveness for slaying their kin the Kauravas (the epic battle described in the *Mahabharata*), saw a herd of grazing cattle, and taking the form of a bull, hid himself among them. The giant Pandava Bhim stood astride the Kedarnath Valley, with a foot on each mountain, and all the cattle except Shiva passed beneath his legs as they made their way home. Bhim reached down to grab Shiva, whom he recognised despite his bovine disguise, but at that moment Shiva dived into the earth, and Bhim was left holding only the hump on the bull's back. Shiva, however, was impressed by the great effort the Pandavas had made to secure exoneration, and finally appeared before them. He granted them *darshan* and atonement, and requested that his hump be worshipped at Kedarnath.

copper libation vessels, and pilgrims, for many of whom this pilgrimage is the realisation of a life-long dream, smear prasaad made of rice, ghee and flower petals on its surface. In times past, some pilgrims ascended a path known as Mahapanth behind the temple and threw themselves from a cliff known as Bhairava Jhamp to gain immediate access to the heavenly abode (this was outlawed by the British in the 19th century).

In the centre of the courtyard before the temple is a large stone Nandi bull, and on either side are stone images of Jai and Vijay, the gatekeepers or *dwarpals* of Shiva.

Other Things to See

Up on a ridge 500m to the east of the temple, coloured flags mark the site of a shrine to **Bhairava** or Bhairab, who, according to tradition, guards over the pilgrimage site during the winter months when the temple is closed. Bhairava is a wrathful form of Shiva. At the rear of the temple is the somewhat surreal sculpture of a giant fist holding an enormous staff, which marks the *samadhi* (final resting place) of the philosopher **Shankaracharya**, who helped revive Hinduism in the 9th century and redirected many of Garhwal's village fertility cults to the worship of Shiva and Vishnu.

From the bridge before the village, a 4km path leading off to the left climbs to the **Chorabari Tal**, also known as the Gandhi Sarovar, a glacial lake over whose waters

the ashes of the Mahatma were scattered. Nearby, emerging from the vast glacier behind Kedarnath, three streams mark the source of the Mandakini, joined farther down by a fourth that falls from the mountainside. The ice surrounding the source of the river is treacherously brittle, and should not be approached.

Places to Stay & Eat

Just past the temple on the right is the *Bharat Sevasram Sangha*, an ashram founded by a Bengali man revered as a saint, Acharya Sreemat Swami Pranavanandaji Maharaj. There are dorm beds or private rooms (by donation), and buckets of hot water cost Rs 10 each.

Punjab Sindh, about 100m before the temple on the right, has dorm beds for Rs 70, and doubles without/with bath for Rs 100/150. There are also VIP rooms for Rs 200. The rooms are very clean but rising damp makes them quite cold at night. Rooms at the back have views of the temple and the peaks.

Baba Kali Kamli Wala Ashram nearby was founded by a Punjabi saint, Baba Vishudhanandji Maharaji. This is a typically drab Kedarnath building, with basic rooms (a mattress on the floor) for Rs 50, or slightly better rooms for Rs 100.

GMVN Tourist Rest House (☎ 6228), a sprawling building to the right of the path past the bridge, is quite comfortable and has dorm beds for Rs 100 and doubles with bath for a pricey Rs 525.

The final approach to the temple through the village is lined with *chai stalls* and *dhabas*, all serving basic veg fare. They aren't that cheap, since supplies have to be brought in on horseback. Temple authorities run a *canteen* at the rear of the shrine.

PANCH KEDAR

According to the Puranic texts, after Shiva plunged into the earth to escape the Pandavas, five *(panch)* parts of his body appeared in five different locations. The hump of his bull form appeared at Kedarnath; his hand *(bahu)* at Tunganath; his face *(mukh)* at Rudranath, his middle *(madhya)* at Madmaheshwar; and his hair *(jata)* at Kalpeshwar.

Although Kedarnath is one of the Panch Kedar, the term usually refers to the other four temples, which lie in the region between Kedarnath and Badrinath. They can be reached by a long (10 to 12 day) trek from Kedarnath, or by taking the rare buses and share jeeps along the rough but scenic Okhimath-Gopeshwar road to various access points and hiking from there.

Madmaheshwar
• alt 3289m

The most remote and least visited of the Panch Kedar lies at the head of the valley of the Madmaheshwar Ganga. It can be reached by a 30km trek starting at Guptakashi, following the Madmaheshwar Ganga to **Kalimath**, at 1463m, and 6km to the north-east. A temple at Kalimath is dedicated to Kali, here worshipped as the destroyer of evil forces. About 3km away is the small village and shrine of **Laki Shila,** where the goddess slew the demons Shumbh and Nishumbh.

The trail then ascends 7km to **Ransi** and a farther 6km to **Gaundhar.** From here it is a steep 11km ascent to Madmaheshwar.

Legend tells that a dog belonging to the hunter Shambhuk fell in a pool here. When it emerged, it shook itself dry, covering Shambhuk in the holy water. This unwitting act of piety resulted in both master and dog attaining moksha (salvation from this life), and both gained immediate admission to the heavenly abode. The temple at Madmaheshwar is a small stone structure with brightly painted woodwork set in meadows. The village offers basic accommodation in *dharamsalas* and simple food.

An alternative route to the temple is via the Deoria Tal, 8km north of Okhimath (see under Tunganath, following). From the lake, a 15km trail branches to the north-west, crossing the Madmaheshwar Ganga and joining up with the trail from Ransi.

Tunganath
• alt 3680m

To get to Tunganath during the pilgrimage season, take the daily 5 am bus from Kedarnath for Badrinath. Heading due east from the settlement of Kund, 6km south of Guptakashi, the bus proceeds to Okhimath, where you can pick up the trail for Madmaheshwar (see the previous section). Murli Singhnegi (☎ 0137286-6741), a graduate of Uttarkashi's Nehru Institute of Mountaineering, is based at the tiny village of **Sari**, 10km from Okhimath towards Deoria Tal, and offers his services for treks in this region.

The main Badrinath road proceeds to the beautifully sited hamlet of **Chopta**, 21km farther east. It wends through dense forests of deodar, emerging at intervals at vast green bugyals, or high-altitude meadows, allowing spectacular views of the peaks without the usual white-knuckle fear of Garhwal's mountain roads. Chopta is generally the first stop on the gruelling bus trip to Badrinath, and you can thaw out with a cup of chai at one of several stalls and enjoy the unrestricted views from the meadows around the settlement.

From Chopta it is an arduous 3km trek climbing above the tree line to Tunganath, where the stone temple, thought to be the highest Hindu shrine in India, is fronted by a Nandi bull. The temple commemorates the appearance of the hands of Shiva.

Basic food and accommodation is available at a *dharamsala* here, though it gets cold at any time of the year. There's a *GMVN Tourist Rest House* at Chopta, with dorm beds for Rs 100 or doubles with bath for a steep Rs 525. There are also some basic places to stay in Chopta village, and a few simple *dhabas*.

Rudranath & Kalpeshwar

The two temples at Rudranath and Kalpeshwar, which commemorate the appearance of Shiva's face and hair respectively, can be reached either from Helang, 14km south of Joshimath, or from Mandal, beyond Chopta, 10km west of Gopeshwar on the Okhimath-Gopeshwar road. The trails are somewhat confusing, so you should find a guide.

From **Mandal**, a 6km trail ascends to the temple of **Anasuya Devi**, from where it is a farther 16km to the village of **Rudranath**, set in a densely forested region. There is a *dharamsala* here, but the locals usually move during the heavy winter snows, so be prepared to camp out. From Rudranath the trail passes through **Panar**, a good well-watered spot, handy for a night halt. Beyond Panar is the tiny village of **Dumak**, 12km from Rudranath, where you should be able to rustle up some dhal bhat and negotiate to spend the night in a *chai stall*. The next village is **Urgam**, at 2134m, from where it is a 2km hike to Kalpeshwar. You'll need to backtrack to Urgam, from where it is 9km to **Helang**, with the trail crossing to the east side of the Alaknanda River. From Helang you can catch a local bus for the 13km trip north to Joshimath.

JOSHIMATH

☎ 01389 • alt 1975m

It was at Joshimath that the 9th century Hindu theologian Shankaracharya meditated and reached enlightenment under a mulberry tree before embarking on his quest to revive Hinduism and establish the four *maths* (seats of learning) and *dhams* (religious centres) in the four cardinal points of the country. Joshimath was designated the first of the maths (named Jyotimath – *jyoti* means light), and Badrinath was established as the first dham, with the

restoration of the image of Vishnu in the temple there.

The most important of Joshimath's many temples is dedicated to Narsingh (Vishnu in his lion form). When winter snows enshroud Badrinath, pilgrims pay homage to Vishnu at Joshimath, and the Rawal or head priest of Kedarnath and Badrinath moves here.

Vaishnavites believe that one arm on the Vishnu idol in the temple is becoming progressively thinner, and that the age of Kali-Yuga, or Evil Times, will be heralded by the shattering of the arm. At this time, a great flood will cause the collapse of the guardian mountains of Jai and Vijay at Vishnuprayag, blocking the way to Badrinath, and a new temple will appear at Bhavishyabadri (Future Badri), in the Tapovan Valley.

Joshimath has a busy market that is a good place to stock up on supplies if you plan to go trekking, and you can arrange guides and porters here and at nearby Auli (see the Information section following). The town is close to the access points for some of Garhwal's most stunning treks, including those to the outer Nanda Devi Sanctuary, and north to Hemkund and the Valley of Flowers. The Curzon Trail, over the Kuari Pass, begins at Tapovan (15km east of Joshimath) or Auli. The ski fields at Auli lie 15km (by road) to the south, or a more direct 3.5km by ropeway.

Information

UP Tourism (☎ 22181) can be found at the Jyotir Tourist Complex, above the bus stand; their office at Auli rents out trekking gear.

None of the banks have foreign exchange facilities, but the manager of the Shailja Guest House and a couple of travel agencies around town will change money at rather unfavourable rates (they know your only option is to return all the way to Rishikesh). The post office is on the Badrinath road, about 250m north of the bus stand.

Organised Tours & Treks

Treks can be arranged at Hotel Nanda Devi, where the offices of the Garhwal Adventure Sport School & Mountain Service (GASSMS)

(☎ 22288), Nanda Devi Mountain Travel (☎ 22170) and Great Himalayan Expeditions (fax 22100) are located. Popular treks include one to the outer Nanda Devi Sanctuary, taking in Lata Kharak and Sena Kharak, with possibly the best views of Nanda Devi available outside the sanctuary, and a number of tribal villages.

Places to Stay & Eat

Hotel Nanda Devi (☎ 22170) near the bus stand has singles/doubles Rs 50/100, or Rs 100/200 with bath. Rooms are clean if spartan, although those with common bath are on the small side of small. Hot water in buckets is Rs 5.

The popular *Shailja Guest House (☎ 22208)* has pleasant rooms for Rs 140/200, and the friendly manager can arrange treks in the area. It is on a lane just off the north end of the upper bazaar.

The hulking *GMVN Tourist Rest House (☎ 22118)* is just above the Shailja Guest House; dorm beds cost Rs 100, doubles are Rs 200 and deluxe doubles with bath are Rs 400. A 5km path to Auli starts just behind the building.

Kedar Holy Home (☎ 22246), on Lower Bazaar Rd, has nice views and decent double rooms for Rs 150.

Hotel Uday Palace (☎ 22004), on Lower Bazaar Rd, has doubles with bath for Rs 475 and an 'executive suite' for Rs 875. The *Dilli Durbar Restaurant* here does north Indian dinners for around Rs 150.

Paradise Café, close to the bus stand, is a popular cheap eatery serving Chinese, south Indian and Punjabi food. *Hotel Marwari* 500m south has a vegetarian restaurant and a range of tooth-rotting Indian sweets.

Shopping

Carpets and woollen shawls can be bought at the Garhwal Wool & Craft Centre, directly opposite the Garhwal Motor Owners' Union on the Badrinath Rd.

Getting There & Away

The GMOU office is open 5 am to 6.30 pm. There are 10 to 15 buses a day to Badrinath

between 6.30 am and 3 pm (Rs 21, three hours). Buses to Rishikesh leave at 4 and 6 am (Rs 125, 10 hours); the 4 am bus continues on to Haridwar (Rs 140). There is one bus a day to Gaurikund (for Kedarnath) at 8 am (Rs 95, 12 hours).

A chartered taxi to Badrinath costs Rs 900, and about Rs 2000 to Rishikesh. Share jeeps for Tapovan leave when overcrowded from near the bus stand (Rs 25). Depending on road conditions, local buses ply between Joshimath and Malari, following the Dhauliganga River and passing through Tapovan and Lata. A permit is required to visit Malari; check with the UP tourist office.

Ropeway to Auli A 4km ropeway carries a cable car between Joshimath and the ski fields at Auli bugyal. The terminus is near the police station at the lower end of Badrinath road. Cars hold 25 people and leave only when full between 9 am and 5 pm. The 30 minute trip costs Rs 200 per person, and there is a generator in case of power failure. The ropeway is supported by 10 towers between Joshimath and Auli, and it is possible to get off at the eighth tower and take the chairlift from there. During the ski season, advance booking through UP Tourism is preferable.

AULI
☎ 013712 • alt 2519m
This ski resort, the best equipped in the country, boasts 5km-long slopes that drop from an altitude of 3049m to 2519m. There's also a 500m-long ski lift. The resort was developed after the conflict in Kashmir closed the resort at Gulmarg.

Open January to March, Auli is 15km from Joshimath. GMVN operates the resort and has a *Tourist Rest House (☎ 2226).* There is no privately run accommodation. Dorm beds cost Rs 60, and deluxe doubles aren't cheap at Rs 750. Skis and boots can be hired here (Rs 200 per day) and seven or 14 day ski packages, including all meals, lodging, equipment, hire and lessons, are offered for Rs 1600 and Rs 2800 respectively. To book, write in advance to the

General Manager (☎ 0135-656817, fax 654408), GMVN, Survey Chowk, Lansdowne Marg, Dehra Dun, UP.

There isn't much in the way of entertainment, winsome ski bunnies or blokes, or wild parties, but the GMVN staff do their best to make your stay enjoyable. All the ski runs end at the resthouse.

If you don't fancy the cable car trip, there is one bus daily during the ski season from Joshimath, which leaves at 8 am (Rs 10, one hour), leaving Auli for Joshimath at 11.30 am.

BADRINATH
☎ 01381 • alt 3100m

Badrinath receives more pilgrims than Yamunotri, Gangotri or Kedarnath, and consequently it is by far the largest of the four dham villages. It is not a particularly attractive town, with its busy bus stand and numerous sturdy grey dharamsalas and ashrams built to withstand the heavy winter snows, but the setting is superlative, lying beneath the snow-capped peak of Nilkantha (6957m), known as the Shining Peak. Below Nilkantha is the black bulk of Urvashi, connected by a saddle with the slopes of Narayan.

To the north is Mukat Peak, also known as Mana Peak, and behind Urvashi is Sunarsali Peak. Above the Badrinath Temple and to the right, the peculiar pyramid-shaped mounds set at regular intervals slow the descent of avalanches. Due to the altitude and the sudden ascent by road you shouldn't attempt too much strenuous hiking on the first day or two.

As the winter snows begin to thaw, temple officials, in consultation with astrologers and the former maharaja of Tehri Garhwal, determine an auspicious day for the opening of the temple, which usually falls towards the end of April or the beginning of May. The temple generally closes in the second week of November after an elaborate ceremony during which the idol is draped in a *choli* (sari blouse) woven by *kanyas* (maidens) – from a chosen family by the name of Molapa who live in the nearby village of Mana.

History

The origins of the temple are somewhat obscure. It is believed that Badrinath may have been an important place of pilgrimage in the Vedic Age (c1500-1200 BCE), and converted into a Buddhist shrine at the time of Ashoka (3rd century BCE). After attaining enlightenment at Joshimath, the Hindu theologian and philosopher Shankaracharya made his way to Badrinath, where he was instructed during a dream to retrieve the *shaligram* (black stone) idol from the temple that had been thrown into the Narad Kund – either by iconoclasts or by those endeavouring to save the idol from them – and reinstate it as the idol of Vishnu. The Buddhist legacy is apparent in the posture of the idol, which is seated in the *padmasana* (lotus position).

Orientation & Information

The settlement flanks both sides of the Alaknanda River; the temple, several ashrams and the interesting bazaar area of Old Badrinath are on the west side of the river. Numerous guesthouses, restaurants, the post office and the bus stand are on the east side. Here the Alaknanda is a fast-flowing mountain torrent. As it flows south-west it is joined by the Mandakini at Rudraprayag, before merging with the Ganges at Deoprayag.

The temple is above the west bank of the Alaknanda, and is reached by a sturdy iron footbridge. At either end of the bridge, moneychangers sit before pyramids of coins, converting pilgrims' rupees into handfuls of coins that are given to the beggars and mendicant sadhus who line the bridge and the steps to the temple (who then return their takings to the moneychangers and exchange them for larger denominations, the moneychangers making a commission on each transaction).

Badrinath Temple

The temple of Badri Narayan is an imposing hive-shaped edifice, reminiscent of the temples built during the reign of the Katyuri rajas, who ruled from Kumaon. The head

Vishnu at Badrinath

The presiding deity at Badrinath is Vishnu. According to Hindu scriptures, Vishnu was reclining by the shores of the Celestial Lake as the goddess Lakshmi massaged his feet when a sage named Narad passed by and rebuked him for indulging in worldly pleasures. Abashed, Vishnu sent Lakshmi away and retreated to the high Himalaya, where he fed himself on berries *(badri)* growing wild in the region and, adopting the Yogdhyani posture, began to meditate for several years.

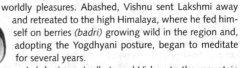

Lakshmi eventually traced Vishnu to the mountain retreat and implored the god to resume his original Sringaric form. Vishnu agreed, on the condition that the valley remain a place of meditation and not of worldly pleasures, and that he be worshipped in both his Yogdhyani and Sringaric forms, the former by gods and sages and the latter by pilgrims.

Lakshmi, as the consort of Vishnu, is usually placed on the left-hand side of the idol. However, during the summer pilgrimage season, the statue of Lakshmi can be seen on the right-hand side of Vishnu's idol – the deities are worshipped as individual entities, not as a couple. During winter, when Badrinath is covered in snow and the temple is closed to pilgrims, leaving the valley to the gods and sages, Vishnu adopts his Yogdhyani form, with Lakshmi on his left-hand side.

Vishnu

priest or Rawal is from the Brahman Namboodiri caste from Kerala, and is also the head priest of Kedarnath. Other priests sit in the cloisters with lists of rituals on offer, ranging from a few rupees to thousands of rupees.

Before the main entrance is a stone Garuda, the vehicle of Vishnu. Six large carved pillars of shaligram support the ceiling of the mandapa, each formed from single blocks of stone. The double doors of the inner sanctum are of silver, flanked by the celestial guardians, Jai (to the right) and Vijay (to the left). In the top panel of each door are raised images of Surya, the sun god.

The small shaligram idol of Vishnu is almost impossible to make out, being heavily garlanded with flowers.

Other Things to See

Just below the temple along the riverbank are the **Tapt Kund** hot springs, in whose sulphurous waters pilgrims bathe before visiting the temple. About 3km north of the village is the small Bhotia settlement of **Mana**, the last village before the Tibetan border, just over 30km away. The village is a jumble of small sturdy stone buildings, quite attractive in a rustic way. From here, according to Hindu lore, a path leads directly to Mt Kailash, the abode of Shiva. Mana was once an important trading village on the trade route between India and Tibet over the Mana La, but with the tensions between China and India the villagers have lost their traditional livelihood and many of the inhabitants now scrape out a living weaving pure wool carpets called *duns*, and tend sheep, goats and yaks. During winter the villagers retreat from the heavy snows to Joshimath and Chamoli.

About 22m north-west of Mana is the **Vyas Gufa** (cave). Locals believe the *Mahabharata* was dictated to Ganesh here by the saint Vyasji. A path leads across the **Bhim Pul** (*pul* means bridge), believed to have been built by the giant Pandava Bhim to enable his brothers to cross the Sarasvati River, to the base of the **Vasudhara Falls**, 4km from Mana. The falls are believed to be the source of the Alaknanda as it falls from heaven. If the top of the falls are obscured by clouds the river actually does seem to fall from heaven. If, however, the weather is clear, there are excellent views of Nilkantha (6957m) to the west. The falls are as far as foreigners are permitted to go without permission from the District Magistrate in Chamoli, which is unlikely to be granted.

Mana can be reached along a road starting at the bus station that eventually flanks the west bank of the Alaknanda River. You can hire a taxi to Mana (Rs 250 return), or it's fairly easy to hitchhike. Soldiers from the camp just before the village may ask to see your passport and check that you don't intend to walk into Tibet.

A short distance beyond Old Badrinath, to the left of the temple, a path divides. The right-hand path mounts the foothills of Nilkantha, passing a few sadhu caves, and ascends a saddle where there are excellent views back over Badrinath, to Chadrapaduka, a walk of some 30 minutes. Here a boulder bears an impression that is believed to be the **footprint** of Vishnu. The left-hand path at the fork just beyond Old Badrinath leads to Bamni village, crossing a small bridge. Above the village, which is less than 1km from Badrinath, is a small **temple** dedicated to the beautiful nymph Urvashi, sent by Indra to distract the sage Arghya from his meditations.

Places to Stay & Eat
Gujarat Bhavan (☎ 2266), on Main Rd, is a few doors up from the Kwality restaurant. Here you'll find spotless singles/doubles with bath for Rs 100/200 (in May and June, doubles only from Rs 200). The manager is very helpful and friendly and there's a dhaba downstairs serving basic fare.

Modi Bhavan nearby also has good double rooms with bath for Rs 150. Hot water in buckets costs Rs 10.

GMVN Tourist Rest House is next to the bus stand and has dorm beds for Rs 100, small doubles for Rs 200, and deluxe doubles with bath for Rs 650.

GMVN Hotel Devlok (☎ 2338) is just about the best in town with doubles for Rs 450 and deluxe doubles in a separate annexe for Rs 650. There's a restaurant here as well and a lounge where you can immerse yourself in day-old English-language newspapers.

If all the above are full then visit the Temple Committee Reception Office (☎ 2204), on Temple Rd near the junction with Main Rd. The office can arrange lodgings in any number of dharamsalas in the town from Rs 50 per double up to Rs 300. It is open daily 8 am to 8 pm.

There are three good restaurants on Main Rd, near the corner with Temple Rd. At the *Kwality*, which has a fine view of the temple over the river, a full meal will set you back about Rs 100. Next door the *Saket Restaurant* does Punjabi, south Indian and Chinese-Indian (Chindian?) food. Another good option is the *Vijay Laxmi*, which has south Indian and Gujarati cuisine. Over on the temple side of the river there are lots of simple old dhabas serving dhal and rice for around Rs 10.

Shopping
There is an enormous amount of religious paraphernalia on sale at Badrinath, from beads, medallions and cassettes to gold embossed plaques of the temple with deities hovering above it. You can even get a video made of your visit to the temple, for highly negotiable prices, complete with religious images and music added. Badrinath is also a good place to buy perky little woollen hats and socks, in a variety of colours, for around Rs 15 each.

Getting There & Away

Buses to Joshimath depart at 6.30, 9 and 11.30 am, and 2 and 4 pm (Rs 21, three hours). The 6.30 am bus continues on to Rishikesh (Rs 149, 12 hours). At 8 am daily there is a direct service to Gaurikund, which is the road head for Kedarnath (Rs 93, 13 hours). You may be able to hire a taxi (depending on availability) to Rishikesh for about Rs 2500, or get a share jeep leaving at around 7 am (or when full) for about Rs 250 per person.

NANDA DEVI SANCTUARY

While not the highest of the snow-clad peaks of the Himalaya, Nanda Devi has been frequently described as the most beautiful, with mountaineers eulogising the splendour of her twin peaks, the higher of the two at 7817m. They are surrounded by a virtually impenetrable ring of lesser peaks, some of which have never been scaled, which encompass a vast wilderness area.

The mountain finds a special place in the hearts of many Garhwalis and Kumaonis; the cult worship of Nanda Devi, the bliss-giving goddess, forms an integral part of the religious life of those who live within sight of the magnificent peaks.

In 1934 the mountaineers Eric Shipton and Bill Tillman, accompanied by three Sherpas, pioneered a route through the Rishiganga gorge, accessed from Lata, 25km from Joshimath. Tillman was the first person to conquer the summit of Nanda Devi, but the goddess has taken a heavy toll on later attempts to violate her sanctity. In 1976, an American woman, 24-year-old Nanda Devi Unsoeld, collapsed and died only 300m short of the summit of the mountain after which she had been named by her mountaineering father, Will Unsoeld.

Unfortunately, this national park is currently closed to trekkers after expeditions took an unsustainable toll on timber for fuel, and it is likely the area will remain closed. Contact GMVN or KMVN for details. For information on treks outside the sanctuary, see the Trekking Around Nanda Devi boxed text in this chapter.

GWALDAM

- alt 1830m

Easily accessible from Almora and Nainital, 78km and 131km respectively to the south, Gwaldam is a ideal base for treks farther north, including to Rup Kund and the Curzon Trail.

From this small market town, set amid apple orchards, you can get the best views of Trisul, whose triple peaks are considered to be the trident of Shiva. There is a small Buddhist temple about 1.5km from the main crossroads.

Gwaldam has a good *GMVN Tourist Bungalow* with dorm beds for Rs 100 and doubles with bath for Rs 450. *Hotel Trishul* has a nice garden and singles/doubles for Rs 100/150.

There are good bus connections to Tharali, 21km north, from where there is a daily bus or jeep to Mandoli, road head for the Rup Kund trek.

RUP KUND

- alt 4478m

Set beneath the towering summit of Trisul (7120m), Rup Kund is sometimes referred to as the 'mystery lake' on account of the large number of human skeletons (over 300) found here. The skeletons are thought to be over 500 years old, and various theories have been proposed as to the calamity that overcame them. The most probable is that they were a party of pilgrims en route to Homkund to pay homage to the goddess Nanda Devi. While crossing the precipitous bank above the lake, the pilgrims evidently lost their footing, with those higher up falling on their brethren below, and the whole cursed party tumbled into the icy lake. Other theories hold that the skeletons are the remnants of an army of the Dogra general from Jammu, Zorawar Singh, who tried to invade Tibet.

The vision of these human remains presents a rather gruesome spectacle, the atmosphere enhanced by the desolate nature of the landscape. Nevertheless, trekkers with a taste for the macabre continue to make the arduous trek to Rup Kund.

Trekking around Nanda Devi

Treks near Nanda Devi (7817m), the second-highest peak in India after Kanchenjunga in Sikkim, are comparable with some of the spectacular treks in the Annapurna or Everest regions of Nepal.

Geographically the summit of Nanda Devi is recognised as the northern border between the Uttarakhand regions of Garhwal and Kumaon.

Treks on the western side of Nanda Devi include the famous Valley of Flowers, the Kuari Pass trek and the trek to the mysterious lake of Rup Kund. South of Nanda Devi are the treks to the Pindar Glacier while to the east of Nanda Devi is the trek to the Milam Glacier – these two treks are outlined in the Trekking in Kumaon boxed text, later in this chapter. Note that trekking in the Nanda Devi Sanctuary to the base of Nanda Devi is currently banned by the Indian government and at present there are no plans to lift this restriction.

The best time to trek in the Nanda Devi region is either in the pre-monsoon period from mid-May to the end of June, or from the mid-September to mid-October during the post-monsoon season. In July and August the region is subject to heavy rainfall although this is the best time to appreciate the rich variety of wildflowers in the Valley of Flowers or the nearby high alpine meadows or *bugyals*.

UP Tourism's regional subsidiary, the Garhwal Mandal Vikas Nigam (GMVN) can organise inclusive treks. Budget for around US$50 per day. If making your own arrangements, porters are normally available at the road head for around Rs 200 per day, while guide rates vary from Rs 300 per day upwards. Food supplies can be bought at Joshimath before commencing the Kuari Pass trek or at Karanprayag if trekking to Rup Kund. If trekking to the Valley of the Flowers or the Hem Kund there are numerous tea stalls en route while there are many hotels at Ghangaria, the base for both the Valley of the Flowers or Hem Kund.

Valley of Flowers & Hemkund

The fabled Valley of Flowers was 'discovered' by the British mountaineer Frank Smythe in the 1930s. Throughout the summer months (mid-Jun to mid-Sept) the valley is an enchanting sight with an impressive array of wildflowers, while the snow-clad peaks including Nilgiri Parbat (6474m) stand in bold relief against the skyline. The valley is nearly 10km long and 2km wide, and is divided by the Pushpawati stream, into which several tiny streams and waterfalls merge. The valley has suffered from large numbers of trekkers and shepherds in the past, leaving the authorities with little option but to create a national park. Day walks into the valley, but no overnight camping, is permitted. It costs Rs 15/100 for Indians/foreigners to enter the Valley of Flowers.

Many local buses operate between Joshimath and Govind Ghat, the starting point for the trek. From Govind Ghat there is a gradual ascent along a well-maintained pilgrim trail to the camp at Ghangaria – the base from where day walks can be made into the Valley of Flowers. From Ghangaria, you can follow the Laxma Ganga to the lake at Hemkund – quite a steep climb. In the Sikh holy book, the *Granth Sahib*, the Sikh Guru Gobind Singh recounts that in a previous life he meditated on the shores of a lake surrounded by seven snowcapped mountains. That lake is now recognised as Hemkund.

Stage 1	Govind Ghat to Ghangaria	(5-6 hrs)
Stage 2	Ghangaria to Valley of Flowers & return	(3-4 hrs)
Stage 3	Ghangaria to Hemkund & return	(5-6 hrs)
Stage 4	Ghangaria to Govind Ghat	(4 hrs)

Trekking around Nanda Devi

Joshimath to Ghat via the Kuari Pass

The trek over the Kuari Pass is also known as the Curzon Trail – however, the Curzon party did not actually cross the pass, abandoning their attempt after being attacked by wild bees.

From Joshimath there is a daily bus service to Auli to commence the trek. On the initial stages there are uninterrupted views up the Rishi Ganga to the Nanda Devi Sanctuary. The trail then winds through a series of pastures with panoramic views of Dunagiri (7066m) and the Chaukhamba massif including Chaukhamba 1 (7138m). The best views of Nanda Devi (7817m) require a day walk along the ridge above the pass. From the Kauri Pass it is a steep descent to the meadow at Dakwani before continuing to the shepherd camp at Sutoli. It's a further two stages across the forested ridges and past small villages high above the Birthi Ganga to the village of Ramni. The final stage descends (steeply in places) to the road head at Ghat where jeeps and buses complete the 30km to Nandaprayag on the Joshimath to Rishikesh road.

Stage 1	Auli to Chitraganta	(6-7 hrs)
Stage 2	Chitraganta to Dakwani via the Kuari Pass	(4-5 hrs)
Stage 3	Dakwani to Ghangri	(7 hrs)
Stage 5	Ghangri to Ramni	(5-6 hrs)
Stage 6	Ramni to Ghat	(5 hrs)

Ghat to Mandoli via Rup Kund

Set beneath the towering summit of Trisul (7120m), Rup Kund is sometimes referred to as the 'mystery lake' on account of the many human skeletons found here. Every 12 years thousands of devout pilgrims make an arduous trek when following the Raj Jay yatra from Nauti village, near Karanprayag. The pilgrims are said to be led by a four-horned ram that takes them from here to Rup Kund. A golden idol of the goddess Nanda Devi is carried in a silver palanquin.

The first stage of the trek climbs from Ghat to the village of Ramni before following a trail through mixed forest and traditional Hindu villages to the large village of Wan. The trail to Rup Kund then ascends through oak, pine and rhododendron forest to the alpine camp at Badni bugyal. The views from this camp are among the finest in the West Himalaya. To the east are the peaks beyond Joshimath, while to the south-east the Great Himalaya Range extends as far as the eye can see across western Garhwal. To the south the foothills descend to the Indian plains, while to the north Trisul (7120m) provides an impressive backdrop.

It's a further stage to the camp at Bhogabasa. From here you can reach Rup Kund with time to return to Badni bugyal the same day. From Badni bugyal there are a number of short cuts across the bugyals and down to the trail between Wan and Mandoli. From Mandoli there are buses and jeeps to Debal and onward connections to Gwaldam and Nainital.

Stage 1	Ghat to Ramni	(5 hrs)
Stage 2	Ramni to Sutol	(6-7 hrs)
Stage 3	Sutol to Wan	(5 hrs)
Stage 4	Wan to Badni bugyal	(5 hrs)
Stage 5	Badni bugyal to Bhogabasa	(4-5 hrs)
Stage 6	Bhogabasa to Rup Kund & return to Badni bugyal	(6-7 hrs)
Stage 7	Badni bugyal to Mandoli	(6-7 hrs)

See the Trekking in Kumaon boxed text for details of treks to the Pindari and Milam glaciers.

Kumaon

• **pop 2,949,199**

Bordered by Garhwal to the west and north, and Nepal to the east, the district of Kumaon covers 21,071 sq km and encompasses three of the eight Himalayan districts of Uttar Pradesh, those of Pithoragarh, Almora and Nainital. Kumaon is known for its hill stations, most well known of which are Almora and Nainital, the first perched along a 5km-long ridge that affords a fine Himalayan panorama, and the second around an emerald green crater lake. However, it also has the less well known, and hence less developed and more tranquil, hill stations of Ranikhet and Kausani.

Mahatma Gandhi was particularly inspired by the forested slopes and stunning 350km-wide vistas at peaceful Kausani, which he believed were unsurpassed. Ranikhet was the favourite of India's first prime minister, Jawaharlal Nehru, who, after visiting the hill station, advocated that more people from the plains should travel to the Himalaya where he was sure they would return home more invigorated and spiritually restored.

Other natural assets include the Corbett National Park and adjacent Sonanadi Wildlife Sanctuary, collectively known as the Corbett Tiger Reserve, and the beautiful alpine scenery along the treks to the Pindari and Milam glaciers.

Apart from its superb natural assets, Kumaon also possesses a number of beautiful temple complexes that are sacred to Shiva, legacies of the Katyuri (8th to 14th centuries) and Chand (15th to 18th centuries) dynasties. These can be found at Baijnath, Bhageshwar and Jageshwar. The patron goddess of Kumaon is Nanda Devi – although the mountain of Nanda Devi, perceived as a manifestation of the goddess, is located in Garhwal, her beautiful twin peaks are eminently visible from Kumaon, inspiring the reverence and awe of its inhabitants.

Kumaon forms an integral part of the important pilgrimage route to Mt Kailash and Lake Mansarovar, in Tibet, with pilgrims crossing into Tibet via the 4334m-high Lipu Pass. British interest in Kumaon's proximity to Tibet was inspired more by concerns of a commercial than spiritual nature: the British coveted the pure pashmina shawls from Tibet and they were keen to exploit the traditional Indo-Tibetan trading routes. In 1815, Kumaon was relinquished to the East India Company, along with half of Garhwal, in payment for British assistance in routing the Nepali Gurkhas.

NAINITAL

☎ 05942 • pop 34,000 • alt 1938m

High Season: mid-Apr to mid-July, mid-Sept to end Oct

This attractive hill station, 289km north-east of Delhi, was once the summer capital of Uttar Pradesh and is expected to be chosen as the temporary capital of the new state of Uttaranchal. The hotels and villas of this popular resort are set around the emerald waters of Naini Lake or *Tal*, hence the name.

Nainital is very much the green and pleasant land that immediately appealed to the homesick Brits, who were reminded of their Cumbrian Lake District. During a hunting expedition in 1839, an English businessman by the name of Barron came across the lake, built himself a small villa on its shores and had his yacht carried up here in 1840. Barron's claim to the area was contested by a local inhabitant, Nur Singh. In a particularly unsporting act, Barron rowed his unwitting adversary out into the centre of the lake and strongly suggested that he relinquish his claims or make his own way back to the shore. Unable to swim, the unfortunate Nar Singh was compelled to comply.

Disaster struck on 16 September 1880 when a major landslide occurred, burying 150 people and creating the recreation area now known as The Flats. Evidence of more recent slips can be seen today, as development puts strains on the unstable western side of the lake.

This is certainly one of the most pleasant hill stations to visit and there are many interesting walks through the forests to points with superb views of the Himalaya. That said, the hundreds of hotels and guesthouses that vie for attention along its eastern perimeters do somewhat spoil the peaceful ambience and it's important to time your visit well.

The high season, when Nainital is packed and hotel prices double or triple, corresponds to school holidays. Christmas and the New Year are also best avoided, as are the festivals of Dussehra (Sept/Oct) and Diwali (Oct/Nov).

Orientation

During the season, the Mall is closed to heavy vehicles for most of the day. Cycle-rickshaws take passengers along the 1.5km Mall between the bazaars at Tallital (Lake's Foot), at its south end, and Mallital (Lake's Head), to the north-west. The bus stand is in Tallital. Hotels and guesthouses can be found here, as well as along the entire length of the Mall and in the Mallital area. Most of the top-end hotels are about 10 to 15 minutes walk to the west of Mallital in the area known as Sukhatal.

Information

There is a post office near the bus stand in Tallital and the main post office is in Mallital. The State Bank of India and Bank of Baroda in Mallital exchange all major travellers cheques. The friendly UP tourist office (☎ 35337) is towards the Mallital end of the Mall and is open 10 am to 5 pm daily except Sunday.

The *Tourist Guide Map of Nainital* (Nest & Wings) is detailed, though out of scale, for Rs 20. Their *Tourist Guide to Kumaon* (Rs 40) is also quite useful. There's also good selection of English-language books, with a special section on the Kumaon region, at Narains, on the Mall or Consul Books in Mallital Bazaar. Books and magazines can be found at the Modern Book & General Store near the Alps Hotel.

Municipal Library The reading room here, right on the lake shore about halfway along the Mall between Mallital and Tallital, is a good place to escape the frenetic activity on the Mall, particularly in the late afternoon, when reflections from the lake create a lovely rippling effect on the walls and ceiling. Bibliophiles will appreciate the old wooden card files and hundreds of old volumes, and there are current newspapers for visitors' perusal. It's open in summer 7.30 to 10.30 am and 5.30 to 8.30 pm, and in winter, 8.30 to 10.30 am and 4 to 7 pm, closed Monday.

Naini Lake

This attractive lake is said to be one of the emerald green eyes of Shiva's wife, Sati. (*Naina* is Sanskrit for 'eye'.) When Sati's father failed to invite Shiva to a family sacrifice, she burnt herself to death in protest. Shiva gathered the charred remains in his arms and proceeded to engage in a cosmic dance, which threatened to destroy the world. To terminate the dance, Vishnu chopped up Shiva's body into pieces, and the remains were scattered across India. The modern **Naina Devi Temple** at the northern end of the lake is built over the precise spot where his eye is believed to have fallen.

Boat operators will take you on a circuit of the lake for Rs 50 in a rowboat (Rs 30 from one end of the lake to the other) or you can hire a small yacht by the hour from the Nainital Boat Club (Rs 60). Alternatively, you can join the small flotilla of pedal boats on the lake and make your way around under your own steam (Rs 30 per hour for a two-seat boat, or Rs 50 for a four-seater).

A day's membership of the Nainital Boat Club (☎ 35318) costs Rs 50, which gives you access to the club bar, restaurant, ballroom and library. The club is less exclusive than it once was. When Jim Corbett lived here he was refused membership because he'd been born in India, and hence was not a *pukkah sahib* ('proper' gentleman).

Snow View & Tibetan Gompa

A chairlift (ropeway), officially called the 'Aerial Express', takes you up to the popular viewpoint at 2270m. The lift is open 7

Trekking in Kumaon

The trekking approaches to the southern and eastern flanks of Nanda Devi are as attractive as those out of Joshimath and Ghat in the Garhwal. The Pindari Glacier to the south of Nanda Devi is one of the most popular Uttarakhand treks. To the east is the trek to the Milam Glacier.

Like the Garhwal the best time to trek is either in the pre-monsoon (mid-May to end Jun) or during the post monsoon season (mid-Sept to mid-Nov). UP Tourism's regional subsidiary, Kumaon Mandel Vikas Nigam (KMVN) offers inclusive treks for around $US50 per day. If making your own arrangements budget for around Rs 150/200 for the Pindari Glacier trek and Rs 200/250 if trekking out of Munsyari to the Milam Glacier. Food supplies should be brought from Naini Tal or Almora as there are limited supplies of tinned goods etc at Song or Munsyari. On the trek to the Pindari Glacier there are many teahouses and PWD resthouses that provide both food and accommodation. However for trekking to the Milam Glacier a tent is necessary on some stages of the trek.

Song to the Pindari Glacier

The Pindari Glacier flowing from Nanda Kot (6861m) and Nanda Khat (6611m) is on the southern rim of the Nanda Devi Sanctuary.

From Almora there's an early-morning bus to Song where you commence the trek. The first stage is a tough one for a first-time trekker, following a well-marked trail through forests of quercus oak and horse chestnut and across open meadows to Dhakri Khal Pass (2830m). Views from the pass are impressive including Trisul (7120m) and Nanda Khat (6611m). The trail then winds down to the Pindari Valley and follows the river course through luxuriant forest to the meadow at Phurkiya. It's an additional stage across meadows to the terminal moraine of the Pindari Glacier at Zero Point (3650m) beneath the impressive backdrop of Nanda Khat (6611m), Changuch (6322m) and Nanda Kot (6861m).

There is a string of very basic KMVN guesthouses along the trail (at Loharkhet, Dhakri, Dwali and Phurkiya) and also PWD guesthouses (at Dakri, Khati, Dwali and Phurkiya), but these can get heavily booked by the hordes of Indian students who hike the trail in May and June. In general you are far better off trekking self-supported.

Stage 1	Song to Dhakri via Dhakri Khal	(6-7 hrs)
Stage 2	Dhakri to Dwali	(6-7 hrs)

am to 8 pm in season (8.30 am to 6 pm in low season) and costs Rs 20 (one way). You can buy a Rs 35 return ticket (from a separate ticket window) but with this you must descend within the hour. Alternatively, it's a pleasant 2km walk up past the Tibetan Gadhan Kunkyop Ling Gompa (see later in this section). At the Mallital end of the Mall, near The Flats, beautifully groomed horses and mountain ponies are available for hire to Snow View and back for Rs 75, offering a pleasant alternative to the steep walk.

At the top there are powerful binoculars (Rs 5) for a close-up view of Nanda Devi (7817m), which was, as the old brass plate here tells you, 'the highest mountain in the British Empire'. Nanda Devi was India's highest peak until Sikkim (and thus Kanchenjunga) was absorbed into the country. There's a small marble temple dedicated to Dev Mundi housing images of Durga, Shiva, Sita, Rama, Lakshmana and Hanuman. From Snow View you can walk west to another viewpoint and then continue on to the main road to Kilbury. From here you

Trekking in Kumaon

Stage 3	Dwali to Phurkiya	(3 hrs)
Stage 4	Phurkiya to Pindari Glacier & return to Dwali	(7-8 hrs)
Stage 5	Dwali to Dhakri	(6-7 hrs)
Stage 6	Dhakri to Song	(5-6 hrs)

Munsyari to the Milam Glacier

The Milam Valley to the east of Nanda Devi has been recently opened to trekkers. Although no special permits are needed to complete this trek you will need to show your passport and register with the Indo-Tibet Border Police (ITBP) at Milam.

The trek includes magnificent views of Nanda Devi (7817m), while the villages in the upper sections of the Milam Valley were the recruiting ground for the famous Pundits, the Indian explorers who mapped much of Tibet in the later decades of the 19th century.

There is an early-morning bus from Almora to the town of Munsyari where you commence the trek. The initial stages follow the course of the Gori Ganga past Hindu villages and mixed forest of chestnut and bamboo. The trail then enters impressive gorges where the Gori Ganga forges its way through the crest of the main Himalaya. It's a further stage to the village of Martoli and the turn-off point for the trek to the base of Nanda Devi East. There are a couple of private guesthouses at Martoli but they are normally only open from late June to August. From Martoli it's an easy walk to Milam with views en route of the remarkable east face of Nanda Devi.

Until 1962 Milam and the nearby villages maintained close trading ties with Tibet. Nowadays this is as far as villagers and trekkers are allowed to go, although you are normally permitted to continue for 3km to view the Milam Glacier (3926m) and the peaks of Rishi Pahar (6992m), Hardeol (7151m) and Trisuli (7074m).

Stage 1	Munsyari to Lilam	(4 hrs)
Stage 2	Lilam to Bodgwar	(6-7 hrs)
Stage 3	Bodgwar to Martoli	(5-6 hrs)
Stage 4	Martoli to Milam	(4 hrs)
Stage 5	Milam to Bodgwar	(8 hrs)
Stage 6	Bodgwar to Lilam	(6-7 hrs)
Stage 7	Lilam to Munsyari	(4 hrs)

could continue up to China Peak (see under Other Walks, following) or head down the road to Sukhatal, passing great views of the lake en route.

A walk up to Snow Peak can take in the tiny **Gadhan Kunkyop Ling Gompa** of the Gelukpa order (of which the Dalai Lama is the spiritual leader). Take the road uphill from the Hotel City Heart, from where a path branches off towards the gompa (the colourful prayer flags are visible from the road). The gompa serves Nainital's small (and mostly itinerant) Tibetan community.

Most of the Tibetan families travel to Nainital in the summer season to sell sweaters and shawls, and in winter descend to the plains.

Other Walks

There are several other good walks in the area, with views of the snow-capped mountains to the north. **China Peak** (pronounced 'Cheena'), also known as Naini Peak, is the highest point in the area (2610m) and can be reached either from Snow View or from Mallital (5km). Climb up in the early morning when the views are clearer.

A 4km walk to the west of the lake brings you to **Dorothy's Seat** (2292m), also known as Tiffin Top, where a Mr Kellet built a seat in memory of his wife, killed in a plane crash. Alternatively, you could take a pony up here for Rs 75. From Dorothy's Seat it's a lovely walk to **Land's End** (2118m) through a forest of oak, deodar and pine. The walk will take about 45 minutes, and in the early morning you may see jungle fowl or *goral* (mountain goats). From Land's End there are fine views out over Khurpa Tal lake.

From the Jama Masjid (Friday Mosque), at the north-west corner of the lake, you can walk in 30 minutes to **Gurney House**, the house in which Jim Corbett resided while in Nainital. This two storey wooden dwelling is now a private residence, but the caretaker may let you look inside.

Other Things to See & Do

Built in 1847, **St John's Church** contains a brass memorial to the victims of the famous landslide. The few bodies recovered were buried in the church's graveyard.

There are good views and spectacular sunsets over the plains from this Hanuman temple, **Hanumangarh**, 3km south of Tallital. Just over 1km farther on is the state **observatory**, which should be open Monday to Saturday 10 am to 5 pm, but check at the tourist office before you head out here. There is a free slide show between 1.30 and 4 pm.

At the Mallital end of the Mall is **Naini Billiards** (open daily, Rs 40 per hour). Coaching is available for Rs 80 per hour.

If you fancy a spot of golf try the 18-hole **Raj Bhawan Golf Club**, founded in 1926 at the summer residence of the UP governor. Green fees cost Rs 400, club hire costs Rs 100 (Rs 50 half set) and caddies cost Rs 30. Contact the secretary SL Sah (☎ 36962) to arrange a pass, as the course lies in a military area.

Nainital Mountaineering Club (☎ 35051), opposite the Hotel City Heart, runs rock-climbing courses at nearby Bara Pattar for Rs 200 per day and can give advice on treks and expeditions in the area. Mr CL Sah at the club can help arrange guides and porters for

around Rs 300 a day, or put you in touch with a guide for nature walks in the environs of Nainital. The club also hires out tents and sleeping bags for around Rs 20 per day (plus Rs 3000 deposit).

Organised Tours

Almost every travel agency run tours to sights around Nainital and farther afield in Kumaon. Agencies include Hina Tours (☎ 35860), Darshan Travels (☎ 35035) and Anamika Travels (☎ 35186), all on the Mall. Fewer tours run in low season but these are often discounted. Tours include:

Lake Tour: Bhimtal, Sat Tal, Naukuchiyatal and Hanumangarh – half day (Rs 80 to Rs 100)
Kausani, Almora, Ranikhet – two days (Rs 250 to Rs 400, including transport, food and accommodation)
Ranikhet – day trip (Rs 150 to Rs 200)
Mukteshwar – day trip (Rs 150 to Rs 175)
Corbett Park – day trip (Rs 650, including park entry fees)

Taxis are also available for the above tours. Prices are around Rs 600 for the Lakes tour and Rs 1800 for a two day Kausani itinerary.

Parvat Tours (☎ 35656), run by KMVN, is at the Tallital end of the Mall. They arrange the standard tours (see the list, previously) and also a four day tour to Badrinath (Rs 600), a six day tour to Badrinath and Kedarnath (Rs 800) and a one or two day tour to Jageshwar (summer only, Rs 150 or Rs 225). Prices include dormitory accommodation, transfers and evening meals.

They can also arrange high and low-altitude trekking for around US$20 per day from Bhageshwar. Luxury bus tickets to Delhi can also be booked here.

Special Events

There is a small festival in mid-September centred on the Naina Devi Temple. There is also an annual autumn festival in the first week of October, which features yachting, dance and musical programs. It is particularly big when the Kumaon festival (see the Festivals boxed text at the beginning of the chapter) is held in the town.

Places to Stay

There are over 100 places to stay, from gloomy budget guesthouses to five-star hotels. During the high season, school holidays and during the festivals of Dussehra and Diwali, prices can triple, and finding anywhere to stay can be a major hassle. Prices below are for the high season and may appear pricey but, unless otherwise mentioned, all hotels discount by *at least* a 50% in the low season.

Places to Stay – Budget

Tallital & the Mall (South End) *Hotel Lake View (☎ 35632)*, on Ramji Rd, run by the gracious Mr and Mrs Shah, has doubles in the season from Rs 300 to Rs 600 (Rs 100 to Rs 300 in low season). All rooms have bathrooms, and hot water is available in buckets for Rs 5. The more expensive rooms are at the front of the building and views extend from the plains, over Tallital, across the lake and to Mallital.

Hotel Gauri Niwas, on Ramji Rd, has double rooms with geysers and lake views from Rs 400 to Rs 600; gloomy windowless rooms at the back are Rs 250. Hot water in buckets costs Rs 5.

Hotel Prashant (☎ 35347), in the same area, has doubles from Rs 400 to Rs 700 in season. The more expensive rooms have good views but the cheaper rooms are a bit shabby. All rooms have bathrooms and running hot water in the morning. There's a good dining hall.

KMVN Sarovar Tourist Rest House (see under Places to Stay – Middle & Top End) has dorm beds from Rs 40 to Rs 75, depending on the season. The spotless dorm has terrific lake views.

Mallital & Sukhatal An excellent budget choice at the north-west corner of Mallital bazaar is *Kohli Cottage (☎ 36368)*. In high season, doubles are Rs 300, Rs 400 and Rs 500, all with bath and 24 hour hot water. Rooms are light and airy, bathrooms are clean and the manager is friendly and helpful. There are lovely views from the roof terrace.

Alps Hotel (☎ 35317) is a bit rickety (it's well over 100 years old) but has enormous double rooms for Rs 200 with a basic bathroom. There's a lovely old broad balcony useful for watching the promenaders wandering the Mall.

The *Youth Hostel (☎ 36353)*, Sukhatal, is set in a peaceful wooded location, about 20 minutes walk west of Mallital. Dorms beds (with lockers) cost Rs 22/42 for members/nonmembers. There are also two double rooms with common bathroom for the same rates. Hot water is available in the mornings. Filling vegetarian thalis (Rs 14) are available in the dining hall, and you can inquire about the Pindari Glacier and other treks here.

KMVN Naina Tourist Rest House (see under Places to Stay – Middle & Top End) has dorm beds for around Rs 50. There's another *KMVN Tourist Rest House*, far from the madding crowd at Snow View, which has rooms for Rs 250/500 in the low/high season.

Places to Stay – Middle & Top End

Tallital & the Mall (South End) *KMVN Sarovar Tourist Rest House (☎ 35570)* is very handy for the bus stand. From 1 April to 15 July, double/four-bed rooms are Rs 800/1500. Between 15 September and 15 November, rates are Rs 600/1000, and during the rest of the year rates are Rs 400/800. Rooms are comfortable, although nothing special, and some have very good views over the lake.

Hotel Elphinstone (☎ 35534) has a wide range of slightly overpriced doubles from Rs 600 and up. All rooms face the lake and have bathrooms (cold water only; buckets of hot water available). There's a pretty garden terrace here, complete with a bust of Queen Victoria bearing a plaque with the inscription 'Victoria the Good'.

Evelyn Hotel (☎ 35457), farther north, is an enormous place, with doubles from Rs 400 to Rs 900. To get to the cheapest rooms entails a strenuous climb up a seemingly endless series of stairs, but the views from up here over the lake are excellent, and

NAINITAL

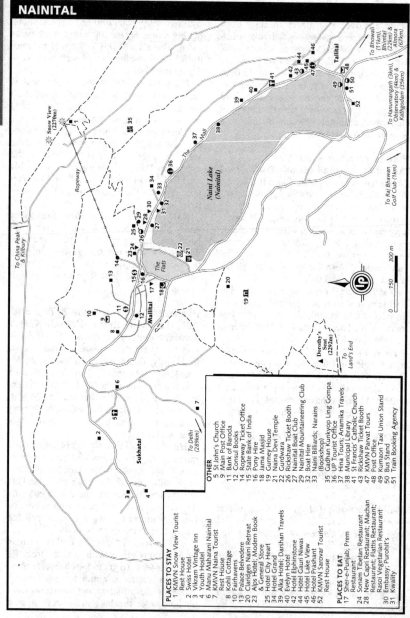

rooms are comfortable. There are several large sunny roof terraces.

Alka Hotel (☎ 35220) has overpriced economy doubles for Rs 1100, and standard doubles for Rs 1500 (Rs 700 and Rs 1000 in the low season). All rooms have running hot and cold water and piped music.

Mallital & Sukhatal The *Hotel Grand* (☎ 35406), the Mall, has singles/doubles for Rs 600/1000, or suites (with a separate sitting area) for Rs 1200. There's running hot water in the morning only. This place is open 15 April to 15 November only. There's a lovely wide shady balcony with potted geraniums, from where there are good lake views.

Fairhavens (☎ 36057, fax 36604), near the post office in Mallital, is a beautifully furnished Heritage hotel and one of the most stylish places to stay in Nainital. Room rates are a reasonable Rs 1250, with a 30% low-season discount.

Lovely old *Palace Belvedere* (☎ 35082, fax 35493) was formerly the palace of the Raja of Awagarh. Take the road that leads up behind the Bank of Baroda. Doubles start from Rs 1090, or with a separate sitting area, Rs 1180. Enormous double suites are Rs 1750. Some of the rooms have very good lake views, or you can look out over the lake from the wicker chairs on the shady veranda. Mr and Mrs Singh are the gracious hosts, and they offer a discount of 30% in the low season. Credit cards are accepted.

Hotel City Heart (☎ 35228) is directly opposite the Nainital Mountaineering Club, just off the Mall. Run by the effervescent Mr Pramod, a bass guitarist in an Indian rock band, doubles are good value, with prices ranging from Rs 450 to Rs 1400. The cheaper rooms have no views, but are large, comfortable and spotless; the more expensive rooms have superlative views of the lake. There's a good roof terrace.

KMVN Naina Tourist Rest House (☎ 36374, Sukhatal) is about 1km from Mallital. Doubles from 1 April to 15 July range from Rs 550 to Rs 800; from 15 September to 15 November, rates are Rs 415 to Rs 600, and in the low season, Rs 275 to Rs 400.

Charming old *Swiss Hotel* (☎ 36013), about 10 minutes walk west of Mallital, in a peaceful location, is run by the Nanda family. It's a very good choice, with comfortable, airy rooms, some with views over a pretty garden. Doubles are Rs 1200, suites are Rs 1500 and four-bed rooms are Rs 1800; all rooms are 25% less in the low season. Rates include breakfast and dinner. Mr Nanda's son is a keen naturalist, and can arrange bird and butterfly-spotting excursions around Nainital.

Vikram Vintage Inn (☎ 36177), beautifully appointed in a secluded location about 20 minutes walk west of Mallital, has singles/doubles for Rs 2000/2500, including breakfast. Reception staff can even arrange a private consultation with a palmist/numerologist (Rs 200 for 30 minutes).

Claridges Naini Retreat (☎ 35105, fax 35103) is in a quiet spot above Mallital and has luxury doubles for Rs 3250 including breakfast and one other meal.

Manu Maharani Nainital (☎ 36242, fax 37350, Grasmere Estate), about 10 minutes walk north-west of Mallital, has luxuriously appointed rooms, most with lake views, for Rs 3500 to Rs 4800 (Rs 2500 to Rs 3500 in low season) and is the best in town.

Places to Eat

There's a wide range of places to eat the Mall, and all the top-end hotels have their own restaurants (visitors welcome).

There are a couple of cheap places in a small cul-de-sac in Mallital's main bazaar, including the *Sher-e-Punjab* and *Prem Restaurant*, with Punjabi and south Indian cuisine.

Sonam Tibetan Restaurant, underneath the Alps Hotel, has decent chicken *momos* (dumplings) and *thukpa* (noodle soup)

There's a *fresh fruit juice stall* by the rickshaw ticket office in Mallital that also does shakes and lassis.

New Capri Restaurant, at the Mallital end of the Mall, has Indian, Chinese and continental cuisine. It's popular, and is often full at lunchtime. Nonveg dishes are around Rs 50.

Rasoi Vegetarian Restaurant, next door, has good thalis and pizza. With prices comparable to the Capri, the *Flattis Restaurant* is another popular eatery, which features mutton and chicken sizzlers.

Machan Restaurant, also nearby, serves excellent pizza (Rs 50) and tagliatelle (Rs 60), as well as decent Chinese and Indian standards.

Embassy is also in this area and is considered one of the best restaurants by locals. Main dishes are between Rs 65 and Rs 100.

Purohit's, next door, has pure vegetarian south Indian cuisine. There's alfresco dining with views across the lake, and filling limited thalis for Rs 35 and Rs 50.

Kwality, also at the Mallital end of the Mall, is set right on the water's edge. It's a bit rowdy at lunchtime, but prices are reasonable, with most veg dishes under Rs 50, nonveg a little more. There is also an ice cream parlour here.

For something special there are two restaurants at the Manu Maharani Hotel: the multicuisine *Kumaon*, and the *Lotus Garden*, serving Chinese cuisine. Main dishes in the restaurants cost between Rs 80 and Rs 140, with sweets (chocolate eclairs!) around Rs 40. If you're longing for a continental breakfast, the buffet breakfast bar has croissants, Danish pastries, cereals, scrambled eggs, etc for Rs 150.

The hotel also boasts Nainital's most stylish bar, the *Viceroy*, where a beer or cocktail costs Rs 100. It closes quite early at 10.45 pm.

Getting There & Away

Air The nearest airport is Pantnagar, 71km south, but it's not currently served by any scheduled flights.

Bus Buses (and shared jeeps) leave from the bus stand at Tallital every 30 minutes for the railhead at Kathgodam (Rs 30, 1½ hours). There's a deluxe (2x2) service to Delhi at 8.30 am (Rs 148, nine hours), a semideluxe (2x2) at 7.30 am (Rs 134) and an ordinary service (3x2) at 6 am and 6.30 pm (Rs 115). Most private agencies book overnight deluxe coach tickets to Delhi (Rs 350 air-con, Rs 250 deluxe) and Haridwar (Rs 250 deluxe).

A daily bus to Song (for the Pindari Glacier trek) leaves Bhowali, 11km from Nainital at the junction of the main routes to Ranikhet and Almora, at 6 am (six hours).

Other services from Nainital to the Indian Himalaya include:

destination	fare (Rs)	departs	duration (hrs)
Almora	33	7, 10 am, noon	3
Bareilly	45	7.15 am, 1.30, 2.30 pm	5
Dehra Dun	119	6, 7 am, 4.30, 8 pm[1]	10
Haridwar	132	5, 6, 7, 8 am, 4.30, 8 pm[2]	8
Kausani[3]	60	7 am	5
Pithoragarh	88	7 am	9
Ramnagar	44	5, 7 am	3½
Ranikhet	31	8 am, 12.30, 2.30 pm	3½
Rishikesh	131	5 am	9

[1] The 8 pm service is deluxe (Rs 212).
[2] The 8 pm service is deluxe (Rs 158).
[3] Additional services for Kausani leave from Bhowali, 11km from Nainital.

Train Kathgodam (35km south) is the nearest train station, and the railway booking agency, near the bus stand, has a quota for trains to Delhi, Lucknow and Kolkata (Calcutta).

The *Ranikhet Express* departs Old Delhi station at 11 pm, arriving at Kathgodam at 6.10 am. It departs Kathgodam at 10.45 pm, arriving at Old Delhi station at 4.45 am (Rs 139/567 in 2nd sleeper/2nd air-con class). Prices include the bus fare to Kathgodam. The office is open 9 am to noon, and 2 to 5 pm; 9 am to 2 pm on Sunday.

Taxi & Jeep Share jeeps leave when full from the bus stand for the bazaar at Bhowali, 11km below Nainital (Rs 15, 30 minutes). Share taxis depart when full for Kathgodam and Haldwani (Rs 30). Sample fares from the Kumaon Taxi Union in Tallital to regional destinations include Almora (Rs 600), Ranikhet (Rs 600), Kathgodam (Rs 300), Ramnagar (Rs 700), Kausani (Rs 1200) and Delhi (Rs 2800).

Getting Around

The official rate for a rickshaw from Tallital to Mallital is Rs 4; tickets can be purchased from booths at either end of the Mall.

LAKES AROUND NAINITAL

Bhimtal

Bhimtal is another pleasant lake, 22km from Nainital. You can take boat trips around the lake (Rs 60 for 30 minutes) or even to a restaurant on an island in the lake. There are only a couple of places to stay, making it much quieter than Nainital.

Zila Parishad Rest House, by the bus stop, has the best value rooms for Rs 210 (Rs 110, August to March). The *Neelesh Inn* (☎ 05942-471170) on the eastern shore has rooms for around Rs 400 and the *KMVN Tourist Reception Centre* on the south side has rooms from Rs 200 to Rs 750 (50% less in low season). You can buy local fishing permits from the Fisheries Office, in the bazaar at the built-up western end of the lake.

Buses to Bhimtal leave Nainital every hour or so between 8 am and 6.30 pm (Rs 12, one hour), and jeeps shuttle frequently between Bhimtal and Bhowali.

Naukuchiyatal

Naukuchiyatal (Lake of Nine Corners) is 4km farther on and quieter still, with similar boating facilities. There are only three hotels here. The very pleasant lakeside *KMVN Tourist Reception Centre* has rooms for Rs 400 or Rs 600 (Rs 200 and Rs 300 in low season) and dorms for Rs 50. The top-end *Lake View Resort* (☎ 05942-47041) has luxurious rooms for Rs 850 to Rs 1800 (25% low-season discount); or you could try the nearby and cheaper *Parichey Resort*.

CORBETT TIGER RESERVE

☎ 05945 • alt 400m to 1100m

Established in 1936 as India's first national park, Corbett National Park is famous for its wide variety of wildlife and its beautiful location in the Siwalik foothills of the Himalaya. It is set in dense sal forest in the Patlidun Valley, traversed by the Ramganga River. With the recent inclusion of the So-nanadi Wildlife Sanctuary to the west, Corbett has grown from 520 to 1318 sq km, and the park and wildlife sanctuary are known collectively as the Corbett Tiger Reserve.

It may seem incongruous for a national park to be named after a famous British hunter – Jim Corbett is best known for his book *The Man-Eaters of Kumaon*, and was greatly revered by local people for shooting tigers that had developed a liking for human flesh. He became known as 'Carpet Sahib' since no one could pronounce his name properly. Over 90 tigers had fallen at the hands of Corbett before the hunter symbolically buried his guns and turned conservationist. He was instrumental in setting up the reserve.

Flora & Fauna

The Patlidun Valley was originally covered in dense forest but clearing and later abandonment of the land has resulted in the emergence of vast grasslands, known locally as *chaur* – the perfect habitat for tigers, wild elephants and other large animals. The Sonanadi Wildlife Sanctuary, unlike Corbett National Park, has no grasslands, and due to the dense forest cover, it is more difficult to spot wildlife there.

Seeing a tiger at Corbett is a bit hit and miss, since the animals are no longer baited or tracked (unlike at Kanha in Madhya Pradesh). Your best chance is to come late in the season (April to mid-June) and stay for several days. Most people settle for fresh pug marks.

More common wildlife includes wild elephants, langur monkeys (black face, long tail), rhesus macaques, civets, peacocks, and several types of deer, including chital (spotted deer), sambar, hog deer and barking deer. There are also mugger crocodiles, the odd-looking gharial (a thin-snouted fish-eating crocodile, often spotted from High Bank, between the Dhangarhi Gate and Dhikala), monitor lizards, wild boar and jackals. Leopards (referred to as panthers in India) are occasionally seen at higher elevations. Don't wear brightly coloured clothing or perfume/deodorant, which will repel animals.

Project Tiger

The Project Tiger program, a joint initiative of the Indian government and the World Wildlife Fund for Nature (WWF), was inaugurated at Corbett National Park in 1973, a year after it was discovered that India's tiger population had dropped from around 40,000 at the turn of the 20th century to only about 1800. Nine reserves were initially included in the program, and there are now 23 reserves across India. By the late 1980s the project was credited with raising the tiger population to around 4300. However, by 1993 it was estimated that the number had fallen to 3750.

It is estimated that there are only between 5000 and 7500 tigers left in the wild. The reason is twofold: habitat loss has increased with human population pressure; and poaching has continued unabated. The trade in tiger bones and flesh, highly regarded in China for their perceived medicinal qualities, is still highly lucrative. Bones are smuggled over the Tibetan border, where they are traded for *shahtush*, the underwool of the endangered Tibetan antelope.

The worrying fall in numbers prompted renewed efforts to save the tiger, culminating in the launch of a new project in 1995 with funding help from the WWF and a UN initiative in 1998. Today it is estimated that Corbett has 128 tigers, up from 91 in 1989. Other Himalayan parks incorporated into Project Tiger include Namdapha Tiger Reserve in Arunachal Pradesh, with an estimated 52 tigers, and Buxa Tiger Reserve in the Bangla hills, with an estimated 31 tigers.

Corbett is also a bird-watcher's paradise, with over 580 species of indigenous or migratory birds, and since the creation of the Ramganga Reservoir, large numbers of waterfowl have been attracted here. The best time of year for bird-watching is from mid-December to the end of March. Common sightings include pied hornbills, hawk eagles, kingfishers, brown fish owls and brown dippers.

Keen anglers can set their wits against the mahseer, a belligerent fighting fish that inhabits the waters of the Kosi River, which runs outside the eastern perimeter of the reserve. Fishing permits can be obtained from the reception centre in Ramnagar for Rs 26.

Orientation & Information

The main reception centre is at **Ramnagar** (☎ 85489, fax 85376), outside the park on its south-eastern perimeter, and there is a second reception centre at **Kotdwar** (☎ 01382-23715), on the south-western edge of the park. The Ramnagar centre is open daily, including holidays, 8 am to 1 pm and 3 to 5 pm and has some useful brochures on what to look for and where to stay. Ramnagar is also the nearest railhead and has several hotels, a State Bank of India (which exchanges travellers cheques) and good transport connections. It's a good idea to bring mosquito repellent, mineral water and binoculars.

Dhikala, in the reserve, 51km north-west of Ramnagar, is the main accommodation centre and the place most travellers visit. Access to Dhikala is from the **Dhangarhi Gate**, about 20km to the north of Ramnagar. Day visitors are not allowed to enter from Dhangarhi Gate so if you want to visit Dhikala you'll have to book accommodation at the Ramnagar reception centre and stay the night, or take the centre's expensive day trip by bus (Rs 1200).

There's a library at Dhikala and interesting wildlife films are shown here (free) in the evenings. The elephant rides at sunrise and sunset (around 6 am and 4.30 pm) are not to be missed and cost Rs 100 each for four people for about two hours. During the day you can sit in one of the *machaan* (observation towers) to unobtrusively watch for animals. Keen bird-watchers should join local expert Harak Singh Aswal for free bird-watching tours around Dhikala on Saturday and Sunday mornings.

Bijrani, only 9km from Ramnagar, is the most popular place for day visits. Only 100 visitors, or 14 vehicles, are permitted daily on a first-come first-serve basis. The reception centre at Ramnagar operates a day trip to Bijrani by bus; see under Getting Around, later in this section. At Bijrani there's an interpretation centre, a short nature trail and a restaurant. It's sometimes possible to get elephant rides from here, although as there are only four elephants, priority is given to those staying overnight. Weekends can get crowded and are best avoided.

It's also possible to make day trips by jeep to Dhela, Jhirna and Kalagarh; access is from Karah gate.

Permits, Fees & Regulations Permits are normally bought at Dhangarhi Gate (for Dhikala) or Amdanda Gate (for day trips to Bijrani). To visit Dhikala you must first make an accommodation reservation at the park reception centre at Ramnagar. They will then give you a booking chit, which you must show at Dhangarhi Gate. If you have booked your accommodation in advance you can theoretically go straight to the park gate (with your booking chit) but it's probably wise to confirm the booking first at Ramnagar. Permits can also be purchased at Karah, Kalagarh, Pakhro, Kotdwar and Sendhikhal gates.

Recent price hikes have made Corbett relatively pricey to visit. With the entrance fee, a jeep ride in and out and even the most basic accommodation, you are probably looking at around US$40 for a two day visit (though you can do it cheaper by sharing the jeep ride or hitching). Charges listed here are for foreign nationals; Indians are charged considerably less. At the gates you must pay an entry fee of Rs 350 for a stay of up to three days, then it's Rs 175 per day. Still cameras are free but a video camera costs a whacking Rs 5000. To take a car into the park costs Rs 100, plus another Rs 200 (full day) or Rs 100 (half day) for a (compulsory) guide. If you hire a jeep you will have to pay these charges yourself.

Reserve regulations include the following:

- Corbett is closed from mid-June to mid-Nov.
- No walking or trekking is allowed in the park at any time (introduced after a British ornithologist was killed by a tigress in 1985).
- Gates are closed at sunset and no night driving is permitted. Visitors must have reached their destination by sunset.
- An officially registered guide is required for all excursions.
- When leaving the park visitors must obtain a clearance certificate, which should be shown at the exit gate.
- From 1 March to mid-June the park's back roads are closed and visitors cannot move about the forest 11 am to 1 pm.

Places to Stay & Eat
The highest concentration of accommodation is at Dhikala, but there are forest resthouses scattered around both the national park and the Sonanadi Wildlife Sanctuary. Bear in mind, though, that if you stay outside of Dhikala and Bijrani (where there are elephant rides), your chances of spotting wildlife are reduced to sightings from the resthouses themselves, as venturing into the reserve on foot is prohibited.

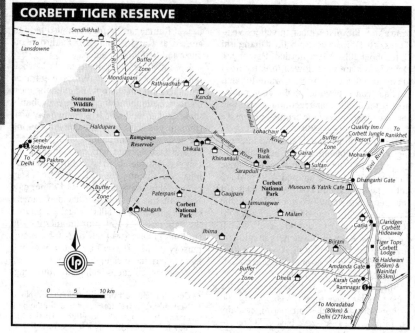

CORBETT TIGER RESERVE

Dhikala   There's a wide range of accommodation here but the higher prices charged for foreigners mean that it's not good value. There's a very basic dormitory (like three-tier train sleepers) in the *Log Huts* (Rs 100) but it's better to go for the triples (Rs 500) in the *Tourist Hutment*. An extra charge (Rs 25) is made for mattresses and sheets in these places. *Cabins* are more comfortable – doubles, with bath, cost Rs 900. All three places can be booked at the reception centre at Ramnagar.

Doubles in the *Old Forest Rest House* (Rs 1500) or the *New Forest Rest House* (Rs 900) are booked through the Chief Wildlife Warden in Lucknow (☎ 0522-283902).

There are also seven *annexe rooms* (Rs 900). Book through UP Tourism in Delhi (☎ 011-332 2251).

There are two *restaurants*, one run by KMVN, and another by a private operator.

Other Forest Resthouses   With your own transport and food, you could stay in the *forest resthouses* at **Sultan** and **Malani** (doubles for Rs 450) and **Sarapduli** or **Gairal** (singles/doubles for Rs 500/900), all in Corbett National Park. There's no electricity at any of these places, although the resthouse at Sarapduli has its own generator. Bring a torch (flashlight). All are accessed from the Dhangarhi Gate, except for Malani, which is accessed from Amdanda Gate.

There is also a *forest resthouse* at **Bijrani**, in the south-eastern corner of the reserve, with singles/doubles for Rs 500/900. Access to Bijrani is via the Amdanda Gate.

There are also *forest resthouses* in the reserve buffer areas of **Dhela**, **Jhirna** and **Kalagarh**, on the southern perimeter of the reserve, and at **Lohachaur**, in the buffer zone to the north of the national park. Doubles at all of these cost Rs 300. You should bring a flashlight and your own food. Bookings for all the above resthouses must be made at the tourist reception centre, Ramnagar.

There are a number of forest resthouses in the **Sonanadi Wildlife Sanctuary** at the western end of the reserve, including those at **Sendhikhal**, **Mondiapani**, **Rathuadhab**, **Haldupara** and **Kanda** (actually just over the boundary in the Corbett National Park). Again there is no electricity and you'll need to bring your own food. Double rates in all of these are Rs 300, and they must be booked through the reception centre at Kotdwar (☎ 01382-23715), open Monday to Saturday 10 am to 5 pm. Write in advance to the Sub-Divisional Officer, Kotdwar Reception Centre, Sonanadi, Kotdwar, UP.

Ramnagar There's a good *KMVN Tourist Bungalow* (☎ 85225) next to the reception centre. It has nice doubles for Rs 300 and Rs 400 and excellent value dorm beds for Rs 60.

Hotel Everest (☎ 85099) has clean and comfortable rooms for Rs 100 to Rs 200 between 15 November and 15 June, and Rs 70 to Rs 125 at other times. Hot water is available in buckets for Rs 5, and room service is available. The hotel is in a side street opposite the bus station.

Hotel Govinda (☎ 85615), near the bus stand, has cheap rooms with common bathroom for Rs 80 and Rs 100, and there's a good restaurant downstairs. The manager is a good source of information and it's worth reading the travellers' tips book here to get some feedback on visiting the reserve.

Private Resorts There are several upmarket resorts along the Ramnagar-Ranikhet road, all outside the reserve precincts. All offer discounts of around 50% when the park is closed.

Tiger Tops Corbett Lodge (☎ 85279, Delhi ☎ 011-644 4016, fax 85278), 7km from Ramnagar, is a very luxurious place with prices to match: singles/doubles are US$170/230 for foreigners, Rs 2500/3500 for Indians. Prices include all meals and two day-visits to the reserve during the season. There are elephant rides, jeep trips and

a swimming pool, and a wildlife slide show in the evenings. Despite the name, it's not part of the company that operates the famous resort in Chitwan (Nepal).

Claridges Corbett Hideaway (☎ 85959, Delhi ☎ 011-301 0211) has accommodation in attractive ochre cottages set in an orchard of mango trees. Air-con double rooms cost from Rs 4000 to Rs 4700, and rates include all meals. Staff can arrange bird-watching and nature-trail excursions, and mountain bikes are available for hire.

Quality Inn Corbett Jungle Resort (☎/fax 85230), in the Kumeria Forest Reserve, has attractive cottages high above the river for Rs 3850, including all meals. This place features its own inhouse elephant (named Ramkali), so rides are assured.

Getting There & Away
For details on getting to Ramnagar from Delhi see the Gateway Cities chapter.

Buses for Delhi depart Ramnagar approximately every hour, with the first service leaving at 5.30 am and the last at 8 pm (Rs 90, seven hours). Tickets can be booked at the Delhi Transport Corporation office or the main bus stand.

Services for other destinations in Kumaon are booked at the Kumaon Motor Owners' Union (KMOU) office, near the petrol pump on the Ranikhet road, on the opposite side to the reception centre. To Nainital, there are services at 7 am and 1 pm (Rs 24, 3½ hours), via Kaladhungi, though it's probably quicker to get on a frequent bus to Haldwani and change there. The Ranikhet services depart at around 7, 9.30 and 11.30 am, and 2 pm (Rs 50, 4½ hours); the 9.30 am bus continues to Almora (Rs 75, 6½ hours). For Almora you could also get on a bus to Batrojkhan and then catch an onward passenger jeep from there.

Ramnagar train station is 1.5km south of the reception centre. The nightly *Ranikhet Express* leaves Ramnagar at 9.45 pm, arriving into Delhi at 4.45 am. Tickets cost Rs 110 for 2nd-class sleeper. It's worth making a reservation a couple of days ahead (ie before visiting Corbett). The Hotel Govinda will arrange tickets for a reasonable Rs 20 commission. For other destinations you will have to change at the busy railway junction of Moradabad, 80km south.

UP Tourism in Delhi runs two/three-night fixed-departure tours to Dhikala from Delhi for Rs 3000/3500, including transport, accommodation, entrance fees, guide and one elephant ride.

Getting Around

There used to be a local bus service from Ramnagar to Dhikala that left at 4 pm (Rs 10, 2½ hours), and returned to Ramnagar at 8 am the next day, but at the time of research it had been suspended.

Jeeps can usually only be rented at Ramnagar and will cost about Rs 500 for a one-way drop to Dhikala, or Rs 1000 for a day safari, plus guide and car charges. Book through any of the hotels or deal directly with a driver.

The park reception centre in Ramnagar offers day trips by bus to Dhikala for Rs 1200 and Bijrani for Rs 600, including the entrance fee. This is the only way to visit Dhikala on a day trip. Local jeep safaris sometimes operate from Dhikala, for around Rs 100 per person.

Safaris on foot are strictly prohibited. The only other mode of transport is the ubiquitous elephant.

RANIKHET
☎ 05966 • alt 1829m
High Season: mid-Apr to mid-July, mid-Sept to mid-Nov

Fifty-eight kilometres north of Nainital, this peaceful hill station offers good views of the snowcapped Himalaya, including Nanda Devi. The name is derived from *rani*, or queen, and *khet*, meaning field, an allusion to a legendary queen who visited the site and, overwhelmed by the green glades and snowcapped vistas, built herself a palace here. Ranikhet was founded by the British in 1869, and is now an important army town and the headquarters of the Kumaon Regiment. It's a pleasant and laid-back place to spend a few relaxing days.

Orientation & Information

Ranikhet essentially comprises two areas. Busy Saddar Bazaar is where buses arrive, either at the UP Roadways stand, at its east end, or the Kumaon Motor Owners' Union (KMOU) stand about 1km away at its west end. Three kilometres behind Saddar is the beautiful wooded area known as the Mall. Development hasn't yet taken its toll up here, and trees still outnumber the few hotels and administrative buildings strung along its shady length.

There's a small UP tourist office (☎ 2227) above the UP Roadways stand. The main post office is on the Mall, about 200m before the Hotel Meghdoot. You can make phone calls and send faxes from the Telecommunications Centre, just above Saddar Bazaar on the way to the Mall. Ranikhet's State Bank of India doesn't change money.

Golf Course

Despite the sign that says 'Defence Land; Trespassers Prosecuted', visitors are welcome to play a round of golf at this nine-hole golf course at Upat (also known as Kalika), 4km outside Ranikhet on the Almora Rd. Set at 1820m above sea level, there are fine 300km panoramic views of the Himalaya. Green fees are Rs 400, caddies are available and club hire is Rs 100. A taxi to the course from Ranikhet will cost Rs 70, or you could catch one of the numerous Almora-bound buses and get off at the golf course.

Ananda Puri (Hairakhan) Ashram

Founded to propagate the teachings of Sri Sri 1008 Hairakhan Wale Baba, more commonly known as Babaji by his devotees (among whom are many Europeans), this ashram is at Chiliyanaula, 3km from Ranikhet. Babaji's devotees believe that he is a *mahavatar* (human manifestation of God) who mysteriously appeared in a cave in the Nainital district as an 18-year-old youth and exhibited an extraordinary knowledge of the scriptures and the Sanskrit language. Babaji left his earthly body in 1984 but his devotees continue to flock to his ashram.

KMVN Himadri Tourist Rest House (☎ 05966-2588) in Chiliyanaula has rooms for Rs 500 to Rs 800; 50% less, low season.

Walks

One kilometre to the south of the West View Hotel is the Shakti temple of **Jhula Devi**, from where you can continue to the orchards of apples, apricots and peaches at **Chaubatia**, 3km distant. From here you can continue another 4km along the ridge top to the artificial lake of **Bhalu Dam**, which supplies Ranikhet's water.

Places to Stay & Eat

Saddar Bazaar On the 2nd floor of a building in Saddar Bazaar is the *Hotel Raj Deep* (☎ 2447), with a huge range of rooms from Rs 75/125 for a single without/with common bathroom to Rs 250 for a double with bathroom and separate sitting area. The rooms are very clean and well maintained and there's a small communal sitting area on the balcony overlooking the bazaar.

Everest Hotel, nearby, has very tatty but excellent value singles/doubles with bath and hot water by the bucket for Rs 85/100.

Moon Hotel (☎ 2382), diagonally opposite, has overpriced triples for Rs 550, and deluxe cottages with hot and cold running water for Rs 850. There's a large cavernous restaurant, with main dishes around Rs 50.

Parwati Inn (☎ 2325), near the UP Roadways bus stand, has deteriorated rapidly in the last few years. Average doubles cost from Rs 350 to Rs 1200 between May and June, and September to October. At other times a 40% discount is offered. All rooms have running hot water in the mornings, and the more expensive rooms have good Himalaya views. The multicuisine *Host Restaurant* here is not cheap, with nonveg dishes from Rs 70.

Tribhuvan Hotel (☎ 2524), back at the west end of town, near the KMOU bus stand, has a wide range of rooms from Rs 200 to Rs 1000. Rooms at the back have a nice balcony

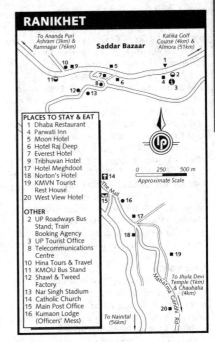

RANIKHET

To Ananda Puri Ashram (3km) & Ramnagar (76km)

Saddar Bazaar

Kalika Golf Course (4km) & Almora (51km)

PLACES TO STAY & EAT
1 Dhaba Restaurant
4 Parwati Inn
5 Moon Hotel
6 Hotel Raj Deep
7 Everest Hotel
9 Tribhuvan Hotel
17 Hotel Meghdoot
18 Norton's Hotel
19 KMVN Tourist Rest House
20 West View Hotel

OTHER
2 UP Roadways Bus Stand; Train Booking Agency
3 UP Tourist Office
8 Telecommunications Centre
10 Hina Tours & Travel
11 KMOU Bus Stand
12 Shawl & Tweed Factory
13 Nar Singh Stadium
14 Catholic Church
15 Main Post Office
16 Kumaon Lodge (Officers' Mess)

0   250   500 m
Approximate Scale

The Mall

To Jhula Devi Temple (1km) & Chaubatia (4km)

To Nainital (56km)

Mahatma Gandhi Rd

and sitting area but the bathrooms are pretty basic for the money (bucket hot water).

There's a good dhaba-style *restaurant* next to the UP Roadways bus stand that serves up cheap and tasty Indian food.

The Mall In a quiet location on the Mall is the pleasant *Hotel Meghdoot* (☎ 2475), stuffed to the brim with lovely potted plants. In low/high season, singles are Rs 200/400 and doubles are Rs 300/600 and Rs 375/750 (the more expensive rooms overlook the Mall). All rooms are carpeted and have bath with running hot and cold water; the double rooms have a separate sitting area. There's a very good restaurant here, with fresh fish taken from streams near Rampur.

Norton's Hotel (☎ 2377), a little farther down the Mall, was established in 1880 and hasn't changed much since. During the season, doubles are Rs 350 and Rs 400, family suites with two beds are Rs 500 and there are cottages with tiled floors and wood panelling for Rs 600. Dorm beds are Rs 65. There's a common lounge and a good-value restaurant. Hot water is free in buckets.

KMVN Tourist Rest House (☎ 2893) is also in the Mall area, but about 1km farther out. Between 1 April and 15 July, doubles are Rs 550 and Rs 800, dropping to Rs 275 and Rs 400 in the low season. Dorm beds cost Rs 60, with a hot water bathroom. The resthouse is set in a quiet area amid forests of deodar, oak and eucalyptus.

West View Hotel (☎ 2261), on Mahatma Gandhi Rd, is about 500m from the resthouse. This lovely old bluestone hotel was originally built for British officers on R&R. Doubles range from Rs 1100 to Rs 2800, with a 30% low-season discount. Most have balconies where you can view stunning sunsets.

Shopping

The Shawl & Tweed Factory, above Saddar Bazaar adjacent to the Nar Singh Stadium parade ground, is housed in an old deconsecrated church. Here you can buy shawls, lengths of tweed, woollen scarves and gents' shawls (known as *pankhis*). Ladies' shawls range from Rs 320 to Rs 480, and gents' from Rs 470 to Rs 500. Lengths of tweed cost around Rs 650 for 3.5m. The factory is run by the Kumaon Regiment Centre, and employees are either war widows or dependents of deceased army personnel.

Getting There & Away

Bus There are regular bus services from the UP Roadways bus stand at the east end of Saddar Bazaar to Delhi (Rs 165, 12 hours). Other services from this stand include:

destination	fare (Rs)	departs	duration (hrs)
Almora	27	5.30, 7, 10 am, 4 pm	2
Haridwar	112	8.30 am, ordinary	
	143	3 pm, express	9
Kathgodam	40	hourly	4
Kausani	31	6 am, noon, 2 pm	4
Nainital	29	8, 10 am	3½
Ramnagar	47	8.30 am, 3 pm	4

There are additional services to Kausani, Nainital, Ramnagar, Almora and Kathgodam from the chaotic KMOU stand, at the west end of Saddar Bazaar.

Hina Tours & Travel, in Saddar Bazaar, operates deluxe (2x2) buses to Delhi (Rs 180, 6 pm), to Haridwar (Rs 250, 6 pm) and, during the pilgrimage season, to Badrinath (Rs 250, 5 am).

Train The railway booking office at the UP Roadways stand has a small allocation of seats on the *Ranikhet Express* from Kathgodam to Delhi. A 2nd-class sleeper costs Rs 165 and this includes the cost of the bus ticket to Kathgodam, 84km away. Bookings should be made at least one day in advance. The office is open Monday to Saturday 9.30 am to 3 pm.

Getting Around

Local buses leave from the UP Roadways stand for the Mall and Chaubatia at 8, 9.30 and 11 am, 1, 2.30, 4 and 6 pm (Rs 4, 20 minutes). From the Mall, they return at 9 and 10.30 am, noon and 2, 3.30 and 5 pm. A taxi from Saddar Bazaar to the Mall costs around Rs 75 one way.

KAUSANI
☎ 05962 • alt 1890

For an even closer view of the Himalaya head to Kausani, 51km from Almora and 76km from Ranikhet, perched on a pine-covered ridge in front of a stunning 350km-wide Himalayan panorama. There are fantastic views of Trisul (7120m), shaped like a trident, Nanda Devi (7817m), Nanda Kot (6861m), Nanda Gond Ganth (6315m) and the Panchchuli, or Five Stoves (6904m), to the far east. Watching the Himalaya gradually turn pink as the sun sets must be one of the highlights of the region. For a closer view you can hire binoculars (Rs 5 for 10 minutes, Rs 50 for two hours) at the Himqueen Restaurant (see Places to Stay & Eat later in this section).

With its fine snow views, this peaceful settlement has a tradition of quiet contemplation. Gandhi stayed at the Anasakti

Ashram here in 1929 and the Hindi poet laureate Sumitranandan Pant grew up here. Today, the fragile peace is largely dependent upon the number of Bangali and Gujarati holiday makers in town.

Up a narrow path between the bus stop and the Himqueen Restaurant is the small **Sumitranandan Pant Gallery** (open Tuesday to Saturday 10.30 am to 4.30 pm), which has a selection of photographs and memorabilia pertaining to the life of the poet. The enthusiastic curator will explain the various exhibits, which are, unfortunately, rather shabbily displayed.

Basic tourist information is available at the post office, near the bus stand. Most of the places to stay are about 10 minutes walk north-west and uphill from the bus stop.

Places to Stay & Eat

Prices listed below are for the high season but all hotels give low and mid-season discounts of up to 50%.

Uttarakhand Tourist Lodge (☎ 84112), at the top of the stairs leading up from the bus stand, has basic but good-value double rooms with bath for Rs 100 on the ground floor, or Rs 150 on the 1st floor. There are also four-bed rooms for Rs 250. Good discounts are offered in the low season, and all rooms face the snows. There's a decent restaurant here.

Shakti and *Neelkanth*, nearby, are also cheap, with rooms and a balcony for Rs 75 to Rs 100, but they face away from the mountains.

Anasakti Ashram has simple rooms available (by donation). Pure veg food is served here, and hot water is available by the bucket.

Amar Holiday Home (☎ 45015), Ashram Rd, about 10 minutes walk uphill from the bus stand, is a good choice. Rooms are set in a pretty garden and Usha, the friendly manager, ensures that guests are comfortable. Unfortunately recent extensions to the Krishna Mount View in front have killed most of the hotel's fine views. Singles are Rs 200 and doubles are Rs 350, Rs 450 or Rs 650, all with bath (hot water in buckets).

Hotel Prashant (☎ 45037) is next door and cheaper. There is a wide variety of

rooms for Rs 100, Rs 150, Rs 200 and Rs 300. but the cheaper rooms are a bit gloomy and there's no view.

Krishna Mount View (☎ 45080), next door, has doubles with Star TV and running hot water for Rs 850 to Rs 1500, though it's popular with Indian groups and can be plagued by shrieking kids. All rooms face the snows. The *Vaibhav Restaurant* here features Mughlai and Gujarati cuisine. Main nonveg dishes are between Rs 60 and Rs 100, and there's a good range of sweets, including *sooji halva*, a wheat and sugar-based dessert (Rs 30).

Other clean and friendly mid-range places nearby include the *Sun'n'Snow Inn*, for Rs 800 to Rs 1000, and the *Hotel Jeetu* (☎ 45023), for Rs 500 to Rs 850.

KMVN Tourist Rest House (☎ 45006) is a couple of kilometres beyond the village. It's very good value and has doubles from Rs 300 to Rs 800 with great views, balconies and hot water. There are also dorm beds for Rs 60. Good low-season discounts are offered.

Himqueen Restaurant, at a bend in the road above the village, is a popular eatery and it also sells interesting *murabba* chutneys and *buransh* rhododendron juice in bottles. Good basic food in a more rustic setting is available nearby at the *Sunrise* and *Ashoka* restaurants.

Getting There & Away

Kausani has no bus station as such and is served only by through buses, en route to or from somewhere else. Buses to Almora pass through approximately every hour between 7 am and 3 pm (Rs 30, 2½ hours), continuing to Nainital (Rs 60, six hours). Otherwise take a Ranikhet bus, get off at Kosi and then take a passenger jeep to Almora (Rs 10). There are a couple of services to Ranikhet between 7 am and 2 pm (Rs 31, four hours). There are through buses every hour or so to Baijnath and Bageshwar.

For Karanprayag and destinations in Garhwal, there's one direct bus at 7 am (Rs 53, three hours) or change at Gwaldam.

The town's one taxi will charge around Rs 250 one way to Baijnath (Rs 400 return).

BAIJNATH
☎ 05962 • alt 1125m

Easily reached by bus or on foot, 19km north of Kausani, is the tiny settlement of Baijnath, which has a stunning – if diminutive – temple complex on the west bank of the Gomti River. If walking from Kausani, don't follow the road, as it's 6km farther; ask for directions along the path downhill through the forest. There are regular buses to Baijnath, or take a passenger jeep to Garur and walk the remaining 2km. From the bridge in Baijnath, a flower-flanked path follows the river for a couple of minutes before reaching the temples.

There are 18 temples in the complex, all of which were constructed during the era of the Katyuris, who once ruled over much of Garhwal and Kumaon between the 8th and 14th centuries. The main temple is in the centre, a square edifice sacred to Shiva, with numerous brass bells hanging from the eaves – donated, according to the Kumaoni tradition, by grateful petitioners to Shiva and his consort Parvati on the birth of a boy child. It is surrounded by a series of temples. Carvings of various deities including Ganesh and Hanuman lie against the face of the main temple, but the most exquisite carving is in the inner sanctum – a beautiful and voluptuous stone image of Parvati, standing about 1.5m high. She holds in her arms many smaller carved images including those of Ganesh and his vehicle, a rat, Shiva astride a Nandi bull, and at the top, on the left, a beautiful carving depicting the marriage of Shiva and Parvati. The temple was badly damaged during the rampages of Aurangzeb, and only the first metre or so is original. It was rebuilt in the 19th century using the original blocks.

Local boys sell fish food to give to huge holy carp, which lurk by the riverside. A few kilometres from Baijnath is the confluence of the Gomti and Garur rivers, another site revered as the place where Shiva married the goddess Parvati.

The new **KMVN Tourist Rest House** (☎ 24101) has excellent value rooms for Rs 150 on the ground floor or Rs 200 with a 1st floor balcony overlooking the temple complex. Prices might rise when geysers are installed. The hotel is a five minute walk out of town. There are a few chai stalls where you can get some snacks.

BHAGESHWAR
☎ 05963

The important pilgrimage town of Bhageshwar, with its ancient stone temples sacred to Shiva, lies 41km to the east of Kausani. The main road, known as Station Rd, is an unattractive strip of commercial chaos, but a labyrinth of windy alleyways leads eastwards down through the interesting bazaar to the Sarayu River.

The town lies in a valley between two small mountains; on the west side is Mt Nhileshwar, which is topped by a temple sacred to Shiva in his form as Nhileshwar – hence the west side of the town is known as Nhil Bhageshwar. A path leads up from the petrol pump on Station Rd to the temple; it takes about 30 minutes to reach the summit, from where there are good views out over the town. Behind the settlement on the east side of the river is a small hill topped by the modern Chandika Temple, sacred to Durga.

Temple Complex

Approaching the Sarayu River, a path branches to the right from Station Rd, passing through the busy bazaar (take the left path at the tree) down to several small ghats at the junction of the Gomti and Sarayu rivers. Here is sited the **Baghnath Temple**, sacred to Shiva. The ancient stone temple, topped by a fluted *amalaka* (disk-shaped flourish) that is protected with a square wooden lattice edifice, is in a sorry state of disrepair, but it appears that at least superficial attempts at restoration are being undertaken.

In front of the temple are a number of small stone **shrines**, many of which still retain sculpted idols. Fragments of sculpture from the site are displayed behind an iron

CRAIG PERSHOUSE

CRAIG PERSHOUSE

LINDSAY BROWN

Top: Yogachoeling Gompa in Ghoom, Bangla (West Bengal) Hills. **Middle:** Colourful Hindu statues in a cave, Darjeeling. **Bottom:** Snow leopard – both endangered and dangerous.

RICHARD I'ANSON

LINDSAY BROWN

RICHARD I'ANSON

From sunrise to sunset, views of the Himalaya are perpetually alive and changing. No two scenes of this famous range are ever the same.

grille in the temple compound, but the identification labels are in Hindi only.

On the opposite side of the path is the smaller **Baneshwar Mahadev Temple**. (Mahadev is the form of Shiva as Supreme Being, reflecting both his functions as creator and destroyer.) An impressive sculpture of a tiger with an elephant's head between its paws protrudes from the roof.

Places to Stay & Eat

Anapurna Hotel (☎ 22109) by the bus stand is clean and pleasant, with good views of the river behind. Singles/doubles with common bath are Rs 80/120 and rooms with private bath are Rs 200.

The charmless *Hotel Rajdoot (☎ 22146),* on Station Rd, about 200m east of the bus stand, has basic but clean rooms for Rs 80/125, or Rs 100/200 with bath (cold water).

Hotel Siddhartha (☎ 22114), diagonally opposite, is better, with doubles and triples for Rs 240 on the 1st floor and doubles on the ground floor for Rs 150, all with bath. Hot water is available free in buckets. The doubles open onto a pleasant balcony with good views out over the river.

The only places to eat are a few basic point-and-eat *dhabas* near the bus station.

Getting There & Away

There are two buses daily to Pithoragarh, at 6.30 and 8.10 am (Rs 76, eight hours), and hourly buses to Almora between 5.30 am and 2 pm (Rs 40, four hours via Takula,; 4½ hours via Kausani). Buses to Ranikhet (via Kausani; Rs 19) leave at 7, 8.30 and 10 am and noon (Rs 56, 4½ hours). For Nainital take an hourly Haldwani bus and change at Bhowali. Buses depart for trekking trail heads at Song at 12.30 and 3 pm (Rs 20, 2½ hours), and Munsyari at 9.30 am (Rs 80, eight hours).

Passenger jeeps also run to Garur (Rs 12), 2km south of Baijnath, from where there are more jeeps to Kausani.

CHAUKORI

* alt 2010m

This village, 47km east of Bhageshwar, is famed for its views of the Himalaya, particularly of the Panchchuli massif, and might be worth a visit if you have some extra time. There's only one place to stay at present, the *KMVN Tourist Resthouse*, which has rooms for Rs 500 to 600 (50% less in the low season), but more places are bound to pop up soon. There are regular buses between Chaukori and both Bhageshwar and Pithoragarh.

ALMORA

☎ 05962 • pop 53,507 • alt 1650m

This picturesque hill station, 68km northeast of Nainital, is one of the few not created by the British. Some 400 years ago it was the capital of the Chand rajas of Kumaon, who moved their capital here in 1563 from Champawat. The Chands successfully repelled the invading Rohillas, and managed to later fend off the Gurkhas in 1815 with the help of the British. To compensate the British for their participation, Almora was ceded to the East India Company.

Nehru spent an involuntary period in Almora when he was incarcerated here during the Quit India campaign. More recent visitors include Dr Timothy Leary, influential author during the psychedelic movement of the 1960s; he was followed by scores of readers, inspired more by the (accurate) reports of cannabis growing wild in the environs of the town than its fine snow views.

The busy town, larger and louder than either Ranikhet or Kausani, extends along a 5km ridge, affording fine views of distant snow peaks. Behind the Mall, along whose length are the majority of hotels and restaurants, is the busy and colourful Lalal Bazaar.

Orientation & Information

The fairly useless UP tourist office (☎ 30180) is on Upper Mall Rd, just before the Hotel Savoy, about 500m to the south of the bus stand. The State Bank of India is on the Mall, opposite the bus stand (open 10 am to noon, Monday to Saturday). It changes American Express travellers cheques only. The Central Telegraph Office (fax 30100), by the post office, is the cheapest place to make international phone calls and send/receive faxes.

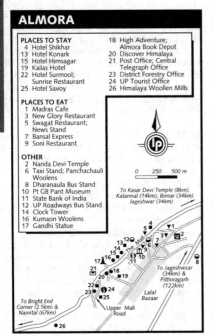

ALMORA

PLACES TO STAY
4 Hotel Shikhar
13 Hotel Konark
15 Hotel Himsagar
19 Kailas Hotel
22 Hotel Surmool;
   Sunrise Restaurant
25 Hotel Savoy

PLACES TO EAT
1 Madras Cafe
3 New Glory Restaurant
5 Swagat Restaurant;
   News Stand
7 Bansal Express
9 Soni Restaurant

OTHER
2 Nanda Devi Temple
6 Taxi Stand; Panchachauli Woolens
8 Dharanaula Bus Stand
10 Pt GB Pant Museum
11 State Bank of India
12 UP Roadways Bus Stand
14 Clock Tower
16 Kumaon Woolens
17 Gandhi Statue

18 High Adventure;
   Almora Book Depot
20 Discover Himalaya
21 Post Office; Central Telegraph Office
23 District Forestry Office
24 UP Tourist Office
26 Himalaya Woollen Mills

0   250   500 m

To Kasar Devi Temple (8km),
Katarmal (14km), Binsar (34km)
Jageshwar (34km)

To Jageshwar (34km) &
Pithoragarh (122km)

Lalal Bazaar

To Bright End
Corner (2.5km) &
Nainital (67km)

Upper Mall Road

The Almora Book Depot, the Mall, has a good selection of books on the Himalaya with particular emphasis on Kumaon. English-language newspapers are available after 11.30 am from the news stand above the Swagat Restaurant, near Hotel Shikhar.

Travel Agencies   Discover Himalaya (☎ 31470, fax 31507), opposite the main post office, arranges porters, guides and ponies and organises high-altitude treks to the Pindari, Milam and Kafni glaciers, as well as rock-climbing and photographic excursions. Ask for Bobby Sah.

High Adventure (☎ 32277), nearby on the Mall near the Almora Book Depot, arranges treks and day tours to local sights, including the stone temples at Bineshwar, near Binsar, and Jageshwar. They also sometimes book coach tours to Nainital (via Kausani) and seats in a taxi service to Delhi.

Things to See
The **clock tower** on the Mall was built in 1842 and carries the motto 'Work as if thou hadst to live for aye, Worship as if thou wert to die today'. There's a **Shiva shrine** in the room below it. Opposite the clock tower in a tiny flower garden is a gilded, cross-legged statue of **Gandhi** surmounted on a squat plinth.

The **Pt GB Pant Museum**, opposite the UP Roadways office, is open Monday to Saturday 10.30 am to 4.30 pm. The heavily moustached Pant was born in Almora and was Uttar Pradesh's first chief minister in the 1960s. (Pt stands for pundit.) The museum has some interesting exhibits on archaeology and ethnography, including a selection of *alpanas* (geometric paintings made by women to decorate the home on auspicious days) and huge *ransingh* horns used during religious processions. Entry is free.

In the Lalal Bazaar, about 10 minutes walk to the north-east of the bus stand, is a small group of **temples**. The Nanda Devi Temple is a relatively modern structure. It houses a very small image of the goddess flanked by images of Saraswati (on her left) and a black image of Mahakali. A mela (festival) is held here for three days in August/September and the Dussehra festival is also celebrated here in grand style. Also in this compound are two stone temples dedicated to Shiva. On the ceiling of the smaller of the two temples is a rosette, and the walls feature carvings of Ganesh, Shiva and Parvati. The bottom courses of masonry feature sculptures of rampant lions, elephants and horses. The other, larger temple, is of a similar architectural style, but its amalaka is protected by a wooden pagoda, and its stone sculpture is more elaborate.

Lalal Bazaar itself is worth a quick visit for its bustling mix of hillmen, silversmiths and *tamta* (hand-beaten copperware) workshops.

The 8km walk up to the **Kasar Devi Temple** is recommended – this is where Swami Vivekananda (one of the founders of the Rama Krishna movement) came to meditate. The area, also known as Paparsali, has the reputation of being something of a 'power centre' and some travellers rent houses and stay for months.

Good views of the Himalaya (especially at sunset) can be had from a hilltop known as **Bright End Corner**, 2.5km south-west of the town centre. The name is a corruption of Brighton End, derived somewhat incongruously from Brighton Beach in England – you couldn't be farther from the waves!

Places to Stay
There's a good range of places to stay but rooms can be noisy if they face onto the Mall.

Hotel Shikhar (☎ 30253), on the Mall, only a few minutes walk from the bus stand, is a huge place, with clean doubles for Rs 150, or a range of doubles with hot water bath starting at Rs 245, and reaching up to to Rs 1000, most with good views. Prices remain constant all year.

Kailas Hotel (☎ 22624) is an extraordinary place run by the charming, if slightly eccentric, Mr and Mrs Shah (who celebrated 55 years of marriage in 1998); this may well be one of your more memorable accommodation experiences in India. Fairly rustic doubles with bath are Rs 150, and there's a five-bed dorm for Rs 40 per bed. Rooms with common bath are Rs 75/120. One room has a primitive water heater that looks like a reject from Dr Frankenstein's workshop – hot water in buckets is a safer bet. Mrs Shah is in charge of the kitchen, and rustles up a mean banana pancake, or you can try the Kumaoni thali (Rs 35) and one of the excellent house herbal teas. Room rates drop in low season. The hotel is a short distance along a path opposite the main post office.

If you'd prefer the comforts of a more modern establishment, the *Hotel Konark (☎ 31217)*, near the State Bank of India, has singles for Rs 150 or Rs 200 and doubles for Rs 150, Rs 200 and Rs 245, all with bath. The staff are friendly and rooms are spotless.

Hotel Himsagar (☎ 30711) is a new midrange hotel with comfortable doubles for Rs 400 to Rs 600, all with hot water bathroom and satellite TV.

Hotel Surmool (☎ 30460) is directly opposite the main post office. Rooms are excellent value in the low season and come with a hot water bathroom for Rs 200 (Rs 400 in summer). Beds in the six-bed dorm are Rs 50.

Hotel Savoy (☎ 30329), on Upper Mall Rd, is a peaceful place just beyond the tourist office. Doubles downstairs, with a squat toilet, are Rs 200, and carpeted rooms upstairs, with hot water bathroom, are Rs 400. There are also suites with a separate sitting area for Rs 500. Rooms are a little tatty, but quite clean and the more expensive rooms open onto a sunny veranda. There's a 25% discount in the low season and a good-value restaurant here.

Places to Eat
Madras Cafe, just off the Mall near the Hotel Shikhar, is a no-frills, reasonably priced vegetarian restaurant, with main dishes under Rs 25. Opposite is the fancier *New Glory Restaurant*, featuring Indian and Chinese cuisine.

Just before the Hotel Shikhar, stairs lead down to the *Swagat Restaurant*. There's an extensive vegetarian menu, which features the sweet milk-based *rabri faluda*. The brightly lit Sikh-run *Soni Restaurant*, just before the State Bank of India, is very popular with locals. Most main dishes are around Rs 40.

The restaurant at the *Hotel Himsagar* is worth a visit, particularly for its excellent Cheese tomato (*panir* cheese in a rich tomato

---

Just Desserts

Almora is a good place to sample *bal mithai*, a form of brown *barfi* (fudge) that is covered in tiny white sugar balls. This sweet is found only in the foothills of Kumaon. Another local favourite is *singauri*, a milk-based sweet with a creamy consistency served in a leaf from the *chyur* tree. It comes in both brown and off-white varieties – the brown form is considered to be tastier.

sauce) and service. The *Sunrise Restaurant* at the Hotel Surmool is also good value.

If you are exploring the Lalal Bazaar, you could take a break (and a cappuccino, cold coffee or lassi) at the *Bansal Express*, just down one of the side streets.

Shopping

Inhabitants of Almora are renowned for their Gandhian loyalties, evident in the production of *khadi* – home-spun cloth, the production of which was strongly encouraged by the Mahatma. Khadi can be purchased at the Gandhi Ashram, near the UP Roadways office.

There are also several woollen mills where you can purchase shawls and jumpers, including Kumaon Woolens, near the Hotel Himsagar, Panchachauli Woolens, near the Hotel Shikar and the Himalaya Woollen Mills, above the KMVN Rest House at the south-west end of the Mall.

Getting There & Away

The UP Roadways office and bus stand is down a small flight of stairs on the Mall, opposite the Pt GB Pant Museum. To Delhi (12 hours) there is an ordinary bus at 3.30 and 4.30 pm (Rs 138) and a semideluxe service at 5 pm (Rs 172). The daily bus to Banbassa, the closest Indian village to the Nepali border, leaves at 7.30 am, and costs Rs 75 (seven hours).

Other services include Nainital (Rs 31, three hours) at 5, 7.30 am, and 2.30 pm, Ranikhet (Rs 26, two hours) at 7, 9 am, 2 and 4 pm, Song for the Pindari Glacier (Rs 52, five hours) at 8.30 am and to Pithoragarh (Rs 62, five hours) leaving at 5, 8 and 11 am. Buses to Pithoragarh also depart from at the Dharanaula bus stand on the east side of the Lalal Bazaar.

Taxi Share taxis leave from just outside the taxi stand and cost Rs 40 to Ranikhet, Rs 50 to Nainital and Rs 100 to Haldwani, the nearest rail head. One-way taxi fares include the Kasar Devi Temple, for around Rs 150, Ranikhet, at around Rs 500, and Nainital, for around Rs 600.

AROUND ALMORA
Katarmal Temple

This fine 800-year-old temple, dedicated to the sun god Surya, is set on a peaceful hillside with excellent views of Nanda Devi. The temple has some fine statues, including the main image of Surya holding two sundials in his arms, and is surrounded by 43 smaller temples. It has a forgotten-by-time feel it.

To get there, take any Kausani or Ranikhet-bound bus or jeep and get off at Kosi, 12km from Almora. From here a 2km (45 minute) uphill trail leads west from the main bazaar and up through several settlements. Ask for directions to 'Surya Mandir'.

Binsar
• alt 2412m

Unobstructed, and possibly unsurpassed, vistas of a 300km stretch of the Himalaya are available from this hilltop, also known as Jhandi Dhar, 34km north-east of Almora. The Chand dynasty of Kumaon (15th to 18th centuries) based their summer capital here, but there are few legacies of this era, apart from the Bineshwar Temple, sacred to Shiva, which was built by Raja Kalyan Chand.

The stone temple lies 3km below the hilltop. Apart from its stunning mountain vistas, Binsar is notable for its profusion of wildflowers and pleasant walks through forest glades of oak and rhododendron. The surrounding countryside makes up the Binsar Wildlife Sanctuary.

Double rooms at *KMVN Tourist Rest House* on the brow of the hill are Rs 300 to Rs 600 (1 April to 15 July; up to 50% off at other times). *Forest Rest House* here can be booked through the District Forest Officer (Wildlife) in Almora (☎ 05962-31753).

There are several buses each day between Almora and Bhageshwar, which will drop you off on request at Kafarkhan, but it's a steep 13km walk from here to the summit of the hill. A taxi will charge Rs 500 one way, or Rs 700 return from Almora.

JAGESHWAR

This little-visited but lovely village is found 34km east of Almora, 3km north of the tiny settlement of Artola, which is on the main Pithoragarh road. Most visitors make the detour to Jageshwar to visit the stone temple complexes here but Jageshwar can also be used as a starting point for walks to Old Jageshwar (4km) or the day hike to Binsar.

Halfway between Artola and Jageshwar, and set on the banks of Dandesavra *nulla* (stream) among dense stands of deodar, are the small **Dandesavra temples**. The largest (and most elaborately sculpted) of these temples dates from around the 10th century CE, which also enshrines a naturally formed lingam.

The **temple complex** at Jageshwar village encompasses 124 temples. The earliest temples date from the 8th century and were constructed during the Katyuri dynasty; the most recent temples in the group date from the closing period of the Chand dynasty (18th century).

The oldest temple in the group is probably the **Mrityunjaya Temple**, the large temple to the right as you enter the compound. The sides of the temple are elaborately carved. The round medallion that protrudes at the front of the temple represents Dattatreya – the three faces of one God. Below is a carving of Shiva, the presiding deity of Jageshwar. He can be seen sitting in the padmasana, or lotus position, suggesting the pervasive influence of Buddhism. Shiva is flanked by his consort, Parvati, and one of their sons, Kartikiya.

The other large temple dominating the compound is to the left, behind numerous smaller temples. This is the **Jageshwar Temple**, which enshrines a sacred lingam. On either side of the doorway are life-sized sculptures of the *dwarpals* – gatekeepers. On the right is the four-armed Nandi, and on the left is Bhrangi, holding a three-headed snake. These represent the bodyguards of Shiva. In the inner sanctum, the lingam is concealed beneath a repoussé silver cover in the form of a snake, which is removed by the temple priest in the morning and evening only. Originally the lingam was protected by a large silver serpent, but this was stolen. As your eyes adjust to the

dark interior, a small shrine to Ganesh, Shiva's son, can be made out.

Walks

One hundred metres past the Jageshwar temples a path leads through forest of deodar, pine and oak to Old, or **Vridha Jageshwar**, 4km distant. Here there is a very old stone temple sacred to Shiva, and fine panoramic views of the Himalaya extending from the Garhwali peaks to the west, across to the snow-covered peaks of western Nepal.

A shorter walk could take you back in the direction of Artola. After a few minutes a trail branches off the Artola-Jageshwar road, leading east over a wooden bridge 3km to the **Jakersam Temple**.

A trail also leads west from the other side of the Artola-Jageshwar road, up to **Kunjakhali**, about 3km from the bridge. One kilometre farther is **Janubaj**, on the bus route to Old Jageshwar. A farther 6km takes you down through pine forest to **Dholchina**, on the main Almora-Sheraghat road, a small settlement where food is available. Beyond Dholchina it is a steep 6km climb through dense forest of oak and rhododendron to the temple of **Bineshwar**, 1km before Binsar.

Places to Stay & Eat

KMVN Tourist Rest House is on the left as you enter Jageshwar. It is set in pretty flower gardens. Dorm beds are Rs 50, ordinary singles and doubles are both Rs 250, and deluxe doubles (with carpet) are Rs 400. Good discounts are available in the low season. All rooms have bath. There is a dining hall here.

The *Forest Resthouse*, set in dense forest 200m farther from the temple complex, has two rooms. Bookings need to be made with the District Forest Officer (DFO) in Almora (☎ 05962-33753). There are several *dharamsalas* in the village where you may be able to get simple accommodation.

Raj Mahel Hotel & Restaurant is opposite the entrance to the temple compound and offers cheap rooms and food (open Mar to Aug only). *Jageshwar Restaurant*, behind the temple group, is open all year, and serves very basic fare (*chapatis* and *sabzi* – vegetables). There are several chai stalls.

Getting There & Away

There is one bus daily from Almora to Jageshwar, which leaves at noon (Rs 25, two hours). It returns to Almora at 7.45 am. Alternatively, you could catch one of the many buses to Pithoragarh and disembark at Artola, from where it is a very pleasant 3km walk to Jageshwar. You may be able to hitch a lift to/from Artola or get a seat in a share taxi. A taxi from Almora will charge Rs 500 one way, or Rs 700 return.

MUNSYARI
☎ 59612 • alt 2290m

The pleasant village of Munsyari, 135km north of Pithoragarh, on the banks of the Gori Ganga, is the trail head for treks to the Milam Glacier and has magnificent views of Panchchuli Range. Porters and guides can be hired and there are several competent trekking agencies in town, including Panch

Chuli Trekking, Nanda Devi Trekking and Devandra Jyoti Treks & Tours. Several shops also sell basic canned goods.

KMVN Tourist Rest House (☎ 2339) has rooms for Rs 250 to Rs 400 and dorm beds for Rs 50. *Martolia Lodge*, near the bus stop, is a good place and the owner is a good source of information on trekking in the region. The *Himani Lodge* and *Puja Lodge* both have rooms for around Rs 100 to Rs 300 and other places are under construction.

Daily bone-shaking buses run early in the morning to Almora and Pithoragarh.

PITHORAGARH
☎ 05964 • pop 42,113 • alt 1815m

Pithoragarh is a large and clean city in the eastern district of Kumaon, and serves as an important halt on the long pilgrimage route to Mansarovar and Mt Kailash in Tibet (although the chances of foreign nationals being granted trekking permits to enter Tibet are negligible). Nevertheless, with sweeping views down over the broad

---

'Eve Rest', Everest or Gaurisanka?

It was at the Survey of India headquarters in Dehra Dun that the highest mountain in the world was first calculated. In 1849 the Great Trigonometrical Survey of India mapped the heights of peaks in the Himalaya Range. Three years later the computed results showed a peak, known to the west as Peak XV, to be the highest mountain in the world. This came as a surprise, as until this time Kanchenjunga near Sikkim was thought to be the peak whose head rose closest to the heavens. Peak XV was rather an ignominious name for the highest mountain in the world, and immediately a search began for its real name.

Western linguists working in Nepal and India reported various local names for the mountain. In Nepal, it was claimed, XV was known as Devadhunga, 'Abode of the Gods'. German explorers, on the other hand, reported that the Tibetan name was Chingopamari. In 1862 the Royal Geographic Society opted for an alternative Nepali name for the mountain: Gaurisanka.

In the meantime, Andrew Waugh, Surveyor General of India, embarked on a mission of his own – to have the mountain named after the head of the Great Trigonometrical Survey, Sir George Everest. He met with much opposition, largely because it was argued that a local name would be more appropriate. Even Sir Everest himself had reservations about the difficulties of rendering his name in local script. In 1865 the Royal Geographic Society decided to back the Everest contingent due to uncertainties surrounding Gaurisanka (in 1902 it was determined that Gaurisanka was another peak, some 50km from Everest).

Incidentally, Sir Everest pronounced his own name 'Eve Rest'.

Sore Valley, and across to the peaks of Panchchuli and those of western Nepal, it is a pleasant place to stay a few days. You may find you'll need to spend a night in Pithoragarh if you're en route to Munsyari for the Milam Glacier trek (see the Trekking in Kumaon boxed text).

Information

The tourist office (☎ 22527) is on Bank Rd at the Shiltham Station Bazaar, about 10 minutes north of the lower bus stands. It's open Monday to Saturday 10 am to 5 pm. The post office is nearby. Between the lower bus stands and Shiltham station is the busy Naya Bazaar, and above it, Gandhi Chowk.

Things to See

The road to the village of Chandak, 7km north of Shiltham Station Bazaar, follows the ridge top and affords fine views across to the peaks of Panchchuli (Five Stoves), to the north, and beyond to the western Nepal peaks of Saipal and Api.

Just before the KMVN Tourist Lodge is the modern **Ulka Devi Mandir**, the temple of the patron goddess of Sera village, below it. From a terrace here there are good views of Pithoragarh to the south, to Mt Thalkedar.

Places to Stay & Eat

Hotel Samrat (☎ 22450) is directly opposite the UP Roadways office. Singles/doubles with bath are Rs 50/100, bucket hot water is Rs 5.

Hotel Uttranchal Deep (☎ 22654) is about five minutes walk from UP Roadways. Doubles with bath are Rs 100 (hot water available in buckets: Rs 5). The staff are friendly and attentive, and there's an extensive room service menu.

Hotel Ulkapriyadarshani (☎ 22345), on Shiltham Station Bazaar, has very basic singles for Rs 75, and doubles from Rs 50 to Rs 95, all with bath. All the rooms are clean, but the cheaper ones are quite dark and shabby.

Hotel Trishul, right by the bus stand, has spartan and somewhat tatty, but clean, singles/double rooms for Rs 30/50 (free buckets hot water).

KMVN Tourist Lodge (☎ 22434) is about 1.5km from the upper bus stand on the Chandag road. Doubles with bath and geyser are Rs 300, and there are dorm beds for Rs 50. Rooms are basic but OK, and there are good views from the ridge on which the lodge is sited. There's a restaurant here. There are numerous jeeps between the bazaar and Chandag that will drop you here.

On Bank Rd are the *Trishul* and *Rawat* hotels, which serve veg and nonveg cuisine. Meals at the Rawat are notoriously spicy.

Getting There & Away

Air At the time of research, scheduled flights to Delhi and Lucknow still hadn't commenced from Pithoragarh's airport. Check at the tourist office to see if anything is planned.

Bus To really confuse things, there are three bus stands; at the bottom of the town is the UP Roadways office, opposite the Samrat Hotel, where buses leave for the plains. This is known locally as the Roadways Station. To Tanakpur (the closest railhead, 151km to the south of Pithoragarh, near the Nepal border), there are buses every 30 minutes between 4.30 am and noon (Rs 72, seven hours).

All these buses continue to the border town of Banbassa (Rs 76, eight hours). There's one service daily to Nainital at 6.30 am (Rs 88, nine hours), and several services to Almora from 5 to 10.30 am (Rs 62, five hours). To Delhi, there are several services via Tanakpur, and one service (at 6 am) via Haldwani.

West 100m is the private bus stand, where you can book buses to Almora and Ranikhet – the 5.30 and 8 am services to Almora continue to Ranikhet (Rs 82, seven hours). UP Roadways has a second office about 10 minutes walk north through the bazaar in the area known as Shiltham Station. Here you can catch buses to the hill villages, such as Munsyari, and share jeeps to the nearby villages of Chandag and Thal. From Thal you can get another share jeep, or bus, 61km farther north to Munsyari.

Train There's a railway booking office at the Roadways (lower) Station, next to the UP Roadways office. It is open daily 10 am to 4 pm and has a small allocation of seats on services departing from Tanakpur, 151km south, near the Nepal border.

BANBASSA

Banbassa is the closest Indian village to the Nepali border post of Mahendranagar, and it is possible to enter Nepal at this point (see the Land section of the Getting There & Away chapter for more details). There are daily buses from Delhi (12 hours) and Banbassa is also connected by rail to Bareilly. From Almora, there's a daily bus leaving at 7.30 am (Rs 85, seven hours).

Bangla (West Bengal) Hills

The hills area of Bangla (West Bengal) encompasses an area of 3149 sq km, bordered by Sikkim to the north, Bhutan to the north-east, Nepal to the west, Assam to the east, and the Indian plains to the south. The region is also a conduit for travel to Sikkim and the north-east.

Most travellers to this region will inevitably visit the large hill station of Darjeeling (2134m). Darjeeling was prised from Sikkim in the mid-19th century by the British and established as a sanatorium for officers of the Raj. It affords spectacular panoramic vistas of the distant snow-clad peaks of the eastern Himalaya, including Kanchenjunga, third highest mountain in the world (and the highest peak in the Indian Himalaya). Even accommodation is remarkable; the imperial legacy of the Raj lives on in wonderful (if somewhat run-down) colonial buildings and hotels. Apart from Darjeeling, a trip to this region can also take in the less visited (and less frenetic!) hill towns of Kalimpong, once an important halting point on the trade route to Tibet, and Kurseong, both of which afford good opportunities for walking in their environs. Down on the plains, to the east of Shiliguri, are the Jaldhapara Wildlife Sanctuary and the Buxa Tiger Reserve.

History

Until the beginning of the 18th century the whole of the area between the present borders of Sikkim and the plains of Bengal, including Darjeeling and Kalimpong, belonged to the rajas of Sikkim. In 1706 they lost Kalimpong to the Bhutanese, and control of the remainder was wrested from them by the Gurkhas who invaded Sikkim in 1780, following consolidation of the latter's rule in Nepal.

These annexations by the Gurkhas, however, brought them into conflict with the British East India Company. A series of wars was fought between the two parties, eventually was leading to the defeat of the

BANGLA (WEST BENGAL) HILLS

Bangla Hills at a Glance

Population: 1,580,000 (year 2000 estimate)
Best Time to Go: hills: Apr to mid-Jun, mid-Sep to Nov; wildlife sanctuaries: Mar to Apr; mountain vistas: mid-Sep to mid-Dec
Trekking Areas: Mirik to Kurseong, Darjeeling area (Apr to May, Oct to Nov)

Highlights
- **Darjeeling** – Lose yourself in the lovely old Raj buildings, tea plantations, and (on clear days) wonderful views of Kanchenjunga.

- **Kalimpong** – Take some great walks, with fine views of the surrounding countryside, and a number of orchid nurseries.

- **Jaldhapara Wildlife Sanctuary** – Visit this sanctuary, home to the endangered one-horned Indian rhinoceros, wild elephants, and various types of deer; open mid-Sept to mid-June.

Gurkhas and the ceding of all the land they had taken from the Sikkimese to the East India Company. Part of this territory was restored to the rajas of Sikkim and the country's sovereignty guaranteed by the British in return for British control over any disputes that arose with neighbouring states.

One such dispute in 1828 led to the dispatching of two British officers to this area, and it was during their fact-finding tour that they spent some time at Darjeeling (then called Dorje Ling – Place of the Thunderbolt – after the lama who founded the *gompa* (monastery) which once stood on Observatory Hill). The officers were quick to appreciate Darjeeling's value as a site for a sanatorium and hill station, and as the key to a pass into Nepal and Tibet. The officer's observations were reported to the authorities in Kolkata and a pretext was eventually found to pressure the raja into granting the site to the British. The raja was promised in return the territory of Debgong, but the British reneged on their side of the bargain, and in return for the loss of his territories, the unfortunate raja received one double-barrelled gun, one rifle, a 20 yard bale of red cloth and two shawls – one of superior, and one of inferior quality. Evidently unhappy with this bargain, the raja appealed to the British in 1841 and was granted an annual stipend of Rs 3000 (raised to Rs 6000 in 1846).

The transfer of Darjeeling to the British, however, rankled with the Tibetans who regarded Sikkim as a vassal state. Darjeeling's rapid development as a tea-growing area and trading centre in a key position along the trade route from Sikkim to the plains of India began to make a considerable impact on the fortunes of the lamas and leading merchants of Sikkim. Tensions rose, and in 1849 two British travellers, Sir

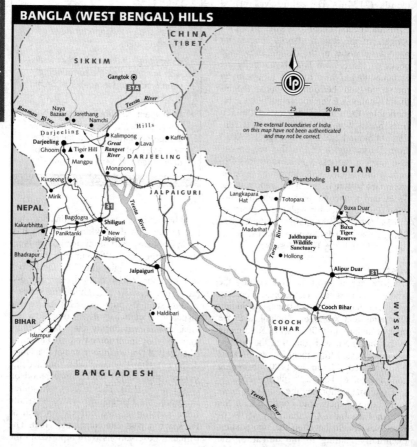

BANGLA (WEST BENGAL) HILLS

The external boundaries of India on this map have not been authenticated and may not be correct.

0   25   50 km

Joseph Hooker and Dr Campbell, who were visiting Sikkim with the permission of the raja and the British government, were arrested. Various demands were made as a condition of their release, but the Sikkimese eventually released both prisoners unconditionally about a month later.

In reprisal for the arrests, however, the British annexed the whole of the land between the present borders of Sikkim and the Bangla plains, and withdrew the annual Rs 6000 stipend from the raja. (The latter was restored to his son, raised to Rs 9000 in 1868 and raised again to Rs 12,000 in 1874.)

The British annexations brought about a significant change in Darjeeling's status. Previously it had been an enclave within Sikkimese territory and to reach it the British had to pass through a country ruled by an independent raja. After the takeover, Darjeeling became contiguous with British territory farther south and Sikkim was cut off from access to the plains except through British territory. This situation eventually led to the invasion of Sikkim by the Tibetans and the British military expedition to Lhasa.

Still not content with their new possession, the British mounted a military expedition into neighbouring Bhutan in 1864, resulting in the Treaty of Sinchula in which the Bhutan Duars and the current district of Kalimpong were annexed to the region.

Development of Darjeeling was rapid and by 1857 it had a population of some 10,000. Most of the population increase was due to the recruitment of Nepali labourers to work the tea plantations established in the early 1840s by the British. Even today, the vast majority of people around Darjeeling speak Nepali as a first language and the name Darjeeling continues to be synonymous with tea.

The immigration of Nepali-speaking peoples, mainly Gurkhas, into the mountainous areas of Bangla eventually led to political problems in the mid-1980s. Resentment had been growing among the Gurkhas over what they felt was discrimination against them by the government of Bangla. Their language was one of those not recognised by the Indian constitution and they were, therefore, denied government jobs, which were only open to those who could speak Bangali.

The tensions finally came to a head in widespread riots throughout the hill country which continued for two years, and in which hundreds of people lost their lives and thousands were made homeless. Tourism came to a halt and the Indian army was sent in to maintain some semblance of order. The riots were orchestrated by the Gurkha National Liberation Front (GNLF), led by Subash Ghising, which demanded a separate state to be known as Gurkhaland. The Communist Party of India (Marxist) was also responsible for a good deal of the violence since it was afraid of losing the support it had once enjoyed among the hill peoples.

A compromise was eventually hammered out in late 1988 whereby the Darjeeling Gorkha Hill Council (DGHC) was given a large measure of autonomy from the state government and fresh elections to the council were held. Darjeeling remains part of Bangla, but now has greater control over its own affairs.

Following the declaration in 1996 that the hill region of UP will become a separate state (Uttarakhand), there were renewed demands for a separate Gurkhaland in the Darjeeling region. However, as the region now has a certain amount of autonomy, and the general consensus is that a separate homeland will eventually be negotiated, things have settled down.

Geography

The Teesta is the major river in the region. Rising in Sikkim, it flows south-west across the northern border of West Bengal, meeting the Great Rangeet River near Kalimpong and carving a dramatic valley down the centre of the three administrative subdivisions of Darjeeling region: Darjeeling, Kurseong and Kalimpong. The elevation profile commences at around 60m above sea level in Jalpaiguri district on the plains, and 117m at Shiliguri, rising through the Kurseong and Kalimpong ranges to over 3500m along the

Festivals of the Bangla Hills

The high concentration of Tibetan gompas in the Bangla hills, particularly in Darjeeling and Kalimpong, ensures that there is a ready succession of colourful Tibetan festivals. Visitors are welcome at these gompa festivals. See the Facts for the Visitor chapter for details of the main Tibetan and nationwide festivals.

April
Bengali New Year This is celebrated on the first day of Vaishaka (mid-April).

August
Accord Day This public holiday in Darjeeling commemorates the anniversary of the foundation of the Darjeeling Gorkha Hill Council.

September/October
Durga Puja Celebrated as Dussehra in the rest of India, Durga Puja is the most important religious festival in Bangla. It is celebrated with the construction of large images of Durga on her vehicle, the lion, which are then carried to nearby rivers and ceremonially immersed.
Flower Festival With the local love of flowers and so many nurseries in the area, Kalimpong holds an annual flower festival in October.

November
Teesta Tea & Tourism Festival Celebrated from 14 to 20 November, this was launched as a joint undertaking by the tourist regions of Darjeeling, Sikkim & Dooars (the corridor encompassed by the area between Shiliguri and the Assam border. Targeted as much to local people as foreigners, it focuses on regional events and cultural exchange. As well as various cultural displays, there are tea garden visits and stays, organised tours, treks and walks through the regions.

---

lesser heights of the Singalila Range, which rises near Darjeeling and culminates in the massive bulk of Kanchenjunga, in Sikkim.

Tourist Offices

There are Government of Bangla tourist offices in most major cities. Accommodation in the Jaldhapara Wildlife Sanctuary must be booked through the Government of Bangla tourist bureau in Kolkata (Calcutta), or the Sub-Regional tourist office in Shiliguri. Bangla tourist offices can also book package tours into the park. See the Jaldhapara Wildlife Sanctuary section for details.

Kolkata (Calcutta)
  (☎ 033-248 5917/5158) 3/2 BBD Bagh (East)
Chennai (Madras)
  (☎ 044-832346) Karim Mansions, 787 Anna Salai

Darjeeling
  (☎ 0354-54050) 1 Nehru Rd
Delhi
  (☎ 011-373 2840) A2 State Emporium Bldg, Baba Kharak Singh Marg, Delhi
Shiliguri
  (☎ 0353-431974) Tenzing Norgay (Hill Cart) Rd

Northern Plains

Shiliguri is not one of India's most salubrious cities, but if you're heading north to Darjeeling or Sikkim, you'll probably find that you'll need to spend at least a day or two here. Lying to the east of Shiliguri, which falls in Darjeeling district, are the districts of Jalpaiguri and neighbouring Cooch Bihar, which borders Assam to the east. In Jalpaiguri are two little-visited wildlife sanctuaries, Jaldhapara Wildlife Sanctuary, with a small population of the endangered Indian one-horned rhinoceros *(Rhinoceros unicornis)*, and the Buxa Tiger Reserve, which is a member of Project Tiger (for more information see the Project Tiger boxed text in the Uttarakhand chapter).

SHILIGURI & NEW JALPAIGURI
☎ 0353 • pop 249,000
Shiliguri lies 8km north of the main railway junction of New Jalpaiguri (known throughout the district as NJP), though there's effectively no break between the two places. This crowded sprawl is the departure point and major trade centre for Darjeeling, Kalimpong, Sikkim, the North-East Region and eastern Nepal. As a consequence, it is packed with trucks and buses. However, it should be dubbed, 'Bicycle-rickshaw City'; there are 40,000 of them and they swarm everywhere. It's not the most pleasant place to stay, but it does have a wonderful climate in winter and is central to many of the main attractions in the region. It is only one hour from Shiliguri to Paniktanki – opposite the Nepal border town of Kakarbhitta.

Orientation
The towns of Shiliguri and New Jalpaiguri comprise essentially just one north-south main road – Tenzing Norgay Rd, renamed in honour of the Everest conqueror (although it is still known locally as Hill Cart Rd). It's about 3km from New Jalpaiguri train station to Shiliguri Town train station, and a farther 5km from there on to Shiliguri Junction train station, behind the Tenzing Norgay Central bus terminal. You can catch the toy train (if it's running) from any of these train stations. Bagdogra airport, which serves this northern region, is 12km west of Shiliguri.

Information
Tourist Offices The Bangla Sub-Regional tourist office (☎ 431974) is up a flight of stairs on Tenzing Norgay (Hill Cart) Rd, on the south side of the river. It's open Monday

to Friday, 10 am to 5 pm. The doorway is easy to miss, but there's a sign across the front of the building. Here, it's possible to book accommodation in the Jaldhapara Wildlife Sanctuary (see later in this section), 135km east of Shiliguri, in Jalpaiguri district.

There are tourist information counters at the New Jalpaiguri and Shiliguri Junction train stations, and the Bangla tourist office and Sikkim Tourism counters at Bagdogra Airport. The police information post is in front of Tenzing Norgay Central bus terminal.

Fishing Permits To obtain fishing permits, check with the Sub-Regional tourist office. Mahseer, one of the world's largest freshwater fighting fish, are found at the confluence of the Teesta and Rangeet rivers. Most fishing permits are on a 'catch and release' basis.

Permits for Assam There's a tiny Government of Assam tourist information office (no phone) down the lane directly opposite the bus terminal, on the east side of Tenzing Norgay (Hill Cart) Rd. It's open Monday to Saturday, 10 am to 5 pm. Brochures are available here, but officers are a bit vague on current permit requirements. (According to the Assam Government tourist office in New Delhi, restricted area permits are no longer required by foreign visitors to enter Assam, but some areas are unstable, so it does pay to make inquiries before travelling.)

Permits for Sikkim Although Sikkim is no longer restricted, permits are still necessary. They are available from Sikkim Tourism (☎ 432646) at the Sikkim Nationalised Transport (SNT) office (☎ 432751) on the east side of Tenzing Norgay (Hill Cart) Rd, diagonally opposite Tenzing Norgay Central bus terminal. Sikkim Tourism is open Monday to Saturday, 10 am to 4 pm.

Money The State Bank of India, on the 3rd floor and a few doors north of the sub-regional tourist office, exchanges American Express and Thomas Cook travellers cheques in US dollars and pounds sterling only. A small encashment fee is levied.

Post & Communications The main post office is on Hospital Rd, near the railway booking office. At time of research, there were no public email or Internet services available, but as Shiliguri is the main server area for the hills, this may change soon.

Medical Services The Paramount Hospital (☎ 530320) is very good and extremely efficient. However, be prepared to pay cash up front for any tests you might need.

Emergency Police: ☎ 20-101; Fire: ☎ 22222.

Places to Stay

There are dozens of hotels opposite the Tenzing Norgay Central bus terminal. *Hotel Hindustan* (☎ 26571) is down a small lane directly opposite the terminal. Singles/doubles are Rs 100/125 or with bath and geyser (boiler), they range from Rs 120/150 to Rs 280/450. Mosquito nets are provided, and there's room service here.

Siliguri Lodge is in a quiet spot next to Sikkim Nationalised Transport. There's a pleasant garden fronting the lodge, and rooms are very clean and airy. Doubles on the ground floor with bath are Rs 155, and in the four bed dorm, it's Rs 45. Decent-sized doubles upstairs are Rs 180 or Rs 250 with bath.

Bangla Tourism's *Mainak Tourist Lodge* (☎ 430986), on Tenzing Norgay (Hill Cart)

Rd, is about 750m to the north. Rooms are Rs 600/700 or Rs 850/1250 with air-con. They have foreign exchange facilities and a restaurant.

Hotel Sharda (☎ 21649) is next door. Singles/doubles are Rs 110/165 (hot water in buckets), or Rs 165/220 with running hot water. They're basic but neat, and mosquito nets are provided.

Hotel Chancellor (☎ 432360), on the corner of Sevoke and Tenzing Norgay (Hill Cart) Rds, is friendly, Tibetan-run and a good budget choice. Small but comfortable singles are Rs 190, and doubles are Rs 200 or Rs 215 with balcony. Three/four-bed rooms are Rs 255/350. Fresh towels, hot water in buckets and mosquito zappers are provided. The front rooms are a little noisy. They are extending and there's a pleasant rooftop patio.

Hotel Vinayak (☎ 431130), in the LM Moulik Complex on Tenzing Norgay (Hill Cart) Rd diagonally opposite the tourist office, is a good mid-range choice. Rooms are spotless, well appointed and have baths. Singles are Rs 200/250, doubles are Rs 300/350, or Rs 600/950 with air-con. There's a good restaurant here, Pamm's, and room service is available.

Hotel Rajdarbar (☎ 534316), on Tenzing Norgay (Hill Cart) Rd between Tenzing Norgay Central bus terminal and the Mahananda River, is a friendly place. All rooms have bath, phone and TV. Rooms start at Rs 250/300, or Rs 450/550 with air-con.

Hotel Blue Star (☎ 431550), on Tenzing Norgay (Hill Cart) Rd just north of the Bangla tourist office, is a budget place that accepts credit cards. Single rooms are Rs 250; doubles from Rs 350.

Ganga Hotel is farther north, but set back, on the same side of the road. It's a little bit grubby but cheap; the bedding is clean, it provides mosquito nets and the management's really friendly. Singles/doubles cost Rs 80/150. The rooms at the front are brighter, but noisier than those at the back.

Hotel Mount View (☎ 425919) is right opposite the Tenzing Norgay bus terminal. It is friendly, clean and also set back from

---

Carbon-Monoxide Poisoning

! Lonely Planet recommends that travellers do not use fires as a means of heating in hotel rooms unless there is excellent ventilation (as there is in most top end hotels). The Indian police have confirmed that a number of deaths from carbon-monoxide poisoning occur each year. Under no circumstances should you burn charcoal or other fuels which give off toxic fumes.

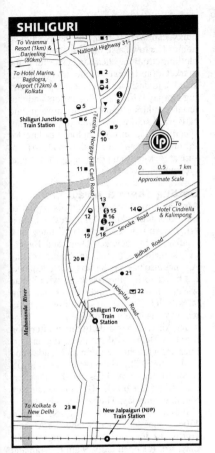

SHILIGURI

PLACES TO STAY
1   Hotel Sinclairs
2   WBTDC Mainak Tourist Lodge; Indian Airlines
3   Ganga Hotel
6   Hotel Mount View
9   Siliguri Lodge
11 Hotel Rajdarbar
16 Hotel Blue Star
18 Hotel Chancellor
19 Hotel Vinayak; Pamm's; Jet Airways
20 Ranjit Hotel & Lodge
23 Hotel Holydon; Hotel Baydanath; Miami Restaurant

PLACES TO EAT
7   Shere Punjab Hotel Restaurant
13 Anand Hotel Restaurant

OTHER
4   Mallaguri Garage
5   Tenzing Norgay Central Bus Terminal; Share Jeeps
8   Assam Tourist Office
10 Sikkim Nationalised Transport (SNT) Terminal; Sikkim Tourism
12 Taxi Stand
14 Share Jeep Stand
15 State Bank of India
17 Bangla Sub-Regional Tourist Office
21 Railway Booking Office
22 Main Post Office

the road. Singles range from Rs 175 to Rs 250, and doubles from Rs 250 to Rs 350. There's also a decent restaurant here.

Hotel Air View (☎ 431542), on Tenzing Norgay (Hill Cart) Rd, is also recommended. Very large doubles cost Rs 180 to Rs 300 with bath and mosquito nets. There's also an excellent, cheap restaurant.

The three star *Hotel Sinclairs* (☎ 22674, fax 432743) is 2km north of Tenzing Norgay Central bus terminal on Tenzing Norgay (Hill Cart) Rd, beyond the overpass. Like its

counterpart in Darjeeling, it is rather overpriced for what it offers. Non air-con doubles are Rs 725/880, and air-con rooms are Rs 1035/1330. There is a foreign exchange facility, a swimming pool, bar and restaurant.

There are a couple of places within walking distance of New Jalpaiguri train station. You're a bit isolated out here, but they're handy for early-morning departures. The *Hotel Holydon* (☎ 23558) has singles with common bath for Rs 125 and doubles with bath (hot water) for Rs 225 and Rs 300. The more expensive rooms at the front are bright and airy. There's a small restaurant. Next door is the *Hotel Baydanath*. Very good singles/doubles with running hot and cold water are Rs 225/300.

There are a couple of hotels just outside Shiliguri that stand out from the rest. *Hotel*

Cindrella (☎ *547136/544130, fax 531173, email cindrella@gokulmail.com)*, at 3rd Mile, Sevoke Rd, is actually quite a way out of town. However it is very quiet and has a pool, gymnasium, health club and billiards. It also offers Internet facilities, foreign exchange and an excellent travel desk and tour agency. Spacious rooms are Rs 1050/1150, or Rs 1350/1550 with air-con. They have a Web site www.cindrellahotels.com.

Viramma Resort (☎ *26222, fax 432497)* is about 1km beyond the National Hwy overpass on the road to Darjeeling. It offers two pools, health club, jogging track, extensive lawns and gardens, a small boating lake, business centre, foreign exchange, restaurant and bar. Standard rooms (with *bed tea* – early morning tea brought to your room) are Rs 450/550, or air-con Rs 750/875. Deluxe doubles are Rs 980.

Hotel Marina (☎ *450371)* is on Highway Rd, in the small town of Biharmore, 4km from Bagdogra airport. It has comfortable doubles/triples with bath and hot-water geyser for Rs 215/265. It's quiet, and there's a restaurant and bar, as well as free bed tea.

Places to Eat

Oriental Room, at Hotel Sinclairs, serves good Chinese and Mughlai cuisine, but service is excruciatingly slow. The best vegan restaurant in Shiliguri, the *Amrapali*, is a fair way out of town at Hotel Cindrella. The budget priced *Shere Punjab Hotel*, opposite the bus terminal serves good food and beer. The very reasonably priced *Anand Hotel* restaurant, to the north of the tourist office, has great chicken rolls – minced chicken with cardamom in batter. The multicuisine air-con restaurant *Pamm's*, at the Hotel Vinayak, is another good place. The *China Garden* restaurant is air-con and serves a good range of Chinese, Indian and continental food. Handy to the train station is the *Miami Restaurant*, next to the Hotel Holydon, featuring south Indian and Chinese cuisine.

Shopping

Shiliguri is famous for its cane work – everything from letter racks to bed-ends, and pot stands to lounge suites. While being bulky, caneware is light and easily shipped home. The town also offers a good range of clothing, from the cheap and cheerful in the markets (and next to the taxi and bus stands), to designer label creations in Tenzing Norgay (Hill Cart) Rd. Tailors and material vendors abound in the area around NJP train station, so even if you are not spending long in town before heading for the hills, you can have clothes made to measure at rock-bottom prices and pick them up on your return to the plains.

Getting There & Away

Air The airport serving the hills region of Bangla is at Bagdogra, 12km west of Shiliguri. Jet Airways and Indian Airlines have regular flights between Delhi and Bagdogra, some via Gauhati, in Assam. Indian Airlines also has regular services to Kolkata. It's better to fly into Bagdogra with Indian Airlines from Delhi, and return to the capital with Jet Airways, as these flights are direct (not via Gauhati in Assam).

Jet Airways has a daily direct afternoon flight to Delhi (US$185) and Indian Airlines has a lunchtime flight on Monday and Friday to Delhi (US$185), via Gauhati (US$50). Indian Airlines also has an afternoon flight to Kolkata (US$80), leaving on Monday, Tuesday, Thursday and Friday.

Indian Airlines (☎ 431509, airport 450666) has an office beside the Mainak Tourist Lodge, on Tenzing Norgay (Hill Cart) Rd. It's open daily, 9 am to 1 pm and 2 to 4.30 pm. Jet Airways (☎ 435876, airport 450589) has an office in the LM Moulik Complex, next door to the Hotel Vinayak on Tenzing Norgay (Hill Cart) Rd. It's open daily, 9 am to 6 pm.

Bus Most North Bengal State Transport Corporation (NBSTC) buses leave from the Tenzing Norgay Central bus terminal. Private buses, including the Hilly Region Mini Bus Owners' Association, with services to Darjeeling, Kurseong, Mirik and Kalimpong (West Bengal Hills), and Jorethang and Gangtok (Sikkim) also have counters at the terminal. Note that if you are travelling to Jorethang in West Sikkim, you will require a trekking permit. See the Inner Line Permits section in the Sikkim chapter for details.

NBSTC buses go to Madarihat (for Jaldhapara Wildlife Sanctuary; Rs 27, 3 hours, six daily), Darjeeling (Rs 26, 3 hours, five daily), Kalimpong (Rs 26, 3 hours, one daily at 7 am) and Mirik (Rs 25, 2½ hours, two daily). There's no NBSTC service between Mirik and Darjeeling, but you can get private buses (Rs 25, 3½ hours).

Three daily rocket services (2x2 pushback seats) leave to Kolkata (Calcutta; Rs 160, 12 hours). There's an ordinary service at 5.30 pm (Rs 145). To Malda, ordinary services depart every 30 minutes between 5 am and noon (Rs 56, 6 hours). There's a night service at 5.30 pm (Rs 65, 7 hours), and a day service at 5.30 am (Rs 57, 5 hours).

To Berhampore (from where you can catch a train to Lalgola on the Bangladesh border) buses leave at 5, 6, 7 and 7.30 am (Rs 95, 8 hours). A daily rocket service for Patna leaves from the NBSTC depot at Mallaguri Garage, a 10 minute walk north up Tenzing Norgay (Hill Cart) Rd (a rickshaw costs Rs 7). Tickets for all destinations in Bihar must be booked here. The bus leaves at 4 pm (Rs 145, 12 hours).

For Gauhati, in Assam, there's a NBSTC rocket service from Tenzing Norgay terminal at 5 pm (Rs 165, 12 hours), and an ordinary service from Mallaguri Garage at 7.30 am (Rs 140).

Sikkim Nationalised Transport (SNT) buses leave from the SNT terminal on the east side of Tenzing Norgay (Hill Cart) Rd. Fares for the 114km journey to Gangtok are Rs 55 in ordinary buses, and Rs 100 for the deluxe service.

Nepal Local buses leave from in front of the Tenzing Norgay Central bus terminal for Paniktanki, opposite the Nepal border town of Kakarbhitta. You can arrange a Nepali visa (US$25; payment in cash only) at Paniktanki. The trip takes one hour, and costs Rs 10. A rickshaw across the border to Kakarbhitta also costs Rs 10. Buses depart Kakarbhitta daily at 4 pm for Kathmandu (Nepali Rs 250, 17 hours). Buses between Darjeeling and Kathmandu also run through Shiliguri and, regardless of which company you go with, you'll have to change buses here. See the Darjeeling section for more details.

Train The *Darjeeling Mail* departs Sealdah in Kolkata at 7 pm (12 hours). Tickets are Rs 170/598 in 2nd sleeper/1st class. The return trip leaves NJP at 6.45 pm, arriving at Sealdah at 8.30 am. The *North East Express* is the fastest train between Shiliguri and Delhi (33 hours). It departs at 5.25 pm and costs Rs 335/908 in 2nd sleeper/1st class, travelling via Patna (16 hours).

For Gauhati (Assam), the *North East Express* leaves at 7 am, arriving at 6 pm (2nd/1st class Rs 135/471). The *Abadh Assam Express* leaves NJP at 7.15 pm, arriving at Gauhati at 5.15 am. Second class sleeper tickets are available on the *Kanchenjunga Express*, which departs at 5 pm, arriving at Gauhati at 5 am.

There's a railway booking office on Bidhan Rd, just off Tenzing Norgay (Hill Cart) Rd. It's open Monday to Saturday, 8 am to 8 pm, and on Sunday and holidays, until 2 pm.

Toy Train If the toy train from Shiliguri/New Jalpaiguri to Darjeeling is running (which it hasn't been for a couple of years due to a major landslide), tickets can be purchased from NJP, Shiliguri Town or Shiliguri Junction train stations. As there are no advance reservations, it may be easier during the busy high season (May to mid-July), to pick up tickets at NJP, where the train originates. When operating, there is a daily service at 9 am and also at 7.15 am in the high season. The journey takes an interminable nine hours to cover the 80 odd km up to the hill station, or four hours to Kurseong, 30km short of Darjeeling. For more details on the toy train, see Getting There & Away in the Darjeeling section.

Bangladesh From New Jalpaiguri to Haldibari (the Indian border checkpoint) takes two hours and costs Rs 15 by train. From here it's a 7km walk along the disused railway line to the Bangladesh border point at Chilahati. From here you can travel by train into Bangladesh. See the Getting There & Away chapter for more details.

Taxi & Jeep The fastest and most comfortable way of getting around the hills is by share jeep. There are a number of taxi stands, including one on Sevoke Rd and one outside Tenzing Norgay terminal, where you can get share jeeps to destinations in the Bangla hills and Sikkim including: Darjeeling (Rs 47, 2½ hours), Kalimpong (Rs 50, 2½ hours), Kurseong (Rs 26, two hours), Mirik (Rs 35, 2½ hours) and Gangtok (Rs 80, 4½ hours). Posted rates for a private taxi are: Darjeeling, Rs 750; Kalimpong, Rs 750; Mirik, Rs 600; and Gauhati, Rs 4000.

Getting Around

There are hundreds of cycle-rickshaws vying for your custom on Tenzing Norgay (Hill Cart) Rd (if they're not already burdened down with pyramids of pineapples). You will have trouble convincing any of them to take you even 500m for less than Rs 5. From Tenzing Norgay Central bus terminal to NJP train station, taxis will charge Rs 120, and auto-rickshaws about Rs 75. A cycle-rickshaw will cost about Rs 20 for the 40 minute trip from NJP train station to Shiliguri Junction, or Rs 30 to Tenzing Norgay Central bus terminal. There are infrequent bus services along this route (Rs 4).

To/From the Airport If you are flying out of Bagdogra airport, you may be able to get a lift from Shiliguri to the airport with airline staff. Check at the Jet Airways or Indian Airlines offices in Shiliguri. A taxi between the airport and Shiliguri costs Rs 150. A less expensive option is to take a taxi to Bagdogra bazaar (Rs 50, 3km) and get a local bus from there into Shiliguri (Rs 4, 9km).

There's a direct bus to Darjeeling from the airport (Rs 75, 3½ hours) which connects with flights. Ask at the Bangla tourist office at the airport; taxi drivers (who charge Rs 150 into Shiliguri) will try to convince you it doesn't exist. From Bagdogra airport to Darjeeling, a taxi will cost Rs 850.

JALDHAPARA WILDLIFE SANCTUARY
• alt 61m

Although most visitors are keen to make a hasty exit from the mayhem of Shiliguri and head north for Darjeeling and Sikkim, if you have the time, it's worth making the 135km trip east to this little-visited sanctuary. It was established in 1941 for the protection of wildlife, particularly the Indian one-horned rhinoceros (*Rhinoceros unicornis*), which is threatened with extinction. The sanctuary has had some success in stabilising depleting rhino numbers, with an estimated population of 35 in the park precincts. Despite this, numbers are slow to rise as poachers still slay these magnificent beasts for the highly coveted rhino horn. The park encompasses an area of 116 sq km, located in the east of Jalpaiguri district between the Torsa and Malangi rivers, with the mountains of Bhutan visible to the north.

The best season to visit Jaldhapara is from October to May, particularly in March and April, when the wild animals are attracted by the growth of new grasses. Apart from rhinos, other animals found in the park environs are (rarely seen) Royal Bengal tigers, wild elephants and various types of deer, including sambar, muntjac (barking deer), chital (spotted deer) and hog deer.

It is possible to take elephant safaris from Hollong, inside the park. Cost is Rs 70 for Indians, Rs 80 for foreigners and there's a discount for students on production of a valid student card. The park entry fee is Rs 10 per person, and Rs 10 per light vehicle. Still camera charges are Rs 5 per day.

Places to Stay & Eat

Within the park is the *Hollong Forest Lodge*, with doubles for Rs 425/850 for Indians/foreigners, plus Rs 120/125 per person (compulsory) for breakfast, dinner and

BANGLA (WEST BENGAL) HILLS

bed tea. Outside the park precincts is the *Jaldhapara Tourist Lodge*, at Madarihat. Doubles are Rs 850 and dorm beds are Rs 190, including all meals. Both these places must be booked in advance through the Sub-Regional tourist office (☎ 0353-431974) in Shiliguri, or the Government of Bangla tourist bureau (☎ 033-248 8271), 3/2 BBD Bagh East, Kolkata, 700001. Bangla Tourism has packages including accommodation, all meals, and a one hour elephant safari.

Getting There & Away

From Tenzing Norgay Central bus terminal in Shiliguri, buses ply to Madarihat, a small village 124km to the east, and 9km from Jaldhapara (Rs 27, three hours). From here, a taxi to Hollong, inside the park, will cost Rs 150. To hire a taxi from Shiliguri to Jaldhapara will cost about Rs 950. In theory, there is a daily train to Madarihat from Shiliguri, which departs at 11.30 am, arriving at Madarihat at 4 pm, but the service is erratic.

AROUND JALDHAPARA
Totopara

Lying on the banks of the Torsa River, 30km from Madarihat, is the village of Totopara, close to the Bhutan border. This is the last remaining settlement of Toto people, an indigenous tribal group whose numbers have dwindled to less than 100. A bus operates between Madarihat and Totopara in the winter months only (Rs 10). During the summer rains, it is impossible to cross the Titi River that lies between the two settlements.

Buxa Tiger Reserve

In an area of natural reedlands and sal forests, the Buxa Tiger Reserve encompasses an area of 761 sq km, of which 369 sq km was designated as a wildlife sanctuary in 1987. The reserve is accessible from the settlement of Rajabhatkawa, a four hour bus trip from Shiliguri, or 3½ hours from Madarihat. As a newly created reserve, there is little infrastructure in place for visitors, but the reserve does possess a wide variety of animal species, including over 230 species of birds and 60 species of mammals. These include a population of some 30 tigers, as well as numbers of wild elephants, deer, gaur (bison), barking, spotted and hog deer, and sambar. Intensive training programs have been undertaken to educate field staff in the importance of conservation-based wildlife management, as opposed to revenue-based forestry.

There are dormitory facilities (Rs 20) at Buxa Duar, a 5km trek from the ranger's office at Santrabari. Close by is an old fort that once protected the most important of the 11 routes into neighbouring Bhutan. During the independence movement, the fort was used by the British as a detention camp for freedom fighters.

Triple rooms are available at Rajabhatkawa, at Rs 40 per bed, or doubles with bath are Rs 225. For bookings, contact the Director, Buxa Tiger Project, PO Aliporedooar, District Jalpaiguri (☎ 03572-2777).

There is one bus daily from Shiliguri to Rajabhatkawa, departing at 10.15 am and arriving at 2 pm (Rs 35), and a daily train service from Shiliguri Junction train station, departing at 11.30 am (Rs 50). The bus is the better bet, as the train arrives after dark at 7.30 pm. From Madarihat, it's 2½ hours by bus to Hashimara (Rs 25), from where you can get a local bus or taxi for the remaining 15km to Rajabhatkawa.

Darjeeling District

• pop 1,335,600

Darjeeling district encompasses three administrative subdivisions: Darjeeling, Kalimpong and Kurseong. The hill station of Darjeeling is the main attraction in this region, but Kurseong and Kalimpong are also well worth visiting, with some interesting walks and treks, particularly from Kalimpong.

Mirik is also being promoted as a hill resort. It's still a relatively laid-back place, although rapid development and excessive tourist numbers are spoiling the environment there.

BANGLA (WEST BENGAL) HILLS

DARJEELING
☎ 0354 • pop 83,000 • alt 2134m

Straddling a ridge in the Darjeeling-Sikkim Himalaya and surrounded by tea plantations on all sides, Darjeeling has been a popular hill station since the British established it as a rest and recreation centre for their troops in the mid-19th century. The industrious Brits, not averse to mixing a little business with pleasure, recognised that the quality of the soil and the mild climate were ideal for tea cultivation, and the forested hill slopes were soon denuded of their cover and planted with this most lucrative revenue earner.

These days people still come here to escape from the heat and humidity of the north Indian plains. You get an indication of how popular Darjeeling is from the 100 or so hotels recognised by the tourist office and the scores of others that don't come up to their requirements, or that haven't applied for status.

In Darjeeling you will find yourself surrounded by mountain people from all over the eastern Himalaya who have come to work, to trade or, in the case of many Tibetans, as refugees. Mother Teresa spent her early years as a nun here with the sisters at Loreto Convent, and writer and naturalist Lawrence Durrell was educated at the prestigious St Joseph's College.

Outside the monsoon season, the views over the mountains to the snowy peaks of Kanchenjunga and down to the swollen rivers in the valleys are magnificent. Even when the peaks are enshrouded with mist (as they generally are during the monsoon), Darjeeling is an interesting and charming place. You can visit Buddhist gompas and tea plantations, ride on the chairlift, spend days hunting for bargains in colourful markets and handicraft shops, or go trekking to high-altitude spots near the border with Sikkim. Alternatively you can soak up the ambience just curled up on a sunny veranda or in front of a cosy fire reading a book, or wandering around and interacting with the local community.

While the fine old buildings that graced what was once affectionately referred to as the 'Queen of Hills' are for the most part still standing, most are in shocking states of dilapidation, with neither the will nor the resources to return them to their former glory. The former queen retains her charm, but she is looking distinctly shabby these days, her royal vestments sullied with fast-food joints, multilevel grey hotel complexes, and convoys of jeeps and tourist buses.

Christmas is a delightful time to be in Darjeeling. Christmas trees, decorations, open fires, merriment and strolling carol singers are the fare for several days, all contributing to the feel of a European or north American Christmas. There is something rather poignant and stirring about hearing traditional carols, such as Silent Night and O Come All Ye Faithful, sung here in a different language and played on local instruments.

Like many places in the Himalaya, half the fun is getting there, and Darjeeling has the unique attraction of its famous toy steam train, the oldest locomotive still running in India. For generations, this miniature train has looped its way up the steep mountainsides from the plains to Darjeeling. Unfortunately, its progress is frequently halted, sometimes for years, by savage landslides that wipe out the tracks, or make the ground too unstable even for the tiny train.

Orientation

Darjeeling sprawls over a west-facing ridge, spilling down the hillside in a complicated series of interconnecting roads and flights of steps. Hill Cart Rd has been renamed Tenzing Norgay Rd (as there's another road by that name in Shiliguri, to eliminate confusion, the name Hill Cart Rd will be used in this section). It's the main road through the lower part of the town, and the train station, the bus and main taxi stand are all on it. The most important route connecting this road with Chowrasta (the town square) at the top of the ridge is Laden La Rd and Nehru Rd. (Nehru Rd is another renamed road, still generally referred to as the Mall.)

Running more or less parallel to, and above, Laden La, and connected to it by

DARJEELING TREKS

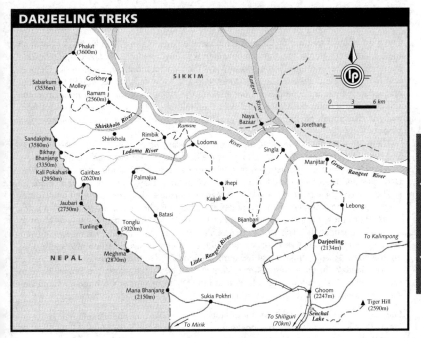

staircases at intervals, is Gandhi Rd, with several mid-range places to stay along its length. Laden La and Gandhi roads converge at a major junction known as Clubside. Laden La continues north until it merges with HD Lama Rd as does Nehru Rd (the Mall), until it meets Chowrasta. Along both are a number of mid-range hotels, photographic supply shops, curio shops and restaurants.

The youth hostel and a number of budget guesthouses are on or near Dr Zakir Hussain Rd, which extends along the top of the ridge about 600m above the bus stand. It can be reached via Rockville Rd, above Gandhi Rd, and once you know the area, also via a myriad of pathways.

The bulk of the top-range hotels, including the Windamere, New Elgin and Mayfair Resort, are clustered around Observatory Hill beyond Chowrasta.

Information

Tourist Offices The Government of Bangla tourist office (☎ 54050) is below the Bellevue Hotel, on Chowrasta. The staff are helpful and have maps and brochures on Darjeeling. You can book here for the bus to Bagdogra airport (Rs 75). The bus leaves from the Police Traffic Point, Clubside, and stops to pick up passengers near the Windamere Hotel. The office is open Monday to Friday, 10 am to 4.30 pm. When this office is closed, tickets for the airport shuttle can be purchased from the Darjeeling Gorkha Hill Council Tourism (DGHC) office (☎ 54879, ☎/fax 54214), in the Silver Fir building, opposite the Hotel Alice Villa, to the north, and downhill, of Chowrasta. The office, which is open daily 10 am to 5 pm, can also arrange activities such as white-water rafting, trekking, etc.

During the busy main tourist season, there are useful tourist assistance booths at

Treks in Darjeeling

The most popular trek out of Darjeeling follows the ridge line marking the border between India and eastern Nepal. The trek can be undertaken any time from the end of the monsoon in late September through till the end of May. The clearest mountain views are in October and November, and although temperatures drop and snow falls are recorded in December and January, there is no problem in undertaking this trek during the winter months. In the spring the haze and clouds associated with the build up of the monsoon are present from mid-March through till the end of May, although by this time the rhododendrons are in bloom.

There are a number of trekking agencies in Darjeeling where you can rent sleeping bags and basic camping gear. There are also many tea house lodges for overnight accommodation, so a tent is not necessary unless you plan to continue onto Phalut. Porters are available from Darjeeling and Mana Bhanjang for around Rs 100 per day; they may also double as guides.

The trek commences from the village of Mana Bhanjang and passes a series of small settlements to the rhododendron forested ridges at Jaubari. On the second stage there is a gradual ascent to the small lake and village at Kali Pokhari before continuing for several hours to the ridge at Sandakphu. This is the place to view the eastern Himalaya with views of Everest, Lhotse and Makalu, while, to the north there is an impressive selection of peaks including the huge Kanchenjunga massif (8598m), the world's third highest peak.

From Sandakphu there are options to continue for two stages along the Singali Ridge to camp at Phalut. The alternative is to descend directly from Sandakphu through rhododendron and conifer forest to the road head at Rimbik and the bus back to Darjeeling.

Stage 1	Mana Bhanjang to Jaubari	(5-6 hrs)
Stage 2	Jaubari to Sandakphu	(6-7 hrs)
Stage 3	Sandakphu to Rimbik	(6 hrs)

Optional trek to Phalut
Stage 3	Sandakphu to Molley	(4-5 hrs)
Stage 4	Molley to Phalut and Gorkhey	(5-6 hrs)
Stage 5	Gorkhey to Rimbik	(6-7 hrs)

both the Darjeeling train station and Clubside taxi stand.

Permits for Sikkim The Foreigners' Registration Office is on Laden La Rd. It's open daily, 10 am to 5 pm. To get a 15 day permit for Sikkim you must first visit the Deputy Commissioner's Office, otherwise known as the DM (District Magistrate), to the north of the town centre on Hill Cart Rd. Then get an endorsement from the Foreigners' Registration Office and return to the DM to collect your permit. The DM's office is open for permit applications Monday to Friday, 11 am to 1 pm and 2 to 4 pm. The whole process takes about an hour. If you want to enter West Sikkim direct from Darjeeling, rather than first going to Gangtok, make sure that Naya Bazaar is one of the places listed on your permit.

Trekking Outfits & Tour Operators
There are several good trekking agents in the Super Market complex, near the Bazaar bus stand on Hill Cart Rd. Himali Treks & Tours books treks and also hires equipment

(see following). It has a half-day mountain-bike tour that leaves from Chowrasta, taking in the Aloobari Gompa and Senchal Lake, and can arrange rafting on the Teesta River. Diamond Tours & Travels has been operating for 11 years, and can arrange treks in Sikkim, make hotel reservations and book luxury bus trips. Kasturi Tours & Travels organises tours to Kathmandu, Gangtok and Bhutan.

Between mid-September and mid-December, the DGHC tourist office offers a sunrise trip to Tiger Hill that leaves early in the morning at 4 am. Tickets cost about Rs 50 and must be booked a few days in advance. Most people go with the independent operators who charge a little less; some operators send a runner to your hotel to make sure you get up! Depending on demand, the tourist office can also organise a local sightseeing tour, a trip to Mirik and a two day tour to Kalimpong and Gangtok.

Other operators include:

Clubside Tours & Travels
(☎ 54646) JP Sharma Rd (off Laden La Rd. Arranges treks and tours in North Bengal, Sikkim and Assam. It specialises in wildlife tours, and can arrange trips to Manas and Kaziranga wildlife reserves in Assam, and Jaldhapara Wildlife Sanctuary.
Dorjee 'Ling' Tours & Travels
(☎ 55099, fax 54717,
email tashi@cal.vsnl.net.in)
Hotel Seven Seventeen on HD Lama Rd. Offers some good local sightseeing tours, as well as longer tours, treks and vehicle rental. It can also arrange instant hotel bookings in Darjeeling, Sikkim, Bhutan and Nepal.
Himalayan Adventures
(☎ 54004/54090, fax 54237)
15 Nehru Rd (The Mall) in the same premises as Das Studios. Specialises in trekking and tours of the entire Himalaya region, it is run by Sheila Pradhan, a real character who can organise some unique experiences.
Himalayan Tours & Travels
(☎ 54544) Has 20 years of experience booking treks in the regions of Darjeeling and Sikkim, and also leads mountaineering expeditions.
Tenzing Himalayan Expeditions
(☎ 54778, fax 52392)
Operated by Tenzing Norgay's eldest daughter, Pem Pen Tsering. The Tenzing family can or-

ganise just about anything in the Himalaya, from a vehicle to Gangtok to private climbing instruction and mountaineering expeditions to Kanchenjunga.
Trek-Mate Tours & Pineridge Travels
(☎ 53912) Adjacent to Pineridge Hotel in Chowrasta. Can tailor treks in the Sikkim and Darjeeling areas to suit your personal requirements, arranges guides and porters and also hires equipment.

Equipment Hire Trekking gear can be hired from the youth hostel, but you must leave a deposit to cover the value of the articles (deposits are returnable, less hire charges, on return of the equipment). Typical charges per day are: sleeping bag Rs 25, rucksack Rs 15 and down jacket Rs 25. There is a good comment and trek notebook here compiled by other travellers. The DGHC Lowis Jubilee Complex, on Dr SK Pal Rd, also hires equipment at minimal charges (a few rupees a day, plus refundable deposit), as does Himali Treks & Tours and Trek-Mate Tours. (See Trekking Outfits & Tour Operators earlier.)

Money ANZ Grindlays and the State Bank of India are both on Laden La Rd, to the north of the post office, and are open 10 am to 3 pm. The ANZ Bank only changes travellers cheques Monday to Friday, 10 am to 1 pm, and charges Rs 100. The State Bank of India has no charge, but often has long queues. Both banks will change most foreign currency. If you want a cash advance on credit card, you will save money by collecting the cash the following day. The same day encashment charge is Rs 250; next day it's Rs 50!

Post & Communications The post office (and poste restante) is centrally located on Laden La Rd. There's a handy parcel posting office next door.

Email and Internet facilities are springing up all over Darjeeling. Now there is a server in Shiliguri, costs are the same as Kolkata, Rs 3 per minute. However, using the Internet or email in this town can be very frustrating as the lines frequently drop out.

The Cyber Cafe (☎ 53950, 53551, email Udayan@cal2.vsnl.net.in), on the 1st floor of the Hotel Red Rose, was the first such facility in Darjeeling, and is still the best. It offers multiple terminals, Web site development, a photocopying service and is also a PCO (so ET can phone home, send a fax and email in one visit).

The Compuset Centre (☎ 54636), one minute from the clock tower next to the Hotel Fairmont, is a friendly place where you can arrange to have emails sent and held for you if you don't have your own email address (compuset@cal.vsnl.net.in); it's closed on Sunday.

Bookshops & Borrowing Libraries The Oxford Book & Stationery Company on Chowrasta (☎ 54325) is the best bookshop here. It's a great shop open until well into the evening. It has a comprehensive selection of books and specialises in Tibet, Nepal, Sikkim, Bhutan and the Himalayan zone. It has a good, reliable mailing system that allows your purchases to be packed and shipped home by sea or air.

Many of the budget guesthouses have borrowing libraries for guests' use.

Photography Das Studios, on Nehru Rd, is a good place to head for advice regarding matters photographic. It stocks up to ASA 400 print and slide film, but although there are several places to process print film in Darjeeling, as yet there is no provision for slide processing. The friendly shop is a good place to browse as it also sells CDs, books, greeting cards and gifts.

Medical Services Puri & Co has a well-stocked dispensary on the Mall, just up from Keventer's. If you need a doctor, inquire here. Opposite the post office at 7 Laden La Rd is the Economic Pharmacy. The Tibetan Medical & Astro Institute is beneath the Hotel Seven Seventeen, at 26 HD Lama Rd; it's open Monday to Friday, 9 am to noon and 2 to 4 pm.

As an alternative to the state hospital, the Mariam Nursing Home (☎ 54327/28) comes well recommended by an English psychotherapist who had occasion to avail himself of its diagnostic services. This small private hospital is located down the hill from the Gymkhana Club, well hidden behind shops and buildings. It boasts a small operating department, various consultancy disciplines and an efficient pathology/diagnostics lab. Travellers tend to be seen by a Dr Siddique who trained in the UK. The consultation fee is Rs 80, and tests range from Rs 40 to Rs 100.

Emergency Police: ☎ 2193; Ambulance: ☎ 2131; Fire: ☎ 2121; Darjeeling Hospital: ☎ 54218.

Tiger Hill
Tiger Hill, near Ghoom, is the highest spot in the area at 2590m, and about 11km from Darjeeling. The hill affords magnificent dawn views over Kanchenjunga and other eastern Himalayan peaks. On a clear day even Mt Everest is visible, looking strangely diminutive against the closer peaks that appear higher from this perspective.

Every day a large convoy of battered jeeps leaves Darjeeling for Tiger Hill at 4.30 am, which means that in the smaller lodges you get woken up at this time every day, whether you like it or not. The return trip costs Rs 50. It can be very cold and very crowded at the top, but coffee is available.

The early morning start and discomfort are worthwhile for the spectacular vision of a 250km long stretch of the Himalayan massifs, with, from left to right, Lhotse (8501m) flanked by Everest (8848m) and Makalu (8475m), then an apparent gap before the craggy Kokang (5505m), flanked by Janu (7710m), Rathong (6630m), the flat-summited Kabru (7338m), Kanchenjunga (8598m), Pandim (6691m), Simvo (6811m) and the cone-like Siniolchu (5780m).

There's a viewing tower and entry costs Rs 2 for the top or Rs 7 for the warmer VIP lounge. Halfway down the hill a temple priest causes a massive traffic jam by anointing the steering wheel of each vehicle on the return trip!

Many take the jeep one way (Rs 30) and then walk back, a very pleasant two hour trip. Tickets can be purchased at the tourist office beneath the Bellevue Hotel.

Senchal Lake

Close to Tiger Hill is Senchal Lake, at 2448m, which supplies (somewhat erratically!) Darjeeling with its domestic water. It's a particularly scenic area and popular as a picnic spot with Indian holiday makers.

Kanchenjunga Views

At 8598m this is the world's third-highest mountain (and since India's annexation of Sikkim in 1975, the highest in India). From Darjeeling, the best uninterrupted views are to be had from Bhan Bhakta Sarani. From Chowrasta, take the road to the right-hand side of the Windamere Hotel and continue about 300m; you can then wander around to Observatory Hill and view the mountain from different angles, or walk up to the shrine on the top of the hill above the Tourist Bungalow. If you happen to be staying up on the ridge at, or near, the Tenzing Norgay youth hostel, all you have to do is go outside to see early morning views almost rivalling those from Tiger Hill. However, as the weather in the mountains can be fickle, nobody should go to Darjeeling just for the views; haze can conceal them for days on end. See the Kanchenjunga boxed text in the Sikkim chapter.

Yogachoeling Gompa

Also known as Ghoom Gompa, this is probably the most famous gompa in Darjeeling, and is about 8km south of town, just below Hill Cart Rd and the train station near Ghoom. The gompa was built in 1875 by Lama Sherab Gyantso, and its monks belong to the Gelukpa order of Tibetan Buddhism. It enshrines an image of Maitreya Buddha (the Future Buddha). The image of the Buddha has a western posture – seated, and with his hands on his knees, rather than in the traditional lotus position, and the eyes of the image are blue. Buddhists believe that the next Buddha will appear in the

west, hence these western manifestations. The gompa also houses a very fine image of Mahakala (Tibetan: Nagpo Chenpo), a wrathful Tantric deity, with its roots in the Hindu god Mahakali. Foreigners are allowed to enter the shrine and take photographs. A small donation is customary and the monks are very friendly.

Bhutia Busty Gompa

Not far from Chowrasta is this colourful gompa, with Kanchenjunga providing a spectacular backdrop. Originally a branch of the Nyingmapa order's Phodang Gompa in Sikkim, it was transferred to Darjeeling in 1879. The shrine here originally stood on Observatory Hill. There's an old library of Buddhist texts upstairs which houses the original copy of the *Tibetan Book of the Dead (Bardo Thodol)*. The manuscript was discovered here by the Swedish scholar, Dr WY Evans-Wentz, who translated the text. There is also a very fine mural depicting Mahakala (Tibetan: Nagpo Chenpo). You will require permission from the caretaker monk to view the mural.

Other Gompas

Halfway between Ghoom and Darjeeling is the **Thupten Sangachoeling Gompa** at Dali. Westerners interested in Tibetan Buddhism often study here. Behind the gompa, a keen gardener has planted over 40 species of rhododendron and yuille trees. Visitors are welcome. There are three other gompas in Ghoom: the large but relatively uninteresting **Samdenchoeling**, the nearby and smaller **Sakyachoeling**, and the **Phin Sotholing**.

Closer to Darjeeling, on Tenzing Norgay Rd, the **Aloobari Gompa** welcomes visitors. The monks often sell Tibetan and Sikkimese handicrafts. If the gompa is closed, ask at the cottage next door and they'll let you in.

Beyond Ghoom in the settlement of Rongbul is the **Gonjan Gompa**, and adjacent to it, the **School of Tibetan Thangka Painting**. The school is run by the Tibetan lama Tsondu Sangpo, and his finely executed work is on display. On Hill Cart Rd, between Ghoom and Darjeeling, is the opulent **Sonada Gompa** over which the Kaloo Rinpoche presides. Kaloo Rinpoche is believed to be an incarnation of the previous Kaloo Rinpoche who founded the gompa, and established retreat centres in France and other parts of Europe, and the USA.

Observatory Hill

Situated above the Windamere Hotel, this viewpoint is sacred to both Hindus and Buddhists. Observatory Hill was once the site of the gompa of Dorje Ling, from which the town takes its name. There's a shrine to Mahakala, for Hindus an incarnation of Shiva, and for Buddhists an incarnation of Padmasambhava (also known as Guru Rinpoche), who established Buddhism in Tibet and founded the Nyingmapa order. The multi-coloured Tibetan prayer flags here double as trapezes for monkeys. Watch out for the monkeys as they can be aggressive.

Dhirdham & Maa Singha Temples

Built in 1939, the Dhirdham Temple is the most conspicuous Hindu temple in Darjeeling. It is just below the train station and is modelled on the famous Pashupatinath Temple (sacred to Shiva) in Kathmandu.

Nearby is a tiny Maa Singha temple presided over by a female priest, or *mataji*, named Kumari Mataji. Her devotees, who include Hindus, Buddhists and westerners, believe she is a prophetess. Her temple is sacred to the goddess Durga, and devotees believe that Durga speaks through mataji.

Bengal Natural History Museum

Established in 1903, this interesting little museum has a comprehensive but dusty collection of stuffed Himalayan and Bangali fauna. The exhibits include over 56 species of mammals, 450 species of birds, 45 species of reptiles, 75 species of fish, and over 290 species of (largely unidentified) butterflies and moths, as well as a library containing over 2000 books and journals.

This magnificent collection is in a very sorry state. Some of the beetles have come off their pins and are lying in the bottom of their display cases with dismembered legs scattered about them, and many of the animals look like they died of mange (though there are a few quite decent dioramas). In a back room, generally not open to visitors, are hundreds of drawers, each full of birds lying on a bed of mothballs – an ornithological mortuary.

The museum is open daily except Thursday, 10 am to 4 pm. Entry is Rs 2.

Padmaja Naidu Himalayan Zoological Park

This zoo was established in 1958 with the objectives of study, conservation and preservation of Himalayan fauna. It is a pleasant zoo, and the animals are well cared for by dedicated keepers (some of whom have worked with the same animals for 20 years). However, it is a zoo, and visitors must realise that any zoo is a compromise.

The zoo houses India's only collection of Siberian tigers, and some rare species such as the red panda and the Tibetan wolf. There has been enormous success in breeding the Tibetan wolf at the zoo, but that of the red panda was not as good until the end of 1996, when a separate breeding enclosure was established next to the snow leopard enclosure. Since then two cubs a year have been bred, with one pair going to the zoo in Sikkim.

The zoo can be reached in a 30 minute walk from Chowrasta. It is open daily except Thursday, 8 am to 4 pm. Entry is Rs 6, and Rs 5 for a 'steel' camera.

Snow Leopard Enclosure

The snow leopards *(Panthera uncia)* were originally housed in the main zoo complex. Due to the disturbance of visitors and the proximity of other animals, these rare and beautiful animals were moved to a large separate enclosure on the way to the ropeway (about 15 minutes' walk beyond the zoo) behind the Himalayan Mountaineering Institute (HMI).

Kiran Moktan at the centre talks at great length and with great affection for his charges. He welcomes interested visitors

Fight for Survival

The beautiful snow leopard can be found across the entire Indian Himalaya, from Kashmir in the west to Bhutan beyond Sikkim's eastern borders. To the north they are found in Tibet, Central Asia and the Altais. Due to the inaccessibility of the terrain and the high altitudes of their habitats (over 3600m), it is almost impossible to be accurate about numbers in the wild – estimated to be between four and five thousand. However, although the snow leopard is a highly endangered and protected species, the smuggling of its pelts continues, resulting in a decline in these numbers.

To ensure the survival of the species, the International Snow Leopard Trust, which controls all breeding programs, was founded in the early 1970s. The Snow Leopard Breeding Program in Darjeeling commenced in 1986 with two leopards brought from Switzerland. The centre had nine cats in 1999, six of which were born at the zoo. The latest arrival, from the Nubra Valley, is a great addition to the gene pool.

In captivity, snow leopards live approximately 14 years, female snow leopards have two breeding cycles a year, but are more likely to conceive in winter. Gestation is from 92 to 100 days and there are usually two cubs per litter, though there can be up to five in the wild.

While it is distressing to see these magnificent animals behind wire enclosures, it's a sad fact that programs such as these enhance the snow leopard's prospects for survival as a species. Certainly, the cats are in wonderful condition in Darjeeling and the dedication of the staff here has to be applauded. Much credit for the program's success in India must be given to its director, Kiran Moktan who is also an accomplished wildlife artist; his works appear in many books (including Lonely Planet) and adorn the postcards here. To watch him playing with, and talking about his charges is a delight.

For further information contact the Conservation Education Director (206-632 2421, fax 632 3967, email islt@serv.net), International Snow Leopard Trust, 4649 Sunnyside Ave Nth, Seattle, Washington 98103, USA.

---

between 9 and 11 am, and 2 to 3.30 pm; it's better to visit in the afternoon when the leopards are more active, but you should not make too much noise. During the mating season, entry of visitors to the enclosure is prohibited. The centre is open daily except Thursday. Entry is Rs 10, (watch your head if entering through the small door set into the high gates!).

Himalayan Mountaineering Institute (HMI) & Museums

India's most prestigious mountaineering institute, founded in 1954, lies about 2km from the town centre on a hilltop known as Birch Hill Park. It is entered through the zoo, on Jawahar Rd West. There are two interesting, and extremely well presented, museums here. The **Mountaineering Museum** has a collection of historic mountaineering equipment, specimens of Himalayan flora and fauna and a relief model of the Himalaya showing the principal peaks. There is a display of badges and pins of mountaineering clubs around the world, and of the traditional dress of the hill tribes of the Himalaya. The **Everest Museum** next door traces the history of attempts on the great peak, with photographs and biographies of all the summiteers.

Sherpa Tenzing Norgay, who conquered Everest with Edmund Hillary in 1953, lived in Darjeeling and was the director of the institute for many years. He died in 1986 and his statue now stands beside his cremation spot just above the institute. The climbing tradition of the Tenzings lives on. Tenzing's eldest daughter, Pem Pem was a climber of some note, Tenzing's son, Jamling Norgay summited Everest in the spring of 1996, and his grandson, Tashi Tenzing summited in 1997.

The institute is open 9 am to 1 pm and 2 to 5 pm (until 4 pm in winter). There's a reasonable vegetarian restaurant, refreshment and chai shop by Sherpa Tenzing's statue.

Tea Plantations

Tea is, of course, Darjeeling's most famous export. From its 78 gardens, employing over 40,000 people, it produces the bulk of Bangla's crop, which is almost a quarter of India's total. About 80% of Darjeeling tea is exported; the domestic market is quite small. Darjeeling tea is mild, and most Indians prefer the bracing jolt afforded by the stronger teas produced in Assam.

The most convenient plantation to visit is the Happy Valley Tea Estate, only 2km from the centre of town, where tea is still produced by the 'orthodox' method as opposed to the 'curling, tearing and crushing' (CTC) technique adopted on the plains. However, it's only worth going when plucking is in progress (April to mid-November) because it's only then that the processing takes place. It's open daily, 8 am to noon and 1 to 4 pm (closed all day Monday and on Sunday afternoon). An employee might latch on to you, whisk you around the factory and then demand some outrageous sum for their trouble; Rs 10 per person is not inappropriate.

See the Shopping section for information about purchasing tea in Darjeeling.

Passenger Ropeway

At North Point, about 3km north of the town, is India's oldest passenger ropeway (cable car). It is 5km long and connects Darjeeling with Singla Bazaar on the Little Rangeet River at the bottom of the valley (there is a very necessary standby generator!) A return trip (including insurance) is Rs 45 and takes about an hour. Cars leave every 30 minutes between 8 am and 3.30 pm (closed Sunday and holidays during the

---

High Tea Hopes

In the last few years modern agricultural practices have improved the viability of the Darjeeling tea estates. The tea plantations were one of the first agricultural enterprises to use clonal plants in their replanting schemes, though most of the tea trees are at least 100 years old and nearing the end of their useful or even natural lives. The ageing plants and deteriorating soil causes grave concern, since tea not only earns the country valuable export revenue, but also provides much employment in the area. With the collapse of the USSR the Darjeeling tea planters lost their best customers and have had to look for new markets. Some have simply switched to growing cardamom, which is more profitable.

Despite the difficulties, the quality of the tea grown has resulted in record prices. The world record for the highest price paid for tea is held by some fine leaves from the Castleton Estate in Darjeeling, for which a Japanese bidder paid US$220 per kg!

Margaret's Hope plantation on the road to Kurseong, produces the tea that eventually finds its way to Buckingham Palace. The plantation's name came about from a rather sad story. An English tea planter took his daughter to England to be educated, but she was not happy there. Her one wish was to return to Darjeeling and the mountains, but she died before she could ever return. In her memory, her father named his property Margaret's Hope.

---

low season). It's a popular trip and you need to book one day in advance, but this can only be done in person at the ropeway station. However, you can phone to check if it's running (☎ 52731).

Lloyd Botanical Gardens

Below the bus and taxi stands near the market, these gardens, which are over 100 years old, contain a representative collection of Himalayan plants, flowers and orchids. The hothouses, although in disrepair, are well worth a visit. The gardens are open between 6 am and 5 pm; entrance is free.

Tibetan Refugee Self-Help Centre

A 20 to 30 minute walk from Chowrasta through leafy glades and tea plantations, brings you down to the Tibetan Refugee Self-Help Centre. It was established in October 1959 to help rehabilitate Tibetan refugees who fled from Tibet with the Dalai Lama following the Chinese invasion. The centre comprises an old peoples' home, orphanage, school, clinic/hospital (☎ 53122), gompa and workshops that produce carpets of pure Ladakhi wool, woollens, woodcarvings and leatherwork. These, and various Tibetan curios, coins, banknotes, jewellery etc, are for sale in the centre's showroom (☎ 52552). Prices are on a par with those in the curio shops of Chowrasta and Nehru Rd, but the proceeds go straight back to the community.

You can wander at leisure through the workshops and watch the work in progress, but the centre is closed on Sunday. The weaving and dyeing shops and the woodcarving shop are particularly interesting, and the people are gentle, warm and friendly. As the centre is self-funding, and a registered charity, donations are always welcome. For more information contact the office at 65 Gandhi Rd (☎ 52346).

Gymkhana Club

Membership of the Darjeeling Gymkhana Club costs just Rs 30 per day, but the activities here are not just equestrian. The word gymkhana is actually derived from the Hindi *gendkhana* (ball house). Games on offer include tennis, squash and badminton (Rs 35 per person per hour including balls or shuttlecocks, racquet and court hire, 6 am to noon); roller-skating (sorry, no blades here!, Rs 5 per hour, 10 am to 1 pm and 3 to 5 pm); table tennis (Rs 5 per hour); and billiards (Rs 15 per person per hour).

Pony Rides

Beware of the pony-wallahs who congregate on Chowrasta. They come along with you as a guide and at the end you'll find you're paying for a second pony and for their guiding time! The usual charge is Rs 60 an hour. You can organise with one of the pony-wallahs to hire by the day or week for pony treks. The cost is negotiable but should be around Rs 200 to Rs 300 per day (plus a guide).

Activities

For white-water rafting on the Teesta River, contact the Manager, River Rafting Centre, DGHC Tourism office, Teesta, Kalimpong (☎ 03552-68261) or DGHC, Silver Fir Bld, The Mall, Darjeeling (☎ 54879/54214, fax 54214). The DGHC can also arrange parasailing.

Contact the Himalayan Mountaineering Institute (HMI) or Tenzing Himalayan Expeditions for advice on tailored mountaineering courses and private tuition. See the Trekking Outfits and Tour Operators entry at the beginning of this section for details of private agencies.

Courses

Three-month Tibetan-language courses for beginners are conducted at the Manjushree Centre of Tibetan Culture (☎ 54159), 8 Burdwan Rd. There are also more advanced six and nine-month courses. The centre can also arrange Buddhist study courses for groups of six or more, and organises talks and seminars on Tibetan culture. For details, contact Norbu at Devekas Restaurant, who has worked at the centre as a volunteer for the past seven years.

You can learn traditional Tibetan woodcarving at the Tibetan Refugee Self-Help Centre (☎ 54686, fax 54237). For more details contact the head office (☎ 52346) at 65 Gandhi Rd.

Reiki, meaning Universal Life in Japanese, is the Usui Tradition of Natural Healing. Short courses and treatments are available in Darjeeling. For details contact Frans & Bronwyn Stiene (email bronwyn@hotmail.com), Reiki House, 1 Nehru Rd, Darjeeling, Bangla (adjacent to Main Bellvue Hotel on Chowrasta Hill in the Mall).

BANGLA (WEST BENGAL) HILLS

DARJEELING

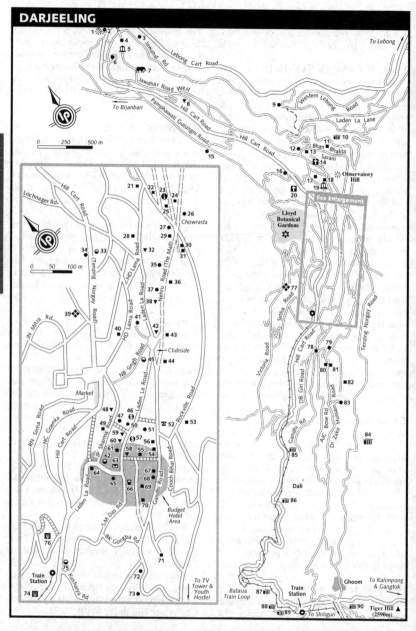

BANGLA (WEST BENGAL) HILLS

DARJEELING

PLACES TO STAY
11   Sailung Hotel
13   Tourist Bungalow
17   Ivanhoe
18   Mayfair Hill Resort
21   New Elgin Hotel;
     Kanchen Restaurant
22   Hotel Alice Villa
24   Windamere Hotel
25   Hotel Sunflower
28   Mohit Hotel
29   Pineridge Hotel;
     Trek-Mate Tours
30   Bellevue Hotel; Tourist
     Office; Indian Airlines
31   Main Bellevue Hotel
36   Hotel Shangrila
40   Hotel Seven Seventeen;
     Tibetan Medical & Astro
     Institute
43   Planters' Club
44   Dekeling Hotel; Dekeva's
     Restaurant
49   Hotel Tshering
     Denzongpa
53   Hotels Valentino; Embassy
     Restaurant
54   Hotel Fairmont
55   Hotel Prestige; Greenland
     Tours & Travel
56   Hotel Springburn
64   Hotel Red Rose;
     Cyber Cafe
69   Hotel Pagoda
70   Hotel Shamrock
71   Sinclairs
78   Hotel Silver Cascade
80   Triveni Guest House
     & Restaurant;
     Aliment Restaurant &
     Hotel
81   Tenzing Norgay Youth
     Hostel; Ratna's
82   Hotel Tower View

PLACES TO EAT
8   Hot Stimulating Cafe
32   Great Punjab Restaurant
38   Glenary's
42   Kev's (Keventer's Snack Bar)
48   New Dish Restaurant
58   Tibetan Restaurants
59   Jain Jaika Restaurant; Park
     Restaurant; Hayden Hall;
     Third Eye
60   Golden Dragon
     Restaurant & Bar

OTHER
1   North Point
2   St Joseph's School
3   Shrubbery
4   Ropeway Station
5   Himalayan Mountaineering
     Institute (HMI)
6   Snow Leopard Enclosure
7   Zoo
9   Tibetan Refugee Centre
10   Bhutia Busty Gompa
12   Raj Bhavan (Government
     House)
14   Gymkhana Club;
     St Andrew's Church
15   Happy Valley Tea Estate
16   Deputy Commissioner's
     Office/ District Magistrate
     (DM)
19   Bengal Natural History
     Museum
20   Loreto Convent & Catholic
     Church
23   Darjeeling Gorkha Hill
     Council (DGHC) Tourism
     Office
26   Pony Stand
27   Oxford Book & Stationery
     Company; Eastern Art
33   Buses, Jeeps & Taxis to
     Kalimpong, Shiliguri & Sikkim

34   Super Market Complex
35   Curio Shops
37   Das Studios; Himalayan
     Adventures
39   Market
41   Manjushree Centre of
     Tibetan Culture
45   Clubside Taxi Stand
46   ANZ Grindlays Bank
47   Clubside Tours & Travels
50   Foreigners' Registration
     Office
51   Clock Tower
52   Telegraph Office
57   State Bank of India
61   Nathmull's Tea
     Merchants
62   Buses to Sikkim (Darjeeling
     Motor Service Co)
63   Main Post Office
65   Economic Pharmacy
66   Joey's Pub
67   Compuset Centre
68   Himalayan Tours & Travels
72   Tibetan Refugee Self-Help
     Centre (Head Office)
73   Nepali Girls' Social Service
     Centre
74   Dhirdham Temple
75   Taxis to Ghoom
76   Maa Singha Temple
77   DGHC Lowis Jubilee
     Complex
79   TV Tower
83   St Paul's School
84   Aloobari Gompa
85   Sonada Gompa
86   Thupten Sangachoeling
     Gompa
87   Samdenchoeling Gompa
88   Ghoom (Yogachoeling)
     Gompa
89   Sakyachoeling Gompa
90   Phin Sotholing Gompa

BANGLA (WEST BENGAL) HILLS

Volunteer Work

The Nepali Girls' Social Service Centre (☎ 2985), Gandhi Rd, undertakes projects that promote the empowerment of women, child survival and development, and environmental protection. Volunteers would be welcome on an informal basis to teach English, art, or musical instruments. Contact the centre for details.

Volunteers may be welcome at the Tibetan Refugee Self-Help Centre teaching English and adult education, but you should write to the head office of the centre in advance. (See the Courses section earlier.)

Hayden Hall is a Christian-based organisation that believes in total, integrated developmental projects at a grass roots level in both the urban and rural areas of this mountain district. Volunteers, prepared to work for a period of not less than six months, are needed with the following backgrounds or qualifications: doctors, nurses, paramedics, weavers, handicraft workers, teachers (pre-school and primary) and those with counselling and motivational skills. For further information contact Father EP Burns or Noreen Dunne (☎ 734101, email hayden@cal.vsnl.net.in), Hayden Hall (near the ANZ Grindlays Bank), 42 Laden La Rd, Darjeeling.

Places to Stay

There is a bewildering number of places to stay in Darjeeling. Those that follow are only a limited selection. Prices given are for high season (roughly from mid-March to mid-July and mid-September to mid-November) but it is well worth checking for discounts anytime, especially during the low season when rates are reduced by up to 75%. Check on taxes and service charges before checking in as they vary greatly and are often included in low-season tariffs.

Darjeeling suffers from chronic power and water shortages, but things appear to be improving. Many hotels now have their own water supply and backup (often noisy!) generators, but some don't, so bring a torch (flashlight). Many of the mid-range to top-end places provide a hot water bottle during the chilly winter months (if there isn't one provided, ask).

Touts

Accommodation touts are paid up to 30% commission for finding guests, and you will ultimately pay for this if you follow them. However, telling them 'No', doesn't always work as they often follow new arrivals to their pre-chosen hotel and then demand payment from the manager saying they brought you. If you are followed, be sure to inform the manager immediately that the tout was in no way responsible for your choice of hotel.

Places to Stay – Budget

Just beyond the post office there's a whole cluster of cheap hotels either on Laden La Rd or on the alleys and steps running off it. Take the stone steps uphill, just beyond the post office, connecting Laden La Rd with Gandhi Rd. Halfway up, a laneway known as Upper Beechwood Rd branches to the right.

The popular *Hotel Shamrock*, run by a no-nonsense Sherpa woman, is along here. Singles/doubles/triples cost Rs 85/170/200, some with bath. Hot water is available free in buckets. There are good views from the upstairs rooms which, with their wood panelling and sloping roofs, have a Swiss chalet ambience.

Hotel Pagoda, next door, has basic but pleasant doubles for Rs 150 to Rs 295 with bath. The cheaper doubles are a bit gloomy. This is a good location, and the staff are friendly. There's a cosy TV room with a fireplace; the fire is lit in winter.

Hotel Prestige (☎ 52699) is back on the stairway leading up from Laden La Rd. All rooms have bath with geyser, and cost from Rs 250 to Rs 600. The upstairs rooms are bright and clean, but those downstairs are quite dark. There's a borrowing library here.

Many travellers head for the area around the youth hostel and TV tower, on or near Dr Zakir Hussain Rd. It's a 25 to 40 minute walk (600m uphill!) from the train station. If you're coming from Chowrasta, Dr Zakir Hussain Rd divides at the TV tower.

Hotel Tower View (☎ 54452), run by a friendly family, is a few steps along the road to the left. There are a range of rooms, from Rs 80 for a single with bath, Rs 120 for a double with great views and common bath (it's right next door), up to Rs 150 with views and bath. There's a convivial lounge area where tasty meals are dished up, and Krishna here is an excellent source of information on sights around Darjeeling. There's also a very good travellers' comment book.

If you take the right-hand road from the TV tower, you'll come to a cluster of budget guesthouses.

The lifeblood of the Himalaya, water both sustains and sculpts the landscape – as snow, ice and vapour in the clouds. These scenes are from Uttarakhand and Himachal Pradesh.

The many places and faces of Bangla (West Bengal) – witnessing and learning about the daily lives of the local people is one of the highlights for many visitors.

The ***Tenzing Norgay Youth Hostel*** is reasonable value for money, if a little characterless. It is perched on a ridge right at the top of the town, is spotlessly clean and undoubtedly has some of the best views in Darjeeling. There's no need to get up early to go to Tiger Hill to watch the sunrise on Mt Kanchenjunga; cling to your bed for an extra 90 minutes and just wander out onto the balcony. There's a good travellers' comment book here, and the staff are informative about treks in the area.

Triveni Guest House & Restaurant (☎ 53878/144) is virtually opposite the hostel. Beds in the dorm are Rs 40, there are singles/doubles for Rs 40/80, or Rs 60/80 with bath. There is a rooftop terrace, an in-house PCO, cable TV and a terrific cheap restaurant.

Aliment Restaurant & Hotel (☎ 55068), nearby and very popular, has rooms from Rs 50/150, and dorm beds for Rs 30. There's a secure storeroom, laundry service, rooftop terrace, good borrowing library (with games and magazines) and a great little restaurant. It is run by a charming, knowledgeable and attentive ex-British Gurkha who can organise local tours and a stay at the family owned orange and cardamom gardens in Mirik.

Ratna's, also near the Triveni, has four charming and cosy doubles for Rs 80, and a comfortable sitting room. This is a great place and rooms are very good value.

Hotel Tshering Denzongpa (☎ 56061, 6 JP Sharma Rd) is an excellent place. It is very friendly and Sherpa-run. Doubles range from Rs 250 to Rs 600. The more expensive rooms have better views.

Hotel Springburn (☎ 52054), on Gandhi Rd past the clocktower and next to Hotel Fairmont, has basic clean rooms for Rs 385. Rooms at the back of the hotel have Kanchenjunga views.

Tiger Hill Tourist Lodge at Tiger Hill, is good for those who have trekked in or can't face the early morning departures to catch the sunrise. It has a four bed and eight bed dorm for Rs 75 per person.

Places to Stay – Mid-Range
An old favourite at this price is the charming, two star ***Bellevue Hotel*** (☎ 54075) on Chowrasta. Fine old wood-panelled doubles range from Rs 550 to Rs 800, and all rooms have baths with hot water in the mornings. Room 49 has the best views, and also has a separate sitting room. For long-term guests there are huge, but rather characterless rooms at the back of the property (some with attached kitchens). For guests only, there's a rooftop terrace, a private Buddhist prayer room and cafe with excellent views out over Chowrasta.

Main Bellevue Hotel (☎ 54178) is behind the Bellevue. This is a lovely old Raj-era building with doubles/triples for Rs 300/700, and a special double with Kanchenjunga views for Rs 800. The hotel is set in a lovely established garden. It has a slightly shabby, yesteryear atmosphere, and a gracious and attentive manager.

The huge, and also old, ***Pineridge Hotel*** (☎ 54074) is opposite the Bellevue Hotel on Nehru Rd. The miles of corridors are painted 'institution green' which gives it a rather oppressive feel, but the rooms are big and bright, if a little shabby. Doubles are Rs 550 and Rs 700, and the deluxe rooms with polished wooden floors are from Rs 850. All rooms have fireplaces, are simply furnished and some have bay windows. Extensive renovations are planned – here's hoping the gracious old-world character is retained.

Hotel Shangrila (☎ 54149) is farther down Nehru Rd. Enormous light, airy rooms with polished wooden floors and pine ceilings are Rs 750 plus taxes (Rs 500 in the low season including taxes). It's a friendly place, but the restaurant downstairs is disappointing.

Hotel Alice Villa (☎ 54181, 41 HD Lama Rd) is a short distance to the north of Chowrasta. Doubles/triples are Rs 990/1450. Rooms in the original building are charming, but those in the ugly new annexe are a bit disappointing. Rates include breakfast and one other meal.

Tea Planters Club (☎ 54349, fax 54348), is above Nehru Rd. Known officially as the

BANGLA (WEST BENGAL) HILLS

Darjeeling Club in the days of the Raj, it is still more often known as the Planters Club on the Mall. The downstairs doubles for Rs 1200 are shabby and gloomy (and chilly). Large, comfortable doubles upstairs are Rs 1800, or there are identical rooms, which are cheaper simply on account of having been allowed to get shabbier, for Rs 1400. There's a billiard room, a musty library, plenty of memorabilia and lots of nice sitting areas. There's a temporary membership charge of Rs 50 per day.

Dekeling Hotel (☎ 54159, fax 53298, 51 Gandhi Rd, email Dekeling Hotel (compuset.@cal.vsnl.net.in), above the Dekevas Restaurant and owned by the same Tibetan family, is a popular place with travellers and probably the best value in town, if you don't mind walking up hundreds of stairs. Doubles are Rs 500 and Rs 800, all with bath and Rs 800/1050 with fantastic Kanchenjunga views. The pleasant wood-panelled attic rooms with common bath are Rs 400 to Rs 600. They have desks and open onto a friendly sitting area. Hot-water bottles and kerosene heaters are the norm in winter and there are plenty of cosy common areas. Like most places, a 50% discount is offered in the low season.

Hotel Sunflower (54391, fax 54390, email sunflower@shivanet.com) is conveniently located on the Mall, with a PCO on the premises. Doubles with phone and TV are Rs 1200 and Rs 1500, with a 60% discount for singles. It has a safe deposit and accepts credit cards.

Ivanhoe (☎/fax 56082, 4 Franklin Prestage Rd) is a heritage hotel nestled in a quiet area below the Mayfair Hotel Resort off Hill Cart Rd. It was once the lead house of a group of five English manors known collectively as Panch Kothi. They were built by an English lady, Mrs Makie (the proprietor of Kokrung Tea Estate), for her five daughters. Huge rooms are Rs 1350/1650.

Hotel Fairmont (☎ 53646, fax 53647, 10 Gandhi Rd) is past the clocktower. All rooms have great views, TV, phone and hot water, and there is also a restaurant. Rooms

in doubles/triples/quads will cost you Rs 1050/1500/2000.

Hotel Seven Seventeen (☎ 54717, fax 54717, email tashi@cal.vsnl.net.in) is the best of several hotels on HD Lama Rd. It's not a great location, but this place is Tibetan-run, warm and welcoming, offering four star service and facilities at two-star prices. There are single rooms for Rs 650, and doubles from Rs 700. There is a restaurant (which serves traditional Tibetan meals on request), a cosy bar and Dorjee 'Ling' Tours & Travels. The Tibetan Medical & Astro Institute is also here.

Mohit Hotel (☎ 54351), on Mount Pleasant Road, is a popular three star property with single/double rooms for Rs 700/900 to Rs 1500. The restaurant has a good selection of Indian, Chinese and continental dishes, and the bar carries imported wines and spirits. There is also a billiard room. The hotel accepts all major credit cards, has foreign exchange facilities, safe deposit, car park and can arrange trekking, tours and vehicle hire.

Hotel Red Rose (☎ 56062, fax 52615, 37 Laden La Rd, email udayan@cal2.vsnl .net.in) is close to the train station. It houses the Cyber Cafe and Udayan Communications and PCO. It's a nice hotel, despite its rather noisy location, and all rooms have a TV, intercom and running hot water. Doubles range from Rs 500 to Rs 1250.

Hotel Silver Cascade (☎ 52026, 9 Cooch Bihar Rd) is up towards the top of the ridge near Aliment Hotel. This recommended place is light, bright and spotless with two restaurants and good singles/doubles for Rs 1000/1400. All rooms have TV, intercom, balcony, heater and 24 hour hot water.

Hotel Valentino (☎ 52228, 6 Rockville Rd) has singles/doubles for Rs 750/950, and deluxe rooms for Rs 1000/1250. Rates include breakfast, and heaters are provided free in winter. The hotel has an Oriental ambience and an excellent Chinese restaurant.

Sailung Hotel (☎/fax 56289) is away from the noise and bustle of the town centre, on the north side of Observatory Rd (a continuation of the Mall). As a corporate holiday home, it only has four guest rooms available to the public (down a mountainside of stairs), but they all have uninterrupted views of Kanchenjunga. Rates are Rs 500 for a double.

Places to Stay – Top End

New Elgin (☎ 54114, fax 54267, email newelgin@cal.vsnl.net.in), is off HD Lama Rd, to the north of Chowrasta, but one road lower. One of Darjeeling's oldest hotels, it has been completely, tastefully and stylishly renovated, but still reflects the ambience of its colonial past. Elegantly furnished singles/doubles cost Rs 1800/2200 – most with open fires, marble bathrooms and hot-water bottles. There's 24 hour room service, a fully stocked bar, a very good restaurant and a laundry/valet service. There are lovely gardens with a gazebo where you can relax and enjoy afternoon tea.

Windamere Hotel (☎ 54041, fax 54043) is a veritable institution among Raj relic aficionados, with Tibetan maids in starched frilly aprons, high tea served in the drawing room to the strains of a string quartet, and a magnificent old bar where the silence is broken only by an old pendulum clock. The hotel, which is now completely nonsmoking (despite the occasionally smokey fires in the rooms), has been owned since the 1920s by Mrs Tenduf-la, a Tibetan lady of advancing years. The rooms are cosy and comfortable, and TVs are conspicuously (and deliberately) absent. Singles/doubles are US$70/110, including all meals. There is also a double suite for US$140.

Mayfair Hill Resort (☎ 56376, fax 52674, email mayfair@cal2.vsnl.net.in) on the lower Mall opposite the Raj Bhavan (Government House), is the most recent addition to Darjeeling's top-end hotels. Originally a heritage property (the summer palace of a maharaja), it has been so extensively renovated that its origins are no longer apparent. It does however, offer luxury in beautiful surroundings, and with fabulous views. The 21 large guest rooms and 10 cottages are beautifully appointed (complete with hairdriers), tastefully fur-nished and boast working fireplaces. There is a restaurant, bar, lounge, marble-decked terraces and gardens. Single/double rates for rooms and cottages are US$82/110.

Places to Eat

There are so many places to eat in Darjeeling that a complete listing would fill a book. The following is a small sample.

Kev's (Keventer's Snack Bar), on Nehru Rd, is still the best place to head for a bacon sandwich. The deli downstairs has sausages, cheeses, ham and other goods.

Supersoft Ice Cream Parlour, virtually next door, has a wonderful selection of tasty treats.

A short walk up the Mall brings you to *Glenary's*, which offers continental dishes, as well as tandoori and Chinese dishes in its upstairs restaurant. However, service is appallingly slow. The bakery downstairs sells excellent brown bread, a range of calorie-laden cakes, great pastries and superb home-made chocolates.

On the lower end of Nehru Rd, under Hotel Dekling, is the popular *Deveka's Restaurant*, famous for its pizzas.

The best Chinese food in Darjeeling can be found at the Hotel Valentino's *Embassy* restaurant (open until 8 pm) and the Chinese-run *New Dish* restaurant (a large airy place with great sunset views) on JP Sharma Rd.

The *Great Punjab Restaurant*, on HD Lama Rd, has, as the name suggests, excellent Punjabi food.

Nonguests are welcome to dine at the *Windamere Hotel* for lunch or dinner, but advance notice is required, and meal times are extremely strict. Afternoon tea is an institution here.

Nonguests are also welcome at the *Kanchen Restaurant* at the New Elgin, also with advance notice.

Opposite the State Bank of India on Laden La Rd is the *Jain Jaika Restaurant* with pure vegetarian cuisine. Upstairs is the *Park* restaurant, with a pleasant outlook over Darjeeling.

A few doors away is the *Golden Dragon Restaurant & Bar*, with rainbow-painted

Tongba – Nectar of the Gods

Only made in the eastern Himalaya, Tongba is the 'beer' of the region. Millet is mixed with water and 'special' yeast and cooked for two hours, then stored in an airtight container for at least 24 hours. (A good tongba is kept much longer.)

Tongba is served in a bamboo container, hot water is added and, after waiting a few minutes for the juices to flow, it is sipped through a bamboo straw.

Note that there is a definite etiquette to be followed. First, always let your tongba sit before drinking. Second, observe others and don't suck through the wrong end of the straw. Third, it is definitely bad form to stir your tongba with the straw. Tongba is refreshed simply by adding more water.

The taste? Well, it's just like warm fermented millet. Very nice in fact – not very strong, and the locals will tell you, 'good for health'. It's a great drink after a hard day's walking through the mountains, but watch out, you may feel a little wobbly after three or four bamboos!

Martin Bradshaw

walls and a seedy 1920s ambience. It's a smoky little den with a very basic menu – beer's the main attraction here. Farther down Laden La Rd, close to the main post office, are a series of tiny *cheap eateries* generally serving Tibetan cuisine.

Most of the guesthouses in the TV tower area have their own dining rooms and can rustle up traditional dishes as well as western favourites such as banana pancakes, jaffles etc. Favourite places are the *Tower View*, *Ratna*, *Aliment* and the *Triveni*.

One place that's just a little bit different is the tiny *Hot Stimulating Cafe*, perched out over the mountainside on the road down to the zoo. You can't see Kanchenjunga from here, but the views over the hills and valleys are beautiful. The Nepalese owners make great food (especially momos) and serve excellent chai and coffee.

Shopping

Curios Most curio shops are on Chowrasta and along Nehru Rd, with another group on Laden La Rd in the post office area. All things Himalayan are sold here – *thangkas* (Buddhist religious art produced on cloth with vegetable dyes, generally with a brocade surround), brass statues, religious objects, jewellery, woodcarvings, woven fabrics and carpets. If you're looking for bargains, shop judiciously and be prepared to spend plenty of time looking.

If you're looking for bronze statues, the real goodies are kept under the counter and cost in multiples of US$100! Woodcarvings tend to be excellent value for money. Most of the shops accept international credit cards.

There is also a market off Hill Cart Rd next to the bus and taxi stands. Here you can find excellent and relatively cheap patterned woollen sweaters, umbrellas and an incredible selection of second-hand clothes mostly from the UK. Most of the clothes have been donated to Tibetan refugee projects and, as there is always a surplus, they sell them to make money. Particularly good value are the sweaters (aran and fairisle knits) and jackets with brand names like St Michael and Moss Bros, are in 'as new' condition.

Habeeb Mullick & Sons (☎ 54109), on Chowrasta, was established in 1890, and has an abundance of curios. Originally they specialised in furs. Distinguished patrons included Queen Sofia of Spain, and Rajiv and Sonia Gandhi. Today the merchandise is more environmentally friendly. There is an astonishing variety of hats, of which the *pièce de résistance* is a 90-year-old Tantric Tibetan hat with carved human bone panels depicting Buddha, which will set you back Rs 7000. There are also tribal artefacts and locally made woollen jumpers (Rs 350 to Rs 550).

At 16 Nehru Rd is the Nepal Curio House (☎ 54010), owned by the third generation of the family who established the business in 1891. The back room specialises in artefacts from the Himalayan region, including thangkas and statues. The owner is happy to explain Buddha's postures, as well as the iconography of the thangkas. You can also purchase Nepali jackets or lengths of *yatha* – coarse handloom woollen Bhutanese cloth.

The Kalimpong Art Gallery, nearby, specialises in Nepali pastel paintings (usually portraits), local jewellery and *khukuri* (traditional Gurkha knives). The tourist models feature brass filigree work and are studded with turquoise and coral, with a bone or wood handle. The more authentic (and more sinister) models are plain and much larger.

Eastern Art, in the Ajit Mansion (Pineridge Hotel complex), has thangkas, brass, silver and gold statues, pure silver jewellery, woodcarvings and copper items, as well as chainstitch Kashmiri carpets), papier-mâché items, wooden masks and brass *aftaba* – elegant long-necked vessels for water or wine, from a few centimetres to half a metre in stature.

Tibetan Carpets For Tibetan carpets, one of the cheapest places in the area is at Hayden Hall, opposite the State Bank of India on Laden La Rd. This women's cooperative sells *casemillon* (wool/synthetic mix) shawls, woollen hats, socks and mufflers.

Virtually next door to Hayden Hall is the Third Eye, an all-women enterprise run by Dechen Wangdi. It gives free training to women weavers and guarantees work at the end of their training. Shipping of carpets can be arranged.

Darjeeling Tea If you're buying tea, First Flush Super Fine Tippy Golden Flowery Orange Pekoe I is the top quality. (First flush refers to the first picking, which takes place in spring.) The price varies enormously; you'll pay anything from Rs 150 to Rs 3000 per kg! The way to test the tea is to take a small handful in your closed fist, breathe firmly on it through your fingers and then open your hand and smell the aromas released from the tea by your warm breath. At least it will look like you know what you're doing even if you don't have a clue! Avoid the tea in fancy boxes or packaging as this is all blended and comes from Kolkata.

If you find that you become hooked on a particular brew, most tea merchants in Darjeeling offer a mail order service. A good place to head is Nathmull's Tea Merchants (☎ 53437, fax 54426), near the post office on Laden La Rd. Mr Vijay Sarda here will hold you in thrall as he waxes lyrical over the virtues of various teas.

Getting There & Away

Air The nearest airport is 90km away at Bagdogra, down on the plains 12km from Shiliguri. See Getting There & Away in the Shiliguri section earlier in this chapter. The agents for Jet Airways are Clubside Tours & Travels (☎ 54646) on JP Sharma Rd (off Laden La Rd), and Pineridge Travels (☎ 53912) on Chowrasta, who are also agents for Necon Air and Bengal Air. The Indian Airlines office (☎ 54230) is beneath the Bellevue Hotel on Chowrasta. The office is open daily, 10 am to 5 pm (closed 1 to 2 pm). Tickets for the airport transfer to Bagdogra can be purchased at the tourist office, next door.

Nepal It is possible to fly from the border (the airstrip is Bhadrapur) to Kathmandu with Everest Air, Royal Nepal Airlines, or Necon Airways. A number of agents can book these flights, which must be paid for in US dollars, including Juniper Tours & Travels (☎ 52625), Clubside Tours & Travels, Pineridge Travels and Himali Treks & Tours (☎ 52154), Super Market complex, above the Bazaar bus stand on Hill Cart Rd.

Bus Most of the buses from Darjeeling leave from the Bazaar bus stand on Hill Cart Rd:

destination	fare (Rs)	departs	duration (hrs)
Gangtok	75	7.30, 8 am 1.15, 1.30 pm	7 hrs
Kalimpong	37	8 am	3½ hrs
Mirik	26	every 40 min 8.30 am to 3.15 pm	3 hrs
Shiliguri	38	every 20 min 6.20 am to 5.30 pm	3 hrs

BANGLA (WEST BENGAL) HILLS

The agent for Sikkim Nationalised Transport (SNT) is the Darjeeling Motor Service Co (☎ 52101), 32 Laden La Rd, open 10 am to 1 pm daily. There is one daily bus to Gangtok which leaves from opposite the office at 1 pm (Rs 65, five hours).

Nepal A number of companies offer daily buses between Darjeeling and Kathmandu, but none of them actually has a direct service; you have to change at Shiliguri. The usual arrangement is that the agents will sell you a ticket as far as Shiliguri, but guarantee you a seat on the connecting bus with the same agency. You arrive at the border around 3 pm (Kakarbhitta is the name of the town on the Nepali side), leave again round 4 pm and arrive in Kathmandu around 9 or 10 am the next day.

Most travellers prefer to do the trip independently, although it involves four changes – bus from Darjeeling to Shiliguri (Rs 38), bus (Rs 10) or jeep (Rs 30) from Shiliguri to Paniktanki on the border, rickshaw across the border to Kakarbhitta (Rs 10), and bus from Kakarbhitta to Kathmandu (Nepali Rs 250, 17 hours). This is cheaper than the package deal, and you get a choice of buses from the border. For more information on the trip from the border to Kathmandu, see the Getting There & Away chapter.

The nearest Nepali consulate is in Kolkata, but visas are available at Paniktanki on the Indian side of the border for US$25 (which must be paid in cash), and these can be extended in Kathmandu.

Taxi & Jeep Most travel agencies book private jeeps and/or Maruti vans. Quoted rates are:

destination	fare (Rs)	duration (hrs)
Gangtok	1200	7
Jorethang	800	2½
Kalimpong	600	3
Pemayangtse	2500	4½
Shiliguri	500	3
Yuksom	2800	5

The section between Darjeeling and Naya Bazaar (21km) is very steep, and during the monsoon it is subject to landslides. If the road is closed, a detour is taken via Teesta Bridge which costs an additional Rs 500.

There is a share jeep stand for Sikkim to the right of the bus ticket office at the bus stand on Hill Cart Rd. Rates (Rs 5 cheaper in the back of the jeep) are: Kurseong (Rs 30, 45 minutes), Kalimpong (Rs 55, 2½ hours), Gangtok (Rs 110, five hours) and Jorethang (Rs 60, two to three hours).

Buses from Jorethang to Yuksom – roadhead for the Dzongri trail – leave at 8 and 9.30 am (Rs 33, three hours). You will require a trekking permit to visit Yuksom. See Permits in the Sikkim chapter for details.

The share jeep office for Kalimpong is at the southern end of the taxi rank, under the stairs to the first level of the Super Market.

Train Shiliguri/New Jalpaiguri is the railhead for all trains other than the narrow-gauge toy train. See the Shiliguri Getting There & Away section earlier for details of standard trains. Reservations for major trains out of New Jalpaiguri can be made at the Darjeeling train station (the toy train terminus) between 10 am and 4 pm daily.

Toy Train The toy train service that used to run daily until the track was washed out by monsoon rains and a major landslide, is slated to re-start soon. If running, it should still leave Shiliguri at 9 am, arriving at Darjeeling at 5.30 pm. An additional service will leave Shiliguri at 7.15 am during the high season. The return journeys from Darjeeling will leave at 7 and 10 am.

Whether the Shiliguri service is running or not, the toy train still goes as far as Kurseong (four hours, 34km) or Ghoom (45 minutes, 8km). From Ghoom, you can walk back via a pleasant ridge track. Trains leave Darjeeling at *approximately* 10 am (check with the station or tourist offices).

Getting Around

There are no local buses between Darjeeling and Ghoom. Share taxis leave from the market near the bus stand on Hill Cart Rd every five minutes (Rs 8). Having a taxi to yourself costs at least Rs 100. A taxi from the bus stand to the central Clubside taxi stand is about Rs 50.

MANGPU

India's only cinchona plantation is at Mangpu, 20km from Darjeeling. Quinine, used in malaria medication, is produced from the bark of this tree. The name cinchona is derived from Countess Chinchon, the Spanish Vicerene of Peru, who was treated with the bark of this tree while suffering a life-threatening fever, and a remarkable cure was effected.

The very humble Mongpu Gompa here is presided over by Drinchen Rinpoche. The rinpoche is a talented artist, and created the image of the Buddha and Guru Rinpoche enshrined in the prayer room. Celebrated writer Rabindranath Tagore used to spend his summer holidays in a house at Mangpu with his friends, and used the setting as inspiration for some of his poems.

MIRIK

☎ 0354 • alt 1767m

Being promoted as a 'new' hill station, Mirik is about 50km from both Shiliguri and Darjeeling. The artificial lake is the main attraction here, and there's a 3.5km path around it. The main tourist area lies to the south of the lake, in the area known as Krishnanagar.

While this is certainly a pretty spot, surrounded by tea estates, orange orchards and cardamom plantations (the views from the top of the hill are stunning), attempts to 'develop' the area for tourism are already threatening to spoil the tranquil ambience. Swimming in the lake is strongly advised against, as it is highly polluted – there is no sewage system in Mirik.

Mirik is the only place in India where the dog population appears to outweigh the human population. All the dogs are nocturnal and extremely vociferous! Take earplugs if you plan to sleep at night.

The post office is in the lane opposite the State Bank of India (which doesn't

exchange travellers cheques; there are currently no foreign exchange facilities here).

Things to See & Do

Perched high above the town is the **Bokar Gompa**, a small and brightly coloured gompa with 70 monks. It can be reached in about 10 minutes by a path leading up from the south end of the lake, about 10 minutes' walk from the taxi stand and set amid banana trees, are three small Hindu **temples** sacred to Hanuman, Kalamata (Durga as the Mother of Time) and Shiva.

Boats can be hired on the east side of the lake for Rs 32 per 30 minutes (two seater), or Rs 42 for a four seater.

A good way to see the sights is by pony. Half-day (three hours) hire costs Rs 200 to Rs 300 (check the condition of the saddle padding before you leave!), around the lake is Rs 50, and to the Swiss Cottages (the top of the hill) Rs 60. Unfortunately, you will have trouble stopping the pony-wallahs (who insist on accompanying you) from whipping your poor beast to make it go faster. They have no understanding of people who treat animals gently and who do not want to go 'too much fast'.

Places to Stay & Eat

Lodge Ashirvad (☎ 43272) is down a small lane opposite the State Bank of India. Downstairs doubles are Rs 130, or from Rs 200 to Rs 250 with bath. There are separate kitchen facilities here for people who wish to self-cater.

Lodge Panchashil (☎ 43284) is next door. Tiny but light and airy singles/doubles with bath are Rs 120/150, or larger doubles/triples are Rs 150/200. The manager is friendly and helpful, and there's a pleasant rooftop terrace here.

Hotel Mhelung (☎ 43300), Samendu Complex, is light and spotlessly clean. All rooms have polished timber floors, room heaters, phones and cable TV. Doubles at the back are Rs 400 or Rs 500 at the front.

Quality Restaurant & Sweet Parlour opposite, offers low-priced meals and a good

Mirik to Kurseong Trek

If you do not have time for the Darjeeling Treks (see the boxed text earlier in this chapter), or just want a taste of Himalayan village life in the Bangla hills; the trek from Mirik to Kurseong may be your cup of tea. It takes seven to eight hours to complete.

The trail starts at the Genesis English School just past the Tourist Lodge. Heading out of town you will pass a number of schools. There are good views of Kanchenjunga about a kilometre from Mirik.

Continuing, you will pass through a number of small villages, stands of pine and bamboo, and orange groves, finally entering Murmah Tea Estate. There is a small shop here at Murmah village. Check out the funky houses, painted like dolls' houses. Most are made of wooden planks with tin roofs these days, but you will see the odd daub house with thatched roof. Notice the village (with the transmission tower) across the river valley to the east. Yes, that is Kurseong, and yes, you will be walking down to the river and all the way back up again! It's a knee jarring walk.

Walk through the tea estate, heading downhill, roughly following the ropeway used to carry tea from and supplies to the estate. A few villages later you will reach the river. Only ford the river if the water level is low, and only with an experienced guide. It is better to cross the bridge visible about a kilometre upstream and then back-track.

After crossing the river, head up the tributary for 500m, then up the steep hill on the right-hand side. Stop for a 'Darjeeling' chai and biscuits in the village of Khomara atop the hill. From the teahouse you have excellent views back across the valley from where you have walked.

There are two main routes to Kurseong from here. The right-hand track is shorter but takes you through fewer villages. We took the left-hand trail. Again you walk through a number of tea estates interspersed with villages and pockets of forest. From the Singell Tea Estate follow the jeep track, taking short cuts when you can, emerging on the main Darjeeling-Kurseong road. Kurseong is about a kilometre after turning right. Turn left for Darjeeling. You may be lucky to catch a jeep or minibus to Kurseong or even back to Darjeeling

A guide is essential owing to the myriad of trails, most of which do not go to Kurseong. Guides can be arranged for around Rs 500 at the Darjeeling Gorkha Hill Council (DGHC) tourist lodge in Mirik. Guides can also be arranged through the DGHC office or a trekking agent in Darjeeling.

Martin Bradshaw

---

selection of local sweets, packet chocolate, biscuits and drinks, in fresh, bright and clean surroundings.

Hotel Jagdeet (☎ 43359), on the main road, has doubles with bath and geyser for Rs 550 and Rs 850 or Rs 1000 for a family room. All rooms are carpeted, and room service is available. There's a popular restaurant-cum-bar next door. They take credit card and may handle foreign exchange.

DGHC Mirik Tourist Lodge (☎ 42237) is slightly farther afield, but within easy walking distance of the lake. Double rooms with heaters are Rs 300 and Rs 350; Rs 30 for a dormitory bed.

DGHC Mirik (Swiss) Cottages (☎ 43270) are perched right at the top of the hill. The property affords stunning, panoramic views of the township and surrounding countryside including Kanchenjunga. Two-storey cottages contain a lounge/dining room and kitchen downstairs, and a large double bedroom, accommodating four people, upstairs. Rates are Rs 750 for two people, or Rs 1000 with kitchen equipment supplied.

Getting There & Away

Buses to Darjeeling leave at 11.30 am, 1.15, 1.45 and 2.15 pm (Rs 20, 3 hours). The journey to Kurseong takes three hours, and costs Rs 28. There are a number of buses to Shiliguri between 6.30 am and 3 pm (Rs 30, 2½ hours). Tickets can be purchased from the wooden shack next to the Restaurant Liberty, near the lakeshore.

There are no share taxis to Darjeeling. To hire a taxi will cost Rs 600 to either Darjeeling or Shiliguri.

There is also a border crossing to Nepal, open to Indian nationals, abut an hour out of Mirik along the road to Ghoom. It may be open up to foreign nationals soon.

KURSEONG
☎ 03554 • pop 18,000 • alt 1458m

Kurseong is 51km north of Shiliguri and 30km south of Darjeeling. The name is said to be derived from the Lepcha word, *kurson-rip*, a reference to the small white orchids prolific in this area. Because of its elevation, it enjoys a mild climate throughout the year, warmer than Darjeeling in the winter, cooler than the plains in summer. It's a good place to break the journey en route to or from Darjeeling. It has a wonderfully peaceful atmosphere and no real tourist infrastructure, so it offers the chance to really get to know the (predominantly Nepali) mountain people.

There are several good **walks** in the environs of the town, including that to Eagle's Crag, which affords fine views down over the Teesta and the southern plains, and a four hour walk along the ridge and through unspoilt forest to Ghoom. The toy train to and from Darjeeling stops right in the heart of the town.

Next to Hotel Delhi (see following) is **Kumai Studio**, the most tourist-friendly shop in town. A combined photographic studio and music, gift and bookshop, it sells fresh film and CDs. English-speaking owner, Sujan Kumai, is very pro-active in tourism and is a mine of information about treks and places of interest in the district.

Places to Stay & Eat

Tourist Lodge (☎ 44409) is undoubtedly the best place in town. It has huge rooms with superb views, heaters and excellent bedding (rooms in the old block also have balconies). Doubles are Rs 525 in the new annexe, and Rs 550 in the original building. There's a restaurant and bar, and discounts are offered in the low season.

Hotel Amarjeet Restaurant & Bar (☎ 44669), on Hill Cart Rd, west of the taxi stand, has doubles with hot water for Rs 300, and there's a bar.

Shyam Hotel (☎ 44240), on Dr Kumar Rd, has doubles/triples for Rs 300.

Luxury Hotel (☎ 44321, 72 TN Rd), east of the station, has singles/doubles for Rs 150/200, and there's a restaurant.

Maya Guest House (☎ 44783), directly opposite the station, is one of the oldest guest houses in Kurseong. Run by a Tibetan family, it serves excellent momos. Very basis singles/doubles are Rs 80/150.

Kurseong Palace, close to the jeep stand, has singles/doubles with hot water and TV for Rs 250/300.

Hotel Delhi Durbar & Restaurant (☎ 44084), in town on the main road to Darjeeling, offers singles with common bath for Rs 70, doubles with bath Rs 150 or Rs 250 with geyser. There are great views from the back rooms.

Getting There & Away

Regular buses run to Darjeeling (Rs 20, 1½ hours); Shiliguri (Rs 26, 2½ hours); and Mirik (Rs 28, three hours). The toy train from Shiliguri to Kurseong (when it is running) takes four hours and it's about the same again to Darjeeling.

KALIMPONG
☎ 03592 • pop 45,000 • alt 1250m

Kalimpong, 74km east of Darjeeling and 72km north of Shiliguri, is a bustling and rapidly expanding, although still relatively small, bazaar town set among the rolling

Helping Hands

St Alphonsus Social & Agricultural Centre (SASAC) just outside Kurseong, is a self-help organisation run by a Canadian Jesuit priest, Father Abraham. Father Abraham and other Jesuit Brothers came to the area more than 50 years ago to set up the St Alphonusus School, which is still going. Seeing a need for the poor people of the region to improve their lot, he left the school to set up SASAC in what had been the Brothers' retreat 8km from Kurseong on the Darjeeling Rd.

Father Abraham's code is not to change the traditional values of the local people, but to build on them. There are no hand-outs and everyone works for their money.

Over the years, he has raised the local subsistence farmers' productivity through improved crop and livestock management. He has set up a model teaching farm based on square-metre farming principles which provides income for the workers and funds new projects. He has assisted in the building of new homes and established a viable sales channel for excess farm produce. He also oversees a cooperative savings scheme and encourages the people to adopt long-term financial and environmental management.

One of his most recent successes, is in the reduction of wood usage (an enormous problem in the hills). Using small interest-free loans through the savings scheme, families have been able to purchase stoves and gas cylinders for cooking, thereby reducing deforestation. When this tiny loan is repaid, he then encourages the women to buy a pressure cooker, which increases the nutritional value of cooked foods and reduces gas usage by 25%. SASAC also has established a plantation and a reforestation scheme.

While offering some basic education, children are encouraged to maintain family values and remain in their community, rather than become another jobless statistic in Kolkata.

There is absolutely no religious pressure in this tight-knit but growing community. While Father Abraham conducts a Catholic Mass, which anyone is welcome to attend (and most do), his 'flock' is made up of mostly Hindus, some Buddhists and half-a-dozen Catholics. He says, 'These people already know how to relate to God. Why would I want to change that? I believe wholeheartedly in *my* faith, but they could teach me a thing or two when it comes to dedication and worship; they do it with so much joy and fervour. Worship is a part of their daily life; it doesn't matter to them if they are in a temple, at a shrine or in a church.'

Anyone wishing to volunteer to work at SASAC, make a donation or purchase a tree for the plantation, should contact Father Abraham (☎ 0354-42059), SASAC, Post Office Tung, District of Darjeeling, Bangla.

foothills and deep valleys of the Himalaya. It was once part of the lands belonging to the rajas of Sikkim, until the beginning of the 18th century when it was taken from them by the Bhutanese. In the 19th century it passed into the hands of the British and thus became part of Bangla. It became a centre for Scottish missionary activity in the late 19th century.

Until the outbreak of the China-India war in 1962, Kalimpong was one of the most important centres of India-Tibet commerce, with mule trains passing over the 3300m Jalep La. The Kalimpong-Jalep La Rd was the largest all-weather route between the two countries.

The main crops grown locally are ginger and cardamom. Kalimpong division was once densely forested, but widespread tree felling has left large areas denuded. There are still some areas where tracts of forest still stand, including along the left bank of the Teesta River, and in the environs of Lava and Richila.

Kalimpong's attractions include three gompas, a couple of solidly built churches, a sericulture (silkworm) centre, orchid nurseries and the fine views over the surrounding countryside. Although not many travellers visit Kalimpong, there's enough here to keep you occupied for a couple of days, and for the energetic, there's some good trekking.

The most interesting part of the trip to Kalimpong is the journey from Darjeeling via the Teesta River bridge.

Orientation & Information

Life is focused on the sports ground and east through the market. The bus stand (known locally as the Motor Stand) and Dambar Chowk, at the north end of Main Rd, is also a busy area, and it's here that most of the cheap hotels are.

Rinkingpong Rd heads south from Main Rd, the central artery through the town. Dambar Chowk, at the head of Main Rd, was originally known as Maharani Chowk, as it was adorned with a huge bronze statue of Queen Victoria. After the removal of the queen, a statue of the local leader of the Gorkha League, Dambar Singh, was erected in her place, but the plaque declaring 'Queen Victoria, Empress of India' remained in place, no doubt to the confusion and consternation of many.

Market days are Wednesday and Saturday, a colourful spectacle as villagers from outlying regions bring their produce into town.

The main post office is on Rinkingpong Rd. It's open Monday to Friday, 9 am to 4 pm and Saturday until 3 pm. Parcels can be sent 9 am to 1 pm.

The Central Bank of India, at the north end of Main Rd, has a very efficient and speedy foreign exchange service, and accepts most major travellers cheques.

There's a reasonable selection of English-language books, including books on the eastern Himalaya, at Kashi Nath & Sons, Rishi Rd. There are a couple of other bookshops at this Dambar Chowk end of Rishi Rd.

Rooms in Bangla tourism forest rest-houses at Lava, Kaffer, Rangpo and Mongpong (see the Around Kalimpong section) can be booked at the Forest Development Corporation (☎ 55783), in the Forestry Compound off Rinkingpong Rd. The office is open Monday to Friday, 10 am to 4.30 pm.

Trekking Outfits & Tour Operators Gurudongma Travels (☎ 55204), Hill Top Rd, runs some very interesting adventure and ecology trips out of Kalimpong. There's a three day trek to the Samthar plateau, 80km from Kalimpong, with magnificent mountain scenery, and taking in traditional Lepcha, Bhotia and Thamang tribal villages. From the plateau, it is possible to descend into the Teesta Valley and cross the river on the 1.5km long Samco Ropeway (see the Around Kalimpong section), from where you can continue under your own steam to Gangtok or Darjeeling. Gurudongma can also offer support services to cycling groups, such as backup vehicles, meals, guides, and accommodation in tents and guesthouses. It also has 10 and 18 speed Indian-made mountain bikes for touring. As well, it conducts rhododendron tours in May.

Himalayan Travels (☎ 55023), at the bus stand, runs half-day tours to points of interest around Kalimpong.

Emergency Police: ☎ 55268; Sub-Divisional Hospital: ☎ 55254.

Temples

There's a small temple complex behind Main Rd (walk down the lane beside the State Bank of India). The **Thakurbari Temple** here was built over 100 years ago, while the newer section was built in 1982. Presiding deities are Shiva, Vishnu and Lakshmi.

The most important temple in Kalimpong is the **Mangal Dham** temple complex, near the Thongsa Gompa to the north of the town centre. It is sacred to Krishna, and was completed in 1993 as a memorial to Kalimpong's most revered guru, Shri 108 Mangal Dasji Maharaj, whose *samadhi* (resting place) is at the temple. The temple is notable for its contemporary temple architecture, employing tonnes of white marble. Its large central sanctum features colourful scenes from the life of Krishna. Some of these feature Nijanandacharya Shri Dev Chandraji (1581-1655), who founded the Krishna Pranami order, and of whom Mangal Dasji is considered an incarnation. Krishna can be seen effortlessly holding up the earth with his little finger, and in one scene, the guru is seen bearing Krishna on his head in a basket.

Gompas

Established in 1922, the **Tharpa Choeling Gompa** belongs to the Gelukpa order of Tibetan Buddhism. It's a 40 minute walk (uphill) from town; take the path to the right off KD Pradhan Rd, just before the Milk Collection and Extension Wing Building.

Lower down the hill, the Bhutanese **Thongsa Gompa** is the oldest gompa in the area and was founded in 1692. The present building is a little more recent since the original was destroyed by the Gurkhas in their rampage across Sikkim before the arrival of the British. It's home to a small community of about 60 monks.

Zong Dog Palri Fo-Brang Gompa, 5km south of the town centre at the end of the ridge, was founded in the mid-1970s by Dudjom Yeshi Dorje, the former head of the Nyingmapa order (he died in 1987), and was consecrated by the Dalai Lama. The walls of the prayer room are richly (and completely) covered in vibrant frescoes executed by a Tibetan artist residing in Darjeeling, and the ceiling is embellished with large *mandalas* (circular images depicting the universe). Close to the ceiling you can see the 25 disciples of Padmasambhava (Tibetan: Guru Rinpoche), the founder of the Nyingmapa order, each inhabiting a stuccoed cave, and engaged in different miraculous feats, such as flying through the sun's rays and bringing the dead to life. Suspended from the ceiling are some magnificent thangkas.

In an upstairs room is an intricate wooden model of the palace of Guru Rinpoche, Zangdok Palri. It includes tiny figures of lamas blowing *radungs*, long-stemmed Tibetan horns, and statues of Padmasambhava and Avalokiteshvara (Tibetan: Chenresig), the Buddhist Bhodhisattva of compassion. (The Dalai Lama is believed by Buddhists to be an incarnation of Chenresig.) There is also a **three dimensional mandala**, one of only three in the world (the others are in Taiwan, and in Spiti in Himachal Pradesh). A larger statue of Chenresig is enshrined in this room. It is depicted with 1000 arms, each of which has an eye in the palm.

Flower Nurseries

Kalimpong is an important orchid-growing area and flowers are exported here to cities in India and overseas. All the nurseries belong to one family, and apart from orchids, they also produce 80% of India's gladioli, as well as cacti. The Sri Ganesh Moni Pradhan Nursery and the Udai Mani Pradhan Nursery are among the most important in the area. There's a flower festival in Kalimpong in October. The best time to see the gladioli is in March and April, while orchids are at their best in the winter months of December to February.

Sericulture Research Institute

The Sericulture Research Institute (open 9.30 am to 4 pm) is on the road to Darjeeling. It cultivates medicinal herbs and plants, including quinine and cinchona which have helped eradicate some strains of malaria. The centre also breeds silkworms and produces silk.

Dr Graham's Home

It takes less than an hour to walk from the town centre up through stands of bamboo to Dr Graham's Home, which was founded in 1900 on the lower slopes of Deolo Hill. The school was established to educate the children of workers on the tea gardens. It started with six children, but there are now about 1300 students.

Originally encompassing only 50 acres (20 hectares), the beautiful grounds, spread over an extensive area on the south-facing ridge, now encompass 477 acres (193 hectares). Enrolment is open to all, but there is a reserve quota for children from economically deprived backgrounds. The chapel above the school dates from 1925, and features fine stained-glass windows. If the caretaker is around, he'll open it for visitors. Visitors are welcome to visit the fine turn-of-the-century school building, and many people bring a picnic lunch to eat in the grounds. Volunteers are always welcome at the school and homes, provided they can dedicate a minimum of six months (see the Volunteer for Dr Graham boxed text for more information).

From the school itself, it is a further 40 minute walk to the summit of **Deolo Hill**, where there are fine views back down over Kalimpong and a *tourist bungalow*. The three reservoirs on the hill provide water to the town.

Nature Interpretation Centre

This centre in the Forestry Compound on Rinkingpong Rd is run by the Soil Conservation Division of the Ministry of Environment & Forests. It consists of a number of well-organised dioramas that depict the effects of human activity on the environment. It's open daily, except Thursday, 10 am to 1.30 pm, and 2 to 4 pm; free admission.

Places to Stay – Budget

Gompu's Hotel (☎ 55818), on Dambar Chowk at the north end of Main Rd, has pleasantly rustic wooden doubles/triples for Rs 200/300 with bath. Hot water is free in buckets. The restaurant and bar here are popular, but slightly pricey; they close at 8 pm.

Lodge Himalshree (☎ 55070), on Ongden Rd, is a small place on the third floor of a building, opposite the Central Bank. It's run by a friendly family, and rooms are plain, but spotless. Doubles/triples are Rs 120/200, or doubles with bath are Rs 250. There's no running water, so water is supplied in buckets.

Deki Lodge (☎ 55095, fax 55290), on Tripai Rd off Rishi Rd, about 10 minutes'

Volunteer for Dr Graham

With a school for 1200 students, a farm, workshops, hospital, bakery, the children's homes and a training program for child nursing and preliminary nursing, there is plenty of need for volunteers. Teachers (especially in English, maths, science, physical education and art), nurses, childcare workers, carpenters, engineers, mechanics, handipersons and those with agricultural skills, are always welcome.

Although Dr Graham's takes 'Gap' students in the year between school and college/university, there is otherwise a requirement for a minimum six-month commitment. Board and lodging is provided. For further information contact Dr Graham's Homes (☎ 033-297211), Berkmyre Hostel, 4 Middleton Rd, Kolkata 700071.

---

walk north of the bus stand, is one of the most popular places to stay. Singles/doubles range from Rs 100 to Rs 550, most with common bath. There's also a triple room with bath and geyser for Rs 450. The common bathroom has 24 hour hot showers. This rambling, happy place has a great atmosphere and is always full of pets. It is run by a friendly family which is a good source of information on treks in the area, and there is secure parking for a couple of cars or several motorcycles.

There are a number of very basic places around the bus stand. The *Janakee Lodge* (☎ 55479) has spartan but clean rooms that vary in price according to which floor they're on; those on the 1st floor are cheaper. Single/double/triple prices range from Rs 130/240/260 with common bath, to Rs 180/270/360 with bath.

Panchvati Lodge (☎ 56165) is a tiny place with a rooftop terrace, homely atmosphere and really pleasant owner. Doubles are Rs 150 with common bath, Rs 200 with bath and Rs 250 for a three bed room.

Classic Hotel (☎ 56335) is in a small cul-de-sac around the corner from the Janakee.

BANGLA (WEST BENGAL) HILLS

It has singles/doubles for Rs 150/250 with bath. Rooms are small, but some have good valley views. There's an extensive Chinese and Indian menu in the downstairs restaurant.

China Garden Lodge (☎ 55945) has good clean doubles with baths for Rs 350. There is also a rooftop 'suite' with balcony and terrace (and Indian loo) for the same price.

Crown Lodge (☎ 55846), on Murgihatta Rd, a few metres off HL Dikshit Rd, is quiet, spacious and clean. It has singles/doubles for Rs 250/350 with bath with geysers (hot water in the morning only). Towels and soap are provided and there's free bed tea. Some of the rooms have pleasant views out over the playing ground.

Chimnoy Lodge (☎ 56264/55557, email heavy.scene@delta.gokulnet.com) is down a few steps from the Crown. It is bright and tidy with pleasant hill views. All rooms have bath with 24 hour hot water and the helpful owner can organise tours and transport. Singles/doubles/triples start from Rs 150/250/350. An extra Rs 50 gives you a TV and views.

Sood's Guest House (☎ 55297/56207) is a nice little place in a garden setting, 500m from town on the main road to Darjeeling. The rooms could do with a fresh coat of paint, but are very reasonably priced. Singles/doubles are Rs 400/600; self-contained cottages are Rs 650. There is a basic badminton court and basketball practice hoop for the energetic.

Hotel Chimal (☎ 55776) is also a little out of town on Ringpong Rd. It offers good doubles with cable TV at Rs 225 to Rs 300.

Places to Stay – Mid-Range

The few mid-range places are all out of the town centre to the south, along Rinkingpong Rd.

Kalimpong Park Hotel (☎ 55304, email parkotel@clte.vsnl.net.in) is the pick of the bunch. Singles/doubles are Rs 1150/1170. All rooms have bath with hot shower. The double deluxe rooms are in the original building, which was once the summer residence of the Maharaja of Dinajpur; room five has beautiful views of Kanchenjunga

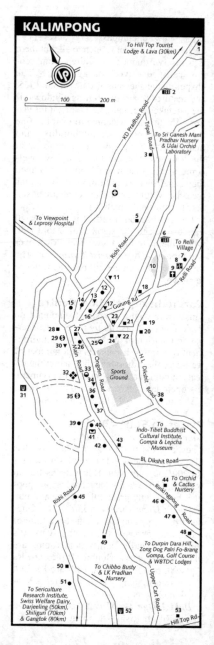

KALIMPONG

KALIMPONG

and Deolo Hill. Most of the other rooms are in the 20-year-old annexe behind the hotel, which is quite comfortable, although not sumptuous.

The Government of Bangla tourist office has two places farther out along the same road. They are also in old colonial bungalows, and have nice gardens and views, but can be a hassle to get to without your own transport. The nicer of the two is the *Morgan House Tourist Lodge* (☎ 55384), about 3km from the town centre. It's a beautiful old ivy-covered Victorian building with leaded windows and a sweeping driveway. Ordinary singles/doubles range from Rs 650/1100 to Rs 1700. All rooms have bath and hot shower, and rates include meals and bed tea. The hotel is in a wonderful position on the top of a ridge with valleys falling away on either side. Above the hotel is Gouripur House, where Rabindranath Tagore lived and wrote a number of his poems.

A cobblestone path through a magnificent flower garden leads from Morgan House to the adjacent Bangla Tourism *Tashiding Tourist Lodge* (☎ 55929). Singles

are Rs 600 and Rs 650, and doubles are Rs 1150, including all meals. The rooms have a lovely outlook but are fairly basically furnished.

Gurudongma House (☎ 55204), on Hill Top Rd, is a lovely quiet place to stay. It's about 2km from the centre of Kalimpong, but General Jimmy Singh will pick up guests from the town centre. Singles/doubles are Rs 600/800, or three to four-person dormitory beds are Rs 210. There's a lovely garden, and rooms are in private cottages with pine trimmings and low Japanese futon-style beds. There are also rooms inside the main house. Meals are available here.

Places to Stay – Top End
If you have the money, there's no better place to stay in Kalimpong than the beautiful old *Himalayan Hotel* (☎ 55248, fax 55122), on Upper Cart Rd, about 300m up the hill past the post office. The hotel is surrounded by superb gardens featuring camellias, azaleas, orchids and poinsettias, and there are views across to the snow-covered peaks of Kanchenjunga. It features old-world furnishings

and is a great place to stay. Room-only rates are Rs 1650/2700 plus 10% tax, and there are also full-board rates.

Hotel Silver Oaks (☎ 55296), on Rinkingpong Rd, is about 100m uphill from the post office. Once the home of a British family who ran a jute plantation, the original eight bedroom building has been extended to a 20 room hotel with delightful gardens and its own bakery. There's 24 hour room service, foreign-exchange facilities and bar. All the spacious, sunny rooms (singles/doubles US$80/92) have views, either of the valley or Kanchenjunga, and are furnished in an old-world style with heavy bureaus, dressers and floral chintz drapery. The Silver Restaurant serves good wholesome fare and is open to nonguests with prior notice.

Places to Eat

Most places to eat close early in Kalimpong, and you'll have trouble getting a bite to eat after 9 pm, particularly in the low season.

New Restaurant is a tiny little eatery at the north end of Main Rd. The *Kalsang Restaurant*, on Link Rd, is a lovely rustic little place run by friendly Tibetans, who will serve butter tea and pork *ghaytuk* (noodles).

Annapurna Restaurant, upstairs on the corner of Gurung Rd, near the Kashi Nath bookshop, is cheap, clean, friendly and serves all sorts of alcohol (beer, rum, whisky). However, the service is unbelievably slow, and you have to ignore the malodorous stairway.

One of the best places to eat in town is the *Mandarin Restaurant*, at the bus stand. The speciality is Mandarin fish, but you'll need to order it two hours in advance. Other tasty dishes include fried chicken balls and Chinese roast pork.

Nonguests are welcome to dine at the *Himalayan Hotel* and *Silver Oaks*, but advance notice is required.

Glenary's has opened two coffee shops and bakeries in Kalimpong, one on Rishi Rd, just beyond the railway booking office, and one on Ongden Rd. They serve cakes, pastries, tea and even Nescafe coffee.

Caramel lollipops are a local speciality. They were originally produced at the Swiss dairy, which was established by Jesuit fathers, but the fathers have returned to Switzerland and the dairy is now closed. Nevertheless, the tradition continues, and you can buy them in most grocery shops. Cheese is still made by locals who trained under the priests. Kalimpong cheese is similar to cheddar, but a bit more tart. You can sample it at *Lark's Provisions* on Rishi Rd.

Shopping

The Bhutia Shop, Dambar Chowk, is run by the friendly Mr K Shila Bhutia, and stocks traditional Bhutia crafts such as woodcarvings, as well as pastel paintings, embroidered bags and other items.

Kalimpong tapestry bags and purses, copperware, scrolls and paintings from Dr Graham's Home are sold at the Kalimpong Arts & Crafts Co-Operative, which was founded by Dr Graham's wife, Katherine Graham. The coop is behind Dambar Chowk and is open Monday to Friday, 10 am to 3 pm, and until noon on Saturday. Shops selling Tibetan jewellery and artefacts can be found in the streets to the east of Dambar Chowk.

Getting There & Away

Air Bagdogra (50km away) is the closest airport, 12km from Shiliguri on the plains. Mintri Transport (☎ 55741), Main Rd, is the agent for Jet Airways, Indian Airlines and Royal Nepal Airlines (the last for flights to Kathmandu from Bhadrapur, over the border in Nepal). Speedways (☎ 55074), farther south down Main Rd, can book flights from Bhadrapur and Biratnagar (both in Nepal) to Kathmandu, with Necon Air.

Bus Mintri Transport operates a daily bus to Bagdogra (Rs 112, three hours). There are numerous booking agents at the bus stand, including Sammy's Corner Bus Booking Office (☎ 55861), with a daily bus at 12.30 pm to Darjeeling (Rs 37, 3½ hours), and buses to Shiliguri departing every 30 minutes between 6.30 am and 4 pm (Rs 45, three hours).

Purnima Tours & Travels (☎ 56193) also has services to Shiliguri, as well as to Gangtok (Rs 36, four hours). Himalayan Travels (☎ 55023) has a service to Kaffer (Rs 28, 4½ hours) at 1 pm daily; and Samco Ropeway (Rs 15, 1½ hours).

Sikkim Nationalised Transport (SNT) is at the west end of the bus stand. The office is open daily, 8 am to 3 pm. If the road is clear, the journey to Gangtok will take about four hours. If a detour is required, it could take up to five hours. Tickets are Rs 36.

Bhutan From Kalimpong it is possible to visit Phuentsholing, just over the Bhutanese border, without a visa. There's a daily bus to Jaigaon, on the Indian side of the border, which leaves at 8.30 am (Rs 49, six hours). There are hotels and guesthouses at Phuentsholing, but not Jaigaon.

Train Although there's no railway line to Kalimpong, there's an India-wide railway booking agency (☎ 55643) on Mani Rd, a tiny lane below Rishi Rd, behind the Lion's Reading Room. It's open for bookings daily, 10 am to 1 pm and 4 to 5 pm.

Jeep There are regular share-jeep departures for Gangtok. The trip takes 2½ hours, and costs Rs 57. They leave when full, generally between 7 am and 3 pm. Private jeeps to Gangtok and Shiliguri cost at least Rs 600. To reserve a jeep for Lava will cost about Rs 600, and to Kaffer, around Rs 1400.

AROUND KALIMPONG
Lava & Kaffer
At 2353m, about 30km east of Kalimpong, Lava is a small village with a small **gompa**, which belongs to the Kagyupa order. Tuesday is market day, and a good time to visit. The tip of Kanchenjunga is visible from Kaffer, at 1555m, and is best viewed at sunrise. There are **forest resthouses** at both Lava and Kaffer (Rs 50 for dorm beds, Rs 450 for doubles; hot water provided in buckets). Also at Kaffer is the **Yankee Resort**, with singles/doubles for Rs 180/300. Buses and jeeps ply regularly between Kalimpong and Lava.

Mongpong & Teesta Bazaar
Sixteen kilometres from Kalimpong where the road divides for Darjeeling and Shiliguri, Mongpong and Teesta Bazaar are becoming centres for **white-water rafting**. It's possible to tackle the rapids between 15 November and 15 February. Contact DGHC Tourism (☎ 03552-62261), Teesta, Kalimpong; DGHC Tourism (☎ 0354-54879 /214), Silver Fir Bldg, The Mall, Darjeeling; or Johnny Gurkha (☎ 03592-55374).

The **Forest Resthouse** here is set beside a meandering length of the Teesta River. Doubles are Rs 450. It's possible to take elephant safaris here. All forest resthouses can be booked at the Forest Development Corporation (☎ 03592-55783) in Kalimpong.

Samthar Plateau
About 80km from Kalimpong is the Samthar plateau, which can be used as a base to visit tribal villages in the environs. Gurudongma Travels (☎ 03592-55204; see the Kalimpong section) has cabins here at the **Farm House Inn** for Rs 200 for singles, or Rs 400/500 in cottages, or deluxe rooms for Rs 600/800. There are also three to four-person alpine tents for Rs 100 per person.

Samco Ropeway
Thrill seekers should head for the Samco Ropeway, a chairlift installed by the Swedish as part of an aid program to help villagers cross the Teesta River. If the idea of dangling from a piece of wire 30m above the water doesn't entice, then give this a miss – it's definitely not for vertigo sufferers! The ropeway is on the main Shiliguri to Gangtok road, at a place known locally as 27th mile. A bus to the ropeway from Kalimpong will take 1½ hours and cost Rs 15.

Sikkim

Until 1975, Sikkim was an independent kingdom, albeit under a treaty allowing the Indian government to control Sikkim's foreign affairs and defence. However, following a period of political crises and riots in the capital, Gangtok, India annexed the country and Sikkim became the 22nd Indian state.

The move sparked widespread criticism, but tensions have now cooled. The central government has been spending relatively large sums of money to subsidise Sikkim's road building, electrification, water supply and agricultural and industrial development, and residents are exempt from central government taxes. Much of this activity was no doubt motivated by India's fear of Chinese military designs on the Himalayan region. Even today, there's a lot of military activity along the route from Shiliguri to Gangtok, and the Chinese do not recognise Sikkim as part of India.

For many years, Sikkim has been regarded as one of the last Himalayan Shangri-las because of its remoteness, spectacular mountain terrain, varied flora and fauna and ancient Buddhist *gompas* (monasteries). It was never easy to visit, and, even now, you need a special permit to enter, although this is easy to obtain (see the Permits section later in this chapter). All the same, access to the eastern part of Sikkim along the Tibetan border remains highly restricted, and trekking to the base of Kanchenjunga, revered throughout Sikkim as the guardian of the land, has to be organised through a recognised travel agency.

The population of Sikkim is approximately 18% Lepcha and 75% Nepali; the other 7% are Bhutias and Indians from various northern states; there is also a small community of refugees from Tibet. About 60% of the population is Hindu and 28% is Buddhist, although the two religions exist, as in many parts of Nepal, in a syncretised form. The ancient Buddhist gompas, of

Sikkim at a Glance

Population: 507,000 (year 2000 estimate)
Capital: Gangtok
Best Time to Go: Mar to May; Sep to mid-Nov
Trekking Areas: Yuksom-Dzongri region (Mar to May, Sep to Nov)

Highlights

- **Gompas** – See the famous Rumtek, near Gangtok, the seat of the head of the Kagyupa order of Tibetan Buddhism; and Enchey Gompa, in Gangtok. In west Sikkim the extraordinarily ornate Pemayangtse Gompa, accessible from Pelling, and the less ostentatious gompas of Tashiding and Sangacholeing are just as beautiful.

- **Yuksom-Dzongri Trek** – Take the fine five or nine day trek into Kanchenjunga National Park from the road head at Yuksom, an interesting historic village.

- **Flora** – Enjoy Sikkim's rhododendrons and orchids, renowned among botanists and flower enthusiasts. Gangtok hosts an international flower festival annually (Mar to May).

which there are many, are one of the principal attractions of a visit to Sikkim.

History

The country was originally home to the Lepchas, a tribal people thought to have migrated from the hills of Assam around the 13th century, although some scholars have suggested that they may have migrated from South-East Asia. The Lepchas were forest foragers and small-crop cultivators who worshipped nature spirits and a complex system of traditional medicine and magic. Nowadays their ability to lead a traditional lifestyle has been severely limited by emigration from Tibet and Nepal. The Lepchas have a homeland in the Dzongu area in the centre of the state, and access to this area is restricted.

The Tibetans started to migrate into Sikkim during the 15th and 16th centuries to escape strife between the nascent Gelukpa order and the Nyingmapa, the oldest Tibetan order. In Tibet itself, the Gelukpa order (of which the Dalai Lama is the head) gradually gained the upper hand. In Sikkim, the Nyingmapa order was introduced by three Tibetan lamas, Lhatsun Chempo, Kathok Rikzin Chempo and Ngadak Sempa Chempo. It was these lamas who consecrated the first *chogyal* or king, Phuntsog Namgyal, at Yuksom, which became the capital of the kingdom (it was later moved to Rabdentse, near Pelling).

In face of the waves of Tibetan immigrants, the Lepchas retreated to the more remote regions. A blood brotherhood was eventually forged between their leader, Thekong Tek, and the Bhutia leader, Khye-Bumsa, and spiritual and temporal authority was imposed on the Lepchas. The name Sikkim is variously translated as 'New House', 'Happy Homeland' or 'Valley of Rice', which perhaps reflects the varied origins of its people as much as any academic confusion.

When the kingdom of Sikkim was founded, the country included the area encompassed by the present state as well as part of eastern Nepal, the Chumbi Valley (Tibet), Ha Valley (Bhutan) and the Terai foothills down to the plains of India, including Darjeeling and Kalimpong.

Between 1717 and 1734, during the reign of Sikkim's fourth chogyal, a series of wars with the Bhutanese resulted in the loss of much territory in the southern foothills, including Kalimpong, then an important bazaar town on the trade route between Tibet and India. More territory was lost after 1780 following the Gurkha invasion from Nepal, though the invaders were eventually checked by a Chinese army with Bhutanese and Lepcha assistance. Unable to advance into Tibet, the Gurkhas turned south where

they came into conflict with the British East India Company. The wars between the two parties ended in the treaty of 1817 which delineated the borders of Nepal. The Gurkhas also ceded to the British all the Sikkimese territory they had taken; a substantial part was returned to the chogyal of Sikkim in return for British control of all disputes between Sikkim and its neighbours. The country thus became a buffer state between Nepal, Tibet and Bhutan.

In 1835, the British, seeking a hill station as a rest and recreation centre for their troops and officials, persuaded the chogyal to cede the Darjeeling area in return for an annual stipend. Tibet objected to this transfer of territory, regarding Sikkim as a vassal state, plus Darjeeling's rapid growth as a trade centre had begun to make a considerable impact on the fortunes of Sikkim's leading lamas and merchants.

Tensions rose and, in 1849, a high-ranking British official and a botanist, who were exploring the Lachen regions with the permission of both the Sikkim chogyal and the British government, were arrested. Although the two prisoners were unconditionally released a month later following threats of intervention, the British annexed the entire area between the present Sikkimese border and the Indian plains and withdrew the chogyal's stipend (the stipend was eventually restored to his son).

Further British interference in the affairs of this area led to the declaration of a protectorate over Sikkim in 1861 and the delineation of its borders. The Tibetans, however, continued to regard these actions as illegal and, in 1886, invaded Sikkim to reassert their authority. The attack was repulsed by the British, who sent a punitive military expedition to Lhasa in 1888 in retaliation. The powers of the Sikkimese chogyal were further reduced and high-handed treatment by British officials prompted him to flee to Lhasa in 1892, though he was eventually persuaded to return.

Keen to develop Sikkim, the British encouraged emigration from Nepal, as they had done in Darjeeling, and a considerable amount of land was brought under rice and cardamom cultivation. This influx of labour continued until the 1960s and, as a result, Nepalis now make up approximately 75% of the population of Sikkim. The subject of immigration became a topic of heated debate in the late 1960s and the chogyal was constrained to prohibit further immigration. New laws regarding the rights of citizenship were designed to placate those of non-Nepali origin, but they served to inflame the opposition parties.

There was also a great deal of grass-roots support for a popular form of government rather than the rule of Sikkim by the chogyal. The British treaties with Sikkim had passed to India at Independence and the Indian government had no wish to be seen propping up the regime of an autocratic raja while doing their best to sweep away the last traces of princely rule.

The last chogyal, Palden Thondup Namgyal, came to the throne in 1963 and struggled to live up to the memory of his revered father, Tashi Namgyal. The Nepali majority pushed for a greater say in government, and impoverished Nepali farmers began attacking the larger landowning gompas. The chogyal resisted demands for a change in the method of government until demonstrations threatened to get out of control. He was eventually forced to ask India to take over the country's administration. He and his American-born wife Hope Cook returned to New York and the last chogyal died of cancer in 1982. Several members of the royal family continue to reside (quietly) in Gangtok.

In a 1975 referendum, 97% of the electorate voted for union with India, with Congress (I)'s candidate, Lendup Dorje Kazi, installed as the first chief minister. Subsequent governments and leaders have been accused of corrupt links with businesses chosen to fulfill government contracts. The current state government is led by the Sikkim Democratic Front (SDF), which helps to ensure elections by threatening to impose social boycotts on people who do not support the party. On the other hand, the SDF has won praise for its environmental policies, banning logging and plastic bags from the state and stopping the hydroelectric scheme on the Rathong River in west Sikkim.

Geography

Sikkim is wedged between Tibet to the north and north-east, Bangla (West Bengal) and Bhutan to the south and south-east respectively, and Nepal to the west. In the north lies the Greater Himalayan peaks, including the third highest mountain in the world, Kanchenjunga (8598m). From this northern region the snow-fed waters of the Lachen and Lachung wend their way southwards, before meeting with the Teesta, which, together with the Rangeet, forms the southern boundary, separating Sikkim from northern Bangla.

From the formidable massifs of the Greater Himalaya project two enormous southward-thrusting spurs: that to the west forms the Singalila Range, which separates Sikkim from Nepal; to the east, the Chola Range forms the boundary between Sikkim and Tibet. Farther south, the Pangola Range separates Sikkim from Bhutan to the south-east. A third spur pierces the heart of Tibet, separating the valleys of the Teesta and Rangeet rivers, which meet at the southern end of the ridge.

In the east lies the Natu La, once a major trade route from Gangtok into Tibet (now China) and the route taken by the British invasion of Tibet in 1904. The pass crosses into the Chumbi Valley – a finger of Tibet that forms a strategic chink in the natural Himalayan armour. Sikkim is thus cradled in the lap of this enormous amphitheatre, enclosed by a series of ever-diminishing ridges that recede towards the plains of north-west India. In the south of the state, river-forged valleys lie only a few hundred metres above sea level.

Permits

Tourist & Trekking Permits The permitted length of stay in Sikkim is 15 days; an extension of 15 days is fairly easy to obtain, especially if you get help from a hotel man-

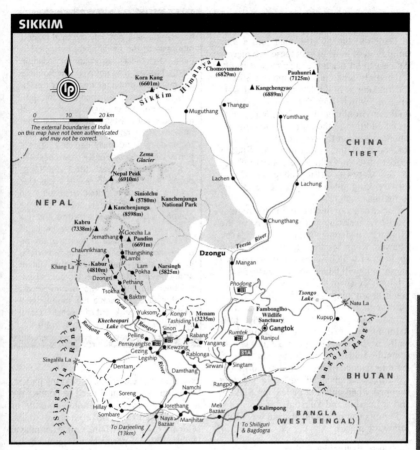

SIKKIM

Chomoyummo (6829m)

Kora Kang (6601m)

Pauhunri (7125m)

Kangchengyao (6889m)

Muguthang

Thanggu

Yumthang

0   10   20 km

The external boundaries of India on this map have not been authenticated and may not be correct.

CHINA
TIBET

Zemu Glacier

Nepal Peak (6910m)

Lachen

Lachung

Siniolchu (5780m)

Kanchenjunga National Park

NEPAL

Kanchenjunga (8598m)

Chungthang

Kabru (7338m)

Jemathang

Goecha La
Pandim (6691m)

Teesta River

Chaunrikhiang

Thangshing
Lambi

Dzongu

Khang La

Kabur (4810m)

Lam
Pokha

Narsingh (5825m)

Mangan

Dzongri

Pethang

Phodong

Tsokha

Baktim

Tsongo Lake

Natu La

Yuksom

Kongri
Tashiding

Menam (3235m)

Fambonglho
Wildlife
Sanctuary

Kupup

Khecheopari
Lake

Rangeet

Sinon

Gangtok

Pelling

Rabang

Rumtek

Ranipul

Pemayangtse

Kewzing

Yangang

Gezing

Legship

Rablonga

31A

Singtam

Singalila La

Dentam

River

Damthang

Sirwani

Rangpo

Soreng

Namchi

Meli
Bazaar

Kalimpong

BHUTAN

Hillay

Jorethang

BANGLA
(WEST BENGAL)

Sombare

Naya
Bazaar

Manjhitar

To Darjeeling
(13km)

To Shiliguri
& Bagdogra

SIKKIM

ager or travel agent in Gangtok – personal contacts count for a lot. Extensions are issued through the Home Office, Government of Sikkim, Tashiding Secretariat, Gangtok. Re-entry into Sikkim within three months is not possible, even if you leave Sikkim before your 15 day permit expires.

While permits can be obtained through the Indian embassy in your home country when you apply for your Indian visa, they can be obtained in India itself, either while you wait or within a few hours. It is considerably eas-

ier to get a permit in Shiliguri, where the office has a photocopier, than in Darjeeling, where you have to walk across town several times to secure the permit. You will need your passport and one photo, plus a photocopy of the front page of your passport (with expiry details and so on), and the page where your Indian visa is stamped; there's no charge. When applying for your permit, you must specify your date of entry into Sikkim.

Permits for Tsongo Lake (valid for a day visit only) and Yumthang (in north Sikkim;

a nonextendible five day/four night permit) can only be obtained from the permit office in Gangtok, but as you must join a tour (minimum of four) to visit these two places, it's best to let the travel agency sort it out.

The only area currently open in Sikkim for trekking is in the Dzongri area of west Sikkim, which has put undue pressure on the environment there. Trekking permits are in addition to the normal tourist permit and are issued at the permit office in Gangtok, or from the Government of Sikkim tourist office in Delhi (see Tourist Offices in the Gateway Cities chapter). Gangtok trekking agencies take care of the formalities.

For areas not included in the regular tourist or trekking permits, apply to the Ministry of Home Affairs, Lok Nayak Bhawan, Khan Market, Delhi, 11003. Each application will be considered on its own merits, and will take at least three visits and a month or so of helpless waiting before you hear anything. The *babus* (bureaucratic bureaucrats) at the ministry have an infamously slow work ethic. If all else fails it might be worth trying in Gangtok as well, as the state government is keen to promote tourism and somewhat resents the interference of the central authorities.

Permits are checked and your passport stamped when entering or leaving Sikkim, and at Legship and Yuksom.

Permits can be obtained from any of the following places:

Foreigners' Registration Offices
  Delhi, Mumbai (Bombay), Kolkata (Calcutta), Darjeeling
Resident Commissioner
  (☎ 011-3015346) Government of Sikkim, 14 Panchsheel Marg, Chanakyapuri, Delhi
Sikkim Tourism Information Centre
  (☎ 033-297516) 4C Poonam, 5/2 Russel St, Kolkata (Calcutta)
  (☎ 0353-432646) SNT Bus Compound, Tenzing Norgay (Hill Cart) Rd, Shiliguri

Kanchenjunga National Park Access into the heart of Kanchenjunga National Park, including the vast Zemu Glacier, is generally only permitted to mountaineering

Kanchenjunga

Kanchenjunga is not only the third highest mountain in the world and the highest in India (after India's absorption of Sikkim in 1975), but also a sacred peak and home to an important protector deity. You'll probably see images of Kanchenjunga throughout Sikkim, either at monasteries, at masked chaam festivals or New Year celebrations. The wrathful *dharmapala*, or protector deity, is normally depicted riding a puma, with a red face and a crown of skulls.

Kanchenjunga means the Five Strong-boxes of the Great Snows or Great Five Peaked Fortress of Snow, depending on who you ask; *khang* is snow, *chen* or *chembo* is big, *dzong* is a fortress and *nga* is five. The name refers to five boxes of treasures that are said to be buried on top of the mountain; containing sacred books, precious stones, an impenetrable suit of armour, salt and medicine. No boxes have yet been spotted, but then mountaineers traditionally turn back a few metres short of the 8598m peak, out of respect for local wishes and to avoid the deity's wrath.

expeditions or experienced trekking parties. For permission, you'll need to contact the Indian embassy in your home country, or apply direct to the Government of India, Ministry of Home Affairs, Grih Mantralaya, Delhi 11003. If permission is granted, the ministry will contact the Sikkim state government, which will arrange a liaison officer for the expedition.

After the permit has been granted, the expedition party needs to obtain permission from the Chief Wildlife Warden, Government of Sikkim, Forest Department, Deorali, Gangtok, Sikkim. This is just a formality, and can be done either before entering Sikkim, or on arrival in Gangtok. Gangtok travel agencies are best acquainted with the system and usually have the most useful contacts. Reputable agents include Tashila Tours & Travels, Yak & Yeti

Travels, Sikkim World Expeditions, Vajra Adventure Tours and Yuksom Tours & Travels. See Organised Tours & Treks in the Gangtok section later in this chapter for further details.

Mountaineering expeditions interested in climbing peaks over 6000m need to obtain clearance from the Indian Mountaineering Foundation (IMF; ☎ 011-467 1211, fax 688 3412), Benito Juarez Rd, Anand Niketan, Delhi 110021. Many peaks are off limits because they are regarded as sacred; climbers have always stopped short of the very top of Kanchenjunga for this reason.

East Sikkim

Due to its proximity to the Tibetan border, entry to most of east Sikkim by foreigners is prohibited. However, this region does encompass the capital, Gangtok, which is included on the standard tourist permit. Within the city and its immediate environs are some fascinating places to visit, including Rumtek Gompa, 24km to the west, the head of the Kagyupa order of Tibetan Buddhism.

GANGTOK
☎ 03592 • pop 90,000 • alt 2500m

The capital of Sikkim, Gangtok (which means 'hilltop'), occupies the west side of a long ridge flanking the Ranipul River. The scenery is spectacular and there are excellent views of the entire Kanchenjunga Range from a variety of points in an around the city.

Many people expect Gangtok to be a smaller version of Kathmandu. It's not, but it is an interesting and pleasant place to stay for a couple of days. Gangtok only became the capital in the mid-19th century (previous capitals were at Yuksom and Rabdentse). The town has undergone a rapid and rather unattractive modernisation in recent years, with buildings and building sites sprawling down the hillside.

Gangtok has also become something of a hill station resort for holidaying Bangalis. The influx peaks during the 10 day Dasain or Durga Puja holiday period at the end of September or early October, when Bangalis converge on the town en masse to enjoy the fresh air and cheap booze. It's a good time to give Gangtok a miss, as prices rise – especially for accommodation and local transport – and finding a room at *any* price can be a major headache.

Orientation

To the north is Enchey Gompa and the telecommunications tower. The palace of the former chogyal and the impressive Royal Chapel (the Tsuk-La-Khang) are lower down along the ridge. Nearby is the huge Tashiding Secretariat complex, and below it, the relatively recently built Legislative Assembly, both designed in a traditional architectural style.

On a continuation of this ridge but much lower is the Namgyal Institute of Tibetology, an Orchid Sanctuary and, not far beyond the institute, a large *chörten* (Tibetan stupa) and adjoining gompa.

All the main facilities – hotels, cafes, bazaars, bus stand, post office, tourist information centre and the Foreigners' Registration Office – are either on, or very near, the main Darjeeling road (National Highway 31A).

Information

Tourist Offices The helpful tourist office (☎ 22064) is at the top (north) end of MG Marg. In the season it's open daily, including holidays, 9 am to 7 pm. Between June and August it's open Monday to Saturday, 10 am to 4 pm. They also run local tours (see Organised Tours & Treks, later).

Money Most travellers cheques can be exchanged at the State Bank of India annexe, behind the tourist office. There is *nowhere* in Gangtok to change Visa travellers cheques, which put the author at the mercy of businessmen offering only two-thirds of the exchange rate.

Post & Communications The main post office is on Paljor Stadium Rd, just past the Hotel Tibet. It's open Monday to Saturday,

Festivals of Sikkim

Tibetan Buddhism is the focus of Sikkim's festivals, although the Lepchas and Nepali Hindus also celebrate certain events. Other festivals also celebrate the flowering of Sikkim's orchids.

February/March
Losar This is the Tibetan new year, and two days prior to it, dances are performed by the monks at Pemayangtse and Rumtek gompas. It falls in early March.

March/April
Bhumchu This Buddhist festival is celebrated at Tashiding Gompa in west Sikkim on the 15th day of the first month (March). More information can be found in the Tashiding section. At Khecheopari Lake, devotees make offerings of flowers, fruit and butter lamps.

March/May
International Flower Festival Corresponding with the best flowering of Sikkim's orchids, this festival takes place in Gangtok. Other species include gladioli, rhododendrons and magnolias.

April/May
Sikkim Festival Held in the White Hall at Gangtok in late April/early May, the main focus of this festival is a flower show and orchids are the chief attraction.

May/June
Saga Dawa This 'triple blessed festival' is to celebrate Buddha's birth, attainment of buddhahood and of *nirvana* (final release from the cycle of existence). Processions of monks carrying sacred scriptures proceed through the streets of Gangtok and other towns. Saga Dawa falls on the full moon of the fourth lunar month (late May or early June).

June/July
Tse Chu This *chaam* (lama dance) depicts the life of Padmasambhava. It takes place at Rumtek Gompa in Sikkim on the 10th day of the fifth month of the Tibetan lunar calendar (July).

---

9 am to 12.30 pm, and 1 to 5 pm. Parcels can be posted from Monday to Friday, 9 am to 2 pm, and on Saturday, from 9 am until noon. The telegraph office is in the same building. At the time of research email access wasn't really possible because the only link was via radio (which makes the whole process exceedingly slow).

Bookshops & Newsagencies The Gangtok General Store Bookshop, on MG Marg, opposite the tourist office, and Jainco Booksellers, a few doors south of the tourist office, both have a good range of English-language titles, with books relevant to Sikkim and the eastern Himalaya. You can get English-language national dailies (the day after publication) at either of these places, and the locally printed *Sikkim Express*, *Sikkim Observer* and *Gangtok Times* are all published weekly.

Medical Supplies Chiranjilal Lalchand is a dispensing pharmacy on MG Marg, opposite the Green Hotel.

Emergency Police: (☎ 22033); Hospital: (☎ 22944).

Festivals of Sikkim

July/August
Drukpa Teshi This festival celebrates the first teaching given by the Buddha. It is held on the fourth day of the sixth month (August) of the Tibetan lunar calendar.

August/September
Panghlapsol This uniquely Sikkimese festival is devoted to Kanchenjunga, the guardian deity of Sikkim, and to Yabdu, the 'supreme commander' of Kanchenjunga. It is celebrated with dramatic dances, with Kanchenjunga represented by a red mask ringed by five human skulls, and Yabdu by a black mask. Dancing warriors in Sikkimese battle dress with helmets, shields and swords, also participate. The highlight of the dance is the entrance of Mahakala (the protector of the Dharma or Buddhist path), who instructs Kanchenjunga and Yabdu to ensure that Sikkim remains peaceful and prosperous. It falls on the 15th day of the seventh month of the Tibetan lunar calendar (late August or early September).

October/November
Dasain This is the Nepali Hindus' version of north Indian Dussehra, Delhi's Ram Lila and West Bengal's Durga Puja. It falls in October, and is also the main holiday period.
Teohar This three day festival of lights is celebrated 15 days after Dasain.

January/February
Chaam Lama dances are conducted at Enchey Gompa in Gangtok on the 18th and 19th days of the 12th month of the Tibetan lunar calendar (January).
Kagyat Dance Held on the 28th and 29th days of the 12th month of the Tibetan lunar calendar (February), this dance festival symbolises the destruction of evil forces. The dances are performed by monks in the gompa courtyard. Prayers are held before the dance. The main centre for the dance is the Tsuk-La-Khang (Royal Chapel) in Gangtok, but dances are also held at Pemayangtse and Phodang gompas.
Losong This Sikkimese New Year (last week of February) is known as Namsoong by the Lepchas. It is also called Sonam Losar (Farmers' New Year), as it falls around harvest time.

Tsuk-La-Khang
The Royal Chapel is the repository of a large collection of scriptures. It's a beautiful and impressive building, and its interior is covered with murals. Lavishly decorated altars hold images of the Buddha, Bodhisattvas and Tantric deities, and there are also a great many fine woodcarvings. The only time it's open to visitors is during Losong (the Tibetan New Year, usually in February) when the famous *chaam* dance portraying the triumph of good over evil is performed. At other times it's worth asking at the gate whether you can see the building.

Namgyal Institute of Tibetology
Established in 1958 and built in traditional style, this unique institute promotes research of the language and traditions of Tibet. It has one of the world's largest collections of books and rare manuscripts on Mahayana Buddhism, many religious works of art and a collection of astonishingly beautiful and incredibly finely executed silk-embroidered *thangkas* (religious art produced on cloth).

It also has painted thangkas depicting the eight manifestations of Padmasambhava (also known as Guru Rinpoche, the Indian priest who established Buddhism in Tibet in the 8th century CE). The institute also has the relics of monks from the time of Ashoka (3rd century BCE Buddhist emperor), examples of Lepcha script, masks, and ceremonial and sacred objects such as the *kapali* (bowl made from a human skull) and the *varku* (a flute made from a thigh bone). The institute also enshrines numerous statues.

There are also a number of religious art and craft works and books on Tibetan Buddhism for sale. It's open from Monday to Friday and every second Saturday from 10 am to 4 pm; entrance is Rs 2. This is a sacred place, and footwear should be removed before entering.

Chörten & Gompa

The gold apex of a huge white chörten, about 500m beyond the institute, is visible from many points in Gangtok and is surrounded by prayer flags and wheels. Next to it is a gompa for young lamas with a shrine containing huge images of Padmasambhava, and his manifestation, Guru Snang-Sid Zilzon.

Orchid Sanctuaries

Surrounding the Namgyal institute and itself enclosed by a peaceful forest, is the poorly maintained **Orchid Sanctuary**, where you can see many of the 454 species of orchid found in Sikkim. The best times to visit are April to May and the end of September to the beginning of December.

There is another, much larger, orchid sanctuary, the **Orchidarium**, off the main road to Rangpo alongside the Rani Khola, a tributary of the Teesta, is accessible by public bus. It's also usually included on tours to Rumtek Gompa.

Up on top of the ridge, near White Hall is a **Flower Exhibition Centre**, featuring orchids and seasonal flowers, as well as bonsai. It's open April to June, and September to November, 10 am to 6 pm daily; entry is Rs 2. **White Hall** was once the residence of the British political officer in Sikkim, and there are pleasant walks here through fine gardens.

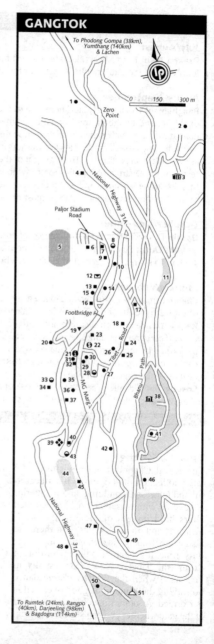

GANGTOK

GANGTOK

Cottage Industries Emporium

High up on the main road above town, the Cottage Industries Emporium specialises in producing hand-woven carpets, blankets, shawls, Lepcha weaves, patterned decorative paper and chogtse tables, exquisitely carved in relief. It's open daily during the high season and in the low season, it's open daily except Sunday and every second Saturday, from 9 am to 12.30 pm and from 1 to 3.30 pm.

Enchey Gompa

Near the telecommunications tower, about 2km from the centre of town, Enchey Gompa was built in 1909, and is home to about 100 Nyingmapa monks. It isn't particularly impressive but the views are nice, and the boy monks running around and playing with the ubiquitous dogs (which seem to know gompas are sanctuaries) are entertaining.

Enchey was built on the site of the hermitage of Lama Druptob Karpo, a Tantric master who performed various extraordinary feats, including flying from South Sikkim to the site of the current gompa. The *chaam* (dance performed by masked lamas) is held on the 18th and 19th days of the 12th month of the lunar calendar (January/February).

The prayer hall is completely covered with exquisite paintings, and is a feast of colour. The roof, which itself is a riot of colour, is supported by four large red pillars, intricately carved with ornate coloured cornices. The orange ceiling is set off by horizontal, bright blue beams. At the *chwa-shyam* (altar) end of the prayer hall is a large Buddha. On the right is Padmasambhava, and on the left, Avalokiteshvara (Tibetan: Chenresig), the Bhodhisattva of Compassion. On the left wall, near the chwa-shyam and behind a glass cabinet is an image of Dorje Phurba (Sanskrit: Vajra Kila). The *dorje* (thunderbolt) and *phurba* (ritual dagger) are important tantric ritual instruments. Dorje is the wild-eyed male part of the image, and Phurba, the female

SIKKIM

part, is locked in his embrace. Beneath his feet, squashed under his taloned toes, is a tiny demon.

In the vestibule are depicted the Great Kings of the four cardinal directions (see the Rumtek Gompa section later in this chapter for details), who protect the gompa and the universe, from demons.

Lall Market

If you've been to markets in Kathmandu or Darjeeling, this one may come as a disappointment due to its limited range of craft shops, but the vegetable market is certainly colourful and there's plenty of activity. Local specialities include *churpi* (amazingly tough dried yak cheese), and the numerous bars around the perimeter are good places to slurp a bamboo tube full of *chang* (fermented millet), the local beer also colloquially called *tongba* (pronounced tomba). See the Tongba – Nectar of the Gods boxed text in the Bangla (West Bengal) Hills chapter.

Organised Tours & Treks

You'll need the services of a recognised tour operator and at least four people in your trekking party if you want to travel to north Sikkim or do the Dzongri Trek (Kanchenjunga). Operators in Gangtok charge between US$25 and US$60 per person per day, and also offer gompa tours, bird-watching tours, and white-water rafting on the Teesta River. Equipment hire (sleeping bags etc) is available from some operators.

Tour operators worth contacting in Gangtok include the following:

Blue Sky Tours & Travels
  (☎/fax 23330) opposite the Hotel Lhakpa on Tibet Rd. As well as treks to west Sikkim, this company also has tours to north Sikkim.
Mahayana Tours & Travels
  (☎ 23885, fax 22707 attn 'Mahayana')
  Room 23, Super Market Complex. Offers a range of treks, including gompa treks and an eight day rhododendron trek from Yuksom to Baktim, Dzongri, Phidong and Tsokha.
Mayur Travels
  (☎ 24462) Paljor Stadium Rd near Potala Tours. Organises local sightseeing trips.

Potala Tours & Travels
  (☎ 22041, email potala@gokulnet.com)
  Paljor Stadium Rd. Offers the usual range of treks at attractive prices.
Sikkim Tours & Travels
  (☎ 22188, fax 22707 attn 'Sikkim Tours')
  Church Rd, near the private bus stand. Lukendra (Luke) here is a keen photographer, and can also organise tailor-made photography and bird-watching tours.
Sikkim Trekking & Travel Services
  (☎ 23638, fax 22707 attn 'Sikkim Trekking')
  Room No 1, Super Market Complex. Not the cheapest, but it's very professional and was the first outfit established in Sikkim; can also organise visits to Bhutan and the North-East Region.
Sikkim World Expeditions
  (☎ 23494, fax 24195)
  Zero Point, NH 31A. Also operates tours to north Sikkim.
Siniolchu Tours & Travels
  (☎ 24457, fax 22707 attn 'Siniolchu',
  email siniolchu@cct.ernet.in)
  Paljor Stadium Rd. Also offers a wide range of tours, including a four day cultural tour of the gompas of Sikkim for US$120 per person with accommodation in tents.
Tashila Tours & Travels
  (☎ 22979, fax 22155)
  NH 31A, opposite the private bus stand. Managed by Alok Raj Pradhan, who can also arrange special-interest tours such as high-altitude rhododendron and primula tours (the primulas are at their best in May and June).
Vajra Adventure Tours
  (☎ 22446, fax 22707 attn 'Vajra')
  Kyitsel House, Arithang Rd. Good quality outfit with their own lodges and camp sites on the Goche La section of the Dzongri Trek.
Yak & Yeti Travels
  (☎ 22714, fax 24643,
  email yakyeti@mailcity.com)
  Hotel Superview Himalchuli, NH 31A, Zero Point. Good value and run by the enthusiastic Satish Bardewa, who also has mountaineering experience.
Yuksom Tours & Travels
  (☎ 23473, fax 22707 attn 'Yuksom')
  NH 31A. Organises treks to west Sikkim and tours to north Sikkim.

Permits Trekking permits for west Sikkim (north of Yuksom) can be obtained from the permit office in the same building as the tourist office. It's open Monday to Saturday, 10 am to 4 pm. To visit Tsongo Lake or north Sikkim, you need to be in a group of four and book a package through a travel agency; agencies will arrange requisite permits. Extensions can be applied for at the Home Office, Government of Sikkim, Tashiling Secretariat, Gangtok; again its easier to get help from a travel agency.

Permits for Fambonglho Wildlife Sanctuary, 25km from Gangtok, can be obtained from the District Forest Officer (☎ 23191), Forestry Secretariat, Deorali, Gangtok. It's also possible to book accommodation in the park precincts here. See the Fambonglho Wildlife Sanctuary section later in this chapter for more details.

To find out more information on the permits you will need when travelling through Sikkim, see the Permits section at the beginning of this chapter.

Equipment Hire Trekking gear such as sleeping bags and tents can be hired at Mountain Adventures (☎ 22454), shop 31, Super Market complex.

Local Tours Local tours run by the tourist office (see Information earlier) operate on a point system, points referring to sites of interest around Gangtok. A seven point sightseeing trip taking in Enchey and Rumtek gompas, the deer park and the Namgyal Institute of Tibetology, among other places, takes four to five hours and costs Rs 150. Half-day tours also cover Rumtek but don't give you much time, and you'd be better off doing this yourself.

Places to Stay
In the winter it's important to inquire about hot water and heating. A bucket of hot water for showering is available at most places (sometimes for a small extra charge), but heating is a rarity. Where an electric heater is available it will definitely cost you more. Very few places have single rooms, and there's often no discount for single occupancy of a double room. Top-end hotels add a 10% service charge.

Don't forget to ask about low-season discounts. They vary between 15% and 30%, usually from around January to March, and in July and August.

Places to Stay – Budget
Hotel Lhakpa (☎ 23002), on Tibet Rd above MG Marg, has very basic four-bed rooms with common bath for Rs 350, doubles with bath for Rs 300, and Rs 400 with geyser. There's a little bar downstairs with a good sound system.

Modern Central Lodge (☎ 24670), on Tibet Rd, is popular but some travellers have reported that the management can be belligerent at times (around cocktail hour). Normally they are very helpful. There is a very useful travellers' comment book, plus free maps with handy transport information. Dorm beds are Rs 30, singles are Rs 60, doubles with toilet are Rs 80 (these rooms are a little dark) or Rs 100 with good views. With bath, rooms cost from Rs 100/120 to Rs 180/200, the most expensive rooms have the best views and geysers in the bathrooms. There's a TV room, snooker room, restaurant, and roof terrace.

Green Hotel (☎ 23354) is on MG Marg, by the tourist office. There's a range of rooms, from Rs 120/150 with bath and hot water in buckets to Rs 200/250 for rooms with bath and geyser. The cheaper rooms are in the old block, and some are a little dark. There's a popular bar and restaurant.

Hotel Lakhar (☎ 22198) is right opposite the SNT bus stand. Rooms with common bath cost Rs 100/200 and doubles with bath and geyser are Rs 300. This is a pleasant place, run by a friendly Tibetan couple, with basic, but spotless rooms.

Blue Heaven Lodge (☎ 23827, Paljor Stadium Rd), is clean and friendly. All rooms have bathroom and constant hot water. Some rooms even have 'honeymoon' beds (just standard double beds but something of a rarity here). Rooms are from Rs 150/200 to Rs 275/350 – the more expensive ones come with a view.

Sunny Guest House (☎ 22179) is at the private bus stand. Doubles are Rs 300 or

Rs 400 and Rs 500 with bath, the latter with a balcony and good views.

Hotel Orchid (☎ 23151), on the highway near the private bus stand, is another reasonable, basic option, although the manager could be more cheerful. Singles/doubles with shared bath are Rs 100/200, doubles with bath are Rs 300 and four-bed rooms with bath are Rs 400.

Places to Stay – Mid-Range

Most mid-range places add an additional 10% service charge to the bill.

Gangtok Lodge (☎ 24670), diagonally opposite the tourist office on MG Marg, is friendly and central. Doubles are Rs 450 with bath (cold water, but there's a geyser in the common bathroom), or with a view, Rs 500. Good discounts are offered in the low season.

Pine Ridge Hotel (☎ 24958), near the Legislative Assembly, is run by the owners of Modern Central Lodge. All rooms have bathrooms and cost Rs 325/450, Rs 525 for a deluxe double. It's a good place but the cheaper rooms are quite small.

Hotel Sonam Delek (☎ 22566), on Tibet Rd, is pleasant. Doubles with common bath are Rs 500 to Rs 800 (with possibly the best views you'll get in Gangtok). A 40% discount is offered in the low season, and there's a good restaurant.

Hotel Superview Himalchuli (☎ 22714) is a great place with excellent views and very helpful staff. It's set just out of the main part of town towards Zero point, in a less congested and more pleasant area. Doubles/triples with bath are Rs 675/775, and there's also dormitory accommodation for Rs 75. There are good low-season discounts, a groovy 1960s-style bar, a garden restaurant, and a telescope for mountain viewing. Yak & Yeti Travels has its office here.

Hotel Mount View (☎ 23647), on Paljor Stadium Rd, has doubles from Rs 400 to Rs 900. All are well appointed, and have baths with 24 hour hot water, and colour TVs.

Denzong Inn (☎ 22692) is in the Denzong Cinema complex, just outside Lall Market. Rooms with bath and geyser are Rs 400/600, and there's an enormous suite for Rs 2000 that could comfortably accommodate four people. The cheaper rooms are nothing special, but some open onto a roof terrace with great Kanchenjunga views.

Places to Stay – Top End

Hotel Tashi Delek (☎ 22991, fax 22362) is centrally located on MG Marg. The tiny ornate doorway opens onto an opulent lobby with Tibetan woodcarving and *objets d'art*. Singles/doubles are Rs 2000/2100, double suites are Rs 4000; add Rs 700 for all meals included. The double deluxe suites have great mountain views; the less-expensive rooms are comfortable, but the views are of the grimy walls of neighbouring hotels. There's a nice terrace restaurant with great views of Kanchenjunga.

Hotel Tibet (☎ 22523, fax 22707) is a popular choice. You'll be welcomed by a doorman in full traditional Tibetan dress. Rooms range from Rs 760/1020 to Rs 1760/2350. There's 24 hour room service, foreign exchange facilities, a travel desk and a small bookshop with books on Tibetan issues. The cheaper rooms are on the road side, and are rather small, as are the mid-range rooms on the valley side. The more expensive rooms are very plush, with traditional Tibetan decor.

Netuk House (☎ 22374, fax 24802) is the home of an old Sikkimese family, the Denzongpas, and part of the 'Heritage Houses of the Himalayas' association, which includes the Windamere in Darjeeling (it also takes bookings for Netuk House). Rates are Rs 1650/2700 with all meals. It is comfortable, quiet and there are fine views from the terrace. Rates are Rs 1650/2700 with all meals.

Nor-Khill Hotel (☎ 25637, fax 23187), above the stadium, was once the royal guesthouse. It's now a beautiful hotel with rooms for Rs 4500/3500 including meals. There's a travel desk, gift shop and foreign exchange, and the hotel is set in attractive gardens.

Places to Eat

Most of the hotels in Gangtok have their own restaurants and some are very good.

The Mysterious Zee

Tibetans are known for their beautiful and ornate jewellery, frequently encrusted with turquoise and coral, forming heavy neck pieces and rings. A lesser known ornament is the mysterious zee, an off-white, elongated 'stone' featuring black swirls in the form of 'eyes', which are threaded on a string and worn around the neck, or mounted on a ring. This seemingly innocuous little item is highly prized by Tibetans, but if you ask where they come from, generally you'll receive an enigmatic smile and silence. The truth is, no one knows where they come from. Some Tibetans claim they are fossilised insects, or segments of fossilised snakes; others believe they are a naturally formed stone found only in Tibet. Some cynics reckon they're highly polished and painted pieces of porcelain.

The zee, which is passed down through the family or traded, can range in size from less than a centimetre to 10cm, and is believed to protect the wearer. There is one belief that zees contain spirits. The miraculous powers of the zee were apparently confirmed when the survivor of a terrible accident in Taiwan was found to be wearing one. They are allegedly ground down and used in Tibetan medicine, and Tibetans have been heard to vociferously claim that they are put to more sinister use in nuclear warheads!

Zees are found wherever there are Tibetan communities, and those in search of the mysterious zee travel from Taiwan, Nepal and even the Middle East to secure one. There are various types of zee. The *sakhu nakhu* (sky earth) zee has a solid black square on one side, and an 'eye' on the reverse side. The *thashuma* zee features a zigzag band around the centre, and the *chunchi* features unbroken bands (called *charies*) and no 'eyes'. Eyes are solid black spots encompassed by a white surround; they come in three types: circular, diamond-shaped, and the highly prized (and rare) 'man's eye', which is oval-shaped. A pitch-black eye with a very white background is considered to be particularly auspicious, and commands high prices. To really confuse matters, odd-numbers of eyes are considered to be especially lucky, and no Tibetan will be caught wearing the extremely unlucky four or six eyed zee.

If you're considering buying a zee, bring your credit card, as a 'genuine' zee can fetch anywhere from Rs 5000 to Rs 25,000. The cheapest 'genuine' zee has two eyes. Zees can be legally purchased in India (including Sikkim), and Nepal, but it is illegal to buy a zee in Bhutan. They should be checked for flaws and chips. Vijdy Sakya at Babu Kazi Sakya & Sons, MG Marg, near the Hotel Tashi Delek in Gangtok, is a wealth of knowledge on zees, and may even have a specimen under the counter to show you.

If you can't afford a genuine zee, a porcelain replica will set you back only about Rs 100, and if you get a good one, no one will be able to tell the difference!

Modern Central Lodge, *Hotel Lhakpa*, *Hotel Lakhar* and *Green Hotel* have restaurants that are popular with travellers. All offer cheap and tasty meals in a variety of cuisines – usually Tibetan, Chinese and Indian – with some western alternatives such as pancakes. Chicken fried rice will set you back about Rs 25 at these places, *tsampa* (Tibetan staple of roast barley flour) is around Rs 15.

Oyster Restaurant, at the Hotel Sonam Delek, is a bit more upmarket. There are continental favourites such as French toast and banana pancakes, as well as Chinese, Indian and Tibetan cuisine.

New Kho-Chi Restaurant & Bar is in a handy location beneath the Gangtok Lodge on MG Marg. There's an extensive Chinese and Indian menu, most dishes under Rs 50.

Metro Fast Food is a cheap south Indian snack bar opposite Gangtok Lodge.

Kikis Garden Restaurant is on the top floor of the Super Market complex. During the season there's a buffet here featuring Sikkimese cuisine.

Blue Poppy Restaurant is at the Hotel Tashi Delek. It does good Sikkimese cuisine but it must be ordered 12 hours in advance. Veg dishes start at Rs 50, and nonveg dishes are around Rs 100. The terrace restaurant is a nice place to relax over lunch.

Snow Lion Restaurant, at the Hotel Tibet, is expensive and the servings aren't very big, but the atmosphere compensates. There's Tibetan cuisine, some Japanese and seafood dishes and good Indian food from their tandoor.

There are also numerous little seedy bars with prices that are refreshingly cheap after Bangla (West Bengal). A beer will set you back about Rs 30. Full-moon and new-moon days are 'dry' days throughout Sikkim. Try chang from a shop in the market – a large bamboo mug full of fermenting millet.

Shopping
The Rural Artisans' Marketing Centre, about midway along MG Marg, has Tibetan carpets from west Sikkim and handloom products. Carpets range in price from Rs 450 for 38 cm sq rugs, to Rs 4000 for 2.73m x 5.46m, and are made from a blend of New Zealand and Indian wool. All profits go to fund rural development programs in Sikkim.

The Charitrust Tibetan Handicraft Emporium (beneath the Hotel Tibet on Paljor Stadium Rd) is a Tibetan Government in Exile initiative, with profits used to fund education programs for economically disadvantaged Tibetan children. Here you'll find brass statues of deities, thangkas, *chubas*, known locally as *bakhus* – the traditional dress worn by Tibetan women – and other Tibetan artefacts. The shop also has a good selection of books on Tibetan religion and culture.

Directly opposite Potala Tours & Travels, on Paljor Stadium Rd, is the Tibetan Curio Store. Here you can find all things Tibetan, including lengths of fine silk brocade ranging from Rs 200 to Rs 1600, colourful prayer flags (Rs 5 for the small ones, or Rs 20 for the large ones); monks' *thermas* (robes); and *damrhus* (small Tibetan drums from which hangs a tassel called a *chophen*). You might like to carry home a brass *jhemta* – the cymbal used in gompas. They range in price from Rs 900 to Rs 1300. Mr Shyam Sunder Bansal here is happy to explain the items in his shop.

Getting There & Away
Air The closest airport is Bagdogra, 120km south on the Bangla (West Bengal) plains near Shiliguri. Jet Airways and Indian Airlines have flights from Bagdogra to Delhi and Kolkata (Calcutta; see Getting There & Away in the Shiliguri section of the Bangla (West Bengal) Hills chapter for details of flights.) Indian Airlines (☎ 23099) has an office on Tibet Rd, near the Children's Park taxi stand. It's open daily, 10 am to 1 pm and 2 to 4.45 pm. The agent for Jet Airways is RNC Enterprises (☎ 23556), on MG Marg, a few doors up from the Green Hotel.

Bus Sikkim Nationalised Transport (SNT) is the main bus operator to/from Gangtok, and they have plenty of services from their well-organised bus stand on Paljor Stadium Rd. Book as far in advance as possible, particularly during the Dasain (Durga Puja) holiday period. The booking office is open 9 am to noon and 1 to 2 pm.

There are daily buses to Shiliguri (Rs 47, five hours), Kalimpong (Rs 50, three hours), Darjeeling (Rs 83, seven hours) and Bagdogra (Rs 60, 4½ hours).

RICHARD I'ANSON

RICHARD I'ANSON

COLIN BARNES

Wherever you go in India, evidence of the spiritual is never far away. **Top left:** Fearsome Enchey Gompa door, Gangtok. **Top right:** Pemayatse Gompa, Sikkim. **Bottom:** Tibetan prayer flags, Tsoska.

Top left: Mosque skyline, Gangtok. **Top right:** Tibetan Mani stone, with the mantra: *om mani pandme hum* (Hail to the Jewel in the Lotus). **Middle:** Festival procession by the lake, Kecheopari Gompa, Sikkim. **Bottom left:** Young boy makes an offering, Sikkim. **Bottom right:** All beings must tread the Wheel of Life.

In addition to the SNT buses, there are private buses that run from the private bus stand (adjacent to Sunny Guest House) to Shiliguri, Darjeeling and Kalimpong. To Shiliguri there are at least 10 buses daily (mostly in the afternoon), and to Darjeeling and Kalimpong at least two daily. They cost much the same as the SNT buses, and should be booked in advance at the private bus stand.

SNT buses for destinations within Sikkim are Gezing (for Pemayangtse) at 7 am (Rs 52, 4½ hours) – buses travel via Singtam, Rablonga, Kewzing and Legship (for connections to Tashiding and Yuksom); Rumtek at 4 pm (Rs 15, 1½ hours); Phodong at 8 am, 9 am and 4 pm (Rs 20, 2½ hours); and Jorethang at 2 pm (Rs 40, four hours).

Train There's a railway reservation counter at the SNT bus stand on Paljor Stadium Rd. It has a small quota of services from New Jalpaiguri (8km from Shiliguri), and is open Monday to Saturday, 9.30 to 11.30 am and 1.30 to 3 pm. See Getting There & Away in the Shiliguri section of the Bangla (West Bengal) Hills chapter for details.

Taxi & Jeep At the private bus stand you can get share jeeps to Shiliguri (Rs 80, 3½ hours), Darjeeling (Rs 90, four hours) and Kalimpong (Rs 80, 2½ hours).

From Children's Park, jeeps leave for destinations in west Sikkim such as Jorethang (Rs 55, three hours), Gezing (Rs 90, 5 hours) and on to Pelling (Rs 120, six hours from Gangtok); and in north Sikkim to Phodong (Rs 35, two hours).

From Lall Market, you can get share jeeps to Rumtek and Tsongo Lake. During the high season, share jeeps for Rumtek leave when full up to 5 pm (Rs 25, one hour), and return between 6 am and 4 pm. In the low season, they leave up to 2 pm. Share jeeps for Tsongo Lake leave in the season only at 9 am and 2 pm (Rs 150, two hours), and return between noon and 2 pm.

For share jeeps to Gangtok from Shiliguri, Darjeeling and Kalimpong, see Getting There & Away in those sections of the Bangla (West Bengal) Hills chapter.

Getting Around
The new city bus service, bitterly opposed by the taxi-wallahs, should now be running along National Highway 31A. All the taxis are near-new Maruti vans; Rs 50 will get you just about anywhere around town. To Rumtek you're looking at about Rs 400 return, including about an hour at the gompa.

AROUND GANGTOK
Rumtek Gompa
Rumtek, on the other side of the Ranipul Valley, is visible from Gangtok though it's 24km away by road. The gompa is the seat of the Gyalwa Karmapa, the head of the Kagyupa order of Tibetan Buddhism. The order was founded in the 11th century by Lama Marpa, the disciple of the Indian guru Naropa, and later split into several orders, the most important of which are Drukpa, Kagyupa and Karmapa. Since 1992 there has been a bitter and sometimes violent dispute over the successor to the 16th Gyalwa Karmapa who died in 1981, with the factions led by two Rumtek abbots, Samar Rinpoche and Situ Rinpoche. There are police stationed at Rumtek to keep the situation under control.

The main gompa is a recent structure, built in the 1960s by the 16th Karmapa as an exact copy of his former gompa at Tsurphu in Tibet, in strict accordance with traditional designs. The prayer room enshrines an enormous (3m-high, including the stand) statue of the Buddha, completely plated in gold. Hundreds of tiny Buddhas kept in glass-fronted pigeon holes represent the number of Buddhas who will come to the world.

The walls are richly embellished with paintings, including those of numbers of Tibetan and Indian scholars (if the robe crosses at the neckline, they're Tibetan; those with the robes around the waist are Indian). However the murals here aren't as fine as the older gompas of Sikkim. Ornamentation is restricted to these vibrant paintings; there is little of the intricate woodcarving that features in many gompas.

In the vestibule to the prayer room are four paintings depicting the Great Kings of the four cardinal directions, who guard the

SIKKIM

The Karmapa Connection

In 1981 the 16th Karmapa died in Chicago, passing down the Sikkim-based administration of the Buddhist Karmapa order to four regents, and sparking a dispute that has caused a painful rift in the exiled Tibetan community.

The stakes are high. The Karmapa sect, reputed to have assets of around US$1.2 billion, has up to one million followers, including many in the USA. The Karmapa himself ranks as the sect's third most important lama, after the Dalai Lama and Panchen Lama, who remains under house arrest in Beijing.

In early 1992, the Karmapa regents announced the discovery of a letter written by the 16th Karmapa that provided critical clues as to the whereabouts of his reincarnation, after which a suspicious car accident proved fatal for one of them. Two weeks after the accident, another of the regents, Shamar Rinpoche, announced that the mystery letter was a fraud. However a search team was already in eastern Tibet on the trail of the Karmapa's 17th reincarnation and by early June, Ugen Thinley Dorje had been found and the Dalai Lama had made a formal announcement supporting his candidature. All this was against a background of a brief occupation of Sikkim's Rumtek Gompa (now the head Karmapa monastery) by Indian troops, and brawling by monks divided over the issue.

Shamar Rinpoche initially opposed the support of Ugen Thinley Dorje, but after talks with the Dalai Lama changed his mind. Several days later, he changed his mind again and, aided by western supporters, began a letter writing campaign. In March 1994, he announced that he had discovered the 'true' reincarnation, a boy named Tenzin Chentse who had been spirited out of China via Chengdu and Hong Kong into India. The fact that the boy was able to obtain travel papers suggests some high-up official involvement. Tenzin continues to live in New Delhi under 24 hour protection.

Meanwhile the Chinese authorities, spouting the official line that he is the only rightful claimant, have formally enthroned Ugen Thinley Dorje at Tsurphu, taking the occasion to announce their 'historical and legal right to appoint religious leaders in Tibet'.

And here lies the rub – with the Tibetan community divided between Chinese-administered Tibet and an exiled government in Dharamsala, the question of where incarnate lamas are to be found is likely to be increasingly prickly. For the Chinese authorities, the more incarnate lamas found in Tibet the better.

Back in Sikkim the arguments roll on. Police keep an uneasy peace at Rumtek, rival factions accuse the other of being foreign spies and even the chief minister of Sikkim, Pawar Kumar Chamling, has stepped into the debate, announcing he supports Ugen Thinley Dorje as the 17th Karmapa.

universe and the heavens from demons. When facing the prayer hall, they are from left to right: Yulkhor Srung (with a white face, and playing a stringed instrument) – the King of the East; Namthose (the antithesis of the King of the East, with a blue face, fangs, bulging eyes and drawing a sword from a scabbard) – the King of the North; Chenmizang (blood-red face, with a serpent coiled around his arm, and holding a stupa in his hand) – the King of the West; and Yulkhor Srung (yellow face, holding a rat and a banner) – the King of the South.

Visitors are welcome to enter the prayer hall, and there's no objection to your sitting in on the prayer and chanting sessions. You'll even be offered a cup of salted butter tea when it's served to the monks.

Behind the main prayer hall is the Great Golden Reliquary Stupa of the 16th Karmapa, Rangjung Rigpae Dorje, who died in 1981. Around the walls are statues of the 16th Karmapa and his 15 predecessors, and before the stupa, paper prayer wheels constantly rotate by means of the heat generated by butter lamps. From the ceiling are suspended numerous richly embroidered thangkas.

Opposite the stupa is the Karmashri Nalanda Institute of Buddhist Studies. Courses for monks only in advanced Buddhist philosophy are run here.

Below the reliquary stupa is the gompa's printing press. The printer (a layperson, not a monk), has been carving wooden blocks with Tibetan script and designs since 1962. The blocks are used for printing prayer books of handmade paper that is made at Rumtek, and prayer flags. You can purchase a set of prayer flags here for Rs 100.

The main chaam known as Tse Chu, is performed on the 10th day of the fifth lunar month (May), and depicts events in the life of Padmasambhava. Another chaam takes place two days before Losar (Tibetan New Year in February/March).

Most activity takes place in the late afternoon. At other times it may be a matter of asking around for someone to open it up for you, which they are quite happy to do.

If you follow the tarmac road for 3km beyond Rumtek, through a gate off to the left you'll find another interesting, but smaller, gompa that was restored in 1983.

Places to Stay & Eat *Sangay Hotel*, 100m down the motorable road from the monastery, is a friendly little place. It's basic but clean, and blankets are provided. Rooms cost Rs 75/150 with common bath and hot water by the bucket. Cheap and basic meals are available.

Hotel Kunga Delek is opposite the main entrance. Small but clean doubles with bath (hot water) are Rs 150.

Martam Resort (☎ 03592-23314) is 5km from Rumtek, in the village of Martam. Rooms cost Rs 1650/2700 with all meals.

It's in a beautiful location in the middle of a paddy field, and staff here can arrange horse riding and treks in the surrounding area.

Getting There & Away There are buses and share jeeps to Rumtek from Gangtok. See Getting There & Away in the Gangtok section for details. If you feel like a bit of exercise, it's a very pleasant 12km walk (downhill) from Gangtok to the National Highway 31A, from where it's easy to get a ride for the 12km (uphill!) trip to Gangtok.

Dechenling Cremation Ground & Ngor Gompa

Leaving Gangtok on the road to Tsongo Lake, after 2km a road diverges to the right. About 250m along this road, a track to the right leads in a short distance to the Dechenling cremation ground. Discreet visitors are welcome to observe the cremation ritual. From the turn-off to the cremation ground the road proceeds to Ngor Gompa, which overlooks the Bhusuk River. It's not of great architectural interest, but is notable as the only gompa in Sikkim belonging to the Sakyapa order of Tibetan Buddhism.

A taxi will charge about Rs 200 return from Gangtok to Ngor Gompa.

Tashi Viewpoint

This viewpoint is 8km to the north of Gangtok, towards Phodong. There are very good views of the east side of Kanchenjunga, as well as those of Siniolchu (5780m), which is considered, along with Nanda Devi in Uttarakhand, to be one of the most beautiful mountains in the world. From Tashi Viewpoint, it's possible to walk to **Ganesh Tok** (*tok* means ridge), in less than an hour. From here, as well as views of Kanchenjunga and Siniolchu, there are fine views back over Gangtok. A taxi to either of these viewpoints from Gangtok will cost about Rs 250 return.

Close to Ganesh Tok is the recently opened **Himalayan Zoological Park**. There are no cages here – it's an open sanctuary covering 205 hectares. The park is part of a controlled breeding scheme for wild animals.

SIKKIM

Fambonglho Wildlife Sanctuary

This sanctuary is 25km from Gangtok, and covers an undulating and ecologically diverse area of 5200 hectares. It is home to a variety of mammals, including barking deer, those ungainly serows, and stocky gorals, various types of wild cats, including marbled leopards and jungle cats, Himalayan black bears, and red pandas. There are also numerous bird species, such as laughing thrushes, various types of owls and pheasants, and Nepal tree creepers.

There is a rich variety of flora, with abundant wild orchids, tree ferns, forests of oak and stands of bamboo, and there are magnificent views of the Sikkim Himalaya, including, of course, Kanchenjunga.

As with all wildlife sanctuaries, don't wear brightly coloured clothing or heavy perfume, as this will frighten the animals away. The best time to spot animals is in the early morning and late afternoon.

The sanctuary is open between October and April, and permission is required from the District Forest Officer (see Information, under Gangtok). Permits are issued routinely for foreigners, but you should carry both this and your Sikkim permit with you at all times while in the park. It's necessary to take an assistant wildlife warden or wildlife guard into the park with you. Entry to the park is Rs 5, and it costs Rs 50 per day to carry a still camera, and Rs 250 for a video camera.

Accommodation is available in rustic *log houses* at Golitar and Tumin, but you'll need to bring food, and water should be carried while you're in the park. Rates are Rs 80 per person.

Tsongo Lake

Lying 35km north-east of Gangtok, foreigners are permitted to visit this high-altitude lake; technically you should be in a group of four, and need to join a tour (US$12). The drive up to the lake is quite spectacular, although the rapid rise in altitude will leave you exhausted if you go climbing around the area. Permits are valid for a day visit only. Numerous agencies in Gangtok offer tours to the lake, and can arrange the requisite permit.

North Sikkim

Previously, foreigners were only permitted to travel as far north as Phodong, 38km by road to the north of Gangtok, which is accessible on the standard tourist permit. However, it is now possible to visit Yumthang, 102km farther north via the villages of Mangan and Chungthang. At the time of writing it was necessary to make arrangements through a travel agency in Gangtok and join a tour with a minimum of four people, at a cost of US$45 per person. The roads are often closed by landslides during the monsoon.

PHODONG

Phodong Gompa, north of Gangtok along a winding but largely tarmac road, belongs to the same order (Kagyupa) as Rumtek, but is much smaller and less ornate. After the 16th Karmapa fled from Tibet and before he installed himself in Rumtek in 1959, Phodong was the most important of Sikkim's three Kagyupa gompas (the third is Ralang Gompa). Here you can feel the timelessness of a part of Sikkim that tourists rarely visit. The gompa sits high up above the main road to Mangan and there are tremendous views down into the valley below.

Phodong is a fairly recent structure, although the original gompa here was founded, like Rumtek, in 1740. The gompa has a community of about 60 monks, many of them born in India after the Chinese occupation of Tibet. They're very friendly and will take you around and explain the salient features of the gompa. The gompa shelters an image of the 9th Karmapa, Wang Chok Dorje, who is said to have founded this gompa. The chwa-shyam is covered in ornate woodcarvings of two entwined dragons. Murals depict ranks of previous karmapas, and on the right wall (when facing the chwa-shyam) is the protective deity of the gompa, Mahakala (Tibetan: Nagpo Chenpo). On the back wall is a depiction of Padmasambhava. The ceiling is supported by six large wooden pillars and has beautifully carved cornices.

Behind the chwa-shyam is the Nagpo Chenpo meditation room, which has some disturbing and striking murals of various demonic deities dismembering miscreants in the bowels of hell. When monks are meditating here, access is prohibited to visitors. Monks can spend months alone in this room, with the disturbing murals as meditational prompts, attended only by a young student monk who brings food. Chaams are performed here in December.

Opposite the gompa is a small community of nuns who belong to the same order. **Labrang Gompa**, 4km farther uphill beyond Phodong Gompa, was established in 1844, and belongs to the Nyingmapa order. Beware of leeches when walking up here.

Places to Stay & Eat

The village of Phodong straddles the main Gangtok to Mangan road, and is about 1km north of the turn-off to the gompas towards Mangan. There are a couple of basic places to stay here.

Yak & Yeti Lodge has rooms with common bath for Rs 80/120, and doubles with attached bath for Rs 150. Hot water is supplied free in buckets, and with one hour's notice, the family here can probably rustle up a bite to eat. Rooms are spotless, and some have good views down over the valley.

Northway Lodge has doubles with common bath for Rs 120, some also with good views, and you can also get basic meals here.

Getting There & Away

Phodong village is 1km beyond the turn-off to the gompa, and buses will drop you here unless you request to be dropped off at the turn-off. From the main road, it's a farther 1km walk up to Phodong Gompa. As the main entrance to the gompa compound is at the back of the gompa, remember to walk around to the entrance via the left-hand side (ie in a clockwise direction). Buses from the SNT bus stand in Gangtok leave for Phodong at 8 and 9 am and 4 pm (Rs 20, 2½ hours). You need to set out early from Gangtok if you want to visit Phodong and Rumtek gompas and return the same day, as the last transport to Gangtok passes through Phodong at about 3 pm. During the season, you may be able to get a share jeep to Phodong from Children's Park taxi stand.

YUMTHANG VALLEY
• **alt 3564m**

The Yumthang Valley lies 140km north of Gangtok. This region has recently been opened to foreigners, but trekking is still prohibited. Indian tourists are permitted to visit and have left a trail of rubbish in their wake. The best time to visit is in April and May, when the rhododendrons are in full bloom. There are **hot springs** here, covered by a wooden shelter, and a few simple *lodges*.

To get here, you'll need to join a tour (minimum of four people required), and local travel agencies can arrange the requisite permits. The road from Gangtok follows the deep valley of the Teesta River, crossing a spectacular gorge over the Rang Rang suspension bridge.

The town of **Mangan** lies 60km from Gangtok; the valley branching off to the north-east is the restricted Lepcha homeland of Dzongu. Another 40km north the road reaches Chungthang where the military presence intensifies; no photography is allowed in this area. As the road winds higher it passes the settlement of Lachlung and the views improve until you reach the pine forests and rhododendrons of Yumthang, surrounded by 6000m peaks. Tour bookings can be made in Gangtok, but at US$45 per day few foreigners bother. See Organised Tours & Treks in the Gangtok section for details.

West Sikkim

West Sikkim is attracting more and more visitors. Its main attractions, other than trekking up to Dzongri at the base of Kanchenjunga, are the two old gompas of Pemayangtse and Tashiding, and trekking in the Pemayangtse area.

The roads are sealed for the most part between Jorethang and Legship, but beyond

Legship, to Tashiding and Yuksom, they are unsealed, and are subject to landslides.

JORETHANG

An important transport hub and administrative centre, Jorethang lies on the east side of the Rangeet River, only 30km north of Darjeeling, and flanked by its twin city, Naya Bazaar. Jorethang actually lies in the administrative district of South Sikkim – the Rangeet River here marks the boundary between south and west Sikkim. The town is pleasantly sited at the confluence of the Great Rangeet and Rangman rivers, surrounded by wooded hills, and with a colourful market along a strip in the centre of the main road. Inhabitants are engaged in fishing, growing ginger and cultivating orange orchards.

A small staircase opposite the bus stand (enter through the gate here) leads – in a steep five minute walk – to a tiny **gompa** belonging to the Nyingmapa order. The prayer room shelters small images of Sakyamuni Buddha flanked by Avalokiteshvara (Tibetan: Chenresig) on the left and Padmasambhava on the right. There are good views of the environs from the terrace in front of the gompa.

Places to Stay & Eat

Hotel Rangeet Valley (☎ 03595-57263) opposite the bus stand, has rooms with attached bath, nets and fans for Rs 130.

Hotel Namgyal, just past the bus stand towards the bridge, is the best place to stay. Some of the doubles have balconies overlooking the confluence of the Rangeet and Rangman rivers. Singles/doubles/triples with bath are Rs 150/300/450, and are spotless.

Getting There & Away

From Jorethang, there are direct buses to Yuksom at 8 and 9.30 am (Rs 50, three hours), and to Legship at 11.30 am and 4.30 pm (one hour), continuing to Gezing (Rs 19, 2½ hours). There are share jeeps to Darjeeling (Rs 60, three hours), Gangtok (three hours), Shiliguri (3½ hours), Gezing (2½ hours) and Legship (one hour).

LEGSHIP

Legship lies 100km west of Gangtok, and 27km north of Jorethang, on the banks of the Rangeet River. It's a chaotic and cluttered little village surrounded by wooded hills, and has a certain ramshackle appeal, with the colourful fruits and vegies piled in pyramids in wooden shacks flanking the main road. A little footbridge spans the river to a small **temple** sacred to Shiva. There's a police checkpoint in Legship.

There's only one place to stay, *Hotel Trishna*, with five doubles with bath and geyser for Rs 200/250.

From Legship you can walk to the hot springs of **Phur Chachu** in about 30 minutes. There is basic accommodation in *wooden huts*, but you'll need to bring your own food. A cave here is revered as the site where Padmasambhava meditated.

GEZING

☎ 03595

The road from Legship leaves the river and ascends high up above the village for 10km to Gezing, an important transport junction, but not a very attractive place. The best time to be here is on Friday, when villagers from outlying regions bring their produce into town and a colourful and busy market dominates the main square. There's a small post office next to the Hotel Kanchanzonga, and travellers cheques (except Visa) can be exchanged at the Central Bank of India, down a lane behind the town square.

There are half a dozen hotels around the town square, all rather grim. The *Hotel Attri* (☎ 50602) is the best, uphill from the main square with the police station on the ground floor. Rooms cost Rs 450 with bath and hot water, and there are good views.

There are SNT buses to Gangtok at 9 am and 1 pm (Rs 48, 4½ hours); and to Pelling (Rs 6, 30 minutes) at 8.30 am, 1 and 2 pm (many more buses on Friday). To Yuksom, buses leave at 1 and 2 pm (Rs 25, four hours); there are also buses to Tashiding, Jorethang and Shiliguri. For Kalimpong, change buses at either Meli Bazaar or Teesta Bazaar; for Darjeeling change at Jorethang.

There are numerous share jeeps to Pelling (Rs 15), and also to Gangtok via Jorethang or Rablonga (both Rs 90, 4½ hours). There is one share jeep daily for Tashiding and Yuksom (Rs 60). A taxi from the town square will charge Rs 150 to Pelling.

PELLING
☎ 03593 • alt 2000m (approx)

Pelling is a pleasant base from which to visit points of interest in the area. It is perched high on top of a ridge, and there are magnificent views of the snowy peaks to the north. From here, the perspective is much the same as from Darjeeling. From Pelling, Kanchenjunga (8598m) looks smaller than the distinctive flat-topped Kabru (7338m) to its left, which is closer. To the right of Kanchenjunga is the pyramid-shaped Pandim (6691m). The massive bulk dominating the foreground to the right is Narsingh (5825m).

There are no foreign exchange facilities in Pelling. The closest place to change money is at the Central Bank of India in Gezing. Many new hotels are being built for Bangali tourists.

Cottage Industries Training Centre

About 150 young people are taught traditional handicrafts such as woodcarving, handloom weaving, bamboo canework and carpet weaving at this centre in Lower Pelling. There is a small showroom here where you can buy goods made at the centre. Opposite the centre is a small woollens centre where you can buy handknits such as jumpers, hats and gloves.

Pemayangtse Gompa
• alt 2085m

Surrounded on two sides by snow-capped mountains, Pemayangtse (Perfect Sublime Lotus) is one of the state's oldest and most important gompas. It was founded in 1705 during the reign of the third chogyal, Chador Namgyal, and its monks enjoyed pre-eminence among the religious community of Sikkim, admittance restricted to those of pure Tibetan race, 'celibate and undeformed'. They were known as *ta-sang* (pure monks), and the head lama of Pemayangtse was invested with the honour of anointing the chogyal with holy water.

The gompa belongs to the Nyingmapa order, the most common of the Buddhist orders of Sikkim. As with all the gompas of this order in Sikkim, it enshrines a prominent image of Padmasambhava. Here he is framed by an extraordinary woodcarving of serpents entwined around a staff, and there is a particularly gruesome image of Dorje Phurba, and a more equanimous image of Avalokiteshvara (Tibetan: Chenresig).

The gompa, damaged in the earthquakes of 1913 and 1960, has been reconstructed several times. It is a plain three storey structure, with an ornate interior. In an upstairs hall, elaborately carved cornices frame the ceiling which is supported by brightly painted beams. The resident monks engage in much drum beating, cymbal clashing, bell ringing, horn blowing and chanting. On the 3rd floor is the *Zandog-palri*, a seven tiered painted wooden model of the abode of Padmasambhava, complete with rainbows, angels and the whole panoply of Buddhas and Bodhisattvas. The model was built single-handedly by the late Dungzin Rinpoche in five years.

In February each year the chaam is performed. The exact dates are the 28th and 29th days of the 12th Tibetan lunar month.

Pemayangtse is about 6km uphill from Gezing on the Pelling road, 2.5km before Pelling. The SNT buses between Gezing and Pelling pass by the turn-off for Pemayangtse, from where it's a steep 10 minute walk up to the gompa. See the Walks around Pelling section following for directions on foot.

Walks Around Pelling

There are some fine walks in the area surrounding Pelling, but unfortunately whenever you leave the main roads, those blood-sucking foes of trekkers worldwide – leeches – are lying in wait to secure themselves firmly to any piece of flesh they can grab on to. See the Cuts, Bites & Stings entry in the Health section in the Facts for the Visitor chapter for ways of dealing with these tenacious little critters.

It takes about four to five hours to walk from Pelling to Tashiding, with some steep ascents along the way, particularly for the last section just before the village. Bring snacks and water, as there's nothing to eat along the way.

Pemayangtse Gompa It takes about 40 minutes to walk to Pemayangtse Gompa (see earlier). Follow the main road back towards Gezing until you come to a crossing where there is a large, white stupa. A sign here points the direction to the gompa. Behind the stupa is a seat made of stone, known as the **Choeshay Gang**, which is supported by the branches of a tree. The seat was built to commemorate the visit to Sikkim of the Tibetan nun Jaytsun Mingyur Paldon, who delivered a dharma lecture to the monks of Pemayangtse.

Rabdentse Palace A 30 minute walk past the turn-off to Pemayangtse (towards Gezing) will bring you to a trail that leads in a few minutes' walk to the scattered ruins of the Rabdentse Palace. Follow the main road until a curve, from where the trail leads off to the left. The palace was founded by the second king of Sikkim, Tenzung Namgyal, in 1670 CE. From here there are fine views across to the village of Tashiding and Tashiding Gompa.

Sangachoeling Gompa A 45 minute walk uphill to the west of Pelling will bring you to the Sangachoeling Gompa (Land of the Sacred Spell), on a ridge above the village. The path commences from behind the soccer field, also known locally as the helipad. It's a beautiful walk along a steep, wooded path, with magnificent glimpses of Kanchenjunga and adjacent peaks to the north at intervals, but be prepared for a bloodletting, as it's riddled with leeches. If you reach a grassy ridge, you've passed the

gompa; double back towards the wooden buildings behind you.

Dubdi Gompa at Yuksom was the first gompa to be founded in Sikkim; however, Sangachoeling was the first to be built. The original building dated from 1697, but the current building was built after the old gompa was destroyed in an earthquake. Unlike Pemayangtse, which only admitted 'pure monks of pure Tibetan race', Sangachoeling had a much more egalitarian admittance policy, and was open to members of all classes and races, including Bhutias, Lepchas and Limbus. It was one of the few gompas in Sikkim that admitted women as nuns.

Sangachoeling belongs to the Nyingmapa order, and shelters fine images of Padmasambhava and the Buddha, among others. The walls are of course completely covered in paintings, but the colours are more muted than usual, and the woodcarving in this gompa is less ostentatious than in some larger gompas.

An upstairs room enshrines some less ornate images, as well as cloth-bound sacred texts. In a small room at the back are some of the original clay statues, some of which still retain fragments of colour. Beside the gompa is a Buddhist cremation ground used by Bhutia and Lepcha villagers.

Rani Dhunga Four hours' walk beyond Sangachoeling is the Rani Dhunga, or Queen's Stone. Here a large stone is worshipped as the image of the female Buddhist deity Rani Dhunga. It's a very steep walk along an ancient trail once traversed by the king and his courtiers. A 10km walk towards Dentam will bring you to the **Changay Waterfalls**. The **Rimbi Waterfalls** are by the roadside on the route to Khecheopari Lake and Yuksom, about 12km from Pelling.

Places to Stay & Eat

There's a lot of building going on in Pelling. Lower Pelling has many new hotels, though some of them prefer only large Indian groups.

Ladakh Guesthouse, close to the Hotel Garuda towards the helipad, is a rustic

Sikkimese house with five rooms, all sharing the bathroom (with geyser). Doubles/triples are 250/350.

Hotel Garuda (☎ 50614) is in the centre where the buses stop. It's a popular travellers haunt with excellent trekking information. You can also store excess gear here while you trek. Dorm beds cost Rs 80, or there are basic rooms for Rs 100/200 with common bath and doubles with bath cost Rs 400. It can get noisy. The food is cheap and occasionally tasty but the service is memorably inept.

Hotel View Point (☎ 50614) is a more modern, well-run hotel in a quiet location on the right side of the helipad in Upper Pelling. Doubles/triples with bath and geyser cost Rs 300/450.

Hotel Kabur (☎ 50685), in Upper Pelling towards Pemayangtse, is a bit overpriced but the family is friendly. Doubles/triples are Rs 550/600 with bath. There's also a slightly pricey restaurant here.

Sikkim Tourist Centre (☎ 50788) is a good mid-range hotel popular with tour groups. The rooms (all doubles) have hot bath and cost Rs 500 (Rs 600 with a view). There's a good restaurant on the top floor and staff can organise tours around Sikkim.

Hotel Mt Pandim (☎ 50756), known locally as the tourist lodge, is 2km outside Pelling, at the foot of the road leading up to Pemayangtse. It's a hulking, slightly run-down place run by Sikkim Tourism with a vaguely Soviet-era atmosphere. At least the views from the garden are superb. Rooms with bath cost Rs 550/650 or Rs 750/850 for deluxe rooms with a view of Kanchenjunga. There's also a restaurant.

Getting There & Away

Although a number of buses pass through Pelling, the choice is far greater from Gezing. It's a 50 minute steep downhill walk to Gezing.

Jeeps leave for Gangtok at 6 am and noon (Rs 100), and to Shiliguri also at 6 am (Rs 100). Tickets should be booked the day before at the *paan* (betel nut and leaves for chewing) stall between the Sikkim Tourist Centre and the Hotel Garuda. To charter a taxi to Khecheopari Lake and Yuksom costs Rs 650 and 700 respectively.

There numerous are share jeeps down to Gezing on market day (Friday) in the morning (Rs 15).

KHECHEOPARI LAKE

Pronounced 'catch-a-perry', and sometimes spelt Khechepari, Khecheopalri or Khechupherei, this place is a popular destination for trekkers. The sacred lake lies in a depression surrounded by prayer flags and forested hills. Resist the temptation to swim, as it's a holy place. If you feel like a dip, you can swim in the river downhill from Pelling en route to the lake. Take care!

By the lake shore is the small Lepcha village of **Tsojo**, and about 1.5km above the lake is the **Khecheopari Gompa**. On the 15th and 16th days of the first month of the Tibetan lunar calendar (around March), a festival is held at the lake. There is a *trekkers' hut* and a *Rest House* at the lake. The trekkers' hut is grimy and dark – not very salubrious. A bed at the Rest House will cost around Rs 80. There are several *chai shops* at the lake. It gets very cold here at night, so bring warm gear with you.

By road the lake is about 27km from Pelling; the walking trail is shorter, but much steeper, and will take about 4½ hours on foot.

From Khecheopari it is possible to continue on foot to Yuksom. The short cut is confusing, so ask for advice whenever you meet anyone en route. It should take three hours to cover the distance between the lake and Yuksom.

There's one bus daily between Pelling and Khecheopari, leaving Pelling at 3 pm (two hours), and returning at 7 am.

TASHIDING

To visit this village, with its beautiful gompa high above it, you require a special endorsement on your tourist or trekking permit. The village lies 16km north-east of Legship along a ridge with dramatic valleys falling away on either side, culminating in the cone-shaped hill on which the gompa is perched.

SIKKIM

Tashiding Gompa

It's a steep 45 minute walk up to the gompa on the flat terrace of the summit. Hundreds of prayer flags create an ethereal ambience, particularly in the early morning.

Tashiding (the Devoted Central Glory) is a much less ostentatious gompa than Pemayangtse. Originally founded in 1716 by Ngadak Sempa Chempo, it belongs to the Nyingmapa order. It was extended and renovated by the third chogyal, Chador Namgyal.

As you enter the gompa compound, the building immediately to your right surrounded by prayer wheels houses the sacred *bhumpa*, or water vessel. During the annual Bhumchu Festival, celebrated on the 15th day of the first month of the Tibetan lunar calendar (March), the water in the vase is mixed with water from the Rathong and Rangeet rivers and distributed to devotees by the head lama of Tashiding. The bowl is then refilled and locked away for one year. When it is again taken out, the lama makes prognostications according to the amount of water still contained in the vessel. A low level of water is a sign of ill tidings, heralding disease, a poor harvest, drought or famine; if the vessel is full to the brim, there will be bloodshed in Sikkim, but if the vessel is half full, there will be an abundant crop and peace will reign in Sikkim. The building is only opened on special festival days.

The original gompa was dismantled, and six of the eight pillars that supported its ceiling were salvaged and installed in the new building, on which construction commenced in 1987. The main prayer hall enshrines an image of the Buddha flanked by four Bodhisattvas on either side.

During the festival of Panghlapsol, celebrated on the 15th day of the seventh lunar month (August/September), the images of Kanchenjunga and Yabdu are brought out to be worshipped, and rich food offerings of bread, biscuits, grains and fruit are placed before them.

At the south end of the ridge, beyond the prayer hall and on a lower terrace, are numerous chörtens. Remember to walk around the chörtens in a clockwise direction.

The gompa is surrounded by numerous auxiliary buildings with elaborate facades and ornate wooden fretwork and carving.

Places to Stay & Eat

Blue Bird Hotel is a simple but welcoming little place with rooms for Rs 40 and good *dhal bhat* (dhal and rice) in the restaurant. *Hotel Laxmi* also has a restaurant and rooms for Rs 50/100. *Siniolchu Guest House* charges Rs 100 for a good room. Meals are served with the family.

Getting There & Away

There is one bus daily to Yuksom (3 pm), and in the morning it passes through at 8 am on the return journey to Legship and Gezing. Share jeeps that pass through Tashiding are often full.

The Ghost of Harbhajan Singh

Many Indian soldiers at the border garrison post of Natu La firmly believe that they are protected by the ghost of Harbhajan Singh, a Sikh private who disappeared on border patrol in the 1960s. Sentries who have fallen asleep at their post at night claim to have been woken by an invisible slap. A bed made for Singh at a makeshift shrine is found curiously ruffled every morning. The Chinese have even spotted a turbaned officer patrolling the mountains high above the Chinese defences – an apparition that immediately sparked a real security alert.

The ghostly guard has become such an institution that the local general now annually sends his jeep to the border to transfer Singh to Shiliguri, where a sleeper berth awaits to take him home to Amritsar for his annual leave. Local people have proved a little more pragmatic, if not downright sceptical – an armed bodyguard (perhaps the one who suggested the ghost be given leave?) travels with the ghost every year to prevent freeloaders from sleeping in the 'empty' berth.

Treks in Sikkim

At present trekking in Sikkim is restricted to the Yuksom-Dzongri region in south-western Sikkim, though trekking agents claim that they will soon be able to arrange treks in both northern and eastern Sikkim.

Yuksom-Dzongri-Goecha La Trek

This is the most popular trek in Sikkim and takes in superb views of Kanchenjunga (8586m). In order to undertake this trek you must get together a group of at least four people and make arrangements through a recognised travel agency in Gangtok, who will also arrange your trekking permit.

Agents usually charge between US$25 and US$60 per person per day, including food, yaks and porters. What they actually provide on the trek will depend on your negotiating skills but make sure everyone is clear about what will be provided – particularly the food. Most do not have good sleeping bags or tents and tend to schedule their stages to stay in the State Government huts that have been constructed on the trek. At the height of the season there's not enough space at the huts and your trekking company will need to provide tents. Whatever the option, it is imperative not to trek too high too quickly and additional days should be reserved before reaching the camp at Dzongri (4025m).

The trek can be undertaken either in the pre-monsoon season from April till the end of June when the rhododendrons are in full bloom, or in the post monsoon season from early October till the middle of November.

From Yuksom (1630m) the trail follows the Rathong Valley through unspoilt forests to Baktim (2740m) where there's a forest resthouse. From Baktim there is a steep ascent to the village of Tsokha (3050m), where a couple of lodges provide overnight accommodation. Above Tsokha the trail enters magnificent rhododendron forests to an intermediary camp at Pethang (3760m). It's a wise idea to either bring tents and spend a night here or spend two nights at Tsokha to acclimatise.

A further stage brings you to Dzongri (4025m) where there are trekkers' huts. From Dablakang, 200m above Dzongri there are excellent views of Kanchenjunga (8586m) and many other impressive peaks on the Singali Ridge that marks the border between Sikkim and Nepal. If spending more than one night at Dzongri, walk up to Dzongri La (4550m, 4 hours return) for great views of Kabru (7317m) and Rathong (6679m).

From Dzongri, the trail drops steeply down to the river where there's a new trekkers' hut; follow the river to Thangshing (3840m) where there is another trekkers' hut. The final stop is at the trekker's hut at Samiti Lake (4200m) from which an early morning assault is made up to the head-spinning Goecha La (4940m) for the best views of Kanchenjunga. Then it's down to Thangshing for the night and back to Yuksom two days later.

Stage 1	Yuksom to Tsokha	(7 hrs)
Stage 2	Tsokha to Pethang	(3 hrs)
Stage 3	Acclimatisation Day	
Stage 4	Pethang to Dzongri	(2-3 hrs)
Stage 5	Dzongri to Samiti Lake	(6-7 hrs)
Stage 6	Samiti Lake to Goecha La and return to Thangshing	(8 hrs)
Stage 7	Thangshing to Tsokha	(6-7 hrs)
Stage 8	Tsokha to Yuksom	(5-6 hrs)

SIKKIM

YUKSOM

Yuksom, 19km north of Tashiding, is as far north as you can travel in Sikkim by road. Although just a small village in a remote corner of Sikkim, it played a significant role in the former country's history, being the site where pioneer lama Lhatsun Chempo, together with Kathok Rikzin Chempo and Ngadak Sempa Chempo (the last of whom founded the Tashiding Gompa), crossed from Tibet into Sikkim and established the Nyingmapa order of Tibetan Buddhism. Yuksom was originally the capital of the kingdom, and Sikkim's earliest monastic community was founded here, on the site on which Dubdi Gompa was later erected. Most travellers wind up here to undertake the trek to Dzongri. From Yuksom there are fine views of both the north and south peaks of Kabru.

Norbugang Chörten

Norbugang chörten is at the end of a track which branches to the left just before Kathok Lake. It was built with materials brought from all over Sikkim, and commemorates the consecration of the first chogyal, Phuntsog Namgyal, by the three pioneer Tibetan lamas.

Dubdi Gompa

Dubdi (the Hermit's Cell), was founded by Lhatsun Chempo and built in 1701, making it one of Sikkim's oldest gompas. There are no longer monks at Dubdi, and it is only opened during special Buddhist festivals. At other times, you may be able to get permission to enter from the caretaker in the village. Check with locals for his current whereabouts. It takes about 40 minutes to walk up to the gompa along a steep path. Go past the hospital to the end of the motorable road, where you'll pass three disused water-driven prayer wheels. After crossing a bridge, take the track to the right. Beware of leeches in summer.

The first building you'll come to is a double storey stone and wood edifice with intricate carving on the facade, although the once-vibrant paint is fading. Inside this hall are enshrined images of Padmasambhava, Lhatsun Chempo, Chenresig and the first king of Sikkim, Phuntsog Namgyal. The walls are covered with paintings of particularly wrathful deities, and there is a painting of the Wheel of Life in an upstairs chamber.

The second building is a lovely single storey stone and wood building. The paintings inside are recent.

Places to Stay & Eat

Hotel Arpan has a few singles and doubles for Rs 80/100, and serves basic meals. It's about 800m from the centre of town on the main road, near the school.

Hotel Wild Orchid has clean rooms for Rs 75/100.

Hotel Dzongrila has basic rooms for Rs 50/100, as well as good food, beer and chang. It's run by a friendly, English-speaking family.

Hotel Demazong is a clean, well-run place with dorm beds for Rs 60, doubles with shared bath for Rs 200, and doubles with bath and geyser for Rs 400.

There are also two **trekkers' huts** and a **Forest Rest House**, which must be booked in Gangtok.

Hotel Tashi Gang is Yuksom's only upmarket hotel, in an unmissable location on a hill. The charming timber-floored rooms have fine views. Standard rooms cost Rs 500/700, while suites cost Rs 1200. There's also a good restaurant and a pleasant garden terrace where a bottle of Dansberg beer costs Rs 50.

Getting There & Away

There is one bus daily (at 7 am) to Gezing (Rs 22) via Tashiding and Legship; and also share jeeps to Gezing and Jorethang (Rs 50, 6.30 am).

Arunachal Pradesh

One of the most remote regions in India, Arunachal Pradesh borders Bhutan, China and Myanmar (Burma). Formerly known as the North East Frontier Agency (NEFA), Arunachal became a state in 1987; the name is variously translated as 'land of the dawn-lit mountains' or 'land of the rising sun'. Arunachal is the most sparsely populated state in India, with barely a million people scattered across 84,000 sq km. The state lies between the swampy Brahmaputra Valley and the high ridgelines of the Himalaya and Patkai ranges, encompassing a broad swathe of rugged highlands hooking around to touch Nagaland in the south-east with a few areas of plains along the Assam border. About 70% of the land is still forested, although rapacious logging companies and locals after a quick buck have already sacrificed a great deal of this crucial resource.

There are 66 or so tribes (though the 1971 census counted as many as 115), ranging from slash-and-burn animist farmers to the Tibetan Buddhist Monpa villages in the west to Thai-speaking people, the Khampti, in the east. The Monpa and the Khampti were the only tribes with a written language before schools were set up by the government. The largest groups are the Adi, in the Along area, the Mishmi in the ranges north-east of Pasighat, and the Nishi around Itanagar. See the Peoples of the Himalaya boxed text in the Facts about the Region chapter for details of the tribes of Arunachal Pradesh.

The *adivasis* (tribal people) are usually friendly, though often visibly surprised to see foreigners. Don't take their hospitality for granted ; if people intimate they would prefer you left them alone, do so. Be polite and ask permission before taking photos .

One sign of Arunachal's status as a virgin destination is the total lack of anywhere to change money; change as much as you'll need (and more) in Gauhati (see Getting There & Away later for details). There is scope for trekking and rafting, but except for

Arunachal Pradesh at a Glance

Population: 1.14 million (year 2000 estimate)
Area: 83,743 sq km
Capital: Itanagar

Highlights

- **Tawang Gompa** – Take the time to see one of the biggest gompas in India, with an ancient library and beautiful golden statue of Sakyamuni. The surrounding region and friendly Buddhist villagers also justify the arduous trip.

- **Apatani Valley** – Visit this unique pocket of sedentary agriculture, centred on Ziro in central Arunachal and surrounded by lands farmed using slash-and-burn methods. It is easy to walk out into the paddy fields where people still wear traditional dress.

- **Namdapha National Park** – Relax in the peace of this vast wilderness. It is difficult to reach in the isolated eastern corner of the state but the charming accommodation and surroundings offer a taste of the otherwise off-limits regions of Arunachal.

a few pricey package tours (organised in advance) these activities are not yet available.

Much of the state, particularly the high altitude regions, is off limits, not just because this is a sensitive border region but because there simply aren't any roads. The Indian army spends vast sums supplying border posts by helicopter. On the other hand, the roads that do exist are kept in excellent condition by the Border Roads Organisation, especially compared with the decayed byways of Assam.

History

Some scholars argue that the tribes of Arunachal appear in the *Mahabharata* as the

ARUNACHAL PRADESH

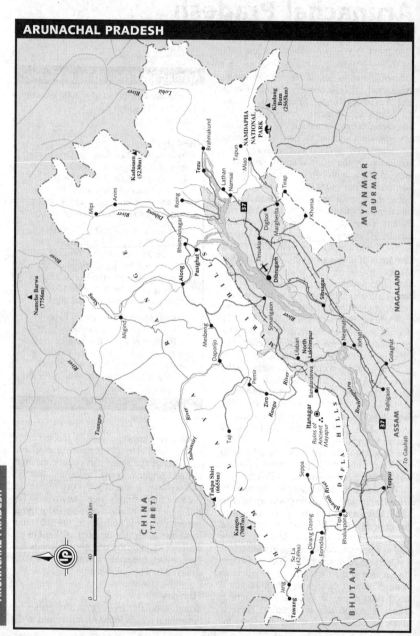

Kirata peoples, who fought under the king of Pragjyotisha (western Assam) in the Battle of Kurukshetra. However, this might be a case of Indian historical nationalism, attempting to place the peoples from every corner of modern-day India into the ancient epic.

In the words of Verrier Elwin, an English anthropologist who became an Indian citizen, 'the history of what is known as (Arunachal Pradesh) ascends for hundreds of years into the mist of tradition and mythology'.

Several archaeological sites have been found in the state, mostly close to the Assam border. The ruins of Malinithan near Pasighat are thought to date from the 10th century, and feature a stepped temple platform built of large stones instead of the usual baked brick. Stone images of the Hindu deities Durga and Nandi as well as celestial maidens have been found here.

After the Ahoms invaded the Brahmaputra Valley from Myanmar (Burma) in 1228 and settled in Upper Assam, a number of Burmese hill peoples followed in their wake and settled in eastern Arunachal, including the Singpho, Khamti, Nocte and Wancho tribes. The histories of the other tribes are, as Elwin put it, obscured in myth.

During Raj times the area that is now Arunachal Pradesh was not developed and British administration basically stopped at the 'Inner Line' – the border with Assam. Between there and the Outer Line (the Tibetan border) the British administered the territory only politically (ie left it alone unless Tibet happened to claim it). As late as 1938 the policy was changed and the British decided to extend their administration up to the international border in some areas. This decision was influenced by the increasing likelihood of war in Asia and by reports that Tibetan officials were collecting taxes from Buddhist communities along the border. The Japanese invasion of Nagaland and Manipur in 1942 hastened matters considerably, and the following year the decision was made to extend British rule throughout the territory. In 1944 the anthropologist Christoph Von Haimendorf visited Ziro and

The Stilwell Road

It's hard to believe now, but during WWII eastern Arunachal Pradesh provided a vital link between British India and the beleaguered forces of Chiang Kaishek in China, who were under threat from Japanese invaders. After the main Burma Road was cut by the Japanese in 1942, thousands of tons of military and medical supplies were hauled through the jungles and tribal areas of Arunachal Pradesh and Myanmar's (then Burma's) Kachin state, before finally reaching China's Yunnan province. Hundreds of Indian and Allied troops died in the construction of the road, named after General Joseph Stilwell, the US commander in the region.

In 1999, 1500 wartime graves were discovered in Arunachal Pradesh and excavations have now started in earnest to unearth one of the great unknown chapters of WWII. After the war the road fell into disuse – today it is used mainly by separatist insurgents as they move to and from camps in northern Myanmar (Burma).

the Apatani Valley to 'prepare the ground for extension of administrative control'; it was the first time Arunachal had been systematically studied. The next big shift came in 1954 when the Indian government decided to extend the reach of the administration farther and created the North-East Frontier Agency (NEFA). The territory was governed from Shillong, then the capital of Assam but now the capital of Meghalaya.

The October 1962 Chinese invasion of the west of the territory brought NEFA to the attention of the central government in the most dramatic fashion possible. Without warning the People's Liberation Army swept through Tawang and Bomdila to as far as Tezpur on the plains of Assam. Before the Indian army could regroup and counterattack, the Chinese withdrew completely, probably having fulfilled their mission of humiliating the Indian government. It is

Verrier Elwin

As the de facto administrator of the North-East Frontier Agency (NEFA) from 1954 until 1964, which later became Arunachal Pradesh, Verrier Elwin (1902-64) was the last Englishman to hold real power in India. Except of course, he was by then an Indian citizen, finishing a remarkable journey from life as an Oxford cleric to becoming a close friend of India's first prime minister Jawaharlal Nehru, and earning respect as the guardian of tribal India.

Elwin's father was a bishop in Sierra Leone, West Africa, his mother was a strict and rather eccentric fundamentalist Christian. After a typically upper class public school education he went to Oxford and became an Anglican clergyman. His calling led him to India in 1927, where he joined a missionary group which embraced the teachings of Mahatma Gandhi, which in turn transformed Elwin into a supporter of the Indian National Congress. But by the early 1930s his activities with the Congress and Gandhi had been curtailed by British repression. Finding himself at a loose end he moved to the tribal lands of the Gond people in modern-day Madhya Pradesh in 1932. Here he began to reject both Gandhi's ideology and that of the church, believing that Gandhi's program of a strict diet, the prohibition of alcohol and home spinning were unsuitable for *adivasis* (tribal people). Likewise he felt the church's missionary efforts did more harm than good to tribal societies. On a personal level he embraced alcohol and tribal women with vigour, which brought him notoriety among prudish critics.

For 15 years he lived among the tribes of central India, marrying a Gond woman in 1941 and writing many books on tribal life, mostly anthropological studies and translations of poetry. After Independence in 1947 his academic reputation continued to grow and, having cut ties with Britain, he chose to stay on in India.

In 1954 he was appointed by Nehru to be tribal adviser to the Governor of Assam, effectively making him the leader of NEFA. His experience of seeing the adivasis of central India ruined by the arrival of moneylenders, missionaries and insensitive government officials led

perhaps significant that the Chinese invasion practically retraced the route that the fleeing Dalai Lama took in 1959 before he found refuge in India. It was certainly one of the stranger invasions of recent decades, one that China has never really explained and India definitely doesn't want repeated.

While the Indian military has maintained huge bases in the west of the territory since the invasion, the central government adopted a policy of gradually opening up the rest of the state without swamping the traditional cultures. Planned by the anthropologist Verrier Elwin (see the boxed text later in this chapter), this policy has seen the tribes of Arunachal fare rather better in modern India that some of the exploited tribes of central India.

In 1971, NEFA was separated from Assam and renamed Arunachal Pradesh.

The first full legislative elections were held in 1978, and the first government fell soon after due to the common Indian habit of political defection. An Adi politician, Gegong Apang, came to power in 1980. Of all the states of the north-east, only Arunachal has not suffered guerilla wars by militants wishing to establish either an independent country or a separate state within India. This can partly be explained by the sheer diversity of peoples, allowing no one group to have political or economic ascendancy, and partly by a reasonably effective state administration and a central government anxious to see the state remain in India.

Some cracks in this unity occurred with the fall of Gegong Apang after 19 years as Chief Minister in 1999. Apang was brought down by a rebellion in his Arunachal Congress party led by Nishi parliamentarians,

Verrier Elwin

him to shut off the territory from the rest of India (except for his carefully chosen cadre of administrative officers). Assamese politicians resented the territory being separated from Assam, and Hindi rather than Assamese being selected as the language of education. Elwin also faced attacks from Indian intellectuals who argued he was trying to keep the tribal people as museum specimens for the benefit of anthropologists. He argued back that tribal people needed to be free from interference and would only benefit from development if it didn't destroy the good points of their culture. He was particularly suspicious of Indian officials who spoke of uplifting and reforming the tribal people – he knew that positive changes could only come from within tribal society.

Recurrent bouts of ill health after years in the backwoods shortened Elwin's colourful life, and he died in 1964.

But Nehru (and, to a degree, later prime ministers) supported Elwin's philosophy of allowing NEFA's tribal people to develop their communities at their own pace, without being overwhelmed by inappropriate development and psychologically undermined by better skilled, better educated settlers. NEFA gradually evolved to statehood in 1987 as Arunachal Pradesh, but the strict regulations curtailing the entry of outsiders remains. Today you can see the relative success of Elwin's policies by the lack of poverty in Arunachal, and by the lack of separatist movements (for which the region is unique) among the tribal states of North-East India.

Elwin's many books on NEFA are quite hard to find these days, although *A Philosophy for NEFA*, *The Art of the North-East Frontier of India* and *Democracy for NEFA* can be found in major Indian libraries. Easier to find is *The Tribal World of Verrier Elwin – an autobiography*, published by Oxford India, and the excellent biography *Savaging the Civilised* by Ramachandra Gufa.

and by MPs from Tirap and Changlang districts (the south-eastern 'hook') demanding a separate state. Apang has been accused of playing off tribes against each other and of using money from logging to stay in power.

The North-East Region of India has long been known for bitter fighting between indigenous peoples and immigrants. In Arunachal, the only group that seems to be resented is the Hinayana Buddhist Chakmas. The Chakmas were settled in Arunachal by Nehru after fleeing the Chittagong Hill Tracts of Bangladesh in the 1960s, when the Kapitai Lake dam drowned their valleys.

In the 1990s Christian evangelical groups have been rapidly winning converts in the state, although exact figures are difficult to get as more than a few foreign missionary groups exaggerate their success to attract money back in their home countries. Nevertheless the Christian community is growing fast; one explanation is that as old tribal loyalties break down under the complex pressures of the modern world, people are seeking a new community. As a response to this, Hindu missionaries such as the Ramakrishna Society are also active, and a new religion combing elements of the tribal faiths called Donyi Polo has also sprung up (see the Donyi Polo boxed text later in this chapter).

Geography

The rugged ranges of Arunachal have created a wide variety of microclimates, according to the altitude and position (whether the land is in a rain shadow or facing the full brunt of the monsoon). The lowlands bordering Assam receive an enormous amount of rain, up to 500cm a year. As Verrier Elwin said, 'the rain comes down

ARUNACHAL PRADESH

all through the year, breaking the usual Indian rule of hot, cold and rainy seasons'. The areas of heaviest rainfall are generally farmed by the *jhum* (slash-and-burn) method. In these areas the steep slopes of the hillsides are cultivated and left to regenerate. In drier areas the valley floor is farmed on a permanent basis, and in places where the upper slopes receive a lot of rain but the valley floor is relatively dry, both methods are used.

The crests of the Himalaya along the Tibetan border between Bhutan and where the Siang River cuts through the range, vary from an average of 6400m at the Kangto Massif near Tawang to an average of 5000m near the Siang. The Himalaya culminate in the 7756m Namche Barwa in Tibet, just north of where the Siang River flows into Arunachal. East of the river the mountains vary greatly in height, from 2700m to 5800m up to the tri-junction of China, India and Myanmar (Burma). The Patkai ranges along the Myanmar (Burma) border gradually descend from 4500m to 1800m where Arunachal meets Nagaland.

Permits

Foreigners are currently permitted to visit Bhalukpong, Bomdila, Seppa and Tawang in the west, Itanagar, the road from Ziro through Daporijo and Along to Pasighat, and Namdapha National Park. It is unlikely travel restrictions will be eased (and they could well be tightened up again if any insurgencies start up, or if the border dispute with China heats up again). The state government charges foreigners US$50 per day just to be in the state, although you'd be lucky to get a permit without being part of a package tour. An all-inclusive package tour costs US$150, which has been strikingly unsuccessful in attracting tourists. That said however, the fees theoretically do entitle you to travel on any public transport and stay in any hotel.

Foreigners must apply in groups of at least four people, though it is a grey area whether or not the four people actually have to travel together (although a group of less

than four must pay a total of US$200 per day). You must apply to the permit offices at least three weeks in advance (a month in advance would be safer) and supply four passport-sized photos and photocopies of the pages in your passport showing your passport number and your Indian visa. The Arunachal Bhawans (offices) have to wait for approval from the Home Secretary in Itanagar and the Ministry of Home Affairs in Delhi. Once approval is granted you then pay the total fees for your visit up-front to the bhawans, in either US dollars or the rupee equivalent. Permits are for 10 days, although if you pay for 15 days you're likely to get a 15-day permit.

If you do manage to get a permit to travel independently, the checkpoints on the various roads entering the state will detain you for possibly as long as three hours while they fill in registration forms. This makes it difficult to catch local buses, who won't want to wait for you. You will also probably be required to register with the authorities in each town you stay in – either the district magistrate's office or the local magistrate. Then you will be put up in a local government bungalow. In Itanagar, Naharlagun, Tawang, Ziro, Pasighat and Bomdila you should be allowed to stay in a local hotel.

Indian tourists need to get an inner line permit from the bhawans, and are permitted to visit any place in the state as long as it is not considered to be of military importance (ie within about 50km of the border, not including Tawang).

Arunachal Bhawans include:

Delhi
   (☎ 011-301 3915) Kautilya Marg, Chanakyapuri
Kolkata (Calcutta)
   (☎ 033-248 6500) 4B Chowringhee Place
Gauhati
   (☎ 0361-562 859) Bhaskar Nagar, off RG Baruah Rd

Organised Tours

At time of research, virtually all foreign visitors to Arunachal Pradesh were part of an organised tour. Reputable agencies that arrange package tours for foreigners (US$150 per day) as well as trekking and angling (US$150 to US$175 per day) include:

Destination North East
  (☎ 0361-511 565, fax 540 376)
  Dighalipukhuri (East), Gauhati
Himalayan Holidays
  (☎ 0360-44632, fax 45050)
  Little Rose Book Stall Complex, Naharlagun
Wild Grass
  (☎ 0361-546 827, fax 541 186)
  Baruah Bhawan, 107 MC Rd, Gauhati

Getting There & Away

Gauhati (also known as Guwahati or Gawahati) in Assam is the region's biggest city and you'll probably pass through here on your way to Arunachal.

You'd be advised to change money here. ANZ Grindlays Bank on GN Bordoloi Rd, Gauhati, is open from Monday to Friday, 10 am to 3 pm. The foreign exchange office at the Hotel Brahmaputra Ashok is another useful option.

Air Borjhav airport is 23km west of Gauhati. Indian Airlines (☎ 0361-564420) has flights to/from Kolkata (Calcutta; US$70, daily), Delhi (US$210, five per week), Agartala (US$45, three per week), Aizawl (US$75, three per week) and Imphal (US$50, two per week). From Tezpur, on the way to Bhalukpong, Indian Airlines (☎ 3712-20083) has two flights a week to Kolkata (US$80). From Dibrugarh, Indian Airlines (☎ 0373-20114) flies to Kolkata (US$95, four times weekly) and Sahara (☎ 0373-31216) flies to Delhi (US$254, four times weekly) and Gauhati (US$55, four times weekly).

Bus Gauhati's Paltan Bazaar bus stand is by the southern exit of the train station. The offices for private bus companies are also in this area and along GS Rd; the most reliable companies seem to be Blue Hills and Green Valley.

Overnight buses go to Shiliguri in Bangla (West Bengal; Rs 225, 13 hours) among many others; plus Bomdila (Rs 205, 18 hours) and Itanagar (Rs 160, 12 hours) in Arunachal.

Within Assam, there are frequent departures for Tezpur (Rs 70, five hours).

Train The most convenient points from which to get to Gauhati are Kolkata (Calcutta) and New Jalpaiguri.

From Kolkata (Howrah), it's 993km and about 24 hours to Gauhati on the *Kamrup Express* or 22 hours on the *Kanchenjunga Express* (Sealdah) at a cost of Rs 245/849 in 2nd/1st class. These trains pass through New Jalpaiguri station at 5.30 am and 6.10 pm, respectively.

Faster and more expensive is the *Rajdhani Express* which leaves Delhi on Monday, Wednesday and Saturday at 5 pm, passing through New Jalpaiguri at 1.50 pm the following day, reaching Gauhati at 8.30 pm. From Delhi it costs Rs 1650/4920 in three-tier air-con sleeper/1st class (Rs 685/1690 from New Jalpaiguri).

Itanagar

☎ 0360 • pop 17,700

The capital, Itanagar, is barely 20 years old and not especially interesting, although you do meet a cross section of Arunachal's peoples. This sprawling new capital is home to both adivasis living in traditional houses and the nascent elite living in standard-issue Indian government estates.

Itanagar is where deals are made and connections sought, where businessmen influence government officials through cultivating 'connections' with financial 'considerations'.

The state capital is also one of those intriguing places where the tribal world and the modern world meet head-on; you can see Nishi tribesmen with cane helmets zooming around on motorbikes, satellite dishes sprouting from the roofs of traditional houses and local men drinking Indian whisky and throwing away their money on lottery games on the street.

Orientation & Information

Orientation is easy – there's one main road. At Zero Point a short road leads off to the Buddha Vihar and the Hotel Arun Subansiri. From here the highway road winds around past the tennis courts for 2km to the Secretariat complex, and ends 1.5km farther on in Ganga Market, where there are several hotels and the bus station.

The nearest tourist office is in Naharlagun, 12km away down the valley on the road to Assam, but it has nothing to offer except reams of brochures. Hotels are the best places to organise travel around the state.

Things to See & Do

There's not much of either, frankly. The **Buddha Vihar** on the hill near the Hotel Arun Subansiri is about all there is to see in the way of monuments. This modern concrete construction serves Itanagar's Monpa and Sherdrukpen communities, and there are a couple of small pictures of Buddha labelled with Thai script donated by the Hinayana Khampti community.

The **Jawaharlal Nehru Museum** near the Secretariat covers Arunachal Pradesh's many tribes with dioramas and collections of wood carvings, textiles, musical instruments and an incredible variety of headwear. On the first floor are exhibits from archaeological sites such as Ita Fort and Malinithan. It's open Tuesday to Sunday, 10 am to 5 pm.

About 6km from Itanagar, **Ganga Lake** lies at the end of a rugged road and a short but steep track. The surrounding forests are quite beautiful. The lake lies in the rugged ranges north of the town; you'll probably need someone to drive you there to negotiate the winding tracks.

Itanagar's sister town of Naharlagun was originally planned to be the capital before the hotter climate and lack of space forced a move to the new town. The daily **market**, known locally as the super market, next to the main road, is an interesting place to wander around, although unless you're buying chickens there's nothing in the way of souvenirs. The nearby **zoo** is rather sparse but the animal enclosures are of a reasonable size; entry costs Rs 2.

Places to Stay & Eat

In Ganga Market the **Hotel Himalaya** has basic doubles for Rs 150. Nearby on the lane leading down to the Arunachal State Transport bus station the **Hotel Blue Pine** (☎ 212042), is a good mid-range option, with singles/doubles with attached bathroom for Rs 290/500. **Hotel Arun Subansiri** (☎ 212677), Zero Point, has some very comfortable rooms for Rs 600/800, with satellite TV. **Hotel Donyi Polo Ashok** (☎ 212626) is the top hotel with air-con rooms for a negotiable Rs 800/1200. It's uphill from the main road on a street branching off near the Secretariat. All these places have quite good restaurants.

Down in Naharlagun, 10km away, the **Hotel Arunachal** (☎ 244960) is a large multistorey place with decent air-cooled rooms for Rs 300/400 and air-con rooms for Rs 500/700. The restaurant is quite good and the menu is a gem; 'scremboiled egg on toast' for Rs 30, 'vegetable steak' Rs 45, 'prawn butterfly' Rs 80, and a choice of 'vienela' or 'strewbawry' ice cream.

Getting There & Away

Buses go to Tezpur (Rs 90, six hours). Green Valley is a reliable operator with 'night super' buses (the usual method of bus in the North-East Region) to Gauhati (Rs 160, 12 hours). See the Getting There & Away section at the beginning of this chapter for details about getting to and from Gauhati.

Getting Around

Other than buses running frequently between Ganga Market and Naharlagun (Rs 8), Itanagar doesn't have much in the way of public transport. A chartered auto-rickshaw between Itanagar and Naharlagun costs Rs 150.

West Arunachal

The route over the Se La to Tawang via Bomdila is the most visited area of the state.

See the Tawang section later in this section for Getting There & Away details.

TEZPUR TO TAWANG

At Tipi, a few kilometres from the state border with Assam at Bhalukpong, there is an **Orchid Research Centre**, best visited in April/May. The centre grows about 7500 orchid plants from across the state in greenhouses scattered around the pleasant lush grounds. At the rear of the centre is the Bharali River.

About halfway between Tezpur (72m) and Tawang (3050m) is the attractive town of Bomdila (2700m), where there are apple orchards and a couple of Buddhist **gompas**. The friendly *Hotel Siphiyang Phong* (☎ 03782-22373) has decent rooms from Rs 400/650. Buses from Gauhati are Rs 205 (18 hours).

From Dirang (900m) with its **fort**, the road winds slowly upwards to the dramatic Se La (4249m), going by a large army camp perhaps ironically titled Shangrila. A lot of the forest here has been destroyed, and erosion keeps the road builders busy. At Se La there is a small Buddhist **shrine** opened by the Dalai Lama.

TAWANG
• alt 3050m

Tawang's main attraction is the Tawang Gompa, the most important in the northeast. While nearby villages have sturdy old stone houses shaded by trees, Tawang itself has been denuded of trees and modernised with ugly concrete buildings. The army live on the upper slopes, locals on the lower slopes with the Central and Nehru markets in between. There is a handicrafts centre at the lower end of town near the hospital.

Tawang Gompa

In the far north-west, this gompa is in a superb location at 3400m, near the border with Bhutan. Said to be the largest monastery in India, Tawang Gompa is beautifully situated on a small hump of a spur about 2km from town. It was founded in about 1645 by Merak Lama, the 6th Dalai Lama, and is currently the active home of Gelukpa monks. The monks hold animated lectures and debates in the open space between the chörtens at the entrance and the *dukhang* (assembly hall) – Verrier Elwin said the atmosphere reminded him of Oxford.

The massive three-storey dukhang has been renovated and was reopened by the Dalai Lama in 1997. The monastery suffered damage in the 1962 Chinese invasion. In any case, the main temple is magnificent, filled with rich brocades and tapestries and centring on a 8m-high golden statue of a stern **Sakyamuni** (the historical buddha). The narrow chin and broad eyes and cheekbones of Sakyamuni set this statue apart Sakyamunis in other gompas.

To the left of Sakyamuni are smaller statues, including one of Merak Lama. On the right is a gold and turquoise-covered **chörten** containing the relics of the founding lama. Behind here is a small **gönkhang** holding veiled statues of the fierce deities.

Next to the dukhang and on the main courtyard is the ancient stone and wood **library**, with a famous collection of manuscripts and thangkas. You might have to ask to see the library.

Places to Stay & Eat

The *Tourist Lodge* is a bit decrepit but OK, with doubles from Rs 400 to Rs 700. The *Inspection Bungalow* uphill from the bus stand is better and much cheaper at Rs 80 per bed. The *Hotel Paradise* in the main market has doubles from Rs 200 to Rs 500 for a 'suite'. There are a few restaurants on the main street serving momos. The local drink is *chang* – rice beer with yak butter melted into it (an acquired taste).

Getting There & Away

Getting to Tawang is no picnic – it's 350km from the nearest airport at Tezpur in Assam and you have to cross the Se La. Indian Airlines (☎ 03712-20083) has two flights a week from Saloni airport (16km from Tezpur) to Kolkata (US$80).

By local bus from Tezpur to Tawang, it takes about 24 hours (Rs 150), and around

12 hours by jeep. From Tezpur, there are also buses to Itanagar (Rs 90, six hours) and Gauhati (Rs 70, six hours).

SEPPA
• alt 600m

The headquarters of the rugged and largely roadless East Kameng district has just been opened to foreigners. The main tribal people here are the Nishi, who like the Apatani, Hill Miri and Sulung tribes trace their descent from Abo Teni, the first man. Traditional Nishi dress for men is a wickerwork helmet with a hornbill beak and a few hornbill feathers attached plus a bun of hair over his forehead and bead necklaces. Men also wear a woollen cloak and a loin cloth, and carry beautifully woven cane knapsacks holding a mean-looking sword on their back. Nishis don't live in villages, instead a number of families share longhouses divided into compartments with a common cooking area, similar to the Dayak longhouses of Borneo.

The ***Inspection Bungalow*** is pretty much the only place to stay (Rs 80 per night); as usual this must be booked at the office of the magistrate in Seppa.

Getting here takes a slow eight hour drive from Bhalukpong (one daily, about 9 am).

Central Arunachal

Only a few places are open to foreigners in the broad belt of the centre of the state, basically along the road from Ziro to Pasighat.

ZIRO
☎ 037892

Ziro is growing rapidly, sprawling out from the central crossroads. There's not much to do, except maybe drink at one of the local bars (but expect a lot of curious onlookers). A 10 minute walk past the big pine-covered hillock brings you to a densely settled agricultural area with irrigated paddy fields separated by small hills planted with pine or bamboo for construction materials.

Ziro is the home of the Apatani people, who are not slash-and-burn farmers like the

---

Donyi Polo

Pasighat is the centre of a new religion called Donyi Polo (*donyi* means sun and *polo* means moon), which is attempting to preserve the Adi tribal myths and traditions in the face of the rapid influx of Christian missionaries. The founders of Donyi Polo felt that if the old tribal faith was to survive, they had to adapt the methods of organised religions, including regular rituals and texts. The congregation meets in a hall called a *dere* on Saturday mornings, where songs and prayers are in the Adi language. Elders who lead the ceremonies sit on a raised platform at the end of the hall.

The doctrine of Donyi Polo is still imprecise, although one old woman explained it this way: Donyi is a feminine deity – when the sun rises so a woman rises to begin preparing food and weaving; while Polo is a masculine deity – when the moon comes out the men start drinking.

---

neighbouring Nishi and Hill Miri tribes, but grow rice on terraces on the basin-like 26 sq km Apatani plateau (the Apatani call their homeland 'the rice bowl'). The plateau is studded with pine-covered hillocks.

Like the Nishi, traditional Apatani dress for men is a cane helmet and a topknot of hair with a brass skewer stuck through it.

Apatani women sometimes wear bamboo plugs the size of walnuts in their noses. Christoph Von Haimendorf visited in the 1940s and noted that Apatani women seemed to aim to wear the biggest possible nose plugs. Nowadays the custom seems to be dying out – one woman said the women feel embarrassed by people staring at them.

The Apatani have village and clan councils called *builangs*, made up of representatives of the elderly and the young with the decision makers consulting both groups. Meetings are held on the *lapang*, a low bamboo platform symbolising the equality of clan members.

You can stay at the ***Blue Pine Lodge***, on the edge of the plateau on the left just as the

ARUNACHAL PRADESH

road enters the basin. It has good doubles for Rs 300 and a few singles for Rs 200. The other option is the *Circuit House*, where beds are Rs 80 per person. Book at the deputy commissioner's office.

DAPORIJO

Daporijo is an overgrown village on the Subansiri River; there's not much to do but look at and be looked at by the local Tagin and Hill Miri adivasis. The town stretches along the river bank, with the small bazaar containing a couple of exceedingly basic hotels. The *Circuit House,* where beds are Rs 80 per person, is the best option.

ALONG

Along is a quiet town mostly inhabited by Adi people on the bank of the Siang River (called the Brahmaputra in Assam). The *Circuit House* (Rs 80 per person) can be booked through the deputy commissioners office (☎ 03782-221).

PASIGHAT

☎ 03796

Pasighat is a larger town than Along, also predominantly Adi, on the banks of Siang. Here the river widens out onto the plains of Assam.

Until 1997 when logging was banned, Pasighat was a prime logging centre. At one point in the mid-1990s there were 35 saw mills operating around the town when local needs barely justified one mill running part time. The saw mills were owned by locals but financed and managed by Marwari businessmen (Marwaris are a powerful caste of merchants originally from Rajasthan, who are notorious for exploiting adivasis and their resources). In the areas of Arunachal Pradesh where shifting jhum agriculture is practised, forests are simply viewed as land which is yet to be exploited.

As with businessmen everywhere, the Marwaris wanted to make as much money as possible in the shortest space of time. As the locals raised the rent on the mill every year, five years was as far as anyone looked ahead. Surrounding areas were basically stripped, despite state laws allowing felling for only local needs. The problem is compounded by the fact that most of the land is common property and much of it is unsurveyed, so the amount of forest lost can only be guessed at.

While the money lasted there was a boom in Pasighat, but now the town is in an economic slump with no solution in sight; pressure is building for a return to the money making logging practices of the 1990s. Indeed logging is continuing in some areas, with tribes clearing the way for transport to the rest of India.

There are some local emporiums selling handicrafts (such as caneware and shawls), a few basic hotels and the *Circuit House* (Rs 80 per person), which is the best place to stay. The circuit house, also known as the Inspection Bungalow, can be booked through the deputy commissioner's office (☎ 22340).

GETTING THERE & AWAY

There are two or three buses leaving very early in the morning from Itanagar to Ziro, Daporijo and Pasighat (6 am to 8 am). It is also possible to take a bus from Dibrugarh to Pasighat or from Tezpur to Ziro.

East Arunachal

The least visited part of the state is still largely off limits for foreigners, although Indian tourists can visit the regional centres of Roing, Anini and Tezu, home to Mishmi adivasis. The southern 'hook' of the state, comprising Tirap and Changlang districts, have long been used as a route for Naga and Assamese militants going to and from bases in Myanmar (Burma), which involves a long and slow trek across the ranges. These districts also see heroin smuggling from the Golden Triangle – another reason not to visit.

The Wancho and Nocte tribes live in villages perched on the top of ridges, and their longhouses are said to be the biggest in Arunachal, with wonderfully springy bamboo floors.

Headhunters of the Hills

The Nocte tribe of Tirap district bordering Nagaland was once a headhunting people of renown, although the custom ceased in British times. The Nocte believed that the soul resides in the neck and can only be released by beheading. The usual method of headhunting was a surprise raid by one village against another, sometimes in revenge for a previous raid and sometimes as a result of disputes over the valuable salt springs in the rugged forested ranges.

There was also an interesting method of announcing a raid: one village would send a messenger carrying two bamboo sticks tied together. One stick was cut to a point at one end while the other was left blunt. The blunt ends signified the intention to take heads. If the village to be raided chose to take up the challenge, it would make both sticks blunt and return them. If, on the other hand, it wanted peace, it would return the sticks as they were, or cut the end of the blunt stick to a fine point and return it.

If a raid was unsuccessful, the hunters would creep quietly back to the village. If they were successful, they came back dancing and singing and began playing the village's log drums. Later the heads would be placed together and the village priest would sprinkle a mix of rice and egg over them to exorcise the spirits, then the heads would be hung from a tree in the village.

In recent years most Nocte have converted to Christianity, which has spread from neighbouring Nagaland, and their grisly trophies have fallen into decay.

NAMDAPHA NATIONAL PARK

Situated in the little-visited far east of the state bordering Myanmar (Burma), this vast forested reserve covers 1850 sq km, ranging from the plains up to 4500m. It is unique in being home to four big cats; tiger, leopard, clouded leopard and snow leopard. There isn't much in the way of treks or trails into the park; it is still a largely trackless wilderness.

Accommodation is available at Deban, in the park, though it must be booked at the office of the Namdapha National Park Field Director in Miao. The *Forest Rest House* and the two *tourist bungalows* are simple but pleasant; doubles cost Rs 95. The cooks are good but you may want to bring extra snacks. Entry to the park costs Rs 10 for Indians, Rs 50 for foreigners.

Miao, 28km from Deban, is a market town. There is an *Inspection Bungalow* and a couple of basic hotels. The Tibetan refugee settlement of Choephelling, where Tibetan carpets are sold, is 3km from Miao on the Deban road.

Buses leave from Dibrugarh for Miao, from where you can hire a taxi to the park.

Language

In all of the main towns of northern India, including the hill stations, English is widely spoken. However, higher up in the mountains this is not the case and any attempt at speaking a little of the local language will be to your advantage.

In Darjeeling and Sikkim, and most parts of Uttarakhand and Himachal Pradesh, Hindi is widely understood (see the following section). It's also the language of the Gujar and Bakrawala shepherds found roaming the hills of the western Himalaya in the summer months.

The people in the outlying villages of the Kashmir Valley speak only Kashmiri; similarly Ladakhi, a Tibetan-based language, is the only language understood in the more remote valleys of Ladakh and Zanskar (see the Ladakhi section later in this chapter). In Himachal and Uttarakhand, Pahari and Garwhali respectively are widely used in the village areas.

HINDI & URDU

As spoken languages there is little difference between Hindi and Urdu. However, Hindi is a Sanskrit-based language, written in Devanagiri script, while Urdu is written in Arabic script.

The list of Hindi words and phrases below should help get you started but for a more in depth guide to the language, get a copy of Lonely Planet's *Hindu/Urdu phrasebook*.

Greetings

The traditional Hindu greeting *namaste* is said with one's hands together in a prayer-like gesture. Namaste means something like 'I salute the divine within you'. A more formal version is *namaskar*.

Muslims, on the other hand, offer the greeting *salaam alekum*, literally 'peace be upon you'. The reply is either to repeat the greeting or say *walekum as salaam* (and also upon you).

Hindus also say *namaste* for 'goodbye', while Muslims say *kudha hafiz* (lit: 'may God bless you').

When addressing a stranger, particularly if the person is of some standing, use the polite suffix *ji* – it's almost like 'sir'. This term can also mean 'yes' in reply to a question. Beware of *acha*, that all-purpose word for 'OK'. It can also mean 'OK, I understand what you mean, but it isn't OK'.

Basics

Excuse me.	*maaf kijiyeh*
Please.	*meharbani seh*
Thank you.	*shukriyaa*
Yes.	*haan*
No.	*nahin*
How are you?	*aap kaiseh hain?*
Very well, thank you.	*bahut acha, shukriya*
What's your name?	*aapka naam shubh kya hai?*
My name is ...	*meraa naam ... hai*
Do you speak English?	*kya aap angrezi samajhte hain?*
A little.	*torah torah*
I don't understand.	*meri samajh men nahin aaya*
How much?	*kitneh paiseh/ kitneh hai?*
What is the time?	*kitneh bajeh hain?*
How do I get to ...?	*... kojane ke liyeh kaiseh jaana parega?*
When does the next bus leave?	*agli bas kab jaayehgi?*
Where is the ...?	*... kahan hai?*
bank	*baink*
bus stop	*bas staap*
chemist/pharmacy	*davai ki dukaan*
post office	*daak khana*
ticket office	*tikat aaphis*
Can I change money here?	*kyaa yahaan paise badlae jaa sakte hain?*

505

LANGUAGE

Where is a hotel?	*hotal kahan hai?*
Do you have a room?	*aap ke paas ek kamraa hai?*
Is there (breakfast/ hot water)?	*(naashta/garam paani) hai?*
big	*bada*
small	*chhota*
today	*aaj*
medicine	*dava-ee*
egg	*aanda*
fruit	*phal*
vegetables	*sabzi*
sugar	*chini*
rice	*chaaval*
water	*paani*
tea	*chai*
coffee	*kaafi*
milk	*dudh*

Trekking

Will you come with me?	*mere saath chalengeh?*
What do you charge per day?	*ek din kaa kyaa lete hain?*
How many days will it take?	*kitne din lagengeh?*
Is there a place to spend the night?	*raat ko rehneh kii jagaa hai?*
Is food/water available?	*khaanaa/paani miltaa hai?*
I have to rest.	*aaraam karnaa hai*

Health & Emergencies

I need a doctor.	*mujhe doktar chaahiye*
It hurts here.	*yahaan daradh hai*
I'm allergic to penicillin.	*mujhe penicilin se elargii hai*
Help!	*bachaao!*
Thief!	*chorr!*
I've been robbed.	*merii chori ho gai hai*
police station	*thaanaa*

Time & Days

today	*aaj*
tonight	*aaj raat*
yesterday/ tomorrow	*kal*
day	*din*

night	*raat*
week	*haftah*
month	*mahina*
year	*saal*

Numbers

Instead of counting in tens, hundreds, thousands, millions and billions, Indians count in tens, hundreds, thousands, hundred thousands, and ten millions. A hundred thousand is a *lakh*, and 10 million is a *crore*. These two words are almost always used in place of their English equivalent. Thus, you will see 10 lakh rather than one million and one crore rather than 10 million.

1	*ek*
2	*do*
2½	*tarhi*
3	*tin*
4	*char*
5	*panch*
6	*chhe*
7	*saat*
8	*aath*
9	*nau*
10	*das*
12	*baranh*
13	*teranh*
14	*chodanh*
15	*pandranh*
16	*solanh*
17	*staranh*
18	*aatharanh*
19	*unnis*
20	*bis*
21	*ikkis*
30	*tis*
35	*paintis*
40	*chalis*
50	*panchaas*
60	*saath*
70	*sattar*
80	*assi*
90	*nabbe*
100	*so*
1000	*ek hazaar*
100,000	*lakh*
10,000,000	*crore*

LADAKHI

Ladakhi is the language used by most people indigenous to Ladakh and Zanskar. Once similar to Tibetan, Ladakhi is now considerably different, and there are disparate dialects throughout the region. Learning a little Ladakhi will add to your enjoyment, and earn you the respect of the local people; if travelling out of Leh or trekking where little English is understood, it is quite necessary. If you only remember one word, make it the all-purpose *jule* (pronounced 'JOO-Lay'), which means 'hello', 'goodbye', 'please' and 'thank you'.

Spelling

Every guidebook, map and tourist brochure can offer up to six or so different ways of spelling a name. For example, there is a famous gompa (or gonpa or gomba) at Tikse (or Thikse, Thiksey or Tiksey). The basic rule is: if it sounds the same, it's the same place.

Basics

Yes.	*kasa*
No.	*man*
How much/many?	*tsam?*
I don't understand.	*hamago*
good	*demo*
rupee	*kirmo*
milk	*oma*
rice	*dras*

meat	*sha*
water	*chhu*
sugar	*khara*

Geography & Climate

In Ladakh, life is completely dominated by the weather and geography. Here are a few words that you may hear:

bridge	*zampa*
ice	*kang*
mountain	*ri*
river	*tsangpo*
stream	*tokpo*
wind	*lungspo*
cold	*tangmo*
lake	*tso*
mountain pass	*la*
snow	*ka*
summer	*yar*
winter	*guhn*

Numbers

1	*chig*
2	*nyis*
3	*sum*
4	*zhi*
5	*nga*
6	*truk*
7	*dun*
8	*gyet*
9	*gu*
10	*chu*

Glossary

acharya – revered teacher; originally a spiritual guide or preceptor

adivasi – tribal person

aipans – geometric folk designs painted on floors and walls of family homes on auspicious occasions

amalaka – stone medallion-shaped flourish featuring fluted edges; it frequently surmounts the *shikhara* of Hindu temples

amrit – baptism

AMS – acute mountain sickness

ananda – happiness; Ananda was the name of the Buddha's first cousin and favourite disciple

anna – a 16th of a rupee; it's no longer legal tender but is occasionally referred to in marketplace parlance (eight annas are the equivalent of Rs 0.50)

Arjuna – *Mahabharata* hero and military commander who retired to the Himalaya

arrack – clear, distilled rice or barley liquor; treat with caution and only ever drink it from a bottle produced in a government-controlled distillery

Aryan – Sanskrit for 'noble'; refers to those who migrated from Persia and settled in northern India

Ashoka – great Buddhist emperor, 3rd century BCE

ashram – spiritual community or retreat

autars – spirits of people who die issueless; they are particularly feared by the Gaddis of Himachal Pradesh

Avalokiteshvara – one of the Buddha's most important disciples; also known as Chenresig

avataar – incarnation of a deity

ayurveda – Indian herbal medicine

baba – religious master, father, and a term of respect

Badri – another name for Vishnu

bagh – garden

bakhu – traditional dress worn by women of Tibetan origin in Sikkim; known as a *chuba* in the western Himalaya

baksheesh – tip, bribe or donation

Bangali – local spelling of Bengali

Bangla – West Bengal

baoli – spring

BCE – before common era

bed tea – early morning tea brought to your room and usually served with biscuits; also known as *Chota Hazri* (little breakfast)

begar – system of unpaid or forced labour

Betel – nut of the betel tree; the leaves and nut are mildly intoxicating and are chewed as a stimulant and digestive

Bhagavad Gita – Song of the Divine One; Krishna's lessons to Arjuna, the main thrust of which was to emphasise the philosophy of *bhakti* (faith); part of the *Mahabharata*

bhakti – devotion

bhang – dried leaves and flowering shoots of the marijuana plant

Bharat – Hindi for India

bhawan – office

Bhim – eldest of the five Pandava brothers and another *Mahabharata* hero, renowned for his great strength and giant stature

Bhodhisattva – one who has almost reached *nirvana*, but who renounces it in order to help others attain it; literally 'one whose essence is perfected wisdom'.

Bön – pre-Buddhist animist religion that was followed in Tibet

Brahma – the source of all existence and worshipped as the creator. Brahma is depicted as having four heads. His consort is Sarasvati.

Brahman – a member of the priest caste, the highest Hindu caste

Buddha – 'Awakened One'; originator of Buddhism who lived in the 5th century BC; regarded by Hindus as the ninth reincarnation of Vishnu

bugyal – high-altitude meadow

carom – snooker-like game in which discs are flicked across a board into pockets

caste – one's hereditary station in life

CE – common era

chaam – ritual masked dance that is performed by monks during religious celebrations at *gompas*

chai – tea

chakra – literally 'wheel', focus of one's spiritual power; disc-like weapon of Vishnu

Chamunda – form of the goddess Durga; a real terror, armed with a scimitar, noose and mace, and clothed in elephant hide

Chandra – the moon, or the moon as a god

Chandragupta – important ruler of India in the 3rd century BCE

chang – Tibetan barley beer

chappal – sandals

Char Dham – the four sacred shrines in Uttarakhand (Yamunotri, Gangotri, Kedarnath and Badrinath) sacred to the goddesses Yamuna and Ganga, and the gods Shiva and Vishnu respectively

charas – cannabis derivative; marijuana

charpoi – Indian rope bed

chatti – pilgrims' lodging

chaval – rice

Chenresig – the Tibetan deity of compassion, also known as Avalokiteshvara; the Dalai Lama is considered to be an incarnation of Chenresig

chillum – pipe

chogyal – Sikkimese king; literally 'one who rules according to chö', or the Way of Law

chola – cloak worn in Sikkim

choli – sari blouse

cholo – a dice game from Tibet

chomo – Tibetan Buddhist nun

chörten – Tibetan word for *stupa*; originally reliquaries (chörten means 'receptacle for offerings'), they are now frequently erected as cenotaphs in memory of a Buddhist saint

choskor – religious enclave, collection of chapels and religious buildings found at Alchi and Tabo

chowk – a town square, intersection or marketplace

chowkidar – caretaker

chuba – traditional dress worn by Tibetan women; in Sikkim, known as a *bakhu*

chwa-shyam – the altar, and most sacred part of the *dukhang* in a Buddhist *gompa*. It is here that the ornate images of the deities are enshrined.

Dalit – preferred term for India's casteless class; *see* Untouchable

damrhu – small Tibetan drum

darshan – offering or audience with someone; viewing of a deity

deodar – a type of coniferous tree found in Himalayan regions

Devi – Shiva's wife. She has a variety of forms

devta – god

DFO – District Forestry Officer

dhaba – basic Indian restaurants

dhaba – hole-in-the-wall restaurant or snack bar

dhal – curried lentil gravy

dham – religious centre

dharamsala – pilgrims' lodging

dharma – Hindu/Buddhist moral code of behaviour, divine law

Dhev-bumi – abode of the gods; the Himalaya

dhobi-wallah – person who washes clothes

dhoop – incense

dhoti – like a *lungi*, but the cloth is then pulled up between the legs; worn by Hindu men

Dhyani Buddhas – a group of five buddhas, each a different colour with different hand positions, symbols and attributes; Vairocana is one of the Dhyani Buddhas

diya – ceremonial floating lamps

dongmo – wooden tube

dongpo – Ladakhi tea churner

dongyur – prayer wheel in Kinnaur

dorje – thunderbolt

Dorje Drakden – protector deity who advises the Tibetan government on matters of state through the Nechung Oracle

Dravidian – a member of one of the aboriginal races of India, pushed south by the Indo-Europeans

Drukpa – Buddhist order

dukhang – the main prayer room or assembly hall of Buddhist *gompas*

dun (doon) – valley

Durga – the Inaccessible; a form of Shiva's wife Devi, a beautiful but fierce goddess riding a tiger; also major goddess of the Shakti cult

dwarpal – gatekeeper

freaks – westerners who have dropped out in India

Ganesh – god of wisdom and prosperity; elephant-headed son of Shiva and Parvati; his vehicle is a rat

Ganga – Ganges River; said to flow through the hair of Shiva; goddess representing the Ganges

ganj – market

ganja – dried flowering tips of marijuana plant; highly potent form of cannabis

garh – fort

Garuda – man-bird vehicle of Vishnu

Gayatri – sacred verse of the *Rigveda*, repeated mentally by Brahmans twice a day

Gelukpa – an order of Tibetan Buddhism founded by the monk Tsongkhapa in the 14th century; the Dalai Lama is the spiritual leader of this order

getruk – a child student of Tibetan Buddhism

ghat – steps or landing on a river; range of hills, or road up hills

ghee – clarified butter used for cooking and religious offerings

GMVN – Gahrwal Mandal Vikas Nigam, the Garhwal tourist authority

GNLF – Gurkha National Liberation Front

gompa – Tibetan Buddhist monastery

gonda – a decorative hat worn by men and women in Ladakh

gönkhang – protector chapel in a monastery

gopis – milkmaids; Krishna was very fond of them

gudma – a large thick woollen garment made in the Kullu Valley, often used as a blanket

Guge – 9th century Kingdom of western Tibet based at Tsaparang and Thöling

gurdwara – Sikh temple

guru – teacher or holy person (in Sanskrit, literally, 'dispeller of darkness')

gufa – cave

Hanuman – monkey god, prominent in the *Ramayana*, follower of Rama

Harijan – name given by Gandhi to India's Untouchables. This term is, however, no longer considered acceptable; *see* Dalit and Untouchable

Hinayana – a type of Buddhism which holds that the path to *nirvana* is an individual pursuit; also known as Theravada Buddhism

HPTDC – Himachal Pradesh Tourism Development Corporation

IMFL – Indian Made Foreign Liquor; beer or spirits produced in India

Indra – the most important and prestigious of the Vedic gods of India. God of rain, thunder, lightning and war. His weapons are the *vajra* (thunderbolt), bow, net and *anka* (hook).

jhula – bridge

jhum – slash-and-burn method of farming

ji – honorific that can be added to the end of almost anything; thus Babaji, Gandhiji

jot – mountain pass (in Garhwal)

jyendue – sacred thread worn by Tibetan Buddhists

jyothirlingam – Lingam of Light – the most important Shiva shrines in India, of which there are 12. The holy lingams in the shrines are said to derive currents of power from within themselves. There are three shrines in the Indian Himalaya, at Kedarnath and Jageshwar, both in Uttarakhand, and at the Baidyanath Temple in Baijnath, in the Kangra Valley of Himachal Pradesh.

Kagyupa – an order of Tibetan Buddhism; divided into the Drukpa and Drigung orders.

kakkars – the five means by which Sikh men recognise each other: *kesh* – uncut hair; *kangha* – the wooden comb; *kachha* – shorts; *kara* – the steel bracelet; and *kirpan* – the sword

kalachakra – literally 'the Wheel of Time', the most complex of Tantric ceremonies

Kali – the Black; a terrible form of Shiva's wife Diva. Depicted with black skin, dripping with blood, surrounded by snakes and wearing a necklace of skulls.

Kali-Yurga – the current age in traditional Hindu thought, evil times

Kalki – the White Horse. Future (10th) incarnation of Vishnu which will appear at the end of Kali-Yuga, when the world ceases to be. Kalki has been compared to Maitreya in Buddhist cosmology

kangyur – the Tibetan Buddhist canon

karma – a law of cause and effect whereby your actions in this life influence the level of your future incarnations, common to both Buddhism and Hinduism

katag – Buddhist ceremonial scarf

Kauravas – adversaries of the heroes of the *Mahabharata*, the Pandavas

Kedar – a name of Shiva

khadi – homespun cloth; Mahatma Gandhi encouraged people to spin khadi rather than buy English cloth

khal – pass in Uttarakhand

khukuri – traditional carved knife used by the Gurkhas

KMVN – Kumaon Mandal Vikas Nigam, the Kumaon tourist authority

Kolkata – Calcutta

kora – Tibetan term for a pilgrim circuit

kot – fort

kotwali – police station

Krishna – Vishnu's eighth incarnation, often coloured blue; a popular Hindu deity, he revealed the *Bhagavad Gita* to Arjuna

kumbh – pitcher

kumbhars – village potters

kund – lake or tank

kurta pajama – traditional dress consisting of a kurta shirt and straight trousers

la – a Tibetan word for mountain pass

Lakshmana – half-brother and aide of Rama in the *Ramayana*

Lakshmi (Laxmi) – Vishnu's consort, goddess of wealth; sprang forth from the ocean holding a lotus; also referred to as Padma (lotus)

lama – Tibetan Buddhist monk or priest

lathi – large bamboo stick; a weapon of the Indian police

LEDeG – Ladakh Ecological Development Group

lhakhang – chapel in a Buddhist monastery

lhamo – traditional Tibetan opera, originally performed over several days

lingam – phallic symbol; symbol of Shiva and his creative powers

Losar – Tibetan New Year

Losong – Sikkimese New Year

lungi – like a sarong

machaan – watchtower (hide) in game reserves from where hunters spied on their prey

Mahabharata – great epic poem, containing about 10,000 verses, describing the battle between the Pandavas and the Kauravas

Mahadev – the Great God; a name of Shiva

Mahadevi – the Great Goddess; a name of Devi, Shiva's wife

Mahakala – Great Time; a name of Shiva the Destroyer

maharaja, maharana, maharao – king

maharani – wife of a princely ruler or a ruler in her own right

mahatma – literally 'great soul'

Mahayana – a type of Buddhism which holds that the combined belief of its followers will eventually be great enough to encompass all of humanity and bear it to salvation

Maheshwara – Great Lord; Shiva

Mahishasura – buffalo demon killed by Durga

maidan – open grassed area in a town or city

Maitreya – Buddha of the future; coming Buddha

mala – rosary beads

mandala – 'circle' in Sanskrit; meditational device and symbol used in Hindu and Buddhist art to symbolise the universe

mandapa – pillared pavilion in front of a temple

mandi – market

mandir – Hindu or Jain temple

mani stone – stone carved with the Tibetan Buddhist mantra 'Om Mani Padme Hum', or 'Hail to the jewel in the lotus'

mantra – sacred word or syllable used by Buddhists and Hindus to aid meditation; metrical psalms of praise found in the *Vedas*

Mara – Buddhist god of death; has three eyes and holds the wheel of life

marg – major road

marg – meadow

masjid – mosque; Jama Masjid is the Friday Mosque, or main mosque

mata – mother

mataji – female priest

math – *gompa*, religious seat of learning

matris – mischievous sprites

maya – the illusory nature of existence

mela – a fair

memsahib – married European lady (from 'madam-sahib')

minjars – silk tassels worn by the inhabitants of Chamba during the annual Minjar Festival that symbolise sheaves of maize

mistri – mechanic

moksha – salvation

mudra – ritual hand movements used in Hindu religious dancing; also symbolic hand gestures adopted by the Buddha

Mughal – the Muslim dynasty of Indian emperors from Babur to Aurangzeb

naga – water spirit and serpent deity

namda – felt

Namgyal – a kingdom, based in Ladakh, which ruled parts of the region from the 16th to 19th centuries

Nanda – the cowherd who raised Krishna

Nanda Devi – the presiding goddess of Uttarakhand; she is revered by all those inhabitants who live within the shadow of the beautiful Nanda Devi mountain, which is believed to be a form of the goddess

Nandi – bull, vehicle of Shiva; Nandi's images are usually seen before temples dedicated to Shiva

Narayan – incarnation of Vishnu the Creator

Narsingh – man-lion incarnation of Vishnu

NEFA – North-Eastern Frontier Agency

Nhilkantha – form of Shiva; his blue throat is a result of swallowing poison that would have destroyed the world

nirvana – the ultimate aim of Buddhist existence; final release from the cycle of existence

nulla (nullah) – ditch or small stream; can also mean valley, as in Solang Nullah, near Manali

nullah – stream or valley

Nyingmapa – a Tibetan Buddhist order formed by the followers of the Indian sage Padmasambhava

Om – sacred invocation representing the absolute essence of the divine principle; for Buddhists, if repeated often enough with complete concentration, it should lead to a state of emptiness

paan – betel nut and leaves plus chewing additives such as lime

padma – lotus

Padmasambhava – highly revered 8th century Indian sage who established Buddhism in Tibet, one of the foremost proponents of Tantric Buddhism

padmasana – lotus position or posture

pahari – literally 'of the hills', can refer to people, language or style of art

Pandavas – set of five brothers who were descendants of the Lunar race and who fought in the great battle of the *Mahabharata*

papu – bright, woollen shoes with curled tips worn during festivals and ceremonies by men and women in Ladakh

parikrama – Sanskrit term for a pilgrim circuit

Parvati – another form of Shiva's wife

pashmina – fine wool from a pashmina goat

pattoo – a thick woollen shawl made in the Kullu Valley and worn by women

pradesh – state

pranayama – study of breath control

prasaad – food offering to the gods

prayag – sacred confluence; in the Garhwal district of Uttarakhand there are five *(panch)* sacred confluences, known as the Panch Prayag, which are formed by the meeting of the tributaries of the Ganges

puja – literally 'respect'; offering or prayers

pujari – person who performs a *puja*; a temple priest

Puranas – set of 18 encyclopedic Sanskrit stories, written in verse dating from the period of the Guptas (5th century AD)

PWD – Public Works Department

Radha – favourite mistress of Krishna when he lived at Govinda (or Gopala), the cowherd

radung – long-stemmed Tibetan horn

raj – rule or sovereignty

raja – king

Rajput – Hindu warrior castes, royal rulers of central India

rakhi – amulet

Rama – seventh incarnation of Vishnu; his life story is the central theme of the *Ramayana*

Ramayana – the story of Rama and Sita and their conflict with Ravana. One of India's most well known legends, it is retold in various forms throughout almost all South-East Asia.

rani – wife of a king

rath – wheeled chariot on which deities are borne during festivals

Ravana – demon king of Lanka (modern-day Sri Lanka); he abducted Sita, and the titanic battle between him and Rama is told in the *Ramayana*

Rigveda – the original and longest of the four main *Vedas*, or holy Sanskrit texts

Ringchen Zangpo – known as the Great Translator; instrumental in resurrecting Tibetan Buddhism in northern India in the 11th century

rinpoche – literally 'high in esteem', a title bestowed on highly revered lamas; they are usually incarnate, but need not be

rishi – originally a sage to whom the hymns of the *Vedas* were revealed; any poet, philosopher or sage

rumal – finely embroidered handkerchief-sized cloth found in the Chamba district of Himachal Pradesh, traditionally used as a covering for sacred texts, but now a popular tourist purchase

SAARC – South Asian Association for Regional Cooperation

sabzi – mushy vegetables

sadar – main

sadhu – ascetic, or holy person; one who is trying to achieve enlightenment; usually addressed as 'swamiji' or 'babaji'

sagar – lake, reservoir

sahib – 'lord', title applied to any gentleman and most Europeans

Sakyamuni – Gautama Buddha, the 'historical Buddha' of the current age

Sakyapa – order of Tibetan Buddhism

sal – a type of hardwood tree found at lower elevations in the Himalayan region

salai – road

samadhi – an ecstatic state, sometimes defined as 'ecstasy, trance, communion with God'. Also, a place where a holy man has been cremated; usually venerated as a shrine.

sangam – confluence; meeting of two rivers.

sarak – road

Sarasvati – wife of Brahma, goddess of speech and learning; usually seated on a white swan, holding a *veena* (a stringed instrument)

Sati – wife of Shiva. She became a sati ('honourable woman') by immolating herself. Although banned, the act of sati is occasionally performed.

Shaivaite – follower of Lord Shiva

Shaivism – the worship of Shiva

shakti – creative energies perceived as female deities; devotees follow the cult of shaktism

Shakti – goddess; Shiva's consort

shaligram – a type of black stone from which idols are often carved; also used in temple architectural elements, such as pillars

Shankar – Shiva as the Creator

Shankaracharya – 9th century Hindu theologian who formulated the philosophy of Advaita Vedanta and postulated the concept of *maya*, or the illusory nature of existence. His reforms heralded the revival of Hinduism in India.

shanti – peace

shikhara – Hindu temple spire or temple

Shiva – the destroyer; also the Creator, in which form he is worshipped as a *lingam*, Shiva is the presiding deity of the Himalaya

singh – literally 'lion'; name of the Rajput caste and adopted by Sikhs as a surname

Sita – in the *Vedas*, the goddess of agriculture; more commonly associated with the *Ramayana* in which Sita, Rama's wife, is abducted by Ravana and then carried off to Lanka

sri (sree, shri, shree) – honorific; these days the Indian equivalent of Mr or Mrs

stupa – Buddhist religious monument composed of a solid hemisphere topped by a spire, containing relics of the Buddha; known as a *chörten* in Tibetan

sudra – low Hindu caste

Surya – the sun; a major deity in the *Vedas*

swami – title given to initiated monks; means 'lord of the self'. A title of respect

tabla – hand drum

tal – lake

tandava – Shiva's dance of destruction
tank – reservoir
Tantric Buddhism – Tibetan Buddhism with strong sexual and occult overtones
Tara – female deity known as Drölma in Tibetan; worshipped by both Hindus and Buddhists
tempo – large auto-rickshaw that operates on fixed route
thakur – titled rulers from Lahaul in Himachal Pradesh
thali – literally a segmented dish, this is a basic all-you-can-eat Indian meal
thangka – rectangular Tibetan religious painting on cloth
thepang – distinctive square woollen cap often worn by Kinnauris
Theravada – *see* Hinayana
thukpa – Tibetan noodle soup
thumpchen – long-stemmed horn played by Buddhist monks; traditionally a Tibetan instrument
tiffin – Raj-era term meaning snack or food
tikka – a mark devout Hindus put on their foreheads
tok – ridge, used in Sikkim
tonga – horse-drawn buggy
topi – cap
torma – Tibetan offering of carved tsampa and butter paste
trisul – trident; symbol of Shiva
tsampa – barley flour, eaten cooked or raw; a staple food in more remote parts of Himachal Pradesh and Ladakh
tso – a Tibetan term for lake; used in Ladakh

tsuglhakhang – literally 'grand temple', normally the main hall in a monastery complex

Untouchable – lowest caste or 'casteless' for whom the most menial tasks are reserved; the name derives from the belief that higher casts risk defilement if they touch one; formerly known as *Harijan*, now *Dalit*
Upanishads – Esoteric doctrine; ancient texts forming part of the *Vedas* (although of a later date), they delve into weighty matters such as the nature of the universe and the soul

Vairochana – the 'embodiment of perfection', one of the five Dhyani Buddhas
Vaishnavite – follower of Lord Vishnu
Vedas – the four Hindu sacred books; a collection of hymns composed in pre-classical Sanskrit during the second millennium BCE: *Rigveda, Yajurveda, Samaveda* and *Atharvaveda*
victorias – horse-drawn carriages
Vikram – Dehra Dun tempos
Vishnu – the third in the Hindu trinity of gods along with Brahma and Shiva; the Preserver and Restorer, who so far has nine avataars

wallah – literally 'man'; can be added to other words; thus dhobi-wallah (clothes washer), taxi-wallah, lassi-wallah etc

yatra – pilgrimage
yoni – vagina; female fertility symbol

Acknowlegments

Thanks

Many thanks to the travellers who wrote to us with useful advice, helpful hints and interesting anecdotes:

Ajai Singh, Andrew & Elaine Mack, Annalisa Hounsome, Antonio Tartaglione, Ariel Talmor, Arno Zuydwyk, Aya Singh & Sons, C & J Woesthuis, Caroline Cupitt, Cindy and Jeroen Woesthuis, Cloin Loth, Dave Fuller, David Hughes, David Wheeler, David Ziringer, Duncan Ross, Emma Pavey, Emma Phillips, Erik Nyhus, Frans and Jan Stiebert, Glenda Quin, Greg Marlow, Herbert Appell, Hermes Liberty, Ian McVittie, Igi Steiger, Iwona Eberle, J. Dyer, James Dunn, James Lochtefeld, Jan Golembrewski, Jan Koster, Jan Stiebert, Joep Verhagen, John Newbould, John Oeveren, John Zande, Josh Saunders, Karl Holubar, Kay Hammond, Kevin Halon, Laurel Burgess, Leif Staver, Lisa Flynn, Mahesh Srivastava, Mahesh Tewari, Marina Collard, Mark Holmes, Mark Nicholls, Michael Koester, Michel van Dam, Michiel Hensema, Mike Smith, Minna Pyhala, Mirjam Malaika, Mirka Bloome, Naresh Sood, Om Shiva Guesthouse, Peter McWaters, Sallie-ann Thorp, Sanjoy Roy, Sharon Peske, Tali Treibitz, Tanya Campbell, Timothy Hall, Uivele Rawat, Vicki Weiss, Wil Sahlman.

LONELY PLANET

Phrasebooks

Lonely Planet phrasebooks are packed with essential words and phrases to help travellers communicate with the locals. With colour tabs for quick reference, an extensive vocabulary and use of script, these handy pocket-sized language guides cover day-to-day travel situations.

- handy pocket-sized books
- easy to understand Pronunciation chapter
- clear & comprehensive Grammar chapter
- romanisation alongside script to allow ease of pronunciation
- script throughout so users can point to phrases for every situation
- full of cultural information and tips for the traveller

'...vital for a real DIY spirit and attitude in language learning'
— *Backpacker*

'the phrasebooks have good cultural backgrounders and offer solid advice for challenging situations in remote locations'
— *San Francisco Examiner*

Arabic (Egyptian) • Arabic (Moroccan) • Australian *(Australian English, Aboriginal and Torres Strait languages)* • Baltic States *(Estonian, Latvian, Lithuanian)* • Bengali • Brazilian • British • Burmese • Cantonese • Central Asia • Central Europe *(Czech, French, German, Hungarian, Italian, Slovak)* • Eastern Europe *(Bulgarian, Czech, Hungarian, Polish, Romanian, Slovak)* • Ethiopian (Amharic) • Fijian • French • German • Greek • Hebrew phrasebook • Hill Tribes • Hindi/Urdu • Indonesian • Italian • Japanese • Korean • Lao • Latin American Spanish • Malay • Mandarin • Mediterranean Europe *(Albanian, Croatian, Greek, Italian, Macedonian, Maltese, Serbian, Slovene)* • Mongolian • Nepali • Papua New Guinea • Pilipino (Tagalog) • Quechua • Russian • Scandinavian Europe *(Danish, Finnish, Icelandic, Norwegian, Swedish)* • South-East Asia *(Burmese, Indonesian, Khmer, Lao, Malay, Tagalog Pilipino, Thai, Vietnamese)* • South Pacific Languages • Spanish (Castilian) *(also includes Catalan, Galician and Basque)* • Sri Lanka • Swahili • Thai • Tibetan • Turkish • Ukrainian • USA *(US English, Vernacular, Native American languages, Hawaiian)* • Vietnamese • Western Europe *(Basque, Catalan, Dutch, French, German, Greek, Irish)*

FREE Lonely Planet Newsletters

We love hearing from you and think you'd like to hear from us.

Planet Talk

Our FREE quarterly printed newsletter is full of tips from travellers and anecdotes from Lonely Planet guidebook authors. Every issue is packed with up-to-date travel news and advice, and includes:

- a postcard from Lonely Planet co-founder Tony Wheeler
- a swag of mail from travellers
- a look at life on the road through the eyes of a Lonely Planet author
- topical health advice
- prizes for the best travel yarn
- news about forthcoming Lonely Planet events
- a complete list of Lonely Planet books and other titles

To join our mailing list, residents of the UK, Europe and Africa can email us at go@lonelyplanet.co.uk; residents of North and South America can email us at info@lonelyplanet.com; the rest of the world can email us at talk2us@lonelyplanet.com.au, or contact any Lonely Planet office.

Comet

Our FREE monthly email newsletter brings you all the latest travel news, features, interviews, competitions, destination ideas, travellers' tips & tales, Q&As, raging debates and related links. Find out what's new on the Lonely Planet Web site and which books are about to hit the shelves.

Subscribe from your desktop: www.lonelyplanet.com/comet

LONELY PLANET

Guides by Region

onely Planet is known worldwide for publishing practical, reliable and no-nonsense travel information in our guides and on our Web site. The Lonely Planet list covers just about every accessible part of the world. Currently there are nine series: travel guides, shoestring guides, walking guides, city guides, phrasebooks, audio packs, travel atlases, diving and snorkeling guides and travel literature.

AFRICA Africa – the South • Africa on a shoestring • Arabic (Egyptian) phrasebook • Arabic (Moroccan) phrasebook • Cairo • Cape Town • Central Africa • East Africa • Egypt • Egypt travel atlas • Ethiopian (Amharic) phrasebook • The Gambia & Senegal • Healthy Travel Africa • Kenya • Kenya travel atlas • Malawi, Mozambique & Zambia • Morocco • North Africa • South Africa, Lesotho & Swaziland • South Africa, Lesotho & Swaziland travel atlas • Swahili phrasebook • Tanzania, Zanzibar & Pemba • Trekking in East Africa • Tunisia • West Africa • Zimbabwe, Botswana & Namibia • Zimbabwe, Botswana & Namibia travel atlas
Travel Literature: The Rainbird: A Central African Journey • Songs to an African Sunset: A Zimbabwean Story • Mali Blues: Traveling to an African Beat

AUSTRALIA & THE PACIFIC Australia • Australian phrasebook • Bushwalking in Australia • Bushwalking in Papua New Guinea • Fiji • Fijian phrasebook • Islands of Australia's Great Barrier Reef • Melbourne • Micronesia • New Caledonia • New South Wales & the ACT • New Zealand • Northern Territory • Outback Australia • Papua New Guinea • Papua New Guinea (Pidgin) phrasebook • Queensland • Rarotonga & the Cook Islands • Samoa • Solomon Islands • South Australia • South Pacific Languages phrasebook • Sydney • Tahiti & French Polynesia • Tasmania • Tonga • Tramping in New Zealand • Vanuatu • Victoria • Western Australia
Travel Literature: Islands in the Clouds • Kiwi Tracks • Sean & David's Long Drive

CENTRAL AMERICA & THE CARIBBEAN Bahamas and Turks & Caicos • Barcelona • Bermuda • Central America on a shoestring • Costa Rica • Cuba • Dominican Republic & Haiti • Eastern Caribbean • Guatemala, Belize & Yucatán: La Ruta Maya • Jamaica • Mexico • Mexico City • Panama
Travel Literature: Green Dreams: Travels in Central America

EUROPE Amsterdam • Andalucía • Austria • Baltic States phrasebook • Barcelona • Berlin • Britain • British phrasebook • Brussels, Bruges & Antwerp • Canary Islands • Central Europe • Central Europe phrasebook • Corsica • Croatia • Czech & Slovak Republics • Denmark • Dublin • Eastern Europe • Eastern Europe phrasebook • Edinburgh • Estonia, Latvia & Lithuania • Europe • Finland • France • French phrasebook • Germany • German phrasebook • Greece • Greek phrasebook • Hungary • Iceland, Greenland & the Faroe Islands • Ireland • Italian phrasebook • Italy • Lisbon • London • Mediterranean Europe • Mediterranean Europe phrasebook • Norway • Paris • Poland • Portugal • Portugal travel atlas • Prague • Provence & the Côte d'Azur • Romania & Moldova • Rome • Russia, Ukraine & Belarus • Russian phrasebook • Scandinavian & Baltic Europe • Scandinavian Europe phrasebook • Scotland • Slovenia • Spain • Spanish phrasebook • St Petersburg • Switzerland • Trekking in Spain • Ukrainian phrasebook • Vienna • Walking in Britain • Walking in Italy • Walking in Ireland • Walking in Switzerland • Western Europe • Western Europe phrasebook
Travel Literature: The Olive Grove: Travels in Greece

INDIAN SUBCONTINENT Bangladesh • Bengali phrasebook • Bhutan • Delhi • Goa • Hindi/Urdu phrasebook • India • India & Bangladesh travel atlas • Indian Himalaya • Karakoram Highway • Mumbai • Nepal • Nepali phrasebook • Pakistan • Rajasthan • South India • Sri Lanka • Sri Lanka phrasebook • Trekking in the Indian Himalaya • Trekking in the Karakoram & Hindukush • Trekking in the Nepal Himalaya
Travel Literature: In Rajasthan • Shopping for Buddhas

LONELY PLANET

Mail Order

Lonely Planet products are distributed worldwide.They are also available by mail order from Lonely Planet, so if you have difficulty finding a title please write to us. North and South American residents should write to 150 Linden St, Oakland, CA 94607, USA; European and African residents should write to 10a Spring Place, London NW5 3BH, UK; and residents of other countries to PO Box 617, Hawthorn, Victoria 3122, Australia.

ISLANDS OF THE INDIAN OCEAN Madagascar & Comoros • Maldives • Mauritius, Réunion & Seychelles

MIDDLE EAST & CENTRAL ASIA Arab Gulf States • Central Asia • Central Asia phrasebook • Hebrew phrasebook • Iran • Israel & the Palestinian Territories • Israel & the Palestinian Territories travel atlas • Istanbul • Jerusalem • Jordan & Syria • Jordan, Syria & Lebanon travel atlas • Lebanon • Middle East on a shoestring • Syria • Turkey • Turkish phrasebook • Turkey travel atlas • Yemen
Travel Literature: The Gates of Damascus • Kingdom of the Film Stars: Journey into Jordan

NORTH AMERICA Alaska • Backpacking in Alaska • Baja California • California & Nevada • Canada • Chicago • Florida • Hawaii • Honolulu • Los Angeles • Louisiana • Miami • New England USA • New Orleans • New York City • New York, New Jersey & Pennsylvania • Pacific Northwest USA • Puerto Rico • Rocky Mountain States • San Francisco • Seattle • Southwest USA • Texas • USA • USA phrasebook • Vancouver • Washington, DC & the Capital Region
Travel Literature: Drive Thru America

NORTH-EAST ASIA Beijing • Cantonese phrasebook • China • Hong Kong • Hong Kong, Macau & Guangzhou • Japan • Japanese phrasebook • Japanese audio pack • Korea • Korean phrasebook • Kyoto • Mandarin phrasebook • Mongolia • Mongolian phrasebook • North-East Asia on a shoestring • Seoul • South-West China • Taiwan • Tibet • Tibetan phrasebook • Tokyo
Travel Literature: Lost Japan

SOUTH AMERICA Argentina, Uruguay & Paraguay • Bolivia • Brazil • Brazilian phrasebook • Buenos Aires • Chile & Easter Island • Chile & Easter Island travel atlas • Colombia • Ecuador & the Galapagos Islands • Latin American Spanish phrasebook • Peru • Quechua phrasebook • Rio de Janeiro • South America on a shoestring • Trekking in the Patagonian Andes • Venezuela
Travel Literature: Full Circle: A South American Journey

SOUTH-EAST ASIA Bali & Lombok • Bangkok • Burmese phrasebook • Cambodia • Hanoi • Healthy Travel Asia & India • Hill Tribes phrasebook • Ho Chi Minh City • Indonesia • Indonesia's Eastern Islands • Indonesian phrasebook • Indonesian audio pack • Jakarta • Java • Laos • Lao phrasebook • Laos travel atlas • Malay phrasebook • Malaysia, Singapore & Brunei • Myanmar (Burma) • Philippines • Pilipino (Tagalog) phrasebook • Singapore • South-East Asia on a shoestring • South-East Asia phrasebook • Thailand • Thailand's Islands & Beaches • Thailand travel atlas • Thai phrasebook • Thai audio pack • Vietnam • Vietnamese phrasebook • Vietnam travel atlas

---

ALSO AVAILABLE: Antarctica • Brief Encounters: Stories of Love, Sex & Travel • Chasing Rickshaws • Lonely Planet Unpacked • Not the Only Planet: Travel Stories from Science Fiction • Sacred India • Travel with Children • Traveller's Tales

Index

Abbreviations

Arunachal Pradesh (AP)
Bangla (West Bengal) Hills (BH)
Himachal Pradesh (HP)

Jammu & Kashmir (J&K)
Ladakh & Zanskar (L&Z)
Sikkim (S)

Uttarakhand (U)
National Park (NP)
Wildlife Sanctuary (WS)

Text

A

accommodation 130-2
  taxes & charges 132-4
Aharbal (J&K) 200
Ahom dynasty 18
air travel 145-51
  glossary 146-7
  to/from India 148-51
  travellers with special
    needs 148
  within India 158-9
Ajay Pal 17
Akhil Bharatiya Gorkha
  League (ABGL) 38
Alchi (L&Z) 236-237
Alexander the Great 16
Almora (U) 417-420, **418**
Along (AP) 503
altitude sickness 110-11
Amar Singh Thapa 17
Ananda Puri Ashram (U) 412-13
Anasuya Devi (U) 390
Animism 59
Apatani people 502
architecture 51-4
  Buddhist 52-3
  domestic 51-2
  Hindu 52
Arghon people 202
arts 49-56
  books 100
  folk art 56
  Roerich Gallery (HP) 316-17
  Tibetan 274, 279
Arunachal Pradesh 493-504, **494**
  books 99-100
  climate 24
  geography 497-8
  getting there & away 499
  history 18, 493-7

Bold indicates maps.

  itineraries 77-8
  people 48, 493 *and be-*
    tween pages 128 & 129
  permits 87, 498
  politics 39-49
Aryan people 15, 347
Ashoka 15, 68
ashrams 131
Auli (U) 391-2
Aurangzeb 17
auto-rickshaws 175
Avalokiteshvara 66

B

Badrinath (U) 392-5
Baidyanath Temple (HP) 288
Baijnath (HP) 288
Baijnath (U) 416
Bajaura (HP) 307
Bajreshwari Devi Temple (HP) 289
Bakrawala people 41
Banbassa (U) 424
Bangla Hills 425-65, **426**
  climate 23-4
  festivals 428
  geography 427-8
  history 17-18, 425-7
  itineraries 77
  permits 429
  politics 38
Baralacha La (L&Z) 232
Barog (HP) 266-7
Basgo (L&Z) 235-6
Beatles, the 370
Bhageshwar (U) 416-17
Bhagsu (HP) 286
Bhakra Dam 25
Bhalukpong (AP) 501
Bhimtal Lake (U) 407
Bhotia people 45-6
Bhuntar (HP) 307-8
Bhutia people 17, 47
bicycling *see* cycling

Bijrani (U) 409
Billing (HP) 288
Bindevasani (U) 369
Binsar (U) 420-1
Bir (HP) 288
birdlife 30-1, 407-8
  Himalayan Aviary (HP) 259-60
birth control 40
Bodgwar (U) 401
Bomdila (AP) 501
Bön 59
books 97-102
  arts 100
  cooking 101
  culture 100
  environment 102
  exploration 102
  history 98
  language 102
  novels 102
  people 100
  religion 101
  travel 98
  travel health 107
border crossings 151-6
Brahma 63
Brahmaputra River 21
Brahmaur (HP) 300-3
British in India 17, 18, 258,
  425-7, 436, 467, 494
Brokpa people 201, 228
Buddha 15, 67
Buddha Jayanti 124
Buddhism 53, 55, 66-70, 206
  architecture 52-3
  art 54
  courses 128, 210, 281
  Karmapa order 482
Burmese in India 494
bus travel 151-6
  safety 165, 328
  within India 159-62
business hours 123-5
Buxa TR (BH) 32, 435-6

Bold indicates maps.

Bold indicates maps.

Boxed Text

MAP LEGEND

BOUNDARIES

- ────────────── International
- ─ ─ ─ ─ ─ Disputed
- ──────── Provincial
- ─ ──── ── Regional

HYDROGRAPHY

- Coastline
- River, Creek
- Lake
- Intermittent Lake
- Canal
- Spring, Rapids
- Waterfalls
- Swamp

ROUTES & TRANSPORT

- Freeway
- Highway
- Major Road
- Minor Road
- City Freeway
- City Highway
- City Road
- City Street, Lane

AREA FEATURES

- Building
- Park, Gardens
- Cemetery

MAP SYMBOLS

- ✈ Airport (International)
- ✝ Airport (Domestic)
- Ancient or City Wall
- Archaeological Site
- Cave
- Cliff or Escarpment
- Embassy
- Gompa
- Hindu Temple
- Hospital
- Monument
- Mosque
- ▲ Mountain or Hill
- ⏛ Museum

Routes & Transport (right column)
- ⇥ Tunnel
- Train Route & Station
- Ⓜ Metro & Station
- Cable Car or Chairlift
- ─ ─ ─ ─ Walking Track
- · · · · · · · Walking Tour
- ─ ─ ─ ─ Described Trek
- ─ ─ ─ ─ Ferry Route

Area Features (right column)
- Market
- Beach, Desert
- Urban Area

Map Symbols (right column)
- ⛫ National Park
- ← One Way Street
- ⚑ Pagoda
-)(Pass
- ★ Police Station
- ✉ Post Office
- 🏛 Stately Home
- △ Chörten or Stupa
- ☎ Telephone
- Temple
- Tomb
- ❶ Tourist Information
- Transport
- 🐘 Zoo

- ☉ **CAPITAL** National Capital
- ◉ **CAPITAL** Provincial Capital
- ● **City** City
- ● Town Town
- ● Village Village
- ○ Point of Interest

- ■ Place to Stay
- Å Camping Ground
- Caravan Park
- ⌂ Hut or Chalet

- ▼ Place to Eat
- Pub or Bar

Note: not all symbols displayed above appear in this book

LONELY PLANET OFFICES

Australia
PO Box 617, Hawthorn, Victoria 3122
☎ 03 9819 1877 fax 03 9819 6459
email talk2us@lonelyplanet.com.au

USA
150 Linden St, Oakland, CA 94607
☎ 510 893 8555 TOLL FREE: 800 275 8555
fax 510 893 8572
email info@lonelyplanet.com

UK
10a Spring Place, London NW5 3BH
☎ 020 7428 4800 fax 020 7428 4828
email go@lonelyplanet.co.uk

France
1 rue du Dahomey, 75011 Paris
☎ 01 55 25 33 00 fax 01 55 25 33 01
email bip@lonelyplanet.fr
minitel 3615 lonelyplanet *(1,29 F TTC/min)*

World Wide Web www.lonelyplanet.com *or* AOL keyword lp
Lonely Planet Images lpi@lonelyplanet.com.au